Praise for *Open Mouse*

W9-BWR-137

[PassPorter's Open Mouse] is the ultimate sourcebook for Disney World visitors with unique problems and needs. Well organized and crisply written, the comprehensive volume covers everything from the needs of nursing mothers to disabled access to autism. Almost anyone with a special need will find both understanding and excellent advice between the covers of this landmark work.

— Bob Sehlinger
Author of "The Unofficial Guide to Walt Disney World"

Amazingly insightful and encouragingly helpful ... delves into a huge gamut of special needs. A must-have for special needs guests visiting Walt Disney World!

— Rich Steck & Judi Janofsky, "Where To Go Next!"
(http://www.wheretogonext.com)

[Open Mouse] is the de facto encyclopedia on special needs at Disney World and it is unlikely that their achievement will ever be duplicated, let alone surpassed.

— Kelly Monaghan, Intrepid Traveler
(http://www.intrepidtraveler.com)

SO INFORMATIVE! You didn't miss a thing, covering every "special need" imaginable. Thank you!!!

— Nancy Buchieri in Georgia

I love this book because it has made me feel comfortable knowing how to navigate dining in the World with my severely food allergic children.

— Kerri Woolbert in Massachusetts

I have never seen such a comprehensive guide for travelers with special challenges before. Thank you for such a thorough investigative guide!

— Lynn Carruthers in Michigan

You covered just about every possibility and that is very comforting for families with special needs kids. This was an excellent investment and a great help to us.

— Kelli W. in Maryland

Benjamin Franklin Award Finalist and ForeWord Book of the Year Award Finalist

What's New in This Edition

Major Enhancements:

✓ **More than 25 brand new pages** filled with valuable information, advice, details, reviews, ratings, and photos.

✓ **More photos** than our previous edition—many of which include the *Open Mouse* authors and peer reviewers in the picture, too!

✓ **"IN FOCUS" profiles** offer a closer look at Disney vacationers with a variety of special challenges.

✓ **New section on epilepsy** available in the Ongoing Medical Treatment section.

✓ **Expanded section on diabetes** also available in the Ongoing Medical Treatment section.

✓ **Enhanced information for the vision-impaired**, including helpful Boarding Tips.

✓ **New Attraction Seating Charts** for the Magic Kingdom, Epcot, Disney-MGM Studios, and Disney's Animal Kingdom attractions.

✓ **Expanded attraction charts** for all parks.

✓ **"Queue-Tip!"** activities from *The Disney Queue Line Survival Guidebook* for passing the time while waiting in line.

✓ **More tips from our peer reviewers** for a wider variety of perspectives and experiences.

✓ **Smoking areas marked on all resort maps** now that Disney resorts have all nonsmoking guest rooms.

Fun Features and Information:

✓ Thousands of small tweaks to further improve our guide.

✓ Current rates, prices, dates, and photos.

✓ Expanded index to make it easier to find things.

✓ More new reader tips, magical memories, and stories.

✓ New peer reviewers to ensure accuracy and thoroughness.

Visit *http://www.passporter.com/wdw/openmouse/guidebook.asp* for a complete list of what's new and changed in this edition!

PassPorter's®
Open Mouse
for
Walt Disney World®
and the
Disney Cruise Line

Easy-Access Vacations for Travelers With Extra Challenges

Deb Wills
and
Debra Martin Koma

PassPorter Travel Press

An imprint of MediaMarx, Inc.
P.O. Box 3880, Ann Arbor, Michigan 48106
877-WAYFARER
http://www.passporter.com

PassPorter's® Open Mouse for Walt Disney World® and the Disney Cruise Line®

by Deb Wills and Debra Martin Koma

© 2007 by PassPorter Travel Press, an imprint of MediaMarx, Inc.

P.O. Box 3880, Ann Arbor, Michigan 48106
877-WAYFARER or 877-929-3273 (toll-free)
Visit us on the World Wide Web at http://www.passporter.com

ISBN-13: 978-1-58771-048-3
ISBN-10: 1-58771-048-X

10 9 8 7 6 5 4 3 2 1

Printed and bound in the U.S.A.

About the Authors

Deb Wills saw Walt Disney hosting his Sunday evening "Wonderful World of Color" television show and promptly fell under the spell of the Disney magic. As a child, she visited the 1964–65 World's Fair in New York and enjoyed the original debuts of attractions like It's a Small World and the GE Carousel of Progress. Her first visit to the Magic Kingdom in 1972 signaled the start of a life-long relationship with the popular vacation resort. After she graduated from college, Deb made many repeat visits to Walt Disney World and the Fort Wilderness Campground in her capacity as a rehabilitation assistant with a vacation travel program for special needs adults. Since then, Deb has paid countless visits to the "World" and has sailed on the Disney Cruise Line 13 times. More than 11 years ago, she began the independent Disney Travel Guide web site known as AllEars.net, and in 1999, began publishing ALL EARS®, a weekly electronic newsletter that goes to more than 86,000 subscribers. When PassPorter publishers Jennifer and Dave Marx approached her with the idea of co-authoring a book about traveling to Walt Disney World with special needs, Deb jumped at the opportunity, realizing that it was the perfect link between her past and present interests. Deb has been a peer reviewer of the award-winning *PassPorter's Walt Disney World* guidebook series since 2000 and in 2004 joined the review group for *PassPorter's Disney Cruise Line and Its Ports of Call*. As a breast cancer survivor, she is active in raising funds and awareness through the Avon Breast Cancer Crusade and Susan G. Komen Foundation. A native of New Jersey, Deb now resides in the Washington, D.C., suburbs.

Debra Martin Koma, a freelance writer and editor, fell in love with Walt Disney World on her first visit there—as an adult. She's returned to her Laughing Place more than 40 times in the ensuing years, enjoying new and exciting experiences with every visit. For the past eight years, she has enthusiastically shared her passion with others as Senior Editor of Deb Wills' web site AllEars.net and the weekly electronic newsletter ALL EARS®, writing in-depth reports on a variety of subjects, including the Epcot International Food and Wine Festival, Disney restaurants and resorts, and overlooked attractions in the theme parks. Debra, who has written for many local and national publications, has also been a peer reviewer of *PassPorter's Walt Disney World* guidebook since 2001. Through her work with PassPorter and AllEars.net, Debra has helped "share the magic" with hundreds of thousands of people. Having grown up with siblings who had a variety of health issues, Debra eagerly signed on when Jennifer and Dave approached her about writing this book, seeing it as a chance to spread a little pixie dust to people who face special challenges when traveling. A native of Pittsburgh, Debra currently resides in Northern Virginia, just outside Washington, D.C., with husband Brian, teenage son Alex, and furry, four-legged son, Dexter.

PassPorter Peer Reviewer Team

Our Expert Peer Reviewers—These experts—each with their own experience with special needs—painstakingly checked our text to ensure PassPorter's accuracy, readability, and thoroughness. Thank you for helping to make PassPorter the best it can be!

Sandra Bostwick is an occupational therapist, college professor, lecturer, and writer. Her educational consulting and coaching practice helps people with challenges excel. She visits Walt Disney World yearly for pixie dust refills.

 Kimberly Button is a former Disney cast member and Disney Cruise crew member and author of *The Disney Queue Line Survival Guidebook*. She has chronic fatigue syndrome, fibromyalgia, chemical sensitivities and food allergies.

Dianne Cook is an RN and a Certified Diabetes Educator, working in a hospital setting for 25 years. Married to Tom for 24 years; they have two boys, Andrew (16) and Matthew (14), and have visited Walt Disney World 28 times.

 Bonny June Eby is a 37-year-old woman with multiple autoimmune diseases. She visits Disney World at least twice a week. She is also mom to a 6-year-old with autism, epilepsy, a feeding tube, cerebral palsy, and other special needs.

Lydia Economou has loved Walt Disney World since her first trip with roommates after college. She is married with three children: Nicholas, Andrew, and Sophia. Her son, Andrew, is lactose intolerant and has asthma.

 Melanie Emmons has struggled with obesity all of her life and has lost about 100 pounds since having lap-band surgery. Her first trip to Disney World was her honeymoon (with her 6'7" husband), and she's returned at least 20 times.

Joanne and Tim Ernest are veterans of more than 20 trips to Walt Disney World and three Disney cruises and are PassPorter moderators. For the past 5 1/2 years, Joanne has suffered from acute peripheral neuropathy.

 Betsy Hicks is a diet counselor and co-owner of Pathways Medical and Holistic Health Center. Her 14-year-old son, Joey, has autism and dietary challenges. Disney has been a yearly part of his therapy for the past five years.

LauraBelle Hime is a PassPorter moderator and the proud owner of annual passes for the last four years. She enjoys touring despite painful fibromyalgia, but the biggest challenge has been her granddaughter Alexis' many allergies.

 Michelle Hohmann has traveled to Disney World and sailed Disney Cruise Line numerous times with her teen daughter, who was diagnosed with ADHD and Asperger's syndrome. She is co-owner of a cruise specialty travel agency.

Masayo Kano is an international traveler from Japan who has loved Disney since her first trips to Tokyo Disneyland in '91 and to Disney World in '93. She's been 10+ times since. She's married to Mamoru, who also loves Disney.

PassPorter Peer Reviewer Team
(continued)

 Deb Kendall has had fibromyalgia for 15+ years. She resides in Texas and has visited Disney World 10 times and Disneyland 100+ times growing up in California. She's learned a new way to enjoy Disney because of fibromyalgia.

Lori Kloman Williamson is a long-time Walt Disney World fan who has made multiple trips since 1971. She has spent a great deal of time traveling to Disney World with her visually impaired husband and best friend.

 Susan Koppel vacationed at Disney before becoming a mom to Alex and Mikie. Her family has experienced Disney with food allergies, GERD, Crohn's, mobility issues, sensory issues, fears, motion sickness, autism, and size issues.

Cathy McConnell is a Disney fan and travel agent who has been on more than 20 trips to Disney World and 12 Disney cruises. She is the mother of a teen son who is profoundly deaf and is active in deaf advocacy groups.

 Chet McDoniel is an Accredited Cruise Counselor with CruisingCo.com/ MouseEarVacations.com. He has no arms and shortened legs. He travels in an electric wheelchair and just loves Walt Disney World and Disney Cruise Line!

Bruce Metcalf works at a major Central Florida theme park where his job includes making life easier for those with challenges. An accident that put him in a wheelchair for three months helped focus his attention.

 Jean Miller, a senior citizen, began her love of Disney while living near Disneyland for a year in the early '60s. A regular visitor to Disney World since its opening, she now spends several weeks each winter at Ft. Wilderness.

Josh Olive is a 6'6", 400-lb. man whose inner child is bigger yet. He's been a BIG fan of Walt Disney World since his first visit in 1979, and he's now a 15-trip veteran.

 Pam Passwater, a senior with psoriatic arthritis and asthma, has visited Walt Disney World 30+ times. As volunteer travel coordinator for St. Louis Dream Factory, she helps seriously ill children plan dream trips to Florida.

Kathy Sauviac is a mother of four with ALS who has extensive personal experience at Disney. She gets around with a power wheelchair while using a ventilator and other equipment. She is accompanied by her service dog, Skye.

 Carol Scopa first visited Walt Disney World in 1975 and visits Mickey and friends at least once every year. A paraeducator, Carol has spent the last 20 years working with children with special needs and learning disabilities.

Mike Scopa is a columnist for MousePlanet, blogger on AllEars.net, and co-host of the WDWTODAY Podcast. Since 1975, he has visited Walt Disney World "between 1 and 100 times" and helps special needs families plan Disney trips.

PassPorter Peer Reviewer Team
(continued)

Beth Shorten, self-proclaimed Queen of Allergies, is a lifelong Disney fan. Disney World is one of the few places in which she feels comfortable dining. Beth is the mother of James, born just before the first edition of this book.

Kitty Smith is a vegan who fell in love with Walt Disney World on her honeymoon 10 years ago. Twelve trips later, she's still in love. She can often be found dishing out veggie dining advice at AllEars.net.

Michelle Spurrier is an early childhood special education teacher. Walt Disney World became the favorite family vacation spot in 1997 for Michelle, her husband, and two sons. Michelle has made 13 trips to Walt Disney World.

Amy Warren Stoll has been to Walt Disney World more than 20 times since her first trip in 1996. She's also cruised with Disney Cruise Line. She hasn't let epilepsy keep her from enjoying her favorite solo trips!

Tim Sullivan is a visually impaired traveler who has been enjoying his trips to Walt Disney World since he was four. He is lucky enough to have a fabulous trio of travel "Princesses" in his wife and two daughters.

Alissa Tschetter-Siedschlaw is a total Disney junkie! She has four kids whose challenges include with Autism Spectrum Disorder, mild cerebral palsy, behavioral issues, anxiety, and g-tube feeds. She is expecting a baby in the fall.

Shawn Varney is a Disney lover with a moderate hearing loss, corrected with digital hearing aids. He and his family have been to Disney more than 10 times. He is married to PassPorter Editor Sara Varney and they have one son, Ryan.

Blossom Zell is a special education teacher, working with students of many disabilities, including autism, PDD, mental retardation, Tourette Syndrome, and ADHD, to name a few. She is the parent of two boys with special challenges.

A special thanks to these important folks "behind the scenes" at PassPorter Travel Press:

Senior Editor and Project Manager: Jennifer Marx
Publishing Vision: Dave Marx
Printer: Malloy, Inc.
Online Coordinator and Newsletter Editor: Sara Varney
Proofreader: Sandy Livingston
Office and Research Assistants: Nicole Larner and Chad Larner
Sorcerers' Apprentices: Kim Larner, Carolyn Tody, and Tom Anderson

© MediaMarx, Inc.

From left to right: Tom Anderson, Dave Marx, Nikki Larner, Chad Larner, Jennifer Marx, Kim Larner, and Carolyn Tody

Sara Varney

Sandy Livingston

Acknowledgments

While you see only the authors' names on the front cover, the book you hold in your hands would not be possible without the countless people who have been there for us during this incredible adventure.

All of you gave us the inspiration and motivation to produce the best guidebook for special needs travelers that we possibly could.

A "world" of thanks to PassPorter's readers, who've contributed thousands of tips and stories since PassPorter's debut. A special thanks to those who generously allowed us to include their contributions in this edition: Bob Sehlinger, Rich Steck, Judi Janofsky, Kelly Monaghan, Nancy Buchieri, Kerri Woolbert, Lynn Carruthers, Kelli W. (page i); Sandy Bostwick (page 5); Sheri Bushong, Therese Taylor, Pat Bubolo (page 6); Melanie Evans (page 13); Carol Scopa (page 15); Ann Berry (page 18); Larry Heidenberg (page 23); Kalli Mulchi, Kathleen Kelly (page 25); Sandy Bostwick (page 27); Alissa Tschetter-Siedschlaw, Sam and Spring Slagle (page 29); Carrie Bass (page 30); Laura Schmitt (page 34); Leanne Phelps (page 36); Robert Feder (page 38); Chet McDoniel (page 41); Masayo Kano (page 45); Kelly LaFramboise (page 59); Amy Warren Stoll (page 63); Patricia Ravert (page 70); Joanne Ernest (page 72); Kitty Smith (page 73); Melissa Goetz (page 80); Tim Sullivan (page 91); Lori Kloman Williamson (page 94); Jennifer Grudnoski (page 95); Abby Harrington, Mae Cavalcanto (page 97); Michelle Steiner (page 100); Leanne Phelps (page 102); Joanne Ernest (page 103); Sandy Bostwick (page 106); Abby Harrington, Kalli Mulchi, and Melanie Evans (page 112); Sue Mickelson (page 136); Betsy Hicks (page 151); Michelle Hohmann (page 180); Pam Passwater (page 184); Joanne Ernest (page 189); Amy Warren Stoll (page 192); Ray Sharpton (page 198); Jean Miller (page 199); Ray Sharpton (page 200); Lori Jones (page 201); Lauren Whitmore, David Kelso, Maggie Ercoli, Ray Sharpton (page 202); Bonny Eby (page 225); Sandy Bostwick (page 229); Kimberly Button (page 238); Kathy Sauviac, Mikki Steiner (page 243); Bonny Eby (page 245); Jean Miller, Pam Passwater (page 252); Kimberly Button (page 259); Deb Kendall (page 261); Kimberly Button (page 264); Masayo Kano (page 266); Carol Scopa (page 268); Bonny Eby (page 281); Donna Jagodzinski (page 287); Jill Blejwas, Tamara Osborne, Maggie Ercoli (page 329); Ellen, Sandy Bostwick, Carol Scopa, Josh Olive (page 330); Kitty Smith (page 335); Amy Stoll (page 349); Betsy Hicks (page 351); Masayo Kano (page 367); Peter Johnson (page 383); Chet McDoniel (page 385); Susie Koppel, Michelle Hohmann, Kitty Smith, Kathy Sauviac, Blossom Zell, Carol Scopa (page 388); Mary Mahaney, Renee Kilgarriff, Susan Koppel (page 389); Tamara Osborne, Laura Schmitt, Joy Jacobs (page 390); Josh Olive (page 394); Cheryl Giffear-Sywkiw, Sam and Spring Slagle, Deb Kendall, Jean Miller, and Joshua Olive (page 410). May each of you receive a new magical memory for every reader your words touch.

To everyone who shared their stories, tips, and experiences, and to those who filled out our survey, we want you to know that we read each and every word and, while we are unable to name all of you here, please know that you had an impact on the writing of this book.

To our incredible review team for all their superb ideas, suggestions, and insightful comments, we can't thank you enough. We were so lucky to find you.

To our friends who provided all manner of support, from information-gathering to photo-taking to providing insight to just plain encouraging us to carry on, we owe you all so much: Cathy Bock, Mary Brennan, Craig Canady, Kenny Cottrell, Jennifer Edwards, Beth Ann Floro, Meli Emmons, Laura Gilbreath, Chet Hall, Gloria Konsler, Jack Marshall, Andrea McKenna, Linda MacLeod, Dotti Saroufim, Di and Marc Schwartz, Jack Spence, Donna Staffanson, and Nancy Tynes.

Our deep appreciation to our publishers, Jennifer and Dave Marx, for having the faith in us to write a book that would meet their standard of excellence.

We also owe a huge debt of gratitude to Walt Disney, for his dreams, and to Disney cast members everywhere, who continue to make his dreams a reality, especially for those travelers who have special challenges.

Appreciations and Dedication

Debra Martin Koma would also like to thank:

♥ My husband and son, who have been patient and understanding (well, most of the time), while I went on numerous "fact-finding missions" to Orlando and spent countless hours huddled in front of my computer: Brian and Alex, you are simply the best. I thank you first of all, because everything starts with you.

♥ My mother, father, and sister: Mom, Dad, and Jackie, thanks for teaching me to be compassionate and for helping to shape the person I am today. You have always had faith in me—for that, I will never be able to thank you enough.

♥ My dear friend and co-author Deb Wills, my other sister: Your warmth, generosity, and kindness, not to mention your boundless energy, are an inspiration to me.

♥ My many teachers, editors, friends, and family members, who encouraged, challenged, and supported me along the way.

Deb Wills would also like to thank:

♥ Debbie Koma: Your patience and guidance during this adventure has been invaluable. You've been there each step of the way and together we have once again made this book a reality! Thank you for your friendship, loyalty, kindness, and unending support. You are my best friend. Here's to our next adventure!

♥ Linda Eckwerth, for her love, patience, and unwavering support of my many projects, including the second edition of this book. You are always there for me and I thank you.

♥ The staff and clients at the facility where I volunteered in Lynchburg, Virginia, during my college years.

♥ The staff and clients at Centers for the Handicapped in Maryland—who taught me what it meant to have a "special need" and with whom I shared the Magic Kingdom and Fort Wilderness in the 1970s.

♥ To Barb Herrera and the many readers who helped create and enhance the various special challenges areas on AllEars.net—you have lightened the load of many travelers and you have my deep gratitude.

♥ My dad, for teaching me what's really important in life and instilling in me the values I have today.

♥ My mom, who passed on her love of Walt Disney to me in the late '50s and who experienced my first Disney attraction with me at the New York World's Fair in 1964. Mom, you weren't with us long enough to see Florida's Magic Kingdom, but I think of you every time I see the Castle and I know you are smiling down on me. I dedicate this book to you!

Contents

List of Maps and Charts

Contents
(continued)

A Letter From the Publishers

We've often said, "Eventually, everyone goes to Walt Disney World." And over the years we've been writing the *PassPorter's Walt Disney World* guidebook, it's become quite obvious that *everyone* does go to Walt Disney World. Time after time, readers write us to ask, "I have/my family member has (insert any and every condition/impairment known to humanity). How can we get the most out of our Disney vacation?" That Disney is the destination is surely no accident, thanks to Disney's sterling approach to hospitality, established a half-century ago by Walt Disney himself. Everyone is Disney's honored guest, and every Disney employee ("cast member") who interacts with guests is schooled in how to treat every one of those guests with respect and to make their Disney experience the best it can be. While you could find other institutions that may outdo Disney hospitality and accessibility in some regards, they exist in a world where attention to an individual's special challenges is spotty at best. Only at Walt Disney World can you visit for a day, a week, or even longer and experience the same high level of respect and accessibility no matter where you go—at the hotel, the theme park, on amusement rides, in the theater, waiting for a parade, at the water park, on the buses, and in the restaurants. Disney "gets it," and knowing that, families that rarely venture from home will make the pilgrimage to Orlando to share in the magic. And we're honored to help!

This amazing book is the result of countless hours of work by a team of amazing writers, editors, and expert peer reviewers. *Open Mouse* is so named because the information in this guidebook opens up the "Mouse" to more travelers with a wider range of special challenges, and as a result, we've needed far more help than usual. Our thanks go to many people, starting, naturally, with Deb Wills and Debra Martin Koma for deciding to take on this Herculean task. Arrayed behind "The Debs" are dozens of people who read and reread every word, and contributed advice, knowledge, vacation tips, and favorite memories to a project that reflects their experience, love, and compassion. Last but not least, there is the hard-working PassPorter team behind the scenes: proofreader Sandy Livingston, who makes sure every "i" is dotted and "t" is crossed; our phenomenal office staff, the brother-and-sister team of Chad and Nicole Larner, who really do play well together; our Online Coordinator and Newsletter Editor Sara Varney, who passes along special articles and tips; and our amazing message board moderators (our "Guides"). Many thanks to all!

Finally, like Walt Disney World and the Disney Cruise Line, this book is also a permanent work in progress. It will never be perfected or completed as long as our readers keep sharing their advice and encouragement and as long as Disney keeps growing and changing. Be sure to let us know how we can serve you better—you're our guests!

Jennifer & *Dave*

Planning Your Special Adventure

Planning

Special Challenges

Getting There

Staying in Style

Touring

Feasting

Resources

Index

"PassPorter's Open Mouse to Walt Disney World and the Disney Cruise Line" is unlike any other travel guide you may have encountered—it's as unique as you are. Oh sure, it's corny and it's been said before: Everybody's special. But you are not just any traveler. You have special requirements that set you apart—challenges and needs that, if they're not addressed, can turn the vacation of a lifetime into an ordeal you'll want to forget.

You are a traveler with special challenges. You are why we wrote this book.

So why do we call this book *PassPorter's Open Mouse*? Well, just like an open house event invites everyone to come and enjoy themselves when they want and how they want Walt Disney World and the Disney Cruise Line welcome all travelers, regardless of the special challenges they may face.

In our opinion, there's no place more open and inclusive than "the World" for travelers needing some sort of special attention. Not only are there features that appeal to young and old alike, but there seems to be a general willingness among the people who work there to go the extra mile ... for everyone, not just for the VIPs. If something doesn't work well, chances are good they'll figure out a way to make it work. If there's an inconvenience, there's bound to be someone who will try to make it less so.

Because every traveling party has at least one member with at least one challenge, we've tried to make this book, like Walt Disney World and the Disney Cruise Line, as open and inclusive as possible. Whether someone in your group has a special dietary requirement, a physical limitation, a medical issue, or something else entirely, we want to make sure you feel comfortable coming to this "open house" or, as we like to put it, "Open Mouse."

Maybe you've always dreamed of taking a vacation to Walt Disney World or cruising with Disney but were reluctant, thinking that once you got there, your special situation would not be accommodated. We can show you how you, too, can enjoy a Disney vacation, no matter what needs or requirements you might have.

The Disney Parks and Disney Cruise Line

If you've never been to the Walt Disney World Resort, you may not realize **just how much ground it actually covers**. We're always amazed when we hear someone say they want to go to "Disney World" when they really mean the Magic Kingdom, the first Disney theme park in Orlando (opened in 1971), the one with the highly recognizable icon, Cinderella Castle.

While the Magic Kingdom is undeniably a major piece of this beautiful Disney puzzle, there is **so much more**. There are four major theme parks: the Magic Kingdom, Epcot, the Disney-MGM Studios, and Disney's Animal Kingdom. There are more than 20 resort hotels with recreation facilities that run the gamut from tame (bicycles) to wild (race car driving). There are also scores of restaurants of every style and cuisine. In addition, there are two water parks, Blizzard Beach and Typhoon Lagoon. There's a shopping and nighttime entertainment complex, called Downtown Disney, which has three components—Marketplace, Pleasure Island, and the West Side. There are four miniature golf courses, and for the more grown up among us, 18-hole professional-quality golf courses. And that's just for starters!

There is so much to see and do at Walt Disney World that even a full week wouldn't be enough time to cover it thoroughly. That's why as you use this book, you'll notice that we emphasize again and again to pace yourself, know your limitations, take your time, and take plenty of breaks— **do not try to do it all**. Don't bite off more than you can chew! Instead, research and plan ahead so that you can be as well prepared as possible for your vacation.

If you've never cruised with the **Disney Cruise Line**, you may not realize that you have a number of choices here, too. First of all, there are two nearly identical ships: the Disney Wonder and the Disney Magic. You have the choice of standard 3-, 4-, or 7-night cruises, as well as specialty cruises, with a variety of ports of call and land excursions. Again, reading up on the subject is the best way to prepare. The more you become familiar with the choices available to you, the better trip you will have.

 Our Coverage of the Disney Cruise Line

For the most part, we integrate our coverage of the Disney Cruise Line throughout this book rather than give it a separate chapter because most vacationers taking a Disney cruise also visit Walt Disney World. If your focus is solely on cruising and you want to read just the relevant sections, flip to the index and look up Disney Cruise Line—you can use it like a mini table of contents!

Planning

Special Challenges

Getting There

Staying in Style

Touring

Feasting

Resources

Index

Should You Go?

We're sure that's the real question you've been asking yourself: **Should I go to Walt Disney World and/or take a Disney cruise?** What if I get there and I find they won't help me? What if I have a horrible time? Or worse, what if my health is compromised as a result?

Rest assured that you **couldn't find a more accommodating spot** than Walt Disney World and the Disney Cruise Line. Hopefully, as you read through this book and find the basic information you need—what's available, what's not—we'll ease your fears and concerns. To give you some insight on how others have managed a successful trip to Walt Disney World and cruised aboard the Disney ships, we've included firsthand tips from people who have made the trip, as well as stories and anecdotes about how a Disney vacation brought a little magic into their lives. Also in this edition, we feature several of our reviewers in mini profiles, highlighting their travel experiences while facing their own challenges.

So why should you, a traveler with special challenges, go to Walt Disney World and/or embark on a Disney cruise? We think there are probably **two main reasons**:

1. **You deserve a vacation**. You struggle with day-to-day challenges, just like everybody does. And maybe your challenges are little more, well, challenging. Why not take a much-needed break at one of the most popular vacation destinations in the world?

2. **Disney is willing to accommodate you**. Disney has been in the vacation business for more than 50 years. Perhaps in your day-to-day living, you find people who haven't encountered a special challenge like yours. With the hundreds of millions of guests who have passed through its gates over the years, Disney has seen almost everything and probably already has a procedure in place for handling situations like yours.

Of the more than 700 travelers who took a survey we conducted, 96.6% had made a trip to Walt Disney World within the past three years. Of these, 46.5% had or traveled with someone who had mobility issues, 22.5% allergies or asthma, and 17.7% autism spectrum disorders. And there were more than 130 travelers who vacationed at Walt Disney World with a variety of special challenges ranging from multiple sclerosis to cerebral palsy to spina bifida to broken bones. It's easy to understand why we say that Walt Disney World is a **welcoming spot** for almost anyone, no matter their ability.

Finding Information

While we hope this book will be your **primary source of information** for your vacation, there are certainly plenty of other resources available.

For a **good general guidebook**, we obviously recommend our parent publication, *PassPorter's Walt Disney World*. It packs a lot of information in a compact package and supplements the information you find in this book. See page 430 for details.

Special travelers to Walt Disney World will also want to avail themselves of **Disney's publications**—there's a small *Guidebook for Guests With Disabilities* printed for each of the four major theme parks. You can request them from Disney in advance by calling Walt Disney World Resort Special Reservations at 407-939-7807 and selecting option 1 (TTY Line: 407-939-7670), or you can pick them up at the theme parks' Guest Relations offices. (Versions of these guides are also available on Disney World's web site at http://www.disneyworld.com—look for the link called "Guests with Disabilities" toward the bottom left of the page.) Guides can also be picked up at Lobby Concierge or Front Desks of Disney resorts. Order vacation planning DVDs directly from the Disney web site or call 407-934-7639.

Walt Disney World Resort Special Reservations is also a good source of information for planning a trip, and they will assist you in making reservations, explaining what types of accommodations are available that meet your requirements. (See phone number above.)

The World Wide Web is another rich source of information for the special traveler. Co-author Deb Wills' well-known unofficial Disney web site, **AllEarsNet** (http://www.allears.net) is comprehensive and current, with thousands of photos from all around the resort, as well as a nearly complete collection of menus from the Disney restaurants. The web site also contains detailed information on traveling with a variety of challenges.

Another source of information is **online discussion groups**. PassPorter has its own set of active message boards at http://www.passporterboards.com, including one especially for special travelers. Another great source for the special traveler is Pete Werner's Unofficial Disney Information Station message boards at http://www.disboards.com. His disABILITIES message board is frequented by travelers who have special health requirements and are willing to share the benefit of their Disney experiences.

Finally, we've included some **relevant web site links** within the following chapters, as well as a hefty collection of web site links in chapter 7.

Planning
Special Challenges
Getting There
Staying in Style
Touring
Feasting
Resources
Index

Planning With Your PassPorter

Your PassPorter is most useful when you keep it handy before and during your vacation. It fits compactly into backpacks and shoulder bags. Or tuck your PassPorter into a **waist pack** (at least 5.5" x 9" or 14 x 23 cm).

Your PassPorter loves to go on rides and cruise with you, but do try to **keep it dry**. A simple resealable plastic bag (gallon size) is a big help.

Personalize your PassPorter! **Write your name** on the inside front cover, along with other information you feel comfortable listing. Your hotel name, trip dates, and phone number help if you misplace your PassPorter. Inside the back cover are calendars and important phone numbers, too.

Two tools you may find helpful for planning are a **highlighter** (to mark "must-sees") and those sticky **page flags** (to mark favorite pages).

If you're familiar with other PassPorter titles, you may be wondering about our famous **organizer PassPockets**. Alas, due to the vast amount of information in this guidebook, we simply couldn't fit in pockets as well—the book would have required a forklift to carry it! And, again due to its size, we're unable to offer a deluxe edition in a binder with pockets either. But if you just love using PassPockets to plan your vacation, you can purchase a binder and a set of pockets separately. For details, see page 430.

Reader Tip: "If you have trouble managing the weight of your airport luggage, consider copying and bringing with you just the pages of this book you'll need for references."—contributed by peer reviewer Sandy Bostwick

The Scope of This Guidebook

Unlike a general guidebook for Walt Disney World or the Disney Cruise Line, this guidebook gives less attention to the basic logistics of travel so it can go into really deep detail on your special requirements. Based on our own experience and that of our fellow vacationers, we cover a wide variety of situations that may arise on a Disney vacation. In fact, we devote an entire chapter to describing each of these special challenges, along with tips, notes, and important information you should know. We then proceed to cover traveling, lodging, touring, and dining, all with a focus on your situation. You'll still find general, descriptive information, but not quite as much as you'll find in our more general guidebooks. You also won't encounter duplicate descriptions. If you decide to supplement this guidebook with another PassPorter, you may rest assured that it adds completely new information.

And while this guidebook is highly detailed, it's impossible for us to cover everything. When you have an unanswered question, we refer you to the PassPorter Message Boards, where you can post your question and read answers and comments from other vacationers. Online updates are available at http://www.passporter.com/customs/bookupdates.htm.

Planning

Special Challenges

Getting There

Staying in Style

Touring

Feasting

Resources

Index

Your Planning Tips and Stories

My two youngest sons have Attention Deficit Disorder. I have been taking them to Walt Disney World on vacation every year since they were preschoolers (some years twice or three times per year). We've tried other vacation destinations, but the boys are easily bored, and no place else can provide the same amount of sensory input as Disney World!

—contributed by anonymous

My six-year-old nephew, who is hearing impaired with multiple allergies and ADHD, had a blast at Walt Disney World. We were concerned that he wouldn't be able to hear well enough to fully enjoy the magic. Disney does such a great job with incorporating visual and sound that Andrew had very little difficulty understanding what was going on. We were surprised by how many cast members knew at least some basic sign language and knew to talk directly to Andrew so he could read their lips. Andrew has so many obstacles to overcome and is always different from the other kids, but not at Walt Disney World. He got to be just another kid having the time of his life. That made all the planning and the worry his mother and I did worth it.

—contributed by Sheri Bushong

Of all the places you can visit with special needs, Disney tops all of them! Not only do they make you feel welcome, but the cast members will try to meet your needs. And yet, regardless of all the help I have received, some of my best memories involve being able to go do things on my own. I have rheumatoid arthritis and recently purchased my own scooter just for Disney vacations. Although I cannot go on all the rides I would like to, some of the best rides have been racing my son from the main house at Saratoga Springs to our room. The new scooter can really go pretty fast. Plus Disney makes every road and pathway so accessible it's easy to navigate. I can't wait to return to my second home. My scooter needs to stretch its legs again!

—contributed by Therese Taylor

While traveling with my son, age 8, who has celiac (gluten intolerance), a life-threatening peanut allergy, and allergies to tree nuts and beans, we were faced with a challenge. I can honestly say the staff at Disney was well-informed and extremely helpful. We never felt as though it was a burden—quite the opposite. My son was made to feel special. His meals were prepared separately by the chef and presented to him by the chef himself. We had very positive experiences at the sit-down restaurants throughout the parks. We travel to Disney every year, but last year was our first visit during my son's birthday. He was made to feel like a king. We enjoyed a character breakfast at 1900 Park Fare, where the chef asked my son what he would like to eat and brought out an enormous variety of foods. Dinner was celebrated at Narcoossee's, and a special birthday cake was prepared for him. Overall, we can say that Disney has allowed us the opportunity to travel and enjoy ourselves while having peace of mind that my son will be safe. We never eat out at home because we do not have that same comfort level. With Disney and the wonderful way the staff is educated and sympathetic to dietary needs, we can enjoy a family vacation with few restrictions. Thank you, Disney.

—contributed by Pat Bubolo

Your Special Travel Challenge

It's true that everybody's unique in one way or another, but some of us have unique requirements based on our physical or psychological challenges. Perhaps we're wheelchair users, or perhaps we are recovering from surgery. Perhaps we're new moms taking care of our infants, or we have children who are physically or emotionally challenged. Maybe we have a hearing or vision loss, or we're on a special diet, or we have fears or other health concerns that require special attention. Walt Disney World is able to accommodate you … in most cases.

In this chapter, we discuss the various special challenges that many of us have, the general services that Disney makes available, and coping strategies for a visit to "The World."

A good way to begin planning your Disney vacation is by contacting Walt Disney World Special (Medical) Reservations at 407-939-7807 (TTY 407-939-7670). Disney's special reservations cast members are trained in the facilities and services available to Disney guests with special needs and can advise you on many aspects of your trip. They will also send you copies of Disney's "Guidebook for Guests With Disabilities" for each of the theme parks or refer you to the online guides at http://www.disneyworld.com.

Even so, Disney's materials only cover certain aspects of the most obvious conditions—they don't thoroughly address all issues. The requirements of parents traveling with infants, for example, or of children and adults with less-than-obvious travel challenges, such as the autism spectrum disorders or even seniors, are not discussed in Disney's material.

That's where the information in this guidebook proves helpful. We have researched a wide variety of topics and have tried to identify the services and accommodations at your disposal while you're vacationing at Walt Disney World. We have also talked extensively with people who have vacationed at Disney or have traveled with family members and/or friends who have required special considerations and can share their tips and accumulated wisdom.

What's Your Special Challenge?
Know Your Code!

Special Challenge	Icon	Page
Attention Deficit Hyperactivity Disorder (ADHD)	*A*	14
Addiction Recovery	*R*	19
Allergies (Food and Other) and Asthma	*G*	21
Autism Spectrum Disorders (ASD)	*U*	25
Chronic Fatigue Syndrome	*C*	32
Cognitive Disabilities	*I*	38
Diabetes	*T*	61
Diet	*D*	34
Down Syndrome	*I*	38
Fears	*F*	40
Fertility	*E*	79
Fibromyalgia	*Ç*	32
Foreign Language	*Ö*	45
Fragile X	*I*	38
Hearing	*H*	49
Heart Health	♥	52
Infants	*B*	55
Medical Treatment	*T*	61
Mental Health	*T*	61
Mobility	*M*	68
Motion Sensitivity	*Q*	73
Physical Therapy	*P*	76
Pregnancy	*E*	79
Rehabilitation	*P*	76
Religion	*W*	82
Seniors	*S*	84
Service Animals	*X*	12
Size	*L*	88
Vision	*V*	91

Don't see your special challenge listed? Go to the next page to learn how we developed this list.

What We Cover

As you glance down our list of special challenges on the previous page, you may be wondering, "**But what about me? Why is my situation not listed?**" It was not our intention to exclude anyone. Space and time constraints prevent us from listing each and every type of traveler who might have a condition that warrants some special attention.

Based on our extensive research, including conversations we had with hundreds of travelers, we've addressed the **most common challenges** experienced by vacationers to Walt Disney World and the Disney Cruise Line. We've therefore included sections on autism spectrum disorders, attention deficit hyperactivity disorder, size issues, hearing and vision impairments, and mobility disabilities.

We have also tried to **group together related conditions**, where appropriate. For example, allergies and asthma often go hand in hand, as do chronic fatigue syndrome and fibromyalgia. In many cases there's overlap, in that various situations share similar characteristics or, more precisely, can be accommodated by the same methods. Vacationers with rheumatoid arthritis, multiple sclerosis, cerebral palsy, muscular dystrophy, and even broken legs all most likely experience some limitations on their mobility and therefore should read the section on mobility. We understand that those with these conditions may also have *other* challenges, and we expect that you know which other sections of the book will apply to you, such as the section on special diets and/or physical therapy.

We hope that, rather than feeling left out, you'll be able to find ample information that applies to you and your specific situation in these pages. We realize that in the real world, one size does *not* fit all ... and we hope we help you see how **a Disney vacation can fit you to a T**!

© Linda MacLeod

Planning

Special Challenges

Getting There

Staying in Style

Touring

Feasting

Resources

Index

Guest Assistance Card (GAC)

Many visitors to Walt Disney World have conditions that may not be **readily apparent** to the casual observer. Those with autism spectrum disorders, attention deficit hyperactivity disorder (ADHD), and heart conditions are just some of the vacationers who may require special consideration for their "invisible ailments." Walt Disney World will provide a Guest Assistance Card (see next page on how to obtain one) that provides certain assistance or accommodations for those who carry it. These accommodations may include the following, based on your special requirement:

✔ Using an auxiliary entrance if you cannot wait in line due to health problems, cognitive disabilities, autism, ADHD, and related fears. You'll likely still wait, possibly even longer than if you'd waited in the queue—you'll just wait in a different location.

✔ Waiting in a shaded spot out of the sun if the attraction's queue has you standing in the sun for an excessive amount of time.

✔ Using your stroller as a wheelchair in queues and through the same auxiliary entrances that wheelchairs and ECVs are allowed to use.

✔ Sitting up front at shows if you have visual impairments.

Important Note: The GAC is not a "front of the line" pass, and you will probably be asked to obtain a FASTPASS if applicable and available.

Wheelchair/ECV users don't need a GAC—your wheelchair/ECV is enough to alert the cast members at attractions to your special needs. If you encounter a cast member who insists that you need a GAC to access the wheelchair loading area, just politely ask that they call Guest Relations. But if you intend to park your wheelchair/ECV at an attraction and walk inside on your own, you may need a GAC to allow you to use the accessible seating and/or boarding areas.

Talk to the cast member stationed outside an attraction to request special assistance. The auxiliary entrance may be the FASTPASS entrance (when it exists). Be aware that many of the auxiliary entrances skip the theming found in the regular attraction queue and may even skip the attraction's preshow.

Bright Idea: Be sure that each person who needs a GAC gets his or her own individual card. This way, if your party splits up, each of the travelers still has their own GAC.

To obtain a **Guest Assistance Card** (GAC), visit Guest Relations when you enter a theme park. Simply state what specific requirements you have and what types of assistance would benefit you.

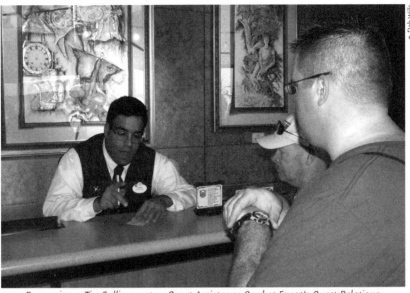

Peer reviewer Tim Sullivan gets a Guest Assistance Card at Epcot's Guest Relations

A letter from your doctor is not required. If, however, you would feel more comfortable with such a letter, be sure it states your requirements, not merely the diagnosis. Also, if you encounter a cast member who does not want to issue you a GAC, ask to speak to a supervisor. The GAC will be valid in all four major theme parks—Disney's Animal Kingdom, Disney-MGM Studios, the Magic Kingdom, and Epcot. Once you obtain a GAC, it will be valid for the duration of your visit for the traveler with challenges and up to five members of their party. Keep in mind, though, that even with a GAC, a particular accommodation may not be available to you at every attraction. If you want to guarantee that you have a seat while you wait, you will have to use a wheelchair/ECV.

Bright Idea: If it is difficult and/or awkward for you to discuss your special challenges or the needs of your special traveler, write a brief letter explaining the situation.

Front of Guest Assistance Card (text intentionally blurred)

Sidebar tabs: Planning · Special Challenges · Getting There · Staying in Style · Touring · Feasting · Resources · Index

Service Animals

We know that individuals with **several types of challenges**, including hearing, mobility, medical treatment, and vision, may use a service animal. We use the icon **[X]** to refer to service animals in this book.

If **flying**, check with specific airlines about their policies—they do vary.

If you use a **service animal**, you are able to take him/her around most of Walt Disney World and on the Disney Cruise, as long as your animal is on a leash or a harness. This includes the parks, hotels, and restaurants.

When you're approaching theme park attractions, follow the same boarding procedures as those given for wheelchair/ECV users. You may need to use an auxiliary entrance when traveling with a service animal. There are, of course, some rides or shows that service animals can't go on or into— **consult with a cast member** if you're unsure. Someone else in your party must stay with the animal. We note these locations in chapter 5, too.

At the water parks, follow the same entrance procedures as described for wheelchair/ECV users. Service animals are not permitted to ride any water attractions or enter any water areas for **health and safety reasons**. A member of your party must remain with the animal at all times.

If your service animal needs to make a pit stop, there are designated areas. Cast members can direct you to the proper location, but it's probably better to check on their whereabouts **in advance**. We note these locations in our individual attraction descriptions in chapter 5, too.

You and your service animal are also welcome in the **First Aid Stations** if you need a place to rest or cool off.

Bright Idea: Ask cast members for water for your animal. Remember they can get dehydrated in the Florida sun, too!

Disney's **kennels** can also help you with your service animals. Kennels are located at Disney's Animal Kingdom (to the right after you pass security, before the turnstiles), Epcot (to the left before the main entrance), Disney-MGM Studios (to the left before the main entrance), Magic Kingdom (at the Transportation & Ticket Center), and Fort Wilderness. You can kennel your service animal for $10/day as a Disney resort guest (higher rate for non-Disney resort guests).

For details on bringing your animal on the **Disney Cruise**, see page 199.

Here's a **packing list** for your service animal: Food, water, bowls, special toys, booties (to protect paws from the hot pavement), medications, immunization records, and veterinary information.

Mental Health Disorders

Bipolar disorder, oppositional defiant disorder, anxiety, depression, Tourette Syndrome, obsessive-compulsive disorder, and Alzheimer's disease are just a few of the mental health and organic brain disorders that a traveler may have. These disorders **may not fit neatly into any of the main categories** we address in this chapter, though some aspects are discussed in Medical Treatment (**[T]**) starting on page 61. We know that these conditions can have an effect on your Walt Disney World and/or Disney Cruise Line vacation. Based on discussions with those who deal with these disorders routinely, here are some tips that can help you enjoy your trip:

✔ Be sure to **bring all your labeled medications**, doctors' names and numbers, and a summary of your medical history—and carry them with you. You may be exposed to the sun more than usual during your stay in Florida, so check before you travel whether your medications increase your sun sensitivity.

✔ Talk with your doctor to see if he/she can **recommend a health care professional** or hospital in the Orlando area, should the need arise.

✔ **Don't overdo it**. Vacations are for relaxing. Have a general plan and be sure to leave time to "chill out."

✔ If you're concerned about **anxiety or troubles while waiting in line**, consider getting a Guest Assistance Card for waiting in an alternative area and try one of our fun things to do in chapter 5. Don't forget that the buses can be standing room only during peak times, especially at park opening and closing.

✔ Remember that taking anyone out of his or her **normal routine** and environment can easily trigger the resurfacing of issues that were thought to have been put to rest. Be on guard for this possibility.

✔ Be aware of **warning signs** or potential triggers to behaviors. If you feel comfortable, discuss these with the people you are traveling with so they can help you if necessary.

Reader Tip: "We did a huge family trip with three elderly people in our group, including my father, who has Alzheimer's. My father's Alzheimer's makes him very stressed in larger crowds. I recommend making an off-season trip, if possible. Also, let your traveler with Alzheimer's know where you're going and what you're doing next. I kept my father in the loop in all our activities and did not treat him like a tagalong. In addition, Alzheimer's patients tend to want to follow a group. Have a person act as a buddy for the day and have them wait outside a restroom to prevent an individual with Alzheimer's from wandering out into the crowd. (Be aware that some restrooms have two exits.) If your Alzheimer's traveler is on a set meal schedule, do not break the routine—it would cause stress and delay the reaction of medications. Finally, make clear plans with a time schedule to prevent a rushed feeling."—contributed by Melanie Evans

Planning

Special Challenges

Getting There

Staying in Style

Touring

Feasting

Resources

Index

Attention Deficit Hyperactivity Disorder (ADHD)

Vacationing with individuals who have attention deficit hyperactivity disorder (ADHD) can be challenging, as most of those with ADHD have no visible disability. To the average onlooker, a child who has ADHD may appear to be out of control, with unfit parents. We realize this isn't the case.

In this book, we use ADHD to represent Attention Deficit Disorder (ADD), Attention Deficit/Hyperactivity Disorder (AD/HD), and Attention Deficit Hyperactivity Disorder (ADHD).

Your Icon:

A

(A=Attention)
Look for this symbol in the book for more details

Planning

"Plan but be flexible" is the mantra for your trip to Disney, but this isn't new to you if you live with someone who has ADHD. This is how you go about each day—with structure, but also with the flexibility to change at the last minute, if needed. This is how to vacation at Disney with a child (or adult) who has ADHD. Research before you go, develop a plan, plan some more, and have a backup (include rain-out options)! Set realistic goals. If possible, plan to take your trip during cooler months for fewer crowds.

Involve your ADHD traveler in the plans for the trip. Watch the Disney planning videos (available from http://www.disneyworld.com or by calling 407-934-7639). Look at photos from past trips, on the Internet, or in books. Give your child one of the kid-oriented Walt Disney World books so they can read about the attractions and decide which ones to try.

Bring along **more doses of any medicines than you think you'll need**. In addition, bring a copy of the prescription in case you need to refill it.

Give consideration to **transportation**. If flying, notify the airline of any special needs. Also request bulkhead seats (no one in front to kick, but remember there is no underseat storage). Be sure to let the attendant know your situation when you board. Once you arrive in Florida, consider a rental car. While Disney transportation works great, there are times you will be waiting for a bus, boat, or monorail. There will be much less waiting involved if you don't have to rely on Disney transportation and can just walk to your car. If you don't rent a car, consider a private car service (see page 109) to take you to Disney instead of the Magical Express bus. You will have a much quieter environment with little or no wait time. Buses will often wait for a minimum number of passengers, and make several stops, and your luggage may not arrive at your resort for several hours.

See our tips on page 193 for **cruising** with autism, which may be helpful to those with ADHD. Also review our section on Fears on page 40.

Disney transportation is efficient but not perfect—during peak times of the year and at park opening and closing times, there will be lines and crowds waiting for buses. If this poses a potential problem, rent a car or take a taxi from the resort hotel (your bell services desk or valet counter can assist with taxis). Taxis are also available in the parking lots at each theme park and at the Transportation & Ticket Center. If you rent a car, remember that Disney resort guests get free parking at the theme parks. **For the Magic Kingdom, consider riding the Disney bus**, as the drop-off is very close to the turnstiles. If you drive to the Magic Kingdom, you'll be much farther away and also have to take a monorail or ferry to reach the entrance.

Always have **water** with you, no matter what the mode of transportation—it's important to stay hydrated.

Know the **check-in time** for your hotel and plan your arrival accordingly. Disney resort hotels allow check-in at 3:00 pm and 4:00 pm, depending on the resort (see chapter 4). If you need to unwind in your room upon arrival, factor in these late afternoon times. If you arrive before the official check-in time, be sure to preregister anyway. This is a great time to restate your special requests. During slow times, your room might even be ready early.

As much as possible during your vacation, **keep your regular routine** regarding wake and sleep times, medication, and eating.

Bright Idea: Bring a few pairs of earplugs from home. They are available from variety, grocery, or other stores and are fairly inexpensive. Disney resort stores do sell them, but they are not cheap! Another alternative is an electronic device with a headset that can play white noise.

Try to **keep all belongings in one place** while you are away from home. A knapsack works well for this.

Bring travel games, word puzzles, activity books, and books on tape. Develop a **list of activities** for those times you do need to wait in lines. We have some suggestions to get you started in chapter 5.

Bright Idea: Bring a pedometer to keep the child focused on how many steps walked—it becomes a game.—contributed by peer reviewer Carol Scopa

Check restaurant menus in advance. (Many menus are available online at http://www.allears.net/menu/menus.htm.) Make advance reservations for any table-service restaurants you plan to visit (see page 333). Scheduling early meals helps to minimize your wait time. You can always call and cancel if you change your mind. If you have special dietary requests, have this noted on your advance reservation. See also Diet on pages 34–37.

Important Note: You may be seated with strangers at the Biergarten in Epcot's Germany pavilion, the table service restaurants in Epcot's Japan pavilion, and the Spirit of Aloha dinner show at the Polynesian Resort. On the Disney Cruise Line, if you wish to be seated by yourselves, be sure to request this when you make your reservations.

[A] ADHD (continued)

Once You Arrive

The **issues and questions** we hear most from parents traveling with children with ADHD involve waiting in line for attractions/characters/shows, special effects in attractions, places where kids can let off some steam, and stimulation overload. Here are our tips for overcoming these issues and making a bit of magic along the way.

Post your itinerary in your resort room so the traveler can look at it when they want. Each day before venturing out, review the rules, expectations, and plans for the day. Point out the attractions or restaurants on the itinerary that they chose, to give them a feeling of empowerment.

Give your traveler with ADHD a **park map** so they can help get to the next attraction, let you know what's coming up, the time of the next show, etc. This gives them something to focus on and minimizes sensory overload.

Bright Idea: Offer a disposable camera so they can take photos of their special memories! (Be sure to put your name and address on it.)

Consider getting a **Guest Assistance Card** if you think it will help you (see pages 10–11).

Be sure all members of your party know that once they are seated in a ride, they **must stay seated for the entire ride**. They cannot stand or exit until the ride is over and fully stopped. In theater settings, sit at the end of a row in case you need to make a quick exit.

Try to dress with **brightly colored clothes** so you can find your traveler who has ADHD if they get separated from you. Take a digital picture each morning to aid with identification (if necessary). Rehearse what to do if you are separated.

Maintain **healthy eating** and any special diets (see Diet on pages 34–37). Use caution with sweets and snacks; bring some favorites from home. Stay hydrated (yes, we've already noted this, but it bears repeating)!

Create a **"time-out plan"** for those times your child may become over-stimulated. We note places where kids can let off steam, as well as quiet spots, in chapter 4 and chapter 5.

When touring the parks, note that even though **flash photography** is not allowed in many attractions, sometimes vacationers ignore the warnings. If your ADHD traveler is sensitive to sudden flashes, be prepared.

Spend time at the resort. Some families will spend one day at the parks and the next day at the resort to break up touring and to minimize the overload factor. Others make sure they spend the afternoons at their resorts and only tour parks in the morning and evening. Still others suggest you take a break in a quiet place after each attraction, then move onto the next activity. NO commando touring!

Character meals (see chapter 6) offer plenty of positive character interactions—more than you get by waiting in line to meet Mickey, especially during crowded times. At character meals, when the characters visit, it's for your table alone. Keep in mind, however, that character meals can be quite loud and boisterous. If your child does not like to be touched, be sure to let the cast member at the podium and your server know before the characters approach your child.

Some restaurants also have **special effects** that may be overly stimulating, such as the Rainforest Café (Disney's Animal Kingdom and Downtown Disney). We've noted these in chapter 6, starting on page 331.

Downtown Disney is not the best place to visit with a child who has ADHD, unless the experience is specifically catered to them. There are simply too many distractions. Bring activities for them to do if needed.

Bright Idea: Cell phones or walkie-talkies can help you stay in touch.

DisneyQuest is a game lover's paradise, but it can also cause problems. It is very noisy, the floor plan is confusing, and there's a lot of visual stimulation. There are multiple levels, and it can be hard to find the elevators and stairs to move from area to area. Be sure to bring a guidemap with you. Don't bring in backpacks or cameras that can be easily left behind and lost. Some parents have reported that their children with ADHD loved DisneyQuest, while others termed it a "nightmare." (See pages 315–320 for more details on DisneyQuest.)

At the **Cirque du Soleil** show (see page 313), keep in mind that there is no intermission and no talking. Also, we highly recommend you go to an early show because it's harder to pay attention when everyone's overly tired. Cirque du Soleil is a great show, but tickets are expensive and not refundable, so be sure it's something everyone can enjoy.

Thinking of the **water parks**? Typhoon Lagoon is more laid-back, but Blizzard Beach has more activities for youngsters. In either park, use caution when going on the lazy river tube ride, where it is easy to get separated. The ride has multiple exits, and it's very hard to keep track of where you entered. This makes exiting and finding your way back a little tricky. (See chapter 5, starting on page 301, for more details.)

[A] ADHD (continued)

PassPorter Picks

✔ Stay on Disney property for better access to your resort for breaks and at the end of the day.

✔ Rent a car to avoid bus lines, especially at theme park closing times.

✔ Use earplugs or a headset to reduce background noise. Be sure to bring a small zipper-type bag for storage.

✔ Use FASTPASS whenever possible to avoid long waits in line at theme park attractions (see page 216).

✔ Take advantage of Extra Magic Hours—fewer crowds and shorter lines for the hour before or a few hours after normal hours (see page 119).

✔ Make advance dining reservations and eat at off-peak times to avoid long waits for meals (see page 333).

✔ Visit the Kidcot Fun Stops at Disney's Animal Kingdom and Epcot, which offer brief hands-on activities for kids with little waiting.

What Is ADHD?

Attention Deficit Hyperactivity Disorder is one of the more common neurological disorders that develops in children and can last into adulthood. Symptoms may include impulsiveness (acting quickly without thinking), hyperactivity (can't sit still and/or talks when others are talking), and inattention (daydreams or is in "another world"). It is difficult for those with ADHD to control their behavior and/or pay attention. Children can have impaired functioning at home and school, while adults have difficulties at work and home.

Those with ADHD have sensory issues; they may be ultrasensitive to smells, lights, loud noises, and/or tactile objects. When their nervous system overloads, it triggers behaviors like "meltdowns." For the individual who has ADHD, sitting still during meals, in an attraction, or waiting in line can be extremely difficult. Sometimes, the impulsive person will blurt out inappropriate comments or display emotions without restraint. The inattentive may become easily distracted, lose or forget things, or become slow and lethargic. They have difficulty processing information as quickly and as accurately as others.

As parent April Higgins told us: "Our son (almost 8 now) is classified as 'ADHD-Wired,' meaning he is not necessarily hyperactive in appearance; it's just that his brain doesn't take a rest. He is constantly thinking, thinking, thinking to a point of confusing himself, demanding completely fulfilled answers to many questions."

Reader Tip: "Children can quickly take over a vacation with whining and demands. When you enter a park, be armed with a plan. We tell our son, 'We are starting in Adventureland and working our way around the park.' A map is very helpful as well. We also have a list of the rides that we all want to see, and we put them in order."—contributed by Ann Berry

Addiction Recovery

Although Walt Disney World is a happy, fun-filled vacation destination, there are several aspects of the place that could prove to be danger zones for folks recovering from a variety of addictions. If you are active in a 12-step program, remember to bring phone numbers of sponsors and group members and any literature you routinely read at home. You may also want to schedule an evening call with a group member or sponsor to "report" how well you did that day. Discipline is the key to success with any 12-step program, even when on vacation.

Your Icon:

(R = Recovery)
Look for this symbol in the book for more details

Recovering From Alcoholism

If you are recovering from alcoholism and need support, meetings of **Alcoholics Anonymous** (Friends of Bill W.) are held daily at 3:00 pm and Sunday at 10:00 am at the Hotel Royal Plaza at Downtown Disney (407-828-2828). There are also meetings held in Celebration on Wednesdays at 8:00 am at the Community Presbyterian Church. For more information on other area meetings, call the A.A. 24-hour hotlines: Osceola County, 407-870-8282; Orange County, 407-260-5408; Spanish-speakers, 407-240-1181; or visit their web site: http://www.osceolaintergroup.org. For Al-Anon and Alateen, phone 407-896-4929.

Friends of Bill W. meetings are offered onboard the **Disney Cruise Line** every day of the cruise except boarding and debarkation days. For meeting details, check your daily Navigator (schedule) for times and locations, or contact Guest Services.

In the theme parks: If you're looking for an alcohol-free paradise, the Magic Kingdom is the place to be. No alcohol is served there at any time during public operating hours, not even at the Magic Kingdom restaurants. The remaining theme parks—Epcot, Disney-MGM Studios, and Disney's Animal Kingdom—serve alcoholic beverages at numerous locations—in counter-service and table-service restaurants, lounges, and at various carts and stands. While these locations are difficult to avoid altogether, you might especially want to stay away from a few of the shops in Epcot's World Showcase (in Italy, Germany, and France), which often feature wine tastings. It also might be wise to avoid World Showcase during Epcot's annual International Food & Wine Festival held every fall—there are many events centered around alcohol, with free beer and wine tastings and many stands selling drinks by the glass.

[R] Addiction Recovery (continued)

At the resort hotels and water parks: Walt Disney World's resort hotel table-service restaurants serve liquor, as do the lounges. Hotel gift shops, some counter-service spots, and food courts have liquor for sale, while some resort rooms have stocked minibars with small bottles of alcohol. There are poolside bars located at all the resorts and the water parks as well.

At Downtown Disney/BoardWalk: Downtown Disney's Pleasure Island is brimming with nightclubs encouraging the consumption of alcohol—alcohol is even sold on the streets. The BoardWalk area has a number of nightclubs, particularly the popular Jellyrolls dueling piano bar, which might encourage alcohol overindulgence. **Note: The official Designated Driver program at Pleasure Island has been discontinued**.

Aboard the Disney Cruise Line: Alcohol is everywhere—at deck parties, shows, meals, and clubs. You can avoid it at the areas geared toward families, such as the movie theater, Studio Sea, and deck 9 aft. The Beverage Station on deck 9 aft offers free coffee, tea, lemonade, punch, and soda.

Recovering From Other Addictions

For those recovering from an addiction to **narcotics**, there are meetings of Narcotics Anonymous in the area. For current meeting information, visit the group's web site at: http://na.org or call the Orlando-area 24-hour helpline at 407-425-5157 (Florida Relay for the Deaf at 800-955-8771).

With hundreds of eateries on Disney property alone, Walt Disney World is a dining extravaganza. If, however, you have or are recovering from an **eating disorder**, you might want to avoid some of the all-you-care-to-eat meals, such as those at 'Ohana at the Polynesian Resort, the Cape May buffet at the Beach Club, or the Whispering Canyon Café at the Wilderness Lodge (see also chapter 6). The organization Overeaters Anonymous has support group meetings in the area. Visit the web site for current information at http://overeatersanonymous.org, or call the Central Florida Intergroup at 800-522-2792.

Those recovering from a **gambling addiction** won't find any slot machines or gaming tables in Orlando, although there are some carnival-style games of chance located around the resort, most notably the Fossil Fun Games in Disney's Animal Kingdom's DinoLand USA. If you're taking a Disney cruise, you'll be glad to know that there is no onboard casino. The only gambling onboard is daily bingo, with cash and merchandise prizes. However, be aware that many of the ports in the Bahamas and Caribbean do have casinos. Disney does not offer gambling-oriented excursions, although some excursions do visit casino hotels. For support, there are meetings of Gamblers Anonymous in the Orlando/Kissimmee area. For information, visit: http://gamblersanonymous.org, or call 800-397-9843.

Allergies (Food and Other) and Asthma

Aaaachooo! Are you beset by allergies? Whether you're reacting to the dust and pollen in the air or the milk in your main dish, allergies or asthma can be a worry. And yet, with planning, allergies needn't get in your way!

Your Icon:

G

(G=Aller**G**ies)
Look for this symbol in the book for more details

Food allergies: For the most part, Walt Disney World has an excellent reputation for meeting the needs of its guests who have special dietary requirements. The key to coping here is in planning and preparation. If you alert the Disney restaurants to your particular allergens, both when you make your advance reservations and 72 hours before you dine, the chefs have a chance to prepare for your needs. Even if you have forgotten to call ahead, all you need to do in most dining situations is talk with your server. Most times, the server will send a chef out to consult with you as to how your foods will be prepared. If you need your dishes to be lactose- or gluten-free, for example, the chef can suggest tasty alternatives. For more details on dealing with most food allergies, refer to our section on Diet (see pages 34–37).

Bright Idea: If you want to call the individual restaurant to make a special request, phone 407-WDW-DINE (407-939-3463) to obtain contact details.

Other allergies: If your allergy/asthma is triggered by inhalants, such as pollen, molds, dust, and grasses, consider the timing of your visit to Central Florida. Obviously, the spring and summer months, when everything is in full bloom, are going to be worse for you than the cooler late autumn and winter months. Keep in mind, though, that Florida is farther south than much of the country, its "spring" starts early, and all kinds of pollens can be present almost any time of the year there. To get the daily pollen counts, consult the local newspaper or TV weather broadcasts, or visit http://www.pollen.com. If you're allergic to bee stings or other insect bites, remember to bring the appropriate treatment with you—Florida has lots of bugs! If necessary, don't forget to carry your epinephrine in case of a severe allergic reaction. (Don't forget to check the expiration date!) To prevent bites, it's a good idea to have insect repellent, long sleeves, and long pants, especially in the evenings. If you do get bitten, Benadryl or some other antihistamine would come in handy.

Bright Idea: If your allergy is severe, wear a medical alert bracelet or necklace that identifies the allergen and treatment. These are available at many pharmacies, through your doctor's office, or from http://www.medicalert.org.

Planning

Special Challenges

Getting There

Staying in Style

Touring

Feasting

Resources

Index

Planning

Special Challenges

Getting There

Staying in Style

Touring

Feasting

Resources

Index

[G] Allergies and Asthma (continued)

Asthmatics and those with a sensitivity to smoke will be happy to note that the Florida Clean Indoor Air Act requires all enclosed indoor workplaces—including resort lobbies, convention spaces, common areas, dining locations, and enclosed backstage areas—to be nonsmoking. There are designated outdoor smoking areas in the theme parks indicated on the guidemaps, though, that you may wish to avoid—do they ever get smoky! There are also lounge areas, as well as some closed-in spaces in queues or ride waiting areas, where you may find yourself in close quarters with other vacationers who are wearing strong scents or smoking despite the smoking restrictions. In addition, some attractions use special effects that have strong odors, including dry ice and smoke. We note these potential problem areas in the following chapters of this guidebook.

Planning Ahead

At the resort hotels: Effective June 1, 2007, all Disney resort hotel rooms are nonsmoking. There are a few outdoor locations around the resort grounds that have been designated as smoking areas, however. Check the resort map or ask a cast member for locations. If you have other allergies or asthma-related concerns, be sure to mention them at the time you make your reservations to determine what accommodations are available to you.

Reader Tip: "I have a terrible allergy to down: goose, duck, or other fowl. I walked into my resort room one time and immediately began to have a terrible allergic reaction. When I looked at the bedding, I found goose down pillows. I called the front desk and asked if they could replace them with hypoallergenic pillows. A cast member from Housekeeping came and exchanged them quickly."

Be sure to **bring your own soaps and shampoos** from home if you have allergies. Disney recently switched vendors for its resort toiletries, and ingredients are not always listed. The new line of products is by H_2Oplus—its web site is http://www.h2oplus.com.

Disney offers special cleaning services to its guests with allergies and sensitivities. If requested, Disney resort hotel housekeeping will clean your room without using harsh chemicals. They can also perform an **"allergy cleaning,"** taking special care to make sure the linens, draperies, etc., are as dust-free as possible. When making your room reservation, be sure to request these services so your needs are noted. Also reiterate your requests upon check-in.

While all Disney dining establishments are smoke-free by law, a few of the **lounges**, which don't serve food, are not required to follow suit. These include the bar or lounge areas of the Lobby Court Lounge and Shula's Lounge at the Dolphin.

Once You Arrive

In the theme parks: Each theme park has a First Aid Station, staffed with a nurse. See our sidebar on page 206 for details on services. In addition, many stores in each theme park (the Emporium in the Magic Kingdom or MouseGear in Epcot, for example) also have over-the-counter medications, such as Benadryl, Tylenol, etc., in an under-the-counter location. Just ask a cast member in the store to point you to the right cashier.

At the water parks: First Aid Stations at Typhoon Lagoon (near Leaning Palms) and Blizzard Beach (near the entrance) help with minor first aid.

At Downtown Disney/BoardWalk: While the clubs and restaurants at Downtown Disney are smoke-free by law, a few of the lounges, which don't serve food, are not required to follow suit. These include the bar or lounge areas of Planet Hollywood, House of Blues, Bongo's Cuban Café, Fulton's Crab House, Rainforest Café, Portobello Yacht Club, and Captain Jack's. Jellyrolls on the BoardWalk also allows smoking.

Bright Idea: If your asthma or allergy requires you to take prescription medication, be sure to bring copies of your prescriptions with you.

Latex Allergies

At Walt Disney World, there are a number of areas where people with a latex allergy should be cautious:

✔ While wristbands used at the water parks and special events, such as evening Extra Magic Hours, are made of plastic, some individuals with latex allergies report experiencing a reaction if the band is wrapped too tightly. To be safe, ask the cast member to put the band on loosely, or wrap the band around a sleeve so it's not touching your skin.

✔ Food preparation at Disney-owned restaurants is done with non-latex gloves. The restaurants that are not owned by Disney, such as the food outlets in DisneyQuest (operated by the Cheesecake Factory) may use latex gloves. If you are not sure, ASK!

Reader Tip: "Because outside food and drink is not permitted in DisneyQuest normally, I usually call their food services directly that day and explain the situation. They usually allow us to bring our own food for my son who has a severe latex allergy."—contributed by anonymous

✔ The clubs' handle grips at the miniature golf courses have latex in them.

✔ There are some latex balloons still sold around the parks.

Reader Tip: "Towel animals left by Disney resort housekeeping almost always have rubber band(s) to hold them together. The rubber band may be 'hidden' in the folds of the towel. Also, one ride that may be of concern is Test Track at Epcot. The tires of the vehicles could potentially be touched by a guest. The ride also involves various tests, including heat and braking, that might cause latex to be released into the air. Guests who are extremely sensitive to latex might be well-advised to skip this ride entirely."—contributed by Larry Heidenberg

For more information, see http://www.allears.net/pl/latex.htm.

[G] Allergies and Asthma (continued)

PassPorter Picks

✔ Consider staying at resorts that are newer and those that are more self-contained, such as the Yacht and Beach Club or the BoardWalk.

✔ If you have food allergies, try a "Disney Vacation Club" resort, such as the Beach Club Villas or Saratoga Springs—these resorts feature kitchenettes or full kitchens so that you can prepare meals.

PassPorter Pans

✔ Avoid resorts that are spread out, forcing you to walk great distances in wooded areas, such as Port Orleans Riverside, Fort Wilderness, and Caribbean Beach. Also be aware that the Wilderness Lodge pipes a faux fire smoke smell into the lobby. Both Wilderness Lodge and Animal Kingdom Lodge have lobby gas fireplaces. If you have a sensitivity to smoke smell, avoid them.

✔ Avoid the outdoor areas of Disney's Animal Kingdom Lodge if you have sensitivity to animals or grasses and pollens. Avoid many of the outdoor areas around Disney's Animal Kingdom park for the same reasons.

✔ Avoid the perfume shops in Epcot's France and Norway pavilions and the Queen's Table shop in the United Kingdom pavilion if you're sensitive to heavy scents. You'll also want to avoid Basin in Downtown Disney and at the Grand Floridian Resort & Spa.

✔ Limit your visits to the stables, petting zoo, and horseback riding trails at Fort Wilderness Resort. You might also want to steer clear of the Affection Section petting zoo in Rafiki's Planet Watch in Disney's Animal Kingdom park.

✔ Be aware that most of the restaurants featuring Asian cuisine use peanut oil in their cooking.

✔ Note that even though all Disney hotel rooms are nonsmoking (as of June 1, 2007), there are a few outdoor smoking areas. In addition, some people may smoke on their balconies.

✔ Avoid the "Heavenly Beds" at the Swan and Dolphin hotels, which may cause problems for those with down or feather allergies. Request hypoallergenic bedding prior to check-in or from Housekeeping.

✔ Be aware that the oils, lotions, and other products used in spa treatments at Walt Disney World and on the Disney Cruise Line often contain very concentrated levels of herb extracts. If you have plant allergies, you may experience a reaction.

✔ Avoid attractions that spray strong scents in your face like It's Tough to be a Bug! See chapter 5 for details.

Autism Spectrum Disorders (ASD)

Having a special challenge that is invisible to the casual observer can be difficult, to say the least. How can you convince folks that you deserve some special attention, when they can't *see* your problem? That's the challenge facing folks traveling with someone who has autism or one of its associated disorders. The good news is your trip can be a very magical and rewarding experience for all.

Your Icon:

U

(U=a<u>U</u>tism)
Look for this symbol in the book for more details

Planning Ahead

Remember to **plan, but be flexible**. Have some structure to your days, but also retain the flexibility to change at the last minute if needed. Read and learn about Walt Disney World, and develop a plan before your trip.

Reader Tip: "Make sure to schedule an off day. I always build in a day where we stay in the room, go to the pool, and just relax."—contributed by Kalli Mulchi

What you do (or don't do) **depends on the ASD traveler**, their schedule, and needs. Is the traveler sensory-seeking or sensory-defensive? Verbal?

Don't forget to also refer to the Fears section (pages 40–44).

As you begin to plan, **watch Disney movies** and the planning videos/ DVDs. These slowly introduce your traveler with ASD to Disney characters, parks, and resorts. Remember, the characters are large and can be imposing in the parks. Introduce your ASD traveler from a distance. Prepare them with stories, talk about the parks, and show pictures.

A Coping Strategy

"Our family has been to Walt Disney World four times with our daughter and our 8-year-old son, who is autistic. He can often be quite rigid and obsessive regarding the favorite attractions he wants to see and the specific sequence in which he wants our family to visit them. Sometimes attractions are being refurbished or are temporarily "down;" other times the family just wants to do something else! We can often avoid a meltdown by preparing him ahead of time. I use guidemaps from previous trips, pictures cut from outdated guidebooks, anything visual to tell a story. For example, I include photos of rides that he wants to ride in Fantasyland. Then I would include a few statements. For example: 'Sometimes I can't do the ride I want,' with an X across the picture of the attraction. Then, 'It's OK to feel sad,' with a picture of a sad face. Then, 'I will do something else that is fun,' with a picture of another attraction, and a happy face. We review the story ahead of time and reinforce it if the situation arises. This helps him to process the information and to respond in a way that is socially appropriate. In other words, no big temper-tantrums!"—contributed by Kathleen Kelly

---

Planning · Special Challenges · Getting There · Staying in Style · Touring · Feasting · Resources · Index

[U] Autism Spectrum Disorders (continued)

If at all possible, **travel in the off-season**, as there will be fewer crowds and cooler temperatures. Also, during the summer months, thunderstorms are the norm each afternoon. If the loud noise will adversely affect your traveler who has ASD, avoid June through August.

Here are several things to help make the vacation go more smoothly:

✔ **Handicapped Parking Permit/Tag**—If you plan to rent/drive a car in Florida, be sure to bring your permit from home. Not only will this grant you access to closer parking spaces at the theme parks and resorts, but you can also valet park for free at participating Disney resort hotels (but don't forget the gratuity).

✔ **Electrical outlet covers**—Some hotels will provide these upon request. Phone ahead and ask to speak to Housekeeping.

✔ **Earplugs**—The sounds in some attractions and fireworks shows can be quite loud and scary, as can the automatic toilets found in most Disney restrooms. Earplugs or headphones can muffle the noise. Some folks even suggest the ear protectors/sound reducers worn by construction workers.

✔ **Favorite snacks and foods**—Avoid potential problems when waiting for food or with a picky eater—be sure to have favorite snacks and foods with you. If necessary, make a grocery stop on your way to Disney. (We list nearby grocery stores on page 407.)

✔ **Favorite comfort "toy"** or item from home to ground the traveler who has ASD. Don't wash it before you leave unless absolutely necessary—it's good for it to smell like home. And don't forget to put your name and contact information on it in case it gets lost!

✔ **A sensory "grab bag"** filled with inexpensive, new toys that stimulate your child. A trip to a dollar store with $20 will do the trick.

✔ **A picture story/itinerary** with stickers that can be placed on things you've done. Share it with your traveler so they know what they will do each day. They can fill in the sections once you've gone on the attraction or dined at the restaurant.

✔ **Personal identification**—In the event the ASD traveler gets separated from you, be sure they are carrying identification and information as to where you are staying and how you can be contacted (see page 100). If you have a digital camera, take a photo each morning before you go out; it will be easier to remember clothing and appearance.

✔ **Penlight**—When attached to a lanyard around a person's neck, it can provide a small amount of light, which is reassuring on dark rides.

✔ **A collapsible stroller**, if the ASD traveler is small enough. You can rent a stroller at the parks, but then you still have to walk to your car or the bus stop and then to your room. Guest Relations can even issue a Guest Assistance Card (see pages 10-11) to allow you to use a stroller as a wheelchair. This means the stroller won't have to be parked outside the attraction, and your child won't have to walk as much. Many travelers with ASD find a stroller a safe haven that helps them cope with all the stimulation at Disney. Families also report that travelers with ASD particularly liked the firm pressure provided by the plastic seats in the park strollers at Disney's Animal Kingdom, Epcot, and the Magic Kingdom.

Bright Idea: Review our section on traveling with Fears on pages 40-44.

Will you drive or fly? If flying, notify the airline of any special needs well in advance of your journey. Also, request bulkhead seats (no one in front to kick, but remember, there's also no underseat storage). Be sure to let the attendant know your needs when you board. Bring extra facial wipes and keep up with medicine dosages and toilet routines. Once you arrive in Florida, consider a rental car. While Disney transportation works great, there are times you will be waiting for a bus, boat, or monorail. There will be much less waiting involved if you don't have to rely on Disney transportation and can just walk to your car. If you don't rent a car, consider a private car service (see page 109) to take you to Walt Disney World instead of a shuttle or Disney's Magical Express. You will have a much quieter environment with little or no wait time. Shuttles will often wait for a minimum number of passengers before they depart and make several stops before you reach your destination.

Bright Idea: Use airplane picture books to acquaint first-time flyers with air travel. Consider making a test run to the airport, too.

Dealing With Sensory Sensitivities

The sensory-rich environment of Disney, with so many sights, smells, sounds, tastes, and movement, can push even the most balanced people to the limit. People with ADHD, ASD, and other behavior issues need to be even more careful. Here are a few strategies that could make a big difference for any person:

✔ Give a bear hug to a child who craves deep pressure to calm them.
✔ Have sensory-defensive children wear new vacation clothes before leaving for the parks. For some, if clothes don't feel just right, the clothing can actually feel painful and itchy.
✔ Have members in your party run interference to make sure crowds don't brush against anyone who can't tolerate light touching.
✔ Find a safe place to sit and place cupped palms over eyes for a few minutes for a calming visual vacation.

                           —contributed by peer reviewer Sandy Bostwick

Side tabs: Planning · Special Challenges · Getting There · Staying in Style · Touring · Feasting · Resources · Index

[U] Autism Spectrum Disorders (continued)

Know the **check-in time** for your resort and plan your arrival accordingly. Disney resorts allow check-in at 3:00 pm and 4:00 pm. If you will want to unwind in your room upon arrival, but not wait for it to be ready, factor in these late afternoon times. If you arrive before check-in time, be sure to let the Front Desk know you're there anyway, as a sort of "pre-check-in." This is a good time to restate your special requests. During slow seasons, your room might be ready early.

When it comes to **choosing accommodations**, the deluxe resorts have less ambient noise to deal with. That said, you still need to travel within your means. When you make your hotel reservation, have the representative note that you need a room "away from all the activity" or "away from the themed pool." This will probably mean a long walk from the main check-in area, though. You might want to consider Pop Century (value resort), Port Orleans French Quarter (moderate resort), or one of the Epcot area resorts (Beach Club, Yacht Club, Swan, or Dolphin) for relatively subdued surroundings. Disney Vacation Club resorts are nice because even the studios offer kitchenettes with microwave, toaster, coffeemaker, and refrigerator, for those times when a quiet meal would be beneficial. Request a ground-floor room (rather than one with a balcony), if appropriate.

Bright Idea: Bring bells for the door to alert you when it's opened.

Check **restaurant menus** in advance for offerings. (Keep in mind menus/chefs can change at any time.) View most Disney menus at http://www.allears.net. Make advance reservations for any table-service restaurant you plan to visit. Minimize wait times by eating when or soon after the restaurant opens. You can always call and cancel if you change your mind. If there are special dietary requests, such as gluten-free foods, have this noted on your reservation. See chapter 6, starting on page 331.

Upon Your Arrival

Keep your regular routine. If your traveler who has ASD is normally up at 7:00 am, then that's when you should get up (you may want to adjust this to reflect your home time zone). If they are used to eating at specific times, do your best to keep that schedule.

Consider whether a **Guest Assistance Card** (see pages 10–11) can provide necessary accommodations for your special needs traveler.

Use FASTPASS at the parks—we can't stress this enough. It will significantly reduce the time you wait in line! One important note, however—some with ASD will not understand why they got in line to get a FASTPASS and then left without riding. Have one member of your group get all the FASTPASSes.

Be sure all members of your party know that once they are seated in a ride, they **must stay seated until the ride is fully completed**. They cannot stand or exit until the ride is over and fully stopped. In theater settings, sit at the end of a row in case you need to make a quick exit.

At **character meet and greets**, show the attending cast member your Guest Assistance Card, if you have one. Ask if you can wait your turn in the shade or away from the crowd.

If you are early risers, morning **Extra Magic Hours** (see page 119) save you time in lines and also offer a cooler time of day to tour the parks.

Physical issues? You'll do a lot of walking. If your traveler with ASD tires easily, **rent a wheelchair or stroller**, depending on their age.

Each theme park has a **First Aid Station**—if you need a quiet place, see if they have a room you can use. See page 206 for more information.

There are **companion restrooms** located throughout each theme park. Look for these especially if you need a place to change diapers or are especially sensitive to sounds. Most, but not all, have changing tables at counter height and no longer than four feet. For locations, see chapter 5.

Ask the cast member outside each attraction about noise levels, ceiling fans, flashing lights, or other **potential problems**. Also ask for seating recommendations. If you want to be near an exit, be the first to go down the row in the theaters.

Reader Tip: "Many autism spectrum children are sensory-seeking, not just defensive. I've traveled with two very different autism spectrum kids and, for both, Big Thunder Mountain Railroad was their favorite. Your child's limitations should guide you."—contributed by Alissa Tschetter-Siedschlaw

Take breaks back at your hotel—don't hesitate to leave while everyone is still going strong. The key is not to let things go too long. Time at the pool or resting in the room works wonders for everyone! However, it's important to know what works best for your traveler. Some on the autism spectrum find transitioning from one situation to another difficult. As readers Sam and Spring Slagle note: "We do not park hop or go back to our lodging in the middle of the day. Our son would be too hung up on the fact that we were leaving the place he was enjoying."

Disney resorts can provide **child bed rails** at no additional cost.

Manipulatives found in certain areas of Disney's Animal Kingdom and Epcot can **provide wonderful tactile stimulation**.

Having dinner in the parks or resort? If it won't disrupt your routine too much, **eat early** (around 4:00 pm) so you don't have long waits.

Planning · Special Challenges · Getting There · Staying in Style · Touring · Feasting · Resources · Index

Planning

Special Challenges

Getting There

Staying in Style

Touring

Feasting

Resources

Index

[U] Autism Spectrum Disorders (continued)

Know where the gardens and **quiet places** are in the parks (see chapter 5). Most people either don't know where they are or avoid them. For you, these can be a great respite. Quiet spots at the resorts are in chapter 4.

Consider **resort character meals** for Disney character interaction instead of the "meets" in the theme parks. At the parks, you can encounter crowds and long waits, especially for the more popular characters. At a character meal, the characters visit each table, without lines or jostling. Once the characters come to your table, their attention can be directed toward you. However, if your traveler is sensitive to loud noises, you may want to avoid character meals, as they can be extremely noisy and crowded. See character meals, starting on page 381.

The **monorail, buses, and boats can be very crowded** or standing room only, especially at park opening and closing. In crowded conditions, you may need to sit or stand beside strangers.

Reader Tip: "I would like to suggest you try Pal Mickey (a speaking, plush Mickey toy available at Walt Disney World) for any child with autism. My son normally 'self-stims' (e.g., hand flapping) when he is overstimulated or excited. I was amazed when I noticed that, after getting Pal Mickey, he was no longer stimming. We bought a bottle strap and used it to hang Mickey around his neck. He was so busy trying to feel Mickey wiggle and listening for him to talk that he was no longer stimming. I was so excited! Just having his own Mickey to hold seemed to give him some needed security."–contributed by Carrie Bass

---

What Are Autism Spectrum Disorders (ASD)?

Autism Spectrum Disorders, also known as Pervasive Developmental Disorders (PDDs), cause impairments in thinking, feeling, language, and the ability to relate socially. They encompass a wide range of symptoms from mild to severe and include diagnoses such as autism or Asperger's syndrome. Unlike people with noticeable physical problems, a person who has ASD may not initially appear any different than one who does not have ASD.

Behaviors that are common to someone who has ASD can include repetitive movements (such as rocking), abnormal responses to sounds and touch, difficulty initiating or maintaining a conversation, tantrums, hitting themselves, and laughing or crying for no apparent reason. These behaviors in a public setting can cause occasional awkwardness, yet most families with a member who has ASD have successful and magical trips to Walt Disney World.

Bright Idea: If you are concerned about others who may make comments on your traveler's behavior, considering printing out small cards that explain autism and your child's condition. Then just hand out a card when necessary. You can get preprinted cards at http://www.autism-society.org.

IN FOCUS: Traveling With Autism

Several years ago, 13-year-old Joey's autism was one of the severest forms, says his mom, peer reviewer Betsy Hicks. He was in horrible pain and extremely self-abusive. Today, after a journey of healing with a holistic approach and many dietary restrictions, Joey is happier and healthier than ever, although his communication is still limited. And visits to Walt Disney World and sailings on the Disney Cruise Line over the last four years have been an important ingredient in his life.

"Joey comes alive at Disney," says Betsy. "He knows every corner and where every ride and show is at all four parks and both water parks. Of course, sometimes that can be a problem, say if something that he likes changes or isn't there any more, but we cope with that when we have to."

© Betsy Hicks

Because of the family's strict diet, Betsy notes that Walt Disney World is the only place she feels dining out is safe. "It helps create a stress-free vacation," she adds.

To further reduce the stress of traveling with a child on the autism spectrum, Hicks offers the following advice:

Betsy and Joey on Cinderella's Golden Carrousel

✔ Start with a personalized story book: I buy cheap scrapbooks and make copies of Disney photos from the Internet or from old brochures. I make "play by play" pages of what's next. I try to keep it vague enough for change, but guided enough to help him understand what comes next. Our last trip involved stopping to visit friends in Clearwater at the beach before going to Disney. The book, helped him understand that he would see Mickey soon. In the back of the book, I make calendars that extend three months prior to the trip. He crosses off each day leading to our vacation during his therapy session. This helps build excitement and teaches patience.

✔ Because children with autism may have difficulty sleeping with all of the excitement, check with your doctor if melatonin is an option. Melatonin is a natural sleep inducer, but it only works for about four hours. I find this invaluable when we travel as being in a different bed, Joey will often wake at 2:00 am. The melatonin puts him back to sleep just long enough to let everyone get a good night's rest and not feel groggy in the morning.

✔ Remember that "fun perspectives" change considerably with autism. For example, it was 3:00 pm and the parade at the Magic Kingdom was just beginning. How wonderful for my daughters, but not for Joey. He enjoys the evening parade, but he's not exceptionally interested in the day ones. Solution? It's all in positioning. What does Joey love to watch? The boats splashing as they come down Splash Mountain. We positioned ourselves on a bridge where the girls could see the parade and Joey could watch the boats. Everyone was happy.

✔ Don't rush. Remember that Walt Disney World is not going anywhere. If you see a quarter of each park and spend the rest of the day at your hotel pool or beach, don't feel cheated. It's better to have a short, enjoyable time than a long, miserable time. This makes returning all the more pleasant.

And, Hicks notes, they will definitely return, since a dose of Disney seems to be terrific medicine for Joey. "When we returned after our last vacation," Hicks notes, "his teacher wrote a long note about how we should take Joey to Disney every weekend, because his learning skills rose considerably."

Chronic Fatigue Syndrome/ Fibromyalgia

Chronic fatigue syndrome, fibromyalgia, and other similar conditions, like rheumatoid arthritis, all have one common symptom—a severe feeling of being tired that has been going on for months. Additional symptoms may include muscle aches, joint pain, and tender body points. But even if you experience these symptoms, a trip to Walt Disney World can still be fun and fulfilling if you remember several important things.

Your Icon:

(C=Chronic)
Look for this symbol in the book for more details

You probably already know the steps you need to take to deal with your symptoms: Eat well-balanced meals, get plenty of rest, and pace yourself physically, emotionally, and intellectually. This will be especially important to remember when touring Disney's theme parks, as there are so many things to look at and long distances to travel. Don't even try to do it all. You won't be able to and you'll just be miserable!

Planning Ahead

As you plan your vacation, consider going during the **cooler months** with lower attendance, like January and early February or early December. Heat just makes fatigue that much worse.

If you fly to Florida, try to book either **nonstop flights** or flights with sufficient layover so you don't have to rush from gate to gate. You can also request wheelchair assistance in traveling from the airport check-in area to the gate and on return. Most airlines will offer preboarding for those needing assistance or extra time. Take advantage of this so you don't have to stand for long periods or struggle to get through the crowded aisles. Be sure to get up and stretch. If you are going to have carry-on luggage, make sure it's on wheels. Ask for assistance getting it in the overhead bin when you board the plane.

If you drive, be sure to factor in **lots of stops** so you can walk around and reduce stiffness in your legs.

When reserving a hotel, request a **room near the elevator** or on the ground floor as well as one that is handicap accessible, if necessary.

Be sure to **bring all medications**, doctors' names and numbers, and a summary of your medical history in case of delays or layovers.

Consider whether a **Guest Assistance Card** (see pages 10–11) can provide necessary accommodations for you or your special traveler.

Consider a **wheelchair or ECV** if you have concerns about stamina. There is a lot of walking at Walt Disney World, both at the theme parks and at the Disney resorts. Renting an ECV/wheelchair can save energy for the attractions. You may also want to consider renting an ECV from a local firm so that you have the wheels with you at the resorts, in the parking lots, etc. Disney buses accommodate wheelchairs and ECVs. See pages 211–213.

Factor in **midday breaks** at your resort. For convenience, we recommend staying at a Disney resort. Consider a soak in the hot tub, or a swim in one of the pools, most of which are heated.

Remember that each theme park has a **First Aid Station** where you can cool off and lie down for a while if you feel overly fatigued. See page 206 for First Aid Station information.

Try to elevate your hands and pump your fists occasionally to avoid pooling of fluids and resulting stiffness and discomfort. Avoid too much salt.

PassPorter Picks

✔ Use **FASTPASS** whenever possible to avoid long waits in line. We note the attractions with FASTPASS in chapter 5.

✔ Take advantage of **Extra Magic Hours**, when one park opens early or stays open late for Disney resort guests. Crowds are often lower, particularly in the mornings, so lines are usually shorter.

✔ Visit popular attractions during **parade times** to avoid long queues.

✔ Make **advance dining reservations**, especially for popular places, to avoid long waits. Dining at off-peak times decreases wait times also.

PassPorter Pans

✔ Unless you have a wheelchair or ECV, avoid attractions with **limited or no seating**, like the 360-degree CircleVision films, which require you to stand for the duration. Review the Attraction Seating Types on page 207.

✔ Avoid long days; **conserve your energy**—going to evening Extra Magic Hours might not be a good idea if you have an early morning planned.

✔ Avoid riding with someone on rides whose momentum may cause them to slide to one side of the car or another, like Big Thunder Mountain Railroad or Primeval Whirl. Instead, consider **riding solo**.

✔ Rides that are jarring can **cause excess pain** and could start a flare-up. Check out the ride or have someone ride it first to check movement.

Diet

Just because you are on vacation doesn't mean you have to change the way you eat. Whether your special dietary needs are lifestyle choices (like low-fat, low-carb, vegetarian, or vegan), health-related (low sodium, no sugar added/diabetic, allergies to fish, nuts, eggs, dairy products, wheat gluten), or religious (kosher/halal), all Walt Disney World table-service restaurants that accept advance reservations (see chapter 6 for details) can **meet your needs**, with many chefs treating your special requests as an opportunity to delight and amaze you.

Your Icon:

D

(D=Diet)
Look for this symbol in the book for more details

Planning Ahead

If you or someone in your party has special dietary needs, make advance reservations by calling **407-WDW-DINE** (407-939-3463) before you leave for your trip. When you do, alert the cast member to your special dietary requests, and they will make a note on the file.

The more time you give the Disney chefs to prepare, the better. Disney restaurants request **72 hours' advance notice**, so that they can plan for your special requirements. If you forget, though, don't despair! Often, if you discuss your issues with your server, you will still be able to dine without breaking your regimen. Servers will often bring a chef out from the kitchen to talk with you personally.

For **dinner shows** like Hoop Dee Doo or Spirit of Aloha Dinner, 24-hour notice is required. Call 407-WDW-DINE as soon as you reach the Orlando area to confirm that your special request is noted on your reservation.

Reader Tip: "My daughter is on a very strict gluten-free, dairy-free diet. To plan out our meals, I ordered the free Disney maps from Disney's web site. I also e-mailed the Magic Kingdom special diets department (wdwmkspecialdiets@email.disney.com). The reply I got came with a listing of the foods we could eat that were certified GF/CF throughout the parks and resorts. This gave me the restaurants, samples of foods, ideas for snacks on Main Street, and other great tips."—contributed by Laura Schmitt

If you are staying **off Disney property**, you can still make special requests of Disney restaurants. Just call the main Walt Disney World switchboard (407-824-2222) and ask to be connected to the specific restaurant.

Bright Idea: If you have a sugar substitute or other ingredient preference, bring a supply. There's no guarantee you'll find your favorites on Disney property.

··>

Upon Your Arrival

Once you arrive in Orlando, if you are staying at a Disney resort hotel, **speak to a cast member** at the resort's Lobby Concierge desk to let them know again what your specific needs are, and request that they call the restaurant for you. The more specific and individual your needs are, the more lead time the restaurant will require. Even with advance notice, however, sometimes the message doesn't get to the right chef. Be sure to talk with your server at the restaurant, who should clue in the chef.

If you have other specific concerns, you can also call the **executive chefs** or Food and Beverage managers at the theme parks directly at the telephone numbers listed below. If no one is available when you call, leave a message and a telephone number so they can get back to you.

> Magic Kingdom: 407-824-5967
> Epcot: 407-560-6395
> Disney-MGM Studios: 407-560-3551
> Disney's Animal Kingdom: 407-938-3288

You can also **obtain restaurant phone numbers** when you make advance reservations or by calling the main switchboard at 407-824-2222.

Bright Idea: Even if you've gotten a listing of ingredients or menus from Disney from previous visits, be sure to check prior to each trip—menus, ingredients, and offerings change often.

Kosher meals can be provided with 24 hours' advance notice at most table-service restaurants. A credit card is required to guarantee the order but will not be charged unless the reservation is canceled within 24 hours or if the party is a no-show. Kosher items are *not* available at these restaurants: the Grand Floridian's Garden View Afternoon Tea, House of Blues, Planet Hollywood, Fulton's Crab House, Portobello Yacht Club, and Rainforest Café. The table-service restaurants at the Swan and Dolphin (Gulliver's Grill, Il Mulino, Shula's Steakhouse, Todd English's bluezoo, and Fresh) do not normally have kosher meals on hand, but call at least 24 hours in advance to inquire whether it's possible to order them. Kosher meals are available without advance notice at these counter-service locations in the resorts and theme parks: Cosmic Ray's at the Magic Kingdom, the food courts at Disney's All-Star Resorts and Pop Century, Riverside Mill Food at Port Orleans Riverside, Liberty Inn at Epcot, Pizzafari at Disney's Animal Kingdom, and the ABC Commissary at Disney-MGM Studios.

Planning
Special Challenges
Getting There
Staying in Style
Touring
Feasting
Resources
Index

[D] Diet (continued)

If you're not planning on eating every meal out, you can **pick up groceries** with items that conform to your diet in a number of places. For example, Gooding's carries Hebrew National brand kosher hot dogs. Lactose-intolerant folks can find lactose-free milk (Lactaid) in some resort convenience stores, but not much else. Your best bet is to visit a nearby grocery store, such as Winn Dixie, or ship items to your hotel in advance.

Bright Idea: If you have specific food allergies or dietary concerns, you may bring your own small snack items into the parks.

Not all restaurants offer sugar-free desserts, or they may have a very **limited choice**. Some spots only have a no-sugar-added brownie as an option. A cheese platter can be a good dessert substitute.

Other pointers contributed by Leanne Phelps, who has several family members with severe food allergies:

✔ **Don't be afraid of buffets**, wondering what ingredients are involved and what cross-contamination might have occurred. Chefs at buffet restaurants are usually just as willing to make special meals as those at table-service restaurants. When you're seated, ask to speak to a chef. Sometimes a chef will point out items from the buffet that you can eat without worry, but usually he or she will ask what types of foods you are interested in and bring you specially prepared food. While you may have to be a little patient, it will be worth the wait.

✔ **Plan for a little extra time**. Even when the restaurants have been notified ahead of time of your dietary need (and especially when they aren't), special meals often take longer to prepare.

✔ **Ask the chef for suggestions**. If you have a special dietary need, you can always ask if a certain menu item could be prepared to meet your needs. However, if you don't have a particular desire, you can ask a chef for ideas. Just mention what ingredients you must avoid.

✔ If you plan to eat often at your **resort's food court**, call in advance to see what accommodations can be made for you. Unlike most food courts in malls and airports, Disney resort hotel food courts can be very accommodating for special diets. Don't hesitate to ask if a Mickey waffle can be made gluten-free or a if dessert can be made sugar-free—many times the answer is yes. If you encounter a cast member who doesn't understand your request, ask to speak to the food court manager on duty.

✔ Some travelers require their food to be **extremely fresh** to avoid bacteria that grows on food that sits for any length of time. If this applies to you, be sure to tell your server. If you would like something from a fast food cart or stand, be very specific about this request, and you can usually watch them prepare your burger or other item on the spot.

Passporter Picks

✔ Even when you don't give advance notice, **servers and chefs** try hard to be accommodating and can be remarkably well-informed. If you have any questions or concerns about the ingredients or preparation of a regular menu item or the availablility of a substitution, don't hesitate to ask your server.

© Deb Wills

✔ Some Disney restaurants are **more accommodating** than others when it comes to special requests. We've found Boma (Disney's Animal Kingdom Lodge), Kona Café (Polynesian Resort), 1900 Park Fare (Grand Floridian), and '50s Prime Time (Disney-MGM Studios) to be especially agreeable to requests for vegetarian/ vegan dishes. Many resort restaurants have come up with excellent no-sugar-added or sugar-free desserts on short notice, too.

Disney chef Tjetjep ("TJ") at Boma

PassPorter Pans

✔ If you're **allergic to seafood**, avoid the following restaurants, which feature primarily seafood on their menus: Flying Fish Café (BoardWalk); Fulton's Crab House (Pleasure Island); Coral Reef (Future World in Epcot); Yorkshire County Fish Shop (United Kingdom in Epcot); Akershus Royal Banquet Hall (Norway in Epcot); Kimono's (Walt Disney World Swan); and Todd English's bluezoo (Walt Disney World Dolphin). While seafood alternatives are often available, cross-contamination is a potential concern.

✔ If you have a **peanut allergy**, avoid the Asian restaurants on property, which tend to use peanut oil in their cooking: the table service restaurants in the Japan pavilion, Yakitori House, Nine Dragons, Lotus Blossom Café (all in Epcot's World Showcase), Tomorrowland Terrace Noodle Station, and Kimono's. Also be careful of Kona Café and 'Ohana in the Polynesian Resort, and the sections of some food courts that serve Asian meals, such as Pepper Market, Pop Century, and Sunshine Seasons (The Land).

Be sure to read chapter 6 on dining, which contains a wealth of information on special diets.

Down Syndrome, Fragile X, and Other Cognitive Disabilities

As we have said throughout this chapter, no matter what your ability or challenge, Disney offers something for everyone. The traveler with Down Syndrome, Fragile X, or other cognitive disabilities is no different.

Because these conditions manifest themselves in so many ways, with such a wide variety of symptoms, we attempt to provide you with general information and tips that help you with your trip. Just remember, even if you aren't able to do or see everything you want to, the magic touches everyone. And a smile on the face of your special traveler will be worth all the planning for your trip to Disney.

Your Icon:

(I=Intellectual)
Look for this symbol in the book for more details

Planning Ahead

Travelers with cognitive disabilities may have **other issues** to take into consideration, including communication and social skills concerns, as well as personal hygiene issues. We recommend that you read the sections on Allergies and Asthma, Autism Spectrum Disorders, Heart Health, Mobility, Ongoing Medical Treatment, and Diet—they may be applicable to your situation. In addition, other sections may also apply—you might want to take the time to browse through the entire chapter.

In all likelihood, a traveler with cognitive disabilities will need closer supervision and guidance while away from home. While one person may have slight difficulty thinking and communicating, another may face major challenges with basic self-care and even physical issues. You really will need to **know the abilities and limitations of everyone** traveling with you ... even yourself!

We say many times throughout this book, but it bears repeating: If at all possible, **travel in the off-season**, as there will be cooler temperatures and lower crowds!

Be sure to **do your research** prior to the trip. Have a good idea of attractions that will and won't be good matches for the special needs traveler.

Bright Idea: Taking anyone out of his or her normal routine and environment can be unsettling. This is especially true for travelers with special challenges. Be aware that old issues thought to be resolved may resurface. To help combat this, before you leave home, practice or role-play various situations that may occur.—contributed by Robert Feder

Perhaps the most important area to take care of is **personal identification**. In the event that members of your group get separated, be sure they not only have a waterproof ID on them, but information as to where you are staying and how you can be contacted. Have a plan in place in case you are separated so you can spring into action and not panic should the situation arise. We offer more details on personal identification on page 100.

Bright Idea: If you have a digital camera or camera phone, take a photo each morning before you go out; it'll be easier to remember clothing and appearance.

If **fatigue and muscle weakness** are a concern, request a room near the elevator or close to the parking lot or bus stop when you make a hotel reservation.

Bring all **medications, doctors' names and numbers, and a summary** of your medical history in case of delays or layovers.

Consider whether a **Guest Assistance Card** (see pages 10–11) can provide necessary accommodations for your special traveler.

Upon Your Arrival

Touring Walt Disney World can involve long days of walking and waiting in lines. **Don't try to do it all**. You simply can't, and trying to do everything will only lead to frustration. Consider mobility issues—if a stroller or wheelchair will help you enjoy more of the day, don't hesitate to rent one (see page 211–213).

If you rely on **Disney transportation**, keep in mind that it can take a long time to get from point A to point B. Plan accordingly. Don't wait until someone has a meltdown or gets overtired and the whole group gets cranky. If one person needs to head back to the room, do it! You'll be glad you did!

There are **many wide open spaces** around Walt Disney World, with lots of people coming and going—lots of characters, colors, and sounds to offer major distractions. Be on alert especially during times when it's easiest to become separated from your group: during parades, when large theater attractions let out, and near character meet and greets.

Planning

Special Challenges

Getting There

Staying in Style

Touring

Feasting

Resources

Index

Fears

Fears evoke unpleasant feelings. Fear of the dark, spiders, heights, crowds, mice, flying, water, coasters; whatever it is, if it makes you feel uneasy, it might even trigger an anxiety attack. A Walt Disney World vacation is supposed to be magical and relaxing—the last thing you want is to be "surprised" by something that makes you feel uncomfortable or anxious.

Your Icon:

F

(F=Fears)
Look for this symbol in the book for more details

Although Walt Disney World is as friendly a place as you can imagine, the special effects or nature of certain attractions may present conditions or objects that make you fearful. Understandably, you want to avoid these situations. Knowledge is your best tool! Research the places you'll visit and things you'll experience so that there are no scary surprises. Here are some tips for doing just that:

Planning Ahead

Some attractions come right out and tell you they might scare you. There are **warning signs** outside the entrance, so heed them! We mention anything that you might want to know about in our individual attraction descriptions in chapter 5.

© Deb Wills

If you or the person who experiences fears is under the care of a **therapist**, be sure to discuss expectations and practice self-talk or calming strategies.

Warning sign

Important Note: Never coerce anyone (adult or child) to go on an attraction. If there is one sure vacation mood-killer, that's it. You can always use the Rider Switch option (see page 204), or consider shopping or slurping on a Mickey bar while the rest of the group sees the attraction.

When in doubt, **ask a cast member about the attraction**. He or she can answer your questions about what you'll find inside the turnstiles. You could also ask those who are exiting the ride for their opinions.

Traveling with others? Have someone you trust **experience the attraction** without you and then report back. You may find it is something you want to try, or it will confirm that you don't. Remember, once you're on a ride vehicle, you are there for the duration. You can't stop the ride midway because you want to get off.

Bright Idea: Almost every attraction and all thrill rides have an "out" before you get on the actual attraction. This allows you to see the preshow and get a feel for the special Disney theming without actually experiencing the ride itself. Don't hesitate to tell the cast member you do not wish to ride. Some great preshows include the Tower of Terror (which could also be scary and dark with thunder) and Rock 'n' Roller Coaster. It's easy enough to see these preshows, then exit.

Remember that sometimes things others find innocent may **terrify you** or your fearful child. For example, when Deb Koma's son was little, he noticed the glowing eyes of the tiger in the tunnel of the Jungle Cruise ride—that was enough to scare him on this very gentle, funny ride. And peer reviewer Sandy Bostwick knows of one child who attended Mickey's Not-So-Scary Halloween Party on the first day of her vacation, then was afraid of everything for the rest of the trip.

Whatever you do, don't make the mistake of riding the Magic Kingdom's Snow White's Scary Adventures with youngsters early in your trip. They will think that it is a fun princess ride and it is **not**—it's dark and quite scary. Some young children are frightened and they will then **associate any ride** that's dark or in a building with their scary experience and refuse to go on another. Trust us on this one!

Concerned with crowds? Definitely travel in the off-season. Enter theaters first or last so you are not in the midst of several hundred people. Being last is generally easier, as you don't have to fight the crowds trying to get the "best seat" and you can exit after almost everyone has left.

Claustrophobic? There are certain areas/rides that you should avoid—like the sound booths at Sounds Dangerous and Conservation Station, the Tower of Terror, Mission: SPACE, the inside waiting areas at Haunted Mansion, and It's Tough to be a Bug. We note these areas in our individual descriptions in chapter 5.

The 3-D presentations in each theme park have special tactile effects that range from a **spray of water** to the sensation of something running over your feet. In addition, special 3-D glasses are provided to wear during the show. If the 3-D effects bother you or a companion, don't wear (or remove) the special glasses. If you hold your child on your lap, he/she will avoid some but not all of the effects—you'll still get sprayed with water, for example.

Not all coasters are the same in intensity or effects. While Rock 'n' Roller Coaster and its three loops in the dark might make you queasy (it does Deb Wills), Big Thunder Mountain Railroad is more family-friendly and might fit the bill for you just fine! But, as peer reviewer Chet McDoniel notes, "On the other hand, since I am unable to hold on effectively in a ride like Big Thunder Mountain, Rock 'n' Roller Coaster is a much less scary attraction for me—the harness holds me well in place."

Planning

Special Challenges

Getting There

Staying in Style

Touring

Feasting

Resources

Index

[F] Fears (continued)

While each of the nighttime shows has lots of fireworks (and bangs), you can still enjoy the show with a lower volume if you **use earplugs** (see page 26) or **watch** from an alternate location. For instance, the Magic Kingdom fireworks can be viewed from any of the Magic Kingdom monorail resort beaches or from a rented pontoon boat. The higher Epcot fireworks can be seen from several of the Epcot resorts, again with lower volume.

Sometimes you can see the attraction itself **without getting on it** to help in your decision whether to ride or not. The big drop on Splash Mountain is clearly visible from the bridge in Frontierland. Continue past the entrance for plenty of viewing areas for Big Thunder Mountain Railroad. Primeval Whirl at Disney's Animal Kingdom is outside, too.

The Disney theme park experience includes fantastic entertainment. Some is improvisational and the cast engages the audience. In other attractions, **audience participation** is possible. For the introverted or shy, we have noted these in the specific attractions/pavilions in chapter 5.

At Disney's Animal Kingdom, cast members sometimes carry around glass containers with **small animals**, insects, spiders, or snakes. This is especially true during the first hour or so the park is open in the Oasis and Discovery Island areas. Cast members with the containers do not approach you; they wait for you to come to them. There are also exhibits in Disney's Animal Kingdom with live small animals. We have so noted in the specific attractions in chapter 5.

© Deb Wills

A cast member with an insect in a glass case

Guests who **don't want to get wet** should stay away from Splash Mountain at the Magic Kingdom and Kali River Rapids at Disney's Animal Kingdom, and be aware that some rides either spray/mist water or have a water component that might get you damp (like Voyage of the Little Mermaid and Honey, I Shrunk the Audience). These are noted in chapter 5.

Fear of water? Avoid the Friendship boats, ferry boats, and other boat transportation. Attractions with water include Pirates of the Caribbean, "it's a small world," The Gran Fiesta Tour Starring the Three Caballeros, Maelstrom, The Seas With Nemo and Friends, Living With the Land, Splash Mountain, and Kali River Rapids.

Service animals are discussed on page 12.

Upon Your Arrival

If the attraction in question is in a theater or if you are "crowd-phobic," try to **sit near an exit** or at the end of the row to make exiting easier.

Remember that once you are on a ride, you **must stay seated** until the ride stops completely—you can not stand or exit until the ride is over.

Bear in mind that this is Florida, and **bugs and small lizards** are virtually everywhere outside. In May and September, tiny "love bugs" (so called because there often two or more mating as they fly) are everywhere—they don't bite or sting, but they can bother the bug-wary.

Certain **restaurants can also present situations** that conjure up particular fears. We note them in our individual restaurant descriptions in chapter 6, but here are a few specific tips:

✔ Be aware of places like the Rainforest Café and Sci-Fi Dine-In Theater, which have scary sound and visual effects. If you have a fear of fire, use caution when going to the Spirit of Aloha dinner or the open cooking grill at 'Ohana, both at the Polynesian Resort. There are other restaurants that have showcase open fires—we note them in chapter 6.

✔ Shy guests might avoid '50s Prime Time Cafe, Whispering Canyon, or 'Ohana, where your server might engage you in some tomfoolery!

✔ If you have fear of bugs and lizards, you might want to avoid Pizzafari, which has depictions of these creatures throughout the seating areas. There are also a lot of bugs in "It's Tough to be a Bug." For the squeamish, note that there's a skeleton in Restaurantosaurus.

✔ If you're claustrophobic, avoid small, crowded places like Plaza Restaurant (Magic Kingdom) and Beaches & Cream (Yacht & Beach Club).

✔ If you're afraid of heights, don't sit near the window at the California Grill (Contemporary) or ride the monorail.

✔ If you have a problem with the dark, avoid very dark restaurants like San Angel Inn (Epcot), Sci-Fi Dine-In (Disney-MGM Studios), and Rainforest Café (Animal Kingdom and Downtown Disney).

✔ If you or someone in your group has a fear of ceiling fans, be aware that many restaurants (and waiting areas) have them.

✔ If you have a fear of birds, avoid Flights of Wonder, Rafiki's Planet Watch, the aviary areas of Pangani Forest Exploration Trail, and the Maharajah Jungle Trek in Disney's Animal Kingdom. Also avoid eating outdoors, particularly around Casey's Corner and near the water in the Magic Kingdom, around World Showcase Lagoon in Epcot, and along the BoardWalk.

[F] Fears (continued)

Obvious fear triggers at both Blizzard Beach and Typhoon Lagoon water parks are the **very fast**, **very high slides and raft rides**. We note other fear factors in our individual descriptions starting on page 305.

DisneyQuest, located in Downtown Disney, has potential scare factors, as does Cirque du Soleil. Much of the action in DisneyQuest's games takes place in **darkened settings**, like Pirates of the Caribbean: Battle for Buccaneer Gold and Buzz Lightyear's Astroblasters. In addition, DisneyQuest has no windows, which might lead to a feeling of claustrophobia. La Nouba, Cirque du Soleil's presentation at West Side, also takes place in a darkened theater. Many of the acts performed during this show are breathtaking, and many involve performers suspended or climbing to great heights. Be aware that Epcot's IllumiNations evening show has huge fireballs in the opening sequence—you can even feel the heat from many viewing areas.

At Pleasure Island, avoid Adventurers Club's main areas (stay upstairs) and Comedy Warehouse's wall with telephones **if you're very shy**.

At the resorts, there are also some potentially scary situations, which we note in chapter 4. Remember to request a room on the lower level when booking if you have **a fear of heights**.

At Fort Wilderness, there are lots of bugs, lizards, and raccoons **walking around**. Both Fort Wilderness and Port Orleans are known to have the occasional gator, but Disney does take steps to control them.

Fear of Giant Mice?

Your favorite Disney characters will come to life as you venture around the theme parks. But while some children (and possibly some adults) eagerly embrace these walk-around characters, others are just as likely to run screaming in the opposite direction. A little work before you encounter any characters may help you avoid the fear and intimidation your child will feel when they realize those little figures of Goofy and Baloo on the television screen are really six feet tall in person.

✔ Talk to your child about the possibility of meeting the characters **before you stand in line** at a character meet-and-greet location. Discuss whether they want to approach the characters or if they'd prefer to enjoy them from afar.

✔ Remind your child that the characters would not hurt them and that **you will be right beside them**.

✔ **If you think it will help**, tell your child that the character is really just a normal person in a costume, pretending to be someone else. (Do this out of earshot of others—you don't want to spoil the magic for anyone!)

✔ For some children, even these reassurances aren't enough—their imaginations are just too good. (Just ask Deb Koma how her son was!) **Tell your child that it will be okay** if they choose to not meet with any characters up close, and mean it! Yes, it's disappointing, but maybe by your next trip, your little one will be ready to meet and greet everyone from sweet Cinderella to cruel old Cruella de Vil.

Foreign Language

It's a Small World, at least that's what the beloved Walt Disney World Fantasyland attraction tells us. And, whether your native language is French, German, Spanish, Japanese, or Portuguese, Disney works to make it even smaller by offering international visitors a number of special aids.

Planning Ahead

The special treatment begins as you start to plan your vacation—**Disney translates its web site** into a number of languages geared toward a variety of cultures:

Your Icon:

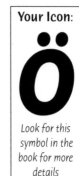

Look for this symbol in the book for more details

For French-speaking visitors:
http://www.disney.ca/vacations/disneyworld/francais

For Spanish-speaking visitors:
http://www.disneylatino.com/disneyvacaciones/waltdisneyworld

For Portuguese-speaking visitors:
http://www.disney.com.br/DisneyViagens/waltdisneyworld/index.html

For Japanese-speaking visitors:
http://www.disney.co.jp/usparks/wdw/index.html

For English-speaking visitors from the United Kingdom:
http://www.disney.co.uk/usa-resorts/waltdisneyworld

For English-speaking visitors from Canada:
http://www.disney.ca/vacations/disneyworld

Once you reach your resort, cast members are ready to provide you with information **in your native tongue**.

International guidemaps

Bright Idea: The Walt Disney World Swan and Dolphin, located within walking distance of Epcot, also have a web site that can be viewed in English, French, Spanish, Portuguese, German, Italian, and Japanese. It not only features the amenities of these two hotels, but information on Walt Disney World attractions and the Orlando area. Visit it at http://www.swandolphin.com.

Reader Tip: "I recently brought my in-laws from Japan to Walt Disney World for the first time. Advance research was my best friend."—contributed by peer reviewer Masayo Kano

[Ö] Foreign Language (continued)

Upon Your Arrival

Begin a visit to each theme park, water park, or Downtown Disney with a stop at **Guest Relations**. Indicated on the theme park guidemaps by a blue "i" symbol, Guest Relations is open during regular park hours and can supply international visitors with a wide range of information. Some cast members are fluent in a variety of languages and will be able to help international guests purchase tickets and make advance reservations dining or other arrangements.

Bright Idea: Look closely at the oval name badges worn by every cast member in the parks and at the resorts. If a cast member is fluent in a language other than English, the name badge will state it.

Guest Relations also has **guidemaps of the parks** in a number of different languages: Spanish, French, Portuguese, German, and Japanese.

Cast name badge with language

International guests can also take advantage of **"Ears to the World" Personal Translator Units**. These are portable devices that provide synchronized, translated narration of the scripts of certain attractions into French, German, Portuguese, Japanese, or Spanish. The units resemble lightweight portable cassette players that can be carried around your neck with headphones. The units are available at no extra charge (although there is a $100 refundable deposit) at Guest Relations in the theme parks. Attractions with this feature include The Circle of Life, Ellen's Energy Adventure, and The American Adventure (Epcot); Hall of Presidents (the Magic Kingdom); and Walt Disney: One Man's Dream (Disney-MGM Studios). We indicate support for this feature in our individual attraction descriptions in chapter 5.

If you'd like personalized attention, guided tours offered in various languages can be arranged through Guest Relations. If you want to be a bit more independent, there are **tape-recorded walking tours** available in a variety of languages in the Magic Kingdom and Epcot—the equipment may be rented from the theme park's Guest Relations office for a small fee with $100 refundable deposit.

For another type of tour, Spanish-speaking guests can buy a Spanish-speaking **Pal Mickey**, a 10-inch plush Mickey Mouse that talks. (He's also available in English.) Using wireless technology, Pal Mickey points out interesting trivia, reminds you of parade times, and offers tips on where to watch fireworks, among other things. Pal Mickey is available for $65 from most resort gift shops and at locations throughout the theme parks.

Menus at most resort and theme park restaurants, both table-service and counter-service eateries, are **available in pictorial format**, and sometimes in French, German, Portuguese, Japanese, or Spanish.

Language assistance is available by calling 407-824-2222, which connects guests with a Walt Disney World operator and a phone interpreter (for Spanish, French, Portuguese, Japanese, German, Italian, and additional languages, subject to availability). In addition, all public telephones throughout the Walt Disney World Resort have instructions posted in French, German, Portuguese, Japanese, and Spanish.

Phone cards for international calls are available from vending machines at many telephone locations around the parks. Most Disney resort lobbies also have these vending machines.

Foreign currency exchange is available for up to $100 per person at Guest Relations in theme parks and up to $50 at Lobby Concierge at Disney resort hotels. The currency exchange desk at the Walt Disney World Dolphin can exchange up to $200 per person. There is also a foreign currency exchange available at the SunTrust Bank on Buena Vista Drive across from Downtown Disney and in Gooding's at the Crossroads shopping center near Hotel Plaza Boulevard.

International Symbols (shown on next page) are used in park maps and on theme park and resort signage.

Disney's International Program

Did you know that Disney invites young people from all over the world to participate in its International Program? Participants can work in a variety of positions throughout the theme parks and resorts as a Cultural Representative, sharing the culture and customs of their countries. Or they can join the International College Program as a student between college semesters. Those in the program live with other participants, making this a multicultural experience for them, too. Look for participants in the International Program in the shops and restaurants located throughout the country pavilions in Epcot's World Showcase. There you can find many natives from the various countries who are more than happy to say a few words in their native tongues or talk about their homelands. Kids can also get in on the fun by visiting the Kidcot Stations around World Showcase—these are staffed by cast members from other countries, who will share some thoughts on their countries and will autograph and stamp the Epcot Passports that are available for purchase in Epcot shops. You can also often find Cultural Representatives during Epcot's Food & Wine Festival in the fall—we've passed the time with natives of countries as diverse as Australia and South Africa who were on hand to discuss aspects of their lands' cultures as they relate to the production of food and wine.

[Ö] Foreign Language (continued)

Here is a **measurement conversion factor chart**:

Multiply...	by	to get...	Multiply...	by	to get...
inches	2.54	centimeters	centimeters	0.3937	inches
feet	0.3048	meters	meters	3.281	feet
miles	1.609	kilometers	kilometers	0.6214	miles
ounces	28.35	grams	grams	0.0352	ounces
pounds	0.4536	kilograms	kilograms	2.2046	pounds
gallons	3.785	liters	liters	0.2642	gallons

More conversions are available at http://www.onlineconversion.com.

And a **temperature chart**:

Farenheit	= Celsius	Celsius	= Farenheit
0°F	−17.8°C	−10°C	14°F
32°F	0°C	0°C	32°F
40°F	4.4°C	10°C	50°F
50°F	10°C	20°C	68°F
60°F	15.5°C	25°C	77°F
70°F	21.1°C	30°C	86°F
80°F	26.7°C	35°C	95°F
90°F	32.2°C	40°C	104°F

If you want to check the **most recent currency exchange rates**, visit http://finance.yahoo.com/currency.

Here is a chart with the **international symbols** you'll encounter in Disney guidemaps and on signage:

	restrooms		stroller/wheelchair rental		must be ambulatory
	companion restroom	P	parade viewing for disabled guests		may remain in chair
	Guest Relations	+	First Aid Station		must transfer from wheelchair/ECV
	ATM location	HC	handheld captioning		must transfer to standard wheelchair
	pay phone	CC	closed (video) captioning		must transfer to chair, then to vehicle
	TTY pay phone	RC	reflective captioning		height requirement
	Baby Center		assistive listening		health warning

Hearing

If you've experienced some or total hearing loss or impairment, you might think that your enjoyment of Walt Disney World and its attractions may be diminished by all the sounds you'll be missing. There is plenty of visual stimulation, and Disney has gone to great lengths to offer a variety of ways to enhance your vacation.

Your Icon:

H

(H=Hearing)
Look for this symbol in the book for more details

Planning Ahead

Disney's **special services for guests with disabilities** can be reached by calling 407-939-7807 (voice) or 407-827-5141 (TTY), a special text typewriter telephone line (there's another at 407-939-7670). The cast members who answer these lines can assist you in arranging much of your vacation.

Important Note: Traveling with a service animal? See page 12.

Special provisions for hearing impaired visitors run the gamut, from the basic to the sophisticated. At the most basic level, cast members at most locations have access to paper and pens/pencils for communicating. Disney also offers special devices, as well as sign language interpreted performances on designated days for certain attractions. We have noted these attractions in chapter 5 starting on page 228.

If you're taking a **Disney Cruise**, submit a Medical Clearance form at least six weeks prior to sailing to let them know that sign language interpreters will be needed for the shows (they send one to the muster drill as well). Request a Room Communication Kit for your stateroom (includes the same things that you get when at the resort–see page 51). Assistive listening devices are available for the Walt Disney Theatre, Studio Sea, Buena Vista Theater, Wave Bands, and Diversions. Closed captioning is available on your stateroom TV; use your remove control menu to activate.

Bright Idea: Bring a waterproof container for storing your hearing aid and batteries, especially when you're aboard a water ride or swimming. If you use a hearing aid, be sure to bring extra batteries with you. Our research around the theme parks and resorts found no place that sells them!

Important Note: A buildup of wax in the ears can make flying extremely painful. Use ear plugs or EarPlanes (http://www.earplanes.com), chew gum, or drink water during takeoff and descent to alleviate the pressure, or seek a physician's care.

Planning

Special Challenges

Getting There

Staying in Style

Touring

Feasting

Resources

Index

[H] Hearing (continued)

Upon Your Arrival

Guest Assistance Packets with **dialogue, narrations, flashlights, and pen and paper** are available from cast members near the performance areas for most shows and attractions. Be sure to ask when you first see a cast member at the attraction (they usually have to find the packets).

Pay phones equipped with amplified handsets are throughout the resort. TTY pay phones are at Guest Relations and at locations indicated on park guidemaps and noted in chapter 5.

Assistive listening devices, for those with mild to moderate hearing loss, are lightweight, wireless devices that amplify sounds. The devices receive infrared signals from overhead transmitters at various locations. The receivers include a set of lightweight headphones with volume control. Available at Guest Relations for a $25 deposit, refundable if returned the same day.

TTY phone

Reflective captioning, in which captions are projected via an LED display onto an acrylic panel positioned in front of you, is used at a number of shows performed in theater settings. Ask a cast member at the entrance of the attraction, as the device takes a few minutes to set up properly. It works like this: You are given a device that resembles a flexible microphone stand with a rectangular piece of Plexiglas attached. The Plexiglas must be positioned so that it reflects the captioning from the back wall. It also must be situated so that you can view the stage and see the words at the base of the stage. Ask to be escorted into the theater before the doors "officially" open so you have time to set up the device. We note the attractions at which reflective captioning is available in chapter 5. (If you use reflective captioning with a 3-D show, the 3-D glasses may make the captions difficult to read.)

Handheld captioning units are another type of portable wireless device that provide a written version of the scripts of certain attractions. The units resemble a handheld video game that can be carried around your neck or shoulder (although they do feel heavy after a while). The device is available at no charge (although there is a $100 refundable deposit) at Guest Relations in the theme parks. You cannot take the device from park to park, though—you must return it to the park where you rented it. We note the attractions at which handheld captioning is available in our individual descriptions in chapter 5. While the synchronization is

not perfect, it provides a great way to know what is being said in the moving attractions. In addition, these units, part of Disney's Assistive Services–Handheld (DASH for short) also serve as closed-caption activators for some attractions. You must be within 20 feet of the screen for this function to work properly.

Handheld captioning unit

Video captioning or closed-captioning is used on monitors in many attractions for preshows. Some of these monitors, indicated on the guidemaps with a "CC" symbol, are "caption ready." You can get remote control activators at guest relations for a $25 refundable deposit. Based on the experience of those we spoke with, this device is the least useful of all.

Performances of **some live shows are interpreted** in ASL (American Sign Language) on a rotating basis:
✔ Disney-MGM Studios shows: Sundays/Wednesdays
✔ Magic Kingdom shows: Mondays/Thursdays
✔ Epcot shows: Tuesdays/Fridays
✔ Disney's Animal Kingdom shows: Saturday

Also on these above days, from 9:20 am to 9:40 am, an ASL interpreter will be in the parks' main **Guest Relations office** to answer questions and help with any other concerns hearing impaired guests may have.

Schedules for interpreted performances vary from week to week, so **check with Guest Relations or Lobby Concierge** for up-to-date information.

You may be able to **request free sign language interpretation** for certain other live entertainment, like Epcot's holiday storytellers. Call 407-824-4321 or 407-827-5141 (TTY) at least two weeks in advance.

Bright Idea: Some cast members are trained in sign language—they'll be identified by a special symbol on their name tags.

© Linda MacLeod

A cast name tag indicating a sign language ability

Staying at a Disney resort hotel might help lessen any concerns you have about your vacation because of the amenities offered that specifically address concerns of those with hearing impairments. Not only does each Disney resort have rooms with closed-captioned television, but there are also **"Room Communication Kits"** available, which include:

✔ Door knock and phone alerts
✔ Bed shaker alarm
✔ Text typewriter (TTY)
✔ Strobe light fire alarm
✔ Phone amplifier

The Guest Relations location at the Main Entrance of both Blizzard Beach and Typhoon Lagoon is the prime source of water park information for guests with a hearing impairment. Guest Relations at both water parks have a **text typewriter (TTY)**. There are also telephones with amplified handsets at various locations, as marked on the water park guidemaps.

Bright Idea: Cirque du Soleil's La Nouba (see page 313) is a great show for people who are hearing impaired because there is so little speaking.

Heart Health

If you're recovering from a heart attack or heart surgery, or if you've been diagnosed with high blood pressure, angina, or other heart-related medical conditions, you might think a Walt Disney World vacation is not for you. With some care and planning, your vacation to Walt Disney World can be among your favorite memories.

Your Icon:

♥

Look for this symbol in the book for more details

Planning Ahead

The first thing to do is **consult your physician**, and get an official medical opinion on how much or how little you should endeavor to undertake.

If you will be flying, be sure to review our general tips for folks traveling with special challenges in chapter 3, starting on page 99. In addition, ask your doctor if any testing is needed to ensure that your condition is stable. Recent studies on the effects of air travel on heart disease have found that **in general, the risks are minimal.** There are, however, some people who should not fly, including those who have had a heart attack (myocardial infarction) or a coronary artery stent within the past two weeks; those who have had coronary bypass surgery within the past three weeks (or longer if there were pulmonary complications); those with unstable angina, poorly controlled congestive heart failure, or uncontrolled arrhythmias.

Bright Idea: There appears to be no evidence that air travel interferes with pacemakers or implantable defibrillators, but check with your airline to verify that their security screening devices will not harm you. To expedite the security screening process, it's a good idea to carry a Pacemaker Identification Card, available from your physician. Also ask the screener to inspect you via a "pat-down" rather than making you walk through the metal detector or be searched with a hand wand. For more tips on going through airport security, visit the web site of the Transportation Security Administration (TSA): http://www.tsa.gov.

As you develop your vacation schedule, plan **low-key days** with frequent breaks. We note quiet spots for breaks in the theme parks in chapter 5.

If necessary, rent an **ECV and/or other equipment** for delivery to your resort—see pages 211–213.

If you need to **monitor your blood pressure** and you're flying to Orlando, remember to pack your blood pressure kit in your carry-on luggage.

Upon Your Arrival

Before your day begins, **check the weather** so that you can plan to be in the cool indoors when the temperature is at its highest. In fact, it's probably best to avoid venturing out in the heat of the day—perhaps sitting in the shade by the pool or meandering in and out of the air-conditioned shops at Downtown Disney would be a better way to spend that time.

The key thing to touring the theme parks is to **pace yourself**. Distances on the park map can be deceptive—things often are farther away than they appear to be, which leads to a lot more walking than you might expect. It's not unusual for us to cover 8, 9, even 10 miles in a day (we can scarcely believe our pedometers). With that in mind, plan your day at a pace that you are comfortable with, not even attempting to cover everything in one day. Perhaps you could even consider renting a wheelchair/ECV to help you conserve your energy. (See "Mobility" on pages 68–72.)

Most of the major thrill rides in the parks carry **health warnings** (see photo for an example)—our advice is to heed them. The coasters, especially attractions like Rock 'n' Roller Coaster or Space Mountain, can really shake a person up, while other attractions, like Mission: SPACE and Stitch's Great Escape, provide thrills that can make even the most-conditioned athlete's heart race!

© Deb Wills

Primeval Whirl warning

The First Aid Stations can **store medications** or special equipment (i.e., blood pressure monitor) while you tour.

While enjoying the water parks, avoid the big water slides, which carry their own health warnings. Just getting to the top of a slide like Humunga Kowabunga can be a huge effort. There are **First Aid Stations** at each water park that can provide a cool place to rest as well as basic first aid.

If you're watching your diet, the Disney table-service restaurants (and some counter-service spots, too) **offer heart-healthy entrees**, indicated with a special symbol on the menu. If you have additional dietary concerns, such as requiring a low-sodium diet, read "Diet" on pages 34–37.

If you're in the Walt Disney World area and have further health needs, a list of some of the **nearby medical providers** can be found in the Ongoing Medical Treatment section of this chapter on pages 61–65.

If you **wear a pacemaker**, know that Disney does not provide explicit warnings for you. Remember to discuss your restrictions with your physician *before* you travel. Taking one of the backstage tours? Be sure to let your guide know before you start out. There may be an area or two backstage you'll want to avoid.

[♥] Heart Health (continued)

PassPorter Picks

✔ The Disney-MGM Studios is a compact theme park, easy to navigate, and many of its attractions are either indoors or in shaded areas.

✔ Consider staying at one of the smaller Disney resorts, such as Port Orleans French Quarter, which does not require long walks to get around its buildings. As an alternative, consider staying at one of the deluxe resorts, which are more self-contained, with ample elevators/escalators and additional amenities. Request a room location close to the lobby, bus stops, elevators, and/or food service areas and explain that it is for a medical condition when you make your reservation.

✔ Dine at some of the restaurants known for their heart-healthy menus, such as California Grill at the Contemporary Resort or Fresh Mediterranean Market at the Walt Disney World Dolphin Resort. There are even a few counter-service spots that offer healthy eating, such as Sunshine Season in Epcot.

✔ Try the smaller pools at your resort, which are usually less noisy and less crowded than the main themed pool.

PassPorter Pans

✔ Avoid the attractions marked with health warnings—they are designated as problematic for a reason!

✔ Blizzard Beach has very little shade, and most of the slides there are "big thrills." This is probably not a good choice if you have heart health concerns—try Typhoon Lagoon instead.

✔ Disney's Animal Kingdom tends to get very hot and humid. Visit early in the day, especially in warmer weather.

⏻ Automated External Defibrillators (AED)

You may have seen signs in airports and many other public places marking the spot of an **automated external defibrillator**. What is it? An AED is a small device that's easy to use and can aid in the treatment of cardiac arrest. Disney has installed AEDs throughout its resort area, both onstage and backstage, and has trained many cast members in their use. As of this writing, AEDs can be found with lifeguards in the pool areas, with mobile security units, and with the nurses at First Aid Stations. In addition, Reedy Creek Emergency Services paramedics can reach the theme parks and Downtown Disney within minutes—they, too, are equipped with AEDs.

Infants

Yes, Walt Disney World is for kids, but is it really for the littlest of little ones? Isn't it a hassle to bring newborns to the World? Sure, some folks will give you strange looks when you tell them that you're taking your infant to Walt Disney World. Baby won't remember the trip and it just means a lot of work for you, they'll argue.

Your Icon:

B

(B=Babies)
Look for this symbol in the book for more details

While it might not be easy for Mom and Dad to juggle a baby, especially if they're also watching a toddler or preschooler, there are times when it's just not practical (or desirable) to leave the baby behind. Maybe you want your other children to see Disney, or you want to visit Mickey yourself. Or you need to keep your baby with you for bonding and/or breastfeeding.

No matter the reason, never fear—just as Disney caters to children of all ages, it makes special accommodations for its youngest visitors.

Planning Ahead

Carefully consider the **time of year** to bring your infant. Ideally, you won't want to visit in the heat and crowds of the summer months. A better time to travel with baby would be in the fall when the crowds have dissipated and things have cooled off a bit or in early December or the January-February time frames when both crowds and temperatures are lower (this is our personal favorite time of year to visit).

If you're flying, seriously consider **purchasing a seat** for your infant. While you can lap-carry infants under age two on domestic flights (international flight policies may differ—check with your airline), a lap is not a safe place for your baby. Most infant car seats are FAA-approved (look for a sticker on the car seat) and fit in airline seats using the buckle to secure the seat in place (no need to use the base on infant seats). Most economy seats are 17 in. wide (43 cm.), so be sure your safety seat is less than 17 in. Note that a safety seat may not fit in a bulkhead row if the arm rests do not go up. Also note that booster seats and safety vests are often not allowed on planes, but the CARES (child restraint system) air belts are acceptable for kids over age 2 and from 22 to 44 lbs. (10-20 kg.)—see http://www.kidsflysafe.com. Inquire with the airline on discounted seats for infants when making your reservation. Visit http://www.flyingwithkids.com for details.

Bright Idea: Infants' ears may be more sensitive to the pressure changes during takeoff and landing, so offer a bottle or pacifier during these times to encourage baby to swallow.

Planning

Special Challenges

Getting There

Staying in Style

Touring

Feasting

Resources

Index

[B] Infants (continued)

Having a car at your disposal (whether a rental or your own) gives you some flexibility. You can head back to the room whenever you want, or you can run out for additional diapers or formula when you need them. If you have a car, be sure to have a car seat for baby's safety. (Florida law requires that all children up to age 3 be restrained in a child safety seat. The penalty for not complying is $60 and 3 points against your driver's license!) If you're renting a car, that means you need to either bring your own car seat or reserve one from the rental agency.

Staying on Disney property and using Disney transportation gets you to and from the parks faster, without the hassle of dealing with parking lot trams and car traffic. You might consider a resort on the monorail line so that getting to and from the Magic Kingdom is easy, particularly if you need to make a midday break. Or consider staying at a resort with a kitchen so that you can have easy access to a microwave and refrigerator.

Renting a **stroller** at Disney saves you the hassle of transporting it from home. But remember, if you rent, you'll only have a stroller at the parks—you won't have one with you for those long walks to the bus or parking lots or around your resort or airport. We recommend bringing your own stroller—best bet is an easily collapsible umbrella-type. If you bring your own, be sure that the height is appropriate for the person doing most of the pushing, otherwise you may be dealing with a sore back at the end of a long day. Another alternative for a small infant is a baby carrier, such as a sling or backpack, for hands-free touring. Just remember that on a very hot day, holding baby so close to your body for long periods of time could overheat both of you! See page 211-213 for stroller rental information.

Caring for an infant while on vacation can add an extra dimension to your experience. The worry and strain of making sure baby's needs are met can wear on parents, especially if they have other little ones in tow. Consider what amenities you can **bring from home** that might make life on vacation easier—a beloved toy, a white-noise machine to help baby sleep, or even an extra pair of hands! That's right—maybe there's a grandparent or aunt or trusted friend who wouldn't mind tagging along to offer extra help and support—maybe they could even watch the infant (and other children) while the new Mom and Dad have a quiet night out alone.

Bright Idea: Not sure how many diapers or how much formula to bring along? Keep a log of baby's diaper and formula usage in the week before your trip to see how much is typically used. Divide by 7 to get the daily amount, and then multiply by the number of days in your trip. Add 10% to the total to be on the safe side. Now you've got just what you need! If luggage space for all those diapers is an issue, consider using a private town car service that includes a stop at a local grocery store. Or pack a cardboard box of your supplies—when you're done, either toss the box or use it to pack all your souvenirs.

Upon Your Arrival

While you may not want to let your infant slow you down, it's probably better if you do. Take things at a **slower pace** than other vacationers, and allow yourself and baby frequent breaks from the hustle and bustle. A midday return to the hotel room for naps all around is a good idea.

If your infant is too small (under 6 months) to slather with **sunscreen**, remember to keep them covered with lightweight, loose clothing that covers their limbs to protect them from the Florida sun. Also make sure your baby stays hydrated—the intense heat and humidity can affect even the littlest park-goers.

Bright Idea: Buy a little battery-powered fan that clips on the handle of the stroller, or maybe even get a small mister to help keep baby cool.

When you're ready for a break, all the restrooms, including men's rooms, have **changing tables** for infants and small children.

Even better than changing tables are **Baby Care Centers**. Each theme park features a bright and clean Baby Care Center located near the First Aid Station. In the Magic Kingdom, the Baby Care Center is behind the Crystal Palace restaurant; in Disney's Animal Kingdom, it's near Creature Comforts on Discovery Island; in Epcot, it's near the Odyssey (on your way to the Mexico pavilion in World Showcase); and at the Studios, it's near the main Guest Relations area at the entrance. In each center, there are private nursing rooms with rocking chairs and low lighting; feeding rooms with high chairs, bibs, and plastic spoons; baby changing tables; restrooms; and a bright child's playroom with kid-sized table and chairs and a television playing videos. There are also the following items available for purchase:

✔ Carnation Good Start Supreme Infant Formula, liquid and powder (the Baby Care Centers are sponsored by Carnation)
✔ baby food and junior food
✔ juice and Pedialyte
✔ baby bottles and nipples
✔ pacifiers
✔ disposable diapers (Huggies)
✔ diaper ointment
✔ baby powder
✔ children's acetaminophen (Tylenol)
✔ moist towelettes (wipes)
✔ sipper cups
✔ teethers

© MediaMarx, Inc.

High chairs at Magic Kingdom's Baby Care Center

Planning

Special Challenges

Getting There

Staying in Style

Touring

Feasting

Resources

Index

Planning
Special Challenges
Getting There
Staying in Style
Touring
Feasting
Resources
Index

[B] Infants (continued)

Although your baby may only be a few months old, there are still plenty of **rides and attractions** sure to entertain them. Cinderella's Golden Carrousel, for instance, is bright with happy music—babies seem to enjoy the gentle spinning and up-and-down of the horses, as long as you hold them tight. We note these "infant-friendly" attractions in chapter 5.

For those rides that baby can't go on, though, Disney offers a "**Rider Switch**" option (also known as "child swap") at most rides that makes life a little easier. It works like this: One adult remains with the non-rider in a holding area (usually near the attraction's exit), while the rest of the party rides the attraction. When the riders exit, a cast member will direct the adult who hasn't ridden directly onto the ride, so that he/she can experience the attraction without additional wait time.

If you're **breastfeeding**, don't stop while you're at Disney—it's not only acceptable according to Disney officials, but it's also permissible by Florida law (a mother can breastfeed her baby in any public or private spot where she is permitted to be—see http://www.lalecheleague.org/Law/Bills14.html). If you wish to nurse discreetly, there are plenty of dim attractions during which you can nurse. At the Magic Kingdom, try Hall of Presidents, Carousel of Progress, Tomorrowland Transit Authority, and Country Bear Jamboree. In Epcot, try the American Adventure, Impressions de France, Spaceship Earth, and Ellen's Energy Adventure. At Disney-MGM Studios, try Voyage of the Little Mermaid and Sounds Dangerous. There are also plenty of other quiet nooks for resting or breastfeeding throughout the parks. We make note of them in chapter 5. You may find it helpful to bring a sling and/or nursing bib for virtually "invisible" nursing wherever you may be. And, of course, the Baby Care Centers make cool, quiet places for nursing.

© MediaMarx, Inc.

Nursing in a sling at Disney-MGM Studios

Bright Idea: If your baby is an early riser, consider getting an early start on your day. Take advantage of Extra Magic Hour (see page 119) if you can.

The counter-service/food court area at most Disney resort hotels has a **microwave**, but be very careful about using it to heat formula or baby food—the microwave can develop hot spots in the food and burn your baby. Instead of a microwave, try a cup of hot water to warm bottles and jars instead. Complimentary refrigerators ideal for storing formula or baby food are available at Disney moderate, deluxe, and Disney Vacation Club resorts or for $10/day at the value resorts.

Bright Idea: If your room has a coffeemaker, heat water in it, then place your bottle or baby food jar in the warm water for a while. As always, check the temperature before giving it to baby.

All Disney resorts and most other hotels provide "pack 'n' play" type **playpens/cribs** for infants at no extra charge—be sure to request one if you need it when you make your reservations. The pack 'n' plays are usually very clean and in excellent condition, but if you get one that is not up to your standards, call Housekeeping for a replacement. The cribs usually come with a fitted sheet, as well as an extra regular bed sheet to use as a mattress pad.

Reader Tip: "We made the mistake of bringing our own full-size double stroller on our last visit. It was very bulky and an annoyance to everyone near us on the Disney buses. On future visits, we will rent a stroller at the parks. It is quite worth the money to avoid such situations!"—contributed by Kelly LaFramboise

The "general store" areas of the Disney resorts have many **baby basics** for sale, including diapers and baby wipes. Of course, you're paying for the convenience. If you have access to a car, it's more economical to drive to Winn Dixie or one of the other retail shops in the Orlando/Kissimmee area.

There's a **children's play area** in each of the Disney resorts' main theme pools, perfect for your little one to splash in. If you're thinking of dipping your infant in any of the resort pools, remember they must be wearing snug-fitting plastic pants over their diapers or special swimming diapers. If you forget to bring them from home, they'll be available for purchase from the pool shop or the resort stores.

Disney does have **child care centers** at many of its deluxe resorts, but children under 4 aren't allowed, so parents of infants have to consider other options if they'd like some time sans baby. The most convenient choice is to have a friend or family member along for the trip watch the child, but if that's not possible, there are a few in-room babysitting services available. Kid's Nite Out is sanctioned by Disney, and its sitters are fully bonded and insured and come prepared to play. Rates vary depending on the age and number of children. Contact Kid's Nite Out at 407-828-0920. There are several other reputable services in the area—one that has been highly recommended to us is Fairy Godmothers (407-277-3724). Babysitters from these firms may also be able to care for children with special needs. Call for specifics. See chapter 7 for more details on child care options.

Should your baby become ill (perish the thought!) while you're on vacation, there are a number of **health care centers** nearby (see page 64).

Disney eateries, both counter and table service, provide **high chairs** for infants (strollers are not always allowed in the restaurants). In addition, your server will be happy to heat a bottle or warm baby food in the kitchen—just be sure to test its temperature after heating.

[B] Infants (continued)

Your infant may be too young to **sample anything from your plate**, but just in case, you should know that children under the age of 3 may share from an adult's plate at no charge. If you choose to order a child's meal from the menu, you will be charged.

The **First Aid Stations at the water parks** offer a quiet spot to cool down for a bit, as well as provide minor first aid care if needed. Remember, though, that Blizzard Beach does not have much shade and is more known as a "thrill" water park. A slightly more sedate experience may be had at Typhoon Lagoon. As mentioned above, if your infant will be playing in any of the water areas, they must be wearing snug-fitting plastic pants over their diapers or special swimming diapers.

You can also bring your infant on a **Disney cruise**, provided she/he is at least 12 weeks old. Request a crib for your stateroom—the Disney Cruise Line will provide a Pack 'n' Play-type porta-crib with a crib sheet, but you'll need to bring your own bedding—we recommend extra-warm jammies rather than blankets for your child's safety. Infant-size life jackets are also provided—request one from your stateroom host or hostess or at Guest Services upon boarding. Although babysitting is not available in guest staterooms, the cruise ships do have Flounder's Reef Nursery, an infant and toddler group babysitting area that is open every evening and certain times during each day. Reservations for this babysitting are taken on cruise embarkation day from 1:30 pm to 3:30 pm. Space is limited and is available on a first-come, first-served basis. The fee is $6 per hour per child, with a two-hour minimum. This service is only available for children ages 12 weeks to 3 years and is not available to children who require one-on-one care or babysitter-assisted medical attention. Children who are not toilet-trained cannot play in the cruise ships' pools, but they can splash in the fountain play area near Mickey's Pool, which is designed exclusively for little ones wearing swim diapers. Speaking of diapers, some infant sundries, like diapers and formula, are available onboard, but it's wise to bring most of what you'll need (baby food, pacifiers, bottles, etc.) from home. If your infant is old enough to sit up in a high chair, let Disney know that you'd like a high chair at your table during dinner, and they will note it on your reservation. If your infant is too young for a high chair, you can bring your infant car seat (the type with a handle) into the dining room and set it on a chair (if stable) or beside your chair while you eat. Diaper Genies are available from your stateroom host or Guest Services.

© MediaMarx, Inc.

Four-month-old Alexander snoozes while his parents eat in Parrot Cay

Ongoing Medical Treatment

Just because you're under a doctor's ongoing care doesn't mean you should stay chained to your home—you deserve a Walt Disney World vacation as much, if not more, than anyone! But let's face it—leaving behind your familiar physicians and caregivers can be a scary prospect. With adequate planning and preparation, you'll find that the Orlando area can provide you with the quality care you need, while allowing you the freedom to visit the Mouse.

Your Icon:

T

(T=Treatment)
Look for this symbol in the book for more details

What do we mean by "Ongoing Medical Treatment"? It's a pretty broad phrase, and to be honest, many of the conditions in this book could be classified as requiring ongoing medical treatment. In this section, we're specifically thinking of those **guests who require special medical treatment** such as periodic dialysis or those who are oxygen-dependent. We're also thinking of those who may be fed via a gastric or naso-gastric tube, or other conditions that require ongoing care such as cystic fibrosis, spina bifida, or cerebral palsy. We also take into account those whose conditions require continuing medication or monitoring, such as diabetes, sleep apnea, epilepsy, Tourette Syndrome, and mental health disorders such as bipolar disorder or depression (see page 13).

Planning Ahead

Obviously, a key factor in making your trip successful is talking with your **health care provider** and working with them to coordinate the services you need in Orlando. Review our general information in chapter 3, starting on page 99.

When **making Disney resort reservations**, request a room that is easily accessible, close to the main facilities and a bus stop if necessary. Also remember to request a refrigerator if you have medication that needs to be kept cold. Disney provides complimentary refrigerators in all moderate, deluxe, and Disney Vacation Club resorts, but there's a $10/night charge at the value resorts. If the refrigerator is required for a medical reason, Disney normally waives the $10/night fee.

Important Note: You can request a "sharps container" to safely discard used needles or other sharp objects that you may use for testing. Containers are provided free (and discreetly) by Housekeeping at all Disney resorts, or by Security at the Swan and Dolphin.

Traveling with a **service animal**? See page 12 for details.

Planning

Special Challenges

Getting There

Staying in Style

Touring

Feasting

Resources

Index

[T] Ongoing Medical Treatment (continued)

Consider resorts that have a **kitchen** to prepare meals and snacks.

While planning your day at a Disney **water park**, keep in mind that Blizzard Beach has very little shade and is a more "thrill"-oriented water park. Typhoon Lagoon is a slightly more manageable park. First Aid Stations at the water parks provide minor first aid care or a place to cool off.

If you're traveling with someone who is **fed by g-tube** and is on a pump for long feeds, try riding the longer attractions, such as "it's a small world," Carousel of Progress, Universe of Energy, The Great Movie Ride, and Spaceship Earth, for uninterrupted fun.

If you're traveling with someone who has **Tourette Syndrome**, which may cause them to impulsively use inappropriate language, bring a doctor's note stating the diagnosis so they are not mistaken for a troublemaker.

If you will need **dialysis**, discuss your options with your local provider. They may help you find facilities and schedule appointments. One clinic in the Orlando area is DaVita Celebration Dialysis in Celebration (800-424-6589 or 407-566-1780), just four miles from Disney property. Note that the Disney Cruise Line does not provide onboard dialysis facilities.

If you're **cruising and require oxygen**, you must complete the Medical Clearance form and let the Disney Cruise Line know the name, address, and phone number of the oxygen supplier.

If you **require oxygen**, consult with your respiratory therapist. They may be able to coordinate shipment of oxygen to your resort or at least be able to offer you advice. Also remember to check with your airline if you are flying to get the latest requirements on traveling with oxygen.

For some **additional background information**, see the list of helpful organizations and facilities in chapter 7, starting on page 396.

Upon Your Arrival

Many of our recommendations for traveling with **heart health or physical therapy** concerns apply to traveling with medical treatment needs:

✔ Use FASTPASS whenever possible to avoid long waits in line. Consider whether a Guest Assistance Card (see pages 10–11) can help.

✔ Observe attraction health warnings and take breaks during the day.

✔ Visit the First Aid Stations in the theme parks if you need the aid of a nurse or if you have medication to be refrigerated while touring. They will also hold medical equipment too bulky to carry around while you tour.

✔ Consider using a wheelchair or ECV to conserve your energy.

These suggestions all are **dependent** on your individual health issues, your stamina, and the frequency of the treatment you require.

Traveling With Epilepsy *by peer reviewer Amy Warren Stoll*

Wear medical identification. Consider medical identification that not only identifies that you have seizures, but also provides access to information for emergency personnel (i.e., a MedicAlert bracelet). Also, write out a list of your medicines, including the dosages and how often you take them. Put this list in an obvious place for emergency workers to find, such as with your photo ID.

If your travels include a cruise, it's very important that you purchase travel insurance. While the ship has facilities to treat minor seizures or even stabilize more serious ones, the possibility of having to be evacuated to a land-based hospital certainly exists, and it would be an expensive predicament to find yourself in. The insurance offered by Disney Cruise Line does NOT provide coverage for preexisting conditions, so talk to your travel agent about your insurance options or visit http://www.quotetravelinsurance.com to compare for yourself. Be prepared to purchase your insurance about the same time that you book your cruise. Most policies must be purchased within a 10- to 21- day window (varies by company) of your trip deposit to waive the preexisting exclusion. CSA Travel Protection also has a plan that can be purchased up until your final payment is made.

Bring your medications. Be sure to bring not only your daily medications, but also any that your doctor has prescribed to be used in the event of "breakthrough" seizures. Bring extra days of medication. Travel delays can happen, and you want to be prepared just in case. Also, pack those in your carry-on, never in your suitcase, and keep them in their original containers.

Do your best to maintain your usual routine. Changing your sleep/wake cycle or taking your medication at a different time will increase your risk of having a seizure, even if you've been seizure-free for quite some time. If you have no choice but to change your routine (maybe you work night shift, for example) visit your doctor before you leave for ways to lessen the effect on your body.

Don't overplan. You may find it difficult to rest well the night before your trip. The excitement and anticipation of your long-awaited trip can sabotage any hope of getting a good night's rest. Thus, don't plan a late night on your arrival day. As tempting as late night Extra Magic Hours are, save them for another day.

Bring your favorites. Do you have certain foods or drinks that you prefer when taking your medicines? Bring them with you to keep in your room. Having these on hand will also make it more convenient to take your meds.

Bring an extra dose of your medication in your park bag so you'll be able to take it on time, even if you're delayed getting back to your room. This may also allow you to be more flexible with your plans as the day unfolds.

Don't be afraid to say "I need a break." If you need to rest, then rest. Surely both you and your travel party would rather spend a few hours back at the room taking a nap, than several hours at the emergency room.

Drink plenty of fluids. The effects of dehydration can trigger a seizure just as easily as a missed dose of medication.

Use the same precautions that you would at home. If you don't swim alone at home, then don't do it on vacation. If you don't drink alcohol at home, don't do it on vacation. If your resort room has a kitchenette, adapt your kitchen safety plan from home to your temporary digs. In general, be on the lookout for potential hazards (moving vehicles, sharp corners, unprotected drop-offs) and take precautions just as you would at home.

Is There a Doctor in the House?

What do you do if you get sick while you're visiting the Most Magical Place on Earth? If your illness does not require immediate care, there are a couple things you can do:

✔ If you're in the parks, visit the First Aid Station (see page 206).
✔ If you're at your resort, call the Lobby Concierge. They'll give you information on the options open to you.

There are three locations of Florida Hospital Centra Care close to Disney property—complimentary transportation is available (note that you will be returned to where you were picked up), and most insurance plans are accepted. Here are the locations:

✔ Lake Buena Vista Centra Care (near Crossroads Shopping Center and Hotel Plaza Blvd.), 12500 South Apopka-Vineland Road, 407-934-2273. Open weekdays 8:00am–midnight, weekends 8:00 am–8:00 pm.
✔ Formosa Gardens Centra Care (near the junction of World Drive and Highway 192), 7848 West 192, 407-397-7032. Open weekdays 8:00 am–8:00 pm, weekends 8:00 am–5:00 pm.
✔ Kissimmee Centra Care (near Medieval Times and Bass Road), 4320 W. Vine Street, 407-390-1888. Open weekdays 8:00 am–8:00 pm.

If you'd prefer to consult with a doctor before you head to a clinic or hospital, you can call Centra Care In-Room Services at 407-238-2000 for a free telephone screening.

Other options recommended by Disney:

✔ Doctors on Call Service (DOCS), 407-399-3627
✔ EastCoast Medical, 407-648-5252—a 24-hour-a-day call center staffed by registered nurses and medical ancillary staff.

But what if you need help *now*? You may think to call 911, but if you're using a cell phone that relays to your home area code, that might not be the most expedient way to get help. Those who have had to deal with this type of situation recommend contacting the nearest Disney cast member first. If you're in the theme or water parks, they'll know the fastest way to contact an emergency rescue team right away. If you're in a resort, call 911 or the front desk, which will contact emergency services for you.

If you're out and about when an emergency arises, or if you have a car at your disposal, you *may* want to go to a hospital emergency room. The closest hospital to Walt Disney World is the Florida Hospital Emergency Department at Celebration Health (407-303-4000). This facility accepts all medical plans for emergency care. To get there, take either Epcot Center Drive or Osceola Parkway east to I-4, I-4 west to exit 64A, then right on Parkway Boulevard, then right on Celebration Place. Watch for "Emergency Room" signs. Driving south on World Drive to the Celebration exit is much farther and takes quite a bit longer. Taking Sherbeth Road from Animal Kingdom/AK Lodge to 192 and then east is slower than taking Osceola Pkwy and I-4. (See chapter 7 for more details.)

That said, it's not always advisable to drive yourself—time saved in the short run must be balanced against the lack of medical staff and livesaving equipment during the drive. Think twice before you "swoop and scoop."

Dental emergency? Call the Celebration Dental Group at 407-566-2222.

Traveling With a Terminally Ill Person

This is probably the hardest section of the book for us to write. Sharing the Magic of Disney during a trip with a terminally ill family member or friend must be one of the **most bittersweet experiences**, one that neither of the authors has had.

Based on our other experience, however, we would recommend that if you are traveling with a person who is terminally ill, you should review our chapter on general travel tips and sections in this chapter on Guest Assistance Cards, Diet, Heart Health, Motion Sickness, Mobility, and Medical Treatment. If the person with a terminal illness is a child, you may want to contact the **Make-A-Wish Foundation** (http://www.wish.org), **Give Kids the World** (http://www.gktw.org), or **Dream Factory** (http://www.dreamfactoryinc.org).

We'd like to **share some thoughts** from an experienced reader who has made this type of trip:

"When touring the parks with someone with a terminal illness, remember that what might be gentle rides for even young children may be physically overwhelming to someone made delicate from their illness.

In Adventureland, Pirates of the Caribbean might be too rough because of the waterfall drop, and the Swiss Family Treehouse involves a lot of walking with no quick exit.

In Fantasyland, both the Many Adventures of Winnie the Pooh and Snow White's Scary Adventures involve sudden turns and bumps. Peter Pan's Flight is gentle, but the side-to-side rocking may be difficult for someone with motion sickness. Buzz Lightyear's Space Ranger Spin might be gentle enough if no one spins the car, but the tunnels would be horrible for someone with motion sickness. Tomorrowland Transit Authority is gentle, but the speed might be unsettling.

There are still many attractions that would pose little problem.

In Adventureland, the Jungle Cruise and the Enchanted Tiki Room (even "under new management") are gentle enough.

I wouldn't recommend any of the Frontierland rides, but the shows would be fine, and Tom Sawyer Island would be a great place to relax. All of the Liberty Square attractions should be fine.

In Fantasyland, 'it's a small world' is the safest ride. In Tomorrowland, the Carousel of Progress is safe but isn't always open.

There are no hidden surprises in Epcot. Avoid Mission: SPACE, Test Track, Cranium Command, Body Wars, Soarin', and Maelstrom; everything else should be fine.

The only really gentle ride-through attraction in the other two parks is the Great Movie Ride, but there are many shows, walk-through attractions, and other touring opportunities to make visits to them worthwhile."

—contributed by Anonymous

Planning

Special Challenges

Getting There

Staying in Style

Touring

Feasting

Resources

Index

Diabetes

According to the National Institutes of Health, more than 20 million Americans (7% of the population) have diabetes, and these numbers continue to rise. While the most common form is Type 2 diabetes (insulin resistant), Type 1 diabetes (insulin dependent) and gestational diabetes (during pregnancy) also exist. No matter what type you have, the complication of diabetes can be devastating. Complications can include heart disease and stroke, high blood pressure, blindness, kidney disease, nervous system disease, amputations, dental disease, and pregnancy complications. It is critically important for a person with diabetes to maintain healthy blood sugar levels.

Diabetes is one of those invisible "challenges." A person with diabetes may be someone you see in a wheelchair and wonder why they are using it. Co-author Deb Wills has Type 1 diabetes.

Talk to your doctor—changes in activity levels, temperatures, and adrenaline from rides can alter your blood sugar. Have a plan for this. Also talk to your doctor if you'll be changing time zones, and get a travel clock with two settings to help you manage your insulin/oral medication.

Stay **hydrated**!

Wear your **MedicAlert necklace/bracelet**.

Pack **three times as many supplies** as you'll normally use at home. You may find yourself testing much more during your trip or run the risk of "equipment malfunctions." And don't forget glucose tabs for those unexpected lows.

Have **current prescriptions** from your doctor. Bring all medicine and supplies in original containers with prescription labels (your pharmacist will label your individual insulin bottles).

Test, test, and test again! Between all the walking and the fun stress of thrill rides, your blood sugar can be affected.

Label everything—meters, kits, etc.—with name and contact details.

When making **dining reservations**, be sure to note you have diabetes.

Consider an **ACCU-CHEK Multiclix Lancet Device** for testing. It works well and requires fewer lancets to pack.

Disney does not offer carbohydrate counts for foods, unless they are prepackaged from an outside vendor. **Bring a carb guide** with you.

Pump wearers, check with the manufacturer about going on thrill or water rides. Some advise you disconnect the pump. Know before you go! Remember to bring a zipper-type bag for storing the pump when disconnected.

Special thanks to the Dunlap family for their help with this section!

Bring your own snacks! Nothing works better than what you already know. Don't experiment with new snacks or testing supplies on vacation.

If you fly, **keep your supplies with you** on the plane, preferably under the seat in front of you for easy access. Try not to put them in the overhead bins. Be sure to have all liquids in a one-quart bag for security.

Security will check all your bags before entering a theme park. Just let them know you have supplies for diabetes treatments in your bag. Co-author Deb Wills hasn't had a problem with this yet.

First Aid Stations are your best friend. They store insulin for you and are safe, clean places to test and give shots. They also have sharps containers.

Counting carbs is perhaps the hardest thing to do while at Walt Disney World. The restaurants and eateries all have ingredients lists, but few offer carb counts. Some prepackaged snacks/desserts come with ingredient listings; chocolate covered banana, no-sugar-added brownie, etc.

Sugar-free Jello is now available in most resort food courts, as well as some counter-service eateries. Most ice cream carts in Disney's Animal Kingdom and certain carts in Epcot have no-sugar-added ice cream.

Reader Tip: "If you have diabetes, ask a cast member in any bakery for assistance in finding sugar-free treats and candy. I couldn't find any diabetic-safe treats in Downtown Disney and wrote a letter to Disney. They replied that cast members have been trained to help people find sugar-free items in all the bakeries, even if they are not labeled that way in the display case. The next time I went to Downtown Disney Marketplace, I asked the cast member behind the counter, and she took me around the entire store showing me what diabetic choices were available ... and there were a lot!"–contributed by Anonymous

Make sure your **know what you can and can't eat**. Don't assume the chefs know all about special diets. Co-author Deb Wills has met several Disney chefs who had no idea about sugar alcohol. Perhaps a no-sugar-added brownie works for you, but it sets Deb Wills' blood sugars on a rocket up.

Tips from the Trenches

Some chefs/restaurants are very helpful with your dietary needs; othes go through the motions. Remember to always request assistance politely. Many eateries have a sugar-free or no-sugar-added dessert, but not all do. Author Deb Wills has given up on Chefs de France.

Several of the table-service restaurants offer artisan cheese platters, which make wonderful desserts. Be sure to ask that any enhancements (syrups, drizzles, or fruit) be off to the side and not on the cheese itself. Deb Wills recently ordered a cheese platter in a fine Disney restaurant only to have honey drizzled over the cheese.

Don't leave your diabetes kit in your stroller or wheelchair when you go into an attraction. The heat and humidity can harm the insulin.

Mobility

Walt Disney World is a **huge complex** encompassing 40+ square miles. When we say there is a lot of ground to cover here, we mean it! You may get along just fine at home, but at Disney, you'll be walking and standing much more than you may be accustomed to. For travelers with mobility issues, Disney has taken your needs into consideration.

If you are a person who uses a wheelchair, cane, or walker on a permanent or temporary basis (accident or surgery/illness recovery); someone who can't stand for long; someone for whom extra walking far exceeds your normal routine; or someone who is unsteady, read on!

Your Icon:

(M=Mobility)
Look for this symbol in the book for more details

Planning Ahead

When you're making your reservations, remember to let any representative you deal with and/or your travel agent know of any special requirements you have. If you need a fully accessible resort hotel room or stateroom, be sure to **book early**, as there are a limited number available. If you need a room close to an elevator for medical reasons, have that noted on your reservation, too. Are you bringing a service animal? This needs to be explained when booking also. Let the Disney representative know you have special needs, and have them make notes on your reservation form. See chapter 4, starting on page 113, for details on making reservations

A week or so before your trip, **confirm all arrangements** you've made to make sure everything is ready.

You can **bring your own wheelchair or ECV** to Walt Disney World, rent one from local vendors, or rent one at a theme park. Your Disney resort may also have wheelchairs available on a limited, no-charge basis for use on the resort's grounds. For more information on renting and getting around via wheels at Walt Disney World, see "Wheels!" on pages 211–213.

If you are flying and bringing your wheelchair (especially motorized ones), be sure to check with airlines **before you purchase your ticket**. Each has slightly different requirements and restrictions. Don't purchase a ticket first only to find out your needs can't be accommodated.

Getting **back and forth from the airport** also requires preplanning, depending on your needs.

Most airlines allow **preboarding for passengers needing extra time**, so you'll be able to get settled in before the rest of the passengers start boarding. When you reach the gate on departure day, be sure to inquire with your airline exactly how this works.

Once you arrive in Orlando, there are several transportation options for **reaching your resort**. If you need an accessible mode of transportation, you have some different options:

1. Use Disney's Magical Express (see page 108), which can accommodate wheelchairs with advance notice—indicate your need at the time you book your Magical Express request.
2. Make reservations with Mears for an accessible shuttle—call 407-423-5566 or visit http://www.mearstransportation.com.
3. While it's expensive, you can rent an accessible van (see chapter 7). This is your only option if you must remain in your wheelchair.

Remember to **bring your handicap parking permit/tag for parking** your vehicle. Those with this tag receive complimentary valet parking at Walt Disney World, where available. If you rent a wheelchair from a local vendor, remember that you need to bring your handicapped parking permit/tag from home, along with the permit registration and appropriate ID. If you park in the regular parking lot at the parks, you will not be able to get the wheelchair on the tram. There are a limited number of wheelchairs available in the parking lot to get you to the turnstiles. We have found these are not often available as the day goes on.

If you or someone in your group **drives to Walt Disney World**, you'll be able to pack anything special you need with you. If you have an accessible vehicle, this will make your experience a little easier, since you are familiar with that mode of transportation.

If you are **able to transfer from your wheelchair** into a car and your budget allows, we suggest town car transportation from the airport. They are basically the same price as a taxi, and you travel in greater comfort with less wait.

Don't let **pride** get in your way. If you exhaust yourself early trying to walk around, nobody will have a magical time at Disney.

Peer reviewer Joanne Ernest at Disney's Animal Kingdom

Traveling with a **service animal**? See page 12.

[M] Mobility (continued)

Upon Your Arrival

Once on Disney property, you'll find that most **Disney transportation is accessible** for wheelchair/ECV users. See "Wheels!" on pages 211–213.

Reader Tip: "I have an autoimmune condition that makes it difficult for me to stand or walk for long periods of time. While I look OK to outsiders, my family knows the signs that I am having difficulty. After a trip where I refused to slow down, we learned our lesson. When we returned to Walt Disney World, we (1) rented a scooter from an outside source, which allowed me to get to and from the hotel without difficulty, and (2) got a Guest Assistance Card that I wore on my lanyard. While many people thought we were using a 'get to the front of the line' card, we decided to ignore the comments and just do what we knew we needed to. Ignoring the looks and comments is not easy, but it's the only way I can enjoy the parks with my children."–contributed by Patricia Ravert

Wheelchair and Electric Convenience Vehicle (ECV) rentals are available at each of the four major theme parks and at the BoardWalk's surrey bike rental desk on a **first-come**, **first-served basis**. Theme park wheelchairs may not be transferred from park to park. See "Wheels!" on page 211 for details on renting ECVs/wheelchairs.

As you experience the Walt Disney World resort from the oldest sections (like the Magic Kingdom and Polynesian resort) to the newest areas (such as Disney's Animal Kingdom and Pop Century) you'll see a gradual **change for the better** in regard to accessibility from minimal to very comfortable.

Each attraction at Walt Disney World has a **symbol** in the guidemap (and the Disney Guidebook for Guests With Disabilities) indicating how you may experience that particular ride. We detail this information in chapter 5.

The various **options** for experiencing the Disney attractions include:
✔ Stay in your wheelchair.
✔ Transfer from your wheelchair to the ride vehicle. This usually involves several steps, and some may be up or down.
✔ Transfer from your ECV to a wheelchair.
✔ Transfer from your ECV to a wheelchair to get through the queue, and then transfer out of the chair to the ride vehicle.

Keep in mind that cast members are not allowed to physically assist anyone in and out of rides.

If you are planning to walk around the park but cannot stand for long periods of time or do not have the stamina to wait in long attraction queues, seriously consider renting a wheelchair or ECV.

Some attractions have **auxiliary entrances**. These are intended to offer those in wheelchairs, with service animals, or with a GAC a more convenient entrance to the attraction. Auxiliary entrances are not intended to bypass waiting lines. Guests with disabilities and a maximum of five members of their party may enter through these entrances. The rest of the party must use the main entrance.

A few attractions have an actual ride vehicle **on display** outside the main entrance so you can see exactly what you'll be boarding. We mention specifics in the descriptions of those attractions in chapter 5. Space Mountain seating can be especially tricky as it is a small space with a T-bar that fits closely on your lap.

Most cast members stationed at the entrance to attractions are on the lookout for guests in wheelchairs/ECVs and will **explain the procedures** for that ride to you. If you spot them first, approach them and explain what your abilities are as far as transferring, walking, or controlling body motion. Based on the information you provide, the cast member will give you instructions. Follow them and you're all set.

Once you get inside an attraction, you may be asked again for the same information by a different cast member. Although it may be annoying, remember that **your safety** is their chief concern and they want to give you the appropriate instructions. If something doesn't sound right to you, though, or you are not clear on the instructions, be sure to ask, ask, and ask!

If you travel with a **service animal**, check with the cast member at each attraction before entering (read about service animals on page 12). We note attraction information for service animals in chapter 5.

If you will be **leaving your wheelchair/ECV**, ask where the ride will unload and where your chair will be at that point. Sometimes you will load and unload in the exact same location. Other times, the chair will be moved to the unload area by cast members.

For the most part, you should be able to go through the full-service Disney restaurants in your ECV/wheelchair. We note where space is tight in chapter 6. However, **counter-service** spots often have narrow queues formed by railings. These spots often are more crowded, which means there's much less room to maneuver. You may want a member of your party to assist with transporting your food, or ask a cast member for assistance. On the plus side, though, some eateries have low counters that are easily accessible and a few lines marked with a wheelchair symbol—you'll find it easier to use those. We have marked the ones we've discovered in our individual descriptions in chapter 6.

Planning

Special Challenges

Getting There

Staying in Style

Touring

Feasting

Resources

Index

[M] Mobility (continued)

Each of the theme parks has a few **companion-assisted** restrooms; not all have changing tables. We've noted where they are for you in chapter 5. Most resorts do not have companion restrooms, however, although all have accessible restrooms.

Merchandise locations are also accessible, but again can be very difficult to navigate, especially when crowded, as they often are at the end of the day. We suggest doing your shopping **early in the day**. By all means, take advantage of merchandise delivery back to your Disney hotel or to the front of the park (see page 120) so that you don't have to carry your purchases around.

A few of the resorts have **"zero-entry"** swimming pools and pool wheelchairs, which allow easier access into the pool. Cast members are not allowed to assist you, but the gradual entrance area makes it much easier to get into the water. See page 116 and chapter 4 for more information.

Many of the hotel swimming pools are equipped with "transfer tiers," but these are most useful to those who have some upper body strength and can lift themselves out of their chairs.

Both Blizzard Beach and Typhoon Lagoon water parks are wheelchair/ECV accessible to a small degree. A number of the rides **require stair walking** to get to the entrance. See chapter 5 for details.

The shops and eateries at Downtown Disney and the BoardWalk are all accessible, yet some are **so crowded with merchandise** they make navigating via wheelchair/ECV nearly impossible. We note which places are least chair/ECV-friendly in our individual descriptions in chapter 5 and 6.

Important Note: When you are getting on (or off) an attraction with mobility issues, you should not rush! Rushing can lead to accidents. The cast member will wait for you.—contributed by peer reviewer Joanne Ernest

Disney Cruise Line offers accessible staterooms, with ramped bathroom thresholds, open bed frames, added phones in the bathroom/nightstand, bathroom and shower handrails, fold-down shower seats, handheld shower heads, lowered towel and closet bars, and emergency call buttons. Note that there are only four stateroom categories that are handicapped accessible: category 3 (one-bedroom suite with veranda), categories 5 and 6 (deluxe balcony), category 8 (deluxe oceanview), and category 11 (standard inside). Categories 3, 5, and 6 will accommodate four passengers in the accessible rooms, while categories 8 and 11 will accommodate two passengers.

One final word. While Walt Disney World is ADA-compliant and the resort is as accessible as possible, there are some areas that are a bit **tricky to navigate**. We have tried to note those throughout this book as appropriate.

Motion Sensitivity

Motion sickness or vertigo occurs when your brain receives conflicting information about your body's position. Your inner ear detects that the vehicle you're in is moving, but your eyes are stationary—it creates a feeling that your spatial orientation, balance, or equilibrium is off and you can feel "carsick" or "seasick." It may make you lightheaded, dizzy, or unsteady. For some, the room may spin or you feel nausea. These are usually temporary conditions and **can often be avoided with proper planning**. (There are some conditions that cause motion sickness that are medical in origin, such as inner ear infections or Meniere's disease, and they require medical treatment.) Whatever your symptoms, all you know is you want to avoid feeling that way, especially when you are at Walt Disney World!

Your Icon:

Q

(Q=Queasy)
Look for this symbol in the book for more details

Sometimes you can **control your environment**. For example, don't go on the Mad Tea Party's spinning teacups. Other times, the environment may be out of your control and you have to find ways to deal with the symptoms (such as when you're on a cruise ship). Here are some tips and advice to follow.

Planning Ahead

Prior to your trip, **talk to your physician** about taking a motion sickness remedy. Some are over-the-counter (OTC), some require a prescription, and some are holistic. Whichever method you choose, try it out a few weeks before you leave home so you'll know exactly how it makes you feel in case there are any side effects.

Co-author Deb Wills has motion sensitivity and has had great success with the over-the-counter medicine called Bonine (generic name: meclizine). In fact, she starts taking it **several days before** she is scheduled to get on the cruise ship. Some folks report Bonine and Dramamine help them on theme park attractions, too!

Reader Tip: "I had good luck with Sea Bands, the bands that apply pressure to certain points on your wrists. No negative side effects. They're reusable and over-the-counter. It seems to help me with what I'd call very slight, occasional motion sickness, especially after the 360-degree films."—contributed by Kitty Smith

Bright Idea: In an airplane, request a window seat and try to be seated over the wings to minimize motion sickness.

[Q] Motion Sensitivity (continued)

Be aware of your triggers and try to avoid those types of attractions. Disney has **warning signs** outside attractions that may affect those with motion sensitivity, and we have noted them in chapter 5. Heed the warnings!

If you've had problems in the past with **big-screen movies**, decide whether entering a Disney attraction featuring a movie is a good idea. A number of them are 360 degrees or extra-large, extra-wide screens, which can cause greater problems.

Some rides **go in circles** and their potential for causing motion sickness is high, from Astro Orbiter, Dumbo, and the Mad Tea Party in the Magic Kingdom to TriceraTop Spin and Primeval Whirl in Disney's Animal Kingdom. You can see all of these rides without having to stand in line—decide for yourself if their spinning would affect you.

The following is a list of attractions that **may cause motion sickness**:

✔ Magic Kingdom: Dumbo, Magic Carpets of Aladdin, Mad Tea Party, Cinderella's Golden Carrousel, Astro Orbiter, Walt Disney's Carousel of Progress (theater slowly moves in a circular motion), Big Thunder Mountain Railroad, Space Mountain, Goofy's Barnstormer, and Buzz Lightyear's Space Ranger Spin (you control the spinning).

✔ Epcot: Mission: SPACE, Body Wars, Test Track, Soarin', the Clamobiles in The Seas With Nemo and Friends, O Canada, and Reflections of China. Also, the Garden Grill restaurant slowly revolves.

✔ Disney's Animal Kingdom: Kali River Rapids (rough water raft ride), Primeval Whirl, Dinosaur, TriceraTop Spin, Kilimanjaro Safari, and Expedition Everest.

✔ Disney-MGM Studios: Star Tours (motion simulator), Twilight Zone Tower of Terror (sudden drops), Rock 'n' Roller Coaster.

There are also some rides where you might **unexpectedly** have a problem, such as the Haunted Mansion and Spaceship Earth. Both of these rides have cars that rotate and travel backward. Also avoid sitting in the backward seat of Magic Kingdom's Tomorrowland Transit Authority if that causes motion sickness for you. Disney buses have sideways seats in addition to forward-facing ones.

If you exit an attraction and aren't feeling quite right, **don't hesitate** to ask a cast member for assistance. They will lead you to a bench to sit and wait a few minutes. Remember, you can always go to the First Aid Station to rest.

Bright Idea: If you feel queasy after an attraction, try small sips of a carbonated drink or nibble crackers to settle your stomach. Another tip is to sniff rubbing alcohol—you can bring small packets of alcohol wipes with you from home. And remember, don't eat right before going on spinning or thrill rides that you think might cause motion sickness, such as Mission: SPACE, Rock 'n' Roller Coaster, or Primeval Whirl.

Feeling a bit **seasick** on your Disney cruise? Go on deck and look out at the horizon. Also, the Infirmary is stocked with anti-motion-sickness over-the-counter medications.

PassPorter Picks

✔ While your group is riding rides that might bother you, browse the shops or **scout out a good place to eat**. If you can bear to watch, take photos of your family/friends riding.

✔ The movies at Body Wars and Star Tours can be experienced **without** the motion simulator running during non-busy times. Inquire with a cast member at the attraction.

✔ On the monorail, bus, or boats, try to **avoid reading**, sit close to the front seat, look out into the distance, and always face forward.

PassPorter Pans

✔ If you frequently get seasick, you might want to **avoid boat transportation** (ferry, launches, Friendships) around the resorts.

✔ The following attractions include **boats that travel along water**. Most are gentle rides, but if you are ultra-sensitive, avoid:

© Deb Wills

Warning sign at Soarin'

- Magic Kingdom: "it's a small world," Jungle Cruise, Liberty Belle Riverboat, Pirates of the Caribbean, Splash Mountain, and the Raft to Tom Sawyer's Island.

- Epcot: Living with the Land, The Gran Fiesta Tour Starring the Three Caballeros, and Maelstrom.

- Disney's Animal Kingdom: Kali River Rapids.

Planning

Special Challenges

Getting There

Staying in Style

Touring

Feasting

Resources

Index

Physical Therapy/Rehabilitation

You are recovering from surgery or an accident, working to maintain your strength or mobility, or just trying to mend what "ails" you. A portion of your healing involves physical therapy—can you stick to your regimen while on vacation? Yes, you may be able to continue (with your health care provider's approval) your rehabilitation during a vacation to Walt Disney World.

Your Icon:

P

(P=Physical)
Look for this symbol in the book for more details

Planning Ahead

Consult with your medical team before leaving home to determine what you can do. Likewise, be sure to find out what you should avoid!

Remember to pack anything you may need for your **exercises** (like exercise bands or workout clothes).

Remember, too, to bring an adequate supply of any medications you may be taking. Also bring along a **copy of your prescriptions**, just in case you need to get a refill!

Some gyms (like Curves) offer travel cards to use at other franchise facilities—check with yours.

Upon Your Arrival

You'll have access to ice machines at the resorts, but if you need heat, you'll want to **pack your own heating pad** or try the instant heat packs available at drugstores. Don't forget zipper-close bags if you need to ice down.

All of the Disney resort hotels have swimming pools. Some even have a **smaller pool** where you can do your exercises (or laps) with less chance of disruption. Some of the pools have zero entryways or transfer tiers to allow for easy transition into the pool. Early morning is usually the best time to visit a pool. While the water parks have lots of activities, they won't be a place for you to do any exercises.

Depending on the exercise(s), you may be able to do them right in your hotel room. If you need more space, there are **fitness clubs** at a number of resort hotels. If you're over 14 and staying at a resort with a fitness club, you can use the facility at no additional charge. (Children 14–17 must be accompanied by parent or guardian.) Most fitness centers have Cybex machines, treadmills, stairmasters, bicycles, and free weights (see next page for a listing of fitness center locations).

Disney Vacation Club (DVC) members may use the fitness club at any DVC resort as long as they are staying at Walt Disney World. A $12 fee will be charged if the DVC member uses a fitness center at a non-DVC resort and they are not staying there.

If you are not staying at a Disney resort with a health club but are staying on Disney property, **you may use a fitness club for $12 per day**.

If you belong to a health club at home, check before you leave to see if there are any **reciprocal privileges** at clubs in the Orlando area.

There are also a number of spas on Disney property where you can receive a **massage** or have access to a sauna, steamroom, or whirlpool (see next page for locations). The purchase of a spa treatment includes use of the adjacent fitness center for the day of treatment. For more details, visit http://www.relaxedyet.com.

Perhaps **renting** a wheelchair or an ECV for touring the parks is the way to go (see Mobility on pages 68–72).

If you want to do some concentrated walking or jogging for cardiac or other rehab, use one of the **walking/jogging/biking trails** at most Disney resorts. Stop by the Front Desk of the Disney resort and ask for a "jogger's map." These will give you a path to follow with approximate mileage. There is a wonderful wooded trail from the Fort Wilderness Campgrounds to the Wilderness Lodge and a riverside trail from Port Orleans French Quarter to Riverside. A large loop can be made to include Epcot, the Epcot resorts and Disney-MGM Studios. The three All-Star Resorts are all back-to-back so you can walk from one to the next to the next and back. Caribbean Beach, Coronado Springs, and Port Orleans Riverside are each large enough to provide their own walking areas. Be aware there are no paths to walk at Disney's Animal Kingdom Lodge.

If you need to contact local doctors/visiting nurses/hospitals during your stay, see **Ongoing Medical Treatment** on pages 61–67.

Planning

Special Challenges

Getting There

Staying in Style

Touring

Feasting

Resources

Index

[P] Physical Therapy/Rehabilitation (continued)

First Aid Stations are available in the theme parks and water parks—see page 206 for details.

Disney Cruise Line has the Vista Spa, an adult-only section of the ship housing the fitness center, aerobics studio, spa treatment rooms, and more. The fitness center is free for your use during the cruise, as is the aerobics studio when classes are not in session (classes may be offered free of charge—check with the spa for details upon your arrival). The fitness center has free weights, Cybex weight machines, treadmills, stair-steppers, ab-rollers, and stationary bikes. The fitness center is usually empty—only on at-sea days does it become busy.

Here is a current listing of **Fitness Centers and Spas** offered at Disney Resort hotels:

✔ Disney's Animal Kingdom Lodge—Zahanati Fitness Center and Spa

✔ Disney's BoardWalk—Muscles & Bustles Health Club

✔ Disney's Contemporary Resort—Olympiad Fitness Center

✔ Disney's Coronado Springs Resort—La Vida Fitness Center

✔ Disney's Grand Floridian Resort & Spa—Disney's Grand Floridian Spa & Health Club

✔ Disney's Old Key West Resort—R.E.S.T. Exercise Room

✔ Disney's Saratoga Springs Resort & Spa—Disney's Saratoga Springs Resort & Spa Fitness Center

✔ Disney's Wilderness Lodge and The Villas at Disney's Wilderness Lodge—Sturdy Branches Health Club

✔ Disney's Yacht & Beach Club Resorts and Disney's Beach Club Villas—Ship Shape Health Club

✔ Walt Disney World Swan and Dolphin Resort has the Mandara Spa (Dolphin) for massage and spa treatments of all kinds. The health clubs at the two hotels have Life Fitness equipment and also offer complimentary fitness classes. Cost to use facilities is $8/day or $20/stay. Hours are 6:00 am-9:00 pm. Note: Both hotels have accessories such as stability balls and core boards. You can also borrow pedometers and jogging strollers here.

Pregnancy and Fertility

It's wonderful—you're expecting your own "little souvenir" just like the cute little girl mentions on those Walt Disney World television commercials. But is it really wise to walk all those miles, standing in long lines in the Florida heat?

Obviously, every expectant woman is different, and it's best to consult with your doctor as to whether you should attempt a trip to Walt Disney World. But once you get the medical go-ahead, here are some things to consider.

Your Icon:

E

(E=Expectant)
Look for this symbol in the book for more details

Planning Ahead

Just because you're going on vacation, don't think you can ignore all the **normal rules and advice** that pregnant women should follow. You'll need comfy shoes that provide lots of support; loose, lightweight clothing; and plenty of sunscreen.

You'll also want to be sure to **stay hydrated**. Pregnant women are supposed to drink more water than usual anyway, and the Florida heat can be unrelenting at times. Because you're drinking more often, you'll need to find the restrooms more often—be sure you have a guidemap with you so you can locate the nearest one when you're traveling in the parks or Downtown Disney.

Remember that park distances on the guidemaps can be deceiving. You'll be doing a lot of walking around, so plan on taking it slow, and be sure to **take frequent rests**. If you can, you may want to even plan a midday break by returning to your hotel for a dip in the pool, or take an afternoon nap in the air-conditioned room.

While you're walking around, remember to be extra careful. The joints of pregnant women tend to become unstable (it's a hormone thing!) and you may lose your footing or your balance more easily. Pay close attention to places with **uneven surfaces**, like the play areas floored with spongy material, and the pathways at Disney's Animal Kingdom. Pay even closer attention when getting in and out of vehicles, especially those you have to step down into or up out of, like some of the boat rides.

Be sure to eat enough—**don't skip meals** just because you're on the go. It's easy to get caught up in having a good time and neglect to eat lunch.

[E] Pregnancy and Fertility (continued)

Also be sure to continue to eat nutritiously. Sure, those yummy cinnamon rolls they sell at the BoardWalk Bakery are awesome, but are they really that good for you? You're on vacation, but you and baby-to-be still need the right nutrients. A better idea is to **pack nutritious snacks** so you don't get overly hungry and eat the wrong things.

Along with eating enough and eating right, remember that you may be experiencing **food cravings** or aversions. Deb Koma says when she was pregnant, she couldn't even look at a hamburger without feeling queasy. Be sure to plan your mealtimes around places that serve food you can actually eat.

If there are any **"creature comforts"** that you can bring along with you, try to squeeze them in your suitcase. Maybe it's your comfy robe and plain crackers to combat morning sickness or the white-noise machine that lulls you to sleep every night.

Upon Your Arrival

When touring the theme parks, you'll see that Disney has **health warnings** on many of its thrill rides and strongly advises that pregnant women not ride these. We suggest you follow this advice, regardless of what stage you are at in your pregnancy.

But don't fret, there's **plenty to do** that doesn't require you getting shaken up or turned upside-down. Disney-MGM Studios, for instance, has many live entertainment shows that are either indoors or in the shade. And don't forget, while others in your group are riding thrill rides like Mission: SPACE or Dinosaur!, there are plenty of shops for you to browse through.

There are health warnings on many of the water slides at Blizzard Beach and Typhoon Lagoon water parks, and we suggest you heed them. A better bet is to **plant yourself in a raft** and float around the gentle "lazy rivers," like Castaway Creek at Typhoon Lagoon. So remember to pack a maternity bathing suit if you plan on pool time.

Reader Tip: "Being seven months pregnant and traveling with my 3-year-old through the parks was a challenge. Make sure you wear comfortable sandals (for swelling and for lots of walking). Pack at least one bottle of water per hour that you will need at the park. Take advantage of the indoor/air-conditioned entertainment. And if you really can't handle it, rent an ECV at the front of the parks."–contributed by Melissa Goetz

Back at your resort, don't hesitate to **call Housekeeping** if there's something that could make your stay in the room more comfortable. For example, you can get extra pillows if you need them for additional support for your pregnant tummy. Keep in mind that many of Disney's value and moderate resorts are spread out, with long walks between services and facilities. You may instead want to consider staying at a more self-contained resort, such as the Contemporary Resort tower or the Wilderness Lodge.

Also, remember that pregnant women must avoid raising their **internal body temperature** too much—check with your doctor before sitting in one of Disney's "spas" (or any hot tubs) or traveling during the hottest months in the summer.

PassPorter Picks

✔ Take advantage of all the quality **live shows** and entertainment around the theme parks. Most of the shows are either indoors or in the shade with plenty of time to sit.

PassPorter Pans

✔ **Avoid the big thrills**, just for this trip. When you return with the fruit of your labor (pun intended), then you can have a family member or friend hold the baby while you spin and coast to your heart's content!

Fertility

Have you been trying to get pregnant? Maybe this trip to Disney is just what you need to relax a little before conceiving. First and foremost, it's important to follow all the rules for pregnant women as you may not realize you're already pregnant (as editor Jennifer Marx discovered on her Disney vacation). Avoid hot tubs like the plague—this applies to women (bad for the egg and embryo) and men (bad for the sperm). If you're on medication, bring enough for the trip plus a little extra (and don't forget a copy of your prescriptions just in case). Don't discount the value of relaxation as a fertility booster either—many women have gotten pregnant on vacations (it's not just a myth). And speaking of making babies, don't forget those little things you may need for "smooth" operations. (We have seen personal lubricants for sale on property, but they aren't generally the fertility-friendly types.) If you're having long-term issues conceiving as Jennifer did, be mentally prepared for the masses of children and babies you will encounter at Walt Disney World. If it becomes overwhelming and positive thinking isn't helping, take a night off for Pleasure Island, where kids are few and far between—just skip or go light on the adult beverages.

Planning

Special Challenges

Getting There

Staying in Style

Touring

Feasting

Resources

Index

Religion

With millions of visitors from all over the world pouring into the Orlando area, houses of worship of every denomination are plentiful. No matter your religious preference, you should be able to find appropriate services in the Walt Disney World area.

Certain religious services were held regularly on Disney property at one time, but that practice was discontinued in 2002. Exceptions are on Easter and Christmas Day—sometimes a few Catholic and Protestant services are held at the Contemporary Resort's Fantasia Ballroom.

Your Icon:

(W=Worship)
Look for this symbol in the book for more details

Bright Idea: If you observe a special diet as part of your religion (e.g., kosher) be sure to read our section on Diet on pages 34-37.

Planning Ahead

Below is a selection of area religious services. For additional information, churches, or services, consult a current **local telephone directory** when you arrive in the Orlando area.

Most of these services can be reached **via taxi** if you do not have the use of your own transportation. Call Mears taxicab service at 407-422-2222.

Bright Idea: As an alternative, consider calling a town car service. Be sure to make arrangements (town car, prearranged taxi) beforehand.

Roman Catholic Services:
Mary, Queen of the Universe Shrine, 8300 Vineland Avenue
Phone: 407-239-6600; Web: http://www.maryqueenoftheuniverse.org
Mass schedule: Sunday: 7:30 am, 9:30 am, 11:30 am, and 6:00 pm
Saturday: 6:00 pm
A priest hears confession daily.

The **shrine** is located 2.5 miles northeast of Lake Buena Vista on the I-4 frontage road. Traveling south on SR 535 from Hotel Plaza Boulevard/Crossroads, drive to the second traffic signal, turn left (Vineland Avenue) and continue approximately one mile.

Bright Idea: If you're taking a taxi to the church, it may be difficult to get one for the return trip. Try walking over to the shopping center next door and getting a cab from there.

Protestant Services:

Community Presbyterian Church, 511 Celebration Avenue
Phone: 407-566-1633; Web: http://www.commpres.org
Directions: To get to **Community Presbyterian Church**, take I-4 West
to exit 65, which will take you to 192 (heading toward Kissimmee). Travel
two traffic lights down, make a left turn onto Celebration Avenue. Follow
Celebration Avenue, and the church is located one-quarter mile down the
road on the right-hand side.

First Baptist Church of Kissimmee, 1700 North John Young Parkway
Phone: 407-847-3138; Web: http://www.fbckiss.org
Directions: To get to the **First Baptist Church of Kissimmee**, go east on
highway 192 (West Irlo Bronson Memorial Highway) toward Kissimmee.
Turn left onto North John Young Parkway. After one block, turn left into
the First Baptist Church.

Islamic Services:

Islamic Center of Orlando, 11543 Ruby Lake Road; Phone: 407-238-2700
Directions: To get to the **Islamic Center of Orlando**, take I-4 East to Lake
Buena Vista exit. Turn left onto SR 535; continue on 535, and the mosque
will be on the right-hand side of the road (about two miles from I-4 exit).

Masjid Al-Rahman Mosque
http://www.iscf.org/About_ISCF_Masajid.asp?masajid=1

Islamic Society of Central Florida— http://www.iscf.org

There is also a designated **meditation/prayer room** open from 11:00 am
to 9:00 pm daily located inside the Morocco pavilion museum in Epcot's
World Showcase. Small rugs are available for guest use.

Jewish Services:

Celebration Jewish Congregation (Reconstructionist), 607 Celebration Ave.
Phone: 407-596-5397; Web: http://www.jrf.org/cjc/index.htm
Directions: To get to **Celebration Jewish Congregation**, take I-4 West to
exit 25A, which will take you to 192 (heading toward Kissimmee). At the
second traffic light, make a right turn onto Celebration Avenue. Follow
Celebration Avenue into town.

Mormon (Church of Jesus Christ of Latter Day Saints) Services:

Orlando Florida Temple (only Mormon Temple in Florida), 9000 Windy
Ridge Road., Windermere, FL; Phone: 407-876-0022
http://lds.org/temples/main/0,11204,1912-1-82-2,00.html

Planning

Special Challenges

Getting There

Staying in Style

Touring

Feasting

Resources

Index

Seniors

Your Icon:

S

(S=Seniors)
Look for this
symbol in the
book for more
details

Congratulations! You've reached senior status and you still want to go to Walt Disney World! We hope we never think we're too old to experience the magic.

We realize that many seniors are fit and healthy and have more energy than we do! But maybe you'd like to take your time and stop to smell the roses. Or maybe you or a senior you're traveling with is among those who have some special challenges. If so, you might have to adapt your plans to meet the demands an **older and wiser body** makes on you. Also, be aware that a vacation with the kids and grandkids can be far more active than you're used to. Even if your health is good, you may encounter unexpected limitations. If you do, don't fight them—every family vacation deserves a happy ending. You'll find pertinent advice throughout this book. And if you experience any unexpected discomfort, the nearest Disney cast member will know how to get you the help you need.

So what really differentiates a mature traveler from a younger vacationer? Obviously, it's hard to make generalizations, but for the purposes of this section, we're assuming that if you're a mature traveler, you're looking for a **different kind of Walt Disney World experience**—maybe one that's more low-key or less hectic than the average Disney-goer's. Even if you're visiting the theme parks with your grandchildren, you still need time that is just for you.

Planning Ahead

If you have specific health concerns, **consult** with your regular physician before undertaking a trip to Walt Disney World. Our tips and suggestions are in no way a substitute for medical advice. And if you do have some special considerations, there are other sections in this chapter that might be of interest to you: Diet, Heart Health, Ongoing Medical Treatment, Mobility, Hearing, and Vision, for example.

So what types of things should you focus on when you're visiting Walt Disney World? First of all, **take everything at your own pace**. Don't get up early to be the first one in the theme parks, unless you *want* to be there at rope drop. Schedule leisurely meals at off-peak hours; you'll avoid long waits and noisy crowds. Make sure you allow yourself plenty of breaks. Possibly head to the resort in the middle of the day for a dip in the pool or just some quiet time in the cool of your room.

Also, there's no reason to keep the whole group together for every activity. **A mix of family togetherness and alone time is key** to everyone enjoying themselves. Seniors may want to spend fewer hours in the park, rejoining the family at a designated time and place. Grandparents can be their kids' heroes by taking the grandchildren back to the room for a midday rest or by babysitting while others spend a late night at the parks. But remember you deserve a break, too, so make sure your kids return the favor!

While all of the Disney theme parks have something to offer the mature traveler, you may find **some activities are more appealing than others**. Epcot in particular is filled with cultural and educational experiences that might be more entertaining to you than the rides in the Magic Kingdom's Fantasyland. Disney's Animal Kingdom, with its myriad live animals and related exhibits scattered throughout the park, is equally interesting.

When booking your room, consider any special health needs you might have and follow our suggestions in the appropriate sections in this chapter. If you need a **larger room**, for example, or if you prefer to be away from the noise of the pools, be sure to request that when making reservations. Some resorts offer "deluxe" categories of rooms that are larger.

Also, choose a resort that reflects the type of vacation you're looking for. If you're staying at a Disney resort looking for **peace and quiet**, that does not mean one of the value All-Stars or Pop Century, which are frequently filled with high school cheerleading and sports groups. Instead, if the budget allows, consider treating yourself to a stay at one of the deluxe resorts, which offer convenience in transportation and location, as well as some enriching experiences. Disney's Animal Kingdom Lodge, for example, has its own game preserve right on the grounds—you can book a room with a savanna view, with giraffes, wildebeest, and other wild animals greeting your morning. And if your budget stretches even further, why not really spoil yourself and stay in a concierge room at one of the deluxe resorts? Amenities there include a special lounge with all-day snacks and beverages.

As a mature traveler, some of your favorite activities may actually be **outside the theme parks!** Be sure to research your trip as much as possible in advance, so that you know about the many golf courses (not to mention miniature golf) scattered around the resort. In addition, many of the resorts offer swimming, tennis, a variety of other court sports, water craft and bicycle rentals, jogging trails, fitness centers, and spas. If fishing is your game, there are a number of catch-and-release programs available.

Planning

Special Challenges

Getting There

Staying in Style

Touring

Feasting

Resources

Index

[S] Seniors (continued)

Upon Your Arrival

Remember that distances around the theme parks **are greater** than you might expect. Consider renting a wheelchair or ECV to help you conserve energy if the heat and activity catch up with you.

Remember to rest frequently, and **hydrate often**! The Florida sun and humidity sap everyone's strength, especially folks who are spending 8–10 hours pounding the hot pavement. (See chapter 5 for quiet spots.)

Don't skip meals! It's easy to forget yourself in the midst of too much fun, but touring the parks on an empty stomach is not a good idea.

Use **FASTPASS** whenever possible; it really is the best way to shorten your time waiting in line. (See page 216 for more details on FASTPASS.)

Take note of where the **First Aid Stations** are located in each park (see page 206). Even if you don't need any of their services, it's a nice, quiet place to cool down if you're feeling overheated or overwhelmed.

If you find that your appetite or your budget isn't as hearty as it used to be, you might not want to dine at the all-you-can-eat meals at Walt Disney World as you won't get your money's worth. A good alternative is to eat your **main meal at lunchtime**, when portions are slightly smaller and prices are slightly less. Some restaurants offer fixed-price menus that represent a good value, and some offer discounts to annual passholders, DVC members, or AAA members. Yet another option is to order appetizers instead of full entrees.

PassPorter Picks

✔ All Disney resort hotels have pools, and most have at least one **"quiet" pool** where you are more likely to enjoy the water without lots of noise. Early morning is usually the best time for a quiet dip. Some pools have zero entryways to allow for easy transitions (see page 116.)

✔ If you'd prefer a **laid-back lounge for a cocktail** before or after your meal, we've enjoyed Martha's Vineyard (Beach Club), the Belle Vue Room (BoardWalk), and Mizner's (Grand Floridian)—these spots usually seem far removed from the "madding crowd."

✔ Certain parts of Tom Sawyer Island can be a **respite** from the hubbub of the Magic Kingdom—if you can manage the uneven, unpaved pathways, head over there and find a spot on a quiet bench, or sip a cool drink while reading at Aunt Polly's Dockside Inn.

✔ If you're curious about how things work, Disney offers a number of **behind-the-scenes tours**, ranging from a few hours to all day.

✔ For **quiet fine dining**, try the table-service restaurants at the deluxe resorts. Among our favorites for a relaxing meal with fantastic food: Artist Point at the Wilderness Lodge, California Grill at the Contemporary, Jiko at the Animal Kingdom Lodge, and Flying Fish Café on the Boardwalk. And there's Victoria & Albert's at the Grand Floridian for special occasions!

✔ While Blizzard Beach has a reputation for being a big-thrill water park, **Typhoon Lagoon** might be more desirable for the mature traveler. Its Castaway Creek lazy river raft ride is a pleasant way to while away a few hours. If you're interested, you can swim with the fishes, or sharks, to boot, in the Shark Reef snorkeling pool. Of course, if the grandkids insist that nothing but Blizzard Beach will do, it also has a lazy river that you can bob along in while the young'uns tackle the fast body slides.

✔ Strolling around both **Downtown Disney** and the BoardWalk is a nice respite from the hustle and bustle of running from ride to ride. There's lots to do in these two areas that get you away from the frenetic pace of the theme parks. Best of all, you can stop in either place for a yummy ice cream cone or cool drink while you sit in shade next to the water and people-watch. The amazing Cirque du Soleil's show La Nouba, at the West Side, is a treat for the eyes that you can only experience in Orlando.

PassPorter Pans

✔ If you're looking for peace and quiet, **avoid the kids' play areas**—they're loud and filled with high-spirited kids running and blowing off steam. These include Tom Sawyer Island, Toon Park, Donald's Boat, Pooh's Playful Spot (Magic Kingdom); Honey, I Shrunk the Kids Movie Set Adventure (Disney-MGM Studios); and the Boneyard (Disney's Animal Kingdom).

✔ Take special care in Disney's Animal Kingdom, where the pathways are often **narrow and uneven**.

✔ Character meals tend to be on the loud and boisterous side, often with additional noisy entertainment for kids. If you want a **sedate meal**, don't dine with the characters.

✔ If the idea of rowdy entertainment turns you off, though, be aware that at night, Downtown Disney's Pleasure Island becomes one nightclub after another, with lots of loud, pounding music playing in the streets, where they also serve alcohol. Over at the **BoardWalk**, the entertainment isn't quite so loud, except Jellyrolls with its dueling pianos. It can draw big crowds that get into the spirit of singing along a little too much at times. Likewise, the smoke-filled ESPN Club bar can be a bit loud with overflow crowds.

Planning

Special Challenges

Getting There

Staying in Style

Touring

Feasting

Resources

Index

Size

Walt Disney World visitors come from countries all over the world, speak a multitude of languages, and come in **all shapes and sizes**. It's clear that one size does not fit all. No one wants to plan an expensive vacation, then worry that they won't fit in the various rides and attractions. Fear not! Walt Disney World has taken your needs into consideration. In fact, folks often comment how "at large" friendly most of Walt Disney World really is.

As you experience the Walt Disney World resort from the oldest sections (like the Magic Kingdom park and the Polynesian resort) to the newest areas (Disney's Animal Kingdom and Pop Century resort), you'll notice how accessibility for people of size has **improved** over the years.

> **Your Icon:**
>
> **L**
>
> (L=Large or Little)
>
> Look for this symbol in the book for more details

Planning Ahead

For people of size, we suggest getting a room with a king-size bed. Not only will you be more comfortable, but there will be **one less obstacle** (the other bed) to maneuver around in your room. You will pay a bit more for a King room category, but the comfort will outweigh the cost.

While all of the value resort room sizes are about the same (260 sq. ft./ 24 sq. m.), the **moderates vary**. Caribbean Beach offers the most space at 340 sq ft. (31.6 sq. m.), compared to 314 sq. ft. (29 sq. m.) at moderates such as Port Orleans Riverside, French Quarter, and Coronado Springs.

The Wilderness Lodge and Disney's Animal Kingdom Lodge have the **smallest rooms** of all the Deluxe resorts at 340 sq. ft. (31.6 sq. m.) and 344 sq. ft. (32 sq. m.), respectively. The Contemporary garden wing has the largest regular rooms at 436 sq. ft. (40.5 sq. m.). The following deluxe resorts offer a deluxe room category that has more space: Disney's Animal Kingdom Lodge, BoardWalk, and Yacht and Beach Club. And, of course, there are the villas of the Disney Vacation Club (DVC) resorts. The DVC studios begin at 356 sq. ft./33 sq. m. (376 sq. ft./35 sq. m. at Old Key West) and offer other amenities such as a small refrigerator, microwave, and coffeemaker. Refer to chapter 4 for resort room categories.

Know the **height requirements and ride restrictions** before you get to Walt Disney World to avoid disappointments and surprises. (You'll find this information in the *Guidebooks for Guests With Disabilities* and online at AllEarsNet.com, http://allearsnet.com/tp/rr.htm.) Also see chapter 5.

Disney Cruise Line offers some of the largest staterooms available on cruise ships. Even non-suite staterooms measure as large as 304 sq. ft. (28.24 sq. m.). Disney Cruise Line also offers accessible staterooms and suites, with ramped bathroom thresholds, open bed frames, added phones in the bathroom/nightstand, bathroom and shower handrails, fold-down shower seats, handheld shower heads, lowered towel and closet bars, and emergency call buttons. The shower areas are small even for "average" sized folks—adults may want to consider using the showers in the Vista Spa's locker rooms, which are larger.

Looking for Walt Disney World Logo clothing? Before you go, check online at http://www.disneydirect.com or at local stores like Wal-Mart. At Walt Disney World sizes, 3X, 4X, and 5X are sold at the **World of Disney** in the Downtown Disney Marketplace.

For **photographs** of Disney ride vehicles and theater seating to identify size issues, visit: http://allears.net/tp/gal_ride.htm.

For **guest reports**, visit: http://allears.net/tp/ridsiz.htm.

Upon Your Arrival

The two main areas of **concern** we hear from people of larger size are:

1. Will I fit through the turnstiles?
2. Will I fit in the ride vehicle or theater seat?

No one has to go through a **turnstile**. The entrance to each park has a gate for wheelchairs and strollers right next to the turnstile. Just motion to the cast member you will enter that way, or ask if you're unsure. The same is true for the entrances of each attraction—most have a gate that swings open. Just ask the cast member. Be on alert at the Magic Kingdom. Those turnstiles and gates are among the smallest in all of Walt Disney World and can be particularly challenging! We note where to watch out in each attraction section in chapter 5.

Some attractions have an actual ride vehicle **on display** outside the main entrance so you can see exactly what you'll be boarding (ask at Test Track and Expedition Everest). We'll mention specifics in the descriptions of those attractions. Space Mountain seating can be especially tricky.

Several attractions in each of the theme parks and water parks have **minimum height requirements** and are so noted in chapter 5.

Sit-down restaurants usually have **chairs without arms**. If you don't see one, ask. Better yet, request one from the hostess/host when you check in. Ask for a booth or table (whichever you prefer) when you check in, too.

Planning

Special Challenges

Getting There

Staying in Style

Touring

Feasting

Resources

Index

Planning

Special Challenges

Getting There

Staying in Style

Touring

Feasting

Resources

Index

[L] Size (continued)

The one theme park dining area where you might encounter a problem is at the **Sci-Fi Dine-In Theater**, where much of the seating is in mock vintage convertibles. A picnic table in the back fits most folks.

Bright Idea: Does the ride vehicle have a seat belt? Be sure and pull it all the way out before you sit down. Seatbelt extenders are available on some attractions. Ask a cast member when you enter the ride.

The **restrooms** all have handicapped stalls, of course, and these provide more room to move around.

If you encounter a problem, do not hesitate to ask a **cast member**. They should be able to get what you need or direct you accordingly.

The **various attraction seating types** are described and illustrated on page 207.

Important Note: Persons small in stature may have difficulty reaching the overhead handholds on Disney buses when there is only standing room. Look for the seat-level bars to hold on to.

PassPorter Picks

✔ Many restaurants have chairs without arms. Ask for one at check-in.

✔ Test Track and Rock 'n' Roller Coaster have much more leg room in the front row; Space Mountain has more room in the back seat.

PassPorter Pans

✔ If you're a tall person, look out for rides that we have designated as having "small spaces" in chapter 5.

✔ Don't take the Segway tour if you're more than 250 lb. (113 kg.). Likewise, you have to be at least 5 feet (152 cm.) tall to drive a Sea Raycer boat and can weigh no more than 320 lb. (145 kg.).

✔ The Magic Kingdom has really narrow turnstiles.

✔ In those Disney Cruise Line staterooms that have pull-down berths, the weight limit is 220 lb. (100 kg.). Some excursions (such as parasailing) have weight limitations also.

✔ Horseback riding at Fort Wilderness has a 250-lb. (113-kg.) limit.

Vision

Visitors to Walt Disney World who have partial or complete vision loss can enjoy just about any experience the resort has to offer, but their experiences will be slightly different. If you have some degree of vision loss, or if you are traveling with someone who does, you'll be relieved to note that Walt Disney World offers a number of services to help maximize your vacation.

Your Icon:

V

(V=Vision)
Look for this
symbol in the
book for more
details

Planning Ahead

Before you head to Orlando, it's a good idea to learn more about the Walt Disney World resort. Some Disney guidebooks are available on **audiotape** through the Library of Congress's National Library Service for the Blind and Physically Handicapped (NLS) at http://www.loc.gov/nls. Contact your local library or bookstores for availability. There are also several services that translate magazine articles into Braille. You might be able to find some travel articles on Orlando through them. Try http://blindreaders.info or the National Federation of the Blind at http://www.nfb.org. International travelers, remember to check with organizations in your region that aid those with vision impairments for further Disney audio book information.

Also, if you require special glasses, it's a good idea to bring an extra pair with you if you have them, or a **copy of your prescription**, in case you need to get an emergency pair.

Remember **sunglasses** and a hat, too, if your eyes are sensitive to the light—the summer sun can be very bright and intense!

Be sure to request an **easily accessible** room when you book your reservation, whether you're staying at a Disney resort or off Disney property. A room that's on the main floor is a good idea. Otherwise, a room that's close to the hotel facilities, such as the food court or elevators, is a good choice.

Disney **restaurant menus** are not available in Braille or audio formats. If you have text-to-voice computer software, you can preview the menus at http://www.allears.net/menu/menus.htm.

Bright Idea: "If you have a cane, consider bringing it with you. Often the only warning someone gets that I have a vision impairment is the 'big white stick!' It alerts cast members that you require assistance before you have to ask."
—contributed by peer reviewer Tim Sullivan

[V] Vision (continued)

Upon Your Arrival

Even though a person with vision loss can tour the theme parks independently, it's probably better to have a **companion** along, especially during busy peak seasons. A companion can help avoid congested traffic areas and provide direction more easily, while also offering verbal descriptions of the sights and attractions. Besides, Walt Disney World is an experience that's enhanced when you share it with a friend.

Bright Idea: When leading a visually impaired person through busy walkways, yield the right-of-way to strollers. Also, agree on what to do if you become separated. It is usually best for the visually impaired person to stop where they are and wait for their companion to come back to them. Peer reviewer Tim Sullvan adds that if you have a cane, you can use it as a "beacon" by holding it vertically in the air so that your companion can spot you more easily.

Among the **aids** that Walt Disney World offers:

✔ **Braille guidebooks** are available at Guest Relations for a $25 refundable deposit (if you return the book the same day). It's a good idea to study the guide for a while before touring a park.

✔ Audiotape guides with **portable tape players** are also available at Guest Relations for a $25 refundable deposit. There are two versions of the audio cassettes: an audio guide (with an overview of the services available to those with vision impairments, as well as an idea of the layout of the theme park) and an audio tour (which describes a specific route, giving distances between attractions and important stopping points along the way). These audio guides are not as useful as the Braille guide, as they are sequential and don't allow you to wander or explore at your own discretion.

✔ Braille and **large-print park guidemaps** are located in Guest Releations at each park. See chapter 5 for Braille map locations in each park.

According to peer reviewer Tim Sullivan, who is vision-impaired, both the Braille guides and the audio guides are a great attempt by Walt Disney World to increase the access and awareness for visually impaired guests, but their formats have **drawbacks**. The Braille guide contains everything that's in the regular guide (in both Braille and large-print), but its size is cumbersome. You could sit for a bit at the beginning of your day to read the guide book ... but that's when most people want to use this time to actually go and see the attractions. In addition, you can only get the guide for the day of your visit (or forgo a $25 deposit). The audio guide is also a really great tool, but it has a *very short* cord connecting the unit to the headset, which makes it all but impossible to wear the guide while walking around, using a cane/service animal/being led by a companion. If you *do* plan to go this route, look into bringing your own headphones that will allow you to wear the audio guide on your belt or in your day pack.

There are several **3-D movies that require special glasses** to see the 3-D effects. They are: It's Tough to be a Bug in Disney's Animal Kingdom; Mickey's PhilharMagic in the Magic Kingdom; Honey, I Shrunk the Audience in Epcot; and Muppet Vision 3-D in the Disney-MGM Studios. These 3-D glasses are wide enough to fit right over your own glasses, but people with vision loss or impairment may not be able to fully perceive the special effects.

There are hands-on displays in some areas that can provide additional sensory input for those with vision loss. In Disney's Animal Kingdom, there are areas along the Pangani Forest Exploration Trail and at Conservation Station that feature "manipulatives," such as animal skulls and bones, for **tactile exploration**. Often the children's areas during some of Epcot's special events (Food & Wine Festival and Flower & Garden Festival) have additional hands-on experiences that are worth investigating.

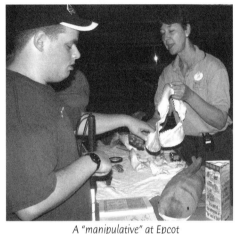

© Deb Wills

A "manipulative" at Epcot

Braille signage is available in Disney **elevators** and marks resort rooms to make it easier to locate your destination.

There are no special provisions at the **water parks**, but you should be able to experience most attractions if you have a companion to assist you.

At Downtown Disney, there is **Braille signage** on the restrooms located at Guest Relations and in Once Upon a Toy, but there are no Braille maps available. Some shops in both Downtown Disney and the BoardWalk may be tricky to negotiate—they are very crowded with merchandise and displays. We have noted other special considerations in our individual descriptions of these areas in chapter 5.

If you use a **service animal**, you'll find that you're able to take it with you around most of Walt Disney World, as long as it's on a leash or a harness. See our information on traveling with a service animal on page 12.

Arrive early for shows and ask cast members if you can be seated before the general population, so you can avoid having to move around with hundreds of people. Most shows have two seating areas for those with disabilities—one low and one high. Ask to be seated in the one that will be accommodate your vision needs.

Planning · Special Challenges · Getting There · Staying in Style · Touring · Feasting · Resources · Index

[V] Vision (continued)

PassPorter Picks

✔ Attractions with a **large amount of dialogue**, such as Spaceship Earth or Hall of Presidents, are easier to follow.

✔ People with vision loss can experience **dark thrill rides**, such as Rock 'n' Roller Coaster or Space Mountain, in much the same manner as those without vision impairment.

✔ The 3-D shows are **multisensory** and can be quite enjoyable.

✔ Consider purchasing **Pal Mickey**, a 10-inch plush Mickey Mouse that talks. Using wireless technology, Pal Mickey points out your location, reminds you of parade times, and offers tips on many other things. Pal Mickey is $65 at most resort gift shops and at locations throughout the theme parks. (There's also a Spanish-speaking Pal Mickey!)

✔ Try to catch some of the **live musical acts** in the parks, like Voices of Liberty in Epcot or the Dapper Dans in the Magic Kingdom.

✔ The props, called **manipulatives**, found in certain areas of Disney's Animal Kingdom and Epcot can give insight through a tactile experience. Animal Kingdom Lodge has similar displays. Often these exhibits are billed for kids, but they can also be useful to those with vision impairments.

PassPorter Pans

✔ For some, the **fireworks shows and parades** are not easily appreciated. Others enjoy the music, sound, and the "impact" of explosions and drums, which can be thrilling.

Reader Story: "It is important to remember that while a visually impaired person cannot enjoy Walt Disney World in the same way as a sighted person, they enjoy it in a different way. What to concentrate on depends on the individual. I have gone multiple times with my husband (who is totally blind) and a friend (who has very limited vision—he can see light and some color). They have different interests. My husband enjoys technology, so his favorite park is Epcot, because of Innoventions and the attractions in Future World. He enjoys listening to the different people at the attractions. My husband also enjoys the thrill rides. His favorite attraction is the Tower of Terror in the Disney-MGM Studios. All of the roller coasters and simulators are the things he wants to do the most. My friend's favorite park is also Epcot, but for a very different reason. He enjoys the food, smells, and shopping in World Showcase and loves talking to the people from other countries, asking about their country of origin. Because he is also a music lover, we try to catch some of the entertainment, such as Epcot Vybe or Off Kilter. He also enjoys going to the different resorts to check out the atmosphere. It is at the resorts where one can take the most time and give good descriptions of what is around."

—contributed by Lori Kloman Williamson

Boarding Tips for the Vision-Impaired

My mother, 60, has advanced retinitis pigmentosa and uses a white cane. She can see the difference between light and dark, but not much else. One of the things we learned fast was to describe to her how a ride loaded—it was frustrating for her when she'd be trying to take a step up into a ride vehicle, only to discover that there's also a slight ledge or barrier she had to step over, as well as step up.

These are the descriptions we used to let her know how to prepare to get on the attraction or ride:

✔ Moving walkway—A continuously loading ride like Haunted Mansion, Spaceship Earth, or the Clamobiles at The Seas with Nemo and Friends

✔ Stop ride—Any other ride that stops the loading vehicle to let you on, such as Journey Into Imagination with Figment!

✔ Step up—A ride vehicle that would require her to step up to get in, such as the parking lot trams

✔ Step over—A ride vehicle that has a ledge or barrier that she'd have to put her feet over in order to load, such as Dumbo the Flying Elephant and the Magic Carpets of Aladdin

✔ Step down—A ride vehicle that requires you to step down to get in the vehicle, such as Pirates of the Caribbean and Test Track

Of course, most attractions were a combination. "it's a small world" is a stop ride with a step down. "Dinosaur" is a stop ride with a step up and step over. "Buzz Lightyear" is a moving walkway with a step over and slight step up.

Using these terms helped immensely in letting my mother know what she was going to need to do to get on the ride safely and efficiently.

—contributed by Jennifer Grudnoski

Planning
Special Challenges
Getting There
Staying in Style
Touring
Feasting
Resources
Index

Planning

Special Challenges

Getting There

Staying in Style

Touring

Feasting

Resources

Index

[V] Vision (continued)

IN FOCUS: Traveling With a Vision Impairment

If you met Tim Sullivan in the parks, you wouldn't realize he has special challenges. In fact, before he began to use his cane all the time at Walt Disney World, you would have wondered why this man suddenly bumped into you. "Can't he see me here?" you might have thought. The truth is, no, he can't.

© Deb Wills

Tim has retinitis pigmentosa, which is tunnel vision, coupled with no low-light vision. As Tim explains, "Straight ahead I'm fine, but to the sides and in dark attractions or at night, I have difficulty. This gives me the most problems in crowds, where I simply do not see all the people. Crowds seem to confuse my vision. Also," he adds, "when a ride is dark, I see little to none of it. My eyes just will not process everything."

Tim and co-author Deb Wills

According to Tim, people with special challenges like his should make their first stop on their first day in any of the theme parks at Guest Relations to get a Guest Assistance Card (GAC). "The GAC is good for your entire visit to Walt Disney World," he notes, and it outlines any assistance you may need while visiting the park. "More importantly," he adds, "it identifies that you in fact have some special needs or challenges that require attention." Tim uses the GAC to provide him an alternative entrance to attractions, where available. This enables him to navigate easier and sometimes even avoid bumps with other guests and bruises from the queue railings. He suggests that you bring some sort of documentation that proves or explains your visual impairment, if you have it. You don't always need it, he notes, but it quickly proves that you do actually need the help you're requesting.

His best advice for touring the parks is to "know that with a visual impairment you will be slowed down, so don't expect to 'see' as much nor do as much. Pick what is most important to you, and make sure you enjoy those things. Take your time moving around the parks and stop and smell the roses—definitely go for quality over quantity."

In addition, Tim offers these touring tips:

Staying late at the parks is a great idea. From my experience, many people tend to go home toward the end of the evening, so the park empties out and you'll have an easier time getting around. Also, with fewer people there, it is easier for you to get onto rides and attractions, increasing your fun level at the park.

Cast members usually don't mind vision-impaired persons touching and feeling various aspects of the "set dressings" for rides. My brother-in-law, who is blind, gets the biggest kick out of some of that stuff. With anything, though, be sure to check with a cast member before fondling everything in sight ... there might be something they do not want you to touch, so better be safe than sorry.

If you go to any of the shows, arrive early and ask the cast members if you can be seated prior to the admission of the rest of the crowd. This will help alleviate some of the craziness that ensues when the masses stampede to get the best seats, but will also ensure that you get the best seating that you will need to suit your vision impairment. The GAC helps here! There are usually specially reserved sections in both the front and rear of the theaters.

Even though I do not always see everything on the rides, there is always something for me to enjoy. Swooping over the streets of London in a pirate ship is magical no matter how much of the ride I can actually see, so make sure you do not bypass anything just because you don't think there will be something for you. Disney always makes sure they attack as many of the senses as they can with their rides.

Your Tips and Stories

I have two autistic children, and I highly recommend watching the Magic Kingdom parade and fireworks in the least crowded places available. We watch the parade at the very end in front of Pirates of the Caribbean by Pecos Bill Cafe and it is great! Last time we went, we stood right along the ropes with only about 20 other people. That way, we didn't have the long wait when trying to claim a spot and fewer people to keep my children as comfortable as possible for their enjoyment. We watched the fireworks from the dock in front of Pecos Bill and Country Bear Jamboree. A lot of people really want to see them in front of the castle, but that is just not an option for our family. The trees were slightly in the way, but not much, and we were the only people standing there along the water. That was actually a very special moment that my husband and I will always treasure with our boys. They loved watching the fireworks and yet we were totally secluded with the feeling that the show was just for us! Then we took our time walking out of the park.

—contributed by Abby Harrington

I went to Disney World when I was eight months pregnant. Everyone thought I was crazy for wanting to go, but it was wonderful! On my doctor's order, I brought a cooler of bottled water each day to keep hydrated and sat down often. There are so many beautiful shady spots to sit that I had never discovered before. In fact, I discovered a lot of things on that trip I had never discovered there before. While everyone was busy riding rides I could not go on, I found new shops and snacks. It was my 2-year-old daughter's first time there, and I really got to enjoy every moment with her instead of rushing to the next ride. I recommend it to any expectant mother.

—contributed by Anonymous

Sometimes "invisible disabilities" are the worst to deal with— when someone looks like everyone else, they should act like everyone else. We have two daughters, Ariel (14) and Hannah (10). Hannah has high-functioning autism. Both parents in our family are active duty military, so for us, planning is everything. We read books, checked things out on the Internet, and planned in advance. We turned the girls into a "research team" and had them work together choosing where we would eat, based on the menus they found posted. We talked about it often with both daughters, but especially Hannah. We made calendars with everything about the day printed on them, so there were no surprises. We also put the same information along with our cell phone number, her first name and photo, and a brief explanation of her disorder on a small card, which we laminated and put on her lanyard. We explained to her that if she became lost, she could find a Disney Cast Member and show them the card. We assured her she wouldn't have to say a thing and they would know just what to do. I think it really put her mind at ease.

—contributed by Mae Cavalcanto

My husband has recently had both hips replaced. This left him little muscle tissue when he sits in a chair. Many rides and shows have nice seats, but very little padding. I purchased a cheap seat cushion—the type you would purchase for a dining room chair (look for a thin one-it fits into a backpack nicely). This added a lot of comfort when sitting in a show that could last 30 minutes, or on a ride like Star Tours, which was a little bumpy.

—contributed by Anonymous

Planning
Special Challenges
Getting There
Staying in Style
Touring
Feasting
Resources
Index

Your Tips and Stories
(continued)

We have two sons, one with Asperger's Syndrome and the other with ADHD and PDD-NOS (pervasive developmental disorder—not otherwise specified). To help them adjust to the trip and ease into our vacation, we always plan to arrive the day before our package starts. This helps with all the sensory issues, different temperature, different smells, different sounds, etc. We book an extra night at the same resort where our package is. When we get to the hotel, we explore the hotel with them so they can see where the restaurants and food court, pools, video game room, store, and the lobby are located. Then we plan dinner to ease into the Disney overload. We will go to Chef Mickey's for dinner, then ride the monorail to see (but not have to hear) the fireworks at the Magic Kingdom. If we are lucky, we see the Electric Water Pageant behind the Contemporary on the Seven Seas Lagoon. If we are staying at Port Orleans, we take the boat up the river to Downtown Disney, explore the shops, have dinner, and ride the boat back to the resort to enjoy the pool.   —contributed by Mary Akers

My granddaughter suffers from fears, mostly fire after their house burned down a few years back. Knowing what to expect on the Backlot Tour and Lights, Motors, Action! Extreme Stunt Show was especially helpful. When she knew what was coming, she was able to handle it, even though I thought my hand was going to fall off a couple of times!   —contributed by Ellen

My daughter Natalie is 10 years old with albinism. She needs to be careful in the sun, and her vision is 20/200, uncorrectable. We have been on vacations many places, including a cruise, but no vacation makes my family feel *normal* like a trip to Walt Disney World. My doctor gave me a letter stating that Natalie needed shade and to sit front and center, when possible. We did not know what this would do for us, but when we arrived at Disney and went to Guest Relations, they gave us a Guest Assistance Card for our entire party for all the parks. We still spent the hottest part of the day at the hotel, but early in the morning, it was a dream. For the first time, my son was not embarrassed and my daughter felt special. Disney is really a place that dreams come true!   —contributed by Anonymous

Last year, I was involved in a serious car accident. At the hospital, a CT scan showed that I had broken my neck. While in the hospital, I thought about our usual Memorial Day trip to Walt Disney World. Should I cancel? Should I go anyway and be there while my husband had a good time? If I went, what couldn't I go on? Obviously, anything that cautioned about neck or back problems. The list was remarkably short. I began to concentrate on what I *could* do and not what I *couldn't* do. I've been to Walt Disney World four times since the accident. There are only 11 attractions that I can't ride. I have had to make adjustments when at Walt Disney World—that's a given—but they are very minor adjustments. We're going to be taking our son and his family to Walt Disney World in a few years. Our new grandson will be able to go on the Kilimanjaro Safaris at Disney's Animal Kingdom, and I won't. Nonetheless, I am looking forward to him and his big sister telling me all about the animals they saw. That's better than the Safari in my opinion.   —contributed by Sheri Niklewski

Getting There (and Back!)

You've decided that you are going to visit the Mouse, and now it's time to make your travel plans.

Just what is the best way to travel to Walt Disney World? Well, so much of that depends on you and your requirements. There are obviously pros and cons to each method of travel, which we address a bit in this chapter. We also tell you other special things you need to know to make the journey with ease and confidence.

In addition to our suggestions and tips, you'll also find special phone numbers and web site addresses to assist you in planning your trip.

No matter which mode of transportation you choose, all travelers should keep the following items on their person or in their carry-on luggage to avoid losing them:

✔ Be sure to bring enough (including extra) of any prescription medications you need, in their original bottles, as well as a copy of the prescription(s), in case you need to get refills. Make a separate list of these medications, including the dosages. If you're a traveler from the United States and the prescription is with a pharmacy chain, getting a refill at a local branch should not be hard. Remember to bring any eyeglass/contact lens prescriptions, too.

✔ Keep a summary of your medical history with you at all times, including the names and phone numbers of your doctor(s). Include a copy of your electrocardiogram if you have heart health concerns. Bring a letter from your doctor(s) describing your health condition and any special relevant information.

✔ Bring lists of contacts and phone numbers in case of emergency.

✔ Carry identification for each person that includes their name, emergency information, and where you are staying in Florida. We've found the Who's Shoes ID to be great for youngsters and for those travelers unable to verbalize or remember their information—for more details, see http://www.whosshoesid.com.

Personal Identification

We recommend everyone traveling keep personal ID on them at all times. This may be something as simple as a driver's license or state-issued ID card. For kids, you may want to have them carry a laminated card or attach ID to their clothing, depending on their age. Here are more specific ways to keep ID on yourself and your travelers:

Cruisers—As early as January 1, 2008, *everyone* (including U.S. citizens) traveling between the United States and Canada, Mexico, Central and South America, the Caribbean, and Bermuda by land or sea (including ferries) may be required to present a valid passport or other documents as determined by the Department of Homeland Security. http://travel.state.gov

Bright Idea: Copy the basic information pages of your passport and keep them separate.

International Travelers—Carry your passport on you at all times, in the event of a problem or emergency. You may want to consider keeping it in a special passport case tucked inside your shirt, and/or use the PassHolder Pouch (see page 401), which fits most passports.

Medical Needs—Medical alert bracelets (or necklaces) are paramount if you have a special medical issue. You can generally find generic bracelets indicating common special needs, such as diabetes, in most drugstores. We recommend you get your ID tag personalized with your contact information, too. You can order these from http://www.medicalert.org.

Other Travelers—There are a variety of products that allow you to wear your identification. You can get bracelets, shoe tags and stickers, and zipper pulls. You can find some of these at http://www.whosshoesid.com.

Looking for an inexpensive, low-tech way to record personal information? Here's a **simple ID card** tailored to a vacation—feel free to copy it as many times as needed. Then just fill it out, laminate it, and stick it in a wallet, purse, pocket, backpack, or PassHolder Pouch. Consider including a recent photo on the back side, too!

Name: _____ Age: _____
Medical Conditions/Medications: _____
_____
Address: _____
Phone: _____ Cell Phone: _____
Hotel: _____ Phone: _____
Hotel Room Registered Under Name: _____
I am traveling with: _____ Cell Phone: _____
_____ Cell Phone: _____
Emergency Contact: _____ Phone: _____

Reader Tip: "I make up ID cards for both of my boys to carry in their waist packs. These cards are about credit card size and include their name, my name, the resort name, resort number, length of stay, home phone, and emergency contact. I also include info about their medication and dosage. I also have a doctor's note (with contact information) indicating that they are under his care for ADHD. I put this inside a plastic sleeve—the kind sold for trading cards or the kind that you get to hold your insurance card in. This keeps the ID from getting ripped or wet. I decorate the cards with Disney stickers, of course!"—contributed by Michelle Steiner

A Special Time to Go

A special vacation starts with carefully choosing the best time to go. Some times are much better than others to visit Walt Disney World. Specifically, the "off-season" is less crowded and more temperate. Everyone has different needs, however, so to help you decide, we charted the **fluctuating factors** for each month below. Most Disney veterans agree that the best time to visit is November–February, being careful to avoid the holidays, when parks fill to capacity. U.S. holiday weekends (such as Memorial Day at the end of May or Labor Day at the beginning of September) are to be avoided whenever possible. The latter half of August and September are uncrowded but very hot and humid. For temperature and rainfall data, visit http://www.passporter.com/wdw/bestoftimes.htm.

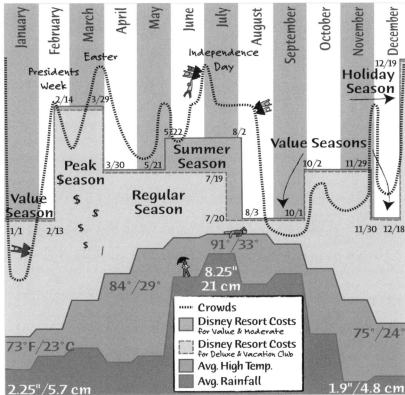

2008 Disney resort cost seasons are as follows:

Value Season is Jan. 1–Feb. 13 (all), Jul. 20–Oct. 1 (deluxe, Vacation Club, and Ft. Wilderness cabins), Aug. 3–Nov. 20 (Ft. Wilderness campsites), Aug. 3–Oct. 1 (value and moderate), Nov. 30–Dec. 18 (all but campsites); *Regular Season* is Mar. 30–Jul. 19 (deluxe, cabins, and Vacation Club), Mar. 30–Aug. 2 (campsites), Mar. 30–May 21 (value and moderate), Oct. 2–Nov. 29 (all but campsites); *Summer Season* is May 22–Aug. 2 (value and moderates); *Peak Season* is Feb. 14–Mar. 29 (all); *Pre-Holiday Season* is Nov. 21–Dec. 18 (campsites only); and *Holiday Season* is Dec. 19–31 (all).

Getting There

Depending on where you live and the size of your group, transportation can be a major item in the vacation budget. The two most popular travel options are **personal vehicle and plane**. Bus and train are options, too. There are pros and cons to every option; only you can decide what works best for you and your specific situation.

By Personal Vehicle

Many travelers choose to drive themselves to Disney for a variety of reasons, not the least of which is **economy**. In addition, having your own vehicle puts you on your schedule and your schedule alone. You don't have to run through airports or figure out train schedules. For large families, driving can be much less expensive than flying, but a long drive can also seriously reduce your magical time at Disney.

Find out how far away you are from Walt Disney World by using a **AAA TripTik** (http://www.aaa.com, membership required) or by visiting Mapquest.com (http://www.mapquest.com). Select "driving directions," which will also give you estimated travel times.

Reader Tip: "Do an Internet research for restaurants or markets that can accommodate your needs in the cities where you will stop for meals or for the night."—contributed by Leanne Phelps

Taking your own vehicle provides a **number of benefits** for the traveler with challenges:
- ✔ You travel on your **own schedule**, avoiding rushes and potential long waits at airports and train stations.
- ✔ You're in **familiar surroundings**, which is especially attractive to those with autism spectrum disorders and other developmental disabilities.
- ✔ Your **own vehicle** is probably more comfortable than standard airline/train seats if you're a person of size.
- ✔ You can **make stops whenever needed** for stretching, restrooms, and food.
- ✔ You **won't be dependent** on Disney transportation once you arrive.
- ✔ It's **easier to pack meals** and snacks.
- ✔ It's easier to **bring your own wheelchair/stroller** and other special items.

There are some **drawbacks** to driving, however, including:
- ✔ A very long drive can **take precious time** away from touring.
- ✔ **More planning is required** to determine routes, tolls, and/or overnight lodging.
- ✔ If you have to do all the driving yourself, it can be **very exhausting**.
- ✔ While the ride down may be exciting, the **ride home can be long and difficult** with tired/cranky travelers.
- ✔ All **long drives can be difficult** for people with ADHD, autism spectrum disorders, chronic fatigue syndrome, and fibromyalgia.

By Plane

Most travelers find that flying is not only the **fastest way** to get to Orlando, but it can sometimes also be the least expensive method. Just like with all components of your trip, know the travelers in your party, be sure to research policies, and contact the airlines with any special requests. Once you've made your plans, be sure to confirm and reconfirm them!

Reader Tip: "If you are bringing your own wheelchair/ECV with you, remember to notify the airline when you make your reservation. Be sure to tell the airline representative whether the chair/ECV is manual or electric. If it is electric, he/she will want to know if you have sealed batteries (they must be sealed to go onboard), and the airline will need to make arrangements for stowing it while in flight. When you check in on the day of travel, remind the gate agent that you are traveling with your wheelchair and ask that he/she notify your destination airport so your chair can be brought to you when you land."—contributed by peer reviewer Joanne Ernest

When trying for **low airfares**, make sure you research all area airports—a slightly longer drive to an alternate airport might save you lots of money on airfare, especially for large families. Also, start checking prices early on so you know when a good deal pops up and can take advantage quickly! Finally, be flexible about what time and day you fly to save even more.

Each commercial air carrier has its own specific information regarding traveling with special needs. Check the airline's web site or phone the airline, and read details carefully before making final plans. The **Transportation Security Administration (TSA)** has more information for people traveling with disabilities and medical on its web site, along with the latest information on carry-on luggage restrictions (including which liquids are permitted onboard): http://www.tsa.gov. Also consult with the TSA site for the latest information on carry-on luggage restrictions, including what liquids are permitted onboard: http://www.tsa.gov/travelers/airtravel/prohibited/permitted-prohibited-items.shtm.

⊕ Special Seats for Special People

Check with your airline about seats for those with special accessibility needs. People of size may request seat belt extenders if necessary (some airlines will not allow you to use an extender if you are seated in an exit row). While you are allowed to lap-carry infants up to 24 months, seriously consider getting them their own seat and bringing an FAA-approved car seat—it's far safer. (Tip: Consider the Sit 'n' Stroll seat/stroller combo at http://www.sitnstroll.com.) Children between the ages of 2 and 4 who weigh between 22 and 44 lbs. can use the CARES in-flight harness restraint, which provides considerably more protection (and has the added benefit of making the child feel more secure in the seat). For more information, see http://www.kidsflysafe.com.

Planning   Special Challenges   Getting There   Staying in Style   Touring   Feasting   Resources   Index

General flying guidelines:

- ✔ Consider wearing **compression stockings** for flights of six hours or more to limit the risk of blood clots.
- ✔ Periodically stand up and **move around** the plane if possible.
- ✔ Flying can be very dehydrating, so **limit your intake** of alcohol and caffeinated drinks, which further dehydrate you. Buy bottled water for the plane after clearing security.
- ✔ Arrange for **wheelchair transportation** to take you to and from your gate if you have mobility or fatigue concerns.
- ✔ Make advance **arrangements for oxygen** if you will need it. Because some airlines do not provide oxygen, you may need to ask your doctor to provide a prescription and fill out an airline medical form at least three business days before your departure. Many airlines do not allow passengers to bring their own oxygen aboard—verify this before booking.
- ✔ If you meet the safety criteria, consider requesting **an exit row**, which offers more legroom. Bulkhead seats also offer more leg room, but you must store carry-on luggage above and may find the seats narrower.
- ✔ Bring your own **meal/snacks**, but don't bring any liquids (purchase liquids after passing through the security checkpoint). Foods meeting your dietary needs may be hard to find in transit. If there'll be an in-flight meal, inquire in advance about special dietary requests.
- ✔ If flying with a **service dog**, request a bulkhead seat so the dog has room to lie down.
- ✔ Occasionally, an airline may ask for a **letter from a doctor** verifying that the special needs traveler is fit to fly. Consider bringing one "just in case."
- ✔ Some airlines serve **peanuts**—check prior to ticket purchase if you have allergies.
- ✔ Ask at the gate about **preboarding** for small children or people needing assistance. Arrive early, and if you have problems, ask to speak to the complaints resolution official on duty.
- ✔ Take all essential **medications and medical supplies** with you in your carry-on luggage.

© Nikki Shenk

Disney's Magical Express can take you from the airport to your Disney resort (see page 108)

Getting Around the Orlando Airport

Orlando International Airport is a large, sprawling hub and one of the better (and cleaner) airports. When you arrive, your plane docks at one of four **satellite terminals**. From there, follow the signs to the automated shuttle train that takes you to the main terminal—there you'll find baggage claim and ground transportation. Once you reach the main terminal (Level 3), follow the signs down to baggage claim (Level 2). Shuttles, taxis, town cars, rental cars, and buses are found on Level 1 (take the elevators opposite the baggage carousels). Each shuttle and bus company has its own ticket booth, so keep your eyes open. If you get lost, look for signs or an information desk that can get you back on track. For more details on the Orlando International Airport, call 407-825-2001 or visit http://www. orlandoairports.net. Page travelers at 407-825-2000.

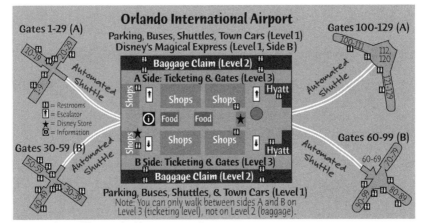

Note: Each satellite terminal has a companion restroom.

⚠ Disabled Air Traveler Hotline

Did you know there's a **toll-free hotline for disabled air travelers** operated by the Department of Transportation? The hotline serves two main purposes: education and assistance in resolving disability-related air travel problems. Hotline operators are well-versed in relevant laws and regulations (Air Carrier Access Act and the regulation 14 CFR Part 382) and can provide callers with general information about the rights of air travelers with disabilities. The hotline operators also respond to requests for printed consumer information about air travel rights of the disabled and can also assist in resolving real-time or upcoming issues with air carriers by contacting the carrier and attempting to resolve the issue. Hotline Duty Officers have, for example, contacted air carriers and convinced them to accept service animals and electric wheelchairs onboard flights or to stow folding wheelchairs in the cabin. Air travelers who want information about the rights of persons with disabilities in air travel or who experience disability-related air travel service problems may call the hotline from 7:00 am to 11:00 pm Eastern time, seven days a week, at 800-778-4838 (voice) or 800-455-9880 (TTY).

⟶

For "Weekend Warrior" Helpers

Are you a helper who will be hoisting wheelchairs/ECVs or their users into cars or trunks? Pushing wheelchairs or assisting a special traveler through airports and on the journey, not to mention during the vacation, can be a challenge. Protect yourself by considering a few basic tips on proper body mechanics. Here are a few general reminders:

1. Start and end the day with a good stretch.

2. When lifting, bend at the knees and let your legs do all the work.

3. Never lift by starting with a rounded back, then straightening. Always use your legs.

4. Never twist your back when lifting. Take small steps with your legs to turn your whole body.

5. Bring any weight as close to your body as possible.

6. When lowering the weight, use your legs, not your back. Think "bottom out, legs bent."

7. Always try to push; don't pull unless absolutely necessary.

—contributed by peer reviewer Sandy Bostwick

© Linda MacLeod

Once you get there, it's "Open Mouse" time at the castle ...

By Bus and Train

You may not have considered **traveling by bus** to Walt Disney World, but several commercial bus lines, such as Greyhound, do offer accommodations for special travelers with adequate advance notice (usually at least 48 hours). Visit Greyhound's web site for details on their services at http://www.greyhound.com or call 800-231-2222.

Traveling by train may be practical for some travelers, especially for those able to take advantage of Amtrak's Auto Train, which allows you to bring your own car without having to drive it all the way to Florida. The Auto Train may be a little more expensive than even flying, but the convenience of having your own vehicle might be worth the expense. The Auto Train leaves from Lorton, VA (just outside of Washington, DC) and arrives in Sanford, FL (about a one-hour drive from Orlando). You board the Auto Train in the late afternoon, eat your meals on board, sleep on board overnight, and arrive the next morning (it's a 16-hour trip) ready to head to Disney. Amtrak offers a variety of accommodations for travelers with special challenges—they even have a section on their web site for special travelers with specific guidelines relating to wheelchairs, service animals, oxygen equipment, etc. Some discounts may be available. For more information on the Auto Train or traveling by train in general, visit http://www.amtrak.com or call 800-872-7245.

Commercial Travel Pros and Cons

As in all types of travel, there are positive and not-so-positive features. When considering commercial travel, here are a few of the benefits to consider:

- ✔ Typically takes **less** travel time.
- ✔ You don't have to **drive** yourself.
- ✔ Can be more **economical** for individuals or small groups.
- ✔ If flying and staying at a Disney resort, you may have access to Disney's new **Magical Express ground transportation** (see the next page).

Before booking this type of travel, here are the **drawbacks** to consider:

- ✔ You may **not be able to walk around** to stretch.
- ✔ There are **baggage limitations**.
- ✔ Seating may be unfamiliar and **uncomfortable**.
- ✔ When **confined to a small space** for a long time, the possibility of meltdown increases for some.
- ✔ You may encounter **longer waits** for security, luggage, check-in, etc.
- ✔ Your personal wheelchair may have to be **disassembled** to be stored in the cargo hold.
- ✔ Your stroller may be **inaccessible** during the trip.

Planning

Special Challenges

Getting There

Staying in Style

Touring

Feasting

Resources

Index

Are We There Yet?

OK, now you've arrived in Orlando ... so how do you actually get to Walt Disney World? If you arrived at the airport, bus, or train station, you'll need transportation to Disney. You can take advantage of Disney's newest program, Magical Express, rent a car, take a shuttle or taxi, or hire a town car.

Disney's Magical Express

Disney's Magical Express offers free transportation between Orlando International Airport and Walt Disney World. If you're a guest of a Disney hotel, you can sign up for this service in advance. You check your bags when you depart from your home airport, then, upon arrival at the Orlando airport, skip baggage claim and proceed directly to a Disney motorcoach (similar to those used by the Disney Cruise Line). Your luggage will then be delivered to your resort. This service is *free* (at press time) for guests staying at Disney hotels (not Swan and Dolphin, Shades of Green, or Hotel Plaza Boulevard hotels) who register at least one day in advance either through their travel agent, online at http://www.disneyworld.com, or by calling Disney Reservations at 866-599-0951 or 407-934-7639. Magical Express can accommodate wheelchairs and ECVs, but there are a limited number of spaces. Make sure to mention if you have a wheelchair/ECV or service animal when making your reservations. Remember to reconfirm your special requirements for your return trip to the airport. There are a few disadvantages to this service:

- It can take several hours for your luggage to be delivered to your resort—be sure to take any necessities in bags that you will keep with you. You can bring your luggage from baggage claim to the bus with you.

- You may have to stop at several other Disney resorts to drop off other passengers before reaching your destination.

Bright Idea: Disney's Magical Express is also available for your return trip to the Orlando International Airport. In addition, if you're flying with a participating airline, you can also use the Resort Airline Check-In Service, which allows you to check your luggage and receive your boarding passes at your resort. As of June 2007, participating airlines are Air Tran, Alaska Airlines, American, Continental, Delta, JetBlue, Northwest, and United (including Ted). Note that international travelers cannot use the Resort Airline Check-In Service, however.

Car Rentals

If you're flying and plan to rent a car once you get to Orlando, we suggest you rent from one of the agencies located right at the airport on Level 1: Alamo, Avis, Budget, Dollar, National, and L&M. (Other companies require taking a shuttle from the airport to an off-site location, which can be a major hassle both ways.) When you reserve your car, be sure to make any special requests, such as a child car seat or hand-control-equipped vehicle. You can check out the individual car rental companies' policies on accommodating special needs by visiting their web sites or by calling their main telephone numbers directly. Note that not all agencies and vehicles can accommodate wheelchair/ECV users or those with mobility issues.

Shuttles and Taxis

Shuttle stands are located at the Orlando International Airport (Level 1), but all other pickup points require advance notice. The major shuttle operator is Mears (800-759-5219). While taxis are available, we don't recommend them for travel due to cost. Large parties may be able to ride in a taxi minivan economically, however.

Town Cars

A number of companies offer taxi, shuttle, or town car service to Disney and the surrounding areas, including Port Canaveral. Of the three options, we suggest the **town car** (if your budget allows) for the following reasons:

✔ The driver **meets you in the baggage claim area**, assists with your luggage, and drives you directly to your Disney resort without stopping at other resorts.
✔ Some services even offer a **free stop at a local grocery store** so you can pick up a few necessities and special food items you probably won't find in the Disney shops.
✔ The town car vehicles are usually late model, very clean, and **very comfortable**.
✔ There is **little wait time**, since the town car drivers are usually waiting to greet you.
✔ You can leave the **driving to someone else** and don't have to worry about getting lost or dealing with traffic.
✔ Your party is the only one in the town car—you **don't have to share the ride** with strangers.

Town car services we've used include (in alphabetical order):
✔ Happy Limo (888-394-4277, http://www.happylimo.com)
✔ Quicksilver (888-468-6939, http://www.quicksilver-tours.com)

Important Note: If you have allergies or asthma, remember to request a smoke-free car that is also free of heavily scented air fresheners.

Packing List

Begin thinking about what you need to pack once you have your transportation decided. Commercial vehicles have restrictions on the size and number of luggage pieces. If you drive yourself, your only limit is the available space in your vehicle. Here is a helpful packing list to guide you—items in **bold** may be handy to carry around in your day bag (some items may not be appropriate for your airplane carry-on due to security restrictions). Tip: Be sure to label all medical equipment as such to avoid extra baggage charges.

The Essentials

❑ Casual clothing you can layer. One "nice" outfit is usually enough, but cruisers will need more dress clothes.

___ Shorts/skirts	___ Pants/jeans	___ Shirts	___ Sweaters
___ Underwear	___ Socks	___ Pajamas	___ _____

❑ Jacket and/or sweatshirt (light ones for the warmer months)

___ **Jackets**	___ Sweatshirts	___ Sweaters	___ Vests

❑ Comfortable, well-broken-in shoes ... plus a second pair, just in case!

___ Walking shoes	___ Sandals	___ Sneakers	___ _____

❑ Swim gear (bring one-piece suits for water slides)

___ Suits/trunks	___ Cover-ups/towels	___ Water shoes	___ Goggles

❑ Sun protection (the Florida sun can be brutal) 👓

___ **Sunblock**	___ **Lip balm**	___ **Sunburn relief**	___ **Sunglasses**
___ **Hats w/brims**	___ **Caps**	___ **Visors**	___ _____

❑ Rain gear ☁ (compact and light so you don't mind carrying it)

___ Raincoat	___ **Poncho**	___ **Umbrella**	___ **Dry socks**

❑ Comfortable bags with padded straps to carry items during the day

___ **Backpacks**	___ **Waist packs**	___ Shoulder bags	___ **Camera bag**

❑ Toiletries 🔑 (in a bag or bathroom kit to keep them organized)

___ **Brush/comb**	___ Toothbrush	___ Toothpaste	___ Dental floss
___ Favorite soap, shampoo, and conditioner	___ Deodorant	___ **Baby wipes**
___ **Aspirin/acetaminophen/ibuprofen**	___ **Band aids**	___ **First aid kit**
___ **Prescriptions** (in original containers)	___ Vitamins	___ Fem. hygiene
___ Hair dryer/iron	___ **Anti-blister tape**	___ Makeup	___ Hair spray
___ Razors	___ Shaving cream	___ Cotton buds	___ Lotion
___ Nail clippers	___ Spare eyeglasses	___ Lens solution	___ **Bug repellent**
___ Mending kit	___ Small scissors	___ Safety pins	___ **Insect sting kit**

❑ Camera/camcorder and more film/tape 📷 than you think you need

___ **Camera**	___ **Camcorder**	___ **Film/tapes**	___ **Storage cards**
___ **Batteries**	___ Chargers	___ **Camera case**	___ _____

❑ Money in various forms and various places

___ **Charge cards**	___ **Traveler's checks**	___ **Bank cards**	___ **Cash**

❑ Personal identification, passes, and membership cards

___ **Driver's licenses**	___ **Other photo ID**	___ **Passports**	___ Birth certificate
___ **AAA card**	___ **Discount cards**	___ Air miles card	___ _____
___ **Tickets/passes**	___ **Insurance cards**	___ **Calling cards**	___ _____

Tip: Label everything with your name, phone, and hotel to help reunite you with your stuff if lost. Every bag should have this info on a luggage tag as well as on a slip of paper inside it.

For Your Carry-On

❏ Your **PassPorter, tickets, maps, guides**, and a **pen** or **pencil**! ✎ Remember to pack any sharp or potentially dangerous items in your checked luggage, not your carry-on.
❏ **Camera** and/or **camcorder**, along with **film, memory cards, tapes**, and **batteries**
❏ Any **prescriptions**, important toiletries, **sunblock, sunglasses, hats, bug repellent**
❏ Change of clothes appropriate to your destination's weather
❏ **Snacks**, ⚓ **water bottle, juice boxes**, gum, favorite books, **toys, games**, blankets

For Young Travelers

❏ Snacks and juice boxes
❏ Books, toys, games, and a night-light
❏ Stroller, carrier, and accessories 🚼
❏ **Diapers, formula, other baby needs**
❏ EarPlanes (http://www.earplanes.com)

For Heat-Sensitive Travelers

❏ **Personal fans/water misters**
❏ **Water bottles** (frozen, if possible)
❏ **Washcloth** to cool off face and neck
❏ **Hats** with wide brims
❏ **Sunshades** (for baby strollers)

For Special Travelers (see page 99 for a list of items to keep in your carry-on)

❏ **Earplugs**
❏ **Handheld games** and game magazines
❏ Personal music player with headphones
❏ **Favorite toy or game**
❏ Special diet snacks or food items
❏ **Chewable anti-nausea tablets**
❏ Disposable thermometers
❏ Handicapped tag from home vehicle
❏ Heating pad
❏ Bengay or Icy Hot (sore muscles)

❏ Special pillows, white-noise machine
❏ **Adequate doses of any medications**
❏ **Prescriptions in case of refills**
❏ Measuring spoon
❏ Extra hearing aid batteries
❏ Special adaptable items
❏ **Medical history/doctor contact info**
❏ Plastic gloves
❏ **EpiPen**, if you have severe allergies
    (remember to check expiration date!)

Everyone Should Consider

❏ Big beach towels (for pools and water parks)
❏ **Penlight** or flashlight (for reading/writing in dark places and to alleviate kids' fears)
❏ **Water bottles**, water bottle strap, and personal **fan/water misters**
❏ **Snacks** for any time of the day (plus gum, if you chew it)
❏ Plastic cutlery for snacks or leftovers ✂
❏ **Quarters** and **pennies** (and a way to hold them) for the coin presses and/or laundry
❏ Plastic storage bags that seal (large and small), plus trash bags
❏ Address book, stamps, and envelopes ✉
❏ Laundry detergent/tablets, bleach, dryer sheets, stain removal wipes, and a laundry tote
❏ Hand sanitizer or antibacterial wipes, disinfectant wipes
❏ Collapsible bag or suitcase inside another suitcase to hold souvenirs on your return
❏ Body Glide (anti-blister and anti-chafing stick)

Your Personal Packing List

❏ _____   ❏ _____
❏ _____   ❏ _____
❏ _____   ❏ _____
❏ _____   ❏ _____
❏ _____   ❏ _____
❏ _____   ❏ _____

Planning · Special Challenges · Getting There · Staying in Style · Touring · Feasting · Resources · Index

Your Traveling Tips and Stories

I suggest parents make identification cards for their kids. Our local school uses Ident-a-Kid (http://www.ident-a-kid.com), and their representatives visit the school every year to update the identification cards. They take a picture and thumbprint of the child (any age) and get their status (height, weight, hair color, eye color, etc.). The parent gets an identification card that looks a bit like a driver's license for the child. We misplaced our son at a Disney on Ice event last March, and even with all the panicking we went through (the longest 10 minutes of my life), I was glad to have that identification card to show to staff. Even another attendee looked at the identification card and watched the exit for us. I buy multiple identification cards each year. My husband and I each keep a card, and I give them to the grandparents also. Best of all, the identification cards were very inexpensive—$7 for one card, $12 for four.

—contributed by Abby Harrington

When traveling by plane, I pack a portable DVD player and snacks for my 12-year-old daughter, who is on the autism spectrum. There have been times when the weather was bad and our flight was delayed several hours. This helped keep her happy.

—contributed by Kalli Mulchi

My 8-year-old daughter has mild to moderate cerebral palsy— she can walk, but tires easily, tends to fall or lose her balance on uneven terrain, and generally lacks fine motor coordination on the right side of her body. If you are making hotel reservations directly through Disney, have a friendly conversation with the cast member to explain your circumstances and request a room that will work for you. I've found that Disney is very sensitive and understanding. I usually call back after making the initial reservation to make a payment/deposit and reconfirm that our requests are noted in the system.

—contributed by Anonymous

We did a huge family trip with three elderly people, including my father, who has Alzheimer's. I toured with all three while the rest of the family hit the larger attractions. My father's Alzheimer's makes him very stressed in larger crowds. I had to deal with dehydration, crowd management issues (my father), and a bad knee (my mother). I had constant worries that the crowds would shove my sister's mother-in-law, who is older than my parents and very tiny. In addition to off-season trips, I suggest calling your local Red Cross to have a Vial of Life mailed for each person in your party. It is free and may save your life. This small tube has your medical information, and you keep in your freezer at home. Some emergency medical responders are trained to look for this vial. It contains your medical history, doctor's information, medications, allergy information, and emergency contact information. It is the size of an M&M candy tube and light to carry. Pack it in your bag, and if something happens, just hand over the tube. This prevents any panic trying to remember doctor's information and medication. When you return home, place it back in the freezer, and update your information periodically.

—contributed by Melanie Evans

Planning

Special Challenges

Getting There

Staying in Style

Touring

Feasting

Resources

Index

Staying and Cruising in Style

Walt Disney World offers 24 themed resort hotels—one is sure to fit your budget and taste. Why would you want to stay at a Disney hotel? There are numerous advantages, but the biggest is that you will be immersed in the magic for your entire vacation! In fact, most Disney hotels offer so many amenities and have so much to do that even if you never set foot in a theme park, you'll still feel you "got away from it all."

There is something for everyone: the budget-minded value resorts with eye-popping, larger-than-life icons; the modestly priced moderate resorts with larger rooms and increased amenities; the posh deluxe resorts with impeccable appointments, multiple dining options, and closer access to the parks; and the Disney Vacation Club (DVC) resorts, which feature accommodations ranging from a studio with a kitchenette to a grand villa with three full bedrooms, several bathrooms, a full kitchen, and living and dining rooms.

In addition, when you stay at a Walt Disney World resort, you have access to special perks, such as:

✔ Disney's Magical Express service—Disney resort guests (excluding the Walt Disney World Swan and Dolphin, Shades of Green, and the Hotel Plaza Boulevard hotels) can arrange for free shuttle service from Orlando International Airport to check-in at their hotel, while their luggage goes straight from the plane to the room. The service will take you back to the airport when your vacation is over, too.
✔ Extra Magic Hours—Visit a designated theme park one hour earlier or several hours later than the general public each day of the week.
✔ Complimentary package delivery from Disney locations to your hotel.
✔ Free Disney transportation to/from the Disney theme parks.
✔ Free parking at the Disney theme parks.
✔ Chargeback privileges that allow you to charge purchases around Walt Disney World directly to your room.
✔ Special Disney character wake-up calls.

Special Lodging for Special Guests

Because Walt Disney World is a family vacation destination, you expect its hotels to be prepared to accommodate all sorts of families' needs. You'll be pleasantly surprised to learn that they are also able to meet most of the requirements of travelers with a **wide variety of special challenges,** too.

Effective June 1, 2007, all Disney resort hotel rooms are nonsmoking.

Disney resort rooms have **standard accommodations** much like you'd find in any hotel: two double or queen beds, a television, a telephone, a small table with two chairs, a small wall safe, a bathroom with shower/tub, and vanity area. We note in the resort descriptions when Disney resort rooms offer other than these standard accommodations.

In addition, all Walt Disney World resort hotels have at least some rooms with the following **special equipment and facilities** for those with particular requirements. These rooms are available by special request (see pages 117–118). In general, the newer resorts (Pop Century, Coronado Springs, Disney's Animal Kingdom Lodge, and Saratoga Springs), or those most recently refurbished, have more and better special accommodations. The following special equipment or facilities are available:

A roll-in shower with bench, handheld shower head, and rail at BoardWalk Villas

© Deb Wills

In the **bathrooms**:
- ✔ Wider bathroom doors
- ✔ Bathroom handrails
- ✔ Roll-in showers
- ✔ Shower benches
- ✔ Handheld shower head
- ✔ Accessible vanities
- ✔ Portable commodes
- ✔ Raised toilet seat with grab bar

In the **guest rooms**:
- ✔ Bed boards and bed rails
- ✔ Adjustable beds, lower beds, and rubber bed pads
- ✔ Open-frame beds
- ✔ Low-level peepholes in doors
- ✔ Refrigerators (charge may apply at value resorts)
- ✔ Closed-captioned televisions
- ✔ Both upper and lower door locks on balcony doors
- ✔ Pack 'n' Play-style portable cribs (request when booking and also at check-in)
- ✔ Room Communication Kits with door knock and phone alerts, bed shaker alarm, Text Typewriter (TTY), strobe light fire alarm, and phone amplifier

Some (not all) **accessible rooms** may have the following:
- ✔ Electrical switches 48" (1.2 meters) above the floor (including thermostat)
- ✔ Touch switch lamp
- ✔ Vanity open below sink (roll under)
- ✔ Lower countertops/cabinets
- ✔ Countertop microwave (in Disney Vacation Club resorts)
- ✔ Low threshold at balcony

Bright Idea: Consider Disney's newest resort, Saratoga Springs Resort and Spa—it was built with many special accommodations "standard." All accessible rooms in this resort are equipped for those with hearing impairments.

Also available on request at some **deluxe resorts**:

✔ Rollaway beds
✔ Down pillows
✔ Heating pads
✔ International electrical adapter

✔ Strollers
✔ High chairs
✔ Electrical outlet covers

Reader Tip: "I'm hard of hearing, and one of my biggest concerns—no matter where I'm staying—is hearing any alarms during the middle of the night (pretty much nothing wakes me up). So be sure to notify the cast member during check-in if you are hard of hearing so they can note it on your room assignment."—contributed by Anonymous

Other special accommodations found throughout the **Disney resorts**:

✔ As mentioned in chapter 5, Disney transportation to and from the resorts is, for the most part, accessible for all vacationers. There are both buses with wheelchair lifts and buses that "kneel" (i.e., they lower to enable easy entry). Ferries, Friendships, cruisers, and monorails also have room and special locations for wheelchairs/ECVs and strollers.
✔ Braille signage (not at all resorts) to identify rooms, shops, restrooms, etc., and on elevator controls.
✔ Standard wheelchairs are available free at each resort on a very limited basis. A deposit is required, but the wheelchair may be used for the duration of your stay. The BoardWalk also rents wheelchairs and ECVs from its surrey bike rental desk—see page 132 for details.
✔ Some resorts have at least one low counter at check-in for someone who's shorter or using a wheelchair/ECV. These are generally found at one of the far ends of the check-in counter.
✔ In the lobby or main building of all resorts, foreign-speaking visitors will find an international phone calling card machine with instructions in Spanish, Portuguese, German, French, and Japanese.
✔ While there are no companion restrooms in any of the Disney resort hotel lobbies that we could find, the Polynesian has one on the second floor across from 'Ohana restaurant, and there are others located in the pool areas of several resorts. We note their locations in the appropriate hotel descriptions on the following pages.
✔ Accessible parking is available at each resort—be sure to have a valid handicapped parking permit or hang tag. If you are staying at a resort with valet parking, it is complimentary with the handicapped parking permit.
✔ Luggage assistance varies depending on your resort category. Although the value resorts offer luggage assistance, it can take up to 60 minutes for luggage to be delivered to your room. (It can also take that long for luggage pickup when you're departing.) The deluxe resorts offer immediate full-service bell services at check-in.
✔ If you have special dietary requirements and plan to eat at your resort's restaurant(s), be sure to call the resort prior to your arrival.
✔ Sharps containers can be requested from Housekeeping. (At the Swan or Dolphin, call Security for a sharps container.)

Bright Idea: Once you arrive, visit the restaurant/food court and ask to speak to a chef—try to do this during off-peak hours if possible. Tell them exactly what your needs are, and be sure to mention any cross-contamination issues, too. Remember, the chefs are most accommodating to your requests when given at least 72 hours' notice. Ask the chef to point out any prepackaged food that would be okay, too!

Planning

Special Challenges

Getting There

Staying in Style

Touring

Feasting

Resources

Index

Special Lodging for Special Guests (continued)

The **resort chefs** we spoke with were very helpful, offering suggestions and asking lots of questions. If you are unsure of anything when dining, ask for an ingredient list or speak with a chef. (We were pleasantly surprised to see Gasparilla's Grill at the Grand Floridian prominently posted the ingredients for many of its baked goods.) See chapter 6 for more details on resort dining.

Here are more **important things you should know** about staying at the Disney resort hotels with special needs:

✔ Most accessible rooms have king beds and only sleep two. There may not be a pull-out or daybed in the room. Be sure to inquire when making reservations.

✔ Disney supplies soap and shampoo in its resorts—it uses a line of products by H$_2$Oplus (http://www.h2Oplus.com), and the ingredients are not always listed. If you use specific soap and shampoo at home due to allergies or sensitivity, bring them with you.

✔ For those with allergies and/or asthma, Disney's housekeeping service will provide special room cleanings and will also use special, less harsh, cleaning agents (see the section in chapter 2 on Allergies).

✔ While many of the deluxe resorts have childcare facilities on-site, these are only open to potty-trained children age 4–12. These "kids' clubs" do not babysit special needs children who require one-on-one attention. Speak to the childcare club cast members in advance, and explain the special needs to determine whether your child can be accommodated. In-room babysitting is available from outside sources. See page 393.

Bright Idea: When you check in, ask if there is any "resort activity" information or schedule available. Also check with the lifeguards for daily pool activities.

✔ Except at Disney's Animal Kingdom Lodge, you'll find at least one path or walkway available for joggers, power walkers, and those wanting to stroll. If you have physical therapy or other exercises to do while at Disney, all deluxe and Disney Vacation Club resorts, as well as Coronado Springs, offer fitness facilities (see page 78). Use of the facility is free to guests staying at that resort, or you can purchase a day pass for $12.

✔ All Disney hotels have swimming pools. A few have zero-entry access areas (see below). Water wheelchairs are available at most resorts with zero-entry access pools—request one from the lifeguard.

What's So Special About a "Zero-Entry" Pool?

Some resorts have primary themed pools with a "zero-entry" shoreline. This is a gradual slope into the pool, just like a real beach. It's ideal for those who are unable to step down into a traditional pool—instead, they can just wade into the water. Most pools with zero-entry also have a water wheelchair available, which can wheel right into the pool—ask a lifeguard about availability. The resorts that currently have zero-entry pools are: Disney's Animal Kingdom Lodge, Grand Floridian Resort and Spa, Polynesian Resort, and Saratoga Springs.

✔ Automatic external defibrillators (AEDs) are located in all pool areas and numerous other locations around the resorts—check the resort map for specific locations.

✔ Most Disney resort hotels have at least one small playground, as well as an arcade.

✔ Bicycle and boat rentals are available at many resorts.

✔ Most of the moderate and deluxe resorts offer outdoor hot tubs (called "spas").

✔ In-room doctor/dental care is available if necessary (see page 64 in chapter 2).

Making Special Reservations

Once you have an idea of where you want to stay at Disney, it's time to **make reservations**. You don't need to use a travel agent, but if you have a great travel agent, by all means consult him or her. Here's the lowdown on making reservations when you have special requests:

If you have **common special requests** (i.e., close to bus stop, etc.), make your reservations for all Walt Disney World resort hotels at 407-WDW-MAGIC (407-939-6244) or 800-828-0228 (Walt Disney Travel Company). When you make your reservations, explain your special requirements and request that they be noted on your reservation form. Remember to state if your request is due to medical reasons—they will try to guarantee that your request is honored. Disney representatives can offer assistance in English, Spanish, Japanese, French, Portuguese, and German. If you have Internet access, you can research rooms and make reservations at http://www.disneyworld.com (click on "Resorts").

If, however, your **special requests are unusual** and/or involve more than the need for an accessible room, ask to speak with Walt Disney World Resort Special Reservations or call directly at 407-939-7807 and press "1" (voice) or 407-939-7670 (TTY). This department works with you to determine what accommodations are available in the hotel(s) you are interested in and then books your reservation. They also note on your reservation what accommodations you need. If you have a travel agent, make sure they know to talk to the Special Reservations folks when making your arrangements.

Remember to **mention all of your special requests** when making your Disney resort hotel reservations. Here are some request ideas:

✔ Unable to walk long distances or have other mobility concerns? Request a room near a bus stop or near central services.
✔ Have a traveler with an aversion to loud noises? Request a quiet room away from pool/elevator and common areas.
✔ Have a wheelchair, or are you a person of size? Request a room with a king bed, which is generally more spacious. (King rooms may carry an additional charge.)
✔ Fear of heights? Request a lower floor.
✔ Traveling with an infant? Request a crib or bed rails. Some resorts have high chairs available, too.
✔ Traveling with someone with medications that need to be kept cold? Request a refrigerator for medical reasons, if not standard in your room.
✔ Does someone in your party have a visual impairment? Request a first-floor room that is near the bus stop and/or food court.
✔ Are you a little person or short of stature? Request a step stool for the room.

Making Special Reservations (continued)

If you have a **particular location or room in mind** (we make suggestions later on), be sure to tell the reservations agent. It's best to make your request as general as possible. You'll have better luck requesting a "ground floor room near a bus stop" rather than simply "room 109." If Disney doesn't know why you want room 109, they can't choose a suitable substitute. Disney will not guarantee a particular room or view, but if your request is "in the system," they will try their best to accommodate you. If you have more than one request, make them in order of priority.

Four to five days prior to arriving at your hotel, call and speak to the front desk and ask for the room assignment cast member. Go over with them what accommodations you requested and **confirm their availability**. If you have specific needs, ask if the room can be blocked for you, so that it isn't given away. The earlier in the day you arrive, the better your chances of being accommodated. We've created an easy, fill-in-the-blanks form for you to use when making phone calls (or when checking in) at: http://www.passporter.com/wdw/resortrequest.htm.

In the rare instance that after all your prearrival work, you arrive and there is no room to accommodate your needs, pull out whatever correspondence you have about the room and **request to be placed in a comparable room** on Disney property that can accommodate your needs.

 ### Checking In

Check-in time at most Disney resorts is either 3:00 pm or 4:00 pm—we specify in the individual resort descriptions. This is a good time to restate your special requests and see if the appropriate room is blocked for you. The problem is, everyone wants to check in at the same time, which makes check-in especially difficult if you have small children or travelers who are unable to wait in long lines for various reasons. Here are some strategies for making check-in a bit easier:

Check in as soon as you arrive, even if it's well before "official" check-in time. Sometimes you may be pleasantly surprised that a room is available. Even if one is not, however, you may still let them know you're on property and then can leave your baggage with Bell Services while you wait wherever you choose—get a meal, visit a theme park, sightsee around the resort, even go swimming. If you check in before your room is ready, some resorts will give you a phone number to call, along with your inactivated room keys. Once the room is ready, they will give you the room number—you don't need to check in again.

If you do encounter a line when you check in, though, there is always a small area with child-size seating and a TV playing Disney videos nearby—a kids' waiting area. Most are in plain view, so while you wait in the queue, you can keep your eyes on the little ones. If you are unable to stand in line for a long time, check with Bell Services and inquire about the availability of a wheelchair.

Once at the front desk, be sure to go over any special requests you made in advance. This is the best time to correct any problems.

Resort Key

Amenities—All rooms have a TV with remote, phone, drawers, rod with hangers, small table, chairs, and simple toiletries. Additional amenities vary and are detailed later. If your room doesn't have a coffeemaker, alarm clock, or iron, request it from Housekeeping.

Check-Out Time—Check-out time is 11:00 am. If you need to check out a bit later, ask the front desk early that morning. If the resort isn't busy, they may grant your request at no extra cost. You can also leave your bags with Bell Services to go play in the parks. Another option is to use Magical Express or the resort airline check-in process (see page 108).

Childcare—Childcare "clubs" are available in some of the deluxe resorts (refer to the chart on page 122), but they only take potty-trained children ages 4–12. Speak to the childcare club cast member in advance to determine whether accommodations for your child are possible. In-room sitting from non-Disney vendors is available. See page 393.

Concierge—All of the deluxe resorts offer concierge services, which give you extra perks like a continental breakfast, afternoon snacks, and itinerary planning services. Tell the valet when you arrive at the resort that you are staying on the concierge level and you may be able to bypass the regular check-in line. Concierge services are associated with certain rooms (often on the higher floors) and come at a higher rate.

Disabled Access—All Disney resorts offer rooms and access for differently abled guests. Call Walt Disney World Resort Special Reservations at 407-939-7807 (voice) or 407-939-7670 (TTY). Be sure to ask that "Special Needs" be noted on your reservation.

Extra Magic Hours—A special program for Disney resort guests as well as guests at the Swan and Dolphin, Shades of Green, and the Hilton, during which a park opens one hour earlier or stays open several hours later than usual. With the lower crowds during these early/late hours, your wait times can be minimal—you can often see and do more in that time than you can throughout the rest of the day. We strongly suggest you take advantage of this feature, especially in the morning. The schedule can change—call 407-939-4636 or check http://www.disneyworld.com for the schedule during your visit.

Food—Every resort has some type of dining option—food courts, cafés, fine dining, and/or room service. All resort eateries are described in detail in chapter 6. If you are looking for snack food or groceries, each resort has an area with a small selection of foodstuffs and drinks. No gum is sold on property. If you have special dietary needs and plan to eat at your resort, it's best to stop by and speak to the chef early in your visit.

Housekeeping Services—Every Disney resort has daily housekeeping services. Request extra towels, toiletries, rubber sheets, extra linens, pillows, and blankets, as well as hair dryers, irons, and boards from Housekeeping. Disney can also provide special cleanings for those with allergies or chemical sensitivities. Request when you make your reservations and again at check-in. Note: Disney Vacation Club (DVC) resorts provide less frequent housekeeping services to DVC members or their guests using DVC points.

Ice and Soft Drinks—All resorts have ice machines within walking distance. Most, but not all, have soda machines. If soda is important, pick up some before you arrive. Another option is to purchase a refillable souvenir mug (offered at most resorts) for free refills of soda, coffee, tea, and cocoa at your resort—see "Refillable Mugs" on page 121.

Information—Check the Walt Disney World information channels on your in-room TV (closed-captioned channels available). These channels offer a nice introduction for newcomers, plus a peek at what's new for veterans. You can also dial "0" from your Disney resort phone to ask specific questions (TTY phones upon request—see "Telephones" on page 121.

Planning
Special Challenges
Getting There
Staying in Style
Touring
Feasting
Resources
Index

Resort Key (continued)

Internet Access—All resorts have high-speed Internet access for $9.95 for a 24-hour period ($10.95 at Swan and Dolphin); some even have public areas with wireless Internet (Wi-Fi). All phones have data ports. Look for a local access number before you arrive (Celebration is a local call, Kissimmee is not). You must include the area code (407) in all local calls. The front desk will receive your faxes for a fee.

Laundry—Every resort has either coin-operated machines in a laundry room near the pool (expect to pay eight quarters/load) or a washer and dryer in your DVC room. One- and two-bedroom and grand villas have stacked washers/dryers in the room that come with a small box of powdered laundry soap. Old Key West, Beach Club Villas, and The Villas at Wilderness Lodge offer complimentary self-service laundry facilities (no coins needed). Laundry bags and forms are available in your resort room for same-day laundering (but it's very expensive). Store your dirty laundry in the laundry bags.

Lobby Concierge—(Formerly Guest Services.) Each resort has a Lobby Concierge desk where you can purchase park passes, make dining arrangements, and find answers to just about any question. You can also connect to Lobby Concierge (and other Disney services) through a button on your in-room phone. At some resorts, Lobby Concierge is combined with the Front Desk staff.

Locations—Room locations, such as a building or room number, can be requested, but are not guaranteed. However, if you note your preferences when you make your reservation and again when you check in, there is a chance you will get the room you want. Resort maps and suggestions are given for each resort in this chapter. If you don't like the particular room you've been assigned, politely ask for another. You can reserve a room in a preferred location for an additional cost—see individual resort descriptions for details.

Merchandise Delivery—Resort guests can have park and Downtown Disney purchases delivered free to their resort, usually by the next afternoon. Inquire before your purchase is rung up. Your package is **delivered to your resort's gift shop** for pickup, not your room.

Money—Cash, Disney Dollars, traveler's checks, The Disney Credit Card, MasterCard, Visa, American Express, Discover, Diner's Club, and JCB are accepted. ATMs are located near the front desk. Make your room deposit over the phone or fax with the above credit cards or by mail with a credit card or check.

Occupancy—All resorts have rooms that hold at least four guests, plus one child under three in a Pack 'n' Play crib. There is an extra charge for more than two adults in a single room. Some Port Orleans Riverside (Alligator Bayou) rooms accommodate up to five guests (they have an optional trundle bed). Some of the deluxe resorts and the Fort Wilderness Cabins can sleep five or more in a room. The All-Star Music family suites allow up to 6, while the two-bedroom villas in the Disney Vacation Club resorts can accommodate up to eight.

Parking—Secured, free, gated parking lots are available at all resorts; the deluxe resorts also offer valet ($10/day, free to those with a handicapped parking permit or tag). The Swan and Dolphin charge to park in their self-serve lot ($9) as well as for valet parking ($12/day or $16/overnight). Shades of Green charges $5 a day for regular parking. Show your resort ID or confirmation at the security gate—parking is reserved for resort guests and those using a resort's restaurants or recreation.

Pets—Pets are not allowed in the parks or resorts (except for a few campsites at Fort Wilderness—see page 148) unless they are service animals. Disney kennels will board pets for $10 per animal per day, and resort guests may board their pets overnight for $13 per night. Although the kennels are designed primarily for dogs and cats, they can also accommodate birds, ferrets, small rodents, rabbits, and nonvenomous snakes. Owners must walk their pets three times a day.

Pools—Every Disney resort has at least one swimming pool, and most pools have some type of disabled access. Some pools have a platform or "transfer tier" for wheelchair users to lift themselves onto and slide into the water. Others have "zero-entry" entrances for wading into the water (see photo on page 152). Hours of operation vary, but usually the "themed" pools close in the evenings while the "non-themed" pools stay open all night. Only guests staying at a resort can use its pool, though some resorts share pools and Disney Vacation Club members using their points have access to all but the Stormalong Bay pool complex at the Yacht & Beach Club and Uzima Springs Pool at Disney's Animal Kingdom Lodge (unless they are staying there, of course). Children in diapers must wear snug-fitting plastic pants or special swim diapers (available at some resort gift shops) when in the water.

Recreation—Every resort has something to do, with many offering a wide variety of outdoor activities. You can visit another resort to use its recreational facilities (with the exception of swimming pools). Hours are seasonal—check upon arrival.

Refillable Mugs—Most resorts sell thermal mugs that can be refilled free or for a small fee at your resort for the duration of your stay. Mugs are about $12 and can generally be refilled at a resort's food court or snack shop. Beverages usually include coffee, sodas, ice tea, and hot chocolate. Milk and juice are occasionally offered as refill options at the beverage station.

Refrigerators—All Disney moderate and deluxe resort rooms are equipped with a small refrigerator, free of additional charge. In the value resorts (All-Stars and Pop Century), a refrigerator can be requested for $10/day (free if required to store medication). Refrigerators can be rented at the Swan and Dolphin for $12/day; the rooms also have minibars.

Room Service—The deluxe resorts and some of the moderate resorts offer room service. Some resorts offer a pizza delivery service after 4:00 pm daily.

Security—A gatehouse guards entry into every resort, and virtually everyone who drives through the resorts' gates is questioned. Show your photo identification and resort identification, or explain that you are checking in, dining, or using the recreational facilities at the resort if you arrive by car. All resort rooms have electronic locks that open with your resort ID for added security. In addition, you can store small valuables in your in-room safe (all Disney resorts have safes) or with the front desk.

Smoking—As of June 1, 2007, <u>all</u> Disney resort rooms, including Disney Vacation Club resorts, are nonsmoking. The policy applies to all guest rooms, patios, and balconies and designates outdoor smoking areas at all resorts affected by the change. Smoking is also prohibited in all lobbies, common areas, restaurants, and convention spaces.

Spa (hot tub)—There's at least one outdoor hot tub at every Disney resort, with the exception of the All-Stars, Fort Wilderness, Polynesian, and Pop Century. Traditional spa facilities (massages and manicures) are available at some resorts (see page 326).

Telephones—Pay phones equipped with a Text Typewriter (TTY) for those with hearing impairments are available in each resort lobby. Resort rooms with special communication kits are equipped with TTY phones also. All rooms have a phone and details on how to use it. Long-distance calls are the cost of the call plus a 50% surcharge. Use calling cards or a cell phone instead.

Transportation—Every resort provides free, accessible transit to and from the parks via bus, boat, monorail, and/or pedestrian path. We list each resort's options and in-transit times in this chapter.

Wheelchairs—Wheelchairs can be borrowed from every resort (inquire at Bell Services). A deposit is required and availability is limited. (See Wheels! on pages 211–213.)

Planning

Special Challenges

Getting There

Staying in Style

Touring

Feasting

Resources

Index

Resort Comparisons

It's clear that Disney tries to address many of your special requirements in the amenities and facilities it provides in its rooms. So **how do you choose** which resort is the best one for you? There are lots of things to consider, obviously. For example, a traveler with allergies or asthma may not want to stay at the Animal Kingdom Lodge, with its wildlife on the resort grounds, or at a resort known for its dense wooded areas—e.g., Port Orleans Riverside or Fort Wilderness, with all the Spanish moss and trees.

In the **hotel descriptions** on the following pages, we've tried to present the information that is most relevant to visitors with special requirements to help you in making your resort decision. In general, we provide a resort description (layout, ambience, theme), check-in experience, guest room types, dining options, amenities (pool, arcade, fitness facility, or other activities), quiet spots, and transportation options. At the end of each resort description, you'll find our overall rating, along with any specific special considerations.

We've also provided the following **overview** of the various resorts' amenities, so that you can make your own quick comparison:

* Kitchen facilities are present only in the villas/ family suites/ cabins of the indicated resorts.	All-Star Resorts	Animal King. Lodge/Villas	Beach Club/Villas	BoardWalk Inn/Villas	Caribbean Beach	Contemporary	Coronado Springs	Dolphin	Fort Wilderness	Grand Floridian	Old Key West	Polynesian	Pop Century	Port Orleans	Saratoga Springs	Shades of Green	Swan	Wild. Lodge/Villas	Yacht Club
Resort Category (D=Deluxe, C=Disney Vacation Club, M=Moderate, V=Value)																			
Category	V	D/C	D/C	D/C	M	D	M	D	–	D	C	D	V	M	C	D	D	D/C	D
Total Rooms	5568	1293	785	910	2112	1041	1967	1509	1195	900	761	853	2880	3056	184	586	758	864	634
Occupancy	4-6	4-8	4-8	4-12	4	5	4	5	4-10	5	4-12	5	4	4-5	4-12	5	5	4-8	5
Kitchen Facilities*	✓	✓	✓	✓					✓		✓				✓			✓	
Monorail						✓				✓		✓							
Restaurants/Cafes	–	2	3	7	1	3	1	3	2	5	1	2	–	1	1	4	3	3	3
Character Meals		✓				✓		✓	✓	✓							✓		
Quick Service	3	1			1	1	1	1		1			1	2				1	
Room Service		✓	✓	✓	✓	✓	✓	✓		✓		✓			✓	✓	✓	✓	✓
Pools	6	1	3	3	7	2	4	2	2	2	4	2	6	7	3	2	2	2	3
Kid Pool	3	1	1	1	1	1	1	1	1	1	1	1	2	2	1	1	1	1	1
Playground	✓	✓	✓	✓	✓	✓	✓	✓	✓					✓	✓	✓	✓	✓	✓
Health Club		✓	✓	✓		✓	✓	✓		✓					✓	✓	✓	✓	✓
Child Care Club			✓	✓					✓	✓		✓						✓	✓

Note: Some rooms, like a king-size bed room that is not a suite, only sleeps 2.

Disney's All-Star Resorts

The All-Star Movies, Music, and Sports resorts are economical, functional, and spread out. The first value resorts at Disney, each has 1,728–1,920 rooms in themed, three-story, T-shaped buildings with elevators. These connected resorts display **larger-than-life icons** to match the theming, like the 35-ft. (10.6-m.) Buzz Lightyear in All-Star Movies, a three-story guitar in All-Star Music, and a 38-ft. (11.5-m.) surfboard in All-Star Sports.

Check-In

The main building of each resort (Cinema Hall, Melody Hall, and Grandstand Hall) houses the front desk/check-in, food court, bus depot, arcade, pool bar, and general store. A short-term check-in parking area is available nearby. Due to the size of these resorts, these central areas are often very noisy, with guests coming and going in all directions. **Check-in time is 4:00 pm**. There is often a long wait to check in to the All-Stars resorts due to the sheer number of rooms they have. To avoid the waits, we suggest you check in as soon as you arrive at Walt Disney World—sort of a "pre-check-in." It's a good time to drop off your luggage, too. Then you can leave to shop or play at the theme parks—check in "for real" later, when the crowds have subsided. See our sidebar on page 118 for other check-in strategies.

Important Note: The front desks here don't have low counters for guests in wheelchairs.

When your room is ready, you will have to walk to it—unless you have a car or your own wheels with you. There is **no internal transportation** system at the All-Stars, and the rooms here are very spread out. You can talk to Luggage Services about the availability of a wheelchair, if needed.

Guest Rooms

The 5,568 rooms at the three resorts are **small** (about 260 sq. ft./24 sq. m.) and fairly standard—they have either two double beds or one king, a TV, and a table with two chairs. Refrigerators are available for $10/night. Room decor varies with the resort's particular theme—Movies features characters from Disney films; Music's motif is, well, musical; and Sports has baseballs, basketballs, footballs, etc.

Guest rooms face a pool, courtyard, or parking lot, with the occasional wooded view. **A $12 premium per night is added to the "preferred" buildings closest to the Main Hall** (reserved at the time of booking). Preferred buildings are Fantasia, 101 Dalmatians, and Toy Story (All-Star Movies), Calypso (All-Star Music), and Surf's Up (All-Star Sports). Those farther away are generally quieter, but you'll also be walking/wheeling a distance to and from the bus stops and all other central services. Of the three All-Star Resorts, the layout of Music is the simplest to navigate.

Standard room layout

Family Suite layout

Disney's All-Star Resorts
(continued)

Guest Rooms (continued)

In 2006, 192 new **family suites** opened at All-Star Music. These 520 sq. ft. (48.3 sq. m.) rooms have two full bathrooms, a kitchenette, queen bed, sleeper sofa, and two convertible twin beds. Each suite sleeps six, plus one child under 3 in a crib. Rates begin at $179.

A major **room renovation** is also underway at All-Star Music.

© Deb Wills

A renovated, standard room at All-Star Music Resort

Despite being among the **smallest rooms at Walt Disney World**, the All-Star rooms can fit an ECV or wheelchair comfortably if you only have two people. If you have four, no matter if they are very small children, things will be tight with the wheelchair/ECV. If you want more room to move around, request a king room—just keep in mind that these tend to be the barrier-free rooms, and they may only have a shower, no tub.

All rooms exit to the outside (no inner corridors), so you are exposed to the elements when you're going to main services or bus stops.

For a **quieter stay**, request rooms facing away from the pool areas on the top (third) floor. Each building has an elevator, as well as partially covered outdoor stairs.

For **convenience** to food, bus stops, and the main pool, request a preferred building.

Important Note: Be aware that at various times throughout the year, large and sometimes boisterous youth groups may be staying at these resorts (think cheerleaders, dance competitions, and Pop Warner football). Inquire about this when you check in.

Dining

Other than limited snacks at the general store, the only places to purchase food at the All-Star Resorts are the **food courts**. Each have several stations offering a variety of selections and a refrigerated section with prepackaged items like sandwiches, salads, fruit, etc. Some kosher foods are always available at the food courts without advance notice. There is also limited pizza delivery in the evenings. One microwave is available for guest use in each food court area.

Amenities

Each All-Star Resort has **two pools: a large themed pool and a smaller pool** that usually is less crowded. There are no water wheelchairs or zero-entry access points for the All-Star pools; however, each has a transfer tier for wheelchair users to lift themselves onto and slide into the water. The bathhouse at the All-Star Sports Home Run pool has a roll-in shower with bench and handrails.

Each All-Star Resort has a **small playground area**, good for letting off some steam. There is also a game arcade located in the main building of each resort, as well as a variety store selling souvenirs and sundries.

There are **no spa or fitness center facilities** at the All-Star Resorts, so if you require a gym for physical therapy or an exercise routine, visit another resort on-site (see page 78). You may use any of those facilities for $12/day, based on availability. The purchase of a treatment at any Disney health club includes use of the adjacent fitness center for the day of treatment.

Disney's All-Star Resorts

(continued)

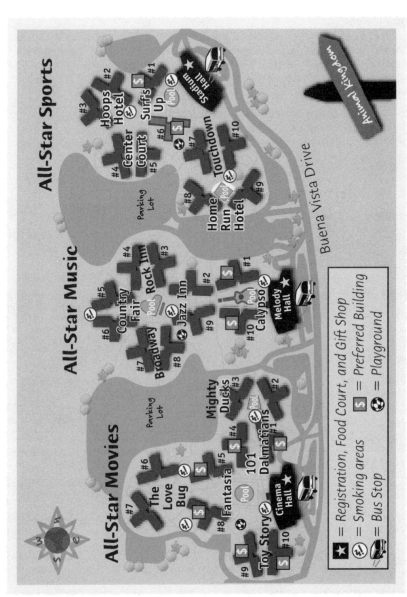

2008 standard room rates begin at $82 in value season, $99 in regular season, $109 in summer season, $119 in peak season, and $129 in holiday season (seasons are indicated on page 101). Family Suites range from $184 in value season to $315 in holiday season. Preferred rooms (see preferred buildings marked on map above) run $12 more per room. Note that prices may increase by $5–$20 per night on some holiday weekends. All rooms at this resort are subject to 13% tax.

Planning

Special Challenges

Getting There

Staying in Style

Touring

Feasting

Resources

Index

Disney's All-Star Resorts
(continued)

Quiet Spots

As big as these resorts are, there are **a few quiet spots** to be found. At All-Star Movies, look for the hammocks behind the palm trees near Fantasia. All-Star Music has picnic tables in the Country Fair courtyard and a small garden with benches in Broadway. All-Star Sports has a large covered pavilion in the back. You'll also find at least one small landscaped area with benches at each resort.

To help you get away from the loud hustle and bustle of the food court, tables and chairs outside may be quieter. These are subject to weather conditions and also tend to be smoking areas. You can always bring your food back to the room.

Transportation

Disney transportation to the parks from these resorts is via **buses**. For other destinations, transfer at a nearby theme park (daytime) or at Downtown Disney (evening).

Waits for buses to and from the All-Stars can be long, especially at park opening and closing times. The queues wind around and can get very crowded—in fact, it is not uncommon to have standing room only on the buses. Sometimes a single bus will service all three of the All-Star Resorts. All-Star Sports is the first stop in both directions in this case.

Estimated Transportation Times

Magic Kingdom	Epcot	Disney-MGM Studios	Disney's Animal Kingdom	Downtown Disney
direct bus ~20 min.	direct bus ~10 min.	direct bus ~10 min.	direct bus ~10 min.	direct bus ~15 min.

Approximate time you will spend in transit from resort to destination during normal operation.

Our Ratings

The All-Star Resorts are great for the budget, but not for amenities. They **rank low to medium**, primarily due to their layout and very basic amenities.

[A][U][S]	Can be very busy and noisy in the pools and central areas.
[C][♥][T] [M][P][E]	Unless you are in a preferred building, have a car, or use a wheelchair, we do not recommend the All-Star Resorts due to their sprawling design.
[D][W]	Food court chefs can accommodate with minimum 72 hours' notice. Kosher foods are available on a regular basis at the food courts here.
[V]	Consider preferred buildings for proximity to main building and services.
[F]	Larger-than-life icons could scare some.
[S]	For a more relaxing experience, consider staying at a moderate, deluxe, or Disney Vacation Club resort.
[L]	Be sure to request a king bed.

Disney's All-Star Movies/Music/Sports Resorts

1901/1801/1701 W. Buena Vista Dr., Lake Buena Vista, FL 32830
Phone: 407-939-7000/407-939-6000/407-939-5000
Fax: 407-939-7111/407-939-7222/407-939-7333

Disney's Animal Kingdom Lodge and Villas

The **most unique resort on Walt Disney World property**, Disney's Animal Kingdom Lodge surrounds you with the sights, sounds, cuisine, and even the animals of Africa. This deluxe resort is horseshoe-shaped and is designed to resemble an African "kraal" village. There are three savannas encompassing 33 acres, which are home to more than 200 mammals and birds. Phase I of Disney's Animal Kingdom Villas, part of the Disney Vacation Club, recently opened, with more rooms coming throughout the rest of 2007. A new DVC building will open in 2009.

Check-In
The self-parking area is a fair distance from the Lodge entrance—there are a few steps or a ramp to reach the main entrance. To avoid this, consider valet parking ($10/night or complimentary with a handicapped parking tag or to DVC members, once the Villas open).

Check-in is at 3:00 pm. Bell Services will assist in taking your luggage to your room. Rooms located at the end of a long hallway, or "trail," can be a significant distance from the front desk or elevator—ask at Bell Services if a wheelchair is available if you need one.

Guest Rooms
This deluxe resort offers **two sizes of rooms**, all very dimly lit and decorated in African-style prints. The standard rooms (floors 1–4) are 344 sq. ft. (32 sq. m.) and come with either two queen beds, one king bed plus a daybed, or one queen bed with bunk beds. The deluxe rooms (floor 5) are 381 sq. ft. (35 sq. m.) and have an additional daybed or fold-out chair single bed. All rooms also have a ceiling fan, table and chairs, TV and armoire, and double sinks in the bath area. In addition, they are equipped with a hair dryer, coffeemaker with coffee packets, wall safe, iron, and ironing board. Newspaper delivery, room service, and voice mail are also available. Concierge service offers additional amenities, as well as a lounge and unique animal-viewing safaris (for an additional fee). The special safaris are sometimes available to non-concierge guests; inquire at check-in. Safaris can accommodate one or two wheelchairs.

Standard room layout

Accessible rooms offer a king bed, roll-in shower, tub, and accessible seat for toilet. You can also request a "Room Communication Kit" with visual smoke alarm, bed boards and rails, egg crate mattress pad, bottle warmer, humidifier, rubber bath mat, and "sharps" container for used needles.

The entire resort is currently one structure, so **all rooms exit into a hallway**, not to the outdoors. As we noted earlier, though, hallways can be very long—if you have a problem walking/wheeling any distance, remember to request a room close to the lobby.

All rooms have a balcony—the minimum size is four feet long. If animal watching is the main reason you want to stay at the Lodge, be sure to reserve a savanna view. Rooms that face the animal savanna have special restrictions—no smoking and no throwing or dropping things off the balcony (for the protection and safety of the animals). There are security cameras that monitor balcony activity.

Disney's Animal Kingdom Lodge and Villas
(continued)

Dining

Disney's Animal Kingdom Lodge's two table-service restaurants, **Boma and Jiko**, are very **vegetarian/vegan friendly**. In fact, Jiko offers special diet menus, including one for gluten-free diners, one for lactose-free diners, and one for vegans. Even so, as we note in chapter 2, it's important to call 72 hours ahead of time to alert the chefs to your special requirements. If you forget to call in advance, we've found that the chefs at Boma are happy to walk you around the buffet, pointing out what you can and can't eat after you explain what foods you need to avoid. Quick service dining at **Mara** or room service are your only lunch options at this resort. See chapter 6 for our in-depth descriptions of dining options.

Amenities

This is a beautiful hotel with many amenities, but there are three major drawbacks: the resort is **isolated**, there are no walking/jogging trails, and rooms are dark and poorly lit. Guests with vision impairments may have problems seeing, especially in the bathroom vanity area.

Numerous activities are offered—inquire at check-in.

Most services are within the main resort, but you have to go outdoors to reach the pool; Mara, the quick-service restaurant; Pumbaa's Fun and Games arcade; and the Zahanati Fitness Center. Disney's Animal Kingdom Lodge also has several public savanna-viewing areas, located inside as well as outside.

There is one large pool, Uzima Springs, which has **zero-entry access**, as well as a water wheelchair available. There's a play area located nearby. There is no leisure pool here.

If you want to **maintain an exercise routine**, the resort has the Zahanati Fitness Center with exercise equipment, steam room, sauna, and massage therapies (for an extra fee).

Zawadi Marketplace is the **retail shop** celebrating the romantic and adventuresome spirit of Africa through the stories and cultures represented in its merchandise. Limited sundries and food are available here. See below for a list of common items of interest to travelers with special requirements, as well as approximate prices.

Typical Grocery/Sundry Items

Found in various resort shops (prices as of April 2007). Not all items available in all stores.

Off insect repellent (6 oz.)	$7.70	Electrical adapter	$8.50
Imodium (6 caplets)	$5.50	Speedo earplugs	$3.25
Cortaid	$2.90	Fruit	$0.99
Pepcid AC (6 tablets)	$5.00	Muffins (no fat-free available)	$2.99
Advil (20 liquid-filled caplets)	$6.75	Bread (whole wheat)	$3.19
Benadryl (24 tablets)	$8.00	Peanut butter	$2.85
Tylenol (30–children's)	$5.50	Sugar-free gummy candy (4 oz.)	$2.75
Bayer aspirin	$3.30	Pop-Tarts	$3.25
Dramamine (4 tablets)	$2.75	Coffee (Folgers brick)	$5.10
Diapers (10)	$8.85	Silk soy milk (1 pint)	$1.49
Swimming diaper	$1.60	Similac formula (1 can)	$11.65
Adult diapers (Serenity Pads, 12)	$11.50	Baby food (jar)	$1.00 +

Disney's Animal Kingdom Lodge and Villas
(continued)

2008 standard room rates begin at $225 in value season, $275 in regular season, $340 in peak season, and $370 in holiday season (seasons are indicated on page 101). Pool view rooms are about $10–$35 higher. Savanna view rooms are $65+ higher than standard rooms. Deluxe rooms (available in both water/pool and savanna view) are $85+ higher than standard rooms. Concierge (Club Level) rates begin at $335 in value season, $390 in regular season, $470 in peak season, and $520 in holiday season. Suites are also available starting in the mid-$600s for a one-bedroom in value season. Note that prices may increase by $20–$30 per night on some holiday weekends. All rooms at this resort are subject to 12.5% tax.

Disney's Animal Kingdom Lodge and Villas
(continued)

Transportation

All Disney **transportation from this resort is via bus**. As you exit the main lobby, the bus station is down to the left. From here, you can get to the theme parks, water parks, and Downtown Disney. The buses that service the Lodge do not stop at other resorts. If you want to travel to other resorts, travel to Disney's Animal Kingdom or another theme park (day) or to Downtown Disney (evening) and transfer to the appropriate bus.

Estimated Transportation Times

Magic Kingdom	Epcot	Disney-MGM Studios	Disney's Animal Kingdom	Downtown Disney
direct bus ~20 min.	direct bus ~15 min.	direct bus ~10 min.	direct bus ~5 min.	direct bus ~15 min.

Approximate time you will spend in transit from resort to destination during normal operation.

Our Ratings

Disney's Animal Kingdom Lodge is one of our favorite places at Disney to relax and get away from it all! It's great for those wanting a quiet, laid-back atmosphere. Co-author Deb Wills could sit on the balcony all morning watching the animals (in fact, she has done just that!). We rate the Lodge **medium-high** with lots of amenities but some drawbacks, as noted.

Our Convenience Scale

[A][B][D] [G][U]	In-room kitchen facilities in the villas are ideal for vacationers who prefer to prepare some meals themselves.
[G]	The savannas are kept very clean, but depending on allergies/asthma, the animals and vegetation could be an issue.
[C][♥][T] [M][P][E]	Request a room near the elevator lobby if you need shorter walking/wheeling distances. Difficult to maneuver wheelchair in rooms that have two beds or bunk beds. Ask for a room with a queen bed plus daybed for a bit more space.
[D]	Very accommodating for special dietary requests with 72 hours' notice.
[F]	There are two gas firepits at Disney's Animal Kingdom Lodge, one just off the main lobby and one outside in the Arusha Rock area. Also, the animals are not very close and are behind barriers, but those with a fear of wild creatures may be uncomfortable in this setting.
[Ö]	Many of the cast members at this resort are from Africa and are more than willing to share the language and culture of their native countries. Japanese breakfast available at Boma.
[L]	For more room, request a king bed or book a deluxe category room. Some rooms have bunk beds—if this would be a problem for you, remember to ask for a room without.
[X]	Very few service animal break areas, due to resort's theming.
[V]	Rooms tend to be dark with low lighting.

Disney's Animal Kingdom Lodge and Villas Resort

2901 Osceola Parkway, Bay Lake, FL 32830
Phone: 407-938-3000 Fax: 407-938-4799

Disney's BoardWalk Inn & Villas Resort

The BoardWalk Inn and its adjacent Disney Vacation Club sibling, the BoardWalk Villas, share a **premium location on Crescent Lake** between Epcot and Disney-MGM Studios. With a seashore theme designed to conjure up the feel of the old-time Atlantic City Boardwalk, these resorts have furnishings in pastel blues, greens, and yellows. The boardwalk that they sit on features fantastic water views, as well as a variety of entertainment and dining options.

Check-In
Ample parking is available at this resort, but the self-parking area is a few minutes' walk/wheel uphill to the lobby. There's also valet parking ($10/day, or complimentary if you're a DVC member staying using points or if you have a handicapped tag). Check-in for both sides of the resort (**3:00 pm at the Inn; 4:00 pm at the Villas**) is done in the common lobby. On the far left of the check-in counter, there's a lower counter to provide easier access for shorter folks or those in a wheelchair.

Bell Services assists in **delivering your luggage to your room**. Because this is a deluxe resort, all rooms exit into a hallway, not to the outdoors (except for Garden Suites; see below).

Guest Rooms
BoardWalk Inn, located on the right as you stand at the entrance with the parking lot/bus stop behind you, has 378 rooms with water, garden, or standard views. Each room is about 435 sq. ft. (40.4 sq. m.) and has one king or two queen beds, plus a 5-foot daybed or queen sleeper sofa. All rooms are nonsmoking rooms. The BoardWalk Inn also has several suites, including 14 separate romantic Garden Suites (about 1,000 sq. ft./93 sq. m.) that resemble two-story cottages, complete with white picket fence. Suites have a separate living room, sleeper sofa, and a wet bar on the first floor, while the open second floor has a king-size bed, a separate shower, and a large whirlpool tub. Garden Suites have an outside entrance.

Standard room layout (Inn)

BoardWalk Villas, on the left, feature 532 studios and one-, two-, and three-bedroom suites that range from 359 to 2,142 sq. ft. (33.4 to 199 sq. m.) Because all villas feature kitchen facilities, these accommodations are ideal for travelers with special dietary needs. Other amenities include a private balcony or patio, hair dryer, iron, ironing board, and vacuum cleaner. All except studios also have a washer, dryer, and DVD player. All rooms also have double sinks, a marble vanity, a table and chairs, sofa, armoire, TV, ceiling fan, toiletries, turndown service (on request), voice mail, and, for most rooms, newspaper delivery. All of the rooms are designated nonsmoking.

If you want to **avoid noise**, especially that of the BoardWalk entertainment venues, request a room overlooking the beautifully landscaped courtyards, away from the promenade and the pools.

Disney's BoardWalk Inn & Villas Resort
(continued)

Dining

The BoardWalk is unique, in that its dining and entertainment options are **located along the promenade** outside the resort. There are a number of table-service restaurants and quick snack spots, but Spoodles in particular is known for its healthier, lighter Mediterranean menu. Flying Fish is, as the name indicates, primarily a seafood restaurant—it's a great choice for diners who want to eat light and healthy, but those with fish or shellfish allergies might want to avoid it. Room service is also available, and there's a great selection of food items in the Screen Door General Store on the promenade. (Dundy's Sundries, just off the main lobby, has a much more limited selection of items.) See page 128 for a list of typical items available that are of particular interest to special travelers. For in-depth descriptions of all the BoardWalk's dining options, see pages 368–369.

Amenities

Trying to maintain an **exercise routine** while on vacation? The BoardWalk has Muscles & Bustles Fitness Center with exercise equipment, steam room, sauna, and massage therapies (for an extra fee). There are also bikes for rent at the resort's recreation center, Community Hall, and surrey bikes on the BoardWalk. In addition, there are two lighted tennis courts. The almost one-mile walkway around Crescent Lake and the path to Disney-MGM Studios are both excellent for walking, jogging, or wheeling.

The main pool, **Luna Park**, has a decidedly carnival feel—in fact, the 200-ft. (61-m.) slide is known as Keister Coaster. Swimmers exit the slide through the mouth of a large clown head—if you have a fear of clowns, you might want to avoid this. Try the two other heated pools or one of the three hot tubs (one near each pool). There's also a wading pool for infants at Luna Park—remember diaper-age children must wear snug-fitting plastic pants or special swimming diapers when in the water. All BoardWalk pools have transfer tiers. Automated external defibrillators (AEDs) are located at each of the pools and at numerous locations throughout the resort.

The **small arcade**, Side Show Games, is located near the health club, and there are also carnival-type games on the BoardWalk itself most nights. If you're looking for a place for your kids to cavort, there's also a playground located adjacent to Luna Park.

Wheelchairs and electric scooters are now available for rent from the surrey bike rental desk at the Boardwalk Resort. Scooters and wheelchairs can be rented for 24 hours or more and can be taken on all the Disney transportation. They are available right at the surrey bike rental counter and can be reserved prior to your arrival by calling 407-938-0349. They will deliver right to any Disney resort at no charge. Rental prices are $30 plus tax for each 24-hour period for the smaller electric scooters (up to 300 lbs.), and $40 plus tax for the larger (prices subject to change). Wheelchairs and scooters are also available for the Disney Cruise Line and are subject to an additional delivery charge. For more information or to make a reservation, visit http://www.buenavistascooters.com.

Quiet Spots

If you need a quiet retreat, the **Belle Vue Room**, off by itself down the hall from the lobby on the Inn side of the resort, is a good bet during the day, when the bar isn't open. There are overstuffed chairs and sofas to relax in. There are also backgammon, chess, and checkers tables (ask a cast member for game pieces). When the bar is open, it may get crowded with noisy groups. There are several quiet sitting areas scattered throughout the resort's buildings, and the gardens near the Garden Suites have benches perfect for resting and soaking in the sun. If you're over on the Villas side of the resort, some floors have oversized seating areas in the middle of the hallway that are usually quiet during the day.

Disney's BoardWalk Inn & Villas Resort

(continued)

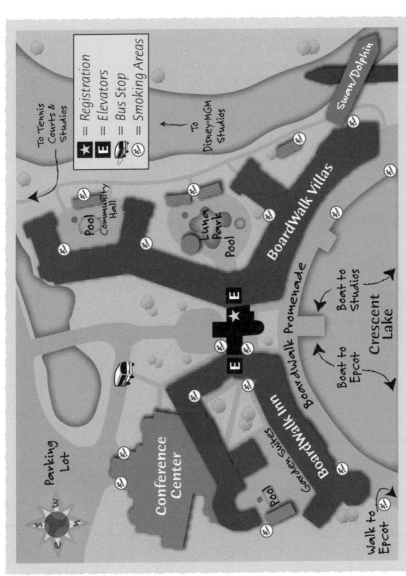

Planning

Special Challenges

Getting There

Staying in Style

Touring

Feasting

Resources

Index

2008 standard room rates at BoardWalk Inn begin at $325 in value season, $370 in regular season, $440 in peak season, and $490 in holiday season (seasons are indicated on page 101). Water view rooms add $75–$110 more. Studio villas at BoardWalk Villas begin at $325 in value season, $370 in regular season, $440 in peak season, and $490 in holiday season. One-bedroom villas are $110–$155 more, two-bedroom villas are $290–$650 more, and three-bedroom grand villas begin in the $1400s. Note that prices may increase by $20–$30 per night on some holiday weekends. All rooms at this resort are subject to 12.5% tax.

Disney's BoardWalk Inn & Villas Resort
(continued)

Transportation

Transportation **options include buses**, which you board in the front of the resort (to the Magic Kingdom, Disney's Animal Kingdom, Downtown Disney, and the water parks) and boats, which depart from the marina (to Epcot and Disney-MGM Studios). You can also walk/wheel to Disney-MGM Studios, Epcot, Yacht & Beach Club, and the Swan & Dolphin (note that there is no shelter/shade or benches along the walkway). If you want to travel to other resorts, travel to a theme park (day) or to Downtown Disney (evening) and transfer to the appropriate bus.

Bright Idea: The buses and boats that service the BoardWalk also make stops at the other Epcot area resorts (Yacht & Beach Club, Swan & Dolphin) on their way to Epcot and the Studios. It is frequently quicker to walk to your destination if you are able to do so.

Estimated Transportation Times

Magic Kingdom	Epcot	Disney-MGM Studios	Disney's Animal Kingdom	Downtown Disney
direct bus ~20 min.	walk (wheel)/boat ~15/~5 min.	walk (wheel)/boat ~15/~20 min.	direct bus ~10 min.	direct bus ~15 min.

Approximate time you will spend in transit from resort to destination during normal operation.

Our Ratings:

The BoardWalk Inn and Villas **rank high** on our convenience scale, although they are not for those on a tight budget. The proximity to two theme parks, numerous dining and transportation options, and other amenities make the BoardWalk area an attractive choice for vacationers who have a variety of needs.

[A][U][S]	The pool area and rooms that front the promenade can be noisy, especially in the evenings.
[G] [D]	In-room kitchen facilities at the BoardWalk Villas are ideal for vacationers with special dietary needs.
[R]	On the promenade, you'll find the Big River Grille and Brewing Works, a brewpub; Jellyroll's, a nightclub; and the ESPN Club—any of these might be a temptation for a person recovering from an alcohol addiction.
[B]	The Villas, with in-room kitchen facilities, are also ideal for vacationers traveling with an infant.
[C][♥][T] [M][P][E]	Request a room near the elevator or lobby if you need shorter walking/wheeling distances. Some units (especially on the Villas side) are extremely far away from the lobby.
[D]	Very accommodating for special dietary requests with 72 hours' notice.
[F]	The clown pool can be scary to some.
[V]	Rooms are bright and cheerful, with plenty of light.

Disney's BoardWalk Inn & Villas Resort

2101 Epcot Resorts Blvd., Lake Buena Vista, FL 32830
Phone: 407-939-5100 Fax: 407-939-5150

Disney's Caribbean Beach Resort

Take a trip to the tropics, mon, and enjoy the lush landscaping and colorful surroundings at the Caribbean Beach moderate resort. The islands, as each grouping of buildings is called, are named after actual islands in the Caribbean (Aruba, Jamaica, Trinidad, etc.) and encircle a 45-acre lake with white sandy beaches.

Check-In
The **Customs House**, Lobby Concierge, and luggage service are located just inside the entrance to the resort. This is where you will be dropped off (or park) for check-in. Check-in time is 3:00 pm.

Luggage service is available. When your room is ready, check with Bell Services at the Custom House. Someone will take you and your luggage to your building (a wheelchair-accessible van is available) if you don't have your own car.

Guest Rooms
This resort has 2,112 rooms and is **so spread out** that it has its own internal bus system, which makes a full circle of the resort every 20–30 minutes. Due to the size of the resort, not all rooms are within easy walking/wheeling distance of the Old Port Royale Town Center, where the food court, restaurant, themed pool, marina, and other guest services are housed, or even to the closest bus stop. We recommend renting a car or ECV if you have any mobility or waiting time concerns.

The rooms are located in two-story buildings and are the **largest of all the moderate resorts**—340 sq. ft. (31.5 sq. m.). There are no elevators to take you upstairs (it's 17 steps to the second floor), so if a ground floor room is necessary for medical/mobility reasons or you have small children or a stroller, be sure to state that when you make your reservation—or consider another resort! Standard views are parking lot or courtyard, or you can request a water (pool or bay) view. We recommend the courtyard view, as it's difficult to enjoy the premium view—most folks don't want to keep the curtains open to see the view due to privacy concerns or fears.

Standard room layout

Rooms have **one king bed or two doubles**, as well as a small table with two chairs, a TV in an armoire, and a ceiling fan. There are no balconies or patios, but there are coffeemakers, refrigerators, and pizza delivery. You can also request a rollaway bed ($15) and an international electrical adapter from Housekeeping.

A **$15 premium** is added to the rate of buildings closest to Old Port Royale (must be reserved at the time of booking). These "preferred" islands are Martinique and Trinidad North. Those farther away will require quite a walk/wheel to and from the food areas. For more "secluded" islands, request Aruba, Jamaica, or Trinidad South.

All rooms exit to the outside (there are no inner corridors), so you will be exposed to the elements when you go to the main services, and passers-by may peer in through your windows. If you are not in one of the preferred islands, you will have a distance to travel to get to Old Port Royale. Your options are to use a car or the internal bus transportation.

Disney's Caribbean Beach Resort
(continued)

Dining

Market Street Food Court offers several food stations with a central cash register area. Offerings include pizza/pasta, a hamburger shop, grab-and-go market, and Bridgetown Broiler. **Shutters**, the full-service restaurant, is open for dinner only with American cuisine inspired by the flavors of the Caribbean. (See chapter 6.) There is also pizza delivery available in the evenings.

Important Note: Chairs here are sturdy and wooden with no arms. For a less congested area during breakfast and lunch hours, seating is available in the Shutters restaurant area.

Amenities

Old Port Royale Town Center, which houses the gift shop, Market Street Food Court, Spanish fort-themed pool, Banana Cabana pool bar, and Shutters, a full-service restaurant, is located about one mile from the Customs House.

In addition to the main themed pool, **each island has its own "non-themed" pool**. While there are no zero-entry pools here, some pools have a transfer tier for wheelchair users to lift themselves onto and slide into the water.

Most of the **"island" pools have ramps** to enter the pool deck area, but Martinique has steps around the pool area. Look behind the pool near the laundry building to find the only ramp. At the other villages, if you find steps leading to the pool area on one side, be sure to check around the "islands." For instance, at Trinidad South, there are steps on the lake side, but flat entrances on the other sides. If you have a car or don't mind hopping on a bus, try another village if one pool is crowded.

Caribbean Beach offers **numerous activities**. You can rent boats and bicycles, jog/walk around the bay, check out the video games in Goombay Games Arcade, swim in the pools, enjoy three playgrounds, or walk to Caribbean Cay, a lush hideaway with tropical plants in the middle of Barefoot Bay. Request jogging information from Lobby Concierge.

There are **playgrounds** at the beaches of Barbados, Jamaica, and Trinidad South.

There are **no spa or fitness center facilities** at Caribbean Beach, so those who require a gym for physical therapy or exercise routine will have to visit another Disney resort. You may use any of the Disney facilities for $12 per day, based on availability. The purchase of a spa treatment includes use of the adjacent fitness center for the day of treatment.

© Deb Wills

Playground at Caribbean Beach Resort

Reader Tip: "You can actually see Epcot's higher fireworks from the beach between Martinique and Trinidad North. Just look across the water toward Aruba."—contributed by Sue Mickelson

Quiet Spots

Quiet spots can be found throughout the resort. There are a number of small, lush areas with a bench here and there to **enjoy the quiet of the resort** or visit Caribbean Cay. The beach walk around Barefoot Bay also has places to sit, rock in a hammock, or just enjoy the quiet. It's especially beautiful and peaceful at sunrise.

Disney's Caribbean Beach Resort
(continued)

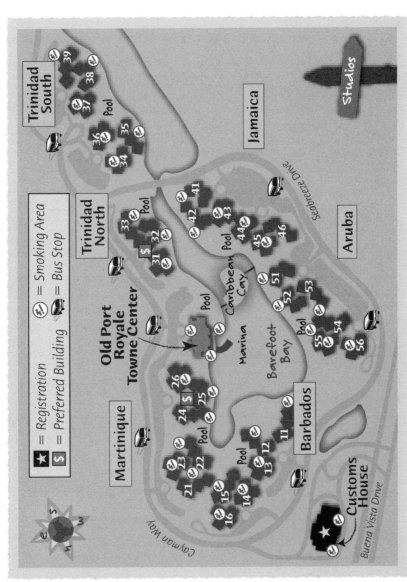

2008 standard room rates begin at $149 in value season, $165 in regular season, $179 in summer season, $189 in peak season, and $205 in holiday season (seasons are indicated on page 101). A water view, king bed, or preferred room adds at least $16 to the above rates. Preferred rooms are in Martinique and Trinidad North, as noted in the map above. Note that prices may increase by $5–$15 per night on some holiday weekends. All rooms at this resort are subject to 12.5% tax.

Disney's Caribbean Beach Resort
(continued)

Transportation
All Disney **transportation here is via dedicated bus** (buses don't stop at other resorts en route). There are seven bus stops, one for each island and one at Old Port Royale.

Estimated Transportation Times

Magic Kingdom	Epcot	Disney-MGM Studios	Disney's Animal Kingdom	Downtown Disney
direct bus ~20 min.	direct bus ~15 min.	direct bus ~12 min.	direct bus ~20 min.	direct bus ~25 min.

Approximate time you will spend in transit from resort to destination during normal operation.

Our Ratings:
Caribbean Beach Resort rates low to medium on our convenience scale. It is a quiet, well-landscaped resort with a beautiful lake where one can relax and enjoy a slower pace. The large, sprawling layout of the resort and separation of the check-in/luggage facility from Old Port Royale make it more important for those with special requirements to have a car or stay in a preferred location.

Our Convenience Scale

[C][♥][T][M][P][S]	Request a preferred building or have a car with you.
[P]	Lots of places to walk/wheel and swim. Also has bicycle and boat rentals.
[S]	Active seniors or those with a car will enjoy the quiet, laid-back atmosphere of this resort.
[F]	There are lots of birds around this resort.
[L]	Rooms are largest of the moderate resort category. Remember to request a king-size bed ($15 extra).

Disney's Caribbean Beach Resort
900 Cayman Way, Lake Buena Vista, FL 32830
Phone: 407-934-3400 Fax: 407-934-3288

Accessible toilet at Caribbean Beach Resort

Disney's Contemporary Resort

One of the two original Walt Disney World hotels, the deluxe Contemporary Resort offers wonderful views of Seven Seas Lagoon, the Magic Kingdom, and Bay Lake. This is a full-service resort, complete with restaurants, pools, convention center, salon, fitness club, and much more. What's more, it's on the monorail loop that serves the Magic Kingdom.

Check-In

Check-in time is 3:00 pm. As you enter the lobby, you will find the check-in counter on your left (there are no low counters, however). There are some comfy chairs across the way, if you need to wait for others in line.

The resort's guest **rooms are spread out** among the large A-frame section (the Tower) and one three-story wing (called the Garden Wing). (The North Wing has recently been demolished—rumor has it there will be another Disney Vacation Club built on this site.) For Tower guests, elevators take you to your floor. Those in the Wing walk/wheel to their rooms. Bell Services will bring your luggage to your room within 15 to 20 minutes of your request. If you choose to take advantage of the ample self-parking, you can drop your luggage off first, park, and then check in (note that the self-parking area is closer to the Wing than to the Tower). Valet parking is available ($10 or complimentary with a handicapped tag). If you are staying in the Garden Wing, ask the valet to keep your car nearby while you check in so you can drive over.

Guest Rooms

Rooms are spacious (about 436 sq. ft./40.5 sq. m.) and have either two queen beds or one king, as well as a daybed. The decor is very, well, contemporary—all rooms were recently renovated and redecorated. Furnishings include a table with chairs, an armoire, flat-screen TV, coffeemaker, hair dryer, a generous-sized bathroom with two sinks, and a massage shower head. Newspaper delivery and turndown service are both available. Rollaway bed ($15) may be added to king-bed rooms. You may also request an international electrical adapter.

Garden Wing rooms have **standard or garden/water views**; Tower rooms have views of Bay Lake or Seven Seas Lagoon. Tower rooms have balconies, while the Garden Wing offers first-floor patios (very few rooms in the Wing have balconies).

The Contemporary offers **concierge service** on the 12th and 14th floors.

Most rooms have two queen beds and a daybed, although there are also king-bed rooms.

If mobility is a concern, reserve a room in the Tower near an elevator, not in the Garden Wing. You'll pay a premium to stay in the Tower, but you'll also have most services available inside the main building. If you stay in the Garden Wing, you will be walking/traveling outside, sometimes in uncovered areas, to get to Disney transportation and resort services.

The **Garden Wing** is close to the pool and the convention center.

Standard
room layout

Disney's Contemporary Resort
(continued)

Dining

The California Grill, on the Contemporary's 15th floor, is **one of the premier restaurants** in Walt Disney World, known not only for great food and wine, but for its exceptional view of the Magic Kingdom. Several vegetarian options are always featured on the menu, but for more specific dietary requests, call 72 hours in advance. Chef Mickey's is a very popular character meal, serving breakfast and dinner. The restaurant is large and open, with characters all around and music that the characters dance to—it is a loud, busy place. The Concourse Steakhouse serves three meals a day and is adjacent to Chef Mickey's. At press time, several of the other dining options at the Contemporary were undergoing changes. A temporary quick service restaurant called Tempo Grab and Go will operate near the Outer Rim lounge on the 4th Floor, while a new table service restaurant called The Wave, is tentatively set to open in late March or April 2008 in the space formerly occupied by the Food and Fun Center. The Concourse Steakhouse on the 4th floor is being converted into a new, permanent quick service restaurant, set to debut in mid-August 2008.

Amenities

On the **first floor** of the Tower are the main lobby, check-in, Bell Services, and Common Grounds (coffee bar with limited hours). The Food and Fun Center food court is being renovated through 2007. The game arcade is now located on the fourth floor. Some areas in the lobby and throughout this resort also have wireless internet (Wi-Fi) access available.

The **fourth-floor concourse** is where you'll find the monorail station (with service to the Magic Kingdom, Polynesian, Grand Floridian, and Transportation & Ticket Center), gift shops, and restaurants.

There are **lots of things to do at the Contemporary**—jogging paths, volleyball, shuffleboard courts, and boat rentals are available. And for the more energetic, there's Sammy Duvall Water Sports Centre (http://www.duvallwatersports.com), which offers a variety of water experiences, including parasailing and skiing.

The **Olympiad Fitness Center** is free to resort guests staying at the Contemporary.

Two adjacent pools serve the resort. There's **no zero-entry pool**; however, there is a water slide and small fountain area for kids. Two hot tubs/spas near the pools can help soothe those aching muscles after a day in the parks. The Sand Bar is located by the pool and is open with seasonal hours.

Go out to the beach and **watch the Magic Kingdom's fireworks**, or head to the fourth-floor concourse, which offers inside views. From Bay Lake-view rooms and the beach, you can watch the nightly Electric Water Pageant.

There is a **wheelchair "restroom,"** rather than just a stall, in the lobby restroom. The lobby's women's restroom also has a "Child Protection Seat" in one of the stalls to allow you to strap an infant securely in place while you're using the facilities.

In 2007, a pilot program called **Disney's Online Concierge** is being tested throughout the Contemporary Resort. The program involves each room having its own computer that provides a variety of services to guests. Guests can use the computer to check flights, order room service, play video games, connect to Disney Internet sites, and contact valet and bell services. The online concierge also sends personal e-mail to the guests with information on the upcoming day's events and weather. If the program proves successful, it will be expanded and may eventually allow guests to make online reservations at Disney restaurants.

Disney's Contemporary Resort
(continued)

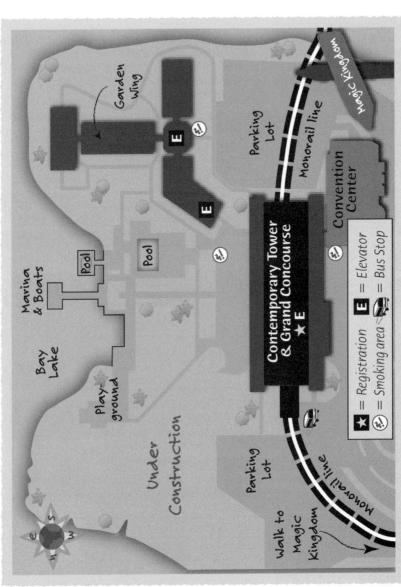

2008 standard room rates begin at $270 in value season, $315 in regular season, $350 in peak season, and $410 in holiday season (seasons are indicated on page 101). Tower rooms are $110–$130 more than the Garden Wing. Concierge Tower rooms start in the low $500s. Suites are also available starting in the $800s. Note that prices may increase by $10–$30 per night on some holiday weekends. All rooms at this resort are subject to 12.5% tax.

Planning · Special Challenges · Getting There · Staying in Style · Touring · Feasting · Resources · Index

Planning
Special Challenges
Getting There
Staying in Style
Touring
Feasting
Resources
Index

Disney's Contemporary Resort
(continued)

There are areas around the grounds by the Garden Wing that offer **quiet places to walk/ wheel** and look out on the waterways. During the day, if there are no conventions, the second floor has a variety of comfy chairs and sofas and is generally unpopulated. In the evening, the second floor area near the elevator is the check-in for the California Grill.

Transportation

There are a **number of transportation options available** at the Contemporary. Disney transportation is via bus, boat, or monorail (which has an accessible station on the fourth floor). The Magic Kingdom is just a 10-minute walk away. Also on the monorail line are the Polynesian and Grand Floridian Resort & Spa. From the bus stop, located to the right as you exit the front of the resort, you can go to the other theme parks, water parks, and Downtown Disney. (Buses sometimes make stops at other resorts en route.) Motorboat launches take you to Fort Wilderness or the Wilderness Lodge (a rare luxury to have any resort-to-resort transportation). Wheelchairs and strollers must be folded. (You must step down into the boat.) Note that water levels and the type of boat in operation will determine whether it is wheelchair-accessible. See page 209 for details.

Estimated Transportation Times

Magic Kingdom	Epcot	Disney-MGM Studios	Disney's Animal Kingdom	Downtown Disney
monorail/walk ~20/~10 min.	monorail x 2 ~15 min.	direct bus ~20 min.	direct bus ~20 min.	direct bus ~35 min.

Approximate time you will spend in transit from resort to destination during normal operation.

Our Ratings

The Contemporary **ranks very high** on our convenience scale—it has a terrific location close to the Magic Kingdom and is on the monorail line. Convenience comes with a price, though—this is a deluxe-priced resort. The resort's varied transportation options (monorail, boat, bus, walking) and numerous other amenities make it an excellent choice for vacationers who have a variety of special challenges.

[A][U][C][B][E][S]	Because it's on the monorail line, getting back to the Contemporary Resort quickly (for a midday break or at the end of the day) is relatively easy.
[C][♥][T][M][P][S]	Request a guest room near an elevator in the Tower.
[D]	The California Grill is known for its versatile menu. Other restaurants are very accommodating with 72-hour notice.
[F]	If you have a fear of heights, stay in the Garden Wing and not the Tower.
[P]	There are lots of places to walk/wheel and swim.

Disney's Contemporary Resort
4600 North World Drive, Bay Lake, FL 32830
Phone: 407-824-1000 Fax: 407-824-3539

Disney's Coronado Springs Resort

Coronado Springs, located between Disney's Animal Kingdom and Disney-MGM Studios, is classified a "moderately priced" resort. Yet because of its convention facilities, it **offers many amenities** normally found only in the deluxe hotels. The architecture and decor reflect the regions of Mexico and the American Southwest.

Check-In
Check-in time is 3:00 pm and takes place in El Centro, the main building, with a spacious lobby and high ceilings. There's one low counter on the far right for wheelchair/ECV accessibility.

The resort is fairly spread out, so getting to your room from El Centro can be as much as a **half-mile trip**. If you need assistance, ask when you check in, and a cast member will give you a lift to your room on a golf cart. Another option for getting around the resort is to hop on a bus at El Centro and ride around the resort to the stop nearest your building. If you require a wheelchair, there are a limited number available for your use at the resort. There's no charge, but a refundable deposit (usually $250) is required.

Guest Rooms
A **sprawling resort** of 1,967 rooms, Coronado Springs has three themed areas of accommodations situated around a 15-acre lake known as Lago Dorado. The main building, El Centro, houses registration and the shops and restaurants. It is located on the south side of the lake. Moving clockwise around the lake, the building areas are the three- and four-story Casitas, which represent the urban areas of the Southwest and Mexico; the rustic Ranchos, themed to reflect rural areas of the Southwest; and the two-story Cabanas, characterized by their sandy shorelines along the beach of the lake. All multistory buildings have elevators. Accessible rooms are located on the first floor of the Casitas 3 building, as well as on the first floor of buildings in the Ranchos and Cabanas.

Rooms are about 314 sq. ft. (29.17 sq. m.) with **two double beds (or one king)**, a television in an armoire with three drawers, table with two chairs, single sink vanity, and bathroom. Other amenities in the room include a four-cup coffeemaker with regular and decaf coffee packets, small refrigerators, a wall-mounted hair dryer, an iron and ironing board, high-speed Internet access, and a small wall safe. Newspaper delivery is available for $1.50/day. A number of junior, one-bedroom, and executive suites are also available.

A number of rooms **connect to the room next door**. Request this type of room if you're traveling with a companion. All rooms here, as at all Disney resorts, are nonsmoking.

Standard room layout

Planning · *Special Challenges* · *Getting There* · *Staying in Style* · *Touring* · *Feasting* · *Resources* · *Index*

Disney's Coronado Springs Resort
(continued)

Buildings in **Cabanas 9B or Casitas 1 or 3 are nearest El Centro** and its bus stop—in fact, the pathway to rooms in the Casitas is fully covered. (To get to other buildings, you'll need to travel outdoors, unprotected from the elements.) Casitas 4, Ranchos 6A or 7B, and Cabanas 8A are near the other bus stops. The Ranchos are closest to the main pool but the farthest from El Centro and its services. We recommend buildings 6B and 8A for the view and proximity to the quiet pool or Cabanas 9B for convenience to El Centro.

© Debra Martin Koma

Roll-in Shower at Coronado Springs

Important Note: This resort frequently hosts large conventions. Inquire about this when you check in so that you can attempt to avoid the large groups.

Dining

Coronado Springs' dining options include the table-service Maya Grill and the nontraditional food court Pepper Market (see page 371). Both of these restaurants will accommodate special requests with 72-hour notice (see "Making Special Dietary Requests," chapter 6). Pepper Market in particular **prepares many items to order** using fresh ingredients—it's easy to speak to the chef on the spot to discuss special dietary requirements. For those who would like a light meal or snack, La Tienda, next to Pepper Market, carries fresh fruit, drinks, sandwiches, salads, and wraps. Other spots to grab a quick bite: Siesta's pool bar and Francisco's lounge. Because Coronado Springs caters to a convention crowd, it also offers limited room service in the mornings and evenings.

Amenities

Unlike the other Disney moderate resorts, Coronado Springs has its **own fitness center**. La Vida Health Club has exercise equipment, a whirlpool, and massage treatments. For those who want to stick to their exercise routine on vacation, there's a nature trail and a pathway encircling the lagoon. There are also boats and bikes for rent at La Marina, and there is a volleyball court.

The Dig Site main themed pool is a **10,800 sq. ft. (1,003 sq. m.) miniature water park**. It's built around a stepped Mayan pyramid and features a 123-foot (37.5-meter) water slide, hot tub that holds up to 22 people, and separate children's pool with water jets. There's also a heated pool in each of the three themed accommodation areas. All the pools have a transfer tier for those who are able to lift themselves onto it and then slide into the water. Automated external defibrillators (AEDs) are located at each of the pools and at numerous locations throughout the resort.

Kids will love the **play area** located at the Dig Site, too, with its swings, slides, and a jungle gym to crawl around on. Nearby is the Iguana Arcade (a second arcade, called the Jumping Bean Arcade, is located at El Centro).

Disney's Coronado Springs Resort

(continued)

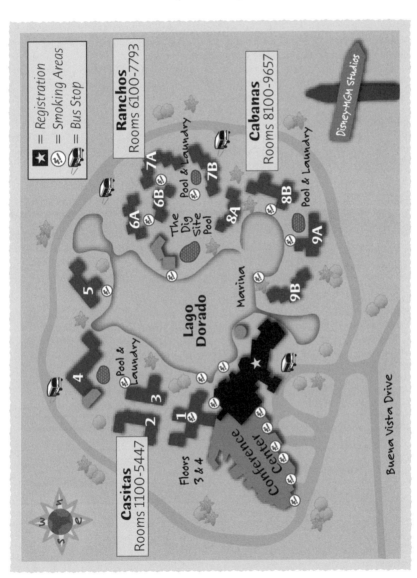

2008 standard room rates begin at $149 in value season, $165 in regular season, $179 in summer season, $189 in peak season, and $205 in holiday season (seasons are indicated on page 101). Water view and king-bed rooms are $15 more. Junior suites are $285–$316 more than standard rooms. One-bedroom suites are $615–$820. Two-bedroom suites are $910–$1,210. Note that prices may increase by $5–$15 per night on some holiday weekends. All rooms at this resort are subject to 12.5% tax.

Planning

Special Challenges

Getting There

Staying in Style

Touring

Feasting

Resources

Index

Disney's Coronado Springs Resort
(continued)

Quiet Spots

If you're looking for a quiet spot to hang out, you've come to the right resort. There are **hammocks located all around Lago Dorado**—they make the perfect place to "chill out." Also, all around the Casitas section are courtyards with beautiful fountains that make nice spots to relax and refresh. The secluded Nature Trail, located behind the Dig Site, is a nice spot for a leisurely exploration, too.

Transportation

All Disney **transportation from this resort is via bus**. There are four bus stops scattered around the resort—the main stop is located down the walkway to your left as you exit El Centro. (Buses often make a stop at Blizzard Beach en route.) A sidewalk connects the resort to Blizzard Beach, and it's a short drive to Disney-MGM Studios or Disney's Animal Kingdom.

Estimated Transportation Times

Magic Kingdom	Epcot	Disney-MGM Studios	Disney's Animal Kingdom	Downtown Disney
direct bus ~15 min.	direct bus ~15 min.	direct bus ~15 min.	direct bus ~10 min.	direct bus ~25 min.

Approximate time you will spend in transit from resort to destination during normal operation.

Our Ratings

Coronado Springs **ranks medium-high** on our convenience scale. Even though it's a moderate resort, it has many deluxe amenities—the fitness center, room service—that make it an attractive choice for vacationers who have a variety of needs. In addition, we've found the cast members here to be extremely helpful and willing to accommodate special requests.

[C][E][♥][T] [M][P][S]	Resort is spread out; request room close to El Centro or bus stop.
[G]	There's a wide variety of flowering shrubs and plants all around the grounds—allergy/asthma sufferers beware.
[P]	There's a health club facility on-site, as well as a nice pathway encircling the lake.
[L]	Request a guest room with a king bed.
[V]	Difficult to navigate alone if using a cane; resort is very spread out.

Disney's Coronado Springs Resort

1000 W. Buena Vista Drive, Lake Buena Vista, FL 32830
Phone: 407-939-1000 Fax: 407-939-1001

Disney's Fort Wilderness Resort & Campground

More than just an ordinary campground, Disney's Fort Wilderness offers a number of **different types of accommodations**, as well as a wide assortment of things to do. Nestled among tall, dark pine and cypress trees dripping with Spanish moss, the 700-acre campground is in a secluded spot on Bay Lake, just minutes from the Magic Kingdom theme park.

Check-In

Check-in at Fort Wilderness (**1:00 pm for campsites; 3:00 pm for Cabins**) is handled pretty much as it is at any Disney resort. The lobby of the registration building has a stone fireplace and rough-hewn rocking chairs, with wood paneling and other homey touches. Once you've checked in, you can drive directly to your campsite if you have your own car. Otherwise, a cast member will take you and your luggage in a minivan to your cabin.

Guest Rooms

All types of camping are available—tent, pop-up, trailer, and motor home (RV)—throughout the 788 campsites. In addition, there are 407 Wilderness Cabins, for folks who enjoy the rustic setting but aren't interested in truly "roughing it." Located on small loop roads connecting to larger thoroughfares, each campsite or Wilderness Cabin is relatively secluded by trees and shrubs and has its **own paved driveway, charcoal grill, picnic table**, and, in the case of campsites, 110V/220V electrical service.

The **Wilderness Cabins**, located on loops 2100–2800, are modified mobile homes with exteriors made to look like genuine log cabins. Measuring approximately 12' x 42' (504 sq. ft./46.8 sq. m.), these air-conditioned cabins are fully equipped for that "home-away-from home" feeling. They can accommodate up to six guests plus a child under 3 in a crib. Each cabin has a bedroom with double bed and bunk bed, full bathroom, full kitchen, and living room with an in-wall full Murphy bed. They are furnished with loveseat, television, and two kid-sized chairs and a table. Three kitchen chairs are around a rustic kitchen table along with an upholstered bench that seats three more. Amenities include a porta-crib and sheet, broom and dustpan, sponge mop, iron, ironing board, vacuum cleaner, extra pillows and blanket, wall-mounted hair dryer, voice mail, and daily housekeeping. No tents are permitted outside a Wilderness Cabin.

Some Wilderness Cabins have **wheelchair accommodations**, with these features:

✔ Wheelchair-accessible door and hallway
✔ Large deck and ramped entry
✔ Roll-in shower
✔ Lower sink/kitchen countertop

The cabins are, however, **extremely dark**. The décor, in shades of dark browns, burnt oranges, and forest greens with dark wood paneling, is made to seem even darker by the cabins' poor lighting. Because you're nestled amongst trees, the rooms are dark even when there is full sunshine outside. In addition, the lightbulbs are low wattage. Those with vision impairments may find it difficult to see in these cabins. (Deb Koma found it hard to see even without vision impairments!)

Cabin layout

Disney's Fort Wilderness Resort & Campground
(continued)

Campsites

There are **three types of campsites**: partial hookups that supply water (in the 1500 and 2000 loops); full hookups with sewer and water (in loops 900–1300 and 1600–1900); and preferred sites (in the 100–800 and 1400 loops) with cable TV, sewer, and water. Preferred sites are closest to the marina and Settlement Depot. Each site accommodates up to ten people and one car; pets are welcome at certain sites. All sites are within walking distance of clean, air-conditioned "Comfort Stations" that have restrooms, private showers, telephones, ice machines (extra fee), and laundry facilities.

Bright Idea: If you use a wheelchair, consider staying near loops 100, 300, 500, 900, and 1400 because the Comfort Stations near these are wheelchair-accessible.

If you're staying without a car, **request to be close to a bus stop**—if your campsite or cabin is at the far end of the loop, getting to the bus stop can be quite a haul. To reduce transit time to the parks, request a site in loops 100–800—these are within walking/wheeling distance of Settlement Depot and the marina. The most popular campsites are on loop 400. If you want a full hookup campsite, we highly recommend loop 800.

Getting around the resort can be difficult, since motor traffic is limited to entering/exiting the park. To get anywhere within Fort Wilderness, you must either walk/wheel or use the internal bus system. Three bus routes—Yellow, Orange, and Purple—serve locations within the resort, and all stop at Settlement Depot and Outpost Depot. A quicker way to get around is to rent an **electric golf cart**. Because they are difficult to get, we suggest you reserve one (up to a year in advance) from Fort Wilderness' Bike Barn at 407-824-2742. Rates are $47+tax per 24-hour period.

Dining

You may **cook many of your meals**, ideal if you have dietary concerns. Bring your own groceries, buy them at Gooding's at Crossroads near Downtown Disney, or buy them from one of the two Trading Posts (a more expensive option) on the campground.

If you choose to **eat out** at Fort Wilderness, there aren't many options for you—there's Trail's End Restaurant (see page 371), which serves food buffet-style, or there's the Chuck Wagon and Crockett's Tavern, which serve snacks. For a special night out, there's the Hoop Dee Doo Musical Revue dinner show or Mickey's Backyard BBQ (see page 382). Special diets can be accommodated at these dinner shows with at least 24-hour notice. Advance reservations are highly recommended for these dinner shows.

Amenities

If you need to maintain an **exercise routine** here, you have a number of choices. Fort Wilderness has no fitness center, but neighboring Wilderness Lodge does, plus there are many trails perfect for hiking, wheeling, or jogging. There are also two lighted tennis courts, plus places for volleyball, tetherball, basketball, and horseshoes. The marina rents boats or surrey bikes, while the Bike Barn rents canoes or standard bikes. In addition, there are horseback rides at the livery for about $42/person. Note that riders must be at least 9 years old and 48 inches tall and can weigh no more than 250 pounds. The campground also has two heated pools, a wading pool, and a beach for sunbathers. Automated external defibrillators (AEDs) are located at each of the pools and at numerous locations throughout the resort. None of the Fort Wilderness pools appear to have transfer tiers. There's also a nightly campfire sing-along with marshmallow-toasting, followed by the screening of a Disney movie.

For the younger set, there are **several playgrounds** around the resort, plus two game arcades: one at the Settlement Trading Post, the other at the Meadows Trading Post.

Disney's Fort Wilderness Resort & Campground
(continued)

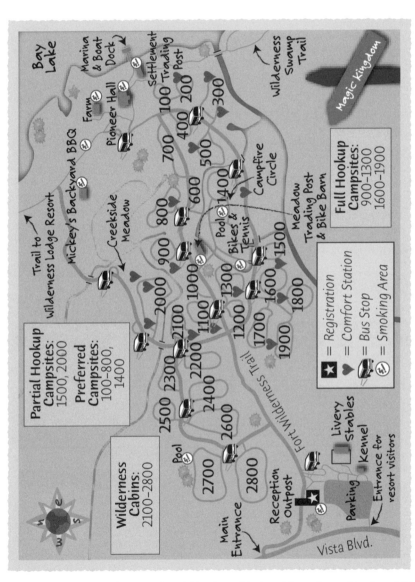

2008 standard campsite rates (partial hookup with electricity and water) begin at $42 in value season, $60 in regular season, $70 in peak season, $81 in holiday season, and $46 in pre-holiday season (seasons are indicated on page 101). Sewer hookup sites add $5–$13 more. Sites with sewer and cable add $14–$17 more to the standard rate. Wilderness Cabins are $255 in value season, $299 in regular season, $340 in peak season, and $380 in holiday season. Note that prices may increase by $1–$20 per night on some holiday weekends. All sites and cabins at this resort are subject to 12.5% tax.

Disney's Fort Wilderness Resort & Campground

(continued)

More Amenities

Seniors might enjoy camping at Fort Wilderness due to its low-key pace and the many activities. Try a bass fishing excursion or a quiet canoe trip. The Electrical Water Pageant, a light and music barge parade on Bay Lake, can be seen from the beach at 9:45 pm.

Those who have **fears of animals** should note that there are many small creatures, such as squirrels, rabbits, raccoons, and armadillos, around the grounds. Pets are also allowed in loops 300, 700, 800, and 1600–1900. The loops are quite dark at night.

Transportation

Because Disney transportation to and from Fort Wilderness requires a transfer from an internal bus to some type of external transport, **a car comes in handy** to save wait and transit times, not to mention aggravation. Boats go to the Magic Kingdom, Wilderness Lodge, and the Contemporary. Bus transportation is a more complicated. Buses for Disney-MGM Studios pick up and drop off at Settlement Depot. Buses for Epcot and Disney's Animal Kingdom/Blizzard Beach pick up/drop off at Outpost Depot. If you need to travel by bus to the Magic Kingdom during park operating hours, take the Orange bus from the Settlement Depot, which will take you to the Wilderness Lodge, and then transfer to a Magic Kingdom bus. To return from the Magic Kingdom during park hours, take the Wilderness Lodge bus, then transfer to the Orange bus to get back to Fort Wilderness. To get to or from the Magic Kingdom after park hours, transfer at the Transportation & Ticket Center. There's a path connecting Fort Wilderness to the Wilderness Lodge. For other resorts, transfer at Magic Kingdom or Downtown Disney.

Estimated Transportation Times

Magic Kingdom	Epcot	Disney-MGM Studios	Disney's Animal Kingdom	Downtown Disney
boat ~15 min.	direct bus ~25 min.	direct bus ~30 min.	direct bus ~30 min.	direct bus ~35 min.

Approximate time you will spend in transit from resort to destination during normal operation.

Our Ratings

Fort Wilderness Resort & Campground **ranks low to medium** on our convenience scale, depending on your individual requirements.

[A][U][C][B][♥] [T][M][P][E][S] [L]	The distance from guest services and difficult internal transportation are drawbacks for persons with mobility concerns and/or who have difficulty waiting. Request a campsite/cabin close to a bus stop. Travelers using wheelchairs/ECVs should avoid this resort if dependent on buses, as it takes quite a while to travel due to multiple loading.
[S]	Some seniors love the peace and calm of this resort; others find the distances from services and transportation system to be drawbacks.
[B][G][D]	The ability to prepare your own meals, either at your campsite or in your Wilderness Cabin, is ideal for vacationers with special dietary needs. But the thick tree cover, along with lots of Spanish moss and numerous woodland creatures, may spark asthma/allergy issues.
[A][U]	Fort Wilderness provides ample opportunity for running off steam and for getting away from the hubbub of the theme parks.

Disney's Fort Wilderness Resort & Campground
4510 N. Fort Wilderness Trail, Lake Buena Vista, FL 3283, 407-824-2900 Fax: 407-824-3508

Disney's Grand Floridian Resort & Spa

A stately **turn-of-the century Victorian hotel**, the gleaming white Grand Floridian sits on Seven Seas Lagoon between the Polynesian and the Magic Kingdom. This is Walt Disney World's most deluxe hotel.

Check-In
Ample parking is available at this resort, but the **self-parking area is across the street**. It's a few minutes' walk/wheel (no incline) to the lobby—you can't park close to your room. There is valet parking, though ($10/day or complimentary with a handicapped tag).

Check-in (3:00 pm) takes place in the Grand Lobby, with its soaring ceiling and exquisite one-ton chandeliers. There's no low counter for wheelchair accessibility at the registration windows, nor is there a companion restroom available in the lobby area. There are, however, a number of comfy sofas and chairs perfect for waiting while another member of your party checks in, as well as a scaled-down kids reception area, complete with TV.

Reader Tip: "On our recent trip to the Grand Floridian for breakfast, we were in the extremely adult lobby area waiting and were very grateful we were not staying there. Joey, with his autism, squeals out loudly and we would have felt very uncomfortable in the posh and almost 'adult only' feel of the resort."—contributed by peer reviewer Betsy Hicks

Once you've checked in, **Bell Services takes you and your luggage to your guest room**, whether you're staying in the Grand Lobby building itself or in one of the outer lodges.

Guest Rooms
There are nearly **900 guest rooms spread out among five lodge buildings** and the Grand Lobby. Rooms are about 400 sq. ft. (37.2 sq. m.) and have marble-topped double sinks and balconies or patios. Most guest rooms, decorated in one of four themes (floral, cameo, swans, or Alice in Wonderland), offer two queen-size beds and a daybed, accommodating five people. The lodge buildings also house the slightly smaller "dormer" rooms, plus suites. Amenities include signature toiletries, turndown service, minibar, refrigerator, wall safe, hair dryer, iron and ironing board, newspaper delivery, 24-hour room service, 4-cup coffeemaker and coffee/tea, high-speed Internet access (for a fee), and bathrobes.

In addition to the standard room amenities, you can also **request these special items**:
- ✔ Bed boards/Bed rails
- ✔ Down pillows
- ✔ Heating pads
- ✔ Cribs
- ✔ Smoke detectors (for guests with hearing disabilities)
- ✔ Microwave (limited number available)
- ✔ Room Communication Kit (for those with hearing impairments)

Four extra-special types of rooms are available. The lodge tower rooms have a separate sitting area, an extra TV and phone, and five windows. Concierge rooms offer personalized services, and continental breakfast, afternoon tea, and evening refreshments in the lounge. Of the concierge rooms, special turret rooms have wet bars and windows all around, while honeymoon suites feature whirlpool tubs.

Standard room layout

Disney's Grand Floridian Resort & Spa
(continued)

Guest Rooms (continued)

The **dormer rooms** on the top floors of the lodge buildings may be a bit smaller (they only sleep 4 rather than 5), but they have vaulted ceilings and a secluded balcony. The best views of Cinderella Castle are found in the lagoon view rooms in Sago Cay and Conch Key lodges, but these buildings are quite a distance from the main building. If proximity to the restaurants and guest services is important, request a room in the Grand Lobby or in Sugar Loaf Key. (These rooms are pricier, though, as they are all suites or concierge level.) Note that the latter sees a lot of traffic, however, and can be noisy. Big Pine Key is near the beach, and its lagoon view rooms offer picturesque views.

Dining

In keeping with the upscale atmosphere of this resort, there are a number of fine dining table-service restaurants, described on pages 372–373, which are happy to accommodate special requests with 72-hour advance notice. Notable among the Grand Floridian's restaurants are Narcoossee's and Victoria & Albert's, Disney's finest restaurant. In addition, there's a 24-hour food stop, Gasparilla's Grill.

You can also arrange for **private dining** here—eat on your balcony, on the beach, or even on a boat in the lagoon. Make arrangements in advance with room service.

If you need **basic groceries and sundries**, there's Sandy Cove on the first floor of the main building (see our sidebar on page 128).

Amenities

If you need to **maintain a fitness routine** while on vacation, there's the Grand Floridian Spa & Health Club, a fully equipped fitness center (with massage and spa treatments, too). There are also two clay tennis courts (for a fee) and a one-mile jogging path to the Polynesian. Finally, you can rent a variety of boats at the marina.

The **playground** is near the Mouseketeer Clubhouse; the arcade is at Gasparilla's Grill.

The main themed pool at the Grand Floridian features a **"zero-entry" shoreline**. This is a gradual slope into the pool, just like a real beach—ideal for those who are unable to step down into a traditional pool. There is also a water wheelchair available, which can wheel right into the pool—just ask a lifeguard for assistance. Besides the main pool, there is also another heated pool, which has a transfer tier, for wheelchair users able to lift themselves out of the chair and then slide down into the pool. There's a hot tub located near each pool and a white sand beach for sunbathing (no swimming allowed). Automated External Defibrillators (AEDs) are located at each of the pools, and at numerous locations throughout the resort.

Grand Floridian's main pool with a zero-entry shoreline

Disney's Grand Floridian Resort & Spa
(continued)

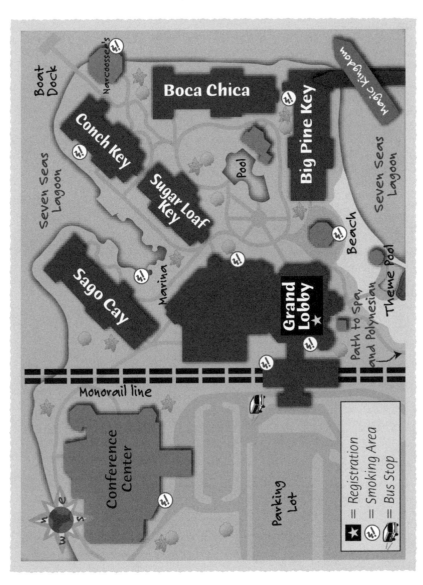

2008 standard room rates begin at $385 in value season, $435 in regular season, $510 in peak season, and $605 in holiday season (seasons are indicated on page 101). Lagoon view rooms are $60–$100 more. Lodge Tower rooms start at $470. Concierge rooms begin at $505 in value season, $580 in regular season, $685 in peak season, and $775 in holiday season. Suites are upward of $900. Note that prices may increase by $10–$30 per night on some holiday weekends. All rooms at this resort are subject to 12.5% tax.

Disney's Grand Floridian Resort & Spa
(continued)

Quiet Spots

If you're looking for a little privacy, try some of the **benches on the second floor** of the main building. There are also quiet spots along the beach.

Another good spot is the **balcony next to the stairs** on the second floor of the main building—it is very secluded and has a table and chairs.

Transportation is varied and fairly easy at the Grand Floridian. A monorail (accessible station on the second floor) goes to the Magic Kingdom as well as the Contemporary, Polynesian, and the Transportation & Ticket Center, where you can transfer to the Epcot monorail. Boats also take you to the Magic Kingdom and the Polynesian, though they only accommodate folded wheelchairs (no ECVs). For other parks, use the buses in front of the resort to the right as you exit. For other resorts, monorail to the Magic Kingdom (daytime) or bus to Downtown Disney (evening) and transfer to a resort bus.

Estimated Transportation Times

Magic Kingdom	Epcot	Disney-MGM Studios	Disney's Animal Kingdom	Downtown Disney
monorail/boat ~3/~10 min.	monorail x 2 ~12+10 min.	direct bus ~10 min.	direct bus ~15 min.	direct bus ~20 min.

Approximate time you will spend in transit from resort to destination during normal operation.

Our Ratings

Grand Floridian Resort & Spa **ranks high** on our convenience scale, but staying here is expensive. The resort has a terrific location on the water, is close to the Magic Kingdom, is on the monorail line, and has numerous other amenities that make it an excellent choice for vacationers who have a variety of special requirements.

[A][U][C] [B][E][S]	Because it's on the monorail line, getting back to the Grand Floridian quickly (for a midday break or at the end of the day) is relatively easy.
[A][U]	More upscale atmosphere may not be appropriate for all.
[C][♥][T][M] [P][E][S]	Request a room near an elevator in the main building.
[D]	Restaurants here are very accommodating with 72-hour notice. Kosher items are *not* available at the Garden View Lounge Afternoon Tea.
[P]	Beautiful health club on-site with lots of places to walk/wheel and swim.
[V]	Rooms are bright and spacious, but buildings are spread out.

Disney's Grand Floridian Resort & Spa

4401 Grand Floridian Way, Lake Buena Vista, FL 32830
Phone: 407-824-3000 Fax: 407-824-3186

Disney's Old Key West Resort

The first Disney Vacation Club (DVC) property, Old Key West, stretches across an area situated between Downtown Disney and Epcot. Built to represent a **relaxed Key West vacation spot**, the resort is a favorite with DVC members but is also popular among non-DVC members.

Check-In
Check-in time is **4:00 pm**. Bell Services will assist in taking your luggage to your room if you need help. All buildings except #64 have parking right out front. If you don't have a car, ask a cast member to transport you via one of the resort's golf carts.

Guest Rooms
The accommodations here are the **largest of the DVC resorts** located at Walt Disney World. It's laid-back and low-key and reminds you of being at a seaside resort. The studios have kitchenettes, while all other villas have full-sized kitchens and "family room" areas. Full-sized washers, dryers, and DVD players are at all villas except the studios. There are laundry facilities near each of the pools.

Its **49 buildings** include studios (376 sq. ft./35 sq. m.) and one-bedroom (1086 sq. ft./101 sq. m.), two-bedroom (1392 sq. ft./129 sq. m.), and three-bedroom (2265 sq. ft./210 sq. m.) villas. Each cluster of buildings shares a parking lot. Views include a golf course, water, and wooded areas, making for a peaceful place of respite.

Buildings 11–14 and 62–64 are **closest to the Hospitality House**. For seclusion, try buildings 47–48 and 52–54. Avoid buildings 30–44 as they feel remote, have more traffic noise, and bus stops are often inconvenient.

Because all Old Key West villas feature kitchen facilities, these accommodations are **ideal for travelers with special dietary needs or an infant**. Other amenities include a private balcony or porch, hair dryer, iron, ironing board, and vacuum cleaner. All rooms also have double sinks, a marble vanity, a table and chairs, sofa, armoire, TV, ceiling fan, toiletries, housekeeping, voice mail, and wall safes.

Accessible rooms are available, but only the three newest buildings (62, 63, and 64) have elevators. Many buildings have three floors, so be sure to request a first-floor unit if necessary. All rooms at this resort, as at all Disney resorts, are nonsmoking. Also remember to request a one- or two-bedroom unit in buildings 30 and above if having the second entrance to the bathroom is important.

You can also **request special items**, such as bed boards and rails, high chairs, shower seat, smoke detector and phone for hearing impaired, toilet seat for wheelchairs, and extra portable cribs.

One-bedroom (unshaded)

Studio layout (shaded)

Entire layout represents a two-bedroom villa

Planning

Special Challenges

Getting There

Staying in Style

Touring

Feasting

Resources

Index

Disney's Old Key West Resort

(continued)

Dining

Dining choices include **Olivia's Cafe**, which serves three meals a day. Many locals frequent this eatery, and we feel it's one of the "best-kept secrets" around Disney. Booths and chairs (with and without arms) are part of the seating plan. For quick service, "Goods to Go" is near the main pool, serving burgers and snacks. The Gurgling Suitcase is adjacent and has drinks and appetizers (but little sitting room). The Turtle Pond Pool has the Turtle Shack snack bar (open seasonally.) Pizza delivery is also available. See pages 374 and 380.

Amenities

If you need to **maintain an exercise routine** while on vacation, there's the R.E.S.T. Beach Recreation Dept., which features traditional exercise equipment, including Nautilus and treadmills. Massage (for a fee) is available by appointment only. Joggers/walkers/wheelers will have a great time exploring the resort as they exercise or even walk/wheel/jog to Saratoga Springs and Downtown Disney. Finally, there are boat and bike rentals.

Playgrounds are located near each of the swimming pools. The Conch Flats Community Hall offers games and organized activities for kids (ask for a schedule). Two arcades, Electric Eel Arcade and the Flying Fisherman, will satisfy video game players.

The **Conch Flats General Store** is small but offers a fairly nice selection of logo goods, souvenirs, watches, and food items and toiletries, as well as packaged liquor (see page 128).

Transportation

Buses stop at the **resort's five bus stops** to take you to all Disney parks and Downtown Disney. In addition, a ferry connects Old Key West to Saratoga Springs and Downtown Disney Marketplace. The ferry is wheelchair-accessible, water levels permitting. Wheelchairs usually need to be folded. Go down to the pool area and you'll find the ramp to the dock.

Estimated Transportation Times

Magic Kingdom	Epcot	Disney-MGM Studios	Disney's Animal Kingdom	Downtown Disney
direct bus ~25 min.	direct bus ~10 min.	direct bus ~10 min.	direct bus ~15 min.	bus/boat ~5/~15 min.

Approximate time you will spend in transit from resort to destination during normal operation.

Our Ratings

Old Key West is a very relaxing resort with all the comforts of home, including flexibility for dining. Although Old Key West has limited transportation options, we **rate it medium to high**.

[C][♥][T][M][P][S]	Request a room near an elevator and close to a bus stop. Buildings 62–64 are the only buildings with elevators.
[P]	Old Key West has a health club on-site and lots of places to walk/wheel and swim, plus many other activities.
[V]	Rooms are bright and spacious, but buildings are spread out.
[S]	Seniors may enjoy the quiet, relaxing atmosphere here.

Disney's Old Key West Resort

1510 North Cove Road, Lake Buena Vista, FL 32830
Phone: 407-827-7700 Fax: 407-827-7710

Disney's Old Key West Resort
(continued)

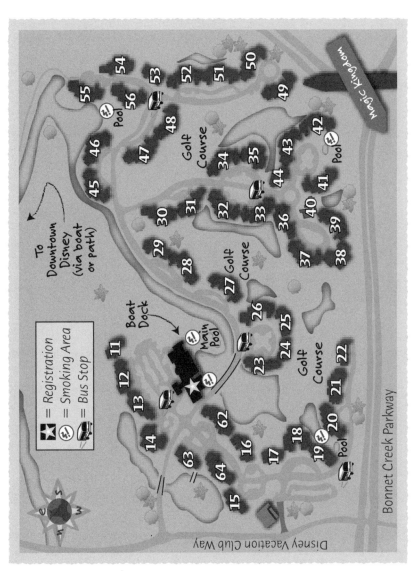

2008 standard studio rates begin at $285 in value season, $315 in regular season, $370 in peak season, and $410 in holiday season (seasons are indicated on page 101). One-bedroom villas are $380–$575. Two-bedroom villas are $530–$875. Three-bedroom grand villas start in the mid-$1100s. All rooms at this resort are subject to 12.5% tax.

Planning · Special Challenges · Getting There · Staying in Style · Touring · Feasting · Resources · Index

Disney's Polynesian Resort

When Walt Disney World opened in 1971, there were only two Disney resorts: the Contemporary and the Polynesian (known as Disney's Polynesian Village Resort at the time). With its **coveted location** on the monorail and the Seven Seas Lagoon facing Cinderella Castle, the Polynesian Resort brings to life a near-perfect tropical paradise.

Check-In

Check-in time is **3:00 pm** in the gorgeous atrium lobby of the Great Ceremonial House. As at many deluxe resorts, the self-parking area is a few minutes' walk/wheel from the main lobby. Consider valet parking ($10/day; free with handicapped tag) instead.

Even though the atmosphere is decidedly tropical, with a splashing waterfall nearly hidden amidst the lush foliage in the center, the echoes make the lobby a **somewhat noisy place**. In addition to the registration desk, located on your right as you enter the lobby, there's an Island Guide desk, immediately on your left when you enter. The guides here can not only answer your questions about the resort but are experts on the cultures of South Pacific island people. Their service is just an extra touch that helps to enhance your visit to this resort.

Once you've checked in and the cast member drapes a colorful, artificial flower lei around your neck, Bell Services will **assist you with your luggage**. Some of the buildings are a few minutes away—Bell Services can transport you via golf cart.

Guest Rooms

There are 853 recently renovated guest rooms distributed among **11 longhouses representing "islands"** in the South Pacific. The longhouses are two or three stories high; the first-floor rooms have patios, and many of the upper-floor rooms have balconies. The room furnishings now feature designer bedding in tropical colors and all new dark wood furniture.

The **standard guest rooms**, at 409 sq. ft. (38 sq. m.), all include the usual furnishings and two queen-sized beds, a nightstand with telephone, table with two chairs, armoire with large, flat-screen TV, in-room safe, iron and ironing board, refrigerator, coffeemaker with coffee packets, and hair dryer in the bathroom. Each room can accommodate five, because it features a daybed. The bathrooms are fairly spacious, with one or two sinks of green marble outside the green marbled shower/tub area and the toilet tucked modestly in a nook behind the sinks. Suites and concierge-level rooms housed in the Tonga and Hawaii longhouses offer personal service and great views.

Amenities for all resort rooms include toiletries, 24-hour room service, housekeeping, turndown service (on request), and voice mail. All first-floor rooms have patios, and all third-floor rooms have balconies. Most second-floor rooms have no balconies, with the exception of Tahiti, Rapa Nui, Tokelau, and Tonga, which were built later.

Exceptional water views looking out at the Castle can be found in Hawaii (concierge building). The first-floor rooms in Tahiti facing away from the water have secluded patios, as do those in Rapa Nui and Rarotonga.

Standard room layout

Disney's Polynesian Resort
(continued)

Guest Rooms (continued)

If you opt for a **standard view**, we recommend Aotearoa for an up-close view of the monorail. For added privacy, request a room on the top floor. It tends to be noisy in the pool areas (near Samoa, Niue, Hawaii, Rarotonga, and Tokelau). Request a room in Tonga (which houses all the resort's suites) or Rarotonga if you want to be close to the Great Ceremonial House and its guest services.

Most of the **wheelchair-accessible rooms** are in Rapa Nui, and all of the rooms with a roll-in shower are here. This building is next door to the Transportation & Ticket Center, making it a fair distance from the Great Ceremonial House services. There are balconies on all of the floors. With one exception, all buildings have their own elevators. There are no accessible rooms in Hawaii, the concierge building.

Important Note: Niue, the smallest building at the Polynesian, is located next to the Great Ceremonial House and is just a few steps from either of the pools, but there is no elevator in the building. To gain access here, you have to enter the Rarotonga building, take the elevator to the second floor, and enter Niue using the connecting walkway.

Dining

Of the dining choices at the Polynesian (detailed on page 374), the **Kona Café** is well-known as a restaurant eager to please those with special dietary needs, particularly vegetarian and vegan diets. 'Ohana is the family style, all-you-can-eat breakfast and dinner restaurant across the way on the second floor, while the 24-hour Captain Cook's Snack Company is on the first. As a special treat, the Polynesian is home to an outdoor, luau-style dinner show, the Spirit of Aloha (see pages 385–386). Special diets can be accommodated at this dinner show with at least 24-hour notice.

Bright Idea: Although there isn't a companion restroom in the lobby, there is one across from the entrance to 'Ohana.

Trader Jack's and Samoa Snacks can be found on the second floor of the Great Ceremonial House, if you need **basic groceries** and sundry items. See page 128 for typical items.

Amenities

For those who want to **keep up with their exercise routine**, the Polynesian does not have its own health club. Guests at the Polynesian may use the nearby Grand Floridian Spa & Health Club free of charge, however. Walkers, wheelers, and joggers can take advantage of the Walk Around the World that partially encircles the lagoon and a 1.5-mile path that winds through the resort (ask at Lobby Concierge for a map). Boaters can rent Sea Raycers and other watercraft at the marina. There are also surrey bikes for rent.

Bright Idea: There's a Sea Raycer out of the water—this comes in handy to help you determine whether you will fit and allows to you practice entering and exiting the vehicle.

In addition to a heated non-themed pool is the Nanea Volcano themed pool, which features a large pool "fed" by a spring, a water slide, warm water areas, underwater music, and a **zero-entry section** (pool wheelchair available—ask a lifeguard). There's also a kids' water play area—remember that children in diapers must wear snug-fitting plastic pants or special swim diapers when in the water. There is no hot tub here, but there is a beach for sunbathing (no swimming allowed). Automated external defibrillators (AEDs) are located at each of the pools and at numerous locations throughout the resort. Note that the pool does not have a transfer tier, but the zero-entry access should make up for that.

Disney's Polynesian Resort
(continued)

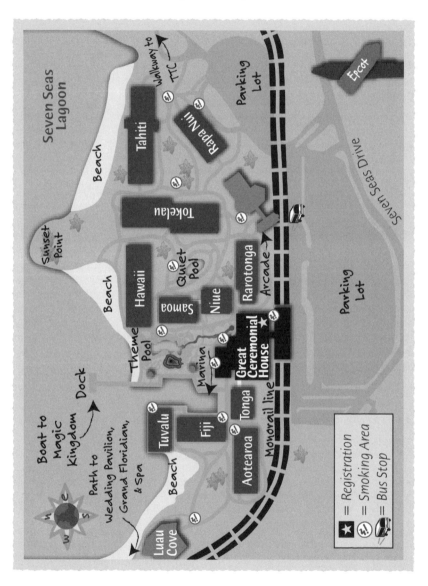

2008 standard room rates begin at $340 in value season, $399 in regular season, $465 in peak season, and $535 in holiday season (seasons are indicated on page 101). A lagoon-view room adds $100–$115. Concierge garden rooms are $480–$720, and concierge lagoon-view rooms are $590–$840. One-bedroom suites are $780–$1,850. Note that prices may increase by $10–$30 per night on some holiday weekends. All rooms at this resort are subject to 12.5% tax.

Disney's Polynesian Resort
(continued)

More Amenities

There's a **playground** near the main pool and a game arcade, Moana Mickey's, by the Never Land Kids' Club.

BouTIKI is the **primary shop** on the first floor in the Great Ceremonial House. Wyland Galleries is also on the first floor.

The **Electrical Water Pageant** passes by the Polynesian around 9:00 pm. If you can't see the lagoon from your room, watch it from the beach or at the end of the dock near the marina.

Magic Kingdom fireworks are viewable from the beach. Kids have a play area while waiting and the noise level is much more manageable.

Quiet Spots

The beach in front of Hawaii and Tahiti has **bench swings and hammocks**.

Transportation

Options abound at the Polynesian. The **monorail** (accessible station on the second floor) can whisk you to the Magic Kingdom, Grand Floridian, and Contemporary, as well as the Transportation & Ticket Center (TTC) in a matter of a few minutes. The launches to the Magic Kingdom and Grand Floridian are *not* wheelchair/ECV accessible—they have steps in and out and can carry a folded wheelchair, but ECVs cannot be boarded at all. To reach Epcot, take a short walk/wheel to TTC and board the monorail. To reach other parks and Downtown Disney, take a bus. If you're feeling ambitious, you can walk/wheel to the Grand Floridian. To reach resorts that aren't on the monorail, take a monorail to the Magic Kingdom and transfer to a resort bus (daytime), or bus to Downtown Disney and transfer to a resort bus (evening).

Estimated Transportation Times

Magic Kingdom	Epcot	Disney-MGM Studios	Disney's Animal Kingdom	Downtown Disney
monorail/boat ~10/~5 min.	monorail x 2 ~10+10 min.	direct bus ~15 min.	direct bus ~15 min.	direct bus ~25 min.

Approximate time you will spend in transit from resort to destination during normal operation.

Our Ratings

The Polynesian Resort **ranks high** on our scale. It has a terrific location on the water, is close to the Magic Kingdom, is on the monorail, and has many other amenities that make it an excellent choice.

Our Convenience Scale

[G]	The variety of lush vegetation may cause asthma or allergy issues.
[A][U][C][B] [E][S]	Because it's on the monorail, getting back to the Polynesian quickly (for a midday break or at the end of the day) is relatively easy.
[C][♥][T][M] [P][E][S]	Request a room near an elevator—remember that Niue does not have its own elevator. Some longhouses are a long walk from the Great Ceremonial House; close buildings are Tonga, Niue, Rarotonga, and Fiji.
[D][G]	Restaurants are very accommodating with 72-hour notice. Kona Cafe is particularly vegetarian/vegan friendly.
[P]	There's no health club but lots of places to walk/wheel and swim.

Disney's Polynesian Resort

1600 Seven Seas Drive, Lake Buena Vista, FL 32830, 407-824-2000 Fax: 407-824-3174

Disney's Pop Century Resort

The **newest of the value resorts**, Pop Century is colorful and sports larger-than-life icons similar to the All-Star Resorts. Pop Century is a much larger resort, though, and once completed (currently only the Classic Years' 2,880 rooms are open), there will be more than 5,700 rooms. As of this writing, there is no opening date for Phase II (we've heard it may open with Family Suites, but there is no official confirmation).

Check-In

Check-in time is **4:00 pm** in Classic Hall, which houses the front desk/check-in, food court, lounge, bus depot, arcade, and general store. The "Everything Pop" area contains the food court, lounge, and general store—these are all open and share the same space, making it quite noisy and busy! The central areas are often very noisy with guests coming and going in all directions. A short-term check-in parking area is available nearby.

As we noted about the All-Star Resorts, you can **expect medium to long lines at check-in** here. To avoid the waits, we suggest you check in as soon as you arrive at Walt Disney World—sort of a "pre-check-in." It's a good time to drop off your luggage, too. Then you can leave to shop or play at the theme parks—check in "for real" later when the crowds have subsided. See page 118 for check-in strategies.

Bright Idea: There is a low check-in counter at either end of the long front desk area to make registration easier for folks in wheelchairs/ECVs.

As in other Disney resorts, there is **special kids' waiting area**, but at Pop Century, this space is just off the lobby, and you are **unable to see it from the check-in line**.

© MediaMarx, Inc.

Pop Century's kids' waiting area

Guest Rooms

The four-story buildings of this resort are **very spread out**. A $12 premium is added to the '60s buildings and portions of '50s and '70s, which are the closest to the main shopping/eating area, Everything Pop!, and must be reserved at the time of booking. Those farther away are generally quieter but also require quite a walk/wheel to and from the bus stops and food areas. Room views include the pool, parking lot, or woods. For quieter rooms, request rooms facing away from the pool/parking areas.

Despite being among the **smallest rooms** at Walt Disney World (260 sq. ft./24 sq. m.), they are quite comfortable and are furnished with two double beds or one king, TV with armoire, and a small table with two chairs. An ECV or wheelchair will fit comfortably if you only have two people—otherwise, it may be difficult to get a wheelchair in the room and close the door. If you have four, no matter if they are very small children, things will be tight with the wheelchair/ECV. If you want more room to move around, request a king room.

Standard room layout

All **rooms exit to the outside** (no inner corridors), so you will be exposed to the elements when walking to bus stops or services.

Disney's Pop Century Resort
(continued)

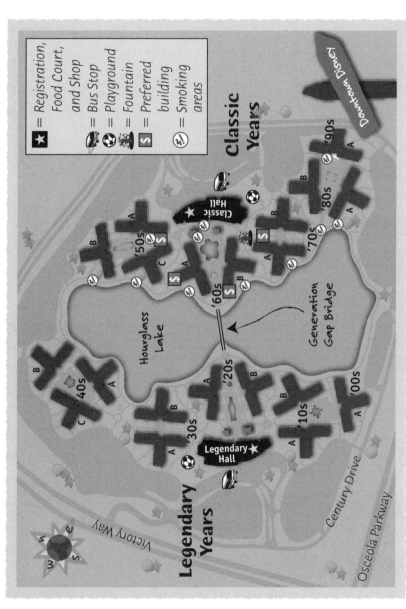

2008 standard room rates begin at $82 in value season, $99 in regular season, $109 in summer season, $119 in peak season, and $129 in holiday season (seasons are indicated on page 101). Preferred rooms (see preferred buildings marked on map above) run $12 or so more per room. Note that prices may increase by $10–$20 per night on some holiday weekends. All rooms at this resort are subject to 12.5% tax.

Disney's Pop Century Resort
(continued)

Other than limited snacks at the general store, the only place where food is available is at the **Everything Pop! food court**. You enter an area with several stations offering a variety of selections. A refrigerated section has packaged items like sandwiches, salads, fruit, etc. Refills for refillable mugs may include lemonade and apple juice. One positive note is that some kosher foods are always available at the food courts without advance notice. Pop Century also has evening pizza delivery service. See chapter 6 for more dining details.

Amenities
Pop Century has **three themed pools**, a small playground area for letting off some steam, and an arcade. The laundry rooms, found at the pool areas, have front loading/accessible washing machines.

Quiet Spots
To get away from the **loud hustle and bustle** of the Food Court, there are tables and chairs outside that may be quieter. You can always bring your food back to the room.

Transportation
All Disney **transportation from this resort is via bus**. (There is currently only one bus stop.) Waits for buses to and from Pop Century can be long, especially at park opening and closing. The queues wind around and can get very crowded—in fact, it is not uncommon to have standing room only on the buses. There is a designated area next to the queue for wheelchair guests to wait, making preboarding easier.

Estimated Transportation Times

Magic Kingdom	Epcot	Disney-MGM Studios	Disney's Animal Kingdom	Downtown Disney
direct bus ~25 min.	direct bus ~20 min.	direct bus ~15 min.	direct bus ~15 min.	direct bus ~20 min.

Approximate time you will spend in transit from resort to destination during normal operation.

Our Ratings
Pop Century is great for the budget, but not for amenities. It's **low** on the convenience scale, primarily due to the layout. However, we do recommend Pop Century as your value resort of choice.

Our Convenience Scale

[A][U][S]	This resort can be very busy and noisy in the pools and central areas.
[C][♥][T] **[M][P][E]**	Unless you are in a preferred building location, have a car, or use a wheelchair, we do not recommend Pop Century due to its spread-out design.
[D][W]	Food Court chefs can accommodate with 72 hours' notice. Note that some kosher items are generally available without advance notice. Guests with peanut allergies should note there is an Asian station in the food court.
[F]	The larger-than-life icons could scare some.
[S]	For a more relaxing vacation, stay at a moderate, deluxe, or Disney Vacation Club resort.
[L]	Be sure to request a king bed.

Disney's Pop Century Resort
1050 Century Drive, Lake Buena Vista, FL 32830
Phone: 407-938-4000 Fax: 407-938-4040

Disney's Port Orleans Resort

Planning

Special Challenges

Getting There

Staying in Style

Touring

Feasting

Resources

Index

Located along the banks of the Sassagoula River, north of Downtown Disney, Port Orleans is actually an amalgamation of two resorts: **Port Orleans Riverside and Port Orleans French Quarter**. Several faces of the Old South are represented at Port Orleans. The French Quarter evokes the feeling of historic New Orleans as it prepares for Mardi Gras; Riverside houses the rustic, moss-covered buildings of Alligator Bayou and the serene, stately mansions of Magnolia Bend.

Check-In

Port Orleans has two front desks, one in each district. Be sure to check with Disney before arrival to find out which district's front desk you should use. Check-in time is **3:00 pm**.

The Mint is your first stop in the **French Quarter**, a large building with wrought ironwork details and a soaring glass atrium that safeguards the district's front desk, guest services, and shop. A step outside reveals narrow cobblestone lanes, complete with "gas" lamps, wrought iron benches, and grand magnolia trees.

A leisurely ten-minute walk or wheel along the Sassagoula takes you to **Riverside**. Banjo music and southern hospitality greet you as you enter Riverside's Sassagoula Steamboat Company, a replica of an old riverboat depot. The depot is the crossroads of this quaint settlement, housing the district's front desk and services. Venture out along meandering paths and wooden bridges to antebellum mansions in one direction or the bayou in the other.

Once you check in, you can drive yourself to your building and park fairly close to your room. Alternatively, **Bell Services will take your luggage** and you to your room.

Guest Rooms

The **French Quarter has six large buildings** with 1,008 rooms. Most buildings have their own gardens in front, charmingly fenced with wrought iron. Riverside itself has two distinct sections—the Southern plantations of Magnolia Bend have 1,024 rooms, as do the more rustic buildings in Alligator Bayou.

Important Note: Large and often boisterous youth groups (cheerleading competitions, Pop Warner football) frequently stay in the Riverside section of this resort. If you're looking for peace and quiet, inquire about this when you check in so that you can attempt to avoid the large groups.

All rooms are 314 sq. ft. (29.2 sq. m.) and have a similar layout, varying only in decor and theme. In the French Quarter, you find **faux French Provincial** furniture, gilt-edged mirrors, and Venetian blinds. Riverside's Magnolia Bend rooms are appointed with cherry furniture and brocade settees.

Standard room
layout

Disney's Port Orleans Resort
(continued)

Guest Rooms (continued)

Rooms in **Riverside's Alligator Bayou** sport beds made of hewn "logs" and patchwork quilts. All rooms accommodate up to four and come with either two extra-long double beds or one king bed (king-bed rooms are located on building corners). Alligator Bayou's 963 rooms house up to five guests at no additional charge by offering a trundle bed (see photo at right), which slides out from under the double bed and fits a child or small adult. Rooms include a TV, armoire, table and chairs, ceiling fan, and a separate vanity area with double pedestal sinks. Every room has a window (corner rooms have two), but none have private balconies. Other room amenities include toiletries (soap and shampoo only), housekeeping, coffeemaker and coffee packets, iron and ironing board, limited room service, in-room safe (most rooms), voice mail, refrigerator, and hair dryer.

© Deb Wills

A Port Orleans Riverside trundle bed

Note that Alligator Bayou buildings **do not have elevators**. If you have mobility concerns, request a ground floor room in one of these buildings.

Port Orleans Riverside is **exceptionally large and sprawling**, and room location can really make a difference in your resort experience. Request the style that suits you best—when you make your reservation, you can specify whether you want a room in Riverside or the French Quarter.

Most rooms in the French Quarter are **within easy distance** of Lobby Concierge, the gift shop, and the food court. If being close to the center of things is important, request Buildings 2–5. The best views are of the Sassagoula River, as the opposite river bank is pristine—consider upgrading to a water view room (specifically request a river view). The buildings in French Quarter do have elevators.

The grand "mansions" of **Magnolia Bend** in Riverside conjure a *Gone With the Wind* feel. The Magnolia Terrace building is a good pick for proximity to recreation and dining. The buildings in Alligator Bayou are smaller (only two stories) and have lush landscaping. Building 14 is near the main building, Ol' Man Island, a quiet pool, and a bus stop—it has no bad views, as it is nestled between buildings and the river. Buildings 15 and 18 are also good choices. For a quieter room, request the second or third floor. Magnolia Bend buildings have elevators.

Bright Idea: If you'd like a brighter room, request one on a corner—it will have two windows.

Because Port Orleans Riverside is so spread out, getting around can take some walking. You may want to **hop a bus to get around** the resort. French Quarter is a much smaller section and easier to get around.

Disney's Port Orleans Resort
(continued)

Dining

Port Orleans' only table-service restaurant is **Boatwright's Dining Hall**. This restaurant in the Riverside district offers breakfast and dinner—see page 375 for details. Two large food courts—Sassagoula Floatworks and Food Factory in the French Quarter and the Riverside Mill at Riverside—offer breakfast, lunch, and dinner. The recently renovated Riverside Mill also now offers several "make-your-own" stations at which you can add your own ingredients to salads and other dishes, as well as a carving station featuring roasted meats. A selection of kosher foods is generally available at the food courts without advance notice, but 72 hours' notice is required for more specialized requests. Limited room service (mostly pizza and sandwiches) is offered after 4:00 pm. There are microwaves in the food courts—they are located near the beverage dispensers.

If you want to keep some snacks or some **simple groceries** in the room, Jackson Square Gifts & Desires (French Quarter) and Fulton's (Riverside) stock sundries and the basics. See our sidebar on page 128.

Amenities

If you're **keeping to an exercise routine** while on vacation, there is no fitness center at Port Orleans, but there is still plenty to do. In Riverside, you can rent bikes, including surrey bikes, from the Dixie Levee marina, and there are two walking/jogging/biking/wheeling routes mapped out around the two resorts. Ask for a map at Lobby Concierge. The Dixie Levee marina also rents pedal boats and other watercraft.

The **French Quarter's Doubloon Lagoon** is a medium-sized themed pool with a huge dragon water slide (you slide right down its tongue). A Mardi Gras band of crocodiles shoots water at unsuspecting swimmers. The French Quarter also has a wading pool and a hot tub nearby. In Riverside, Ol' Man Island in the middle of the district offers a "swimmin' hole", complete with a water slide, a waterfall cascading from a broken sluice, and a fun geyser. A hot tub and kids' wading area are also available here. There's a transfer tier at both themed

© Debra Martin Koma

Wheelchair transfer tier at Doubloon Lagoon

pools for wheelchair users able to lift and lower themselves into the water. Riverside also has five other heated pools throughout Magnolia Bend and Alligator Bayou.

The **two spas (hot tubs)** near the themed pools are great after a long day at the parks. The spa in the French Quarter is a bit secluded (look near the laundry) but large enough for several people to soak comfortably. Automated external defibrillators (AEDs) are located near all the pools and are scattered throughout the resorts.

There's a **playground** near each of the two themed pools. An old-fashioned fishin' hole on Ol' Man Island in Riverside lets you hang a cane pole over a pond stocked with catfish, perch, bass, and bluegill (catch and release only). For more adventure, you can book a fishing excursion down the Sassagoula. Enjoy an evening carriage ride through the two sister resorts. Carriages depart from in front of Boatwright's in Riverside between 6:00 pm and 9:30 pm. (Cost is $35 for a 30-minute ride for up to four adults or two adults and two to three children.)

Disney's Port Orleans Resort

(continued)

Port Orleans Riverside

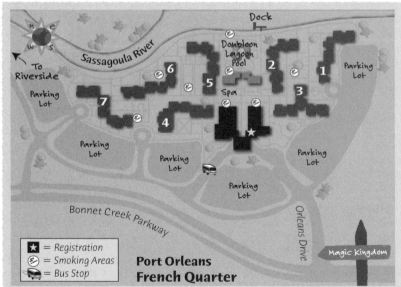

Port Orleans French Quarter

2008 standard room rates begin at $149 in value season, $165 in regular season, $179 in summer season, $189 in peak season, and $205 in holiday season (seasons are indicated on page 101). Water view and king-bed rooms are $16–$26 more. Note that prices may increase by $5–$15 per night on some holiday weekends. All rooms at this resort are subject to 12.5% tax.

Disney's Port Orleans Resort
(continued)

Quiet Spots
The resort's grounds are beautifully landscaped with **small parks and gardens**, plus plenty of benches overlooking the Sassagoula River.

Transportation
Disney transportation to the theme parks, water parks, and Downtown Disney is via **bus**. Buses usually stop first at French Quarter's one bus stop, then go to the four stops in Riverside. To get to other resorts and destinations, take a bus to Epcot (when open) or to Downtown Disney (evening) and transfer to the appropriate bus. An accessible boat also picks up from Riverside and the French Quarter and goes to and from Downtown Disney Marketplace until 10:00 pm. Boats run about every 20 minutes (weather permitting) and are relaxing but leisurely.

Estimated Transportation Times

Magic Kingdom	Epcot	Disney-MGM Studios	Disney's Animal Kingdom	Downtown Disney
direct bus ~10 min.	direct bus ~10 min.	direct bus ~15 min.	direct bus ~15 min.	direct bus/boat ~15/~20 min.

Approximate time you will spend in transit from resort to destination during normal operation.

Our Rating
Port Orleans Riverside **rates medium** on our convenience scale, but French Quarter is **medium-high**, due to its compact size and charming atmosphere.

Our Convenience Scale

[A][U][S]	It can be very busy and noisy in the pools and food court areas.
[C][♥][T][M] [P][E][S] (Riverside Only)	If mobility issues are a concern and you do not have a car or a wheelchair, request a building close to services—this resort covers a lot of ground. Also, Alligator Bayou buildings do not have elevators—consider requesting a room on the ground floor.
[D][G][W]	Food court chefs are happy to accommodate with 72 hours' notice. Riverside food court usually has kosher items available.
[G]	There are many, many trees covered with Spanish moss around the Riverside area—allergy/asthma sufferers beware.
[F]	Alligators have been spotted in the Sassagoula River here. Lots of other small animals (i.e., bunnies and squirrels) also roam this resort. Big faces hang down from the ceiling in the food court and could be scary. There are also many ceiling fans here.
[M]	The playground at Riverside is all sand, making it difficult for those with mobility issues.
[S]	Seniors will enjoy the French Quarter district.
[V]	Low lighting in Alligator Bayou rooms may not be good for those with vision impairments.

Disney's Port Orleans Resort
2201 Orleans Dr. and 1251 Dixie Dr., Lake Buena Vista, FL 32830
Phone: 407-934-5000 (French Quarter) or 407-934-6000 (Riverside)
Fax: 407-934-5353 (French Quarter) or 407-934-5777 (Riverside)

Planning

Special Challenges

Getting There

Staying in Style

Touring

Feasting

Resources

Index

Disney's Saratoga Springs Resort and Spa

This is **Disney's newest resort**, located on the site of the former Disney Institute, adjacent to the Lake Buena Vista Golf Course and across Village Lake from Downtown Disney. The 65-acre Saratoga Springs Resort and Spa has 828 units, making it the largest Disney Vacation Club property to date.

Modeled on **Saratoga Springs**, **New York**, the historic vacation escape famous for its healthful spa waters and thrilling horse races, this resort features Victorian-styled buildings peppered with thematic details such as a horse weather vane and a "stable" gate.

Check-In

The resort's check-in area (**check-in time is 4:00 pm**) is found in the Carriage House, an airy and bright space. Once you've checked in, you can drive over to your cluster of buildings. There's ample parking next to each building, although you can't park right in front of your room as you can at Old Key West Resort. Alternatively, Bell Services assists you with your luggage and takes you to your room. Another option is to board the bus that stops in front of the Carriage House and take it to the bus stop closest to your building.

Guest Rooms

Each of the sections of Saratoga Springs ties in to one aspect of the "Health, History, Horses" motif. **Congress Park** is named for the real city's central greenspace, a favorite of both athletes and artists. Other sections are The Springs, The Paddock, The Carousel, and The Grandstand. Victorian-style buildings border on the lake looking out to Downtown Disney. Rooms are decorated in soft shades of seafoam green, sand, cream, and pale yellow with dark wood furnishings and accents with a decidedly equine motif.

The Saratoga Springs Villas, with their **kitchen facilities**, are ideal for cooking meals for yourself. Studio villas (355 sq. ft./33 sq. m.) host up to four guests with one queen bed, a sofa bed, double sink, microwave, toaster, coffeemaker, and a small refrigerator. The one-bedroom (714 sq. ft./66.3 sq. m.) and two-bedroom (1,075 sq. ft./100 sq. m.) villas host up to four or eight guests, respectively, and offer master suites with king beds and whirlpool tubs,

DVD players, sofa beds, full kitchens, and washers/dryers. The two-story grand villas (2,113 sq. ft./196 sq. m.) sleep up to 12 and feature three bedrooms, four bathrooms, a full kitchen, and dining room.

Ask to be close to the footbridge, which leads to the Carriage House, if **mobility** is a concern. There are no "preferred" or premium-priced guest rooms. Rooms in the Springs are closest to the Carriage House and themed pool areas, with views of Saratoga Lake or gardens/parking. The Paddock is spread out and distant from other facilities.

One-bedroom (unshaded)

King

Queen

Studio layout (shaded)

Entire layout represents a two-bedroom villa

Disney's Saratoga Springs Resort & Spa
(continued)

Dining

The kitchen facilities in the villas are perfect for those with **special dietary needs**, allowing you to prepare at least some of your meals for yourself. The Artists' Palette is a modified food court designed to resemble an artist's workspace. Open all day, it features a variety of prepackaged items, as well as some made-to-order offerings, such as pizzas, salads, and sandwiches. The Artists' Palette also stocks some basic groceries and sundries. See the sidebar on page 128 for an idea of typical items and prices. Turf Club Bar and Grill is the table-service restaurant, serving sandwiches and moderately priced fare, with indoor or outdoor seating.

Amenities

For those who wish to maintain an exercise routine while on vacation, the Saratoga Springs Spa has a **fully equipped fitness center** (as well as a full range of spa treatments for an extra fee, of course). There are also two clay tennis courts, a jogging path, basketball, shuffleboard, and bicycles for rent at Horsing Around Rentals. Additionally, right next door is the Lake Buena Vista Golf Course.

The High Spring Rock pool features a **"zero-entry" shoreline**. This is a gradual slope into the pool, just like a real beach— ideal for those who are unable to step down into a traditional pool. There is also a water wheelchair available, which can wheel right into the pool—just ask a lifeguard for assistance. In addition, there's a special transfer tier at the pool with an accessible platform for wheelchair users able to lift themselves out of the chair. There are two hot tubs located near the main pool—one is equipped with a special wheelchair lift. Congress Park has a playground, as well as a pool with wheelchair transfer tiers and a fairly large outdoor hot tub. The Carousel section did not have a pool or playground at this writing. The Grandstand pool does not have transfer tiers. However, it does have a new magnetic gate—a person must be tall enough to pull it up to open. This pool also has a fountain area for the kids to play in, as well as pool bar. All pools have guest laundry.Automated external defibrillators (AEDs) are located at each of the pools and at numerous locations around the resort.

© MediaMarx, Inc.

Saratoga Springs' zero-entry shoreline

Planning

Special Challenges

Getting There

Staying in Style

Touring

Feasting

Resources

Index

Disney's Saratoga Springs Resort & Spa
(continued)

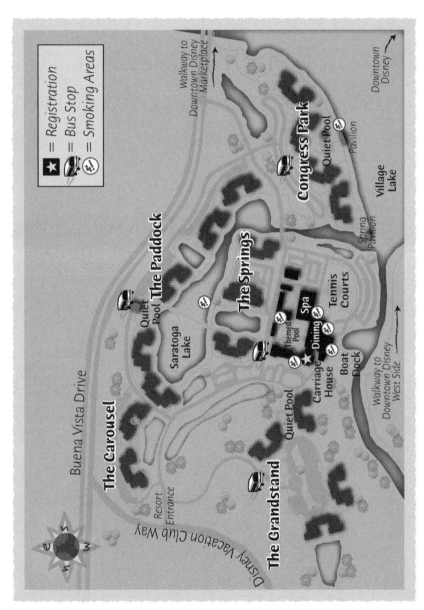

2008 standard studio rates begin at $285 in value season, $315 in regular season, $370 in peak season, and $410 in holiday season (seasons are indicated on page 101). One-bedroom villas are $380–$575. Two-bedroom villas are $530–$875. Three-bedroom grand villas start in the mid-$1100s. All rooms at this resort are subject to 12.5% tax.

Disney's Saratoga Springs Resort & Spa
(continued)

Quiet Spots
There are a few quiet spots here. There's a barbecue pavilion, a fireworks pavilion, formal gardens, and gazebos/fountains, all perfect for sitting and relaxing or reading in the sunshine. The Turf Club Lounge patio can also be quiet during off-peak times.

Transportation
Direct buses to the four theme parks, water parks, and Downtown Disney stop at the resort's bus stops. These buses also provide internal transportation within the resort. An accessible boat (if water levels allow) from the dock near the Carriage House goes to the Marketplace at Downtown Disney, stopping at Old Key West en route. Walking/wheeling paths connect the resort with Downtown Disney Marketplace and West Side (West Side pathway crosses the footbridge near the boat dock). There is also a path connecting this resort to Old Key West (see map on previous page).

Estimated Transportation Times

Magic Kingdom	Epcot	Disney-MGM Studios	Disney's Animal Kingdom	Downtown Disney
direct bus ~25 min.	direct bus ~10 min.	direct bus ~15 min.	direct bus ~20 min.	walk/bus/boat ~15/~10/~7

Approximate time you will spend in transit from resort to destination during normal operation.

Our Ratings
Saratoga Springs Resort and Spa **ranks medium** on our convenience scale. While the kitchen facilities available in the rooms here make it an excellent choice for vacationers with infants or special dietary needs, we find the resort remote from the theme parks with restricted transportation options. Also, buildings are spread out, and most are located far from the main resort services.

[C][♥][T][M] [P][E][S]	If mobility issues are a concern, request to be in a guest room near an elevator.
[D][G]	Food court chefs are happy to accommodate with a minimum of 72 hours' advance notice.
[♥][P]	This resort has gorgeous spa and fitness facilities. When construction is completed, it will be beautifully landscaped and pleasant to walk/wheel around.
[S]	If you're interested in golf, you're just a few minutes away from a golf course here.

Disney's Saratoga Springs Resort & Spa
1960 Broadway, Lake Buena Vista, FL 32830
Phone: 407-827-1100 Fax: 407-827-1151

Disney's Wilderness Lodge & Villas

The rustic setting, log interior, and enormous lobby of the Wilderness Lodge transport you from the hustle and bustle of the theme parks to a quieter, more **serene location**. Along with its neighboring Disney Vacation Club (DVC) Villas, this is one of those Disney resorts that is so complete an experience, you don't have to enter a theme park during your vacation and yet you'll still feel like you got away from it all. It was designed by the same architect responsible for Disney's Animal Kingdom Lodge.

Check-In
Self-parking at the Lodge is a distance from the lobby entrance, up a short incline. There is also complimentary parking for DVC members staying on points. Consider valet parking ($10/day or complimentary with handicapped tag). Check-in for both the Lodge (a deluxe resort) and the DVC Villas is **3:00 pm**. Services, including registration, for both the Lodge and the Villas are shared. Valet parking is free to DVC members staying on points.

The Lodge is the **main building** with left and right wings that surround the courtyard and themed pool area. The Villas are off to the right, connected to the main building by an outdoor covered walkway.

Guest Rooms
The Lodge has 728 guest rooms and suites that were refurbished with new furniture, carpeting, and bedspreads in 2006–2007. Some **open into the main lobby**, but most are along the wings with wooded or pool/water view. Standard view rooms may overlook the roof or parking areas. Regular rooms (about 340 sq. ft./32.5 sq. m.) have two queen beds, though a few have bunk beds in lieu of the second queen. All Lodge rooms have a balcony or patio, small table and chairs, TV, wall safe, refrigerator, coffeemaker and coffee packets, and hair dryer in the bathroom. Double sinks in the bathroom vanity area are standard, as are newspaper delivery and voice mail. Turndown service is available on request.

Standard Lodge room layout

If you think you'd like a **little more space**, request a king room—these double as the barrier-free rooms and have a large shower but no tub. Concierge service is available and features separate adult and kid "lounges." You'll bypass the front check-in desk when you stay concierge. Note that all handicapped and king rooms only sleep 2—there are no daybeds or pull-out beds available.

© Deb Wills

The Villas have **136 studio, one-, and two-bedroom villas**. The studios have a kitchenette, while the one- and two-bedroom villas offer full kitchens, a common area, and a stacked washer and dryer. Access to the main lobby from the Villas is via a long, inclined ramp.

For **quieter rooms**, request the top floor or a woods view. Lower floors facing the courtyard and pool can be a bit noisy.

The kitchenette of a Wilderness Lodge studio

No rollaway beds are available at the Lodge.

⟶

Disney's Wilderness Lodge & Villas
(continued)

Dining

Wilderness Lodge hosts one of Disney's finest restaurants, **Artist Point**, which features many game items and cuisine specialties of the Pacific Northwest. They are especially accommodating to special requests with 72-hour notice. The Lodge's counter-service spot, Roaring Fork, can be quite crowded, but in the seating area, there is a microwave for warming foods. Whispering Canyon Cafe, just off the main lobby, has noisy, all-you-can-eat, family-style fun. An a la carte menu is also available. There's a good assortment of grocery items in the Wilderness Lodge Mercantile (see page 128). For a more in-depth look at the resort's dining options, see chapter 6.

Amenities

There are **plenty of activities** at the Wilderness Lodge—and even more if you visit neighboring Fort Wilderness Resort and Campground. Boats (some accessible, some not) and walking paths connect the two resorts. At the Wilderness Lodge, you can rent boats or bicycles, enjoy the Sturdy Branches health club, play at the Buttons and Bells arcade, swim in Silver Creek or the pool at the Villas (both have transfer tiers), or explore the art and artifacts located throughout the resorts.

Central services are easily located off the **main lobby** and include front desk, Lobby Concierge (guest services), Whispering Canyon Café (serves three meals a day), Artist Point (a full-service dinner featuring the tastes of the Pacific Northwest), Roaring Fork (a fast-food spot), and Territory Lounge, as well as Trout Pass Pool Bar. Whispering Canyon Café is a restaurant that's open to the lobby. It can get quite boisterous at the Canyon when the tomfoolery begins! Pony races for the kids (and sometimes adults) are not uncommon.

Bright Idea: Ask for a kids' activity book at the front desk, and don't forget to look for all the Hidden Mickeys.

The Lodge also offers a **resort tour** some mornings. For a special treat, inquire at check-in about being a Flag Family. Steep stair-climbing is required to participate.

The famous **Fire Rock Geyser** spouts off hourly, and the Electric Water Pageant is visible from the beach every evening.

© Deb Wills

The beach at Wilderness Lodge & Villas Resort

Disney's Wilderness Lodge & Villas

(continued)

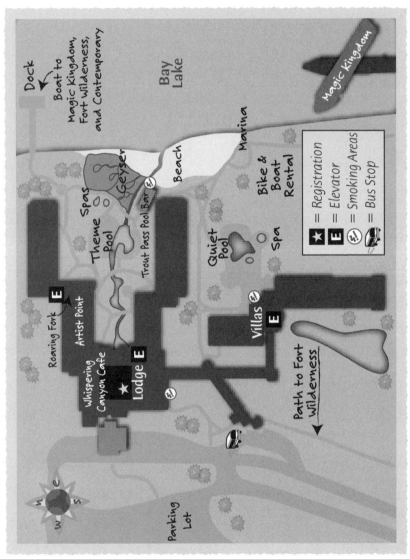

2008 standard room rates begin at $225 in value season, $275 in regular season, $340 in peak season, and $370 in holiday season (seasons are indicated on page 101). Woods view rooms are $25–$30 more. Courtyard view rooms are $50–$60 more than standard rooms. Standard concierge rooms start in the high $300s. Studio villas are $315 in value season, $360 in regular season, $425 in peak season, and $480 in holiday season. One-bedroom villas are $425–$635. Two-bedroom villas are $610–$1,120. Note that prices may increase by $10–$30 per night on some holiday weekends. All rooms at this resort are subject to 12.5% tax.

Disney's Wilderness Lodge & Villas
(continued)

Transportation

Even though the Wilderness Lodge is near the Magic Kingdom, it's **not on the monorail line**, nor can you walk/wheel to the Magic Kingdom or the Transportation & Ticket Center (TTC). Disney-provided transportation is via boat (to the Magic Kingdom) or bus (to all other locations). Feedback on the transportation runs hot and cold, so if waiting is an issue, we suggest renting a car. Boat transportation (some accessible boats) is available to Fort Wilderness and the Contemporary. Boat transportation to the Magic Kingdom is occasionally not accessible due to water levels. When this occurs, take a bus to TTC.

Estimated Transportation Times

Magic Kingdom	Epcot	Disney-MGM Studios	Disney's Animal Kingdom	Downtown Disney
boat ~8 min.	direct bus ~10 min.	direct bus ~15 min.	direct bus ~15 min.	direct bus ~25 min.

Approximate time you will spend in transit from resort to destination during normal operation.

Our Ratings

Wilderness Lodge is a great place to relax and enjoy the theming. Kitchen facilities available in the villas make it an excellent choice for vacationers with infants or special dietary needs. We rate it **medium-high** on our convenience scale—our only reservation is that even though all services are centrally located, the resort is remote from most Disney locations other than the Magic Kingdom and Fort Wilderness.

Our Convenience Scale

[A][U][S]	Main pool area can get very crowded. A smaller pool is available at the Villas. Roaring Fork—the quick-service spot—can be crowded and noisy.
[C][♥][T] [M][P][E]	Request a room near an elevator if you have mobility concerns. All non-suite lodge rooms (not villas) that are accessible have king beds only; there are no daybeds, pullouts, or rollaways.
[D]	Chefs are very accommodating with 72 hours' notice.
[P]	Fitness facility is on premises, as well as plenty of walking/wheeling trails and other activities.
[L]	Be sure to request a king bed—definitely not a bunk bed room, which has even less floor space.
[V]	Rooms may seem dark and poorly lit, partially due to the dark wood furnishings.

Disney's Wilderness Lodge and Villas Resort

901 W. Timberline Drive, Lake Buena Vista, FL 32830
Phone: 407-824-3200 Fax: 407-824-3232

Planning

Special Challenges

Getting There

Staying in Style

Touring

Feasting

Resources

Index

Disney's Yacht & Beach Club & Villas Resorts

The Yacht Club and Beach Club are **sister resorts**, perched on the bank of Crescent Lake, directly across from Disney's BoardWalk. The Beach Club Villas, a Disney Vacation Club (DVC) resort, joined these resorts in 2002. All are within walking/wheeling distance of both Epcot and the Disney-MGM Studios.

Like the BoardWalk across the lake, these resorts were designed to evoke the feel of the **seashore in the early 1900s**. The Yacht Club is the gray clapboard half of the building, with a dilapidated ship on its beach. The Beach Club's side is sky blue, with a white sandy stretch of beach. Adjacent to the Beach Club, in a separate seafoam green structure, are the Beach Club Villas.

Check-In

The Yacht and Beach Club have **separate entrances and separate front desks**. Neither has a low counter for check-in. Beach Club and Beach Club Villas guests check in at the Beach Club's front desk. Check-in time at both resorts is 3:00 pm.

Parking is available, but the lot is a lengthy (though level) walk/wheel from the lobby. Valet parking is available ($10/day or complimentary to DVC members staying at the Villas using points or to those with a handicapped parking permit). Bell Services will assist you with your luggage, but note that some rooms are located quite a long distance from the front desk. Ask if a resort wheelchair is available to save you the steps.

Guest Rooms

Standard rooms (634 at the Yacht Club, 580 at the Beach Club) are 380 sq. ft. (35.3 sq. m.) and are decorated in pastel colors. The Yacht Club has a decidedly more nautical feel to the decor (anchors, compasses, and the like), while the Beach Club and Villas are rather more casual seaside in tone. Rooms have one king-size or two queen-size beds, a daybed, double sinks, a makeup mirror, a small table and chairs, refrigerator, coffeemaker with coffee packets, and an armoire with a television and a minibar. Some slightly smaller rooms have a king-size Murphy bed and an extra sink and counter. Some rooms have balconies or patios. Other room amenities include room service, hair dryers, iron and ironing board, newspaper delivery, turndown service (on request), wall safe, toiletries, and voice mail. Both the Yacht Club and the Beach Club offer a concierge service with slightly larger rooms on the fifth floor. In addition, 40 special suites (20 in each resort) range in size from a junior suite to a two-bedroom suite to the ultimate Presidential Suite.

Standard room layout

Upon request, the Yacht and Beach Club can provide the following **special items**:

- ✔ Rollaway beds ($15 plus tax per day)
- ✔ Bed boards and rails
- ✔ Cribs
- ✔ International electrical adapter
- ✔ Smoke detectors for hearing impaired
- ✔ Heating pads
- ✔ Down pillows

Disney's Yacht & Beach Club & Villas
(continued)

Guest Rooms (continued)

The 205 **Beach Club Villas**, with their kitchen facilities, are ideal for those who prefer to cook at least some meals and snacks for themselves. Rooms are studio, one-, and two-bedroom villas. Studios accommodate up to four guests with one queen-size bed, a double-size sofa bed, and a kitchenette (with a sink, microwave, and a small refrigerator). The one- and two-bedroom villas accommodate up to four or eight guests respectively, and offer full kitchens, DVD players, king-size beds, and whirlpool tubs in the master bedroom, double-size sleeper sofas in the living room, and washers/dryers. Amenities for all villas include room service, iron and board, hair dryer, newspapers, high-speed Internet access, turndown service (on request), in-room safe, toiletries, and voice mail. All rooms at these resorts, as at all Disney resort hotels, are nonsmoking.

One-bedroom (unshaded)

Studio layout (shaded)

Entire layout represents a two-bedroom villa

Upon request, the Beach Club Villas can provide the following **special items**:
- ✔ Bed boards and rails
- ✔ Full-size cribs
- ✔ Extra portable cribs
- ✔ Down pillows
- ✔ High chairs
- ✔ Electric mixer
- ✔ Booster seat
- ✔ Shower seat and toilet seat for disabled
- ✔ Smoke detector and telephone for hearing impaired
- ✔ Electric adapters
- ✔ Tea bags and decaf coffee

If mobility is a concern, request a room closer to the lobby for **easier access**. Also, there's a bank of elevators near each resort's lobby to serve most rooms. If your room is at the far end of a hall, though, look for a single elevator or stairway. If you're heading to Epcot, the exit near Beach Club's quiet pool is most convenient.

The Yacht Club has **accessible water and pool view rooms**, as well as accessible lagoon view club-level rooms, but its garden view club-level rooms are not accessible. At the Beach Club, there are no water/pool view or lagoon view club-level accessible rooms, but the garden view club-level rooms are accessible.

Stormalong Bay, the mini-water park between the Yacht & Beach Clubs, is very popular, and can be **quite noisy**, even into the night. Request a room away from it if noise is a concern.

All rooms on the first floor have patios. Most rooms on the top floor have full balconies, as do some on other floors. Be aware that some balconies are **standing room only**, however. If a full-size balcony is important, request it.

Some rooms have a **king-size Murphy bed**. These are slightly smaller than other rooms. If you desire a slightly larger room, consider the Beach Club's fifth-floor concierge level.

Disney's Yacht & Beach Club & Villas
(continued)

Dining
Because the Yacht and Beach Clubs **share restaurants**, there are a number of great dining options here (see pages 378–379). The Yacht Club Galley and the Crew's Cup Lounge are especially good for those looking for lighter fare. In addition, the Beach Club Villas, with their kitchen facilities, give you the chance to prepare some meals and snacks in the room. The resorts' shops (Fittings and Fairings at the Yacht Club; Beach Club Marketplace at the Beach Club) offer a good selection of grocery and sundry items. (See page 128.) Also, the Beach Club Marketplace offers made-to-order and prepackaged sandwiches, salads, and sweet treats. Room service is always available.

Amenities
If you need to **maintain an exercise routine** while on vacation, there's the Ship Shape Health Club, a complete fitness club offering a spa, sauna, and massage therapies. The resorts also have two lighted tennis courts and a sand volleyball court. The Bayside Marina rents watercraft and surrey bikes as well.

Three sandy-bottom swimming pools along with whirlpools, bubbling jets, a water slide in a shipwreck, and two hot tubs (spas) form the three-acre mini-water park known as **Stormalong Bay**. Stormalong Bay is for Yacht and Beach Club and Villas resort guests only (resort ID required). There is no zero-entry access at Stormalong Bay, but there are several spots where you can wade into shallow pool areas of $2\frac{1}{2}$ to 3 feet of water. There is also a transfer tier for wheelchair users who are able to lift and lower themselves into the water. Lifeguards here suggest that if you're mobility-challenged, but can handle a few steps up, you might be able to go down the slide at the kids' pool. Quieter pools with transfer tiers are located at the far ends of the resorts. The Villas has its own pool, called "Dunes Cove," and a hot tub. Automated external defibrillators (AEDs) are located at each of the pools and at numerous locations throughout the resort.

Near Stormalong Bay, there's a **playground**, while the game arcade, Lafferty Place, is located adjacent to the pool area.

Quiet Spots
Quiet spots abound around these resorts. Just off the Beach Club Lobby is The Solarium, near the entrance to the Villas is The Drawing Room, and near the Villas' quiet pool is The Breezeway. Over at the Yacht Club, there are chairs on the first floor, just behind the shop, that are often vacant and usually very quiet. Other chairs in the hallway on the way to the quiet pool offer another quiet area.

Reader Tip: "The beach swings are a very appealing place to get away, especially during sunset."—contributed by peer reviewer Michelle Hohmann

© Deb Wills

The Breezeway at the Beach Club

Disney's Yacht & Beach Club & Villas
(continued)

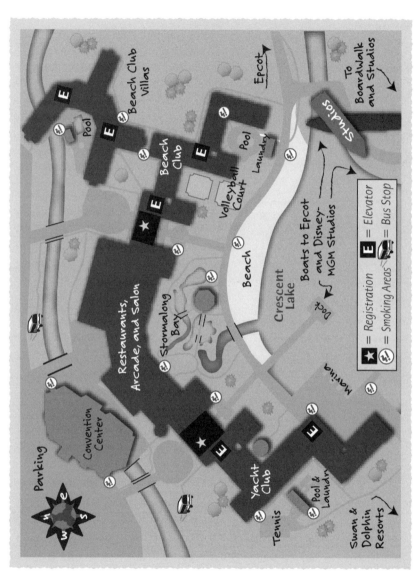

2008 standard room rates begin at $325 in value season, $370 in regular season, $440 in peak season, and $490 in holiday season (seasons are indicated on page 101). Water/pool view rooms are $70–$75 more. Beach Club Villa studios are $325 in value season, $370 in regular season, $440 in peak season, and $490 in holiday season. One-bedroom villas are $425–$645. Two-bedroom villas are $610–$1,140. Note that prices may increase by $10–$30 per night on some holiday weekends. All rooms at this resort are subject to 12.5% tax.

Disney's Yacht & Beach Club & Villas
(continued)

Transportation

There are a **number of transportation options available** at the Yacht and Beach Club resorts. Accessible Friendship boats (which also stop at the BoardWalk and the Swan and Dolphin) leave from the marina for Epcot and Disney-MGM Studios. Buses to the Magic Kingdom, Disney's Animal Kingdom, and Downtown Disney leave from the front of the Beach Club and Yacht Club—they also service the other Epcot area resorts. The BoardWalk, Dolphin, and Swan are all within walking and wheeling distance, as is the International Gateway to Epcot. Although the inclines on the bridges to BoardWalk and Swan/Dolphin are a challenge, you can avoid the incline on the path to Epcot via a waterside bypass. You could also walk or wheel to Disney-MGM Studios along the path beside the BoardWalk Villas. Reach other destinations by transferring at a nearby theme park (day) or Downtown Disney (evening).

Estimated Transportation Times

Magic Kingdom	Epcot	Disney-MGM Studios	Disney's Animal Kingdom	Downtown Disney
bus ~20 min.	walk/boat ~10/~10 min.	walk/boat ~20/~15 min.	direct bus ~20 min.	direct bus ~15 min.

Approximate time you will spend in transit from resort to destination during normal operation.

Our Ratings

We rate the Yacht Club and Beach Club and Villas **very high** on our convenience scale, even though they are among the more expensive Disney resorts. The kitchen facilities available in the Villas make them an excellent choice for vacationers with infants or special dietary needs. In addition, the resort is centrally located, convenient to both Epcot and Disney-MGM Studios, as well as the Walt Disney World Swan and Dolphin hotels and the BoardWalk Inn and Villas. Transportation and dining options abound, and among the restaurants located in the vicinity are some of the most accommodating for travelers with special diets.

Our Convenience Scale

[A][U][S]	Stormalong Bay pool area can get very noisy and crowded. Smaller quiet pools are available. Beaches and Cream restaurant, located near the pool, can also be quite crowded and noisy.
[C][♥][T][M][P][E]	Request a room near an elevator if you have mobility concerns.
[D]	Chefs are very accommodating with 72-hour notice.
[♥][P]	Excellent fitness facilities available on the premises; in addition, there are great walking paths and numerous other activities.
[L]	Be sure to request a king bed.

Disney's Yacht and Beach Club and Villas Resorts

1700/1800 Epcot Resorts Blvd., Lake Buena Vista, FL 32830
Phone: 407-934-7000/8000 Fax: 407-934-3450/3850

Shades of Green Resort

Planning

Special Challenges

Getting There

Staying in Style

Touring

Feasting

Resources

Index

Shades of Green is a **U.S. Armed Forces Recreation Center** right in the heart of Walt Disney World. It is exclusively for active and retired military personnel, as well as reservists, National Guard, Department of Defense civilians, and U.S. Public Health Service officers. The resort reopened in 2004 after an extensive renovation and expansion.

Guest Rooms
The rooms are **among the largest** at Disney at 450 sq. ft. (42 sq. m.). The 586-plus rooms are all nonsmoking, as are most central areas. Rooms are located in two buildings, one three stories and the other five stories. The building to the left of the lobby is closest to the parking garage, fitness center, and Mangino's restaurant. The building to the right of the lobby surrounds the Millpond and Magnolia pools. Also nearby is a playground, Evergreen's Sports Bar and Grill, and hot tub. There are rooms facing the pools. If you have mobility concerns, ask to be in a room closest to the lobby. There are ADA-compliant rooms—inquire at booking. Eleven family-style suites that sleep six or eight are also offered.

Dining
Garden Gallery offers a la carte and buffet breakfast and dinner (different theme nightly). Evergreen's Sports Bar and Grill serves salads, sandwiches, and burgers, while Mangino's serves dinner Italian-style. Room service offers breakfast and dinner service. Express Café near the bus area has food to go, and there is also a Starbucks coffee stand.

Amenities
For activities, there are **two pools** (Millpond and Magnolia), as well as a kids' pool and hot tub. An arcade is also near Millpond Pool. One 9-hole and two 18-hole golf courses are adjacent to the resort, owned and operated by Walt Disney World. AAFES General Store sells snacks, sundries, and limited Disney items. There is also a Starbucks located in front of AAFES. Note that the Disney Channel is not broadcast on Shades of Green televisions.

Quiet Spots
The resort has lots of **landscaped paths and walkways**, with benches sprinkled throughout. The expansive lobby area also offers areas to sit and relax, gaze into the fireplace, or sit outside on the deck overlooking the central grounds and, in the distance, the golf course.

Transportation
Shades of Green has its **own transportation** (separate from Disney's) to all of the major Disney theme parks which is provided at the **bus stop** located outside the lobby on the lower level. Be sure to read the bus schedule you receive at check-in. Note that service to Downtown Disney doesn't begin until 6:30 pm. Buses have ramps for wheelchair access. Parking is $5.

Our Ratings

[A][U][S]	The pool area can get very crowded and noisy.
[C][♥][T][M] [P][E][S]	If you have mobility concerns, we suggest renting a car and requesting a room near an elevator.
[D][G]	Chefs are accommodating with 72-hour notice. One reviewer noted that chefs were not helpful during a recent trip, however.
[G]	There is a fireplace in the lobby.
[F]	Alligators are sometimes present on grounds and near pools.

Shades of Green Resort
P.O. Box 22789, Bay Lake, FL 32830, Phone: 407-824-3400 Fax: 407-824-3665
For more information: 888-593-2242, 407-824-3400, http://www.shadesofgreen.org

Swan and Dolphin Resorts

With its sculptures of swans and heraldic dolphins, the Walt Disney World Swan and Dolphin resorts tower above nearby Epcot. Some find their design striking; others find it surreal. Westin and Sheraton, both of which are divisions of Starwood Hotels, jointly manage this pair of luxury hotels popular with **business and international visitors**.

Check-In

Each of these resorts has its own **separate check-in area**. Both areas have been recently refurbished but are very open with loud echoes, particularly the Swan with its noisy splashing fountain. Check-in time at both resorts is 3:00 pm.

Self-parking is available for $9/day, but the lot is a **few minutes' walk from the hotel entrance**. Valet parking is available for $12/day or $16 for overnight (prices include tax). Parking is complimentary with a handicapped tag.

Once you've checked in, **Bell Services** will assist you with your luggage, but note that some rooms are located quite a long distance from the front desk. Ask if a resort wheelchair is available to save you the steps.

Guest Rooms

Rooms feature either one king-size bed or two double-size beds, separate vanity and bath areas, two 2-line phones, minibar, hair dryer, iron and ironing board, in-room safe, coffeemaker, newspaper, and high-speed Internet access ($10.95 for 24 contiguous hours). In-room movies and Nintendo are also available for an extra charge. Some rooms have balconies, and 195 suites offer a bit more room. Guest rooms at both resorts sport a modern design (by Michael Graves) and "Heavenly Beds" with pillow-top mattresses and down comforters. The resorts also offer conference facilities, plus many of the same amenities and benefits found at Disney resort hotels.

Reader Tip: "The Dolphin had the nicest handicapped room we've used at Disney. Large and spacious, just steps from the elevator, and with a huge shower/bath area. It was planned for the disabled."–contributed by peer reviewer Pam Passwater

Important Note: These resorts frequently host large conventions.

Dining

Between the two resorts there are quite a number of **dining options**, from the 24-hour Picabu (Dolphin), to the full-service Il Mulino (Swan) and the upscale seafood extravaganza Todd English's bluezoo (Dolphin). In addition, the Swan and Dolphin are just a short walk/wheel from the BoardWalk and the Yacht and Beach Club Resorts and their eateries (see pages 368–369 and 378–379). Notable for its willingness to cater to special diets is Fresh Mediterranean Market, which features a healthful buffet and made-to-order items. Note that kosher items are not generally available at Swan and Dolphin restaurants, but can be ordered with 72 hours' notice. Note, too, that the Swan and Dolphin feature restaurants with a great emphasis on seafood: Kimonos (sushi) and Todd English's bluezoo.

Amenities

Each hotel has a **heated pool**, perfect for swimming laps. Located between the two resorts is the three-acre Grotto Pool, which has a waterfall and slide. There's also a kiddie pool for the little ones and four whirlpools. There's also a small playground located at each resort, not too far from the pools.

Planning

Special Challenges

Getting There

Staying in Style

Touring

Feasting

Resources

Index

Swan and Dolphin Resorts
(continued)

Amenities (continued)

Each resort has a **game arcade**—the Dolphin's is a bit larger and is located near Picabu.

Guests receive most of the **same benefits** enjoyed at the Disney-owned resorts, including package delivery, but they cannot charge Disney purchases to their room.

If you need to **maintain a fitness routine** while on vacation, both the Swan and Dolphin feature fully equipped fitness centers ($8/day). Several walking/wheeling/jogging routes, ranging from one to four miles, have been mapped out—ask at the fitness center for a map. There are also four lighted tennis courts between the two hotels, as well as basketball and volleyball areas. And if you're not up to a round of real golf at one of Disney's golf courses, the Fantasia Gardens Miniature Golf is just a short walk away.

The Dolphin is home to the luxurious **Mandara Spa**, which offers massage and spa treatments, as well as salon services.

Transportation

Disney **buses** take you to Disney's Animal Kingdom, the Magic Kingdom, the water parks, or Downtown Disney. The bus stop is at the front of either resort (exit the hotel and walk/wheel down the sidewalk to the left). Note, however, that buses stop at other Epcot area resorts (BoardWalk, Yacht Club, and Beach Club) en route. There are accessible Friendships, which also stop at the Epcot area resorts, that run to Disney-MGM Studios and Epcot from the dock located between the two hotels. Walking/wheeling to Epcot or Disney-MGM Studios is also an option from these two very conveniently located hotels.

Our Ratings

We rate the Swan and Dolphin resorts.**high** on our scale. The convenient location, close to two theme parks, and numerous dining and transportation options make them a very good choice for guests with a variety of needs. Also, many discounts and special rates (for AllEars.net readers, teachers, AAA, Disney Annual Passholders, etc.) are available.

[A][U][S]	The Grotto Pool area can get very crowded and noisy. Smaller pools are available.
[C][♥][T][M][P][E]	Request a room near an elevator if you have mobility concerns.
[D][G][W]	Kosher items available only with 72 hours' notice. Some restaurants are reluctant to cater to special diets, but Fresh is extremely accommodating.
[L]	Be sure to request a king bed.
[Ö]	Japanese breakfast featured at Garden Grove. Many international visitors frequent these hotels.

Walt Disney World Swan and Dolphin Resorts

1500 Epcot Resorts Blvd., Lake Buena Vista, FL 32830
Phone: 407-934-3000 (Swan) or 934-4000 (Dolphin)
Fax: 407-934-4499 (Swan) or 407-934-4099 (Dolphin)
For reservations, call 888-828-8850 or 407-934-6244
For more information, visit http://www.swandolphin.com

Disney Vacation Club

The Disney Vacation Club (DVC) is Disney's version of vacation ownership, a sort of **mouse-friendly timeshare**. Unlike traditional timeshares (where you purchase a set place for a set time of year), the DVC works on a point system, providing flexibility regarding accommodations and when you want to travel.

Currently, there are **eight DVC resorts**: Old Key West (see pages 155–157), BoardWalk Villas (see pages 131–134), Villas at the Wilderness Lodge (see pages 174–177), Beach Club Villas (see pages 178–182), Saratoga Springs Resort and Spa (see pages 170–173), Vero Beach (along the Florida coast), and Hilton Head Island (South Carolina). Phase I of Disney's Animal Kingdom Villas is now open in the main lodge, with additional rooms opening throughout the end of 2007. Accommodations offered range from studios to one-, two-, and three-bedroom villas. Housekeeping is limited.

DVC accommodations can be **rented** just like all the other Disney resort hotels or can be reserved by members. For those traveling with special needs, more at-home amenities are offered in DVC resorts, making them a great choice. Studios have a kitchenette and access to laundry machines, while the one-, two-, and three-bedroom villas have full kitchens, washer and dryer, whirlpool tub, and space!

Disney Vacation Club
200 Celebration Place, Celebration, FL 34747-9903
Phone: 800-500-3990 Fax: 407-566-3393
DVC information kiosks are at most Disney parks and resorts.
Sales offices and models are at Disney's Saratoga Springs.
DVC web site: http://www.disneyvacationclub.com

© MediaMarx, Inc.

The master bedroom of a one-bedroom villa at Saratoga Springs Resort

Other Hotels

Below are a few hotels and motels near Walt Disney World (but not on property) that either our editors and publishers Jennifer and Dave Marx stayed in and recommend or at which our readers report good experiences.

Hotel Name (in alphabetical order)	Starting Rates	Year Built	Year Renovated
Nickelodeon Family Suites	**$180 +**	**1999**	**2005**

This 800-suite resort offers close proximity to Walt Disney World (just 3 mi./5 km.). The hotel offers unique and very convenient "Kidsuites" with a living room, kitchenette, master bedroom, and kids' room. The kids get a bunk bed, TV, Nintendo (fee applies), and a small table and chairs. If you don't have kids, you can get a room with a different configuration, such as the SweetHeart Suite (whirlpool tub and 50" TV), the CinemaSuite (60" TV with stereo surround), Residential Suite (full kitchen), or the Two-Bedroom Suite. Guests get a full, hot breakfast buffet from 6:30 am to 11:00 am. Kids eat free when they dine with adults. The resort also has a large pool, water playground, two hot tubs, and a small miniature golf course. There is a free scheduled shuttle bus to Walt Disney World, but we found it more convenient to drive. The resort was being revamped with a Nickelodeon theme in spring 2005. Visit http://www.hifamilysuites.com or call 407-387-5437 or 877-387-5437. Hotel address: 14500 Continental Gateway, Orlando, FL 32821.

Radisson Resort Orlando-Celebration	**$79 +**	**1987**	**2005**

Jennifer and Dave enjoyed their stay at this 718-room, 6-story deluxe hotel just 1.5 mi. (2.5 km.) from the gates of Walt Disney World. Guest rooms accommodate up to four guests with either one king-size bed or two double-size beds. Recently refurbished rooms come in either pool or courtyard views and feature modern Italian furniture and marble bathrooms. Amenities include a 25" TV, mini refrigerator, stocked minibar, in-room safe, coffeemaker, iron and ironing board, hair dryer, makeup mirror, voice mail, data ports, and free high-speed Internet access (most rooms). For a $7 daily service fee, you get enhanced shuttles to attractions, 24-hour access to the fitness center, use of lighted tennis courts, free local and toll calls, and free newspaper delivery. The resort has two pools, a water slide, a wading pool, and two hot tubs, as well as lighted tennis courts, fitness center, playground, and arcade. Food service includes a full-service restaurant (open for breakfast and dinner), a deli with Pizza Hut items, a sports bar, a pool bar, and room service. Note that kids under 10 eat free when accompanied by a paying adult. There is a free scheduled shuttle bus to attractions. For the best rates, visit http://orlando.guestselectresorts.com or call 407-396-7000 and ask for the "Y-PASS" rate code. 2900 Parkway Boulevard, Kissimmee, FL 34747.

Sheraton Safari Resort	**$125 +**	**1994**	**1998**

While this isn't equivalent to Disney's Animal Kingdom Lodge, this safari-themed resort is a winner with kids and adults alike. The 489-room, 6-story hotel is located just 1/4 mi. (1/2 km.) from the Disney property (you can't walk to it, but it is a short drive or ride on the scheduled shuttle). Guest rooms come in standard (one king-size or two double-size beds), Safari Suites (with kitchenette and separate parlor), and deluxe suites (with full kitchens and large parlors). Standard rooms accommodate up to four guests or five guests with the rental of a rollaway bed. All rooms have a balcony or patio, TV with PlayStation, two phones with voice mail, data ports, high-speed Internet access, hair dryer, makeup mirror, coffeemaker, iron and ironing board, and in-room safe. The resort features a large pool with a 79-ft. water slide, wading pool, hot tub, fitness center, and arcade. One full-service restaurant (Casablanca's) offers breakfast and dinner (kids under 10 eat free with paying adults), along with the Outpost Deli (for lunch and dinner), the ZanZibar Watering Hole, and room service (6:30 am–10:00 pm). Visit http://www.sheratonsafari.com or call 407-239-0444 or 800-423-3297. Hotel address: 12205 S. Apopka-Vineland Road, Orlando, FL 32836.

Disney Cruise Line

The Disney Cruise Line combines many of your favorite things from the Disney theme parks and transforms them into two magnificent cruising ships for a **unique vacation experience**. The Disney Magic and the Disney Wonder boast outstanding customer service, unique dining and entertainment experiences, Disney characters, and, of course, magic.

Whether you're sailing on the Magic or Wonder, each evening you'll receive in your stateroom the **Navigator** newsletter, packed with information on the next day's activities for all age groups, including children. This guide provides you with dining hours and locations, special activities, and show descriptions and times. Extra copies of the Navigator are available at Guest Services. The Magic and the Wonder are almost identical, so all descriptions here apply to both, unless otherwise noted.

Adults without children sometimes hesitate to go on a Disney cruise because they equate Disney with "family," but co-author Deb Wills loves the **adult-only areas** of the ship and Castaway Cay and has never felt inundated with young ones.

Cruise veterans will find the Disney **staterooms larger than most other cruise lines**. Standard in each room category are a television, phone, and in-room safe. Bathrooms contain hair dryer and tub. Almost half of all staterooms offer a verandah, where you can sit and enjoy your morning coffee or evening beverage.

Before You Go

You can **book your Disney Cruise vacation** yourself through Disney Cruise Line. Call 888-325-2500. Outside the United States, call 407-566-6921 (representatives offer assistance in English, Spanish, Japanese, French, Portuguese, and German). For information via TTY, call 407-566-7455. You can also reserve your cruise through http://www.disneycruise.com or contact a travel agent.

Whatever you decide, when you book your cruise, you'll also be **selecting your stateroom**. Before you call, make sure you have a list of any special needs/requirements and preferences to discuss with the reservation agent. This is when you'll note everything from special dietary requests, to accessible staterooms, to the need for a special communications kit.

If you have any special medical needs or dietary requests, or require an accessible room, you need to submit a **special medical form**. Request this from your travel agent or Disney directly. The earlier you book your cruise, the better your chances of obtaining an accessible cabin in the category you desire.

You will be asked if you prefer the **early or late dining seating**. Early dining is usually 5:45, 6:00, or 6:15 pm, and late dining is usually 8:00, 8:15, or 8:30 pm. If eating at a specific time is necessary for you, be sure to mention this when you book your reservations. Early seating times fill quickly. Remember any time zone changes when deciding on early or late seating. It is quite possible that you will be sitting with "strangers" at meal time.

Bright Idea: If you wish to have your own table (no others seated with you), be sure to request this in advance. Once onboard the ship, check with Guest Services to see if your request was granted. If not, you will have the opportunity to request dining changes at that time.

Staterooms on the Disney Cruise Line

Inside Staterooms (Categories 10–12)
Inside staterooms are the **least expensive**. There are no windows (don't reserve if you are claustrophobic), which makes the rooms fairly dark. Category 10 rooms are 214 sq. ft. (20 sq. m.), and categories 11 and 12 are 184 sq. ft. (17 sq. m.). Category 12 sleeps only three people. Categories 11 and 12 do not have the split bathroom (separate toilet and bath). Room locations range from deck 2 to deck 7 (most on the lower decks).

Outside Stateroom With Porthole (Categories 8–9)
These are not the small portholes you might associate with a ship—these are large round windows that let in a **good amount of light** (except deck 1's outside staterooms, which have two tiny portholes). No verandahs though. Category 8 rooms have 214 sq. ft. (20 sq. m.) and are on decks 5–7, but most are in the front of the ship (avoid if you have motion sensitivity).

Outside Stateroom With Verandahs (Categories 4–7)
Staterooms are 268–304 sq.ft. (25–28.2 sq. m.). Your verandah is your own **private deck** for watching the sights. Categories 5–7 are the same size. Co-author Deb Wills enjoys the category 7 room for the enclosed verandah, as well as the lower price. Most category 7 verandahs have solid balconies, so you cannot see out when sitting.

Outside Stateroom Suites With Verandas (Categories 1–3)
These are huge rooms with extra amenities, such as concierge service and expanded room service. All suites are on deck 8 and are pricey!

A standard category 9 stateroom

Bright Idea: To view the location of accessible staterooms, visit the Disney Cruise Line "Deck Plans" page at http://disneycruise.com or check the stateroom chart in "PassPorter's Field Guide to the Disney Cruise Line and Its Ports of Call" guidebook.

Reviewer Tip: "When we booked our cabin, we were told my electric wheelchair would most likely fit in the room and, if not, we could leave it in the hallway. When we checked in, they said it would not fit, but the stateroom host would stow it. The stateroom host told us he had no place for it and would have to leave it by the elevator. Fortunately, we were able to upgrade. With something important like this, call and call again! Even then, be flexible once you board the ship."—contributed by peer reviewer Joanne Ernest

An accessible stateroom (category 11) has a lot of space

An accessible, roll-in shower

Planning · Special Challenges · Getting There · Staying in Style · Touring · Feasting · Resources · Index

Embarking on the Disney Cruise Line

Documentation

Your **cruise documents** will arrive approximately two weeks prior to sailing. Be sure to fill these out before you leave home. If you fill them out online, be sure to print them out, sign, and bring with you to the port. Double-check that you have the proper ID with you. Current photo ID and valid birth certificates are accepted for U.S. residents at the time of writing, but only until 12/31/2007, when passports are required for all persons (adults and children, U.S. resident or otherwise) reentering the United States from the Caribbean.

As of January 23, 2007, citizens of the United States, Canada, Mexico, and Bermuda are required to **present a passport** to enter the United States when arriving by air from any port of the Western Hemisphere. As of January 1, 2008, citizens traveling between the United States and Canada, Mexico, Central and South America, the Caribbean, and Bermuda by land or sea may be required to present a passport. Note: Your passport expiration date must be a minimum of six months after your travel dates.

Packing

Be sure to **pack a day bag** with anything you might need from the time you depart for the cruise terminal until dinner, including all medications. Depending on where you are coming from and your mode of transportation, it is possible you will not see your luggage from early morning to that evening! Bring a toiletries case that will hang over the bathroom door.

Small personal coolers are allowed for medications, baby food, or dietary needs.

Check-In

Check-in is the time to **reconfirm** that Disney Cruise Line has a record of any special needs requests you made in advance. If you need special assistance boarding, discuss this with the crew member at the terminal when you check in. Alas, there are no accessible counters at check-in. Boarding is done by number so you can wait comfortably until your group is called—lines are minimal at boarding time.

Safety Drill

Before ships leave Port Canaveral, a **mandatory safety drill takes place at about 4:00 pm**. In your stateroom closet, you'll find bright orange life jackets. Check the jackets when you arrive in your stateroom. If you need different sizes, contact your stateroom host/hostess right away. An announcement over the stateroom and ship loudspeakers (complete with sounding alarm) will notify you of the drill. You must put on your life jacket and report to your designated location. The life jackets partially pull apart and must be pulled on over your head. Your assembly station is mapped on the back of your stateroom door, and your station location is noted on your life jacket. While most locations are on the outer decks of the ship, some are inside, such as at Animator's Palate. It gets quite crowded and noisy in these areas. Once you arrive at your station, a crew member will take attendance (be sure to check in when called). You will be required to wait until the "all clear" is sounded. This can be 15–20 minutes. Keep your life jacket on until you return to your stateroom. If standing or stairs are a problem, go to Guest Services when you board and ask for assistance. Those with mobility issues may be dismissed a few minutes earlier to access elevators. For guests who have a hearing impairment, if you filled out the medical form requesting an interpreter, one should be available to assist with the safety drill.

If you **require assistance** during the safety drill, stop by Guest Services soon after you board and let them know your situation. People with mobility issues will be assisted (and will be able to use the elevators and areas of the ship normally restricted to crew—some stairways are steep). A limited number of larger-size life jackets are available upon request. Ask your stateroom host or hostess, or call Guest Services once you board.

Dining on the Disney Cruise Line

Where to Eat

You have a **choice of places** to dine and snack throughout your cruise: buffet, table-service restaurant, snack bars, room service. You are assigned a dining table location and rotation for dinner. Your servers stay with you as you move to different dining rooms each night.

Special dietary requirements are accommodated on the Disney Cruise ships, provided you make your requirements known before you cruise. Be sure to submit a special medical form for any special dietary needs, including Kosher foods. A notation will be made on your reservation and you may be instructed to meet with the Food and Beverage team the afternoon you board ship (check the Welcome Navigator for time/location). This information will be passed to your servers, who will be with you each evening throughout your cruise (except if/when you dine at the premium restaurant, Palo). Be sure to remind your servers (and the head waiter) of your dietary requests on the first evening.

If you wait until you are onboard to request a special meal, your **choices will be very limited**. Basics such as vegetarian (two choices) or grilled chicken/fish are always available at the table-service restaurants, but obtaining foods without sauces or making other special requests, isn't always possible due to the "en masse" kitchen preparation. For example, co-author Deb Wills could not eat a tuna entree as it could only be prepared with shellfish, to which she is allergic.

Bright Idea: When you're breakfasting at Triton's/Lumiere's/Parrot Cay, Egg Beaters egg substitutes are available upon request. Because these take longer to prepare, be sure to order them as soon as you are seated.

Kosher meals are available at the table-service restaurants only when requested in advance of your cruise. Sugar-free or no-sugar-added desserts are offered during lunch and dinner in the table-service areas. Inquire at the buffets.

Kids' menus are available at table-service restaurants (adults can order from them, too). Basic items usually include hot dogs, macaroni and cheese, pizza, chicken strips, grilled cheese, soda, milk, or juice. Smoothies are $3.50 extra.

Room service is available 24 hours a day, whether you are at sea or in port (except on debarkation morning). Although the menu is very limited, you don't have to leave your cabin to eat. Special dietary items are limited with room service, though. Selections include chef salad, soup, fruit, sandwiches, burgers, mac and cheese, peanut butter and jelly, and pizza.

Deb Wills has cruised while on **Weight Watchers** and, after seven days, remained the same weight as when she set foot onboard. She did splurge a bit at Palo, but she made sure to get some exercise in and was able to maintain her diet.

© MediaMarx, Inc.

Co-author Deb Wills (right) and Linda Eckwerth at Palo

Planning

Special Challenges

Getting There

Staying in Style

Touring

Feasting

Resources

Index

Entertainment on the Disney Cruise Line

What to Do

The cruise just wouldn't be Disney's without **characters and first-rate shows**. The entertainment starts during the Sail Away Party (5:00 pm) on decks 9 and 10. The party is very high energy, noisy, and crowded. That said, it's one of our favorite parts of the cruise experience. And there's nothing so thrilling as hearing "When You Wish Upon A Star" from the ship's horn as you pull out of port!

The nighttime **theater shows** are high-quality entertainment, too, and are very popular. Early diners attend the later shows, and late diners the early shows. If you require special accommodation, arrive early and speak to a cast member. Those with mobility concerns but not in a wheelchair should sit closest to the rear of the theaters. There is a hidden ramp that goes to the front of the theater and is accessible; inquire with a crew member.

People of all ages love the Disney characters. In addition to appearances during the day, **characters are available for photographs** each evening in the atrium just outside Triton's/Lumiere's. Lines tend to be very long at these times, especially when Mickey and Minnie are in their formal attire. It also can get very crowded and noisy during these photo sessions.

The **Vista Spa** is a delightful adults-only area where you can get pampered and keep in shape. You can get spa treatments and salon services, take exercise and nutrition classes, and work out in the fitness center (the perfect place to maintain an exercise routine).

Travel Insurance

While no one likes to think their vacation might get canceled at the last minute, it can happen. If you have **medical issues**, you may be especially vulnerable to needing to cancel a planned trip or for emergency medical evacuation once aboard. In addition, weather concerns (traveling from the north in winter, cruising the Caribbean during hurricane season), can delay your arrival to the port.

Most **travel insurance policies** will offer trip cancellation/interruption, delay protection, emergency medical, and baggage coverage. The Disney Cruise Line offers a policy that starts at $49 per person. However, if you use the Disney Cruise Line policy and do not book your airfare with them, that portion of your trip may not be covered. Also, some preexisting conditions are not covered, so be sure to inquire.

You can also call your insurance agent or visit http://www.insuremytrip.com, http://quotetravelinsurance.com, http://www.accessamerica.com, or http://www.csatravelprotection.com. Don't delay if you want travel insurance, as some insurance policies must be **purchased within a week of paying your deposit** for the cruise. Co-Author Deb Wills had a good experience when she needed to use her Access America policy for a last-minute cruise cancellation.

Reader Tip: "Buy your travel insurance within a few days of making your initial cruise deposit. The travel insurance companies will only cover preexisting conditions if you purchase their coverage within 7 to 21 days (varies from company to company and plan to plan) of making your initial deposit. I've searched and have yet to find a company that will cover preexisting conditions, at any price, if you purchase the plan outside the 7- to 21-day window."—contributed by peer reviewer Amy Warren Stoll

Special Requirements on the Disney Cruise Line

Special Requests

When you're making your special requests for the cruise, remember that everything is handled by the Disney Cruise Line reservations staff on *land*. In other words, these are not the same people who will be traveling with you on the ship. That's why it's so important to **double-check that all requests** have been recorded once you receive your final boarding documents. Then, once you are onboard, and before the ship sails, visit Guest Services (deck 3 midship) to verify that all your requests have been noted. The crew members onboard will do everything possible to accommodate you, but they must get the information from Disney Cruise Line reservations first—otherwise, they won't know just what it is that you require and make sure it's around.

Allergies

For many cruisers, traveling south means **different vegetation and flowers**. If you are sensitive to pollen, grasses, etc., be sure to bring your allergy medication with you. Bedcovers in the staterooms are changed after every cruise, along with your bed linens. If you require any special cleaning, discuss this when you make your reservations.

Disney **restricts smoking** to certain areas of the ship and enforces it. No smoking is allowed in the main dining areas or staterooms. Smoking is allowed in the dance club, adults-only lounge, and open areas, such as decks 9 and 10. No smoking is allowed in the Mickey pool area. Guests can smoke on their verandahs, however, and the smoke can travel.

ADD/ADHD/ASD

The **Disney Cruise Line DVD** is a great way to become familiar with the ship and your upcoming voyage—you can request the free DVD by calling 888-325-2500 or visiting online at http://www.disneycruise.com.

All outside railings facing the water have solid bottoms to **discourage climbing**.

Be sure to bring **earplugs and/or sound cancellation headphones for loud areas** (such as the open decks and buffet areas).

All verandah staterooms have a second lock high up on the verandah door that must be unlocked to access the verandah.

Be sure to visit Guest Services once you board if you will need special accommodations during the **mandatory safety drill**.

You might encounter **lines and/or waits** in these spots:
- ✔ At check-in at the terminal. Lines are usually short unless the cruise is "sold out."
- ✔ Waiting to board the ship prior to embarkation time. While Disney boards by numbered groups, some folks still get in line. There is no real reason to do this unless you want to make sure you get a reservation at Flounder's Reef or Palo, the adults-only restaurant.
- ✔ During the safety drill. You will be required to wait at your designated location until all staterooms have checked in and the "all clear" is given.
- ✔ On excursions. While Disney excursions are very organized, you often have to gather and wait several times. Also, some excursions may have a fair amount of travel time, so ask before booking.
- ✔ For character photographs. Lines can be long during the evening hours when everyone wants a photo with Donald and Daisy or Mickey and Minnie.
- ✔ At Guest Services, especially during your last 24 hours onboard.
- ✔ At the buffet meals.

Special Needs on the Disney Cruise Line
(continued)

Addiction Recovery

There are **Friends of Bill W. meetings** onboard the Disney Cruise Line. The 7-night cruise has meetings every day except boarding and debarkation day. The 4-night cruise has meetings on day 2 and 3 (again, not on boarding or debarkation day). The 3-night cruise has meetings on the second day (again, not on boarding or debarkation day). Check your daily Navigator for times and locations, or contact Guest Services onboard to obtain meeting information.

Important Note: Remember, alcohol is everywhere onboard and there is always a "drink of the day." Drinking age is 21.

Chronic Fatigue

Try not to let the jam-packed personal Navigator alarm you! While there is plenty to keep you entertained and active during the cruise, you can also choose to **just kick back** and watch the water go by if you desire. You don't even have to leave the ship until you return to port if you choose.

If you have a room in category 7 or above, you can sit and smell the sea air right from your **stateroom's verandah**. Order room service for meals and you're all set. Category 8 allows you to sit at the window and watch the water. Deck 4 offers lounge chairs under shade facing the water—this area is generally quiet. The Tropical Rainforest at the Vista Spa is a great place for quiet and relaxation, complete with soothing heat and steam.

Use caution when selecting excursions. Some of them take the entire day, with much of the time used to get back and forth from the ship.

Fears

If you or someone you are traveling with doesn't like heights, book an inside stateroom and stay away from the edges of the decks. Fear of water? Avoid the outside decks.

Foreign Language

The Directory of Services book found in your stateroom has brief information sections in the back written in **Spanish, French, German, and Japanese**. Dining room menus are also available in those languages. Have your reservation noted and remind your servers the first evening.

 Crowded Areas

- ✔ Topsiders/Beach Blanket Buffet Lunch on embarkation day
- ✔ Before and after the evening dinner seatings
- ✔ Before and after a stage show ends
- ✔ Character meet and greets
- ✔ Atriums during photography sessions
- ✔ Shutters, where photographs are displayed (especially the last 24 hours)
- ✔ Debarkation at a port—at the initial time you are able to leave the ship
- ✔ Embarkation at a port—as the time to be back onboard nears
- ✔ Kids' and family pools, especially on "at sea" days when it's hot
- ✔ Safety drill assembly stations
- ✔ Elevators, especially midship

Special Needs on the Disney Cruise Line
(continued)

Hearing Impaired

Assistive listening systems are available for the Walt Disney and Buena Vista theaters, WaveBands/Rockin' Bar D, and Studio Sea. A $25 refundable deposit will be charged to your stateroom. Inquire at Guest Services.

Closed-captioning is available for stateroom TVs and select onboard video monitors. American Sign Language interpretation is available for live performances on designated cruises. You must make arrangements at booking. Inquire regarding a schedule.

Communication kits are available for your stateroom and contain door knock and phone alerts, phone amplifer, bed shaker, strobe light smoke detector, and TTY.

Guest Assistance Packets containing show scripts, flashlights, and pen/paper are available at Guest Services. You can sign out these packets and keep them until the night before debarkation, then return them to Guest Services.

Infants/Children

Traveling with young ones? You can **request Pack 'n' Play-type cribs**, bed rails, and high chairs from your stateroom host/hostess. Crib blankets are not provided (nor recommended for young infants).

© MediaMarx, Inc.

Formula for infants (milk-based Isomil and Similac) are sold in the Treasure Ketch (deck 4). You can also purchase diapers, wipes, diaper ointment, pacifiers, and a few other items—baby food is not available for purchase nor is it offered in the restaurants. The ship's stores have limited hours and are closed when in port. It's best to bring your own supplies—there is a limited supply of diapers and formula onboard.

If your child is between 12 weeks and 3 years, or not toilet-trained, you can use **Flounder's Reef Nursery**, the ship's full-service childcare center. (If your child

A Pack 'n' Play-type crib aboard the Disney Cruise Line

is older, see the Oceaneer Club and Lab sidebar on the next page.) Located on deck 5, near the Buena Vista Theatre, Flounder's is equipped with a playroom and toys, Disney movies, baby bouncers, and rocking chairs, as well as a separate sleeping area with cribs

© MediaMarx, Inc.

for infants and mats for toddlers. There is also a small diaper-changing room. Babies in Flounder's Reef may be given apple juice and saltine crackers, as appropriate for their age. No other food is given to them.

Flounder's Reef play area

Flounder's Reef is **$6/per hour** for the first child and $5/hour for each additional child, with a two-hour minimum. Flounder's is open daily, usually from 1:00 pm to 4:00 pm and 6:00 pm to midnight. Times can vary depending on port, so be sure to check your Navigator for times. Be sure to reserve Flounders online as soon as you're able.

Planning

Special Challenges

Getting There

Staying in Style

Touring

Feasting

Resources

Index

Special Needs on the Disney Cruise Line
(continued)

Oceaneer Club and Lab

The Oceaneer Club (ages 3-4 and 5-7) and the Oceaneer Lab (ages 8-9 and 10-12) are activity centers designed just for kids. Special age-appropriate programs run here throughout the day and evening, and there is no additional fee—it's included in the price of your cruise. Children must be potty-trained; however, exceptions are made for special needs children. If your special needs child is not potty-trained, they will be admitted to the club unless they require one-on-one care or have more demanding needs. You will have a pager and will be called to take care of the child's toileting needs. If there are special medical needs, you must file a medical form when you make your reservation.

On the first afternoon of the cruise, visit the children's area (deck 5 midship) to speak with the counselors and (if desired) sign in your kids. As you're filling out the registration form (it's quite lengthy!), be sure to talk with the counselors to explain any special needs your child has. We've been told some parents do not mention "special needs" for fear their child won't be accepted—rest assured the staff makes every effort to accommodate every child and strives to make sure every child has a special cruise. Be sure to include all special considerations, including allergies, illnesses, limitations, medical conditions, medications, fears, etc. The more information you share, the better the staff can assist your child. You may stay with your child in the club or check on him/her whenever you like. The clubs can be very loud, so be sure to bring earplugs if you or they have a sensitivity to noise.

The club issues pagers to parents so you can be contacted quickly in case a problem arises. Parents are paged when children require bathroom assistance (staff cannot change diapers or help children with the toilet). If your special needs child is in the kids' program while in port, be sure to leave a responsible adult aboard the ship.

Make sure you understand the rules and the schedule for the clubs. For safety reasons, there are times of transition (when the groups are changing locations) when you will not be able to sign your child in or out.

If you are unsure how your child will react in the club, start out slowly. Leave them there for just a short amount of time. Next time, they can stay a little longer. Remember, be flexible!

If at any time your child wants to leave the club, they can let the counselors know, and you will be paged. Children as young as 8 can sign themselves out of the clubs with parental permission. Children 10-12 are automatically allowed to do this unless the parents specify they cannot.

There are various age groupings for kids' activities. While the Disney Cruise Line is very strict and will not allow you to move your child up to an older age group, you may be able to move down, depending on your child.

The Disney Cruise Line is unable to provide one-on-one care for any child with special needs, and counselors are not allowed to administer any medications. If your child will be in the club and it's med time, you will have to give the medication yourself.

Special Needs on the Disney Cruise Line
(continued)

Medical Treatment

Disney has a well-equipped **medical facility** on deck 1 staffed by two doctors and three registered nurses from Vanter Cruise Health Services (http://www.vanterventures.com). The center is open daily in the morning and early evening, and a physician and nurse are on call 24 hours a day. The Disney Cruise Line contracts out for the medical care. Any usage fees you incur will be charged to your stateroom and must be paid before you leave the ship. You will be provided a form to file with your insurance company after the cruise. There is a very limited pharmacy onboard for emergencies and unexpected illnesses. All regular medications must be brought with you. In extreme circumstances, Disney will arrange to have a passenger taken back to the nearest port to receive medical care (costs will vary).

If you need to have your **blood pressure checked**, stop by the first aid center during normal working hours.

Bright Idea: We strongly urge you to take out travel insurance when you book your cruise (see page 192). Be sure to inquire about coverage for preexisiting conditions.

A small refrigerator, actually more like a beverage cooler, comes in each stateroom. It's set at approximately 55° F/ 13° C. It is 8" deep x 12" wide x 16.5" high. This is not a suitable storage area for your medications. Request a real refrigerator when making your reservation and confirm just prior to sailing. The onboard medical center has a limited supply of **compact refrigerators for medications**.

Housekeeping will provide a **container for "sharps,"** or used needles—just ask your stateroom host or hostess upon arrival. Use caution, as the sharps containers are soft plastic and somewhat difficult to use.

Mobility/Accessibility

Sixteen **handicap-accessible, barrier-free cabins** are available in categories 3, 5, 6, 8, and 11. These rooms are larger than normal and also feature open bed frames, additional phones in the bathroom/nightstand, bathroom and shower handrails, fold-down shower seats, handheld shower heads, lowered towel and closet bars, and emergency call buttons. Those with mobility concerns who do not use a wheelchair should book a stateroom near an elevator.

© Deb Wills

Peer reviewer Chet McDoniel in an accessible category 8 stateroom

Most **standard wheelchairs do not fit through the regular cabin doors** onboard. Some standard chairs can easily fold, and if so, they can be taken inside the room.

A pool transfer tier can be found at the Quiet Cove pool (multistep, not automatic).

Companion restrooms are located at deck 3 aft by Parrot Cay, deck 4 forward by the Walt Disney Theatre, deck 9 forward by Vista Spa, and deck 10 aft by Palo.

The **Walt Disney Theatre** has places for wheelchairs in the back. If you can transfer from your chair, you can request seating in the front row. Ask the crew member when you arrive at the theatre. They'll take you inside and get you set up before everyone else enters. For some shows, depending on whether the performers need the space, you may remain in your wheelchair and basically park "in front" of the front row (it doesn't hurt to ask).

Special Needs on the Disney Cruise Line
(continued)

Mobility/Accessibility (continued)

The handicapped viewing area for the **Sail Away Party** is on deck 10 overlooking the pool. It's a great place for everyone to watch the party, but be aware there is _no_ shade! There is also a "participation" area for the party on deck 9 near the gazebo on the left side. Check with crew members 30 minutes prior to the activity for exact location.

Elevators are small and often crowded. Avoid the midship elevators in particular.

To **access** Lumiere's/Triton's (deck 3) go through the back entrance—the main entrance has steps. Access to the raised seating at Rockin' Bar D/WaveBands (also deck 3) is via ramp located in the bar area.

Wheelchairs are available on a very limited basis from Guest Services. If you will need a wheelchair or ECV while onboard or in ports, bring your own or rent one (call 866-416-7383 or visit http://brevardmedicalequip.com) with delivery and pickup right at the ship.

The **Port of Nassau is semi-wheelchair friendly**. There are some sidewalk cut-outs and some accessible shops. If you book an excursion through Disney Cruise Line, they will _not_ transport your electric wheelchair, but they may be able to provide a manual one for you to use. At this time, there are _no_ excursions that can accommodate powered chairs.

The Disney Cruise Line makes every attempt to **dock directly** at the port's pier, allowing gangplank loading and unloading (accessible for wheelchairs), but there may be times when this is not possible. In those cases, cruise guests are "tendered" from the ship to the shore. Tendering involves transportation via small boats. You must be able to transfer from your wheelchair to the tender boat and out again, and your wheelchair must be folded and transferred to the tender. In certain situations, it will be impossible for guests in wheelchairs to transfer due to safety concerns.

A limited number of **beach wheelchairs** are available at Disney's private island, Castaway Cay, on the left at Shuttle's Cove (the first tram stop). Beach wheelchairs are also available at Serenity Bay (the adults-only beach). Note that the beach wheelchairs are very difficult to push on sand. The lifeguards will keep your personal wheelchair at their stations. If you need help reaching the first tram stop, ask a crew member after you get off the ship.

Bright Idea: If you plan to get out of your wheelchair at the beach, bring a cover to reflect the heat (and protect against the salt water).

Getting around **Castaway Cay can be a challenge** from a mobility standpoint, as much of the surface area is sand. The only companion restroom on Castaway Cay is in the First Aid building across from the family beach (but quite a distance from the adult beach). Tram service on Castaway Cay is available, but because the space is smaller than normal Disney buses, be aware that some motorized scooters and wheelchairs may not fit. (Right behind the driver, in the first "row" of seats, there is a section of seating that can be pulled up for a wheelchair to fit in. No lifting is involved. A manual ramp is pulled out from the floor in that seating section by the driver.)

The **Disney Cruise Line buses** are chartered through Mears. Each bus can accommodate two electric wheelchairs. If there are more than two in your party, be sure to discuss this when you book the transport. The restroom onboard the buses is wheelchair-accessible.

Reader Tip: "The worst area for wheelchairs is exiting or entering on deck 10. The 'humps' in the doorways are almost impossible for a scooter. The doorway ramp is higher than my scooter can transverse and it gets stuck on the doorway at its highest point. I must have someone help me as I get off my scooter to help lift it off the ledge."–contributed by Ray Sharpton

Special Needs on the Disney Cruise Line
(continued)

Service animals are allowed onboard (you'll need to file a special medical form—see page 188); however, they may not be allowed off the ship at certain ports. Special paperwork must be filled out once you make a reservation—this includes separate paperwork for the Bahamas. Check with your travel agent or Disney representative for specifics. Service animals are allowed in all public areas of the ship, except some areas of the Vista Spa. Stop at Guest Services once onboard to find "rest areas" for your service animal. If you book a category 6 or better stateroom, Disney can provide "turf" for your service animal to use on the verandah. Many of the break areas are not in guest areas, and while you may accompany your animal while on break, many cast-member-only areas, are a tight squeeze for a wheelchair. See page 12 for more details on bringing service animals.

Seniors

Reviewer Tip: "We are seniors who do not travel with any children, and we really love the Disney Cruise Line. We have done two cruises—a 7-night and an 11-night—and we have three more booked. We find that children are not around where we go and do not bother us. In the dining room, they are well-behaved. We sailed once on the Queen Mary II and find that Disney is far superior in terms of service."—contributed by peer reviewer Jean Miller

Motion Sensitivity

Disney Cruise Line ships have two huge stabilizer fins that diminish the worst of the ship's motion. Beyond that, we recommend you consider one of the following remedies.

Bright Idea: Try the remedies long before you leave home to evaluate potential side effects.

✔ **Purely natural**—Go topside, take deep breaths, get some fresh air, and look at the horizon. The worst thing you can do is stay in your stateroom. Drink lots of water and have some mild food, such as saltine crackers—avoid fatty and salty foods, and eat lightly.

✔ **Herbs**—Ginger is reported to help reduce seasickness. It comes in pill and cookie form—even ginger ale can help. It's best to begin taking this in advance of feeling sick.

✔ **Bonine, or "Dramamine Less Drowsy Formula"**—These are brand names of meclizine, which has far fewer side effects than original formula Dramamine (which we don't recommend for adults). Take it a few hours before departure for maximum effectiveness. Note that Bonine is only for those 12 years or older; use original formula Dramamine for kids ages 2 to 12. The onboard medical facility provides free chewable meclizine tablets (25 mg.) from a dispenser next to its door on deck 1 forward. Guest Services (on deck 3 midship) may also have some meclizine if you can't make it down to deck 1.

✔ **Sea-Bands**—These are elastic wrist bands that operate by applying pressure to the Nei Kuan acupressure point on each wrist by means of a plastic stud, thereby preventing seasickness. Some people swear by them; some say that they don't work. Either way, they are inexpensive (unless you buy them on the ship) and have no medical side effects.

✔ **Scopolamine Transdermal Patch**—Available by prescription only. It is the most effective preventative with the least drowsiness, but it also comes with the most side effects, such as dry mouth and dizziness. For more information about scopolamine, speak to your doctor and visit http://www.transdermscop.com.

✔ **Ship Location**—A low deck, midship stateroom is generally considered to be the location on a ship where you'll feel the least movement. If you know you're prone to seasickness, consider requesting a stateroom on decks 1-2, midship. But if once you're onboard, you find yourself feeling seasick, the best thing to do is get out of your stateroom, go to deck 4 midship, and lie down in one of the padded deck chairs. You can feel the ship's motion most at Animator's Palate and the Walt Disney Theater.

✔ **Choose Excursions Wisely**—Those prone to motion sickness may want to avoid shore excursions that rely heavily on smaller boats such as ferries and sailboats.

Special Needs on the Disney Cruise Line
(continued)

Pregnancy

Women past their 24th week of pregnancy are **not allowed to sail** on the Disney Cruise Line. Prior to this, cruising is actually very comfortable for pregnant women as there isn't a huge amount of walking and it's easy to graze all day long. Be aware that you should not take any medications for nausea without your doctor's permission (Sea-Bands are just fine, however). Check with your doctor prior to the cruise as well as the Vista Spa staff for the treatments available while pregnant.

Religion

Those on 7-night cruises can attend an **interdenominational service** in Diversions (deck 3 forward) on Sunday at 9:00 am. Erev Shabbat (Jewish Sabbath Eve) services are held in Diversions Fridays at 5:30 pm. You can attend services in Cape Canaveral on 3- and 4-night cruises on Sunday. Western Caribbean cruises can attend afternoon services on Sunday in Key West. See http://www.marinersguide.com/regions/florida/capecanaveral/churches.html.

⚠ Chill Out Time

If you're looking for a place to just sit and be for a while, here are some places that we've found onboard:

✔ Grab a padded lounge chair on deck 4—you can enjoy the scenic views and stay shaded, too (great for naps).

✔ Deck 7 aft has a secluded and usually quiet deck.

✔ Enjoy the warmth of the sun on deck 10 (pools are on deck 9).

✔ Peace and quiet can be yours for lunch at Lumiere's/Triton's when most of the passengers are out exploring the port of the day.

✔ Ask for a Hidden Mickey Challenge from Guest Services and see how many you can find.

✔ Take an early morning or late night stroll around deck 10. It's breezy up there, so bring a jacket.

✔ Treat yourself at the Vista Spa (see page 192).

✔ Serenity Bay on Castaway Cay is an adults-only beach where the only noise you'll hear is the lapping of the waves. Lounge chairs and umbrellas available on a first-come, first-served basis.

✔ Cove Cafe (for adults only) is quiet and relaxing until cocktail hour. The area just outside the cafe is "smoking optional."

Bright Idea: If you book a Land/Sea package, we definitely recommend doing the theme parks first and the cruise second for maximum relaxation.

Reader Tip: "The inside cabins don't have a window, so it is very dark with the lights out. I always keep the remote control close by and have the TV station tuned to the live camera at the front of the ship. This not only shows me the time of day, but what the weather is like outside."—contributed by Ray Sharpton

Special Needs on the Disney Cruise Line
(continued)

Size

Check your life jacket once you're in your stateroom on the afternoon of embarkation day. If you need a larger size, ask your stateroom host or hostess prior to the safety drill at 4:00 pm.

Ask your head server for chairs without arms in the main dining areas. Folding chairs are available upon request for the back of the theaters.

Most stateroom bathrooms can be uncomfortable as the sink and toilet are very close together. Elevators are small and often crowded—avoid the midship elevators when possible, as they are very narrow.

Reader Tip: "My husband, who is a very large man, found it better to use a restroom outside our stateroom. He could go into the handicapped stall and it gave him lots more room than trying to use the restroom in our inside stateroom, which was a very tight fit."—contributed by peer reviewer Lori Jones

Visual Impairments

Services for those with visual impairments are limited onboard the cruise ships. All elevators do have Braille buttons; however, **Braille menus are not available**. A limited number of children's books in Braille are available for participants in the Oceaneer Club.

Palo, Spa, and Excursion Reservations

Once your cruise is paid in full, you can access your reservation online, and at specific intervals, you can make your reservations for Palo, the spa, and excursions. Concierge Cruisers: reservations can be made up to 105 days before embarkation. Castaway Club Members: 90 days prior to embarkation. All other sailors: 75 days prior to embarkation.

More Information

Looking for more information? There's a full-length PassPorter guidebook dedicated to the Disney Cruise Line and its ports of call! Visit http://www.passporter.com/dcl/guidebook.htm and see page 431.

We also recommend the unofficial Magical Disney Cruise Guide, which is located online at http://allearsnet.com/cruise/cruise.shtml.

One other web site that is very informative regarding the Disney Cruise Line is http://www.castawayclub.com.

Visit http://www.disneycruise.com or call 888-325-2500.

© MediaMarx, Inc.

A cruiser keeps their personal wheelchair in the hallway to save room in their stateroom

Planning
Special Challenges
Getting There
Staying in Style
Touring
Feasting
Resources
Index

Your Lodging Tips and Stories

My son is on the autism spectrum, and we travel with him at least once a year to Walt Disney World. One of the best things we have done is to stay at the same hotel every time. It takes our son a couple of days to adjust and transition to vacation time. By staying at the same hotel, we've eliminated a lot of that transition time. We love the Walt Disney World Dolphin Resort, and we have stayed there every time we have gone (he's 5 years old and this August will be his seventh trip). He knows the hotel so well and remembers small details about the room or lobby that my husband and I forget. We can normally arrange to get a suite there, which allows my son to have his own room to sleep in. He now associates going to Walt Disney World with the Dolphin and actually calls Walt Disney World the "Dolphin Fish."　　—contributed by Lauren Whitmore

Traveling with an autoimmune condition, such as Lupus (SLE), we have found that staying at the monorail resorts is the way to go. Reactions and/or fatigue can occur at any time, so the monorail allows for quick returns to and from many locations.
　　—contributed by David Kelso

My two youngest sons have ADD and I have been taking them to Walt Disney World at least every year since they were preschoolers. Luckily we discovered Fort Wilderness. It has been an amazing and invaluable find. It's quiet, simple, and old-fashioned "outdoorsy" fun. Even if you don't camp, there are (nice) cabins to rent. Each evening at Fort Wilderness, they have a campfire, marshmallow roast, and a Disney movie. There's a marina to rent watercraft, and you can rent golf carts or bikes as transportation during your stay. Fort Wilderness is a perfect contrast to the fast-paced parks and a wonderful alternative to typical hotel rooms for familes with special needs children. During our last visit, my youngest son commented, "Fort Wilderness is the best place in The World."　　—contributed by Anonymous

I request a handheld shower head and shower chair in a standard (non-handicapped) room when I vacation with my 24-year-old developmentally delayed daughter. That way we can accommodate four guests rather than the two guests that usually fit in a normal handicapped room.　　—contributed by Maggie Ercoli

I recently used the handicap rooms on the Disney ships with a physician medical letter. This allows me room to park my scooter inside the room without walking a long distance down the hallways to the elevator areas. In the staterooms, the walk-in/roll-in shower is so much easier for me to use and it has a fold-down chair to sit in also. It seems so much safer for me to not step over a bath tub for fear of slipping and maybe hurting myself.　　—contributed by Ray Sharpton

I've cruised twice on the Disney Wonder with my ECV and I'll be making it three times the last week of August. I can walk, but not long distances due to arthritis. I've found the category 6 handicapped staterooms are fantastic, large, and easy to maneuver in, with generous balcony space for a wheelchair or my scooter. Unfortunately, the stateroom door rim is high and difficult to get over. Additionally, there are real problems getting out on deck space, through and over doors. For instance, on deck 4 aft, there is a button on the inside of the door, but no button on the outside, so you have to wait for someone to open the door for you. Deck 9, however, is fine. There should be more doors that are accessible.　　—contributed by Anonymous

Touring the Parks

Perhaps you've never considered a trip to the Walt Disney World Resort before—maybe you thought your challenges would be too limiting. We're here to show you how it *can* be done.

Yes, Walt Disney World is a big place, and yes, taking on its theme parks can seem a daunting task. What about the crowds? What about the lines? How can I get around? What if I don't fit in the seat? These are all valid questions and concerns for anyone, but especially for you if you have special health- or lifestyle-related requirements.

We've tried to take the guesswork out of touring the Disney theme parks. We've not only rated each attraction, but we've assessed them for their user-friendliness. We've looked at the size and type of seating, the nature of the attraction, the location of the queues, fear factors, and any special accommodations that the attractions offer. In addition, we've talked to real people who've experienced these rides and shows themselves, to learn firsthand what works and what doesn't. From their shared knowledge, we've also compiled tips and stories that we hope will help enhance your vacation.

In this chapter, we familiarize you with some Disney buzzwords and discuss some key Disney features that can help make your experience more enjoyable. We also talk about your transportation options and other mobility concerns. Finally, we break down the attractions at the four major theme parks, as well as the water parks and other fun places to visit in the Disney universe.

© Linda MacLeod

Monorail over Epcot

Planning

Special Challenges

Getting There

Staying in Style

Touring

Feasting

Resources

Index

Touring With Special Challenges

The single most important thing to remember before you ever enter a theme park is **preparation**, as emphasized in chapters 1 and 3. This is particularly true for travelers who have special challenges. Have a general plan of where you're going and when, how you're going to get there, when and where you're going to eat, and what you're going to do if things don't go as planned.

In practical terms, we strongly recommend you make a **rough schedule** of your days. Include which park(s) you want to visit and which attractions you want to experience. Reading this chapter is the first step. We also urge you to make advance reservations if you plan to dine in the World (see chapter 6) and figure out transportation in advance (see pages 208–210).

To help you get started, here are some Disney **buzzwords** and other terms that you'll find helpful to understand as you read through this chapter:

Admission Media—Park passes (tickets). See pages 214–215 for pass details and rates.

Attraction—An individual ride, show, or exhibit (see page 228).

Baby Care Center—A special facility found in each major park, near the First Aid Station, where you can nurse, feed, and change a baby. It also has most baby care supplies on hand. See page 206. (Note: All restrooms, including men's rooms, have baby changing facilities.)

Cast Member—A Disney employee (identified by their white, oval nametags).

Child Swap—A system available at most rides that allows one adult to wait with a non-rider (or special needs traveler) while the other person rides an attraction (see below).

Rider Switch (also known as "Child Swap")

If someone in your party can't or doesn't want to experience an attraction, but others do, take advantage of Rider Switch. It's available at most of the attractions at Walt Disney World.

Here's how it usually works: The entire party proceeds through the standard queue area. Part of the group experiences the attraction while a companion waits with the individual or service animal who will not ride (due to age/height restrictions, fears, or special needs, etc.). After the first group is done, the person who waited can then proceed to the attraction without going through the queue again, while the others wait.

We've noted attractions where Rider Switch is most useful in our individual attraction descriptions. Ask the first cast member you encounter at the attraction to determine the exact procedures for the specific attraction.

Companion Restroom—A larger-than-average-size restroom that allows visitors of both genders to enter so travelers who need help can be accompanied by a companion. Companion restrooms are indicated on park maps and in the Guidebooks for Guests With Disabilities. Note that not all companion restrooms have changing tables or urinals—very few do, in fact.

ECV—Electric convenience vehicle. A three- or four-wheeled motorized scooter. These can be rented at the theme parks and elsewhere. (See Wheels! on pages 211-213.)

Extra Magic Hour—Disney resort hotel guests can enter designated parks one hour early or stay up to three hours later on certain days (see page 119).

FASTPASS—Disney's timed-ticket system (see page 216).

First Aid Station—See sidebar on next page.

Guest Relations—The primary information counters located at each park.

Lockers—Available near the entrance of each park and the Transportation & Ticket Center. Cost is $5/day plus $2 refundable deposit. Save your receipt for a new locker at another park on the same day.

Queue—A waiting area or line leading to an attraction or character greeting.

Rider Switch—See the sidebar on the previous page.

Restrooms—Available everywhere and indicated on all maps. A limited number of companion restrooms are also available in each theme park (see above).

A typical queue

Seating Types—Different vehicles and shows have different types of seating (see details on page 207).

Single Rider Line—Available only at certain attractions. This system allows riders to bypass the regular standby line if they're willing to ride separately from their group. This works well if the rider is traveling with a special needs traveler who does not wish to experience a ride and doesn't need a companion.

Smoking—Prohibited in most park areas. Designated smoking areas are noted on maps.

Standby Line—The regular queue for an attraction.

Strollers and Wheelchairs—Single and double strollers, as well as manual wheelchairs, are available for rent at all parks and many other locations. (See Wheels! on pages 211-213.) For some special needs children, strollers may be used as wheelchairs with a Guest Assistance Card (see page 10).

Tip Board—Information boards located around the theme parks that give attraction wait times, show times, and opening/closing information.

Times Guide—A sheet listing attraction hours and show times, available freely at the turnstiles and around the theme parks.

Touring With Special Challenges
(continued)

First Aid Stations and Baby Care Centers

First Aid Stations are on hand for you in each of the four theme parks and the two water parks. First Aid Stations are staffed by licensed practical nurses or registered nurses who can assist with most non-emergency needs. (If you have an emergency, contact the nearest cast member or call 911!) They are also able to refrigerate medication or cool-down vests for service animals, and will store small medical equipment that you need to have handy, like nebulizers. The stations also have small private rooms/cubicles with cots if you need to lie down to recover from motion sickness, the heat, etc. These cots are also ideal for changing older children or adults. Most stations have companion restrooms, as well as a TTY phone nearby. The First Aid Stations are located:

✔ Magic Kingdom: To your left as you face the Crystal Palace Restaurant, just off Main Street U.S.A.

✔ Epcot: In the Odyssey Center, between Future World and World Showcase.

✔ Disney-MGM Studios: Near Guest Relations on your left, just after you pass through the turnstiles.

✔ Disney's Animal Kingdom: In Discovery Island, just behind the Creature Comforts shop.

✔ Typhoon Lagoon: Just to the left and slightly behind Leaning Palms.

✔ Blizzard Beach: Near entrance between Lottawatta Lodge and Beach Haus.

Baby Care Centers are located in each of the four theme parks. At the Baby Care Centers, you can change, nurse, or feed your baby; purchase supplies (diapers, baby powder, formula, etc.); pick up lost children; have a quiet snack (you provide the food) with young children; cool down from the heat, etc. Baby Care Centers have a small kitchen where you can heat bottles or food, as well as high chairs, rocking chairs, and a small play/TV area for young children who are waiting for mom. Some stations, like the one in Epcot, have changing tables that can accommodate larger or older children. The Baby Care Centers are located near the First Aid Stations listed above.

Note: Early in 2007, the Magic Kingdom opened the "Wish Lounge" especially for travelers vacationing with a wish-granting organization. Inquire at the First Aid Station regarding access.

The changing room at Magic Kingdom's Baby Care Center

Attraction Seating Types

To experience an attraction at Walt Disney World, you may have to walk, stand, fasten a seat belt, wear a harness, etc. We describe the basic terms here so you understand them as you read our individual attraction details:

Bench Seat—A seat with no arms that may fit anywhere from two to 20+ people in the row. Bench seats may or may not have backs. Examples are Kilimanjaro Safaris and Country Bear Jamboree (with backs) and Flights of Wonder (without backs). Some bench seats have grooves or low handlebars.

Bench seats with backs at Beauty and the Beast

Harness—A padded mechanism that comes down over your shoulders to keep you in place in your vehicle. Examples: Rock 'n' Roller Coaster and Mission: SPACE.

Low/high lap bars—A low bar is one that is pressed into your lap to restrict your movement. A high bar rests (more gently) on your lap or may not even be lowered at all. Examples: Big Thunder Mountain Railroad (low lap bar) and Haunted Mansion (high lap bar).

The overhead harness at Stitch's Great Escape!

A low lap bar on Big Thunder Mountain

Seat belt—Lap or lap-and-shoulder belt very similar to car seat belts. Examples: Twilight Zone Tower of Terror, Dinosaur, and Dumbo The Flying Elephant have lap belts; some Test Track seats have lap-and-shoulder belts.

Small space—This term means different things to different folks, but basically, it indicates space is limited in some manner. Examples: Mad Hatter's Tea Party, Dumbo The Flying Elephant, and Astro Orbiter.

A lap seat belt on TriceraTop Spin

Standing—An attraction that requires you to stand for a significant portion of the presentation. Some 360-degree movies that require standing offer "lean rails" for you to rest against. Examples: Reflections of China and O Canada!

Lean rails for standing at Reflections of China

Theater seating at One Man's Dream

Theater seating—The type of seating you would find in a movie theater. Seat sizes vary in width and leg room. Wheelchair/ECV areas are provided in attractions with theater seating. Examples: Honey I Shrunk the Audience and Mickey's PhilharMagic.

For more information, see Wheels! on page 211.

Getting Around the Resort and Parks

We've said it before, but it bears repeating—Walt Disney World is *huge*! The entire resort—theme parks, water parks, hotels, the whole works— encompasses 40+ square miles! That's a lot of ground to cover, so be sure you're prepared for some major walking or wheeling before you go.

Bright Idea: To reach the Magic Kingdom, be sure to take the Disney resort bus. You will be dropped off much closer than if you parked your car.

Just how you get around the World really depends on your individual situation. Those reliant on wheelchairs or ECVs, for example, may find having a **vehicle at your disposal** to be indispensable. Driving yourself from place to place allows you the freedom to come and go on your own schedule—especially important if you're traveling with an infant or with someone who tires easily. Having your own vehicle (your personal car or a rental) also affords you the ability to venture off Disney property easily—perhaps to buy more formula and diapers or special dietary items, or to attend religious services. Should you decide to rely on Disney's complimentary transportation, however, here's what's available:

© Debra Martin Koma

Bus transportation is available within Walt Disney World every 15 to 30 minutes. Bus destinations are posted on signs as well as on bus marquees (illuminated signs atop each bus). Buses can accommodate a wheelchair/ECV as long as it will fit on a standard bus lift (32" x 48"). Buses can hold up to two non-collapsed wheelchairs/ECVs—if you can fold your wheelchair and sit in a regular seat, more chairs can be accommodated. If you have a longer or wider wheelchair than will fit on the lift, or if you have three or more wheelchairs/ECVs in your party, contact the front desk at your Disney resort for travel options. Bus drivers will assist you in boarding the bus through the rear entrance and ensure that your chair is secured appropriately. There are currently three types of wheelchair/ECV access in use on Disney buses: 1. The oldest buses have stairs that convert to form a lift (see photo). These are a tight fit for most wheelchairs/ECVs,

Our friend Nancy Tynes, using a Disney bus lift

and oversized scooters/ECVs will not fit. The wheelchair/ECV user backs onto the platform and sets the brakes. The front of the ramp folds up so you don't roll off, and then it rises to floor level. If you are in a wheelchair pushed by someone else, they back onto the platform pulling the wheelchair toward them, and they stay on the ramp, too. 2. Some buses have a ramp that slides out of an enclosure in the base of the bus floor. The wheelchair/ECV user backs onto this ramp into the bus. 3. The newest buses have a ramp that flips outward. These ramps are wider and are also found on "kneeling buses," which allow them to go down lower, making the ramp less steep and easier for wheelchair/ECV users to back onto. These buses that "kneel" actually dip down in front, too, making it easier for everyone to climb aboard the stairs. Strollers are permitted on all types of buses, but they should be folded prior to boarding, unless being used as a wheelchair for a special needs child.

Important Note: Disney bus drivers are required to board passengers in wheelchairs/ECVs first. Be sure to wait in the designated wheelchair queue, or wait in a place where the driver can see you. Wheelchairs/ECVs will be the last off the bus.

Monorail transportation (a futuristic, elevated railway with a single track) is available between the Transportation & Ticket Center (TTC), the Magic Kingdom, and Epcot from about 7:00 am until 1.5 hours after each park closes. Service to the resorts is available until two hours after the Magic Kingdom closes. The resort monorail services the Contemporary, Polynesian, and Grand Floridian resorts. Monorails are wheelchair/ECV accessible, but there's a small step up from the platform to the train car. A monorail pilot will place a ramp on the platform so you can wheel into the accessible car (which is appropriately marked). Note that the ramps leading to the monorail stations at the Magic Kingdom, Epcot, and TTC are quite steep—it may be difficult to push a manual wheelchair here (Epcot's and

Taking a stroller on the monorail

Contemporary's stations have an elevator). Strollers are also permitted on the monorail, and they do not need to be collapsed. Note that side-by-side double strollers fit best in the wheelchair-accessible cars. Ask a cast member if you need assistance.

Important Note: The ramp for boarding the monorail car may be steep for your ECV/wheelchair. Ask the monorail cast member to be sure the exit doors on the opposite side of the monorail car are closed, in case you require a lot of acceleration to board.

Boat service is available in a number of locations around Walt Disney World. All wheelchairs, ECVs, and strollers can be accommodated unless otherwise noted below.

The Magic Kingdom Ferry takes you between the TTC and the Magic Kingdom. Small motor launches connect the Magic Kingdom area resorts (Disney's Fort Wilderness, Contemporary, Wilderness Lodge/Villas, Grand Floridian, and Polynesian). Wheelchairs and strollers must be folded up and carried onboard. No ECVs are allowed. You must step up or down into the boat (depending on water levels).

Larger motor cruisers run from the Magic Kingdom to Fort Wilderness and the Wilderness Lodge. ECVs can be accommodated on motor cruisers unless the water levels are too low.

The Disney Vacation Club and Port Orleans Ferry (think extra large pontoon boat) has two routes—one run connects Old Key West and Saratoga Springs to Downtown Disney; the other run connects Port Orleans Resort to Downtown Disney. These boats accommodate strollers. Ask if wheelchairs should be folded. A maximum of two electric vehicles can board because of weight, but ask about ECVs. Transfer out of the chair is not normally required.

Friendship boat in the World Showcase Lagoon at Epcot

Friendship boats operate in the Epcot area. One run goes from Epcot, BoardWalk, Yacht & Beach Club, Swan & Dolphin, then Disney-MGM Studios (and also does this route in reverse). The other Friendship routes are inside Epcot between two areas of World Showcase. Friendships are usually accessible with normal water levels, however when levels are higher or lower than usual, it may not be possible to board a wheelchair or ECV. In these cases, signs are posted on the docks.

Walking is by far the most common way to get around the parks themselves. There's very little in the way of intra-park transportation. Be sure to bring comfortable, well-broken-in shoes if you're going to be hoofing it.

Getting Around the Resort and Parks
(continued)

Parking at Walt Disney World

Parking lots are huge, and during peak times of the year, they can fill up. The rows are very, very long, and unless you have a handicapped parking permit, you won't have a choice of where to park. Cast members direct cars very systematically to an exact space. Each lot is assigned a name, and all rows are numbered, so be sure to write down your lot and row numbers before leaving the area! Tram service is provided from parking areas to the park.

Bright Idea: Take a photo of the row number with your digital or cell phone camera, or leave yourself a voice mail with the location of your car.

Parking is free if you're staying at a Disney resort or have an Annual Pass; otherwise it's $10/car or $11/camper or RV. If you have a disabled parking permit, ask the cast member where disabled parking is located. (If you don't have a disabled permit but are traveling with a wheelchair/ECV, ask the cast member for the best place to park.) In the theme parks, follow the blue line painted on the road to the disabled parking area.

Parking lot trams are used in the four major theme parks but do not service the disabled parking area. Even though the designated disabled parking area is the closest parking to the park entrance, it still may be quite a way to the actual turnstiles, not to mention the wheelchair/stroller rental location, so use the passenger drop-off area instead if you're able (follow signs to the drop-off location). If you have an easily folded wheelchair and can climb in unassisted, the tram may be a better option for you than parking in the disabled parking area. Note that cast members *cannot* assist you in boarding, however. A limited number of courtesy wheelchairs (designated by blue flags, backs, and seats) are sometimes available in the disabled parking area, but we've seldom seen them as the day goes on. If you're taking the tram from the parking lot, you'll need to step up into it and sit on hard bench seats. Be sure that small children are seated in the middle of tram benches and that strollers are collapsed. The trams will take you near the entrance of the park (or, in the case of the Magic Kingdom, to the TTC), but you'll still need to walk a bit to get to the turnstiles and stroller/wheelchair rental spot. When departing

the theme park, you reverse the procedure, returning to the parking lot via tram again. There is only one tram stop per section, so be sure to listen carefully when your section and row are announced. Note that there's no tram service at Downtown Disney, Blizzard Beach, Typhoon Lagoon, or Wide World of Sports.

© Deb Wills

A Walt Disney World tram

Wheels!

The wheel: Whatever did we do before its invention? Wheels make getting around so much easier, particularly for those of us with small children or stamina or mobility issues. Whether you need a stroller, a wheelchair, or an ECV to help you navigate, here's what you need to know about wheels in the Walt Disney World Resort.

Any wheeled vehicle you use to get around Disney has to have **at least three wheels**. Why? Disney's policy is that guest-operated, two-wheeled vehicles, no matter the type, are not permitted on the transportation systems or inside the parks, including Downtown Disney and Disney's Wide World of Sports. This is primarily directed at the use of Segway Human Transport Vehicles (which guests are not permitted to use anywhere on Disney property, except during Disney-monitored tours) but also applies to bicycles and scooters. For safety reasons, two-wheeled vehicles are only permitted on established bike paths or other areas that allow the use of recreational bicycles. In most circumstances, maneuverability is difficult, and others may not easily see or avoid these vehicles, creating a potential safety concern.

Various other options exist for those who need to use a **wheelchair or ECV/scooter**. At the theme parks and Downtown Disney, you can bring your own or rent one on a first-come, first-served basis. In addition, several medical supply companies in the Orlando area rent these types of vehicles—they even will deliver them to your resort, with Disney's full cooperation.

The main advantage to **bringing your own** stroller or wheelchair/ECV is that you can keep it with you. You'll be able to use it both at the parks and the resorts, getting to and from your transportation, plus you'll have it with you at the airport or train station if that's how you're traveling. Note that you may be able to rent a complimentary wheelchair at your resort, for a refundable ($250–$300) deposit. See chapter 4 for more details.

If you choose to **rent from a Disney theme park**, consider this:

1. Disney only has a limited number of strollers/wheelchairs/ECVs for rent each day, and you're not able to reserve these in advance. If you get to the theme park too late (which could mean mid-morning), you may be out of luck and not get a stroller/ wheelchair/ECV.
2. Disney rental ECVs have four wheels and may seem cumbersome and low-powered to people accustomed to riding a more maneuverable three-wheeled scooter.
3. You will only have use of the wheels while you're in the theme park, which means you'll need to walk to the bus/tram stop or to your car and then from the bus stop to your room at the resort or hotel.

If you decide to rent from one of the Disney theme parks, however, here are the current prices at the time of writing:

Single Stroller	$10 per day (for one child 38 inches and 50 pounds or under)
Double Stroller	$18 per day (for two children 38 inches and 50 pounds each or under)
Wheelchair	$10 per day
ECV	$35 per day plus $5 refundable deposit. You must be 18 years old or older to rent ECVs.

Wheels!
(continued)

If you plan to visit more than one park in a day, **hang on to your receipt**. When you get to the second park, show your receipt and you can get another stroller/wheelchair/ECV, if one is available, at no additional charge. When you turn in your wheels, you can request a transfer wheelchair to get to your car.

You also have the option of renting a stroller, wheelchair, or ECV for multiple days—Disney calls it a **"Length of Stay Rental."** You'll pay once for as many days as you want, plus you'll get a small (10%) discount. Then when you return the next day, just show your receipt to the cast member and you'll be shown through the queue with little or no wait. The **"Length of Stay" rentals do not guarantee** a stroller, wheelchair, or ECV. (Length of Stay rentals may not be available during peak seasons.)

Bright Idea: "Express Stroller Rental" is sometimes offered outside the turnstiles at park opening—look for the sandwich board sign and cast member for quick stroller rentals without waiting in the standard line.

You can rent strollers, wheelchairs, and ECVs from the following locations:

Magic Kingdom: Rentals are located to your right, inside the entrance turnstiles. Wheelchairs can also be rented at Mickey's Gift Station at the TTC. Replacement strollers and wheelchairs can be obtained at the Tomorrowland Arcade, Tinker Bell's Treasures, and Frontier Trading Post. Replacement strollers are also available to railroad passengers at stations of the Walt Disney World Railroad. Rentals are located under the train station.

Epcot: Wheelchairs can be rented at The Gift Spot, on your right just before the main entrance; wheelchair/ECV and stroller rentals are at the shop to the left of Spaceship Earth and at the International Gateway. Replacements can be obtained at the Glas und Porzellan shop in the Germany Pavilion in the World Showcase.

Disney-MGM Studios: Rentals are located on your right after you pass through the turnstiles at Oscar's Super Station. Replacements can be obtained at the Writer's Stop at the end of Commissary Lane. Just show your receipt. Replacement strollers can also be obtained at Tatooine Traders.

Disney's Animal Kingdom: Wheelchairs can be rented at The Outpost shop on the left *before* you enter the park. Wheelchair, stroller, and ECV rentals are on your right just after you pass through the turnstiles. Replacement strollers can be obtained at Creature Comforts and Mombasa Marketplace. Complimentary loaner strollers are provided for all at the Conservation Station as you exit the Wildlife Express train.

Wheelchairs and electric scooters are also now available for rent from the surrey bike rental desk at the **Boardwalk Resort**. Scooters and wheelchairs can be rented for 24 hours or more, and can be taken on all the Disney transportation. They are available right at the surrey bike rental counter and can be reserved prior to your arrival by calling 407-938-0349. They will deliver right to any Disney resort at no charge. Rental prices are $30 plus tax for each 24-hour period for the smaller electric scooters (up to 300 lbs.), and $40 plus tax for the larger (prices subject to change). Wheelchairs and scooters are also available for the Disney Cruise Line and are subject to an additional delivery charge. For more information or to make a reservation, visit http://www.buenavistascooters.com.

Wheels!
(continued)

You can also rent strollers, wheelchairs, and ECVs at **Downtown Disney**. Charges for rentals here vary slightly from the theme parks:

Single Stroller (no double strollers)	$10 per day plus credit card imprint.
Wheelchairs	$10 per day plus credit card imprint.
ECVs	$35 + $5 refundable deposit. An imprint is taken of a major credit card; if you fail to return the ECV, your credit card will be charged for its replacement. You must be 18 years or older to rent an ECV.

You can rent strollers, wheelchairs, and ECVs from Guest Relations at the **Marketplace**, located near Once Upon a Toy. You can rent single strollers and wheelchairs (not ECVs) from Guest Relations at Downtown Disney's West Side, located near the bridge that connects the West Side with Pleasure Island.

Renting a stroller/wheelchair/ECV from a **local company** means that you'll have the wheels with you for the duration of your vacation. For about the same cost per day as Disney, these companies will not only rent you the chair/ECV, but will even deliver and pick up the wheels to your requested destination. There are many vendors located in the Orlando area (check the local phone book)—here are a few vendors for which we have firsthand knowledge:

© Deb Wills

Our friend Linda used an ECV to tour the parks comfortably while recovering from a back injury

For Wheelchairs/ ECVs:	Care Medical: 407-856-2273 or 800-741-2282 Walker Medical: 407-518-6000 or 888-SCOOTER (726-6837) Apria: 407-291-2229 or 800-338-1640 Randy's Mobility: 863-679-1550
For ECVs ONLY:	Scootarama: 877-RENT-ECV (736-8328)
For Strollers:	Family Rentals: 407-909-0042 Medical Travel (Special Needs Strollers): 800-778-7953

Other Wheels

Shoes with wheels on them (most common brand name is "Heelys") are popular these days with kids, but Disney's official policy is that they're not allowed in the theme parks. Wagons, skateboards, scooters, inline skates, rolling suitcases, backpacks with or without wheels larger than 24" long x 15" wide x 18" high, and any trailer that is pushed or towed by an ECV, wheelchair, or stroller, are also prohibited. Coolers with wheels cannot be rolled through the park, but can be stored in a locker.

Park Passes

When it comes to park admission, it's safest to budget **$76**/day for ages 10 + (**$64**/kids ages 3-9), the single-day/single-park base price for the major parks (based on the last price in increase in August 2007). The "Magic Your Way" multiday passes emphasize flexibility and savings, so you can do more at a lower price. Here's the deal on passes (prices include tax):

■ **Magic Your Way Tickets**	*Actual 2007-2008 Rates*

Magic Your Way tickets are available for 1-10 days. Guests can stick to basic admission or add one or more options at the time of purchase (see explanations below). Magic Your Way replaces single-day passes and all varieties of Park Hopper passes. A Magic Your Way **Base Ticket** *($76-$240) is good for entry to a single major park (Magic Kingdom, Epcot, Disney-MGM Studios, or Disney's Animal Kingdom) for each day of the ticket. Multiday Base Tickets bring substantial discounts (see chart on the next page), so it pays to buy your admission all at once. Multiday Base Tickets expire 14 days after the first use, but they do not have to be used on consecutive days. Buy only as much admission as you'll actually need for your visit to Disney. Note that multiday Base Tickets are imprinted with the guest's name, so they are not transferable. The* **Park Hopping** *option (add $47.93) lets you visit more than one major park on the same day, for the length of your ticket. Available with any Base Ticket, this option is costly unless you spend four or more days at the parks, but it's indispensible if you plan to visit all four parks in fewer than four days, and it can maximize the enjoyment of any longer stay. The Magic Your Way* **Water Parks Fun and More** *option (add $53.25) adds a limited number of single-day, single-park admissions for the minor parks (Blizzard Beach, Typhoon Lagoon, Pleasure Island, DisneyQuest, and Wide World of Sports) to any Base Ticket. Each Magic Plus option is worth $10-$38, depending on where you use it. Purchase this feature with 1- to 3-day Base Tickets and you receive three Plus Options, 4- to 5-day Base Tickets receive four options, 6-day Base tickets receive five options, 7- to 10-day Base Tickets receive six options. Regardless of how many Plus options you receive, the cost to add this feature is always the same. As long as you make a minimum of two visits to the more costly minor parks, you'll get your money's worth. The* **Premium** *option (add $101) is a combination of a Base Ticket, Park Hopping, and Magic Plus options (but at no additional savings). The* **No Expiration** *option (add $15-$180) is best suited for those who plan to save the unused portion of a multiday ticket for a future vacation. The 14-day life span of a Base Ticket is generally enough for any one vacation. Prices for the various tickets are listed in the comparison chart on the next page.*

■ **Annual Pass**	*Actual 2007-2008 Rates*

Unlimited admission to the four major parks for a full year, plus special privileges. An Annual Pass ($477/$421) costs less than two 3-day Magic Your Way Base Tickets with Park Hopping. Annual Passes also kick in great discounts on resorts (based on availability) and other privileges, such as a newsletter and events. There are also annual passes for the water parks ($106/$86), Pleasure Island ($60), DisneyQuest ($95/$76), and water parks plus DisneyQuest ($137/$105). You cannot share an Annual Pass (or any other multiday pass).

■ **Premium Annual Pass**	*Actual 2007-2008 Rates*

A Premium Annual Pass ($617/$543) offers the same privileges as the regular Annual Pass plus unlimited admission to the minor parks (including DisneyQuest) for $140 more. Five minor park visits cover the added cost. A Premium Annual Pass costs less than two 3-day Premium Magic Your Way tickets with a No Expiration option, and it is good for a full year.

Special Needs Admissions: No special tickets, discounted or otherwise, are available for those with special needs. Kids under 3 are admitted into the parks for free (and get a free ride if the ride allows someone that small). Anyone 10 and over is considered an adult in the eyes of the ticket booth. Passes for kids ages 3–9 cost up to 20% less than adult passes. Also, the option-filled pass you buy for yourself is usually more than your child needs, especially if you use childcare programs.

Old Ticket Media: Prior to "Magic Your Way," Disney issued "Park Hopper" passes. If you have an old Park Hopper with unused days on it, you may use those days. (You can no longer upgrade ticket media if it has been used.)

Upgrades and Exchanges: Within 14 days of your pass's first use, you can upgrade or apply the unused value to a better pass. Visit Guest Relations (parks) or Lobby Concierge (resorts) for details.

Advance Purchase Discounts: Discounts of between $2 and $19 are possible on tickets of five days or longer duration, if you purchase them in advance at Disney's web site or include them in the cost of a vacation package. This is significantly less than the value of advance purchase discounts available in the past.

AAA: Members can expect some sort of discount (historically 5%) on some passes. You must purchase tickets directly from AAA to get the discount.

Florida Resident Discounts: Florida Resident Seasonal Passes work like Annual Passes, but with blackout dates in busy seasons, plus some special deals for residents only.

Disney Vacation Club Discounts: Discounts of about $100 are available on Annual Passes for members of the immediate family residing in the same household. See page 186.

Military Discounts: Discounts of roughly 7%–8% may be available on admission—check with your Exchange shop or MWR (Morale, Welfare, and Recreation) office. Some offices may need to preorder your tickets, so we advise you check with them well in advance. Keep an ear out for special programs for active military personnel—in recent years, Disney offered all active military personnel a free five-day park hopper, with discounted admission for up to five family members or friends. To check on current specials and buy tickets, phone 407-824-1403 or visit Shades of Green (see page 183) upon arrival.

Online Ticket Brokers—These folks sell legitimate, unused tickets at good rates. Try http://www.mapleleaftickets.com (800-841-2837). Be wary of others hawking tickets, including eBay and timeshares.

Pass Comparison Chart: Options and prices for your number of days in the parks.

Pass Type Days:	1	2	3	4	5	6	7	8	9	10	11	12	13	14
Base (single day/park)	$76	$148	$216	$225	$229	$231	$233	$236	$238	$240				
Base + No Expiration		$164	$238	$274	$293	$300	$334	$374	$402	$431				
Base + Park Hopping	$123	$196	$264	$274	$277	$279	$281	$283	$285	$288				
Base + Park Hop. + No Exp.		$212	$285	$322	$341	$348	$382	$422	$451	$479				
Base + Water Parks & More	$129	$201	$269	$279	$282	$284	$286	$289	$291	$293				
Base + Water Parks + No. Exp.		$217	$291	$327	$346	$354	$388	$427	$456	$485				
Premium	$177	$249	$317	$327	$330	$332	$334	$337	$339	$341				
Premium + No Exp.		$265	$339	$375	$394	$402	$436	$475	$504	$533				
Annual Pass										$477	⟶			
Premium Annual Pass											$617	⟶		

For more details and updates, visit http://www.allears.net/pl/ticket.htm.

Planning · Special Challenges · Getting There · Staying in Style · Touring · Feasting · Resources · Index

Touring Advice

In interviewing fellow Disney vacationers, we heard several recurrent themes as to what makes touring Walt Disney World with special challenges most enjoyable. We'd like to share some **hard-earned advice** with you in the hopes that it will make your trip easier and more pleasurable.

1. Plan and be prepared! Visit http://www.disneyworld.com (look for the **Guests With Disabilities** link) or write ahead to Disney to obtain copies of the current guidemaps and the current Guests With Disabilities Guides (there's one for each of the major parks) so that you're familiar with procedures.

2. Know the **abilities and limitations** of everyone in your group, including yourself. Don't push, don't try to experience everything—because you just can't do it. Take midday breaks.

3. Take advantage of **Disney's programs** that help you save time and waiting, such as Extra Magic Hour, FASTPASS, and Rider Switch.

4. Be sure everyone in your party knows the "**rules of the road**." Once you are seated in a ride, you <u>must stay seated</u> until the ride ends—you cannot leave a moving vehicle. When you enter a theater, sit at the end of the row in case you need to make an early exit from the building.

5. Don't be afraid to **ask a cast member for help**. They are there to make your experience the best it can be and are more than willing to offer advice and aid. While they can't physically assist you, they can suggest the best ways for you to experience attractions and can point you in the direction of additional aids, such as special parade viewing areas.

Disney's FASTPASS

Just what is this FASTPASS you've been hearing so much about? For the Disney-goer with special challenges, it is probably the single most important program that Disney offers in its theme parks. FASTPASS is basically a timed-ticket system that allows you to wait in line "virtually," while you go off shopping or eating or riding something else. It works like this: Insert your park admission pass into a FASTPASS machine located near the attraction. Your FASTPASS pops out, marked with the time later in the day that you can return to ride/experience the show, bypassing the regular, or "standby" line. You can go about your business until your time "window" opens, thereby avoiding long waits in line. You generally can hold only one FASTPASS at a time, but check the FASTPASS itself, which will tell you how soon you can obtain another. This feature is especially attractive to those who can't tolerate standing in one place for long periods, such as children with ADHD or those with chronic fatigue. One of the best things about FASTPASS (besides how it eliminates wait times!) is that it's free to all Disney park guests. We've indicated which attractions have FASTPASS throughout this chapter and encourage you to take advantage of it as much as possible. FASTPASS is sometimes not used in the off-season or on slow days, but during busy seasons, FASTPASSes for certain attractions can be gone as early as noon!

Character Meet and Greets

One of the highlights of a visit to Disney World is **meeting the characters** you've seen so often on TV and movie screens. But getting to meet the characters isn't always so easy, especially for children with special challenges who may not be able to tolerate waiting in long lines for a variety of reasons. As one mom writes: "What to do with a kid who is absolutely nuts over Disney (typical for autism spectrum disorder children), but who also finds the sounds, smells, touches, and inescapable crowds about as appealing as dental surgery?" Here are some tips to minimize wait times for those popular characters:

1. If there is a particular character you want to meet, speak to a cast member at Guest Relations when you enter the park. They have a **special number** to call to determine if, when, and where specific characters will appear.

2. Check the **times guides** for special character greeting times in each theme park. Arrive at the designated spot a few minutes early to get in the front of the queue if possible. If you have several members in your party, perhaps one can wait in line while another walks around with the impatient, tired, or fidgety child.

3. If you're waiting at a **character greeting location**, speak to the cast member handling the character. They may, at their discretion, choose to help you through the queue more quickly. They may also alert the character to your child's special requirements.

4. **Be flexible**. If your child is unable to wait for Pooh or Mickey today, perhaps trying again later or another day will make all the difference. Also, if your child gets to the front of the line and realizes that the *big* Tigger standing in front them is too intimidating, do not force them to embrace the character. Try again later or another day. In fact, some children are satisfied to see their favorite characters from a distance. Also, realize that characters are on a schedule. Mickey may need a "cheese break" while you are in line. Cast members will tell you how long it will be until the character returns.

5. Visit a **show or parade** that features the character(s) your child wants to see, rather than waiting in a long line.

6. Take your child to a **character meal**. In this setting, a variety of Disney characters come around to your table and spend several minutes, giving you their undivided attention. Keep in mind that character meals in the resorts tend to be less hectic than those in the theme parks. Characters at these special meals also have handlers. Speak to the handler about your special traveler's challenges—they will then be able to alert the character.

Adults, these characters are there for you, too! Don't be shy or embarrassed about having your photo with your lifelong favorite Mr. Smee, Mickey, or Chip and Dale.

You can **learn more about Disney characters**, including how to find them, meet them, photograph them, and get their autograph, in *PassPorter's Disney Character Yearbook* e-book (see details on page 432).

Understanding and Using the Attraction Descriptions and Ratings

If you've used a PassPorter guidebook before, you know that our custom-designed attraction charts include background, tips, restrictions, queue conditions, accessibility details, enhanced ratings, and much more. We use a special attraction chart to organize all this information, allowing you to find what you need for touring the theme parks at a glance.

Description Key

Icons[3]	Ratings[4]

1 Attraction Name [D-3[2]]	FP	🕴	#	#	#
Description offering an attraction overview, what to expect with a focus on how the queue, waiting area, and the attraction itself can affect your special challenges. We also offer our suggestions for the best seating/viewing/riding, tips, and height/age restrictions. Tips for each special challenge, when available, follow letter icons (see page 8). We also include peer reviewer tips and favorites, as they relate to their special needs, where appropriate.	Type[5]
	Scope[5]
	Ages[6]
	Thrill Factor[7]
	Avg. Wait[7]
	Duration[7]

[1] Each chart has an empty **checkbox** in the upper left corner—use it to check off the attractions you want to visit (before you go) or those you visited during your trip.

[2] **Map coordinates** are presented as a letter and a number (i.e., A-5). Match up the coordinates on the park's map for the attraction's location within the park.

[3] Icons indicate when an attraction has FASTPASS (**FP**) or a height/age restriction (🕴).

[4] Our **ratings** are shown on the far right end in the three boxes, on a scale of 1 (poor) to 10 (don't miss!). The first is co-author **Deb Wills'** rating, the second is co-author **Deb Koma's** rating, and the third is our **Readers'** ratings. We offer our personal ratings to show how opinions vary, even between people like us who like many of the same things. Use our ratings as a point of reference. For example, we both love the details and the little things that make Walt Disney World unique, and we are fondly nostalgic over the oldest attractions. But where Deb Wills dislikes spinning, gets dizzy over inversions, and is sensitive to overly loud noises, Deb Koma enjoys all the coasters and thrill rides and finds herself drawn repeatedly to rides that shake her up and turn her upside-down.

[5] The boxes on the right below the numeric ratings give basic information. The first box is **attraction type**. The second box is always **attraction scope**, which we rate with the guest with special needs in mind as follows:

     E-Ticket   A major crowd-pleaser—don't miss it! (Expect long lines.)
     D-Ticket   Excellent, try not to miss it.
     C-Ticket   A good attraction enjoyed by most.
     B-Ticket   OK, but don't fret if you don't have time for it.
     A-Ticket   A simple diversion, often overlooked.

[6] **Age-appropriate ratings**. For example, we may say "All Ages" when we feel everyone, from infant on up, will get something out of the experience. More common is "Ages 4 & up" or "Ages 8 & up" for attractions we think will be best appreciated by vacationers who are at least 4 or 8. This is *only* our guideline and not a Disney rule.

[7] **Thrill/scare factor**, **average wait**, and **duration** follow the age ratings, though we eliminate these if they don't apply or expand them if deserving. We did our best to format this information so you can understand it without having to check this key, too!

Magic Kingdom

For many, the **Magic Kingdom**, which opened on October 1, 1971, is Walt Disney World. With its gleaming Cinderella Castle as a focal point, the theme park is known for both its gentle kid-pleasing rides, like Dumbo The Flying Elephant, and its high-energy thrill attractions, such as Space Mountain.

This dream-made-real is home to **seven themed lands** and scores of attractions that appeal to all ages, covering 107 sprawling acres. With all there is to experience in this wonderland, the thought of trying to navigate this theme park can be daunting, especially for people who must deal with special challenges. But armed with a little knowledge and aided by careful planning, a trip to the Magic Kingdom will make you feel like a little kid again.

Guest Relations is located in two spots in the Magic Kingdom: on your right before you pass through the turnstiles and on your left as you enter the park, in the City Hall building. This is where you can obtain current guidemaps, times guides, and Guidebooks for Guests With Disabilities; obtain a Guest Assistance Card (see pages 10–11); rent hearing or vision devices; obtain the current schedule for sign language-interpreted attractions; and ask any special questions you might have. There is also a TTY phone here.On Mondays and Thursdays from 9:20 am to 9:40 am, a Sign Language Interpreter is usually available at Guest Relations to answer your questions, too. Wheelchair/ECV users enter City Hall via one of the ramps on either side of the building.

To help you plan your days, you should know that the Magic Kingdom is **laid out like a wheel**, with the hub centered directly in front of Cinderella Castle (see map on pages 222–223). Pathways act as the spokes leading to the following themed areas:

Main Street, U.S.A.—A glimpse of a younger, simpler America. Many of the shops lining Main Street, U.S.A. are interconnected—you could walk or wheel its length without going outdoors. Folks using wheelchairs/ECVs or strollers, however, may find the shops hard to navigate, as they are cluttered with merchandise displays, not to mention lots of browsing shoppers. Unless you're trying to stay out of the weather, you'll usually find it easier to move down Main Street's sidewalks or the street itself. Beware of the grooves and trolley rails in the street, which can wreak havoc with a stroller or wheelchair/ECV.

AMBIENCE

PARK LAYOUT AND NAVIGATION

Planning

Special Challenges

Getting There

Staying in Style

Touring

Feasting

Resources

Index

More
Magic Kingdom

Adventureland—Home to attractions that tap into the adventurer in all of us, including the famous ground-breaking Audio-Animatronics of Pirates of the Caribbean and the Jungle Cruise. This land has several wide open spaces that are easy to navigate, although its outdoor plaza shops are difficult to get around. If you're in a wheelchair, be aware of the ramp leading to Adventureland from the hub—its incline is misleading and may require that someone push you or that you enter Adventureland from Frontierland via Liberty Square.

Frontierland—The spirit of the Old West lives on in attractions such as Big Thunder Mountain Railroad and Splash Mountain. The streets of the frontier get very congested, though, particularly around parade times, so you may find it hard to pass through if you're on wheels. One other word of warning—the gulls in this area have gotten particularly aggressive. Beware if you have a fear of birds—or if you just want to keep your french fries safe!

Liberty Square—Colonial times revisited via a trip on an old river boat and a stay with the presidents of our nation. It's fairly easy to move about outdoors, but Liberty Square's shops are a problem with narrow entryways and cramped quarters.

Fantasyland—A child's dream come true, with attractions featuring such popular childhood characters as Peter Pan, Snow White, and Winnie the Pooh. Fantasyland crowds can be extremely difficult to navigate, even if you're on foot. Crowds here are worst on Saturdays and Sundays.

Mickey's Toontown Fair—A kid-sized place that allows youngsters to visit with their favorite Disney characters. Geared to the grade-school set and younger, the streets here are fairly easy to get around, although getting through some of the structures can be difficult if crowds are thick.

Tomorrowland—A look at the future through retro eyes, featuring thrills like Space Mountain and Stitch's Great Escape! This very popular area is most congested around Buzz Lightyear's Space Ranger Spin entrance and over near Space Mountain.

⚠ Wait Times

Each park has a tip board in a central location that tells you approximate wait times for each attraction. A cast member stationed there updates the board frequently, but sometimes the tip board, or even the wait times signs posted at individual attractions (see photo to right) may not be accurate. This happens for a variety of reasons, including minor problems that actually shut the attraction down temporarily. If you want to verify the expected wait time, don't hesitate to ask the cast member at the attraction's entrance.

© Deb Wills

Snow White wait time

Getting to the Magic Kingdom

The Magic Kingdom attracts locals and tends to be **busiest on Saturday and Sunday**. To avoid crowds as much as possible, we suggest going on a Monday. Tuesday and Wednesday may be good days, too, depending on the Extra Magic Hour schedule (see page 119). The most popular attractions, like Space Mountain, are best if done first thing in the early morning to avoid long lines. Parents of young children are better off doing Fantasyland or Toontown Fair first—they get busier later in the day. Go to big thrill rides during parades. Shop in the afternoon to avoid crowds. Remember to check the tip board on Main Street for ride wait times. And most importantly, remember to take breaks throughout the day and drink plenty of water.

By Car—For many special needs travelers, it may be more convenient to travel by car. Take I-4 to exit 67 (West) or exit 62 (East) and continue about 4 miles to the toll plaza. All-day parking is $10 (free to Disney resort hotel guests and Annual Passholders), and the pass is valid at other Disney parks' lots on the same day. Cast members will direct you to the accessible parking area if you need it.

By Monorail—From the Contemporary, Polynesian, or Grand Floridian resorts, take the monorail directly to the park. Each of these deluxe resorts have elevators that will take you to the monorail platforms. If you're using a wheelchair or ECV, cast members will assist you in boarding. From Epcot, you'll have to take the monorail to the TTC and transfer to the Magic Kingdom express monorail or the ferry boat. There are accessible ramps for boarding each of these transportation methods.

By Boat—From the TTC, a ferry will take you over to the Magic Kingdom. The Polynesian, Grand Floridian, Fort Wilderness, and the Wilderness Lodge & Villas also have motor launch service to the Magic Kingdom. The motor launches used on the Grand Floridian/Polynesian route and occasionally used on the Ft. Wilderness/Wilderness Lodge route cannot accommodate ECVs, and wheelchairs must be folded. Use available buses or the monorail instead. Motor cruisers are used on the Fort Wilderness/Wilderness Lodge to Magic Kingdom route—wheelchairs can be transported, as can ECVs, unless water levels are too low. Note: If you are staying at a Disney resort <u>not</u> serviced by the monorail, the bus is often the easiest and fastest way to get to the Magic Kingdom, since you are taken directly to the park, bypassing the TTC.

By Bus—From all other resorts, buses take you directly to the Magic Kingdom. From the Disney-MGM Studios or Disney's Animal Kingdom, you must take a bus to the TTC, then transfer to monorail or boat. From Downtown Disney, the easiest route is to take a bus to the Polynesian and take the monorail.

By Land—You can walk or wheel from the Contemporary along a path paved with Walk Around the World bricks.

BEST TIMES TO GO

GETTING THERE

Planning

Special Challenges

Getting There

Staying in Style

Touring

Feasting

Resources

Index

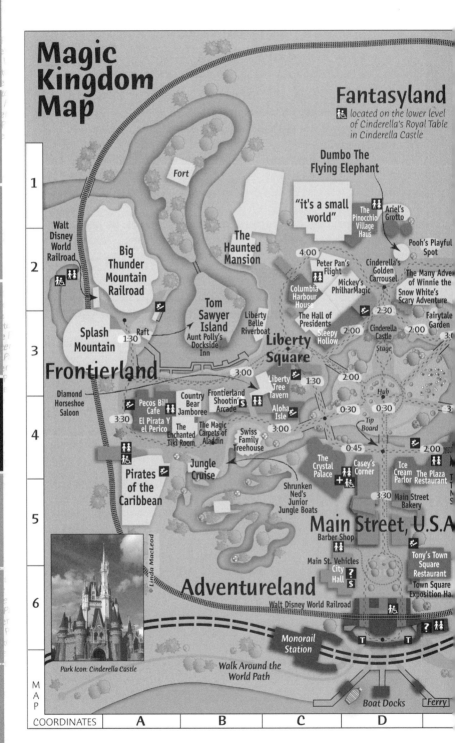

Magic Kingdom Map

Fantasyland

located on the lower level of Cinderella's Royal Table in Cinderella Castle

Dumbo The Flying Elephant

"it's a small world"

The Pinocchio Village Haus

Ariel's Grotto

Pooh's Playful Spot

Walt Disney World Railroad

Big Thunder Mountain Railroad

Fort

The Haunted Mansion

4:00

Peter Pan's Flight

Columbia Harbour House

Mickey's PhilharMagic

Cinderella's Golden Carrousel

The Many Adven of Winnie the

Snow White's Scary Adventure

Tom Sawyer Island

Aunt Polly's Dockside Inn

Liberty Belle Riverboat

The Hall of Presidents

Sleepy Hollow

2:00

Cinderella Castle Stage

2:30

2:00

Fairytale Garden

Splash Mountain

1:30

Raft

Liberty Square

3:0

Frontierland

3:00

Liberty Tree Tavern

1:30

2:00

Hub

Diamond Horseshoe Saloon

Pecos Bill Cafe

El Pirata Y el Perico

Country Bear Jamboree

Frontierland Shootin' Arcade

Aloha Isle

0:30

0:30

3

3:30

The Enchanted Tiki Room

The Magic Carpets of Aladdin

3:00

Swiss Family Treehouse

Tip Board

0:45

2:00

Pirates of the Caribbean

Jungle Cruise

The Crystal Palace

Casey's Corner

Ice Cream Parlor

The Plaza Restaurant

Shrunken Ned's Junior Jungle Boats

3:30 Main Street Bakery

Main Street, U.S.A

Barber Shop

Adventureland

Main St. Vehicles City Hall

Walt Disney World Railroad

Tony's Town Square Restaurant

Town Square Exposition Ha

© Linda MacLeod

Monorail Station

Walk Around the World Path

Park Icon: Cinderella Castle

Boat Docks

Ferry

MAP COORDINATES | A | B | C | D

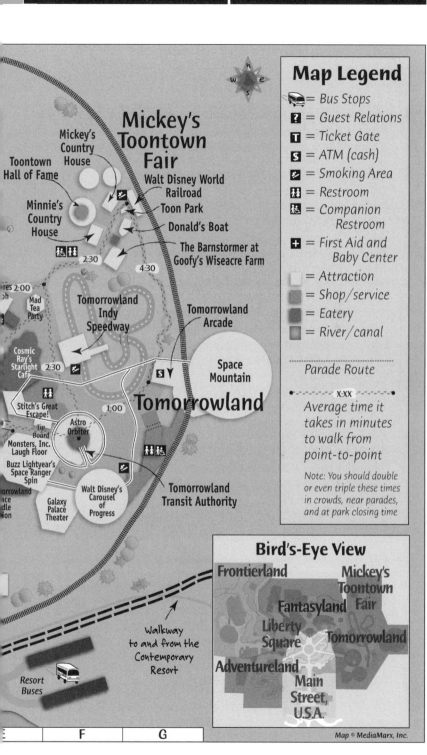

Map Legend

🚌 = Bus Stops
❓ = Guest Relations
T = Ticket Gate
S = ATM (cash)
🚬 = Smoking Area
🚻 = Restroom
♿ = Companion Restroom
➕ = First Aid and Baby Center
▭ = Attraction
▭ = Shop/service
▭ = Eatery
▭ = River/canal

Parade Route

•·······X:XX·······•
Average time it takes in minutes to walk from point-to-point

Note: You should double or even triple these times in crowds, near parades, and at park closing time

Mickey's Toontown Fair

Mickey's Country House
Toontown Hall of Fame
Minnie's Country House
Walt Disney World Railroad
Toon Park
Donald's Boat
The Barnstormer at Goofy's Wiseacre Farm

2:30
4:30

res 2:00
oh
Mad Tea Party
Tomorrowland Indy Speedway
Tomorrowland Arcade

Cosmic Ray's Starlight Cafe 2:30

Space Mountain

Tomorrowland

Stitch's Great Escape!
1:00
Astro Orbiter
Tip Board
Monsters, Inc. Laugh Floor
Buzz Lightyear's Space Ranger Spin
orrowland
ace
dle
ion
Galaxy Palace Theater
Walt Disney's Carousel of Progress
Tomorrowland Transit Authority

Bird's-Eye View

Frontierland
Fantasyland
Liberty Square
Adventureland
Mickey's Toontown Fair
Tomorrowland
Main Street, U.S.A.

Walkway to and from the Contemporary Resort

Resort Buses

F   G

Map © MediaMarx, Inc.

Planning · Special Challenges · Getting There · Staying in Style · Touring · Feasting · Resources · Index

Making the Most of Magic Kingdom

TIPS

After passing through Magic Kingdom's turnstiles, the **wheelchair/ ECV and stroller rentals** are on your left, under the railroad station. There are only limited numbers of wheelchairs and ECVs, and reservations are not taken, so be sure to get there early to rent. (Or consider renting from an off-site vendor—see pages 211-213.)

Bright Idea: If you're getting to the Magic Kingdom via the Transportation & Ticket Center, you can rent a wheelchair from Mickey's Gift Station there. Wheelchairs are kept out of sight, so just ask—it may be more convenient than renting at the Magic Kingdom itself.

It would be easy to waste a lot of time zigzagging across the park. Instead, **plan your day** and move around the park in a way that best conserves not only your time but your energy. We suggest you start in Tomorrowland and work your way around the park counterclockwise—many visitors head to the most popular attractions like Space Mountain or Splash Mountain, or they tend to start in Adventureland, not realizing that several attractions aren't open in Adventureland until 10:00 am! Check daily times guides—not all attractions may open with the park.

SPECIAL CONSIDERATIONS

The **First Aid Station** is located to the left of the Crystal Palace, just off Main Street, U.S.A. See page 206 for services available there. The "**Wish Lounge**," for families traveling courtesy of a wish-granting organization, is nearby. Ask at the First Aid Station for access.

The Magic Kingdom's **Baby Care Center** is next to the First Aid Station. There you'll find changing tables, high chairs for feeding, a kitchen for heating bottles and food, a communal nursing room with about four rocking chairs, and a cast member who can sell you basic baby care items like diapers.

The nursing room has several rocking chairs and subdued lighting

© MediaMarx, Inc.

No alcohol is sold in this park—not even in restaurants.

You'll find a large **Braille map** on a stand located in Main Street U.S.A.'s City Hall (Guest Relations). There's also a Braille map of the park near the tip board on Main Street, U.S.A., near the hub.

Entertainment at the Magic Kingdom

The daily 3:00 pm parade is, at the time of writing, the 20-minute **Disney Dreams Come True parade**, featuring favorite Disney characters. There's also an evening parade on certain nights, the dazzling lights of **SpectroMagic** (co-author Deb Koma's favorite!). There are several special viewing areas for those in wheelchairs/ECVs: Town Square in Main Street, U.S.A.; on the Tomorrowland side of the Partners statue near Cinderella Castle; and across from the Liberty Tree Tavern in Liberty Square. Speak to a cast member to gain access. These areas fill up quickly, so arrive early to get a spot. During peak periods, access may be limited to the special needs traveler plus one member of their party. If you're traveling without a wheelchair and want to use these areas, you will need a Guest Assistance Card (see pages 10–11). If you don't like to be close to others, these viewing areas may not be a good choice. Wheelchairs are usually parked within inches of each other. Alternatively, you can view the parade from Frontierland, where it may be less crowded. If you wait here, it takes about 15 minutes for parades to arrive from Town Square. "For the 3:00 pm parade, the wheelchair section in Liberty Square is the only one in the shade!"–contributed by peer reviewer Bonny Eby

Schedules for **American Sign Language (ASL)-interpreted shows** are made a week at a time. Ask at Guest Relations for the current schedule. The afternoon parade has sign language interpretation at the Liberty Square viewing area on certain dates. You must be in the small area next to the Liberty Bell about 20 minutes beforehand.

Live entertainment is performed along the streets throughout the day. New in 2006 were "Captain Jack's Pirate Tutorial," "Woody's Cowboy Camp," and "Family Fun Days Parade." None of these live shows has a special viewing spot, nor are they ASL-translated. Check your times guide or visit http://pages.prodigy.net/stevesoares. The Castle Forecourt Stage Show, "Dream Along With Mickey," is performed in ASL on certain dates (check with Guest Relations). There's nowhere to sit and no designated wheelchair viewing area, but if you arrive 15 minutes before show time, wait in the right section of the audience. Interpreters stand on a platform near the stage.

The 12-minute **Wishes fireworks show** takes place on most nights. Although you can view the fireworks from around the park, the best viewing spot is directly in front of the castle, standing in the middle of Main Street between Casey's Corner and the Ice Cream Parlor.

Veterans may participate in the **Flag Retreat** in Town Square around 5:00 pm daily. Inquire early in the day at Guest Relations in City Hall.

ENTERTAINMENT

Special Challenges

Getting There

Staying in Style

Touring

Feasting

Resources

Index

Finding Your Place at the Magic Kingdom

SEATING

Attraction Seating Chart

See page 207 for explanations of each type of seating listed below.

Astro Orbiter	small space with loose lap belt
Barnstormer at Goofy's Farm	high bar
Big Thunder Mountain Railroad	bench seat and low bar
Buzz Lightyear's Space Ranger Spin	bench with back and low bar
Carousel of Progress	theater
Cinderella's Golden Carrousel	straddle horse or bench with loose lap belt
Country Bear Jamboree	padded bench with backs
Dumbo The Flying Elephant	small space with loose lap belt
Enchanted Tiki Room	padded bench with back
Fairytale Garden	backless bench or standing
Galaxy Palace Theater	bench
Hall of Presidents	theater
Haunted Mansion	high bar
"it's a small world"	bench with backs
Jungle Cruise	bench
Liberty Square Riverboat	standing or bench
Mad Tea Party	very small space
Magic Carpets of Aladdin	small space with loose lap belt
Many Adventures of Winnie the Pooh	high bar
Mickey's PhilharMagic	theater
Monstes, Inc. Laugh Floor	bench with backs
Peter Pan's Flight	high bar
Pirates of the Caribbean	bench (with backs)
Snow White's Scary Adventures	bench /small space
Space Mountain	straddle bench/small space with low t-bar (see page 244)
Splash Mountain	bench and high bar (small space)
Stitch's Great Escape!	harness
Tomorrowland Indy Speedway	small space with loose lap belt
Tomorrowland Transit Authority	bench (with backs)
Town Square Exposition Hall	theater
Walt Disney World Railroad	bench (with backs)

Finding Your Place at the Magic Kingdom

Attractions With Restrictions/Warnings

Big Thunder Mountain Railroad	40 in. (102 cm.). For safety and comfort, you should be in good health and free from heart, back, or neck problems, motion sickness, or other conditions that could be aggravated by this adventure. Expectant mothers should not ride.
Goofy's Barnstormer	35 in. (89 cm.).
Haunted Mansion	Attraction may be too intense for very young children.
Snow White's Scary Adventures	Attraction may be too intense for very young children.
Space Mountain	44 in. (112 cm.). For safety, you should be in good health and free from high blood pressure, heart, back, or neck problems, motion sickness, or other conditions that could be aggravated by this adventure. Expectant mothers should not ride.
Splash Mountain	40 in. (102 cm.). For safety, you should be in good health and free from high blood pressure, heart, back, or neck problems, motion sickness, or other conditions that could be aggravated by this adventure. Expectant mothers should not ride.
Stitch's Great Escape!	40 in. (102 cm.). For safety, you should be in good health and free from high blood pressure, heart, back, or neck problems, motion sickness, or other conditions that could be aggravated by this adventure.
Tomorrowland Speedway	Children under the age of 12 months should not ride. 52 in. (132 cm.) to drive, otherwise ride with a person who meets height requirement. For safety, you should be in good health and free from high blood pressure, heart, back, or neck problems, motion sickness, or other conditions that could be aggravated by this adventure. Expectant mothers should not ride.

RESTRICTIONS

Planning
Special Challenges
Getting There
Staying in Style
Touring
Feasting
Resources
Index

Finding Your Place at the Magic Kingdom

SPECIAL PLACES

Attractions With Hearing Devices

Assistive Listening	Hall of Presidents, Mickey's PhilharMagic, Galaxy Palace Theater, Stitch's Great Escape!, Jungle Cruise, Enchanted Tiki Room, Country Bear Jamboree, Carousel of Progress, Judge's Tent (in Toontown), Castle Forecourt Stage, and Sunny Eclipse (at Cosmic Ray's)
Handheld Captioning	Haunted Mansion, "it's a small world," Peter Pan's Flight, Snow White's Scary Adventures, The Many Adventures of Winnie the Pooh, Walt Disney World Railroad, Tomorrowland Transit Authority, Carousel of Progress, Buzz Lightyear's Space Ranger Spin, Pirates of the Caribbean, Jungle Cruise, Enchanted Tiki Room, Stitch's Great Escape, and Dream Along With Mickey
Reflective Captioning	Hall of Presidents, Mickey's PhilharMagic, and Country Bear Jamboree
Video Captioning	Judge's Tent (in Toontown), Carousel of Progress intro, and Stitch's Great Escape preshow
ASL Interpretation	Jungle Cruise, Liberty Belle Riverboat, Castle Forecourt Stage show, Storytime with Belle, and Disney's Dreams Come True parade.
Ears to the World (Translation Devices)	Walt Disney World Railroad, Enchanted Tiki Room, Jungle Cruise, Hall of Presidents, Liberty Belle Riverboat, Haunted Mansion, Tomorrowland Transit Authority, and Carousel of Progress

Warnings, restrictions, and stroller parking are clearly marked throughout the park

Finding Your Place at the Magic Kingdom

Quiet areas for a break or time-out:
- The Fairy Tale Garden, to the right and behind the castle, has several shows of Storytime with Belle, but between performances, it's a wonderfully quiet, shaded spot.
- Down by the old Swan Boat dock (along the rose garden path near the castle) is quiet and secluded, and the way to get there is solitary and peaceful.
- The Tomorrowland Terrace Noodle Station counter-service restaurant (leading up to Tomorrowland) is actually very quiet during off-peak hours—stop there before the lunch rush or mid-afternoon for a shady break. This eatery is open seasonally.
- Town Square Exposition Center theater has some quieter areas on either side of the theater, some with tables and benches.
- Indoor restaurant seating areas between Pecos Bill's and El Pirata Y El Perico are often quiet at off-peak times.
- The pathway between Mickey's Toontown Fair and Tomorrowland along the railroad tracks is a relaxing area.
- Outside the park, follow the "Walk Around the World" path west past the monorail station to benches, lawns, and a sandy beach (no swimming).
- A cool, but not necessarily quiet, spot is just to the left of the Tomorrowland Light & Power Co. (the video game arcade next to Space Mountain). There are benches there and the doors to the arcade are usually open—on a hot day, the cool air-conditioned air just pours over you. This is a wonderful spot if you can stand the background noise of the arcade and the nearby Tomorrowland Indy Speedway.
- Under train station on the benches, out of the hot sun.

Peer Reviewer Tip: "No quiet spot nearby? You can temporarily place a coat or blanket over a stroller to make a 'safe place' for your child."—contributed by peer reviewer Sandy Bostwick

Companion restroom locations in the Magic Kingdom
- At the First Aid Station near Crystal Palace in Main Street, U.S.A.
- In the lower level of Cinderella's Royal Table restaurant in the castle
- Near Splash Mountain in Frontierland
- In Mickey's Toontown Fair at Pete's Garage
- To the right of Space Mountain in Tomorrowland
- At the Transportation & Ticket Center's East Gate
- Next to Pinocchio Village Haus

Note: These companion restrooms are the least maneuverable of all the parks and have no changing tables or urinals.

SPECIAL PLACES

Planning

Special Challenges

Getting There

Staying in Style

Touring

Feasting

Resources

Index

Charting the Attractions at Main Street, U.S.A.

Deb Wills' Rating
Deb Koma's Rating
Readers' Rating

☐ Main Street Vehicles [D-5]   `2` `2` `5`

A one-way ride between Town Square and Cinderella Castle (either direction) in vintage vehicles. Horseless carriages, trolleys pulled by Belgian horses, and even a fire engine. These vehicles are fun to ride in if you're willing to wait in the slow, long lines. *[A][U][C]* There are often long waits for the vehicles, standing in unshaded areas. *[G]* Avoid horse-drawn vehicles if allergic to horses. *[F]* Horses are quite large—those with a fear of animals might want to avoid. *[M]* Guests must transfer from ECV/wheelchair (the trolley can take a folded wheelchair; the jitney cannot). All vehicles require at least two steps up. *[Q]* You must sit sideways on the omnibus, fire engine, and two jitneys. *[L]* The omnibus has narrow doors and stairway.

Vehicles
A-Ticket
All ages
Gentle ride
Long waits

☐ Town Square Exposition Hall [D-6]   `3` `4` `5`

Don't pass by this museum dedicated to cameras—it's also the Camera Center! Walk inside to see early Mickey Mouse cartoons playing, and check out the interactive kiosks, photo cutouts, and character greetings! *[B]* Darkened area (in theater) for discreet nursing. *[L]* Theater seats may be tight for larger body types. *[M]* May remain in wheelchair/ECV. Use ramp to your right as you face the building.

Exhibit
A-Ticket
Ages 3 & up
Simple fun

☐ Walt Disney World Railroad—Main Street Station [D-6]   `5` `5` `7`

Circle the Magic Kingdom on a steam train, with stops at Main Street, U.S.A., Frontierland, and Mickey's Toontown Fair. You'll catch glimpses of all but Liberty Square and Fantasyland along the 1.5-mile journey. Ride the full route, or disembark at any stop. Attraction is closed during the fireworks. *[C][S][L][V]* Use the railroad to travel around the park without wasting energy. *[M]* ECV/ wheelchair users take the ramp next to the station, then go to the front of the train near the engine. Do <u>not</u> use the exit ramps from inside the train station. The engineer will assist in loading you into the first car—there is a bench seat for your chairless companions. Note that ECV users must ride the full circuit. Only two wheelchairs/ECVs per train. *[B]* Fold personal strollers before passing through the turnstiles. Replacement rental strollers may be available at other stops (hold on to your nametag!) but are not guaranteed. *[Ö]* Ears to the World can be used here. *[H]* Certain segments have handheld captioning. *[F]* There are two short, dark tunnels between the Main Street and Frontierland stations.

Train Ride
B-Ticket
All ages
A bit loud
Gentle ride
Short waits
20-min. ride (roundtrip)

ⓘ What Is and Isn't an Attraction?

We define an "attraction" as an individual ride, show, or exhibit. These are the destinations at the park and almost invariably come with a queue. We cover virtually all the attractions that Disney lists in its own guidemaps, plus a few that aren't listed that we think are deserving of the "attraction" title (such as Ariel's Grotto). Like Disney, we don't consider things like talking trash cans (yes, they exist!) to be attractions, as they rarely have a queue. We also don't consider parades or fireworks to be attractions, either—we cover these under the Entertainment sections in the park introduction pages. Character greeting areas are less straightforward—if Disney considers one to be an attraction or we feel it offers more than simple character greetings, we include a description of it. For a list of character greeting locations, refer to the guidemap upon your arrival and see page 217 for more tips.

Charting the Attractions at Adventureland

| | Deb Wills' Rating | Deb Koma's Rating | Readers' Rating |

"The Enchanted Tiki Room–Under New Management" [B-4] — 6 6 6

This Disney fixture has enchanted visitors for years. Infused with new life a few years ago with the addition of Iago and Zazu, it's a showcase for Audio-Animatronics. Many parts of the show take place above you, so you must look up to view. Shaded outdoor queue (standing only), and you are entertained by a short preshow. **[U][B][F]** There are periods of darkness, thunder, lightning, and some scary-looking tiki gods chant loudly. **[G][U]** There is often an unpleasant odor in this room. **[M]** Wheelchair users must enter preshow area at a designated gate to the right of the turnstiles at the direction of a cast member. You'll be shown to the special seating area. **[Ö]** Ears to the World available. **[H]** Handheld captioning and assistive listening are available. **[V]** Very dimly lit.

| Show |
| D-Ticket |
| Ages 4 & up |
| Dark, loud at times |
| Short waits |
| 2-min. intro 9-min. show |

Jungle Cruise [B-4] — FP — 8 8 7

A silly sail along the "Rivers of the World" in a craft reminiscent of The African Queen. Even though you cruise by Audio-Animatronics animals and restless natives, the only real danger is that you'll split your side from the skipper's corny jokes. You may get slightly damp. The shaded outdoor queue snakes for what seems like an eternity some days, with no place to sit while you wait. Boat has bench-type seats. **[A][U][F]** There are periods of darkness as you ride through a tunnel; there are also realistic-looking Audio-Animatronics snakes and other animals. **[A][U][F][I]** Be aware that sometimes there is a loud, sudden gunshot noise that may startle some. **[A][U][C][♥][T][I][M] [P][E][S]** Use FASTPASS to minimize wait times. **[Ö]** Ears to the World available. **[H]** Assistive listening is available. Sign language-interpreted performances on designated days; check with Guest Relations for schedule. Arrive at least 10 minutes in advance; through the wheelchair entrance to the left of the standby queue. **[M]** Wheelchair/ECV users must use the ramped pathway to the right of

| Boat Ride |
| D-Ticket |
| Ages 3 & up |
| Dark, fake snakes and wild animals |
| FASTPASS or long waits |
| 10-min. ride |

the Swiss Family Treehouse exit to access the attraction's area. Enter the attraction through the designated queue to the left of the FASTPASS machines. If able, you must transfer from your chair to the boat; otherwise wait for an accessible boat. **[Q]** This is a real, though gentle, boat ride, so those with extreme motion sickness may want to avoid. **[C][M][S][L][V]** You must step down to get into the boat–since the boat is floating, this can be tricky.

© Brian Martsolf

An accessible Jungle Cruise boat

The Magic Carpets of Aladdin [B-4] — 5 5 5

Ever wanted to fly on a magic carpet? This is your chance! You control the height and front-to-back rocking motion on this ride that's very similar to Dumbo. Watch out for the spitting camels. Outdoor queue is partially shaded–waiting for your turn to fly can get quite hot. Carpets have two rows of bench seats with loose lap belts. **[U][F][Q]** Although you control it, your carpet can soar high and spins around at a fairly good speed. **[M]** Wheelchair/ECV users enter using the regular queue. If able, you must transfer from your chair to the carpet, otherwise wait for an accessible vehicle. ECV riders who cannot transfer to the vehicle must transfer to a standard wheelchair. One carpet accommodates a single wheelchair and a companion. **[L]** Each row of the carpet can accommodate two average-sized adults; people of larger size may require their own seat.

| Ride |
| D-Ticket |
| Ages 3 & up |
| Flies high |
| Long waits |
| 1½-min. ride |

Charting the Attractions
at Adventureland
(continued)

	Deb Wills' Rating	Deb Koma's Rating	Readers' Rating

Pirates of the Caribbean [A-4]

	10	**10**	9

Yo Ho! A Pirate's Life for me! The inspiration for the recent blockbuster movies, this slow, dark ride takes you through a subterranean world of buccaneer Audio-Animatronics and now features Captain Jack Sparrow, Barbossa, and Davy Jones. Lines can be slow, but most of the wait is in the cool indoors. Guests must be able to step down into boat and up out of boat. One medium drop; you may get splashed. Inclined moving walkway at exit. **[U][F][I]** Queue can be very crowded and create claustrophobic feelings during busy seasons. This boat ride is completely in darkened surroundings. There are some depictions of mild violence and loud noises, such as cannon shots. New smoke effect at beginning of ride is odorless. **[H]** Handheld captioning is available. **[M]** Wheelchair guests enter using the regular queue. You must transfer from your wheelchair to the boat; folding wheelchairs will be stowed on the boat. ECV guests and those in non-folding wheelchairs must transfer to a wheelchair provided at the ride. Manual wheelchair users may find the steep ramps difficult. An elevator is available to take you back up to the main floor at the end of the ride. **[M][S][V]** Parts of queue very dimly lit, with uneven floor. **[L]** Boats have bench seats with backs and ample room for all body types. **[X]** Break area for service animals nearby; ask a cast member.

Boat Ride
E-Ticket
Ages 6 & up
Dark, slight drop, scary to young kids
Medium waits
10-min. ride

Shrunken Ned's Junior Jungle Boats [B-4]

	2	**3**	3

Got a couple of bucks? Then you might want to pass a few minutes steering these remote-controlled miniature Jungle Cruise boats around the little lagoon. You must buy tokens—one token for $1.00, two tokens per play. **[F]** Shrunken heads, skeletons. **[M]** Wheelchair/ECV accessible. **[A]** Outdoor fun, may be good place to let off some steam.

Arcade
A-Ticket
Ages 6 & up

Swiss Family Treehouse [B-4]

	4	**6**	4

If you've seen the classic Disney movie "Swiss Family Robinson," then you'll really appreciate the details of this representation of the shipwrecked family's treehouse home. **[A][G][U][C][B][♥][T][I][M][P][E][S][L][V]** This attraction involves <u>lots</u> of stairs (137 steps, to be exact) and is <u>not</u> wheelchair/ECV or stroller accessible. **[B]** Leave strollers in the designated area to the left of the treehouse entrance, or cast members will move them. **[F]** Once at the top of the treehouse, you have a terrific view of Adventureland below, but those with a fear of heights might find it unsettling.

Walk-Thru
B-Ticket
Ages 4 & up
Lots of stairs
Allow 15–30 min. to walk through

© Debra Martin Koma

Water play area in Adventureland

Charting the Attractions at Frontierland

Big Thunder Mountain Railroad [A-2] FP | 10 | 10 | 9 |

This high-speed (35 mph) coaster is a runaway mine train with lots of twists and turns, sudden stops, and sharp drops. The outdoor part of the queue is partially shaded, but the waits here can be quite long, with only a few rocks or fences here and there to lean against. Seats are bench-style with a low bar. **[A][U][I][S]** This is a big thrill ride, so it could cause overstimulation. **[A][U][C][♥][T][I] [M][P][E][S]** Use FASTPASS to minimize wait times. **[C][♥][T][Q][P][E][S]** You can really get shaken up on this rough roller coaster, so those with motion sickness, heart-, neck-, or back-related issues, as well as pregnant women, should avoid. **[X]** Service animals are NOT permitted. **[B]** Use Rider Switch. **[F]** There are some dark moments along the way as the train passes through tunnels. Anyone with a fear of heights, falling, or bats should also avoid this ride. **[M]** Wheelchair/ECV users, use FASTPASS. If FASTPASS is unavailable, enter through the exit on the right and speak with a cast member. You must transfer out of your wheelchair/ECV to ride. Keep in mind that if an emergency evacuation is necessary, you'll have to deal with stairs or else wait until someone can help you. **[B][L]** You must be at least 40 in./102 cm. to ride. **[L]** People of larger size may need their own row; lap bar may be uncomfortable. Tall folks have minimal back support during ride. **[V]** Parts of queue very dimly lit.

Coaster
E-Ticket
Ages 6 & up
Rough, fast ride with lots of twists and turns
FASTPASS or long waits
5-min. ride

Country Bear Jamboree [B-4] | 8 | 5 | 5 |

Audio-Animatronics bears perform country-western music in this hokey show, accented by jokes and dancing. Wait indoors, with occasional overflow outside. **[A][I][U]** Theater has padded bench seats. Show can be loud; may overstimulate. **[L]** The turnstiles to this attraction are <u>very</u> narrow. Ask a cast member to let you in via the wheelchair entrance if necessary. **[B]** Leave stroller in the designated area to the left of the entrance, or cast members will move it. Dark theater for discreet nursing. **[F]** Show takes place in a darkened theater. Also, talking animals may scare some. **[H]** Assistive listening and reflective captioning available. **[M]** Wheelchair/ECV users, enter through door on the left side of the building. You may remain in your chair during the show.

Show
C-Ticket
Ages 2 & up
Loud
Medium waits
15-min. show

Frontierland Shootin' Arcade [B-4] | 2 | 5 | 3 |

OK, pardner—set your rifle sights on these targets from the Old West! You get about 35 shots for 1 dollar. **[A][U][I]** Can be loud; may overstimulate. **[M]** Wheelchair accessible rifles located on the left side of the counter, up the ramp.

Arcade
A-Ticket
Ages 9 & up

Frontierland Station–Walt Disney World Railroad [A-3] | 5 | 5 | 7 |

Ride the full route, or disembark at any stop. Attraction is closed during the fireworks. **[U][♥][C][M][S][L][V]** Use the railroad to travel around the park. **[B]** Fold personal strollers before climbing the entry stairs. Replacement rental strollers may be available at other stops (hold on to your nametag!) but are not guaranteed. **[Ö]** Ears to the World available. **[H]** Certain segments have handheld captioning. **[M][S][L]** If you have difficulty climbing stairs, you can be admitted via the wheelchair ramp; see a cast member for assistance. Wheelchair/ECV users should also see a cast member for admission via the wheelchair ramp at the exit on the right, which is fairly steep. ECV users must ride back to Main Street. Only two wheelchairs/ECVs per train. **[F]** There are two short, dark tunnels between the Main Street and Frontierland stations.

Train Ride
B-Ticket
All ages
A bit loud
Gentle ride
Short waits
20-min. ride (roundtrip)

Planning
Special Challenges
Getting There
Staying in Style
Touring
Feasting
Resources
Index

Charting the Attractions at Frontierland
(continued)

	Deb Wills' Rating	Deb Koma's Rating	Readers' Rating

☐ Splash Mountain [A-3]   FP 🧍   10 9 9

Everybody has a Laughing Place, and this log flume with Br'er Rabbit, Br'er Fox, and other characters from the Uncle Remus stories might be yours! First 10 minutes of the ride are calm with small drops, taking you through an Audio-Animatronics wonderland. But watch out for the five-story drop near the end—it's a doozy! There's a play area near the exit called the Laughin' Place for youngsters too small or fearful to ride. Queue is outdoors, mostly uncovered until you get quite close to the ride. There's a good chance you'll get wet on this ride—in fact, the seats are often wet from previous riders. Bring a towel, poncho, or something to sit on if this bothers you. Note that you must step down to get into log. **[A][U][I]** This is a big thrill ride, so it could cause overstimulation. **[A][U][C][♥] [T][I][M][P][E][S]** Use FASTPASS to minimize wait times. **[X]** Service animals are _not_ permitted. Break area for service animals behind parade gates; ask a cast member. **[♥][T][Q][E][S]** Because of the steep drop and other dips and turns, those with motion sickness, heart- or back-related issues, as well as pregnant women, should avoid this ride. **[B]** Use Rider Switch. **[B][L]** You must be at least 40 in./102 cm. to ride. **[M][S][V]** Parts of queue very dimly lit, with uneven floor. **[L]** The logs have smallish bench type seats, which may be uncomfortable for people of size, including taller people. **[F]** Parts of queue very closed in. Some dark moments along the way and, of course, the big drop—anyone with a fear of heights or falling should avoid this ride. **[H]** Remember to remove your hearing aid and put it in a watertight container. **[M]** Wheelchair/ECV users should use FASTPASS. If FASTPASS is unavailable, speak with a cast member. Otherwise, enter through the regular queue. There are stairs at the point where the queue enters the building, so wheelchair/ECV users, as well as those with crutches or canes, will be diverted around this area. (Others who need to avoid stairs will need a Guest Assistance Card.) You then must transfer out of the chair to the boat, then step down into the boat (and step up to get out at the end of the ride). Keep in mind that if an emergency evacuation is necessary on this ride, you might have to deal with stairs or else wait until someone can help you.

Boat Ride With Thrills
E-Ticket
Ages 9 & up
Sharp drop!
FASTPASS or long waits
12-min. ride

☐ Tom Sawyer Island [A-3]   5 6 5

There are caves, tunnels, and an old fort on this little island themed to Mark Twain's popular Tom and Huck novels. You have to take a raft (no seats, must stand) to reach the island. Closes at dusk. **[A][U]** Good place to run around and blow off steam. **[G][U]** There is often a musty or unpleasant odor in the tunnels. **[C][♥][T][E][V]** The island trails and tunnels involve lots of walking and some climbing, although there are places to stop and rest along the way. **[F]** Tunnels and caves here are _very_ dark and close—avoid if you have claustrophobia. There are also a few rickety bridges that might bring on a fear or two. **[S]** Seniors may want to avoid the island simply because there are so many youngsters running around and there is a lot of walking involved. **[B][M][P]** You must be ambulatory to get around the island easily—there are stairs, bridges, and narrow tunnels not made for strollers or wheelchairs. In addition, the rafts transporting guests to the island cannot take ECVs. Instead, wheelchair users may wait at the island's dock, maybe play a game of checkers, or wheel over to Aunt Polly's Dockside Inn for a drink or snack, if it's open. **[L]** Some of the tunnels are very narrow—larger body types might not be able to squeeze through comfortably.

Playground
C-Ticket
All ages
Some dark tunnels and caves
Short waits for raft
Allow at least an hour

Charting the Attractions at Liberty Square

Planning
Special Challenges
Getting There
Staying in Style
Touring
Feasting
Resources
Index

	Deb Wills' Rating	Deb Koma's Rating	Readers' Rating

■ Diamond Horseshoe [B-3] — 4 4 5

At press time, this character meet and greet spot was serving light fare/ snacks from 11:00 am to 4:00 pm daily. This change may be temporary for the busy summer season—we have no word on if character meet and greets will resume here.

Character Meet
A-Ticket
All ages

■ The Hall of Presidents [C-3] — 7 7 6

Audio-Animatronics at their best—all of this country's presidents take the stage and are represented, down to the most minute detail, following a patriotic 180-degree film of our history. Shows every half-hour. Theater holds 700. **[A][U]** Long show may be boring for children with short attention spans or no patience. **[B]** Dark theater for discreet nursing. **[F][V]** Show takes place in a darkened theater. **[Ö]** Ears to the World can be used here. **[H]** Assistive listening and reflective captioning are available. **[M]** If using a wheelchair/ECV, enter the lobby through the right side of the turnstiles and ask to be directed to the special seating area. **[L]** Theater-style seats may be tight squeeze for larger body types.

Show
C-Ticket
Ages 10 & up
Dark theater
Short waits
23-min. show

■ The Haunted Mansion [B-2] — 10 10 9

Travel on a slow-moving track through the other-worldly home of 999 Grim Grinning Ghosts. There's no gore, but plenty of things that go "boo!" Outdoor queue is mostly uncovered, but lines move steadily. Some standing once indoors for the preshow. Be aware that at times your "Doom Buggy" ride vehicle turns side to side and travels backward and occasionally stops. **[A][U][C][F][♥][T][I] [S][V]** Ask cast member to bypass preshow to avoid claustrophobic feelings or standing for a long time. Doom Buggy vehicle wraps around you and can create a very closed-in feeling. After the preshow, boarding area is very dimly lit and lines merge so that you are very close to, even touching, others. **[A][U][I][V]** You must board and exit using a moving walkway. **[A][U][B][F][♥][T][I][S]** The entire ride is <u>very</u> dark, and although the scares are meant to be mild, some sensitive souls may find them too intense. **[Ö]** Ears to the World available. **[H]** Handheld captioning is available. **[B]** Leave stroller in the designated area to the right of the entrance. Use Rider Switch. **[M]** Wheelchair/ECV users should speak to a cast member for boarding instructions. The moving walkway can be slowed or stopped to make boarding/getting off easier. **[L]** Vehicles may be a tight squeeze for larger body types—consider riding alone in a vehicle.

Track Ride
E-Ticket
Ages 6 & up
Very dark, some scares
Medium waits
3-min. intro
7-min. ride

■ Liberty Square Riverboat [B-3] — 5 5 5

This steam-powered sternwheeler features a narration by "Mark Twain," as you travel around Tom Sawyer Island. Sometimes characters ride along with you. Cruises depart on the half-hour. You wait on a shaded dock, with benches nearby. Beware of standing downwind, as you may feel the warm steam from the smokestacks. **[C][♥][T][P][E][S][L]** There's limited seating on the boat, so be prepared to stand. **[H]** Sign language-interpreted on designated days; check with Guest Relations. Arrive at least 15 minutes in advance. Enter through wheelchair entrance on either side of landing. Interpreter will be on first level. **[M]** If using a wheelchair/ECV, enter through the exit ramps on either the left or right side of the landing. Speak with a cast member before boarding. Note there are stairs between decks. **[Q]** This is a real boat ride, even though it's gentle. **[Ö]** Ears to the World available.

Boat Ride
C-Ticket
All ages
Gentle rides
Med. waits
20-min. ride

Charting the Attractions at Fantasyland

| | Deb Wills' Rating | Deb Koma's Rating | Readers' Rating |

☐ Ariel's Grotto [D-1]

	3	**3**	**3**

If the Little Mermaid is your favorite character, this is the place to meet her! Spend some one-on-one time and have your photo taken with Ariel here. The ceiling inside the "cave" area drips water. **[A][U][C][♥][T][M][P][E][S]** The wait to see Ariel can be quite lengthy. Outdoor queue has very limited shade, some umbrellas; there is a comfortable-height low wall around a portion of the queue where you can lean or sit. Once inside the "cave," it is air-conditioned. **[M]** If using a wheelchair/ECV, use the regular queue. A recent renovation enables wheelchair/ECV guests to pull up next to Ariel for photographs.

Character Meet
A-Ticket
All ages
Long waits

☐ Dream Along With Mickey [D-2]

	6	**5**	**5**

This live show is performed on the Castle Forecourt Stage in front of Cinderella Castle several times a day. **[C]** Unless you're lucky enough to find a bench to sit on, you'll have to stand or sit on the ground for the duration of this show. **[F]** Some Disney villains appear onstage—might be scary to young children. The show concludes with daytime fireworks whose sudden loud sounds could be startling. **[H]** Handheld captioning and assistive listening are available. Sign language-interpreted performances on designated days; check with Guest Relations for schedule. Arrive at least 15 minutes before the show and stand in the <u>right</u> section of the audience. There is no seating. **[M]** No special Wheelchair/ECV viewing area is available.

Live Show
C-Ticket
All ages
Few scares
15-min. show

☐ Cinderella's Golden Carrousel [D-2]

	5	**5**	**6**

Ride this beautiful merry-go-round that dates back to the early 1900s redone with scenes from Cinderella and music from Disney movies. The queue area is mostly shaded, and the line moves fairly quickly. You must step up onto the carousel platform and pull yourself up on a horse with a loose lap belt. The height of the horses will change from start to finish. A horse that's easy to mount in the beginning may be very high at the end. **[A][U][I]** Noise level on this merry-go-round is high—could cause overstimulation. **[B][F]** Height of the carousel horses might be a bit scary to some. **[B]** Leave stroller in the designated area, or cast members will move it. **[M]** Wheelchair/ECV guests enter at the exit to the right of the main entrance; a cast member will direct you on how to board. Tip: Send a quicker member of your party ahead to claim your horse/seat. Note you may get on and off at different spots. You must transfer out of your chair and sit on either a horse (they all move up and down) or in the one stationary chariot. The chariot, which is wooden with padded seats, is located in the middle of the horses, not on the outside row. You must be able to step into it; could be awkward. It has two rows with room for two adults in each row. **[Q]** Those who are very motion sensitive might want to avoid this ride. **[X]** Check with a cast member before bringing on a service animal. **[S][L][V]** Height of horses may make getting on or off difficult.

Ride
B-Ticket
Ages 2 & up
High horses can be scary
Short waits
2-min. ride

© MediaMarx

Cinderella's Golden Carrousel is a kid favorite

Charting the Attractions
at Fantasyland
(continued)

Deb Wills' Rating
Deb Koma's Rating
Readers' Rating

Planning

Special Challenges

Getting There

Staying in Style

Touring

Feasting

Resources

Index

☐ Dumbo The Flying Elephant [D-2]   5 5 5

A classic carnival ride featuring the famous Disney elephant flying in circles over Fantasyland. The queue is mostly in the shade, but the waits here can be long, with no place to sit. Guests must take a small step into the vehicle. **[U][F][Q]** Although you control it, your elephant can soar high and spins around at a fairly good speed. Those who are afraid of heights or who are very motion sensitive might want to avoid this ride. **[B]** Leave stroller in the designated area away from the entrance, or cast members will move it. **[M]** Wheelchair/ECV users enter via the ramp to the right of the standby queue. You must transfer from your chair to the elephant. **[L]** Elephants can comfortably accommodate one large person and one child; people of larger size may require their own seat.

Ride
D-Ticket
All ages
Spins high in the air
Long waits
2-min. flight

☐ Storytime with Belle [E-3]   7 6 5

Belle of Beauty and the Beast fame reenacts her story with the aid of audience members. There's even a chance for character meet and greet afterward. Limited seating on concrete benches without backs. **[A][U][I]** Show can get very crowded, with people standing or sitting very close to one another. **[F]** May be called on for audience participation (both adults and children). **[H]** Sign language-interpreted performances on designated days. Arrive at least 20 minutes before the show and sit or stand in the right section of the audience.

Live Show
B-Ticket
All ages
No scares
15-min. story

☐ "it's a small world" [C-2]   9 7 6

This ride first debuted at the World's Fair in 1964 and has been charming visitors ever since with its dolls from around the world, not to mention its unforgettable song: "It's a world of laughter, a world of tears ..." Most of the queue is in the shade. With so much music and movement, this ride can be overstimulating. **[B]** Leave stroller in the designated area to the left of the attraction, or cast members will move it. **[H]** Handheld captioning is available. **[M]** ECV users must transfer to a wheelchair to negotiate the queue. Boats that can accommodate wheelchairs are available. Inquire with a cast member at the attraction.

Boat Ride
C-Ticket
All ages
That song!
Short to med. waits
11-min. cruise

☐ Mad Tea Party [E-2]   4 6 6

Spin like crazy in giant teacups in this ride themed to Alice in Wonderland's Mad Tea Party. Turning the metal wheel in the center makes you spin faster. Mostly shaded queue area. Seating in teacups is very cramped, even for average-sized adults. **[A][U]** The noise level in this ride is high—it could cause overstimulation. **[B]** Leave stroller in the designated area, or cast members will move it. **[M]** Wheelchair/ECV guests enter at the exit to the right of the operator's control booth. Tip: Send a quicker member of your party ahead to claim your teacup. Note that you will get on and off at different spots. You must transfer out of your chair to ride. Those who have trouble maintaining an upright position on their own should not ride, since the spinning creates a great centrifugal force. **[Q]** This is the ultimate spinning ride. Those who get dizzy easily should definitely avoid it! **[L]** The small teacup entrance and center wheel may make teacups a tight squeeze for people of larger size. **[X]** Service animals are not permitted on this attraction. **[V]** Use caution exiting vehicle—step down is difficult to detect.

Ride
C-Ticket
Ages 4 & up
Spinning!
Short waits
2-min. spin

Planning
Special Challenges
Getting There
Staying in Style
Touring
Feasting
Resources
Index

Charting the Attractions
at Fantasyland
(continued)

	Deb Wills' Rating	Deb Koma's Rating	Readers' Rating

▢ The Many Adventures of Winnie the Pooh [E-2] 🄵🄿	**6**	**6**	**7**

Take a tour through the Hundred Acre Wood in a bouncing hunnypot as you pass by Pooh, Tigger, Piglet, and friends in scenes from several of their well-known stories. A preschooler pleaser! Luckily, the long lines here are mostly in shaded areas, but there's no place to sit while you're passing the time. **[A][U][C][♥][T][I] [M][P][E][S]** Use FASTPASS to minimize wait times. **[A][I][U]** Fans in queue. **[H]** Handheld captioning is available. **[F]** Most of the ride is in darkened surroundings; there's even a simulated rainstorm that can be scary to young children. **[B]** Leave stroller in the designated area, or cast members will move it. **[M]** ECV users must transfer to a wheelchair to negotiate the queue. There are some wheelchair-accessible hunnypots; these can be ridden without bouncing movements—ask cast member about turning movements off. Note that vehicle can tip backward. **[L]** Each row of the hunnypot vehicles seats two average adults comfortably. People of larger size might prefer own seat; lap bar might be uncomfortable.	**Track Ride**
	D-Ticket
	All ages
	Some dark spots could be scary
	FASTPASS or long waits
	3-min. ride

▢ Mickey's PhilharMagic [D-2] 🄵🄿	**10**	**8**	**9**

The newest 3-D movie with other sensory effects is named after Mickey but is really Donald Duck's show. Scenes take you through popular animated classics, like Aladdin and The Lion King, all set to the corresponding music. Most of the queue area outdoors is shaded; indoors the waiting is cool and comfortable with low lighting. Can get crowded in waiting area. **[A][U][I]** Show is very loud—could cause overstimulation. **[A][U]** Enter row first to be closest to exit. Gusts of air are blown into your face several times; also, there is the simulated scent of apple pie. Water is also sprayed on you several times. To prevent this, search for the sprayer on the seat back in front of you before the show starts, then cover it with your hand. **[A][U][C][♥][T][I][M][P][E][S]** Use FASTPASS. **[A][U][F][I][Q][S][V]** You must wear special 3-D glasses; they fit over regular glasses. Those with vision impairments may not fully appreciate the effects. **[G]** Artificial scents blown in face. **[B]** Leave stroller in the designated area, or cast members will move it. **[F]** Most of the show is in darkened surroundings; some special 3-D effects are intense and loud. **[H]** Reflective captioning; assistive listening. 3-D glasses make captioning hard to see. **[M]** Wheelchair/ECV accessible. Once inside, head toward the right for accessible seating. Notify a cast member for help. **[L]** Theater-style seats may be tight squeeze for people of larger size.	**Show**
	E-Ticket
	Ages 5 & up
	Dark, loud; some effects may be scary
	FASTPASS or med. waits
	10-min. show

Queue-Tip!

Try this Winnie the Pooh quiz to pass the time while waiting to ride:

What color is Pooh's shirt?

Where does Pooh live?

What is Pooh's favorite food?

What is Pooh stuffed with?

Who are some of Pooh's pals?

—contributed by peer reviewer Kimberly Button,
author of the *The Disney Queue Line Survival Guidebook*

Charting the Attractions
at Fantasyland
(continued)

Planning

Special Challenges

Getting There

Staying in Style

Touring

Feasting

Resources

Index

	Deb Wills' Rating	Deb Koma's Rating	Readers' Rating

Peter Pan's Flight [C-2] **FP** | 8 | 7 | 8

Off to Neverland in a pirate ship, you'll soar over scenes from the movie Peter Pan—London, Mermaid Lagoon, and don't forget the evil Captain Hook. The long lines here are mostly in the shade. **[A][U][C][♥][T][I][M][P][E][S]** Use FASTPASS to minimize wait times. **[B]** Leave stroller in the designated area, or cast members will move it. **[F]** Most of the ride is in darkened surroundings; there's evil Captain Hook and the crocodile in many scenes, possibly scary to young children. Also, your ride vehicle is suspended from the top and sides—those with a fear of heights might be uncomfortable. **[M]** Wheelchair/ECV users should use FASTPASS; otherwise speak with the cast member at the entrance for direction. You must be able to step on the moving walkway and into the moving vehicle to ride—the walkway will not be stopped. There may be an area that is more accessible, however, if you speak with a cast member. **[H]** Handheld captioning is available. **[L]** Each "ship" holds two average-size adults comfortably. People of larger size might prefer own vehicle; lap bar. **[X]** Service animals are _not_ permitted.

Track Ride
D-Ticket
Ages 3 & up
Dark, heights, could be scary
FASTPASS or long waits
4-min. ride

Pooh's Playful Spot [D-2] | 5 | 5 | 5

This outdoor play area, across from The Many Adventures of Winnie the Pooh, features a slide, playhouse, and pop-jet fountains. Pooh and friends sometimes hold meet and greets here. Parents must supervise children; the area is not always monitored by cast members. **[A][U]** Great spot to burn off some energy! **[A][U][F]** You may get wet or squirted in some areas. **[M]** Wheelchair accessible, but spongy flooring may be difficult to move around on. **[C][♥][T][E][S][L][V]** Flooring is uneven and may be difficult to walk on. Lots of small spaces between equipment.

Playground
A-Ticket
Ages 2–5
Allow about 15–20 minutes

Snow White's Scary Adventures [D-2] | 5 | 6 | 5

Traveling in a three-rowed mining car, you go through the highlights of Disney's classic "Snow White and the Seven Dwarfs," complete with the scariest Wicked Witch ever. **[A][U][I]** The noise level in this ride is high—it could cause overstimulation. **[B]** Leave stroller in the designated area away from the entrance, or cast members will move it. **[F]** Most of the ride is in darkened surroundings; some of the effects are intense and loud, especially the Wicked Witch, who repeatedly pops out at you. **[H]** Handheld captioning is available. **[T][Q]** This ride makes many sudden turns and jerks. If you have back and/or neck problems, you might want to avoid this ride. **[M]** Wheelchair/ECV users enter at the marked gate at the far right of the attraction. You must transfer out of your chair to ride. **[L]** People of size might prefer to ride in their own row. The back seat of the car is better for larger adult sizes. **[X]** Check with a cast member before bringing a service animal on this attraction.

Track Ride
C-Ticket
Ages 5 & up
Dark, scary for small children
Short waits
3-min. ride

Tip: The popular **Bibbidi Bobbidi Boutique**, a beauty salon for little princesses (and princes), is opening a new location in Cinderella Castle opposite Cinderella's Royal Table in September 2007. See page 314 for information on the salon's location in Downtown Disney.

Planning

Special Challenges

Getting There

Staying in Style

Touring

Feasting

Resources

Index

Charting the Attractions at Mickey's Toontown Fair

Deb Wills' Rating | Deb Koma's Rating | Readers' Rating

☐ The Barnstormer at Goofy's Wiseacre Farm [F-2] 🕴

6	8	6

Short but kid-friendly coaster that swoops through Goofy's barn. The long, winding outdoor queue is partially shaded, with many diversions (such as the cornfields). Each plane has bench seats with a high bar. **[A][U][C][♥][T][Q][P] [E][S]** *Even though it's billed as a "kiddie coaster," you can really get shaken up on this ride, so those with motion sickness, heart- or back-related issues, as well as pregnant women, should avoid it.* **[B]** *Leave stroller in the designated area, or cast members will move it. Use Rider Switch.* **[M]** *Talk with a cast member at the entrance for directions on boarding. ECV users must transfer to a wheelchair to negotiate the queue. You must then transfer from your chair to ride.* **[L]** *You must be at least 35 in./89 cm. to ride. The vehicles don't have much leg room, and may be too small for some taller/larger adults. Avoid seats with "roofs," which may make entry and exit awkward.* **[X]** *Service animals are <u>not</u> permitted.*

Coaster
D-Ticket
Ages 4 & up
(35" and up)
Fast turns
Med. waits
1-min. flight

☐ Donald's Boat [G-1]

3	3	4

Interactive water play area. Allow 20-30 minutes. See our sidebar on page 268 for water play areas. **[A][U]** *Great play area for blowing off some steam.* **[A][U][F]** *You may get wet or squirted.* **[H]** *Remove hearing aid and place in watertight container.* **[M]** *Wheelchair/ECV accessible, but spongy flooring is difficult to move around on. Upper level of boat accessible by stairs only.*

Playground
A-Ticket
All ages

☐ Mickey's Country House and Judge's Tent [F-1]

5	5	6

See Mickey's home with whimsical details, including his sports equipment and gardening tools. After meandering through his house, meet the Big Cheese himself. The lines to meet Mickey are long, but they are mostly in the cool indoors of his tent. Lines are shorter later in the afternoon and evening. Can get very crowded. **[A][U]** *Visit during parade times or later in the day to avoid long waits.* **[H]** *Assistive listening is available in the Judge's Tent character greeting area. The Judge's Tent monitors have captioning.* **[M]** *Wheelchair/ECV accessible. Go through the regular queue, through the house, and into the Judge's Tent.* **[V]** *Visit with face characters (those who can talk, not in costume covering head).*

Walk-Thru
B-Ticket
All ages
Long waits
Allow 20 min.
to 1 hour

ⓘ Noisy Restrooms at Walt Disney World

Some adults and children who are sensitive to loud noises may be fearful of self-flushing toilets found in the theme park restrooms. The "red eye" sensor located behind the toilet on the back wall detects movement and will automatically flush—sometimes while you're still seated! To cope, try one of the following:

✔ Cover the sensor with a sticky post-it note until you are finished.
✔ If you're assisting someone, cover the sensor with your hand.
✔ Wear earplugs or headphones.

Remember to remove any paper you've placed over the sensor when you're through—and don't use regular stickers, which may not be easily removed. Note that there are also several new automatic hand dryers in some restrooms at Disney's Animal Kingdom. These new dryers are super loud, so avoid them if such noises are an issue. Paper towels are still available in all restrooms.

Charting the Attractions
at Mickey's Toontown Fair
(continued)

Column ratings: Deb Wills' Rating | Deb Koma's Rating | Readers' Rating

Minnie's Country House [F-1] | 5 | 5 | 6

Miss Minnie's home is full of hands-on activities, including a microwave that pops popcorn and a refrigerator that blasts cool air. Minnie's not usually here, but still, this house is worth a look. Allow 20 minutes to 1 hour. **[M]** Wheelchair/ECV accessible. Go through the regular queue, through the house. **[X]** Break area for service animals nearby; ask a cast member.

| Walk-Thru |
| B-Ticket |
| All ages |
| No scares |
| Short waits |

Toon Park [F-1] 🧍 | 4 | 4 | 6

Kids' play area. Parents must supervise kids; not always monitored by cast members. **[A][U]** Great for blowing off steam. **[L]** Must be <u>under</u> 40 in./89 cm. to play. **[M]** Wheelchair/ECV accessible, but spongy flooring is hard to move around on.

| Playground |
| A-Ticket |
| Ages 1–4 |

Toontown Hall of Fame [F-1] | 4 | 3 | 6

Meet Minnie Mouse and other favorite Disney characters here. Most of the lines here are long, but at least they are in the cool indoors. Visit when Toontown opens at 10:00 am to see the characters sing and dance before dropping the rope. **[A][U][I][C]** Waits to meet the characters can be quite long. **[M]** Wheelchair/ECV accessible. Go through the regular queue.

| Character Meet |
| A-Ticket |
| All ages |
| Long waits |

Walt Disney World Railroad–Toontown Station [G-1] | 5 | 5 | 7

Hop out here to see Toontown or walk over to Fantasyland and Tomorrowland. Or stay on board for the Main Street, U.S.A. station—a great shortcut to the exit. Closed during fireworks. **[U][C][M][S][L][V]** Use the railroad to travel around the park. **[B]** Personal strollers must be folded before boarding. Replacement rental strollers may be available at other stops (hold on to your nametag!), but are not guaranteed. **[F]** Two short, dark tunnels between the Main Street and Frontierland stations. **[Ö]** Ears to the World available. **[H]** Certain segments have handheld captioning. **[M]** Wheelchair/ECV users enter on far right of station. Only two wheelchairs/ECVs per train.

| Rail Ride |
| B-Ticket |
| All ages |
| A bit loud |
| Gentle ride |
| Short waits |
| 20-min. ride |

Turnstiles

Traditional turnstiles (with the rotating arms that you have to push forward to enter) are located at the entrance of all the theme parks to count daily visitors. Magic Kingdom's turnstiles are the narrowest—probably because it was the first park built and standards were different at the time. You'll find the same type of turnstiles at the entrance of some Magic Kingdom attractions. (At the other parks, you only encounter an occasional old-fashioned turnstile at the individual attractions—the other parks use photo cells embedded in the attractions' entryways to count visitors.) People of larger size, as well as those with mobility issues, strollers, and service animals, do <u>not</u> have to enter through a turnstile. There are alternate entrances at all attractions—ask a nearby cast member for help. Tip: If you're helping someone through the turnstile, be aware of where the arms are going to strike him or her to avoid a painful experience.

© Debra Martin Koma

A old-style turnstile

Charting the Attractions at Tomorrowland

Deb Wills' Rating
Deb Koma's Rating
Readers' Rating

■ Astro Orbiter [F-4] | **3** **7** **3**

Like Dumbo, this ride spins you 'round and 'round in rocket ships that you can control. The differences are the space-age theme, the faster speed of spinning, and the fact that you must ride an elevator to reach the vehicles. The long queues for the elevator here are outdoors but shaded—if you must wait for this ride, try first thing in the morning or in the evening when it's cooler. Vehicles have loose lap belts. **[A][U][Q]** Although you control it, your vehicle can soar high and spins around at a fairly good speed. Those who are very motion sensitive might want to avoid this spinning ride. **[F]** To reach this ride, you must take a very small elevator up—it holds about 10 adults in a VERY cramped space. In addition, there's a slight odor that many find offensive in this elevator. The ride itself is very high and has a commanding view of Tomorrowland. Those with a fear of heights might want to avoid it. **[A][U][C][♥][T][I][M][S]** Queues for this attraction can be quite long as you wait to board the small elevator up to the ride itself and stretch into mostly unshaded areas. **[M]** Wheelchair/ECV users enter through the regular entrance. The cast member will direct you past the turnstiles onto the elevator. You must transfer from your chair to the vehicle. **[L]** Vehicles can comfortably accommodate two average-sized adults sitting one in front of the other; people of larger size may require their own vehicle.

Ride
C-Ticket
Ages 5 & up
Flies high!
Long waits
1½-min. flight

■ Buzz Lightyear's Space Ranger Spin [F-4] *FP* | **9** **10** **8**

Shoot at electronic targets in this ride that's like a giant arcade game featuring characters from Disney's Toy Story. Your vehicle spins at your command, and your laser "ion cannon" is homed in on the evil Emperor Zurg for a chance to save the universe! While much of the queue is indoors, during busy times, the lines can stretch outside into unshaded areas. **[A][U][I]** The noise level in this ride is high, almost like being <u>inside</u> a giant arcade game—it could cause overstimulation. **[A][U][I][V]** You must board and exit using a moving walkway. **[A][U][C][♥][T][I][M][P][E][S]** Use FASTPASS to minimize wait times. **[H]** Handheld captioning available. **[M]** Wheelchair/ECV guests should use FASTPASS; otherwise go through the standby queue. ECV users must transfer to a wheelchair to negotiate the queue. Ask a cast member for a wheelchair-accessible vehicle. Note that some wheelchairs might be a tight fit. If this is the case, you can switch to a standard wheelchair if available. The moving walkway can be slowed or stopped. Ask a cast member for assistance. **[Q]** Although you control the spinning of the vehicle, you do need to rotate from side to side to aim at targets—motion sensitive folks may find the spinning disorienting. **[I][T][V]** Swirling red lights in tunnel and flashing white lights (where they're taking your photo) near end of ride. **[L]** Vehicles can comfortably accommodate two average-sized adults; people of larger size may require their own vehicle. Sitting in the middle of the seat may be more comfortable, but makes aiming/shooting awkward. **[X]** Service animals should not ride.

Ride
D-Ticket
Ages 4 & up
Mild "space flight" effects
FASTPASS or med. waits
4-min. flight

Side tabs: Planning | Special Challenges | Getting There | Staying in Style | Touring | Feasting | Resources | Index

Charting the Attractions
at Tomorrowland
(continued)

	Deb Wills' Rating	Deb Koma's Rating	Readers' Rating

■ Walt Disney's Carousel of Progress (seasonal) [F-4] `10` `10` `6`

This attraction debuted at the World's Fair in 1964-65. It tracks the path of modern technology from the turn of the century to the present day, with Audio-Animatronics that tell the tale. Theater turns with the passing of each scene, although the stage remains stationary. Limited operating hours. The outdoor queue is partially shaded, but waits are not usually very long. **[B]** Dark theater for discreet nursing. **[H]** Assistive listening and handheld captioning are available. The preshow portion of Carousel of Progress is closed-captioned. **[M]** Wheelchair/ECV users enter through the regular entrance, where the cast member will direct you to the seating area. **[L]** Theater-style seats may be tight squeeze for larger body types. **[X]** Break area for service animals nearby; ask a cast member for details. **[Ö]** Ears to the World available here.	**Show**
	C-Ticket
	Ages 6 & up
	No scares
	Short waits
	22-min. show

■ Galaxy Palace Theater (seasonal) [F-5] `2` `2` `4`

Partially covered outdoor theater is home to a variety of live shows throughout the year. Bench seats are hard. **[M]** Wheelchair/ECV users may remain in chairs. Ask cast member for special viewing area. **[H]** Assistive listening available.	**Live Show**
	B-Ticket
	All ages

■ Stitch's Great Escape! [E-4] FP ☀ `3` `3` `5`

This attraction features Stitch the alien before the events in the movie "Lilo & Stitch" occur. The attraction contains some of the most sophisticated Audio-Animatronics technology ever developed and features characters straight out of Lilo & Stitch. Covered queue area, but during busy times, queue can extend into main, unshaded pathway. Standing preshow. Theater-style seating, but an overhead harness rests on your shoulders during the show. Harness may bounce at times. **[A][U][C][♥][T][I][M][P][E][S]** Use FASTPASS to minimize wait times. **[G]** Simulated chili dog smell is quite strong. **[X]** Check with a cast member before bringing a service animal on this attraction. **[A][U][F]** Most of the show takes place in darkness, with loud sudden noises and tactile effects. Cries and screams from others in audience can also be unsettling. Note that you are restrained by harness—could create feelings of being trapped. **[B]** Use Rider Switch. **[Ö]** Ears to the World can be used here. **[H]** Assistive listening and handheld captioning are available at this attraction. The preshow portion of this attraction is captioned. **[M]** If in a wheelchair/ECV, ask a cast member to seat you in an accessible area, where you can remain in your chair and still use the harness so that you experience the special effects. Peer reviewer Kathy Sauviac adds, "This can also be done without the harness if you want to skip the special effects but still accompany your party. My wheelchair, because of the equipment on the back, wouldn't fit under the harness, but I was still allowed into the attraction." **[L]** Theater-style seats may be a tight squeeze for larger body types. Seats are hard, molded plastic and are 20" wide. **[B][L]** Height restriction of 40 in./102 cm.	**Show**
	E-Ticket
	Ages 7 & up
	Could be scary for young kids
	FASTPASS or long waits
	6-min. intro 12-min. show

Reader Tip: "I have a steel rod in my back due to scoliosis of the spine. I read that if you lift your shoulders before the shoulder harness engages on Stitch, that it will not be so tight. Well, I did that and the shoulder harness still adjusted down a little after the attraction started. Because of the hard molded seats, I was not able to find a comfortable position to sit in and was in horrible pain for the entire time. Never never never again will I go on this ride. Very OUCHY!"–contributed by Mikki Steiner

Planning

Special Challenges

Getting There

Staying in Style

Touring

Feasting

Resources

Index

Charting the Attractions
at Tomorrowland
(continued)

Deb Wills' Rating

Deb Koma's Rating

Readers' Rating

☐ Space Mountain [G-3]　　　　**FP** ☂

| 7 | 8 | 9 |

This very rough, high-speed coaster is entirely in the dark with lots of jerky twists and turns and sharp drops. The outdoor portion of the queue often stretches out into exposed sunshine, while the indoor queue is very dark. Watch your step as you step down into the vehicle! These are some of the most difficult vehicles to get in and out of in the Magic Kingdom. **[A][U][C][♥][T][I][Q][P][E][S]** You can really get shaken up on this rough roller coaster, so those with motion sickness, heart- or back-related issues, as well as pregnant women, should avoid this ride. **[A][U][C][♥][T][I][M][P][E][S]** Use FASTPASS to minimize wait times. **[F]** This coaster is completely in the dark. Anyone with a fear of heights or falling should also avoid this ride. Launch tunnel is very closed in; may cause claustrophobia. **[M]** Wheelchair/ECV users should use FASTPASS. If FASTPASS is unavailable, speak with a cast member at the entrance. The standby line is not accessible, so if you do not have a FASTPASS, the cast member will issue you a written one. ECV users must transfer to a wheelchair to negotiate the queue. You must then transfer out of your chair to ride. You need to be able to step down into the vehicle to ride, and there is a steep, moving walkway at the exit. Keep in mind that if an emergency evacuation is necessary on this ride, you'll have to deal with a catwalk and ladders or else wait until someone can help you. If you want to stay in your wheelchair, you can see the preshow and postshow sections and avoid the ride altogether. Manual wheelchair users may find the steep ramps difficult. Be sure to lock brakes on wheelchairs/ECVs on the moving walkway. **[B]** Use Rider Switch. **[I]** Some flashing lights and jerky movements may trigger seizures/migraines. **[L]** You must be at least 44 in./112 cm. to ride. Riders straddle t-bar, and the space is small. Entry/exit may be awkward. People of larger size might find lap bar uncomfortable. **[X]** Service animals are <u>not</u> allowed. **[V]** Queue is very dimly lit.

Coaster
E-Ticket
Ages 8 & up
Twists and turns all in the dark
FASTPASS or long waits
2½ -min.

© Debra Martin Koma

Space Mountain vehicle

☐ Monsters, Inc. Laugh Floor [E-4]

| 6 | 6 | 7 |

Featuring characters from the popular Monsters Inc. film, this show integrates new technology that allows interaction with the audience (similar to Turtle Talk with Crush—see page 260). Anticipate playful banter and teasing in a theater seating 400. Spotlights shine on random unsuspecting guests—video is shown onscreen. Seats are hard plastic benches with backs. Queue is indoors. **[F]** Dark theater, friendly monsters. Guests may be called on to participate. **[L]** People of larger size may find the seats uncomfortable. **[H]** Assistive listening available here. Preshow has video captioning. Portions of the show have handheld captioning. **[M]** Wheelchair/ECV users may remain in their seats.

Show
D-Ticket
All ages
Dark, playful monsters

☐ Tomorrowland Arcade [G-3]

| 2 | 3 | 3 |

Located at the exit of Space Mountain, this noisy arcade is a great place to wait while other members of your group are riding the coaster. Most games are 50 cents to $1.00 per play. **[A][U]** The noise level in this arcade is high—could cause overstimulation. **[M]** While the arcade itself is wheelchair/ECV accessible, only some games are.

Arcade
B-Ticket
Ages 6 & up

Charting the Attractions at Tomorrowland
(continued)

	Deb Wills' Rating	Deb Koma's Rating	Readers' Rating

Tomorrowland Indy Speedway [F-3] 🕴 | 5 | 5 | 4 |

What kid doesn't want a chance to drive before they're 16? This ride gives them that chance. The top speed is only 7 mph and the gas-powered cars are on a track, but that doesn't matter—this is one popular attraction. Cars have a loose lap belt. Tip: "If there is a member in your party who cannot stand being bumped from behind, have another member drive in a car behind them as a buffer from strangers."– contributed by peer reviewer Bonny Eby **[A][U][♥][T][Q][P][E][S]** Another car may bump you from behind on this ride, so those with motion sickness, heart- or back-related issues, as well as pregnant women, should avoid this ride. **[A][U]** Can be extremely noisy. **[G]** Exhaust fumes from cars can be irritating. **[M]** Wheelchair/ECV users go through regular queue to the access gate, where a cast member will direct you. You must be able to transfer out of your chair into the vehicle, and you must be able to depress the gas pedal and steer if driving. **[L]** You must be at least 52 in./132 cm. to drive the car. The cars may be too small for people of larger size. **[V]** You must steer a car on a track for this ride—those with vision impairments may not be able to judge distances between cars. **[X]** Service animals should not ride.

Ride
C-Ticket
Ages 4 & up
Some bumps and sudden stops
Long waits
4-min. drive

Tomorrowland Transit Authority [F-4] | 6 | 7 | 6 |

Get a grand tour of Tomorrowland on this elevated people-mover that takes you through Space Mountain and several other Tomorrowland attractions. No waiting usually, but you must take a moving conveyor belt that travels up a steep incline before boarding. Steep moving ramp decline after ride. **[A][U][I][V]** You must board and exit using a moving walkway. **[B]** Dark stretches for discreet nursing. **[F]** Long stretches of this ride pass through complete darkness. Offers sneak peek into Space Mountain, for those who think they may be too afraid to ride. **[Ö]** Ears to the World available. **[H]** Handheld captioning is available. **[M]** You must be ambulatory to ride—there's a sharply inclined moving walkway to enter, then there's a moving platform. You must then board your vehicle, which is moving at the same speed. **[Q]** If traveling backward bothers you, be sure to choose a forward-facing seat. **[L]** Vehicle has two rows facing each other. People of larger size may require their own row.

Ride
B-Ticket
All ages
Dark in spots
Very short waits, if any
12-min. grand tour

© Deb Wills

A Tomorrowland Transit Authority vehicle

Planning

Special Challenges

Getting There

Staying in Style

Touring

Feasting

Resources

Index

IN FOCUS: Traveling With Multiple Challenges

Right Cerebral Cortex Polymicrogyria—that's a mouthful isn't it? Especially when you consider that it's the diagnosis for such a little girl. But that's the complex disorder of the brain that causes MJ Eby, age 6, to have cerebral palsy, autism, feeding issues, seizures, hallucinations (related to her birth parents' genetic schizophrenia), scoliosis, fetal alcohol spectrum disorder (FASD), hearing and vision problems, and more.

Bonny and Andrew Eby, MJ's adoptive parents, knew she was going to be a special needs child, but didn't realize the actual extent of her disabilities when they adopted her. Bonny, who has several health issues of her own and subsequently spends much of her time in a wheelchair, too, says, "We are glad we didn't know the extent of the issues we would face with MJ, because we most likely would have opted out. Then we would have missed out on knowing the most amazing individual on earth."

According to Bonny, regular visits to Walt Disney World over the last few years have been a lifesaver for MJ, who communicates mostly with pictures and sign language.

"She just loves Disney World, especially the live shows, like Finding Nemo—The Musical," notes Bonny. "And trading pins—she loves to trade them, and she's received more than 4,000 pins from Disney Cast Members and from guests from all over the world."

Although Walt Disney World is one of the most accommodating places the Ebys have visited with MJ, it's not without its challenges. Her biggest challenge in the parks continues to be the limited availability of companion restrooms with changing tables large enough to accommodate the growing MJ. As MJ nears her 7th birthday (and 60 pounds), it is no longer appropriate for her daddy to take her into the men's room for changing (there are a couple of men's restrooms with changing tables, but those are few and far between). Due to her disabilities, Bonny is unable to lift and change her daughter on her own.

Despite that, Bonny realizes that their visits to Walt Disney World are some of the best medicine that MJ can get. "MJ has started talking a LOT more, although words are still jumbled often," Bonny says, adding that she can usually decipher them. Walt Disney World provides a safe place for MJ's hyper-sociability (caused by the FASD and autism) and most of all, it is the one place that she gets to be just a kid rather than a set of diagnoses. "The cast members treat her like she is a princess and she often finds other special needs kids to play with," Bonny points out. "For MJ, Walt Disney World is therapy and play all in one."

MJ's Picks:

1. The characters! Being on a feeding tube, MJ does not like to be in restaurants when Mommy and Daddy eat, but she does love character meals!

2. MJ loves to have her arms painted by the face-painting artists in the parks. (This is a great alternative to faces for kids like MJ—just ask; they will gladly accommodate you).

3. The playgrounds (Pooh's Playful Spot, The Boneyard, Honey I Shrunk the Kids)

MJ gets her arm painted

4. Finding Nemo—The Musical at Disney's Animal Kingdom (the one thing we do every week without fail).

⟹

Epcot

At three times the size of the Magic Kingdom, Epcot is huge! It is divided into two worlds: Future World encompasses the front section of the park, while the 11 pavilions in World Showcase circle a manmade lagoon. If you have any stamina or mobility concerns, we highly recommend touring Epcot in a wheelchair/ECV (especially in the hotter months).

Future World has been **slowly evolving** from the original collection of rides it opened with in 1982 to more high-tech, innovative attractions like Soarin', Turtle Talk with Crush, and Mission: SPACE. There is much more to Epcot than simply the attractions though. Live entertainment is the norm and six museum-quality galleries offer glimpses of art and artifacts. Generally speaking (if you bypass Mission: SPACE and Test Track), Epcot is the most laid-back of all the parks—it lends itself to "take it one step at a time" touring no matter what the ages or special challenges of any of its guests.

There are three **Guest Relations** locations at Epcot. You'll find one on the far right, before you pass through the park turnstiles. The main Guest Relations location is to the left and rear of Spaceship Earth. The third is outside the turnstiles at the International Gateway. Guest Relations is where you can obtain a current Guidebook for Guests With Disabilities, obtain a Guest Assistance Card (see pages 10-11), obtain a schedule for sign language-interpreted attractions, and ask any special questions. Hearing and vision devices can be rented from Guest Relations near Spaceship Earth. On Tuesdays and Fridays from 9:20 am to 9:40 am, a sign language interpreter is usually available at Guest Relations to answer your questions.

After you pass through the **Epcot front entrance turnstiles**, the wheelchair/ECV and stroller rentals are on your left. There are only limited numbers of wheelchairs and ECVs, and reservations are not taken, so get there early. (Or rent equipment from an off-site vendor—see page 213). If you enter through the International Gateway, go left after the turnstiles to rent your wheels. There are very few rentals available at this location—if they are out, ask them to call Guest Relations at the front of the park for availability.

The pathways in Epcot are wide and **easy to navigate**. Unlike some of the other parks, Epcot's layout is very straightforward with little confusion as to what direction you need to travel. The pavilions are mostly friendly to travelers who use wheelchairs/ECVs, those with mobility issues, health issues, youngsters, and seniors; however, during crowded times (park closing, holidays, festivals), stores and outdoor pathways become congested, making movement difficult.

Getting to Epcot

Epcot's **Future World is more crowded when the park opens** because World Showcase does not open until 11:00 am. If there are long lines, either get a FASTPASS or circle back later, once crowds have moved into World Showcase. The exceptions are Soarin', Test Track, and Mission: SPACE, which are so popular that they always have long lines. Parts of Future World close at 7:00 pm, so crowds are more concentrated in World Showcase. The variety of ethnic restaurants available also makes World Showcase popular in the evenings. Remember to check the tip boards for ride wait times; there's one in Innoventions Plaza and another on the way to Mission: SPACE.

Epcot is unique in that there are **two separate entrances**, making it the only park to which you can travel via all modes of transportation: car, bus, boat, walking/wheeling, or the monorail. The front entrance has the Disney resort bus stops, car parking lot, taxi and charter bus zones, and the monorail. At World Showcase's International Gateway, you can arrive by land or boat. If you enter through World Showcase before 11:00 am, cast members will direct you to Future World (past Canada and the United Kingdom).

By Car—Special needs travelers may find it more convenient to travel via car. Take I-4 to exit 67 (westbound) or exit 62 (eastbound) and continue to the Epcot toll plaza.

By Monorail—From the Magic Kingdom, Contemporary, Polynesian, or Grand Floridian, take the monorail directly to the Transportation & Ticket Center and then transfer to the Epcot monorail. If you're using a wheelchair or ECV, cast members will assist you in boarding. Note that the entrance and exit ramps to the monorail platform are steep. There is a bypass elevator; ask a cast member for access.

By Boat—The Friendship boats make a huge loop from Epcot to the BoardWalk, Yacht and Beach Club, Swan and Dolphin, and Disney-MGM Studios. The boat is a gentle ride, giving you a chance to sit and get out of the weather, but it does take some time, depending on where you board. Friendship boats are wheelchair/ECV accessible. Strollers can be pushed on without folding; enter at the rear of the boat. Ask a cast member if you need a small ramp for access.

By Bus—From all other resorts, buses take you to the Epcot bus depot. Some bus stations are a long walk/wheel from the front gate.

By Land—From the BoardWalk Inn & Villas, Yacht and Beach Club/Villas, Swan, Dolphin, and the Disney-MGM Studios, Epcot is within walking/wheeling distance. Follow the pathways toward the International Gateway, which emerges between France and the United Kingdom.

Making the Most of Epcot

TIPS

If members of your party don't mind getting split up, take advantage of the **single rider line** found at Mission: SPACE and Test Track. These lines are often faster than FASTPASS and definitely quicker than the standby line. Test Track cars sit three across, while Mission: SPACE pods hold four. If there are vacant spaces, cast members will fill them with individuals from the single rider line. The drawback is you will be separated from your group.

Kidcot Fun Stops (suggested ages 6–10) are located at each World Showcase Pavilion as well as in The Land pavilion, The Seas with Nemo and Friends, Test Track's gift shop, and Innoventions. In World Showcase, international cast members will talk with children about their native lands, engage them in a craft, stamp their World Showcase Passports (kids of all ages) if they have one, and sign a personal message in the language of the country. Kid's Guides with facts and pictures of Epcot are available at Guest Relations or the turnstiles and can be stamped and signed, too.

Seniors love Epcot, so allow extra time. Consider a guided tour like Undiscovered Future World or Behind the Seeds (see page 325).

Theaters are large, so once a show ends, there is a lot of **congestion** as folks exit the immediate area and decide where to go next.

Friendship boats provide transportation across World Showcase—docks are located in front of Morocco and in front of Italy (see map on next page). There are often long waits for the boats, and unless you need a rest or particularly enjoy the boats, you'll get to your destination more quickly by walking/wheeling. Friendship boats are accessible to wheelchairs, unless water levels are too high or low.

SPECIAL CONSIDERATIONS

The **First Aid Station** (with companion restroom) is located at the junction of Future World and World Showcase, in the Odyssey Center, near Mexico. The Baby Care Center is right next door. See sidebar on page 206 for services available there.

Braille maps are located outside the Electric Umbrella in Future World and on the International Gateway Path in World Showcase, as well as at Guest Relations in Future World.

Alcohol is sold throughout Epcot, both inside and outside buildings and restaurants; this is especially true during the International Food and Wine Festival in the autumn.

Planning · Special Challenges · Getting There · Staying in Style · Touring · Feasting · Resources · Index

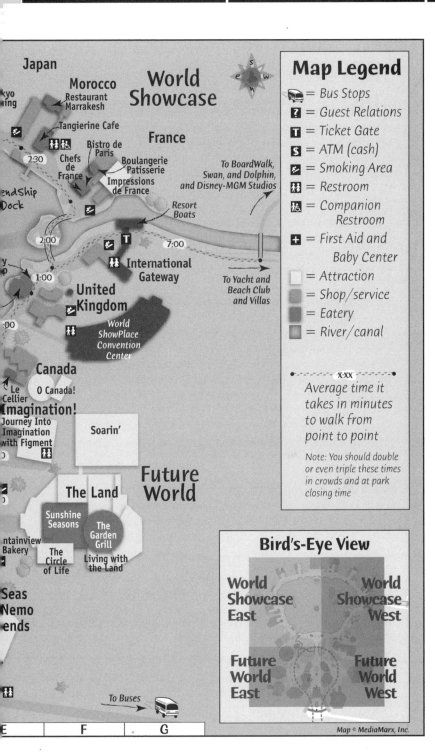

Japan

Morocco
Restaurant
Marrakesh

Tangierine Cafe

World
Showcase

France

Bistro de
Paris

Chefs
de
France

Boulangerie
Patisserie

Impressions
de France

endship
Dock

Resort
Boats

To BoardWalk,
Swan, and Dolphin,
and Disney-MGM Studios

2:30

2:00

7:00

International
Gateway

To Yacht and
Beach Club
and Villas

1:00

United
Kingdom

World
ShowPlace
Convention
Center

Canada

Le
Cellier

O Canada!

Imagination!
Journey Into
Imagination
with Figment

Soarin'

Future
World

The Land

Sunshine
Seasons

The
Garden
Grill

ntainview
Bakery

The
Circle
of Life

Living with
the Land

Seas
Nemo
ends

To Buses

E   F   G

Map Legend

= Bus Stops

? = Guest Relations

T = Ticket Gate

S = ATM (cash)

= Smoking Area

= Restroom

= Companion
Restroom

+ = First Aid and
Baby Center

= Attraction

= Shop/service

= Eatery

= River/canal

x·xx

Average time it
takes in minutes
to walk from
point to point

Note: You should double
or even triple these times
in crowds and at park
closing time

Bird's-Eye View

World
Showcase
East

World
Showcase
West

Future
World
East

Future
World
West

Map © MediaMarx, Inc.

Planning

Special Challenges

Getting There

Staying in Style

Touring

Feasting

Resources

Index

ENTERTAINMENT

Entertainment at Epcot

Live entertainment can be found throughout the park. You can spend your entire day watching each of the live performers. Enjoy musical acts, improvisation, and incredible a cappella singing! (Check times guide for details.) As your trip gets closer, check the unofficial Walt Disney World Live Entertainment web site for times: http://pages.prodigy.net/stevesoares/index.htm.

Disney characters are found throughout Epcot. The Epcot Character Spot (across from Innoventions West) has continuous meet and greets of a variety of costumed favorites. (Check the times guide for details.) Characters also frequent the pavilion most representative of their origins in World Showcase; Beauty and the Beast in France; Winnie the Pooh, Mary Poppins, and Alice in the United Kingdom; Snow White in Germany; and so on. See page 217 for more details.

Schedules for **sign language-interpreted shows** are made a week at a time. Epcot days for ASL translations are generally Tuesdays and Fridays. Times may vary. The best thing to do is check at Guest Relations, and they can print out the latest schedule for you.

Peer Reviewer Tip: "As retirees, we spend one to two months a year at Walt Disney World, and many days, we go from one live entertainment venue to the next!"—contributed by peer reviewer Jean Miller

Bright Idea: "Our top pick for entertainment is Off Kilter at the Canada pavilion in Epcot. If you haven't had the opportunity to hear Celtic rock music with a world class bagpiper (as well as bass and lead guitars, keyboards, and drums), you don't want to miss this opportunity. There's a cleared space in front of the stage for dancers of all ages. We recently returned from our sixth trip to Walt Disney World with disabled adults, and two of them said that <u>the</u> best part of the entire trip was watching Off Kilter, getting their pictures taken with them, and visiting with them."—contributed by peer reviewer Pam Passwater

© Pam Passwater

Pam Passwater (far left) with her Dream Factory group, posing with Off Kilter

Finding Your Place at Epcot

Attraction Seating Chart

American Adventure	theater
Circle of Life	theater
Gran Fiesta Tour	bench with back (boat)
Ellen's Energy Adventure	bench with back
Honey I Shrunk the Audience	theater
Impressions de France	theater
Journey Into Your Imagination	moving, bench with back, high bar
Living with the Land	bench with back (boat)
Maelstrom	bench seat (boat); bench with back (theater)
Mission: SPACE	harness, low bar (small space)
O Canada!	standing with lean rails
Reflections of China	standing with lean rails
Spaceship Earth	moving, bench with back, small space
Soarin'	seatbelt
Test Track	automobile seating with shoulder/lap belts
Turtle Talk with Crush	bench without back
The Seas with Nemo and Friends	high bar (clamobile)

Attractions With Restrictions/Warnings

Honey I Shrunk the Audience	Intense special effects.
Journey Into Your Imagination	A few intense special effects.
Maelstrom	Guests with health restrictions and expectant mothers may wish to bypass the ride.
Mission: SPACE	44 in. (112 cm.). For safety, you should be in good health and free from high blood pressure, heart, back, or neck problems, motion sickness, or other conditions that could be aggravated by this adventure. Expectant mothers should not ride. Claustrophobic guests should avoid.
Soarin'	40 in. (102 cm.). Guests with fear of heights or prone to motion sickness should use caution.
Test Track	40 in. (102 cm.). For safety, you should be in good health and free from high blood pressure, heart, back, or neck problems, motion sickness, or other conditions that could be aggravated by this adventure. Expectant mothers should not ride.

SEATING AND RESTRICTIONS

Planning

Special Challenges

Getting There

Staying in Style

Touring

Feasting

Resources

Index

Finding Your Place at Epcot

Attractions With Hearing Devices

Assistive Listening	Ellen's Energy Adventure, Innoventions (certain sections), Circle of Life, Honey I Shrunk the Audience, Test Track (briefing room), America Gardens Theatre, Impressions de France, Maelstrom theater, O Canada!, American Adventure, Biergarten (Germany), Reflections of China, and Turtle Talk with Crush
Handheld Captioning	Ellen's Energy Adventure, Journey Into Imagination With Figment, Living with the Land, Spaceship Earth, Gran Fiesta Tour, and Maelstrom (ride)
Reflective Captioning	Circle of Life, Honey I Shrunk the Audience, Impressions de France, Maelstrom (film), O Canada!, American Adventure, and Reflections of China
Video Captioning	Honey I Shrunk the Audience, Mission: SPACE, Soarin' (preshow), and Test Track (Briefing Room)
ASL (certain days and times)	Turtle Talk with Crush, The Seas (lock-out chamber and manatees), House of Innoventions, and World Showcase Players
Ears to the World (Show Translators)	Spaceship Earth, Innoventions, Ellen's Energy Adventure, Mission: SPACE, Test Track (Briefing Room), Circle of Life, Honey I Shrunk the Audience, Journey Into Imagination, Reflections of China, American Adventure, and O Canada!

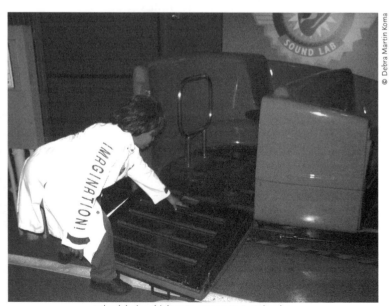

© Debra Martin Koma

Wheelchair vehicle at Journey Into Imagination

Finding Your Place at Epcot

Those wishing or needing a **quiet area** for breaks, time-outs, or baby nursing should consider:

- The right side of Living Seas near the entrance to Coral Reef restaurant.
- Turning right into World Showcase, just past the store, is an alcove with benches and some shade.
- During the day and early evening, the IllumiNations viewing areas by the United Kingdom and France are generally unoccupied.
- On the right side of Morocco is a quiet area with shade and benches.
- Short but lush vegetation trail to the right of the Mexico pavilion.
- In the Canada pavilion, the benches on the second level are in a quiet area.
- In the United Kingdom, the garden in the back (when there are no shows).
- In the back of France or near its gardens.
- In Japan's gardens near Yakitori House.
- Ellen's Energy Adventure has a line of benches (some shaded).
- The far left side of Test Track near the entrance to the Cast Access area. You can still hear the noise of Test Track, but it's generally not populated here.

Companion restrooms are located in the following areas:

- Near Spaceship Earth (East side only, large changing table)
- Future World East opposite Test Track
- Future World West opposite The Land (changing table)
- Refreshment Port (right side, changing table)
- First Aid Station near Odyssey Pavilion (no changing table)
- Norway (near Viking ship—no changing table)
- Germany (right side)
- Morocco (right side)

SPECIAL PLACES

Planning
Special Challenges
Getting There
Staying in Style
Touring
Feasting
Resources
Index

Charting the Attractions at Future World (East)

	Deb Wills' Rating	Deb Koma's Rating	Readers' Rating

■ Spaceship Earth [D-7]

9 | **8** | **8**

Epcot's shimmering geosphere icon, standing 180 feet tall, closed for renovations earlier in 2007, and, at press time, was to reopen in mid-November. New scenes were added, others enhanced and an interactive screen was installed on ride vehicles. A new postshow area, Project Tomorrow, has hands-on exhibits. Additional changes to ride and vehicles are unknown at press time. Companion restrooms are nearby. While we cannot be sure of the renovated attraction's specifics, here are our notes on the attraction <u>before</u> renovation in the event the attraction is similar. **[A][U][F][T][I][Q][V]** Fluorescent lighting similar to strobes in "tunnel" area may trigger seizures in those prone. **[A][U][F]** Ride vehicles may unexpectedly pause briefly; periods of darkness, narrow and enclosed spaces. **[G][F]** Smell of wood burning in Rome scene. **[B]** Dark ride for discreet nursing. **[Ö]** Ears to the World available. **[H]** Handheld captioning available. **[M]** Main queue is not accessible for wheelchairs/ECVs; use entrance on side. Transfer from wheelchair to vehicle. Check with cast member for loading procedures. If an emergency evacuation is necessary, you'll have to deal with stairs or else wait until someone can help you. **[F][Q]** Vehicle gently rotates and then travels backward downhill during last part of ride. **[A][Q][P][E][V]** Slow-moving load/unload platform. **[X]** Check with cast member before entering with service animals. The smell of burning wood might upset some service animals. **[L]** Each row can fit one large adult and one small child; a large adult may need to sit in their own row.

Track Ride
E-Ticket
Ages 5 & up
Dark, steep incline, some backward travel; gentle
Short waits except at park opening
15-min. ride

■ Innoventions East [C-6]

5 | **6** | **6**

"The Road to Tomorrow"—Disney partners with high-tech vendors who exhibit cutting-edge technologies via demonstrations, hands-on activities, and video games. This is a walk-/wheel-around exhibit area with few benches. It is very loud and can be crowded. Take the House of Innoventions tour, try the UL Testing Lab demos and hands-on, and visit the Disney Internet Zone. There's also a Kidcot Fun Stop here, as well as the Environmentality Corner, where you can make your own paper! Check with cast member at each exhibit for special accommodations. **[A][U][F][I][S]** Very noisy with lots of stimuli. **[Ö]** Ears to the World available for Intro to Innoventions. **[H]** Assistive listening available at some exhibits. Sign language-interpreted performances at House of Innoventions on designated days; check with Guest Relations for schedule. Arrive at least 20 minutes in advance; meet interpreter at entrance. **[X]** Check with cast member before entering specific exhibits with service animals.

Playground
B-Ticket
All ages
Very noisy
Short waits
Allow 30–60 min. to explore

Charting the Attractions
at Future World (East)
(continued)

Deb Wills' Rating   Deb Koma's Rating   Readers' Rating

☐ Universe of Energy (Ellen's Energy Adventure) [B-7]   7 | 7 | 7

Talk show host (and comedian) Ellen DeGeneres dreams of winning "Jeopardy!" but the Energy category stumps her. Bill Nye the Science Guy saves the day. Standing preshow (sets the story) in cool, dark room with handful of benches. Travel in slow-moving, 97-passenger hard plastic vehicles (long bench seats with backs) past primeval dinosaurs, view widescreen dramatic film. Shows start every 17 minutes. Indoor queue with uncovered outdoor queue overflow. **[A][U][B][F][♥]** Dinosaur area is dark, loud, and may be scary. **[C][♥][T][E][S]** Sit in air-conditioning to rest and enjoy. Enter row last so you don't have to move all the way down the bench to enter and exit. **[B]** Dark ride for discreet nursing. **[Ö]** Ears to the World available. **[H]** Assistive listening and handheld captioning available. **[X]** Break area for service animals nearby; ask a cast member. **[Q]** Movie segment in preshow might cause motion sickness. **[M]** Must transfer to standard wheelchair at entrance (no ECVs allowed, motorized wheelchairs are OK). May remain in wheelchair for show, but some wider-/longer-than-average wheelchairs may be a tight fit. After preshow, move right into loading area and wait for cast member assistance.	**Film/Ride** D-Ticket Ages 4 & up Dark, loud, dinosaurs Med. waits 8-min. intro 37-min. ride

☐ Wonders of Life (seasonal) [B-7]   S | 5 | 7

Once a thriving pavilion focusing on health and fitness, Wonders of Life is now open only a few weeks a year. Eateries and exhibits are permanently closed. If the pavilion opens during your visit, main attractions are Body Wars (similar to Star Tours on page 278), Cranium Command (standing preshow, bench seats for show), and The Making of Me (bench seating).	**Pavilion** C-Ticket

© Deb Wills

Hands-on activities at Kidcot Fun Stops entertain kids

Planning · Special Challenges · Getting There · Staying in Style · Touring · Feasting · Resources · Index

Planning
Special Challenges
Getting There
Staying in Style
Touring
Feasting
Resources
Index

Charting the Attractions
at Future World (East)
(continued)

Deb Wills' Rating
Deb Koma's Rating
Readers' Rating

■ Mission: SPACE [B-6] FP ᐟ 2 9 8

The International Space Training Center prepares you for a mission to Mars! Long, winding queue weaves inside and outside. Four-person ride vehicles simulate liftoff and space flight in a very enclosed space with individual harnesses. Upon entering the pavilion, a cast member will ask you to choose between the original high-intensity version ("Orange") or the low-intensity adventure ("Green"); you are given a card with your adventure color. (You can also opt to go through the queue and then exit before riding.) The high-intensity version is extremely intense as the simulator spins you rapidly on a centrifuge. Some guests detect the movement and/or become queasy and dizzy; others do not. Heed the warnings: Do not look side to side or close your eyes. Focus on the screen in front of you. The Orange version may aggravate unknown health conditions. The Green Adventure is the same ride without the centrifuge spinning. It is milder, although some folks (like Deb Wills) still report dizziness and disorientation. Deb Koma, on the other hand, loves the thrill of the Orange version! Green or Orange version: Must be in good health; free from high blood pressure, heart, back, or neck problems and motion sensitivity. Postshow area is wheelchair accessible, but spongy flooring makes it difficult to navigate. Postshow has games and hands-on fun for all ages, but is very loud and crowded. Play area for small kids (huge tubes to climb on). **[A][U][C][♥][T][M][P][E][S][L]** *Use FASTPASS to minimize wait times, or try the single rider line.* **[A][U][C][F][♥][T][I][M][Q][P][E][S][V]** *If uncomfortable with enclosed dark spaces, simulators, spinning, or loud sounds, you should not ride.* **[B]** *Use Rider Switch.* **[Ö]** *Ears to the World available in preshow. Mission: SPACE video kiosk available in English, Spanish, Japanese, German, Portuguese, and French.* **[F]** *You should not ride if you're claustrophobic.* **[H]** *Closed-captioning for preshow.* **[X]** *Service animals not allowed.* **[M]** *Transfer from wheelchair to training capsule.* **[B][L]** *Height requirement is 44 in./112 cm. Vehicle is very small. Seat room is ample, but the "rocket" closes down, similar to a car trunk. Persons large through the stomach note the "rocket" may not be able to lock—if it's not locked, you won't go on your mission.* **[V]** *Very dimly lit.*

Thrill Ride
E-Ticket
Ages 8 & up
Disorienting
FASTPASS or long waits
7½-min. preshow
5-min. ride

A Green Team "less intense training" card

⚠ Holidays Around the World

Each year from Thanksgiving to New Year's, Epcot celebrates Holidays Around the World. The entire park is decorated in red and white poinsettias, garland, fir trees, lights—and there's even special entertainment! Each World Showcase country has a holiday storyteller who performs a cute and informative short skit (standing only for most performances) on the customs of various lands and cultures, after which you can ask questions.

Charting the Attractions at Future World (East)
(continued)

	Deb Wills' Rating	Deb Koma's Rating	Readers' Rating
	8	9	9

■ Test Track [B-5]   *FP* ＊👤

Experience General Motors' car testing procedures. Travel up to 65 mph in open-air vehicles (two rows of three). Queue area is very loud and slow-moving; lots of loud banging and collision simulations. Standing preshow takes place in a small room. Shoulder/lap belts on ends, only lap belts in middle seat. Fast, banked sharp curves, sudden stops, bumps, abrupt temperature changes. Must be in good health and free from high blood pressure; heart, back, or neck problems; and motion sickness. Companion restroom nearby. Exit into GM Showroom. You can bypass the ride by entering through the gift shop and auto showcase area. Just outside is the Cool Wash Coca-Cola misting station (operating during warmer months) as well as a butterfly garden (a great place to take a breather). **[A][U][C][♥][T][M][P][E][S][L]** Use FASTPASS to minimize wait times or ask for the single rider line. **[A][R][U][C][F][♥][T][I][M][Q][P][E][S][V]** Rough/fast ride with various lighting and environmental changes. **[A][R][G][U][F][♥][T][I][M][S][V]** Mechanical arm shoots mist toward vehicle in corrosive testing room. **[Ö]** Ears to the World available for Briefing Room. **[F]** Unless there are three in your party, you will be seated with strangers. **[H]** Assistive listening and video captioning available for Briefing Room. **[X]** Service animals not allowed. **[M]** Accessible FASTPASS machine on far right. Check with cast member for directions. Transfer from wheelchair to vehicle. **[M][L]** There is a stationary vehicle in a private area if you want to practice boarding. Ask a cast member. **[♥][E]** Guests with these conditions should not ride. **[Q]** Use caution if prone to motion sickness. **[C][M][S]** If you cannot step down into the car, ask to be loaded at the seat belt stop where it might be easier, with a shorter step. You can also transfer from wheelchair to vehicle easier at this stop. A grab bar is available upon request—it can be secured in the car for someone who needs to pull themselves out of the wheelchair and into the car. **[B]** Use Rider Switch. **[B][L]** Height restriction 40 in./102 cm. Larger people may not be completely comfortable in this ride, as it has bucket seats. Middle seats are the least comfortable, back row has very little leg room, front row has leg room to spare. If no one is in the middle seat, a larger person might be OK in one of the outside seats, but if it's a full car, a larger person literally might not fit. The seat belts are very ample, but it might help to lift your bottom off the seat to get the seat belt closed. Otherwise ask a cast member for assistance.

Thrill Ride
E-Ticket
Ages 7 & up
Fast, jerky, bumpy
FASTPASS/ single rider line, or very long waits
3-min. intro 5-min. ride

Queue-Tip!

Try passing the time in Test Track's long queue by hunting for the following items: red tool chest, wrench, calendar dated June 1927, car radio, high voltage sign, baby in a car seat, crash dummy, airbag, yellow sign with mama and baby ducks.

—contributed by peer reviewer Kimberly Button,
author of the *The Disney Queue Line Survival Guidebook*

Sidebar tabs: Planning / Special Challenges / Getting There / Staying in Style / Touring / Feasting / Resources / Index

Charting the Attractions at Future World (West)

| | Deb Wills' Rating | Deb Koma's Rating | Readers' Rating |

Innoventions West [D-6]

| | 5 | 6 | 6 |

Part two of Epcot's high-tech trade exhibit. Demos (Where's the Fire), hands-on activities, and games. Send an e-mail to your family and friends, or try to ride a Segway. This is a walk-around exhibit area with very few benches. It can be very loud and crowded in some areas. **[A][U][F][I][S]** Some areas very noisy with lots of stimuli. **[Ö]** Ears to the World available for Innoventions introductions. Send a postcard in one of six languages: kiosk available in English, Spanish, Japanese, German, Portuguese, and French. **[X]** Check with cast member before entering specific exhibits with service animals. **[H]** Assistive listening available at some exhibits.

Playground
B-Ticket
Ages 6 & up
Noisy
Short waits
Allow
30–60 min.
to explore

Club Cool [D-6]

| | 4 | 5 | 8 |

Cool down and quench your thirst in this unique tasting room sponsored by Coca-Cola. Taste international flavors of sodas and check out Coca-Cola merchandise. You can also design your own beverage holders. **[A][U]** Noisy—loud, pop music playing. **[A][U][T][M][P][E][S][V]** Floor is sometimes wet/sticky. **[G][D][E][T]** No list of ingredients and no sugar-free beverages. **[M]** Accessible soda stations, but description signs too far away. Ramp located behind cash register.

Walk-Thru
A-Ticket
Ages 2 & up
Noisy, cold,
sticky floor
Unlimited

The Seas with Nemo and Friends [E-7]

| | 9 | 9 | 9 |

The original Living Seas pavilion has had an "extreme makeover" and is now The Seas with Nemo and Friends. Explore with the help of Nemo, Marlin, Dory, and Crush! Enter pavilion via Clamobiles entrance straight ahead, or bypass with entrance on left side through gift shop. Visit Bruce's Shark World (great photo opportunities), see manatees, and enjoy the aquarium with sea turtles, sharks, rays, and more. **[M]** Restroom stalls too small for door to close with some wheelchairs. **[X]** Use caution if traveling with service animal. Marine life is in full view (floor to ceiling windows). **[F]** Sharks and other marine life seen via Clamobiles and in the aquarium. **[V]** Queue and entire building very dimly lit.

Pavilion
E-Ticket
All ages
Medium to
long waits
Allow one
hour

Clamobiles [E-7]

| | 8 | 7 | 8 |

Enter the low-lit beach and boardwalk area as you meander to the Clamobiles (bypass available—ask cast member or enter through gift shop). Seats are two across in Clamobiles as Nemo and friends swim among the real marine life in the country's largest saltwater aquarium. Dark ride but tame. **[F]** Dark, with low ceiling, and enclosed vehicles—could cause claustrophobia. **[M][V]** Ramped entry queue is dimly lit, winding, and can be difficult to navigate in larger ECVs (including Disney rentals) or wheelchairs (sharp turns). **[M]** One accessible Clamobile is available; you may need to transfer to a regular wheelchair. **[Q]** Visuals give illusion of being underwater; can be disorienting. **[V]** Long, winding queue; very dimly lit.

Ride
D-Ticket
All ages
Med.–long
waits
4-min. ride

Turtle Talk with Crush [E-7]

| | 10 | 10 | 9 |

Crush interacts with audience in "real time." Bench seating with no backs; kids are encouraged to sit down front. While you wait, play Mr. Ray's Pop Quiz in waiting area or enjoy the live stingray exhibit. **[H]** Assistive listening. Sign language on select days; obtain schedule from Guest Relations. Check with cast member upon entering. **[M]** Alternative entrance available. You may be told to return later at a special time if there are too many wheelchairs/ECVs at a particular show.

Show
D-Ticket
All ages
Medium to
long waits
17-min. show

Charting the Attractions
at Future World (West)
(continued)

Deb Wills' Rating
Deb Koma's Rating
Readers' Rating

The Land [E-6] — 9 8 7

Explore agriculture and our environment. Very popular Soarin' attraction, gentle boat ride, movie, innovative food court, and sit-down character meals. Elevator (very small) inside to the left of Garden Grill restaurant. **[B]** Strollers must be parked outside. **[M]** Wheelchair entrance on right. Look for the huge wheelchair-accessible stall in far rear of women's restrooms.

Pavilion
E-Ticket

The Circle of Life [F-6] — 8 6 6

The Lion King's Timon and Pumbaa host this environmental film with a message for us all. Spectacular photography. Music can get loud. Standing indoor queue area with limited bench seating. Theater seating inside. **[A][U]** Enter row first to be closest to exit. **[C][F][♥][T][M][P][S][V]** Steep steps up/down theater. **[B]** Dark theater for discreet nursing. **[Ö]** Ears to the World. **[H]** Reflective captioning available and assistive listening for movie. **[M][P]** Cast member will direct you to seating area. Wheelchair/ECV area is in back of theatre—open area without seats. Others in party will be encouraged to sit in row ahead. One person may remain with wheelchair but must stand. **[L]** Theatre seats may be too narrow for some body types.

Film
D-Ticket
Ages 3 & up
Short waits
12-min. film

Living with the Land [F-6] — FP — 7 6 7

A gentle, narrated boat ride through Epcot's agriculture farm. Learn about hydroponics and aquaculture from prerecorded audio (no cast member is onboard with you). Step down into boat. **[A][U][C][♥][T][M][P][E][S][L]** Use FASTPASS to minimize wait times. **[A][I][U]** Brief segments of ride simulate rainforest mist, desert air, and smells—may bother those with sensory issues. **[F]** When crowded, queue design could trigger claustrophobic feelings; dark in areas (especially beginning), simulated thunderstorm. **[H]** Handheld captioning. **[M][P]** Follow signs to wheelchair entrance to right of ride entrance. Must transfer from ECV to standard wheelchair. All boats have ramp for wheelchairs (one wheelchair per boat).

Boat Ride
D-Ticket
Ages 4 & up
Dark
FASTPASS or medium waits
13-min. ride

Soarin' [F-6] — FP 🧍 — 10 10 9

Soarin' takes you on a simulated, hang glider flight over the grandeur of California, the Golden State. You are lifted up to 40 feet (12.2 meters) inside a giant projection screen dome (think IMAX). Sights, smells, gentle motion, and even wind make you feel aloft. Sit side by side on one of the three rows (10 seats per row). Bench seats, legs dangle, seat belts. Entrance queue and the exit path are <u>very</u> long with slopes. Tip: Get your FASTPASS as early in the day as you can—this is VERY popular attraction! Standby queue now features interactive games to help pass wait time. **[A][U][C][♥][T][M][P][E][S][L]** Use FASTPASS to minimize wait times. **[A][U][F][♥][T][M][Q][P][S][V]** Your row of seats will rise up and simulate flight (think of hang gliding). **[H]** Video captioning for preshow. **[G]** Scents of pine, orange, and the seashore. **[B]** Use Rider Switch. **[F]** Heights, flying, sensation of falling, feet dangle. **[Q]** Could produce motion sickness. **[X]** Service animals are not allowed. **[M]** Must be able to transfer to ride vehicle; wheel right up to ride to transfer. No option to remain in wheelchair/ECV and view from floor. Peer reviewer Deb Kendall notes: "My favorite ride is Soarin'. It's easy to access and transfer with an ECV. It is so fun to feel like I am in the clouds flying over California. **[C][♥][T][Q][S][E]** Should not ride.

Simulator
E-Ticket
Ages 7 & up
Simulated heights
FASTPASS or long waits
Very long waits
5-min. ride

(side tabs: Planning, Special Challenges, Getting There, Staying in Style, Touring, Feasting, Resources, Index)

Charting the Attractions
at Future World (West)
(continued)

	Deb Wills' Rating	Deb Koma's Rating	Readers' Rating

☐ Honey, I Shrunk the Audience [E-5]   *FP* | 8 | 8 | 8 |

Dr. Wayne Szalinski (Rick Moranis) demonstrates his newest invention, receives the Inventor of the Year award, and, well, someone gets shrunk again! Standing preshow on slanted floor to view 12 flat-screen monitors (some monitors in second row have subtitles). Theater seating with slight padding. Loud noises, intense special effects (some tactile), theater vibrates. May be too intense for children and some adults. Video monitor on left side of 3-D screen to view without 3-D glasses. **[A][U][C][♥][T][M][P][E][S][L]** Use FASTPASS to minimize wait times. **[A][U][B][F][♥][T][I][Q][S]** Effects include wind, water, movement, loud noises, other tactile effects. **[F]** When cast member finishes the intro in the theater, smoke comes out of the podium. Film features lions, snakes, mice, and other scary moments. **[A][U][F][I][Q][S][V]** Wear special 3-D viewing glasses—they fit over regular glasses. **[Ö]** Ears to the World available. **[♥][T][M][Q][P][E][S][L]** Preshow area has a 10- to 15-degree slope. Stand in back of preshow area to lean against partial wall (just in front of wheelchair area). **[X]** Check with cast member before entering with service animals. Break area for service animals nearby; ask cast member. **[H]** Reflective captioning available—see cast member at entrance. Assistive listening and video captioning (preshow) available. 3-D glasses make captioning hard to see. **[M]** Wheelchair entrance on left. Transfer to seat to experience all special effects. Only one person can accompany wheelchair to special seating area. **[Q]** Theater vibrates when "shrunk." Mild motion sensitivity may occur when Adam "picks up" the theater. **[L]** No chairs without arms in theater.

3-D Film
E-Ticket
Ages 8 & up
Very loud, dark, snakes, mice
FASTPASS or med. waits
5-min. intro 13-min. film

☐ Journey Into Your Imagination With Figment [E-5] | 7 | 7 | 3 |

Figment, the lovable purple dragon, stimulates your imagination with sight, sound, smell, and musical fun! This is a gently moving ride in four-person, hard plastic vehicles, but special effects may be intense. Vehicles stop periodically. After ride, exit into Image Works. Located inside the Imagination pavilion. **[A][U][C][B][F][♥][T][I][Q][S][V]** Vehicle vibrates in sound lab; loud noises, flashes of light, darkness. Smell lab has mild skunk scent, air blows in your face. **[C][♥][T][I][M][Q][P][E][S][L][V]** Vehicle boarding area flat; cars do stop for loading. **[B]** Dark ride for discreet nursing. **[Ö]** Ears to the World available. **[H]** Handheld captioning available. **[X]** Break area for service animals nearby—ask cast member. **[M]** Wheelchairs enter on left. Wheelchair-accessible vehicle available. Some longer-or-wider-than-average wheelchairs may be a tight fit. If able, transfer to an available manual wheelchair. **[L]** Each row can fit one large adult and one small child, or a large adult will need to sit in their own row; back row slightly wider than front.

Track Ride
C-Ticket
Ages 5 & up
Portions are dark with loud noises and flashes
Med. waits
6-min. ride

☐ ImageWorks: Kodak "What If" Labs [E-5] | 5 | 6 | 7 |

Hands-on sound and image exhibits, digital photo, and unique photographic gift items. Located inside the Imagination pavilion. **[A][U][C][B][F][♥][T][I][S]** Very noisy. **[A][U]** Lots of activities are good for burning off some excess energy. **[M]** If crowded, it can be hard to maneuver around. Some hands-on activities have lower kiosks for wheelchair/ECV users or small children.

Playground
B-Ticket
All ages
Allow 10-15 minutes

Side tabs: Planning, Special Challenges, Getting There, Staying in Style, Touring, Feasting, Resources, Index

Charting the Attractions at World Showcase

(listed in clockwise order)

	Deb Wills' Rating	Deb Koma's Rating	Readers' Rating

Mexico [B-4]

7 | 8 | 8

Pavilion
D-Ticket
All ages
Low light

© Debra Martin Koma

Travel south of the border and enjoy unique exhibits, a Mexican shopping plaza, San Angel Inn restaurant, and a twilight setting with a volcano in the distance. Restrooms inside pavilion's restaurant on the right. Entertainment in courtyard standing only. Cool, darkened setting is good for getting out of the sun, but it can get crowded. **[F][S][V]** Very low lighting in marketplace and restaurant. **[Ö]** Many cast members working here are from Mexico and are fluent in Spanish. **[X]** Break area for service animals nearby; ask cast member. **[M]** Access pavilion via ramp on right of main entrance. Hard to maneuver wheelchair in shopping areas, especially when crowded.

Trying on sombreros in Mexico appeals to all ages, even co-author Deb Koma's aunt Carol

Gran Fiesta Tour Starring The Three Caballeros [B-4]

7 | 7 | 5

Boat Ride
C-Ticket
All ages
Dark, but gentle
Short waits
7-min. cruise

The "Three Caballeros" (Donald Duck, Panchito, and Jose Carioca) joined this boat ride in 2007, along with an updated film. The gentle ride follows the Three Caballeros as they tour Mexico on a magic serape. Various sights found in and around Mexico are featured, mixing live action with animation. You must step down into boat. A few boats have wheelchair ramps. Some mist in beginning of ride. Very dark in spots. Fiber-optic fireworks in ceiling near end. **[B][F]** Skeleton-costumed band; simulated fireworks display. **[B]** Dark ride for discreet nursing. **[H]** Handheld captioning available. **[M]** Wheelchair/ECV users use regular queue. **[Q]** Boat ride is gentle, but still rocks a little.

Norway [B-3]

5 | 6 | 7

Pavilion
C-Ticket
All ages
Allow 30 min.

A visit to Scandinavia includes a Maelstrom boat ride, eateries, shops, live entertainment, and trolls. Shops are difficult to maneuver as they go from large to small spaces. A replica of a Gol Stave Church from Oslo is open to explore. The Stave Church has two entrances, one with stairs, the other with level access; inside it has an exhibit on Vikings. Wheelchairs/ECVs fit through the church door, but the door is heavy. A wheelchair-bound guest traveling alone will have trouble opening this door by themselves. Entertainment is in the courtyard; standing room only. A companion restroom is to the right of the Viking ship. **[C]** The Stave church is quiet and cool, though there is no place to sit. **[F]** A very large troll statue is in the shop. **[Ö]** Many cast members here are from Norway and speak Norwegian. **[M][L][V]** Small hallways make the Stave Church difficult to walk through.

Bright Idea: All of the outdoor merchandise around World Showcase in particular can be very tempting to many children (and even some adults). Remember to carry some small surprise items with you, maybe special treats you brought from home, to serve as distractions from the pricey souvenirs on display.

Charting the Attractions
at World Showcase
(continued)

	Deb Wills' Rating	Deb Koma's Rating	Readers' Rating

☐ Maelstrom [B-3]   **FP** | 8 | 8 | 7 |

Travel to a Norwegian fishing village via a mythical forest with trolls, storms, and polar bears. There's a short, steep drop; short backward ride; and Vikings. May get splashed on ride. Boat seats have backs but no padding. One ride sequence has boat going toward a pulsating, spinning light, similar to a strobe light. If boats back up waiting to unload, they bump each other and you get jostled. Exit the boat into a small theater for brief movie about Norway—seats have slat backs and padded seats. To bypass theater, walk right through. **[A][U][C][B][F][♥][I][S]** Movie is VERY loud, especially in the beginning. **[A][U][C][♥][T][M][P][E][S][L]** Use FASTPASS to minimize waits. **[A][U][B][F][♥]** Special effects may be scary. Large trolls/polar bears, lightning, and darkness. **[B]** Use Rider Switch. **[F][Q][V]** Boat turns and travels backward briefly. **[H]** Handheld captioning for ride. Assistive listening and reflective captioning for movie—ask cast member at entrance. **[M][S][V]** Two steps to load/unload boat. Rails separating boarding area limit space available to assist person boarding/exiting the boat. **[M]** FASTPASS machines hard to access. Wheelchair is brought from loading to unloading zone. If an evacuation is necessary, you need to be able to handle stairs, or else wait for help. Theater not very wheelchair-friendly; ends of rows recessed for wheelchairs. Back row does not allow access for wheelchair. Go to the far side of the theater (near exit) and reposition your wheelchair. **[Q]** Boat ride can be rough at times. You may experience slight problems with movie—sit in back of theater, not sides or front.	**Boat Ride**
	D-Ticket
	Ages 5 & up
	Small drops, backward, dark
	FASTPASS or med. waits
	15-min. ride

☐ China [B-3] | 6 | 7 | 6 |

Majestic architecture, exhibits, gardens, shopping, live entertainment, and eateries transport you to China. Land of Many Faces gallery offers unique exhibits. Entertainment in courtyard—standing or sitting on the ground only. **[Ö]** Most cast members in this pavilion are natives of China and speak Chinese. **[H]** Pay phone with TTY in plaza. **[M]** Wheelchair/ECV accessible.	**Pavilion**
	C-Ticket
	All ages
	Allow 20 min.

☐ Reflections of China [A-3] | 6 | 6 | 7 |

The 360-degree CircleVision movie allows you to see China's people, cities, and cultures. Waiting area indoors with benches (see photo below). Live entertainment in preshow area by Chinese musicians—check times guide. Theater has no seating, only lean rails. You must stand for the entire presentation. **[C][♥][T][M][Q][P][S][L][V]** Lean rails available. **[Ö]** Ears to the World available. **[H]** Reflective captioning—see cast member. Assistive listening available. **[Q]** You may experience motion sickness—if 360-degree movies make you a little dizzy, stand near the back of the room or don't go. **[M]** Position in rear of theatre.	**360° Film**
	D-Ticket
	Ages 6 & up
	Could cause dizziness
	Short waits
	13-min. show

Benches in the preshow area

© Debra Martin Koma

Queue-Tip!

While waiting to board Maelstrom, look for the following items in the mural above the loading area: cruise ship, lighthouse, polar bears, sea monster, boy climbing on rocks.

—contributed by peer reviewer Kimberly Button,
author of the *The Disney Queue Line Survival Guidebook*

Charting the Attractions at World Showcase

(continued)

	Deb Wills' Rating	Deb Koma's Rating	Readers' Rating

Germany [B-1]

	3	5	7

Fantasy, folklore, and the sounds of Oktoberfest. Live entertainment in restaurant, seating based on availability for non-dining guests. Watch the outdoor clock tower on the hour. Don't miss the model train village. Companion restroom on the right side of the pavilion. **[R]** Wine tastings sold. **[Ö]** Most cast members in this pavilion are natives of Germany and speak German.

Pavilion
B-Ticket
All ages

Italy [C-1]

	4	6	6

Shops, architecture, and restaurant represent the beauty of Italy—Venice in particular. Entertainment in courtyard, limited patio furniture seating, standing or sitting on the ground only. **[R]** Wine tastings sold. **[F]** Improv group selects participants from the audience. **[Ö]** Most cast members in this pavilion are natives of Italy and speak Italian. **[H]** Sign language-interpreted performances on designated days. Check with Guest Relations for schedule.

Pavilion
C-Ticket
All ages

The American Adventure [D-1]

	7	8	7

The American Adventure is located directly across the lagoon as you enter from Future World. Enjoy an Audio-Animatronics show, outdoor amphitheater, fast food eatery, and tiny gift shop. Spirit of America Fife and Drum Corps may play outside. Live entertainment preshow by a cappella group Voices of Liberty in the lobby of the pavilion with limited benches, standing, or sitting on the floor. You can listen to the singers without seeing the show. American Heritage Gallery located to the right of the building lobby. **[H]** Pay phone with TTY in Liberty Inn. **[X]** Break area for service animals is nearby—ask cast member. **[M]** Gift shop has little room to maneuver.

Pavilion
D-Ticket
All ages

The American Adventure Show [D-1]

	9	7	7

American history buffs will love this multimedia show with Mark Twain and Ben Franklin as your guides. Film montage was updated in mid-2007! Two escalators and a set of stairs lead to main theater; for elevator (on right as you enter Rotunda), see cast member. Theater seating. Located inside The American Adventure. **[C][♥][T][M][E][S]** Theater is cool with comfortable seating. **[B]** Dark theater for discreet nursing. **[F]** Mild violence (not graphic) from war scenes, dark at times. Bright camera flash in Civil War photography scene, thunder and lightning in Chief Joseph scene. **[Ö]** Ears to the World available. **[H]** Reflective captioning available—see cast member at entrance. Assistive listening also available. **[M]** Wheelchair area in back of theater, maximum 12 wheelchairs per show. Wheelchairs will be brought upstairs in elevator to listen to preshow singers from above. While waiting to enter theater, you will be in a roped-off area with other wheelchair/ECV guests. Floor is sloped 10-15 degrees. May be difficult to hold wheelchair, so set brakes. When you enter theater, wheelchair seating immediately on left. Don't go past this area, as rest of floor is sloped. Cast will assist getting you settled in theater prior to crowds arriving. **[Q]** May experience motion sensitivity during scene with Frederick Douglass. **[L]** Theater seats may be too narrow for some body types. **[S][V]** Dimly lit; floor is steeply sloped.

Show
E-Ticket
Ages 5 & up
Dark at times
Med. waits
15-min. preshow with singers
30-min. show

Charting the Attractions
at World Showcase
(continued)

	Deb Wills' Rating	Deb Koma's Rating	Readers' Rating

America Gardens Theatre (seasonal) [D-1]

| | | | 8 | 7 | 6 |

Home to a wide variety of special entertainment, from '60s bands to the Candlelight Processional. Check times guide for shows. Front area may be reserved for those with special dining packages. Open-air bench seating; very little shade, sun/heat may be intense. Located at The American Adventure pavilion. **[B]** Quiet spot for discreet nursing on days when no performances are being held. **[H]** Assistive listening available. **[M]** See cast member for wheelchair area.

Show
D-Ticket
All ages
Waits vary
Usually 25 min.

Japan [D-1]

| | | | 8 | 7 | 7 |

The bright Torii gate welcomes you. Beautiful area–hill gardens with water, rustic bridges, flowers, and koi pond. The Bijutsu-kan Gallery hosts traveling exhibits. Mitsukoshi Department Store and several eateries. Entertainment in courtyard; traditional drums are very loud–standing or sitting on the ground only. Tip: Between Japan and Morocco are areas with benches and shade. **[R]** Sake wine tastings sold. **[C][♥][T][M][E][S][L][V]** Small elevator near shop entrance brings you to restaurants. Very limited maneuvering room, crowded waiting area. **[F]** Elevator can trigger claustrophobia. **[Ö]** Most cast members in this pavilion are natives of Japan. Peer reviewer Masayo Kano notes, "This pavilion has two really great things: Miyuki (very impressive candy maker) and Matsuriza (drummers). I just love them, and their performance makes me proud that I'm Japanese!"

Pavilion
C-Ticket
All ages
Short waits
Allow 20 min.

Morocco [E-1]

| | | | 6 | 8 | 7 |

Architecture, shops, entertainment, and foods of this North African country are showcased here. Gallery of Arts displays science, music, and technology. Entertainment lagoon side on stage, few benches (no backs). Companion restroom on far right side of pavilion. **[Ö]** Most cast members in this pavilion are natives of Morocco and speak Arabic. **[H]** Pay phone with TTY available. **[M]** Shops, alleys, and café, hard to negotiate in wheelchair. **[W]** There is a designated meditation/prayer room (Islamic) open daily from 11:00 am to 9:00 pm located inside the museum; small rugs are available for use.

Pavilion
C-Ticket
All ages
Short waits
Allow about 20 min. to explore

France [F-2]

| | | | 7 | 7 | 7 |

Journey back to the France of 1870-1910 through Impressions de France movie, restaurants, and shops. Live entertainment in courtyard–very limited bench seating. **[R]** Wine tastings sold. **[G]** Designer fragrances and perfumes in several shops. **[C][F][♥][T][M][P][E][S][L][V]** Second-floor gallery in Plume et Pallette shop only accessible by stairs. **[Ö]** Most cast members in this pavilion are natives of France and speak French.

Pavilion
D-Ticket
All ages

Impressions de France [F-2]

| | | | 7 | 7 | 7 |

Palais du Cinema is home to a French travelogue set to classical music. Beautiful views of Normandy, Loire Valley, Paris, etc. Theater seating. Music can be loud. Located in France pavilion. **[C][♥][T][M][E][S]** Waiting area has no seating but is in cool indoors. **[B]** Dark theater for discreet nursing. **[H]** Reflective captioning available–see cast member at entrance. Assistive listening also available. **[M]** Enter left side of hallway; cast member will assist you. **[L]** Theater seats may be too tight for some body types.

Film
D-Ticket
Ages 5 & up
Dark theater
Short waits
18-min. film

Charting the Attractions
at World Showcase
(continued)

Deb Wills' Rating   Deb Koma's Rating   Readers' Rating

☐ United Kingdom [E-3]   7 9 7

The British Isles represented by music, improvisational performers, shops, gardens, pub, eateries, and architecture. Entertainment in courtyard—limited benches, standing, or sitting on the ground. Hedge maze in back for kids. Tip: Tables and umbrellas located to the right of Yorkshire Fish and Chips (unless reserved). **[R]** Pub featured prominently. **[G]** Designer fragrances and perfumes in Queen's Table Shop adjacent to Tea Caddy. **[F]** Improv troupe selects folks from the audience. **[H]** Sign language-interpreted performances of World Showcase Players on designated days; check with Guest Relations for schedule.	**Pavilion** C-Ticket All ages

☐ Canada [E-4]   7 7 7

Many international influences on our neighbor to the north are showcased with a Native Indian village, French chateau, and beautiful English gardens. Live entertainment, shops, movie, and eateries. Entertainment in courtyard with bench seating or standing—music can be very loud. **[M]** Wheelchair ramp in front of pavilion. **[Ö]** Some cast members in this pavilion speak French.	**Pavilion** C-Ticket All ages

☐ O Canada! [E-4]   7 7 6

A new version of this 360-degree CircleVision movie debuts in late 2007, with breathtaking views of the Canadian countryside, including British Columbia, Calgary Stampede, and the Changing of the Guard. Waiting area is small but inside and cool. Theater is standing with lean rails, no seating! You may experience motion sickness—if 360-degree movies make you a little dizzy, stand near the back of the room or avoid. **[F]** You might feel claustrophobic in waiting area. **[Ö]** Ears to the World available. **[H]** Reflective captioning—see cast member at entrance. Assistive listening also available. **[M]** Position wheelchair/ECV in rear of theater. To gain access to movie, wheelchairs must enter through Victoria Gardens past Le Cellier restaurant over a wooden walkway through a canyon. Although level, this area is extremely narrow. When a wheelchair is on this walkway, there will not be room for any opposing foot traffic. **[Q]** Motion sensitivity possible.	**360° Film** C-Ticket Ages 5 & up Dark, a little dizzying 18-min. film

---

⊕ Epcot's Festivals

Epcot is home to **two major festivals**, one in the spring and one in the fall, in addition to being the showcase for December holiday decorations. Every spring, Epcot hosts the International Flower & Garden Festival, while each fall brings the International Food & Wine Festival. Both offer unique displays, exhibits, and seminars (most free with admission). During the Flower & Garden Festival, Disney boasts thousands of blooms throughout the park. If you have allergies (including to molds) or asthma or are sensitive to smells, use caution touring Epcot during the festival. The Flower and Garden Festival usually has a kids' play area where they can let off a little steam. Crowds tend to be higher during the festivals, especially on weekends. During the Food and Wine Festival, World Showcase is very crowded, especially on weekends. Alcohol is sold at almost every food kiosk, and there are many seminars offering free wine and beer tastings. Check with individual booths for ingredient listings, which may or may not be available.

Planning   Special Challenges   Getting There   Staying in Style   Touring   Feasting   Resources   Index

IllumiNations: Reflections of Earth

IllumiNations: Reflections of Earth is the multimedia nighttime show that concludes each day at Epcot. Fireworks, lasers, lights, torches, water fountains, and music mesmerize you for 15 minutes. Very limited seating; standing or sitting on the ground is the norm. Fire, explosions, and, depending on wind (check direction), smoke. Viewing areas for wheelchairs/ECVs include in front of each Showcase Plaza shop, in front of Canada and Italy. These spots tend to fill very quickly, so arrive at least 45 minutes early. After the show, there are huge crowds exiting the park; sit on a bench and enjoy the music while waiting for the park to empty. Noise can be a major distraction for service animals here—some may shy away from it.

Bright Idea: Bring snacks and other items to help pass the time while waiting for the show. It's also a good time to call family and friends so the kids can talk about their trip.—contributed by peer reviewer Carol Scopa

Fountain/Water Play Areas

What kid doesn't like to play in a water fountain? Your little ones can delight in a number of fountains and water play areas around the World. Two magical water fountains are located in Epcot—one in Future World East on the way to Mission: SPACE and another on the pathway connecting Future World to World Showcase. The base of these areas is made from a soft, spongy material, and the water spurts up at odd angles unpredictably. There's another such fountain at Downtown Disney in the Marketplace. These are great places for little ones to cool off and let off some steam, especially in the summer. Just be sure they take off their shoes and socks first—remember to bring a change of clothes and towel for them, and a plastic bag to put the damp stuff in. (Or maybe they can wear a bathing suit underneath their regular clothes.) They *will* get wet—and love it!

Other locations for fun water play (note that during periods of cooler weather or drought, the fountains may be turned off):

✔ Magic Kingdom: Donald's Boat in Mickey's Toontown Fair, Tiki God Statues in Adventureland, Ariel's Grotto and Pooh's Playful Spot in Fantasyland

✔ Epcot: Cool Wash mister near Test Track; Jumping Fountains near Imagination Pavilion (see photo)

✔ Disney-MGM Studios: Honey I Shrunk the Kids playground; Coca-Cola bottle mister near the Backlot Tour

✔ Animal Kingdom: The Boneyard

© Deb Wills

Epcot's Jumping Fountains water play area

Disney-MGM Studios

Walt Disney first had the idea for a park based on the movies more than 40 years ago, but it wasn't until May 1989 that the Walt Disney Company unveiled the **Disney-MGM Studios**. Here, guests of Walt Disney World can witness the inner workings of movie and television production facilities.

Through its exciting attractions, Broadway-caliber shows, first-rate entertainment, and hands-on participation, the Disney-MGM Studios not only entertain but educate. The Studios have nearly doubled in size in the last ten years and continue to expand, but it still remains a fairly compact theme park, easily experienced in a day.

AMBIENCE

Disney-MGM Studios isn't as easy to navigate as other parks due to its free-form layout (see map on pages 272-273). There are two Guest Relations locations here—the first is on your left before you pass through the turnstiles; the second on your left after you enter the park. Guest Relations is where you can get guidemaps for disabilities, obtain a Guest Assistance Card (see pages 10-11), rent hearing or vision devices, obtain the current schedule for sign language-interpreted attractions, and ask any special questions. On Sundays and Wednesdays from 9:20 am to 9:40 am, a sign language interpreter is usually at Guest Relations to answer questions. You'll also find a TTY phone here. Here are the five areas of Disney-MGM Studios:

PARK LAYOUT AND NAVIGATION

Hollywood Boulevard—The main street of this 1930s town, the street is fairly easy to negotiate, but its shops, which are interconnected like those in the Magic Kingdom, are very congested.

Echo Lake—Attractions and eateries circle this quiet lake, which features the towering Dinosaur Gertie. Although accessible, there are several areas with steps—be sure to check out where the ramps are.

Sunset Boulevard—The very popular street that's home to the park's two biggest thrill rides, Rock 'n' Roller Coaster featuring Aerosmith and the Twilight Zone Tower of Terror, and the nighttime Fantasmic! amphitheater show. Be prepared to fight the crowds. The open-air food court here, Sunset Ranch, features more healthy options than most places, but its setup is very crowded and difficult to get around in.

Streets of America—Includes facades of the streets of San Francisco, New York, and other cities. The Streets of America is home to a huge amphitheater for the Lights, Motors, Action! Extreme Stunt Show.

Mickey Avenue—A variety of soundstages and the Animation Courtyard make up this area, which is fairly easy to get around.

Getting to Disney-MGM Studios

Disney-MGM Studios can be **enjoyed in one day**, although it is best to visit the most popular attractions earlier to avoid long lines. Take advantage of Extra Magic Hour mornings, if possible. The most popular attractions—Rock 'n' Roller Coaster and the Twilight Zone Tower of Terror—generate very long lines. Make a beeline for these rides first thing, unless you've just eaten breakfast!

Several of the shows have **limited seating capacity** (such as Voyage of the Little Mermaid) and can require a lengthy wait if busy.

Wherever possible, get a **FASTPASS**. Check the entertainment schedule in the park's times guide for show times, and check the tip boards for wait times.

Take the **length of the show times** into account when planning your route, and keep in mind that viewing several shows can take a considerable amount of time.

Bright Idea: Plan to be at shows when the doors open if you need a special viewing location, or if you will be watching an ASL performance.

Many attractions and restaurants empty immediately before and during a **parade**, affording shorter lines or the chance to get a table without advance reservations.

By Car—For many special needs travelers, it may be most convenient to travel by car. Take I-4 to exit 67 (west) or exit 62 (east) and continue on to Disney-MGM Studios. All-day parking is $10 (free to Disney resort guests and Annual Passholders), and the pass is valid at other Disney parks' lots on the same day.

By Boat—From Epcot's International Gateway, BoardWalk, Yacht & Beach Club, and Swan and Dolphin, take a "Friendship." These boats are fully accessible for wheelchairs/ECVs and strollers.

By Bus—Take a direct bus from all resorts (other than those mentioned above), Epcot's main entrance, and Disney's Animal Kingdom. From the Magic Kingdom, catch a bus at the Transportation & Ticket Center. From Downtown Disney, Typhoon Lagoon, or Blizzard Beach, take a bus or a boat to a resort and transfer to a Disney-MGM Studios bus.

By Land—You can walk or wheel from the BoardWalk, Swan & Dolphin, and Yacht & Beach Club, and even Epcot's International Gateway. Follow the paths marked along the canal beside the BoardWalk Villas.

Making the Most of Disney-MGM Studios

The **First Aid Station** is located near Guest Relations on the left, just after you pass through the turnstiles. The Baby Care Center is right next door. See sidebar on page 206 for services available there.

After you pass through the turnstiles, you can **rent strollers, wheelchairs, or ECVs** from Oscar's Super Service on the right. (See "Wheels" on page 211.)

We think **seniors will enjoy this park**, which is filled with nostalgia for an era gone by. Caricatures of old-time actors line the walls of the Hollywood Brown Derby restaurant, and movie memorabilia adorns Sid Cahuenga's shop near the entrance of the park. There's even an attraction that pays tribute to Walt Disney—One Man's Dream—whom many of today's seniors must certainly recall.

There are quite a few **live shows** in the Studios, most either in air-conditioning or in the shade. Take advantage of them!

Character greeting spots abound here, but the lines can be long. Check your daily times guide for exact times and locations, then plan to be there several minutes early to avoid long waits in line.

Several shows at Disney-MGM Studios (such as Indiana Jones Epic Stunt Spectacular, and the Backlot Tour feature **audience participation**. Even one of the restaurants, the '50s Prime Time Café, is known for its interaction with the clientele. If you're the shy, retiring sort, you may want to avoid these, or at least take steps to avoid being called on. (See sidebar on page 279.)

Disney-MGM Studios has several uniquely Disney themed **dining experiences**, but they are not without special concerns. The Sci-Fi Dine-In Theater, for example, has a very dark setting and projects snippets of old science fiction movies on a drive-in style screen. Also, seating is in restrictive "booths" made to resemble old autos. Investigate the atmosphere of the restaurant before dining.

A large **Braille map** mounted on a stand is located just outside Guest Relations on your left, after you enter the park. Another is located behind Hollywood Junction (tip board) at the intersection of Hollywood and Sunset Boulevards.

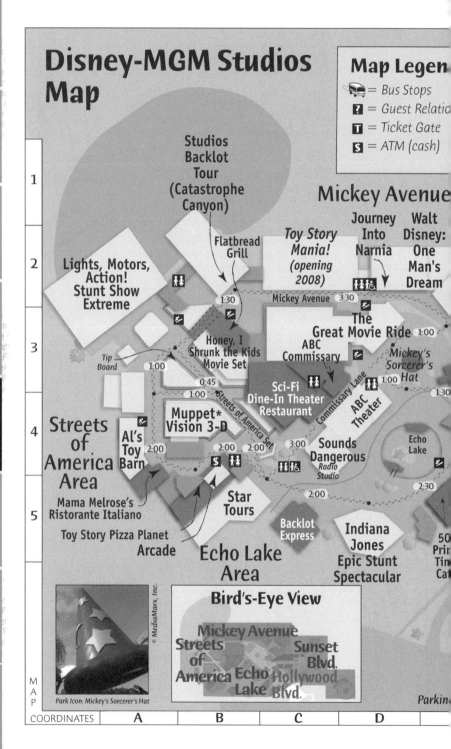

Disney-MGM Studios Map

Map Legend

- 🚌 = Bus Stops
- ❓ = Guest Relatio
- 🎫 = Ticket Gate
- $ = ATM (cash)

Studios Backlot Tour (Catastrophe Canyon)

Mickey Avenue

Flatbread Grill

Toy Story Mania! (opening 2008)

Journey Into Narnia

Walt Disney: One Man's Dream

Lights, Motors, Action! Stunt Show Extreme

Mickey Avenue 3:30

1:30

The Great Movie Ride 1:00

Honey, I Shrunk the Kids Movie Set

ABC Commissary

Mickey's Sorcerer's Hat

Tip Board

1:00

0:45

1:00

Sci-Fi Dine-In Theater Restaurant

ABC Theater

Echo Lake

1:30

Streets of America Area

Al's Toy Barn

2:00

Muppet* Vision 3-D

Streets of America Set

2:00 2:00

3:00

Sounds Dangerous Radio Studio

Mama Melrose's Ristorante Italiano

Star Tours

Backlot Express

Indiana Jones Epic Stunt Spectacular

50 Pri Tin Ca

2:30

2:00

Toy Story Pizza Planet Arcade

Echo Lake Area

Bird's-Eye View

© MediaMarx, Inc.

Park Icon: Mickey's Sorcerer's Hat

Mickey Avenue

Streets of America

Echo Lake

Sunset Blvd.

Hollywood Blvd.

Parkin

M A P

COORDINATES | A | B | C | D

Side tabs

Planning · Special Challenges · Getting There · Staying in Style · Touring · Feasting · Resources · Index

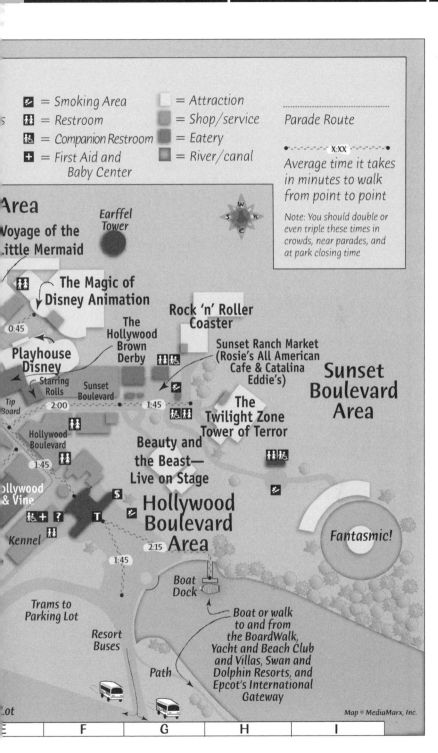

⚡ = Smoking Area
🚻 = Restroom
🚻 = Companion Restroom
➕ = First Aid and Baby Center

☐ = Attraction
☐ = Shop/service
☐ = Eatery
☐ = River/canal

Parade Route

●---------- X:XX ----------●

Average time it takes in minutes to walk from point to point

Note: You should double or even triple these times in crowds, near parades, and at park closing time

...Area

Voyage of the Little Mermaid

Earffel Tower

The Magic of Disney Animation

Rock 'n' Roller Coaster

0:45

The Hollywood Brown Derby

Playhouse Disney

Starring Rolls

Sunset Boulevard

2:00

1:45

Sunset Ranch Market (Rosie's All American Cafe & Catalina Eddie's)

Sunset Boulevard Area

Tip Board

Hollywood Boulevard

1:45

Beauty and the Beast— Live on Stage

The Twilight Zone Tower of Terror

...ollywood & Vine

$ T

➕ ?

Kennel

Hollywood Boulevard Area

2:15

Fantasmic!

1:45

Boat Dock

Trams to Parking Lot

Resort Buses

Path

Boat or walk to and from the BoardWalk, Yacht and Beach Club and Villas, Swan and Dolphin Resorts, and Epcot's International Gateway

Map © MediaMarx, Inc.

...Lot

E   F   G   H   I

Planning

Special Challenges

Getting There

Staying in Style

Touring

Feasting

Resources

Index

ENTERTAINMENT

Entertainment at Disney-MGM Studios

The afternoon parade here is **Disney's Stars and Motor Cars** and features themed vehicles bearing many Disney characters. Two special viewing spots for those in wheelchairs/ECVs are located at the end of Hollywood Boulevard—one in front of the giant Sorcerer's Hat, the other in front of Keystone Clothiers shop. Speak to a cast member for access. An ASL translation is done in front of the ABC TV Theater on designated days, across from Min & Bill's Dockside Diner. Arrive at least 15 minutes early and stand or sit in the designated viewing area on the steps in front of the building.

Fantasmic! is an extremely popular nighttime fireworks and laser display held in an amphitheater near the end of Sunset Boulevard. Obtaining a seat often means getting there more than an hour before show time. If there are two shows, try to attend the later one—it will be much less crowded. (Or consider using the Fantasmic! Dinner Package—see page 357). Other special considerations at Fantasmic!: The walk to the theater is a LONG, uphill walk. If you're attending in a wheelchair/ECV, you enter through the regular queue and stay to the right. Talk to a cast member for directions to the special wheelchair seating area. Cast members will direct those in wheelchairs/ECVs to the back row, but if you wish to sit in the front row, just ask. Tip: There are only a limited number of wheelchair seats, so be sure to arrive early! There is limited accessible seating there. A companion-assisted restroom is available in the amphitheater—there is no changing table, however. A TTY phone is located at these restrooms, also. Assistive listening and reflective captioning are both available. The area reserved for those who need reflective captioning is located on the far right side, back corner of section Mickey 1, in front of the tech booth. Talk to a cast member about using these devices here. Those seated in the front rows of this show often get wet—sit back farther if this is a potential problem. Guests sensitive to loud, sudden noises, minor explosions, and special smoke and light effects may wish to avoid as it includes all of these. The amphitheater can hold nearly 10,000 when it's filled to standing-room-only capacity—crowds at the show's conclusion can be crushing as they try to exit. Strollers must be parked in a designated area.

Disney-MGM Studios is also known for its roaming characters who perform a variety of **improvisational skits** on the street, often enlisting the involvement of unsuspecting guests. Known as Streetmosphere, these actors are usually quite humorous, but if you are shy you might prefer to avoid them. See page 279.

New to the Studios is the **High School Musical Pep Rally**, based on the popular Disney Channel movie. The show is performed several times a day in front of Sorcerer Mickey's hat. Cast members throw basketballs into the audience at the start of the show. You can sing or dance along—it's a very fun, high-energy, 15-20 minute show. Be sure to arrive early to get a spot up front if you're in a wheelchair. There's no special viewing area.

Finding Your Place at Disney-MGM Studios

Attraction Seating Chart

Backlot Tour	standing/bench
Beauty and the Beast	bench (with backs)
The Great Movie Ride	bench (with backs)
Honey I Shrunk the Kids	playground
Indiana Jones Epic Stunt Spectacular	bench (no backs)
Journey Into Narnia	standing
Lights, Motors, Action! Extreme Stunt Show	bench (no backs)
The Magic of Disney Animation	theater/stool
Muppet*Vision 3-D	theater
One Man's Dream	walking/wheeling and theater
Playhouse Disney Live!	floor seating
Rock 'n' Roller Coaster	harness
Sounds Dangerous	theater
Star Tours	theater with seat belt
The Twilight Zone Tower of Terror	bench with back and seat belt
Voyage of the Little Mermaid	theater

Attractions With Restrictions/Warnings

Fantasmic!	May be too intense for children and some adults.
The Great Movie Ride	Special effects may be too intense for children and some adults.
Rock 'n' Roller Coaster	48 in. (122 cm.). For safety, you should be in good health and free from high blood pressure, heart, back, or neck problems, motion sickness, or other conditions that could be aggravated by this adventure. Expectant mothers should not ride.
Sounds Dangerous	Some intense special audio effects.
Star Tours	40 in. (102 cm.). For safety, you should be in good health and free from high blood pressure, heart, back, or neck problems, motion sickness, or other conditions that could be aggravated by this adventure. Expectant mothers should not ride.
The Twilight Zone Tower of Terror	40 in. (102 cm.). For safety, you should be in good health and free from high blood pressure, heart, back, or neck problems, motion sickness, or other conditions that could be aggravated by this adventure. Expectant mothers should not ride.

SEATING AND RESTRICTIONS

Planning

Special Challenges

Getting There

Staying in Style

Touring

Feasting

Resources

Index

Finding Your Place at Disney-MGM Studios

HEARING DEVICES

Attractions With Hearing Devices

Assistive Listening	Beauty and the Beast, Fantasmic!, Indiana Jones Epic Stunt Spectacular, Muppet*Vision 3-D, Playhouse Disney, Sci-Fi Dine-In Theater Restaurant, Sounds Dangerous, The Magic of Disney Animation, Voyage of the Little Mermaid, One Man's Dream (theater only), Lights, Motors, Action! Extreme Stunt Show
Handheld Captioning	Backlot Tour, The Great Movie Ride, Playhouse Disney, Sounds Dangerous, Beauty and the Beast, and One Man's Dream
Reflective Captioning	Fantasmic!, Muppet*Vision 3-D, The Magic of Disney Animation (theater), Little Mermaid, and One Man's Dream Theater
Video Captioning	Backlot Tour (queue ramp and prop warehouse only), Muppet*Vision 3-D (preshow only), Playhouse Disney (queue only), Star Tours (boarding area only), One Man's Dream, and Tower of Terror (preshow only)
ASL Interpretation	Disney's Stars and Motor Cars Parade, Beauty and the Beast, Indiana Jones, and Backlot Tour.
Ears to the World	Sounds Dangerous, Muppet*Vision 3-D, One Man's Dream, Backlot Tour preshow, and Tower of Terror preshow

© Debra Martin Koma

Bed/changing table at the First Aid Station at Disney-MGM Studios

Finding Your Place at Disney-MGM Studios

SPECIAL PLACES

Planning

Special Challenges

Getting There

Staying in Style

Touring

Feasting

Resources

Index

Those wishing or needing a **quiet area** for breaks, time-outs, or baby nursing should consider:

- Behind Sid Cauenga's One-of-a-Kind shop, near the park entrance.
- The Writer's Stop, around the corner from Sci-Fi Dine-In Theater.
- The little corridor leading to Radio Disney studio, next to Sounds Dangerous.
- Near the Magic of Animation building.

A number of **companion restrooms** are available at the Disney-MGM Studios:

- At the First Aid Station
- Near the Twilight Zone Tower of Terror
- Across from the Star Tours ride
- To the right of Lights, Motors, Action! amphitheater
- Inside Lights, Motors, Action! amphitheater
- In Fantasmic's amphitheater
- Near Rock 'n' Roller Coaster
- Next to soundstages on Mickey Avenue

© Debra Martin Koma

Stroller rental at Disney-MGM Studios

Planning · Special Challenges · Getting There · Staying in Style · Touring · Feasting · Resources · Index

Charting the Attractions in the Echo Lake Area

	Deb Wills' Rating	Deb Koma's Rating	Readers' Rating

Indiana Jones Epic Stunt Spectacular [D-5] FP

| | 8 | 8 | 8 |

Get a behind-the-scenes look at how the amazing stunts from the Indiana Jones movies were done. Adults may be chosen to participate in the show. Outside queue is unshaded. Seating in the amphitheater is on hard metal bleacher-like backless benches. **[A][U][I]** The noise level in this show is high—could cause overstimulation. **[A][U][C][♥][T][I][M][P][E][S]** Use FASTPASS to minimize waits. **[F]** After sunset, the amphitheater is very dark for some portions of the show. Also, there are lots of sudden, loud noises, explosions, fire, and some staged fight scenes. **[H]** Assistive listening available. Sign language-interpreted performances on designated days; check with Guest Relations for schedule. Arrive at least 25 minutes before the show and proceed to the main entrance. Speak to a cast member and sit in the <u>center</u> section of the audience, to the right of the show control booth. **[M]** Wheelchair/ ECV users should use FASTPASS; speak to the cast member at the entrance to be directed to special seating area.

Live Show
E-Ticket
Ages 4 & up
Loud, fire, violence
FASTPASS or med. waits
30-min. show

Sounds Dangerous [C-4]

| | 4 | 6 | 6 |

Comedian Drew Carey takes you through a humorous program showcasing state-of-the-art sound effects. Queue is mostly shaded, with video monitors providing preshow fun. **[A][U][F]** Much of this show is in complete darkness. You must wear earphones to experience the audio effects, which include the buzzing of bees and the hum of an electric razor. Those sensitive to loud noises may wish to avoid. **[B]** Dark theater for discreet nursing. **[Ö]** Ears to the World available. **[H]** Handheld captioning and assistive listening. **[M]** Wheelchair/ECV users use regular queue; speak to the cast member at the entrance to be directed to special seating area. **[L]** Theater-style seats are very small—may be tight for people of larger size; ask cast member for seats with armrests that can be raised. (They should be located near the rear on the left as you face the screen.)

Film
C-Ticket
Ages 7 & up
Takes place in darkness, very loud noises
Short waits
12-min. film

Star Tours [B-5] FP 🚶

| | 9 | 10 | 8 |

Inspired by the Star Wars movies, this popular attraction combines a flight simulator with action-packed video for a rough ride. The indoor queue weaves all around—during very busy times, there is even a line outside (mostly shaded). The giant AT-AT machine above you just before the entrance sprays mist during hot weather. A companion restroom is opposite the entrance. A TTY phone is at these restrooms. **[A][U][I]** The noise level in this ride is high—could cause overstimulation. **[A][U] [C][♥][T][I][M][P][E][S]** Use FASTPASS to minimize wait times. **[F]** Dark/violent at times. **[C][♥][T][Q][P][E][S]** You can really get shaken up on this simulator, so avoid it if you have motion sickness, heart- or back-related issues, or if you're pregnant. Roughest ride is in the back row! **[F][♥][T][I][M][E][S]** During non-peak times, cast members may run the movie without running the simulator. Be sure to ask! **[H]** Video at boarding area is closed-captioned. **[I][T][U][V]** Strobe-like lights flash throughout attraction. **[M]** Wheelchair/ECV users should use FASTPASS; otherwise speak to the cast member at entrance. ECV users must transfer to wheelchair to negotiate queue. Must transfer out of chair to simulator seat. Manual wheelchair users may find the steep ramps difficult. **[B]** Use Rider Switch. **[B][L]** Height restriction: 40 in./102 cm. Seats (with retractable belts) may be tight for people of size; armrest may be uncomfortable. **[T][I][M]** Cast members can provide a 5-point harness for those who require more than just a seat belt. **[X]** Service animals not permitted. Break area for service animals nearby.

Thrill Ride
E-Ticket
Ages 8 & up
Rough, rocky, may cause motion sickness
FASTPASS or long waits
3-min. intro 5-min. flight

Charting the Attractions in the Streets of America Area

	Deb Wills' Rating	Deb Koma's Rating	Readers' Rating

Honey, I Shrunk the Kids Movie Set Adventure [B-3]

5 5 6

Kids' play area themed to the popular movie series. Listen for the ant sounds and the sniffing dog's nose! Note that there's no seating inside. **[A][U]** Great place to run around and let off steam. **[F]** Some tunnels are very closed-in spaces and completely dark. Also, giant ants and bugs are depicted—avoid if you have a fear of insects. There is a possibility of getting sprinkled with water from the dripping Super Soaker. **[M]** Not recommended for ECV users. Wheelchair users go through regular queue to the access gate. **[C][♥][T][M][E][S][L][V]** Flooring is uneven, and the spongy surface may be difficult to negotiate. Lots of small spaces between slides and other equipment. **[B]** Leave stroller in the designated area away from the entrance to the playground, or cast members will move it.	**Playground**
	B-Ticket
	All ages
	Giant bugs, dripping water
	Short waits
	Allow 30 min.

Muppet*Vision 3-D [B-4]

9 8 9

Kermit, Miss Piggy, and other Muppet friends take you through a demonstration of 3-D technology with added sensory effects. Indoor waiting area is dimly lit—there's really nowhere to sit while you're waiting, but you are entertained by the Muppets in a preshow video on overhead monitors. Floor in preshow slopes downward sharply. **[A][U][I]** The noise level in this show is high—it could cause overstimulation. Sensory effects like spraying water and air blowing in your face may be disconcerting. Also, real bubbles float gently down from ceiling. **[A][U][F][I][Q][S][V]** You must wear special 3-D glasses; fit over regular glasses. Those with vision impairments may not fully appreciate the effects. **[F]** Avoid this show if you're sensitive to loud noises. **[Ö]** Ears to the World can be used here. **[H]** Handheld and reflective captioning and assistive listening available here. Film portion of preshow is also closed-captioned. 3-D glasses make captioning harder to see. **[M]** Wheelchair/ECV users enter through the standby queue to the access gate at the turnstiles. The cast member in the waiting area will direct you to the seating area. **[L]** Theater-style seats may be tight squeeze for larger people.	**3-D Film**
	E-Ticket
	Ages 4 & up
	Loud, some violence
	Med. waits
	10-min. intro 18-min. film

Get Involved ... or Not!

Disney-MGM Studios is well-known for its band of actors who roam the park's streets looking to involve visitors in their improvisational comedy acts. Known as Streetmosphere, these performers take on personalities ranging from old-time movie stars to ordinary plumbers and workers. They're lots of fun, if you're into that kind of thing, but if you're on the fearful/introverted side, you might want to avoid them. Here are a few other places or groups that encourage the audience's participation. In some you may be called on at random, in others you have to volunteer. Either way, you decide if you want to become part of the act!

In Epcot: World Showcase Players; Turtle Talk with Crush
In the Magic Kingdom: Storytime with Belle and Monsters, Inc. Laugh Floor
In Disney's Animal Kingdom: Flights of Wonder and DeVine
In Disney-MGM Studios: Indiana Jones; Backlot Tour; '50s Prime Time Cafe; and Lights, Motors, Action! Extreme Stunt Show
Outside the Theme Parks: Whispering Canyon Cafe; 'Ohana; Spirit of Aloha; Hoop Dee Doo Musical Revue; Comedy Warehouse; and Adventurers Club

Charting the Attractions
in the Streets of America Area
(continued)

	Deb Wills' Rating	Deb Koma's Rating	Readers' Rating

☐ Streets of America Movie Set [B-4]

	3	4	6

Facades of buildings along popular city streets (New York, San Francisco) provide an interesting movie set backdrop. Other details, like city noise sound effects, add to the atmosphere. *[M]* Wheelchair/ECV accessible. *[X]* Service animal break area is located backstage to the left of the Courthouse here—speak to a cast member for assistance.

Walk-Thru
A-Ticket
All ages
Take as long as you want!

☐ Toy Story Pizza Planet Arcade [B-5]

	3	3	6

Designed to resemble the pizza place in Disney's original "Toy Story," this arcade is adjacent to a counter-service restaurant. Typical video game arcade, with most games requiring two to four tokens (which cost 25 cents each). *[A][U][I]* The noise level in the arcade is high—it could cause overstimulation. *[M]* Wheelchair/ECV accessible.

Arcade
A-Ticket
Ages 5 & up
No scares
Few waits

☐ Lights, Motors, Action! Extreme Stunt Show [A-2]

	8	8	8

Imported from Disneyland Paris, this show wows you with an epic display of the stuntperson's art. Cars, motorcycles, and Jet Skis roar across the set while a giant video screen shows how the special effects action is turned into movie magic. A 5,000-seat amphitheater packs in the audiences. Seating in the amphitheater is on hard metal, backless bleachers. Very loud show. There is a companion

© Deb Wills

A car flies in Lights, Motors, Action!

Show
E-Ticket
Ages 3 & up
Loud!
35–40 min. show

restroom located in this theater (no changing table). *[A][U][I]* The noise level in this show is high—could cause overstimulation. *[F]* There are lots of sudden, loud noises, explosions, and fire. There is also a chance of accidents/injury to performers. Ask to be seated in a low area if heights bother you. *[H]* Assistive listening available. *[M]* Wheelchair/ECV users should speak to the cast member at the entrance to be directed to the elevator (to your left after you pass through the main entrance). The accessible section is about halfway up the theater. Note that it may be hard to see over the railing if you are seated in the lower accessible section. *[V]* Action is projected on a giant video screen.

🔔 Fantasmic! Dinner Package

The Fantasmic! Dinner Package includes a fixed-price dinner at one of the participating Disney-MGM Studios restaurants (Hollywood Brown Derby, Mama Melrose Ristorante Italiano, or Hollywood & Vine) and reserved seating in the Fantasmic! amphitheater (usually on the far right side of the theatre) at no additional charge. This means that instead of waiting in line for 60–90 minutes outside the theater, you can walk right up to the theater 30–45 minutes before show time and still have a good seat. (Note that these seats are still first-come, first-served.) Ask about the package when you call to make your reservations.

Charting the Attractions in the Mickey Avenue Area

Deb Wills' Rating
Deb Koma's Rating
Readers' Rating

▌ Journey Into Narnia [D-2] | 5 | 5 | 6 |

See an in-depth movie trailer for "The Lion, The Witch, and The Wardrobe," accented by an appearance of the White Witch, and concluding with a pass by a variety of costumes and props used in the film. Rest of attraction is a walk-through. **[F]** Dark room, sudden appearance of witch. **[C][♥][T][M][P][S][L][V]** Standing room only for film. **[H]** Assistive listening and video captioning available. **[M]** Wheelchair/ECV users may remain in chairs.

Film/ Walk-Thru
B-Ticket
All ages
Allow 15 min.

▌ The Magic of Disney Animation [F-2] | 5 | 5 | 8 |

Tour what used to be Disney's Florida animation studio. This attraction now features a short film in a small theater with an animator and Mushu, from Disney's "Mulan," explaining the animation process. There's a hands-on program at the end of the tour, during which an animator talks you through the process of drawing your own Disney character, which you can keep as a souvenir. Seating for latter portion is at artist desk on stool—spectators can sit on benches. Outdoor queue is mostly shaded. **[A][I][U]** Peer reviewer Bonny Eby comments, "Our daughter LOVES the hands-on area here—it has some interactive computer things, a character meet and greet, and a 'museum' of animation!" **[H]** Reflective captioning and assistive listening available. Film portions are also captioned. **[M]** Wheelchair/ECV users enter through the standby queue. Ask the cast member to be directed to an accessible seat during the drawing section. **[X]** Break area for service animals nearby; ask cast member.

Film/ Walk-Thru/ Hands-On
C-Ticket
Ages 4 & up
No scares
Med. waits
Allow 45 min.

▌ Walt Disney: One Man's Dream [D-2] | 9 | 9 | 8 |

Trace Walt Disney's path in this exhibit of hundreds of artifacts from his youth and early days in the business and throughout his career. After perusing the displays, view the film, which features Walt himself talking about his amazing journey. **[B]** Dark theater for discreet nursing. **[Ö]** Ears to the World available. **[H]** Handheld and reflective captioning and assistive listening available. Movie is also closed-captioned. **[M]** Wheelchair/ECV users enter through the regular queue. **[L]** Theater-style seats may be tight squeeze for people of larger size. **[X]** Break area for service animals nearby; ask cast member.

Walk-Thru
D-Ticket
Ages 10 & up
Short waits
Allow 30 min. for exhibit; 20-min. movie

▌ Playhouse Disney—Live on Stage! [E-3] | 7 | 7 | 8 |

Perfect for preschoolers, this show spotlights characters from the Disney Channel's popular daytime programs: Bear in the Big Blue House, JoJo and Goliath, Stanley, and Pooh and friends (although we hear that the Little Einsteins may soon join the cast). Outdoor queue is mostly in the sun. **[A][U]** Sit at far ends of sections for easy exit if necessary. Separate unmarked entrance for those with Guest Assistance Card—ask a cast member. Note that real bubbles float gently down from ceiling and streamers are shot into the audience. **[B]** Music and dancing—baby should love this! **[H]** Handheld captioning and assistive listening available. Film portions in the queue area are also captioned. **[M]** Wheelchair/ ECV users enter through the regular queue. Ask a cast member for directions to special seating area. **[C][L][M][P][S][T]** You must sit on the carpeted floor for this show—there is only limited bench seating at the rear of the theater.

Live Show
C-Ticket
All ages
No scares
Med. waits
20-min. show

Side tabs: Planning | Special Challenges | Getting There | Staying in Style | Touring | Feasting | Resources | Index

Charting the Attractions
in the Mickey Avenue Area
(continued)

Deb Wills' Rating | Deb Koma's Rating | Readers' Rating

☐ Studios Backlot Tour [B-2]

8 **8** **7**

Learn how sea battles are filmed, tour Disney's backlot, and brave Catastrophe Canyon, a special effects tour de force. Audience members can be chosen to participate in the first part of the tour. Outdoor queue is shaded, which is good, since waits can be quite long. You're entertained by a video on overhead monitors while you wait. The first portion of the tour is all standing with nowhere to sit, and you may get splashed. Tram tour portion also includes the danger of getting wet—those seated on the left (as you face front) get wettest. You can use the restroom after the standing portion of the tour. After the tour, browse through the American Film Institute (AFI) Showcase Exhibit. (At press time the exhibit theme was "Villains," which may be scary for some.) **[A][U]** Queue may be overstimulating during long waits, as the loud movie clips repeat and many people are crowded into a very small area. **[A][U][F][I]** Parts of the tour have sudden, very loud effects. The Catastrophe Canyon portion is not only loud, with explosions, but also with rushing water and fire. **[F][Q]** Tram shakes and trembles during Catastrophe Canyon portion. **[Ö]** Ears to the World available at preshow. **[H]** Film portions are closed-captioned. Sea battle and tram tour in sign language on designate days—check with Guest Relations. Meet interpreter at entrance. **[M]** Wheelchair/ECV users enter through the regular queue; stay to the right. The access gate is to your right. You may stay in your wheelchair/ECV and ride in an accessible vehicle, or fold wheelchair and stow on the tram ride. You may remain in wheelchair/ECV at the AFI exhibit.

Show/Ride
D-Ticket
Ages 6 & up
Explosions, fires
Long waits
40-min. tour

☐ Toy Story Mania [D-2] [coming in 2008]

? **?** **?**

Toy Story Mania will open in the soundstage formerly occupied by Who Wants To Be A Millionare—Play It! The ride will immerse guests in a 3-D interactive experience as they travel in vehicles along a midway-themed route. Riders interact with Mr. Potato Head in the queue and aim at animated targets with a Toy Story theme to score points, while an intelligent game technology adjusts skill levels accordingly. Every ride will be different We can only guess at this time, but imagine the ride will be similar to the Magic Kingdom's Buzz Lightyear Space Ranger Spin in terms of special challenge considerations (see page 242).

Ride
D-Ticket
Ages 4 & up
We estimate a 4-5 minute ride

☐ Voyage of the Little Mermaid [E-2]　　*FP*

9 **7** **8**

A mingling of live action, puppetry, and film make this show a must-see for any Ariel fan. The popular Disney animated film is reenacted with fun results! You may feel mist or even rain. Most of this queue is outdoors, but in the shade. Indoor waiting area dimly lit and gets very crowded—could cause claustrophic feelings. **[A][U][I]** Parts of this show have very loud special effects. Also, there are flashing light effects and some smoke. **[A][U][C][♥][T][I][M][P][E][S]** Use FASTPASS to minimize wait times. **[F]** Parts of this show are in the dark. Also, Ursula the Sea Witch can be very menacing. **[H]** Reflective captioning and assistive listening. **[M]** Wheelchair/ECV users should use FASTPASS; otherwise speak to the cast member at entrance. This is a difficult show to park ECVs; some areas have parallel parking. **[L]** Theater-style seats may be tight for people of larger size.

Live Show
E-Ticket
Ages 3 & up
Dark, strobe effects
FASTPASS or long waits
17-min. show

Queue-Tip!

If you get caught in a line in this park, look at your guidemap for the following: Kermit the Frog balloon, dinosaur, Coke bottles, boat, guitar, dragon, fountain, mermaid.
—contributed by peer reviewer and author Kimberly Button

Charting the Attractions in the Sunset Boulevard Area

	Deb Wills' Rating	Deb Koma's Rating	Readers' Rating

Beauty and the Beast–Live on Stage [G-4] · 8 8 8

A reenactment of Disney's animated film about a girl who finds love with an enchanted prince, featuring dazzling costumes, music, and sets. Entertaining preshow by a cappella group "4 for a Dollar." Seating is on hard metal bleachers with backs. Theater is covered, but open, with big, noisy fans in the back. **[A][U][I]** There are some sudden loud noises in this show. **[F]** Some dark, menacing scenes and staged violence. **[G][U]** Some smoke effects—usually only reaches front rows. **[H]** Handheld captioning and assistive listening are available. Sign language-interpreted performances on designated days; check with Guest Relations for schedule. Arrive at least 25 minutes before the show and sit in the <u>right</u> section of the audience. (Preshow is <u>not</u> interpreted.) If you are in a wheelchair and cannot transfer out, however, there is no special seating here. **[M]** Wheelchair/ECV users enter using the ramp on the right; seating is in rows in the front and the back—we suggest the front row, although the stage is slightly elevated and you will have to look up a bit. **[X]** Break area for service animals nearby; ask a cast member.

Live Show
E-Ticket
Ages 5 & up
Loud sound effects
Med. waits
10-min. intro 30-min. show

The Great Movie Ride [D-3] · 8 7 8

Take a trip through movie history on this tram tour that combines film with amazing Animatronics and some live-action surprises. Queue snakes around indoors, while you watch movie clips projected on huge screens. During busy times, queue may overflow to the unshaded outdoors. **[A][U][I]** The noise and excitement levels during this ride can be high at times. Alien scene may be too intense for some. **[A][U][I]** Queue area can also be overstimulating during long waits, as the loud movie clips repeat multiple times, and many people are crowded into a very small area. There are explosions, gunshots, and fire in some scenes. **[C][♥][T][M][E][S]** If there are long waits in the queue area, there's nowhere to sit—only rails to lean against. **[F]** Certain scenes during this ride are in very dark surroundings, and there are some sudden, loud noises. There's also an extraterrestrial alien scene, a realistic wicked witch, representations of mummies, skeletons, snakes, and other animals, and some staged violence. **[G]** Some smoke effects, usually only affect front of tram. **[H]** Handheld captioning is available at this attraction. Assistive listening is available for the preshow portion only. **[X]** Certain elements may be distracting to service animals—check with cast member before bringing onboard. **[M]** If in a wheelchair/ECV, see a cast member when you enter the queue with the large movie screen. You'll be directed to an alternate entrance. For more room, request your wheelchair be left at the loading dock instead of folded up with you in the vehicle. There is a wheelchair-accessible car at the rear of the tram. **[V]** Long, winding queue, very dimly lit.

Film/Ride
D-Ticket
Ages 4 & up
Some dark scenes, aliens, loud noises
Long waits
3-min. intro 18-min. ride

© Debra Martin Koma

Seating on the Twilight Zone Tower of Terror
(see next page)

Planning · Special Challenges · Getting There · Staying in Style · Touring · Feasting · Resources · Index

Charting the Attractions in the Sunset Boulevard Area
(continued)

	Deb Wills' Rating	Deb Koma's Rating	Readers' Rating

☐ Rock 'n' Roller Coaster Starring Aerosmith [G-3] *FP* 🧍

Ratings: **9** | **10** | **9**

	Coaster

This high-speed coaster goes from 0 to 60 mph (96.5 kph) in 2.8 seconds! There are lots of twists and turns, inversions, and sharp drops—all completely in the dark. Music is fed, very loudly, through speakers in headrest. Harness holds you in place. The shaded outdoor queue winds around—once inside, you must stand during a brief preshow video featuring Steven Tyler and his Aerosmith cohorts. A companion restroom is located in the plaza. **[A][U][I]** The noise and excitement levels in this ride are very high—it could cause overstimulation. **[A][U][C][♥] [T][I][M][P][E][S]** Use FASTPASS to minimize wait times. **[♥][T][Q][P][E][S]** There are several inversions during this ride—you can really get shaken up, so avoid it if you have motion sickness; heart-, neck-, or back-related issues; or if you're pregnant. **[F]** The ride is completely in the dark. Anyone with a fear of heights or falling should also avoid this ride. **[M]** Wheelchair/ECV users should use FASTPASS; otherwise enter through the standby queue. ECV users must transfer to a wheelchair—speak with a cast member to obtain one. You must transfer out of your wheelchair to ride, but you have only 30 seconds to accomplish this. If you'd like to practice boarding beforehand, you can use a stationary vehicle kept in a private area. If you anticipate difficulty boarding, ask the cast member about a special boarding car, which may be available. Keep in mind that if an emergency evacuation is necessary on this ride, you'll have to deal with stairs and narrow walkways or else wait until someone can help you. **[B]** Use Rider Switch. **[B][L]** You must be at least 48 in./122 cm. to ride. Front seats of the "limos" seem to be roomier, as do odd-numbered rows. Adjustable u-bar restraint seems to accommodate most body types. **[X]** Service animals are not allowed. **[V]** Very dark; exiting preshow may be disorienting.

Sidebar:
- E-Ticket
- Ages 8 & up
- Very dark, very loud, very fast!
- FASTPASS or long waits
- 2-min. preshow 1.5-min. ride

☐ The Twilight Zone Tower of Terror [H-4] *FP* 🧍

Ratings: **10** | **10** | **9**

	Thrill Ride

A haunted hotel houses a "malfunctioning" elevator that drops you again and again, unpredictably. The outdoor queue is partially shaded, but progresses up a hill through a tangle of unkempt trees. Preshow and boiler room waiting areas are both very dark! A companion restroom is located opposite the entrance. There is a TTY phone located at these restrooms, also. **[A][U][C][♥][T][Q][P][E][S]** There are intense special effects, including some lightning. There are also a number of sharp, sudden drops, so avoid if you have motion sickness; heart-, neck-, or back-related issues; or if you're pregnant. **[A][U][C][♥][T][I][M][P][E][S]** Use FASTPASS to minimize wait times. **[Ö]** Ears to the World available during the preshow. **[H]** Film portions of preshow are captioned. **[F]** The ride is almost completely in the dark, except for a moment when the doors open, allowing you to look out onto the theme park below. Anyone with a fear of heights or falling should avoid this ride. **[M]** Wheelchair/ECV users should use FASTPASS; otherwise speak to a cast member at the attraction entrance. ECV users must transfer to a wheelchair—speak with a cast member to obtain one. You must transfer out of your wheelchair to ride. **[B]** Use Rider Switch. **[B][L]** You must be at least 40 in./102 cm. to ride. Seats have retractable belts. While the belts are long enough, the space allotted on the bench may be a tight squeeze for people of larger size. To give yourself a little more room, do NOT sit near a wall—request an aisle seat. Be aware that as you lift out of your seat during the ride, you may land on hardware uncomfortably. **[X]** Service animals are not permitted.

Sidebar:
- E-Ticket
- Ages 8 & up
- Dark, sudden drops, very scary
- FASTPASS or long waits
- 10-min. intro 5-min. ride

Side tabs: Planning · Special Challenges · Getting There · Staying in Style · Touring · Feasting · Resources · Index

Disney's Animal Kingdom

Planning
Special Challenges
Getting There
Staying in Style
Touring
Feasting
Resources
Index

Disney's Animal Kingdom, which opened in 1998, is the newest and largest of the Walt Disney World theme parks. It was initially called a "New Species of Theme Park," and it is just that! Part zoo, part theme park—lush landscaping, detailed architecture, animals, birds, shows, and rides all make up Disney's Animal Kingdom.

Just through the turnstiles, the Oasis provides a peaceful transition from daily life to the beauty of the park. As you emerge from the Oasis, before you stands the 145-foot -tall (44-meter) **Tree of Life**, a magnificent icon. The branches span 160 feet (49 meters). Twenty artists carved more than 300 animals into the 50-foot-wide (15-meter) trunk, branches, and roots. You'll spot different animals depending on your location.

AMBIENCE

Guest Relations is located to your left both outside and inside the park turnstiles (see park map on pages 288–289). Visit here to obtain the Guide Book for Guests With Disabilities, a Guest Assistance Card (see pages 10–11), hearing or vision rental devices, the schedule for sign sanguage-interpreted attractions, and ask any questions. On Saturdays from 9:20 am to 9:40 am, an ASL interpreter will usually be in Guest Relations to answer questions.

PARK LAYOUT AND NAVIGATION

Oasis/Discovery Island—A lush tropical area with paths to transition you from parking lot to park. Once you arrive in Discovery Island, you'll set your eyes on the Tree of Life, home of the 3-D film It's Tough to be a Bug! You'll find animal- and bird-viewing areas, with shaded areas and benches for sitting.

Africa/Rafiki's Planet Watch—Swahili architecture shapes Harambe village, complete with eateries, marketplace, and the Kilimanjaro Safaris! Board a train to visit Rafiki's conservation exhibits and petting area.

Asia—The mythical Kingdom of Anandapur surrounds you with the crumbling ruins of an ancient village, hand-painted walls, temples, a maharajah's palace, and the commanding view of Mt. Everest, home to the thrilling Expedition Everest and the Yeti!

DinoLand U.S.A.—A tribute to dinosaurs real and imagined! Kids play in a dig site, enjoy Chester and Hester's tacky and wacky fossil fun games and rides, and visit the Broadway caliber show, "Finding Nemo—The Musical."

Camp Minnie-Mickey—Reminiscent of the Adirondacks, this especially kid-friendly area includes the amazing Festival of the Lion King, Pocahontas and her Forest Friends, and Character Greeting Trails.

Getting to Disney's Animal Kingdom

BEST TIMES TO GO

Disney's Animal Kingdom can be enjoyed in one day, although it is best to **visit the most popular attractions earlier** and use FASTPASS to avoid long lines. Take advantage of Extra Magic Hour mornings, and don't forget to check the tip board for ride wait times.

Co-author Deb Wills particularly enjoys Disney's Animal Kingdom on **Extra Magic Hour mornings**, as the animals are generally awake and moving around. Especially during off-peak times, get a breakfast goodie and coffee from Kusafiri Bakery and then find a quiet animal viewing location in the Discovery Island Trails.

Wherever possible, **get a FASTPASS**. Check the entertainment schedule in the park's times guide for show times. Take the length of the show times into account when planning your route, and keep in mind that viewing several shows takes a lot of time.

The most popular attractions—**Kilimanjaro Safaris, Expedition Everest, and "Finding Nemo—The Musical"**—generate very long lines early and during peak season, throughout the entire day. Get a Kilimanjaro Safaris FASTPASS and visit the nearby Pangani Forest Exploration Trail while you wait. Or get your Expedition Everest FASTPASS, then visit the Maharajah Jungle Trek.

Remember that once a show ends, there will be **lots of congestion** as folks exit the immediate area and decide where to go next.

GETTING THERE

By Car—For many special needs travelers, it may be most convenient to travel by car. Take I-4 to exit 65 (east or west) and follow signs to Disney's Animal Kingdom parking. All-day parking is $10 (free to Disney resort guests and Annual Passholders), and the pass is valid at other Disney parks' lots on the same day.

© Debra Martin Koma

Disabled parking sign at Disney's Animal Kingdom

By Bus—Take a direct bus from all resorts, Epcot's main entrance, Transportation & Ticket Center, and Disney-MGM Studios. From Downtown Disney, Typhoon Lagoon, or Blizzard Beach, take a bus or a boat to a resort and transfer to a Disney's Animal Kingdom bus.

Making the Most of Disney's Animal Kingdom

TIPS

The park has its share of **small and large hills and uneven paths**. To simulate the "real" outdoors, pebbles, rocks, animal tracks, sidewalk cracks, and roots were formed in the concrete pathways throughout the park. ECV riding is doable, but those pushing a wheelchair or unsteady on their feet may have difficulty. Also, those using a cane might find it catches or jams on the uneven terrain.

Disney's Animal Kingdom is the **hottest of all the parks**, especially in the summer. Some shows and rides are outside. Be sure to wear protective clothing and sunscreen, and stay hydrated!

For animal protection and conservation, **no straws or drink lids** are available. Should you require a straw for drinking, you must bring your own, or you can purchase a souvenir cup with a built-in straw ($7).

A large **Braille map**, mounted on a stand, is located near the Disney Outfitters store, across the bridge from the Oasis and near the Tip Board. There is also a Braille map inside Guest Relations.

Access to most of the attractions is via **regular queue**; however, some of the queues have tight corners, making wheelchair and especially ECV maneuvering tricky. The prime example of this is the Dinosaur attraction.

Need your **medicine refrigerated**? Take it to the First Aid Station, and they'll take care of that for you. The First Aid Station also has a companion-assisted restroom. There is a TTY phone located here, also. The **First Aid Station** and Baby Care Center are located behind the Creature Comforts shop in Discovery Island (see page 206).

Throughout the theme park are hands-on items called **manipulatives**. Guests with vision impairments or needing tactile stimulation can instead feel the size and shape of animal heads, bones, etc. Three areas that have these manipulatives are the Pangani Forest Exploration Trail, Maharajah Jungle Trek, and Rafiki's Planet Watch—these can sometimes be found at the kid's activity stations, too!

Service animals are allowed, but the closeness of animals throughout the park could cause problems for some. Be aware!

Reader Tip: "The parrots in The Oasis take exception to my dog. They become very loud. This could cause a problem for many service animals and disturb nearby humans, too!"—contributed by Donna Jagodzinski

SPECIAL CONSIDERATIONS

Planning | Special Challenges | Getting There | Staying in Style | Touring | Feasting | Resources | Index

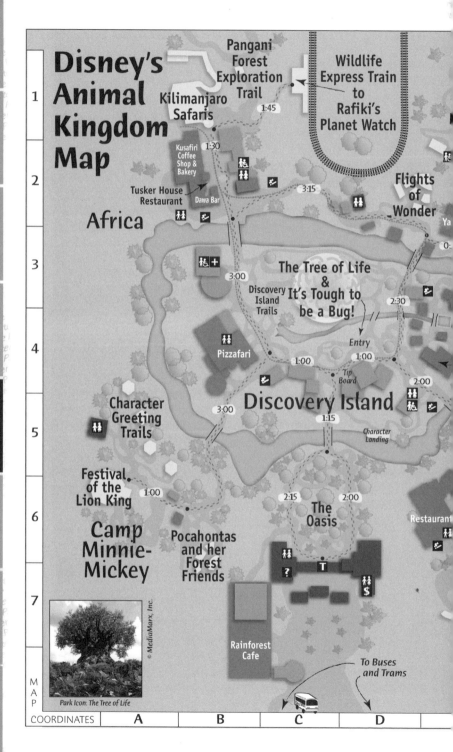

Disney's Animal Kingdom Map

Pangani Forest Exploration Trail

Kilimanjaro Safaris

1:45

Wildlife Express Train to Rafiki's Planet Watch

1

2

Kusafiri Coffee Shop & Bakery

1:30

3:15

Flights of Wonder

Tusker House Restaurant

Dawa Bar

Africa

The Tree of Life & It's Tough to be a Bug!

3

3:00

Discovery Island Trails

2:30

Entry

1:00

4

Pizzafari

1:00

Tip Board

2:00

Character Greeting Trails

3:00

Discovery Island

1:15

5

Character Landing

Festival of the Lion King

1:00

2:15

2:00

6

Camp Minnie-Mickey

Pocahontas and her Forest Friends

The Oasis

Restaurant

7

Rainforest Cafe

To Buses and Trams

© MediaMarx, Inc.

MAP

Park Icon: The Tree of Life

COORDINATES | A | B | C | D

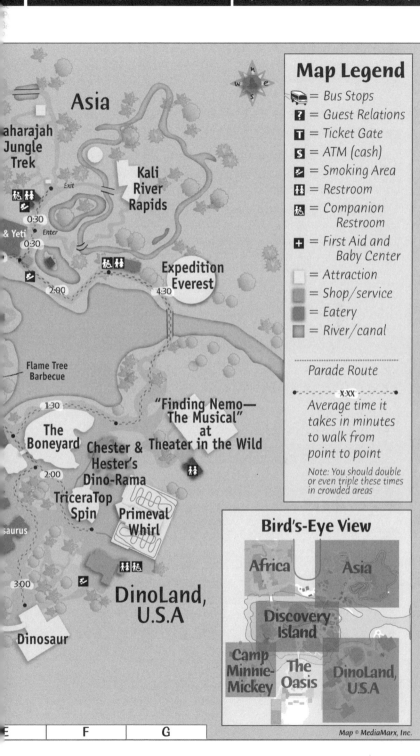

Asia

Maharajah Jungle Trek

Kali River Rapids

Exit
0:30
& Yeti
Enter
0:30

2:00

Expedition Everest
4:30

Flame Tree Barbecue

1:30

The Boneyard

Chester & Hester's Dino-Rama

TriceraTop Spin

Primeval Whirl

"Finding Nemo—The Musical" at Theater in the Wild

2:00

saurus

3:00

DinoLand, U.S.A

Dinosaur

Map Legend

= Bus Stops
? = Guest Relations
T = Ticket Gate
S = ATM (cash)
= Smoking Area
= Restroom
= Companion Restroom
+ = First Aid and Baby Center
= Attraction
= Shop/service
= Eatery
= River/canal

Parade Route

•— x:xx —•
Average time it takes in minutes to walk from point to point

Note: You should double or even triple these times in crowded areas

Bird's-Eye View

Africa   Asia

Discovery Island

Camp Minnie-Mickey   The Oasis   DinoLand, U.S.A

Map © MediaMarx, Inc.

E   F   G

Planning

Special Challenges

Getting There

Staying in Style

Touring

Feasting

Resources

Index

Planning

Special Challenges

Getting There

Staying in Style

Touring

Feasting

Resources

Index

ENTERTAINMENT

Entertainment at Disney's Animal Kingdom

Live entertainment includes a talking palm tree (Wes Palm), a wandering vine (DeVine), and musical and acrobatic acts.

Schedules for **sign language-interpreted shows** are made a week at a time. Check at Guest Relations for the most recent schedule. Sign language interpretation is usually offered on Saturdays.

Festival of the Lion King and **"Finding Nemo—The Musical"** are the most popular live shows—you shouldn't miss them! Check the times guide and try to make the first or last show of the day.

The afternoon **Mickey's Jammin' Jungle Parade** is a bright, festive treat for the eyes, as giant-sized whimsical puppets meander through the park. Some of the puppets interact with the audience! There are special viewing areas for those in wheelchairs/ECVs:
- Near the Dawa Bar in Harambe, Africa
- Across from Beastly Bazaar on Discovery Island

Kid's Discovery Clubs offer brief (and sometimes hands-on) learning experiences. A kid's guidemap is sometimes available, too.

SEATING

Attraction Seating Chart

Dinosaur	narrow seat with bars at hips, seat belt
Expedition Everest	low bar
Festival of the Lion King	bench seats (no backs)
"Finding Nemo—The Musical"	bench seats (with backs)
Flights of Wonder	bench seats (no backs)
It's Tough to be a Bug	bench seats (with backs)
Kali River Rapids	narrow seats with seat belts
Kilimanjaro Safari	bench seats (with backs)
Pocahontas and Her Forest Friends	bench seats (no back)
Primeval Whirl	small area, low bar, bench seats (with backs)
TriceraTop Spin	small space with loose lap belt
Wildlife Express to Rafiki's	bench seats (with backs)

Finding Your Place at Disney's Animal Kingdom

Planning

Attractions With Restrictions/Warnings

RESTRICTIONS
Special Challenges
Getting There

Dinosaur	40 in. (102 cm.). Intense special effects. For safety, you should be in good health and free from high blood pressure, heart, back, or neck problems, motion sickness, or other conditions that could be aggravated by this adventure. Expectant mothers should not ride.
Expedition Everest	44 in. (112 cm.). For safety and comfort, you should be in good health and free from heart, back, or neck problems, motion sickness, or other conditions that could be aggravated by this adventure. Expectant mothers should not ride.
It's Tough to be a Bug	Special effects may be too intense for children and some adults.
Kali River Rapids	38 in. (97 cm.). For safety and comfort, you should be in good health and free from heart, back, or neck problems, motion sickness, or other conditions that could be aggravated by this adventure. Expectant mothers should not ride.
Kilimanjaro Safaris	For safety, you should be in good health and free from high blood pressure, heart, back, or neck problems, motion sickness, or other conditions that could be aggravated by this adventure. Expectant mothers should not ride.
Primeval Whirl	48 in. (122cm.). For safety, you should be in good health and free from high blood pressure, heart, back, or neck problems, motion sickness, or other conditions that could be aggravated by this adventure. Expectant mothers should not ride.

Staying in Style

Attractions With Hearing Devices

HEARING DEVICES
Touring

Assistive Listening	Kilimanjaro Safaris, Rafiki's Planet Watch, Wildlife Express Train, Conservation Station, Kali River Rapids (queue only), Pocahontas and Her Forest Friends, Festival of the Lion King, Flights of Wonder, "Finding Nemo—The Musical," It's Tough to be a Bug, and Dinosaur (preshow)
Handheld Captioning	Festival of the Lion King, Pocahontas and Her Forest Friends, Kilimanjaro Safaris, Wildlife Express Train, and Conservation Station
Reflective Captioning	It's Tough to be a Bug and "Finding Nemo—The Musical"
Video Captioning	Kilimanjaro Safaris (queue), Pangani Forest Exploration (Gorilla Falls Overlook), Rafiki's Planet Watch, Dinosaur (preshow)
ASL (on certain days)	Mickey's Jammin' Jungle Parade, Festival of the Lion King, Pocahontas and Her Forest Friends, and Flights of Wonder
Ears to the World	It's Tough to be a Bug and Kilimanjaro Safaris

Feasting
Resources
Index

Finding Your Place at Disney's Animal Kingdom

SPECIAL PLACES

You can't get there from here! Unlike the other parks, Animal Kingdom offers **no real orderly sense of direction**. Discovery Island is the closest thing to a "hub," and paths from all the lands lead back here. Africa, Asia, and DinoLand U.S.A. are connected by a path. To reach Camp Minnie-Mickey, you have to return to Discovery Island, and Rafiki's Planet Watch is only accessible via the Wildlife Express train in Africa. Be sure to have a guidemap with you! Signage provides attraction names and directions, so look for it.

Those looking for a **quiet area** for breaks, time-outs, or baby nursing/napping should consider:
* Inner parts of the Discovery Island trails are rarely populated and offer benches.
* Upcountry Landing, when not used for character greets.
* Path from Africa to Asia, via back side of Tree of Life—near Flights of Wonder are tables and chairs facing the water, quiet viewing area.
* Far right part of the Character Greeting Trails, near the restrooms.
* Area behind Drinkwallah.
* Cretaceous Trail in DinoLand U.S.A.

Companion restrooms available at Disney's Animal Kingdom:
* Opposite Flame Tree Barbecue, just before DinoLand U.S.A. entrance on right
* Rafiki's Planet Watch (no changing table)
* In the Mombasa Marketplace in Harambe, Africa (no changing table)
* Near Chester and Hester's Dinosaur Treasures in DinoLand U.S.A. (no changing table)
* First Aid Station on Discovery Island near Creature Comforts shop
* Near Maharajah Jungle Trek, on left just before entrance
* Inside Maharajah Jungle Trek, to the right as you exit the Bat House (no changing table)
* Near Expedition Everest in Asia

Charting the Attractions at The Oasis and Camp Minnie-Mickey

	Deb Wills' Rating	Deb Koma's Rating	Readers' Rating

☐ The Oasis [C-6] | 8 | 8 | 7 |

Lush tropical vegetation allows you to decompress as you enter this new species of theme park! Winding paths with viewing areas—give the birds and animals a chance to appear. Have your camera ready. **[G]** Heavy vegetation, grasses, molds, pollen, and animals are present. **[F][V]** One spot along one of the paths has a small "cave" to pass through, but it can be bypassed. **[M][P][E][S]** Watch for roots and ruts in the paths; they have been artificially placed to appear lifelike. **[V]** The heavy vegetation makes the natural lighting dim in spots, especially some of the viewing areas.

Walk-Thru	
B-Ticket	
All ages	
Allow 20 min.	

☐ Camp Minnie-Mickey Character Greeting Trails [A-5] | 6 | 5 | 6 |

Visit Disney characters among the trees in an Adirondacks-like setting. Each trail is marked with characters appearing; each character has their own queue. Have your camera ready. Note: They don holiday apparel in December! **[A][U][C]** Waits can be long at times; go while Festival of the Lion King is being performed. **[F]** Large characters may be scary to some. **[M]** Queues difficult to navigate in larger wheelchair/ECV.

Outdoors	
B-Ticket	
All ages	
Med. waits	

☐ Festival of the Lion King [A-6] | 9 | 9 | 9 |

This Broadway-class show in the round based on The Lion King is not to be missed with its beautiful music, singing, dancing, acrobats, stilt walkers, and floats. The theater is enclosed and offers bench seating (no backs) and air conditioning. Outdoor queue is uncovered with little shade. See the first or last show of the day for shortest waits. Audience members in the front rows (typically children) may be briefly included in the "show." Must climb stairs or sit in first row (reserved for wheelchair travelers and guests). Entertainers will interact with those in the front rows, and some audience participation occurs. **[A][U]** Lots of action from all directions, especially front rows. **[C][♥][T][M][E][S][L]** No backs on seats. **[F][U]** One act involves fire twirling. **[H]** Assistive listening and handheld captioning available. Sign language-interpreted performances on designated days; check with Guest Relations for schedule. Arrive at least 25 minutes in advance; see cast member. **[M]** Wheelchair seating areas in front; see cast member when arriving. Arrive at least 30 minutes prior to show time, and cast member will seat you first before general seating. **[X]** Check with cast members for seating locations.

Live Show	
E-Ticket	
Ages 2 & up	
Long waits	
30-min. show	

☐ Pocahontas and Her Forest Friends [B-6] | 5 | 7 | 4 |

Live forest animals (like ducks, raccoon, skunk, and snake) take the stage with Pocahontas in this show geared toward kids. Wait in an outdoor queue with limited tree shade. Outdoor theater has sheer netting over most bench seats without backs. First four rows are darker colored and for kids only. Certain performances are animal training sessions (check guidemap for times). **[F]** Small animals, snake, and birds on stage. **[Ö]** Preshow instructions given in English followed by Spanish. **[H]** Assistive listening and handheld captioning available. Sign language-interpreted performances on designated days; check with Guest Relations for schedule. Arrive 20 minutes in advance and sit on left side of audience. Notify cast member that you are there. **[M]** Ask for wheelchair/ECV seating in the front of the theater for kids.

Live Show	
C-Ticket	
Ages 3 & up	
Live animals, snakes, and birds	
13-min. show	

Side tabs: Planning · Special Challenges · Getting There · Staying in Style · Touring · Feasting · Resources · Index

Charting the Attractions at Discovery Island

	Deb Wills' Rating	Deb Koma's Rating	Readers' Rating

☐ It's Tough to be a Bug! [D-4]   *FP*

	9	8	9

In the dark caverns at the base of the Tree of Life is a special 3-D attraction. Hosted by Flik the ant from It's a Bugs Life, the show also includes the evil Hopper. Special effects may be too intense for some and include: "spiders" dropping from ceiling, dry ice "smoke," stink bug smells, tactile effects, and spraying water. Effects may be less intense in the back. Queue winds through Tree of Life roots (with carvings). Once through turnstiles, queue area inside is dimly lit and can get very crowded, but it is air-conditioned. Theater with bench seating (with backs) is dark and has a high ceiling. The show gets very loud! Please use caution, especially with children. This can be a VERY scary attraction! Heed the warning signs. If unsure, don't go in! **[A][U]** Enter row first to be closest to exit. **[A][U][D][B][F][♥][T][P][E][S]** Show takes place in very dark theater and includes spiders, things falling from ceiling, smells, insects, tactile effects in seats, and a menacing villain. **[A][U][C][♥][T][M][P][E][S][L]** Use FASTPASS to avoid waiting in line. **[G]** Dry ice smoke. **[F]** 3-D effects (remove 3-D glasses to alleviate fear), insects, loud buzzing sounds, "stings," darkness, and claustrophobia in preshow area. **[Ö]** Ears to the World translation. **[H]** Assistive listening with rental device. Reflective captioning available; ask cast member at entrance. 3-D glasses make captioning difficult to see. Also seating area is on far left, making 3-D effects difficult to see. **[X]** Check with cast member regarding service animals—they are allowed, but make sure your animal can tolerate the noise level and sudden appearance of characters and props. **[M]** Wheelchair/ECV accessible through main queue. When exiting, use exit ramp on left. Wheelchair seating in back or front at the ends of the rows. Front row is easier to transfer to seat. Let cast member know your preference at the entrance. **[V]** Darkened queue and theater. You must wear 3-D glasses, which fit over other glasses, to experience special effects.

3-D Show
E-Ticket
Ages 6 & up
Dark, smells, spiders, "stings"
FASTPASS or med. waits
8-min. show

☐ The Tree of Life and Discovery Island Trails [C-3]

	8	8	8

Lush gardens with animal viewing areas surround the Tree of Life and its 325 carvings. This area is often overlooked, especially first thing in the morning. Have camera ready. **[A][U][B]** Semi-secluded areas for quiet time. **[G]** Lots of greenery and animals—those with allergies should be aware. **[C][♥][T][P][E][S]** Look for shaded benches on out of the way paths. **[M]** Wheelchair/ECV accessible on regular pathway.

Walk-Thru
B-Ticket
All ages
Allow 30 min.

© MediaMarx, Inc.

A rental wheelchair in front of The Tree of Life

Charting the Attractions at Africa

▪ Kilimanjaro Safaris [B-1]   *FP* | 10 | 10 | 9 |

	Ride
Enjoy the beauty of the 100-acre animal reserve aboard modified open-air covered trucks with hard plastic bench seating with minimal padding. Driver will point out wildlife, and there is a story line about poaching (which may be modified in the near future). No stopping for photo ops, so have camera ready or just enjoy the view. Children should sit on the inside portions of the bench. Very bumpy, jerky, rough ride on rugged terrain. Each ride is a different experience. Outdoor queue is very long but covered with a few ceiling fans. Loading area ramps downward. There is a small, netted area to place items in, but it's awkward to get things in and out. **[A][U][C][♥][I][E][S][L]** Use FASTPASS to minimize wait times. **[G]** Heavy vegetation, grasses, molds, pollen, and animals are present. **[B]** Strollers must be left in designated area, partway into the queue. From stroller park to beginning of loading area is about 40 feet (12 meters). **[F]** When crowded, queue design could trigger claustrophobic feelings. Rickety bridge simulates jeep falling. **[Ö]** Ears to the World available. **[H]** Assistive listening and video captioning (queue area) are available. May not be able to hear driver identifying animals or the themed commentary on poaching. **[X]** Check with cast member regarding service animal on vehicle; may be allowed as long as they stay in a "lay down" position. Break area for service animals nearby; ask cast member. **[C][B][♥][T][Q][P][E][S]** Very rough ride with bumps and jolts. **[M]** Follow signs to designated loading area (you will unload at the same place to retrieve your wheelchair). Must transfer from ECV to either vehicle seating or standard wheelchair.	E-Ticket
	Ages 3 & up
	Bumpy, live birds and animals, "close escapes"
	FASTPASS or long waits
	19-min. vehicle ride

▪ Pangani Forest Exploration Trail [B-1] | 8 | 8 | 7 |

	Walk-Thru
Gorillas, meerkats, hippos, and birds all make their home along the self-paced walking trail that's just under half a mile long. Between the heavy vegetation and some covered viewing areas, there is some shade. Still, it can get quite hot in here during summer months. Be sure to listen and ask questions of the animal guides. Some hands-on exhibits in the Naturalist's hut. Some areas can become very congested (underwater hippo area, first gorilla area). **[A][U][C][♥][I][E][S][L][T]** Lots of walking. **[G]** Heavy vegetation, grasses, molds, pollen, and animals are present. **[C][B][M][S][V]** Doors in/out of Research Center are awkward and heavy (no automatic opening). **[F]** Research Center has hands-on and small exhibits with spiders, snakes, and lizards. Some birds in aviary may be on the ground or low on branches. **[A][U][C][F][♥][T][I][M][Q][P][E][S][L][V]** As you leave the enclosed gorilla area, you will cross a wobbly, wooden bridge. A second, smaller wobbly bridge follows the bachelor gorilla group area. **[Ö][H]** Video with closed-captioning in Research Center. Go left as you enter, instead of straight to the glass viewing. **[X]** Check with cast member at entrance before bringing service animals. Some service animals not allowed in aviary and must use bypass. **[M]** Wheelchair/ECV accessible along main path. **[V]** Manipulatives available for exploring at several points along trail.	D-Ticket
	All ages
	Spiders in enclosed cases
	Short waits
	Allow at least 30 min.

Planning
Special Challenges
Getting There
Staying in Style
Touring
Feasting
Resources
Index

Charting the Attractions at Rafiki's Planet Watch

	Deb Wills' Rating	Deb Koma's Rating	Readers' Rating

☐ Wildlife Express Train to Rafiki's Planet Watch [C-1]   5 4 5

	Train Ride
The only way to reach Rafiki's Planet Watch is via this slow-moving train where all seats face outward/sideways. There are two rows of seats and room for one wheelchair per car (you'll need to back in). There is a long walk once you exit the train until you get to Rafiki's Planet Watch. If there is a long wait for the train going out, expect at least that much wait returning. Narration and animal buildings as you travel to Rafiki's Planet Watch. Covered queue with ceiling fans; however, line can extend outside. **[B]** Stroller (unless collapsible) must remain at train station and you must carry child; use a courtesy stroller at destination. **[H]** Assistive listening with rental device. **[M]** Mainstream queue, some turns are tight, especially 180-degree ones. At turnstile, go left for wheelchair entrance and then straight ahead, wait for cast member. You may stay in your wheelchair/ECV.	A-Ticket
	All ages
	Glimpses of backstage
	Short waits
	15-min. ride (each way)

☐ Rafiki's Planet Watch [off map]   6 7 5

	Exhibit
Conservation and animal care themed exhibits and activities. Outdoor Affection Section allows hands-on interaction with small domestic animals. Animal Cam shows animal care area; huge colorful mural full of Hidden Mickeys! Most exhibits indoors, includes hands-on, tasting animal food, characters, and Song of Rainforest sound booths (narrated by Grandmother Willow). Might see animal surgeries. **[A][U][F]** Sounds of Rainforest booths have very low lighting and require headset. Sounds include birds, animals, mosquitoes, and thunderstorms. **[A][U]** A good place to cool down and run around. **[G]** Hands-on animal area inside and outside. **[G][D][E][W]** Selected animal foods available for tasting. **[H]** Assistive listening. Video captioning in interactive area of Conservation Station. Arrive at least 5 minutes in advance to see animal presentation at the indoor stage. Rainforest booths feature all sounds through earphones. **[X]** Service animals not allowed in Affection Section; break area for service animals nearby—ask cast member. **[M]** Wheelchair can enter Rainforest booths, but will have to back out. Must transfer from Disney rental ECV to manual wheelchair for Affection Section.	C-Ticket
	All ages
	Backstage, educational fun
	Live animals
	Short waits
	Allow at least 60 min. for a good exploration

© Debra Martin Koma

The Braille Map of Disney's Animal Kingdom, located on Discovery Island

Charting the Attractions at Asia

Also see Expedition Everest on next page.

	Deb Wills' Rating	Deb Koma's Rating	Readers' Rating
	6	8	7

☐ Flights of Wonder [D-2]

The outdoor Caravan Stage is home to more than 20 species of free-flying birds including macaws, cranes, hawks, and owls. The whimsical show also has a conservation theme, so it's educational as well as fun. May be abbreviated or canceled due to inclement weather. Bench seating with no backs. Bleachers on left/right side offer elevated viewing. Mostly shaded theater. For an up-close look, head to the stage area when the show is over! Great photo ops too. Outdoor queue is uncovered. No food or beverage allowed in theater. Adults with video/still cameras may be chosen during the show to come on stage and photograph. **[A][U][C][♥][I][E][S][L]** No queue area per se—just wait outside theater for opening. **[B]** Leave strollers at entrance. **[F]** Audience participation. **[F][V]** Birds fly low over the audience. **[H]** Assistive listening. Sign language-interpreted shows on certain days; check with Guest Relations. Arrive at least 20 minutes in advance; sit in the <u>left</u> section. **[M]** Wheelchair/ECV accessible—special seating on far left in front and also in back.

Live Show
C-Ticket
Ages 3 & up
Live birds overhead
Med. waits
25-min. show

☐ Kali River Rapids [F-2]   *FP* 🧍

	6	9	8

Water raft ride through a jungle jeopardized by illegal logging. There may be flames, but there are also geysers and you will get wet! Wear a poncho to reduce getting soaked. Small storage area in the raft's center to keep items dry, but it really doesn't (bring trash bag or large resealable bag). Must wear shoes to get on ride, but then you can remove them and place in bag to keep dry. High speed in places with a drop. A portion of the ride goes through a simulated burning forest, you will feel the heat and smell fire. Outdoor covered queue is incredibly themed, with intricate details—don't rush through. Once past the turnstiles, the loading area is a large rotating disc that moves at same speed as rafts. Step down into raft and seatbelt yourself in. Rafts seat 12, in six separate seats for two. Special effects may be too intense for some. **[A][U][C][♥][I][E][S][L]** Use FASTPASS. **[G]** Flower scents in the beginning and fire and smoke in parts. **[B]** Use Rider Switch. **[F]** You <u>will</u> get wet! **[H]** Assistive listening in queue. Take extra precaution to ensure hearing aids are removed and kept in dry place. **[X]** No service animals. **[M]** Transfer from ECV/wheelchair to raft. Separate loading area for wheelchairs. The raft will be docked with plenty of time to load. Raft is flagged and you are returned to same location at end. Cast members will hold cane while you're on the ride. **[C][♥][T][Q][P][E][S]** Should not ride. **[B][L]** Minimum height 38 in./97 cm. **[L]** Two persons of size will not fit comfortably on one seat, but a person of larger size will be comfortable sharing the seat with a child or petite person.

Raft Ride
E-Ticket
Ages 7 & up
Med. drop, flames, geysers, and you will get wet!
FASTPASS or long waits
5-min. cruise

☐ Maharajah Jungle Trek [E-1]

	9	8	7

Lush path with beautiful Asian/Indian architecture and tigers, bats, birds, tapirs, and komodo dragon. There is no glass between you and the bats; but there is a barrier that stops them from entering the viewing area. Multiple viewing areas for tigers. Listen to and ask questions of the guides. Parts of open-air trail are covered; some areas can become very congested (tiger areas) and you may have to wait. Companion restroom after bathouse. **[A][U][C][♥][I][E][S][L]** Lots of walking. **[G]** Heavy vegetation, grasses, molds, pollen, and animals present. **[F]** Bathouse bypass available. **[X]** Service animals may be allowed; check with cast member at entrance. Some service animals not allowed in aviary and must use bypass. Break area for service animals nearby; ask cast member. **[V]** Manipulatives available.

Walk-Thru
D-Ticket
All ages
Bats!
Short waits
Allow at least 30 minutes

Planning · Special Challenges · Getting There · Staying in Style · Touring · Feasting · Resources · Index

Charting the Attractions
at Asia (continued) & DinoLand U.S.A.

Deb Wills' Rating   Deb Koma's Rating   Readers' Rating

☐ Expedition Everest [G-3]   FP 🏃 | 10 | 10 | 9

A high-speed train ride with coaster thrills, fast backward movement, and drops. Come face-to-face with Yeti (abominable snowman)! Two seats in each row, and each seat has an individual low bar. Lengthy queue provides interesting storyline—lots to see while you wait. Queues (both FASTPASS and standby) weave inside and out. Single Rider Line also available for shorter waits. **[A][U][C][♥][I][E][S][L]** Use FASTPASS to minimize wait times. **[A][R][U][C][F][♥][T][I][M][Q][P][E][S][V]** Rough/fast ride. **[F]** Portions of ride in dark, fear of heights, falling. **[B]** Use Rider Switch. **[X]** Service animals not allowed. **[M]** Transfer from wheelchair to vehicle. **[♥][Q][E]** Guests with these conditions should not ride. **[V]** Parts of queue are very dimly lit.	**Coaster** E-Ticket Ages 8 & up (44 in./ 112 cm.) FASTPASS or <u>very</u> long waits

DinoLand U.S.A.

☐ The Boneyard [F-5]   5 | 5 | 6

Kids can let off steam by climbing and sliding in the Boneyard. Flooring is spongy mat-like material. There are some places to sit. Bring a towel and dry clothes. Keep close eye on child, as there are several paths to wander. Virtually no shade except for the mammoth dig site, which is covered with a couple of large fans and has rocks for adults to sit on. Good photo ops. Some bridges are made of net and very wobbly. Take ramp or stairs across walkway to dig sit to sift through sand. Shovels/pails provided for kids, wheelchair ramp into sand. **[A][U][F]** Lots of kids in a confined area. **[G]** Sand pit could cause problems. **[C][T][I][M][P][E][S][L][V]** Spongy floor makes walking/wheelchair travel difficult. Not recommended for those in an ECV. **[C][B][♥][T][E][S][L]** Very hot during summer months; be sure to bring water with you. **[F]** Small "cave" with a low ceiling behind T. Rex.	**Playground** B-Ticket Ages 1 & up Allow at least 20 min.

☐ Dinosaur [E-7]   FP 🏃 | 7 | 7 | 8

Travel back 65 million years to the Cretaceous period in search of an Iguanadon. Save him before the meteor shower gets everyone! Outside queue covered with ceiling fans, inside winds around with tight corners. Standing preshow. Ride in 12-person vehicles; each rider has seat belt. Very dark, turbulent, rough ride with loud noises and flashes of lights (especially at beginning and end). Big dinosaurs jump out at you. Sharp turns, sudden stops, herky-jerky motion—think of a bucking bronco ride! Intense special effects. Must be in good health, free from heart, back, or neck problems and motion sickness. **[A][U][C][♥][I][E][S][L]** Use FASTPASS to minimize wait times **[A][U][C][F][♥][T][I][M][Q][P][E][S][V]** Loud/rough/fast ride with various lighting changes and sudden movements. **[C][B][♥][T][Q][E]** Guests with these conditions should not ride. **[C][L][M][S][L]** There are 16 steps down to the loading bay and 16 back up after the ride, or use bypass elevator (see cast member). When you exit the preshow briefing room, pass through a hallway into the loading bay. As you enter, look to your left for the elevator. Transfer from wheelchair to vehicle. **[B]** Use Rider Switch. **[F]** Queue has insect/reptile photos. When crowded, inside queue design could trigger claustrophobic feelings; darkness, loud noises, dinosaurs jump out at you but don't touch you. **[H]** Assistive listening and video captioning (TV monitors to far right in "Briefing Room") available in preshow. **[X]** Service animals not allowed. **[L]** Seats are narrow due to seatbelt hardware, can hurt when jostled. If you are large-breasted, this ride may actually be painful. Minimum height 40 in./102 cm. **[V]** Parts of queue are very dimly lit.	**Thrill Ride** E-Ticket Ages 7 & up Dark, scary, **very loud**, dinosaurs FASTPASS or med. waits 3.5-min. ride

Charting the Attractions
at DinoLand U.S.A.
(continued)

Deb Wills' Rating   Deb Koma's Rating   Readers' Rating

☐ "Finding Nemo—The Musical" [G-4]   10   10   8

"Finding Nemo—The Musical" opened in January 2007 in a newly renovated and now enclosed and air-conditioned theater (replacing Tarzan Rocks). See your favorite Finding Nemo characters come to life through unique puppetry and colorful costumes. Outdoor queue with no cover and very long waits. Must climb up/down stairs for seating. Hard bench seats with backs. Theater is in two sections; runway comes up the middle of the first section. Characters come down runway and also up the aisles and in the area between the upper and lower sections. Some seats adjacent to stage with no barriers; must not touch stage or performers. Restroom located just outside theater on right—you can easily go there before show starts and re-enter theater. **[B]** Park strollers in designated area outside theater. **[A][U][I][B][F][♥][E][S]** Music can be very loud at times; consider sitting further back for less intensity. **[H]** Reflective captioning and assistive listening available. **[F]** There is a song featuring sharks. Sudden loud noises. **[M]** Talk to a cast member at entrances for wheelchair seating area.

Live Show
E-Ticket
Ages 4 & up
Loud
Very long waits
(check times)
35-min. show

☐ Primeval Whirl [G-6]   FP 🧍   5   10   8

Herky-jerky "mini" coaster whose cars spin, make sudden turns, and short, sudden drops. "Time machines" are designed to seat four, with two sections for two people and a low bar for safety. Must be in good health, free from heart, back, or neck problems and motion sickness. Small person seated next to large person will get jostled. **[A][U][C][♥][I][E][S][L]** Use FASTPASS. **[A][U][C][F][♥][T][I][M][Q][P] [E][S][V]** Rough spinning ride with sudden movements. **[B]** Use Rider Switch. **[X]** Service animals not allowed. **[B][♥][Q][E]** Guests with these conditions should not ride. **[M]** Wheelchair/ECV users must transfer to ride vehicle. If unable to brace yourself with legs and arms, you may not be able to stay seated. **[B][L]** Minimum height 48 in./122 cm. **[L]** Persons of larger size can comfortably sit in one of the double seats. If you have a smaller person with you, you may be able to share the seat. Use caution with lap bar being too snug and hurting during ride.

Coaster
D-Ticket
Ages 7 & up
Fast, drops
FASTPASS
2.5-min. ride

☐ TriceraTop Spin [F-6]   5   3   7

Dumbo-like ride that circles a hub as four-person cars shaped like dinosaurs go up and down. Vehicles have a loose lap belt. **[A][U]** Must stay in vehicle for entire ride. **[F]** Heights, spinning. **[X]** Service animals not allowed. **[M]** Accessible car available. You are required to transfer from ECV to standard wheelchair. Some longer-or-wider-than-average wheelchairs may not fit. **[Q]** Ride goes in circle and up and down. **[L]** Each row can fit one large adult and one small child, or a large adult will need to sit in their own row.

Ride
C-Ticket
Ages 2 & up
1.5-min. ride

☐ Dinorama Fossil Fun Games [F-6]   2   5   7

Cheesy carnival games of skill or chance. Cost is $2 a game, which include: Raptor Race, Meteor Strike, and Fossil Fueler, occasional walk-around Dinosaur. **[A][U]** Very loud area with lots of stimulation. **[M]** Wheelchair/ECV accessible—see a cast member for where to go for each game.

Arcade
A-Ticket
Ages 2 & up
Allow 15 min.

Planning   Special Challenges   Getting There   Staying in Style   Touring   Feasting   Resources   Index

Touring the Water Parks

On a sultry summer day, or even a warmish winter one, Disney's two water parks sure are inviting. Choose from either Typhoon Lagoon, which opened in June 1989 with its back story of a tropical storm gone wild, or Blizzard Beach, which debuted in April 1995 with the theme of a freak snowstorm taking over a resort in Florida. While they may not have as many amenities for visitors with challenges as the theme parks or resort hotels, they do offer some provisions that will make your visit easier. Note that many attractions require walking up and down stairs.

Guest Relations, located in front of the entrance to each water park, will provide you with a park guidemap (available also in Spanish, French, Portuguese, German, and Japanese), as well as information on services for guests with disabilities. Also at Guest Services, you'll find a text typewriter (TTY).

You can **borrow a standard wheelchair** from Guest Services, although they have a limited number available. Just leave a driver's license or other valid ID as a deposit.

Ticket booths have one lower accessible counter. Lines can be very long at opening time, so either buy in advance or use the Ticket Vending Machines located near the booths.

Most water park attractions require you to **transfer from your wheelchair** either by yourself or with the assistance of a member of your party. Water park cast members are not permitted to physically assist guests.

Bring a cover for your wheelchair so the seat doesn't get so hot.

Water wheelchairs may be available for use in the shallow water areas. Ask a lifeguard. Note that all wheelchairs are only permitted in water up to the axle on the main wheels.

Most **food and merchandise** locations at the water parks are accessible, although some eateries have very narrow queues that are difficult to negotiate. If you have someone with you, have them order and carry your food, or ask a cast member for assistance.

If you have **special dietary concerns**, contact the water park's food and beverage manager before your visit.

The **First Aid Stations** at the water parks are not as large as at the theme parks and only have very basic supplies; however, each does have a companion restroom and the ability to refrigerate medications or cool-down vests for service animals.

Drinking fountains are wheelchair accessible, but you may also request cups from the nearest restaurant or refreshment stand.

Cast members have access to **paper and pencils/pens** if necessary to communicate.

Phones with amplified handsets are available in each park; see guidemap for location.

Be sure to **remove hearing aids** and keep them in a dry place, such as a plastic bag.

Smoking is permitted in designated areas only. Consult a map if you wish to avoid them.

Note that **wait times** increase as the day wears on. Also, the water parks will refuse additional visitors if they reach capacity. This can happen as early as 10:00 am during the weekends or peak seasons. Consider going early in the day.

Water parks will close if **lightning is visible** in the distance.

Touring the Water Parks
(continued)

Typhoon Lagoon Attractions With Restrictions/Warnings

Crush 'n' Gusher	Must be at least 48 in. (122 cm.) tall to ride—you should be in good health and free from heart conditions, back, or neck problems, or other conditions that could be aggravated by this adventure. Expectant mothers should not ride.
Bay Slide	Must be UNDER 60 in. (152 cm.).
Castaway Creek	Adult supervision required.
Humunga Kowabunga	Must be at least 48 in. (122 cm.). Expectant mothers and those with neck or back problems are strongly discouraged from experiencing any water slide attraction.
Keelhaul Falls	Expectant mothers and those with neck or back problems are strongly discouraged from experiencing any water slide attraction.
Mayday Falls	Expectant mothers and those with neck or back problems are strongly discouraged from experiencing any water slide attraction.
Gang Plank Falls	Expectant mothers and those with neck or back problems are strongly discouraged from experiencing any water slide attraction.
Storm Slides	Expectant mothers and those with neck or back problems are strongly discouraged from experiencing any water slide attraction.
Ketchakiddee Creek	UNDER 48 in. (122 cm.) only.
Shark Reef	Guests under age 10 must be accompanied by an adult.
Wave Pool	Adult supervision required.

Blizzard Beach Attractions With Restrictions/Warnings

Chair Lift	32 in. (81 cm.). No infants or lap-riding.
Cross Country Creek	Adult supervision required.
Downhill Double Dipper	48 in. (122 cm.).
Slush Gusher	48 in. (122 cm.).
Summit Plummet	48 in. (122 cm.). Expectant mothers and those with neck or back problems are strongly discouraged from experiencing any water slide attraction.
Tike's Peak	UNDER 48 in. (122 cm.) only.

Planning

Special Challenges

Getting There

Staying in Style

Touring

Feasting

Resources

Index

Touring the Water Parks (continued)

If you have a **prosthesis**, you must follow a number of special requirements. Cover any exposed metal, sharp edges, or nonskid material before going on any water slide. Coverings, which must be smooth cloth and strong enough to keep the prosthesis from protruding, must be preapproved by water park management. Pick up a specific prosthesis information sheet at Guest Services, but in general, the guidelines are:

✔ If your prosthesis is below the knee, you may ride all the attractions with or without the prosthesis.

✔ If your prosthesis is above the knee and non-bending, you may ride everything with the prosthesis (except where noted for individual attractions). Note that some slides require you to cross your legs at the ankles.

✔ If your prosthesis is above the knee and bends, you may not ride Typhoon Lagoon's Humunga Kowabunga or Blizzard Beach's Summit Plummet.

✔ If your prosthesis is hip level, you may not ride Humunga Kowabunga or Summit Plummet.

✔ If your prosthesis is an upper limb or arm, you can ride all the attractions with or without the prosthesis.

Service animals are welcome at the water parks as long as they remain harnessed/leashed at all times. Follow the same entrances as those using wheelchairs. Animals are not permitted to ride any of the water attractions or enter the water anywhere at the park. Someone must be with the animal at all times. There are designated break areas for service animals as follows (ask a cast member for assistance):

At Typhoon Lagoon	At Blizzard Beach
backstage gate at Shark Reef	backstage gate at main entrance
backstage gate at Ketchakiddee Creek	backstage gate near Runoff Rapids
backstage gate at main dressing rooms	

Although there is some shade around the parks, be sure to apply **sunscreen** frequently, and wear a hat, sunglasses, and long sleeves for extra protection from the sun.

The water is **heated** in all attractions, except Typhoon Lagoon's Shark Reef.

The **pavement** can get very hot—wear flip-flops or surf shoes for extra protection. If the pavement in an area is very wet, be on the lookout for low-level squirting water jets.

Lockers and towels can be rented at Typhoon Lagoon's Hi 'N Dry Towels or Blizzard Beach's Snowless Joe's. It's $5 for a small locker and $7 for a larger size with a $2 refund when you return your key. Towels are $1. Life jackets are free with a refundable deposit and ID. Note that fanny packs are not allowed on rides. Tip: Bring your own towels (from home or your hotel) to save the towel rental fee.

Water Park Dining—Leaning Palms is the main counter-service eatery at Typhoon Lagoon; Lottawatta Lodge is at Blizzard Beach. Both feature sandwiches, wraps, burgers, and salads. If you have special dietary concerns, contact the Food & Beverage manager at least 24 hours before your visit to the water park (see chapter 6 for our guidelines on requesting special meals). There are also a variety of snack spots (sugar-free ice cream is available at some locations) and beverage kiosks (nonalcoholic beer available). There are pictorial menus, as well as menus translated into Spanish, Portuguese, French, German, and Japanese. There are also picnic areas with shade and tables—you can bring your own food and beverage into the park (especially if you have special dietary needs), although no alcoholic beverages or glass containers are permitted.

Typhoon Lagoon Water Park

Typhoon Lagoon spreads out across 56 lush acres located near Downtown Disney. Most water slides here (Crush 'n' Gusher is the exception) have no elevators and require walking up and down stairs.

Disney's back story of this water park claims that a **terrible storm** blew through the once-calm resort of Placid Palms, leaving wild waters in its wake, not to mention the shrimp boat Miss Tilly impaled on a mountaintop called Mount Mayday. There are plenty of thrills to be found here, and we think that Typhoon Lagoon is slightly friendlier to visitors with special needs than Blizzard Beach.

The focal point of Typhoon Lagoon is its **2.5-acre wave pool**, which sits below Mount Mayday. Circling the park's perimeter is a slow-moving "lazy river" known as Castaway Creek, perfect for tubing. Cascading down the mountain are an assortment of body slides and raft rides. We describe these attractions beginning on page 305.

By Car—Take exit 67 off I-4, take the first exit, and turn right on Buena Vista Dr.—the park is on the right. From Downtown Disney, turn right to Buena Vista Dr.—the park is on the left. Free parking. Parking for park-goers with disabilities is directly across from the entrance plaza. A valid disability parking permit is required.
By Bus—All Disney resorts have direct buses to Typhoon Lagoon. From the Magic Kingdom, Epcot, Disney-MGM Studios, and Disney's Animal Kingdom, take a bus or monorail to a nearby resort and transfer to a Typhoon Lagoon bus (which may also be the Downtown Disney bus). Allow about 30–60 minutes if you travel by bus. Buses deposit park-goers at stops to the left of the Guest Services plaza.

Guest Relations is to the left at the entrance to Typhoon Lagoon.

The small **First Aid Station** (see page 206) is just to the left and slightly behind Leaning Palms (as you're facing it). There's also a companion restroom.

Lost children are entertained at a special desk near Singapore Sal's shop.

International phone card vending machines are located near the restrooms behind Singapore Sal's.

AMBIENCE

LAYOUT

GETTING THERE AND AROUND

Planning

Special Challenges

Getting There

Staying in Style

Touring

Feasting

Resources

Index

Planning · Special Challenges · Getting There · Staying in Style · Touring · Feasting · Resources · Index

Making the Most of Typhoon Lagoon

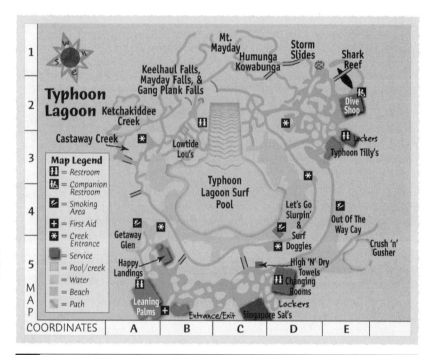

Map Legend
- 👫 = Restroom
- ♿ = Companion Restroom
- 🚬 = Smoking Area
- ➕ = First Aid
- ✳ = Creek Entrance
- ⬛ = Service
- ⬜ = Pool/creek
- = Water
- = Beach
- = Path

Typhoon Lagoon · Ketchakiddee Creek · Castaway Creek · Lowtide Lou's · Mt. Mayday · Humunga Kowabunga · Keelhaul Falls, Mayday Falls, & Gang Plank Falls · Storm Slides · Shark Reef · Dive Shop · Lockers · Typhoon Tilly's · Typhoon Lagoon Surf Pool · Let's Go Slurpin' & Surf Doggies · Out Of The Way Cay · Crush 'n' Gusher · Getaway Glen · Happy Landings · Leaning Palms · High 'N' Dry Towels · Changing Rooms · Lockers · Singapore Sal's · Entrance/Exit

COORDINATES | A | B | C | D | E |

⚠ Tips for Wheelchair Users at Water Parks

✔ Since prolonged exposure to water can remove oil/grease from wheel bearings, avoid getting your wheelchair axle wet.

✔ Sand can cause a lot of damage, so stay on the paved pathways.

✔ Use care as you wheel around—if one of your wheels goes off the sidewalk, you can tip over!

✔ Remember to use lots of sunscreen, or cover up.

✔ Ask to use the water wheelchair that's available.

Slide warning signs are prominently displayed at Typhoon Lagoon

Charting the Attractions at Typhoon Lagoon

Deb Wills' Rating
Deb Koma's Rating
Readers' Rating

■ Typhoon Lagoon Surf Pool [C-4]   10 10 9

One of the world's largest inland wave pools! There is a two-hour cycle of waves: 90 minutes of high surf waves that come every 90 seconds, followed by 30 minutes of gently bobbing waves. A small chalkboard at the edge of the beach near the front of the park gives the day's wave schedule. The surrounding white sand beach offers plenty of places to relax in the sun—shady areas are harder to find. Surf waves are very turbulent and strenuous. Bathers can lose their footing, bump into one another, and scrape body parts on the pool bottom. Water depth changes rapidly. High waves can create an undertow effect. **[F]** The six-foot-high waves can be intimidating. **[C][♥][T][M][P][S][L][V]** The shoreline of the pool is just like a real beach, very gradually sloping downward. Just wade into the water—no step down required. **[M]** Water wheelchairs may be available—ask a lifeguard or at the High 'N' Dry Towel and Locker Rentals. Regular wheelchairs can enter from the pathway and zero-depth entry points located at Blustery Bay below the Clock Tower and at Whitecap Cove near Surf Doggies and the Coffee Wagon. Wheelchairs only permitted into the wave pool up to the axle on the main wheels. ECVs are NOT permitted in the water—transfer to a regular wheelchair. **[B]** Children wearing diapers must either wear snug-fitting plastic pants or swim diapers.

Pool
E-Ticket
All ages

■ Castaway Creek [Entry points: A-3, A-2, D-2, D-3, D-5]   9 10 8

Take a tube for a relaxing, 2,100-foot (640-m.) trip around the park. Adult supervision is required. There are several entrance/exit points, so it may be confusing. Entrances are marked with distinctive symbols—be sure everyone knows what to symbol to look for. There are a few tubes with bottoms for children who cannot hold themselves upright—request from a cast member. **[A][F][I][U]** Water is squirted on swimmers in several spots. **[C][♥][T][M][P][S][L][V]** There is one accessible entrance with a platform, or "transfer tier," located at Seahorse Landing #5 (across from Let's Go Slurpin'), but you must be able to lower yourself into the water or a tube or have a friend or family member assist you. **[B]** Children wearing diapers must either wear snug-fitting plastic pants or swim diapers. **[L]** People of size may be uncomfortable in the tubes.

Lazy River
D-Ticket
Ages 3 & up

© Debra Martin Koma
Transfer tier at Castaway Creek

■ Crush 'n' Gusher [E-3]   🏃   5 7 8

Crush 'n' Gusher is a water coaster that sends you both up and down along a series of flumes and spillways through a rusted-out tropical fruit facility. Choose from three routes: Banana Blaster, Coconut Crusher, and Pineapple Plunger. Rafts accommodate 1-3 riders. **[A][U][C][F][♥][T][P][S]** Fast drop! May be too intense for some adults and children. **[C][M][P][S][T][♥]** Follow the sign for wheelchair/ECV access—it leads to an elevator, which takes you to the top of the slides. A cast member will return your wheelchair/ECV to the pool area below to await you after you slide down. **[B]** Use Rider Switch. **[E]** Pregnant women are not permitted to ride. **[B][L]** 48 in./122 cm. height restriction. **[L]** Peer reviewer Josh Olive notes, "If you have concerns about your size on this water coaster, don't worry! At 6'6" and 400 lbs., I barely even slowed down on the uphill portions. It's a fantastic ride!"

Raft slide
E-Ticket
Big drop!
Ages 7 & up

Charting the Attractions at Typhoon Lagoon
(continued)

	Deb Wills' Rating	Deb Koma's Rating	Readers' Rating

■ Ketchakiddee Creek [A-2]

Deb Wills' Rating: 5 · **Deb Koma's Rating:** 6 · **Readers' Rating:** 7

Fun geared to 2- to 5-year-olds, with slides, geysers, and fountains. *[A][F][I][U]* There are several spots where water is squirted on swimmers. *[B]* Children wearing diapers must either wear snug-fitting plastic pants or swim diapers. *[B][L]* Height restriction: 48 in./122 cm. tall or under.

Playground · B-Ticket · Ages 2-5

■ Bay Slides [A-2]

Deb Wills' Rating: 5 · **Deb Koma's Rating:** 5 · **Readers' Rating:** 7

Gentle water slide just for the little ones, ends in its own special corner of the surf pool. *[B]* Children wearing diapers must either wear snug-fitting plastic pants or swim diapers. *[B][L]* Height restriction: 60 in./152 cm. tall or under.

Jr. Slide · C-Ticket · Ages 2-5

■ Keelhaul Falls [B-1]

Deb Wills' Rating: 5 · **Deb Koma's Rating:** 6 · **Readers' Rating:** 7

Take a one-person tube through caves and waterfalls. *[A][U][C][F][♥][T][P][S]* May be too intense for some adults and children. *[♥][T][S][L]* To ride, you must be free of head, neck, back, and heart problems. Also, you must carry your own raft. This ride is for strong swimmers. *[A][U][C][♥][T][P][S][L][V][M]* You must climb many steps to reach the top of this slide. It is NOT wheelchair/ECV accessible. Also, during busy seasons, waits (all standing, little to no shade) can be quite long. *[B]* Use Rider Switch. *[F]* This ride takes you through darkened areas and moves at a white-water pace. *[Q]* May experience motion problems as tube can rotate as you go through turns. *[E]* Pregnant women are not permitted to ride. *[B][L]* Children under age 4 must take a smaller tube.

Tube Slide · C-Ticket · Ages 4 & up

■ Mayday Falls [B-1]

Deb Wills' Rating: 6 · **Deb Koma's Rating:** 6 · **Readers' Rating:** 7

Another one-person tube ride, this takes you past rocky falls at a slightly slower pace than Keelhaul Falls. *[♥][T][S][L]* To ride, you must be free of head, neck, back, and heart problems. Also, this ride is for strong swimmers. *[A][U][C][♥][T][P][S][L][V][M]* You must climb many steps to reach the top of this slide, and you must carry your own raft. It is not wheelchair/ECV accessible. Also, during busy seasons, waits (all standing, little to no shade) can be quite long. *[B]* Use Rider Switch. *[F]* This ride takes you through darkened areas and moves quickly. *[Q]* May experience motion problems as tube can rotate as you go through turns. *[E]* Pregnant women are not permitted to ride.

Tube Slide · C-Ticket · Ages 7 & up

■ Gang Plank Falls [B-1]

Deb Wills' Rating: 5 · **Deb Koma's Rating:** 9 · **Readers' Rating:** 6

Families can ride together on this quick white-water rafting adventure. *[C][♥][T][P][S][L][V][M]* You must climb many steps to reach the top of this slide, and a member of your group must carry your own raft. It is not wheelchair/ECV accessible. If you can manage all the steps, however, there is a spot where you may be loaded into the raft with your group to experience this ride. Ask a cast member for direction. *[F]* There are several spots where water is sprayed at you or dumped on you. *[Q]* May experience motion problems as tube can rotate as you go through turns. *[E]* Pregnant women are not permitted to ride.

Raft Slide · C-Ticket · Ages 4 & up

Charting the Attractions
at Typhoon Lagoon
(continued)

Deb Wills' Rating
Deb Koma's Rating
Readers' Rating

Humunga Kowabunga [C-1]

| | | | 1 | 6 | 7 |

The highest body slide (actually three of them) at this park, it only takes 10 seconds to shoot to the bottom. You must go down feet first, with your ankles crossed—remember to cross your arms over your chest. *[A][U][C][F][♥][T][P][S]* Fast (30 mph/48 kph) drop! May be too intense for some adults and children. *[A][U][C][♥][T][P][S][L][V][M]* You must climb many steps to reach the top of this slide. It is not wheelchair/ECV accessible. Also, during peak seasons, waits (all standing, little to no shade) can be quite long. *[B]* Use Rider Switch. *[E]* Pregnant women are not permitted to ride. *[B][L]* 48 in./122 cm. height restriction.

Body Slide
E-Ticket
Ages 9 & up
Very fast, steep drop

Storm Slides [D-1]

| | | | 4 | 5 | 7 |

Three different body slides (Rudder Buster, Stern Burner, and Jib Jammer) take you through caves and tunnels at a fast pace. *[A][U][C][F][♥][T][P][S]* May be too intense for some adults and children. *[A][U][C][♥][T][P][S][L][V][M]* You must climb many steps to reach the top of this slide. It is NOT wheelchair/ECV accessible. Also, during busy seasons, waits (all standing, little to no shade) can be quite long. *[B]* Use Rider Switch. *[E]* Pregnant women are not permitted to ride.

Body Slides
E-Ticket
Ages 8 & up

Shark Reef [E-1]

| | | | 9 | 10 | 8 |

Snorkel among the colorful tropical fish and live (but safe) sharks (hammerheads) and rays, too. There's also the chance for a longer scuba-assisted snorkeling experience for a fee. *[C][G][♥][T][P][S][L]* Those with heart problems should not attempt to snorkel, nor should those prone to seizures or with asthma. This attraction is for experienced swimmers, although life jackets are provided. If you are not a strong swimmer, you may still snorkel and float across the pool. *[L]* Children under 10 must be accompanied by an adult. *[M]* Underwater viewing area is wheelchair accessible via path that goes under the shipwreck. Wheelchair users may snorkel if they are able to get into the water on their own or have a companion to assist them. *[F]* Viewing area under shipwreck is dark and very closed in, with eerie underwater sounds piped in. *[Ö]* Foreign language instructions are printed and hanging from posts at the platform before entering the reef.

Pool
E-Ticket
Ages 6 & up
Cold, salty water

© Debra Martin Koma

Shallow areas like this at Typhoon Lagoon are ideal for a water wheelchair

Blizzard Beach Water Park

Blizzard Beach brings the chills and thrills of a Colorado winter to the warm Florida sun. Ski jumps, toboggan rides, and slalom runs zip you past snow that never melts in Disney's most action-oriented water park. There are no elevators here, and many water slides require walking up and down stairs.

AMBIENCE

According to legend, a freak winter storm developed over the western end of Walt Disney World Resort and covered the area with a thick blanket of powdery white snow. Soon plans were underway for **Florida's first ski resort**. Ski lifts were put up, toboggan runs were laid down and an entire resort area blossomed around the mountain of snow. Yet another sudden temperature change returned temps to their normal Florida levels, and the powdery snow quickly turned into slippery slush. The ski resort became known as Disney's Blizzard Beach, the most slushy, slippery, exhilarating water park anywhere!

GETTING THERE

By Car—From westbound or eastbound I-4, take exit 65 (west on Osceola Parkway), exiting at Buena Vista Drive. Free parking.

By Bus—All resorts and Disney's Animal Kingdom have direct buses to Blizzard Beach. From Disney-MGM Studios, take the Coronado Springs bus. From Epcot, take the Disney's Animal Kingdom Lodge bus. From the Magic Kingdom and Downtown Disney, take a bus or monorail to a Disney resort and board a bus to Blizzard Beach. We recommend you take Disney transportation when you can, because the parking lot can fill up on busy days.

The **First Aid Station** is near the park entrance in between Lottawatta Lodge and Beach Haus. There are companion restrooms here and also behind the locker area. Lost person area located between Lottawatta Lodge and First Aid. See page 206.

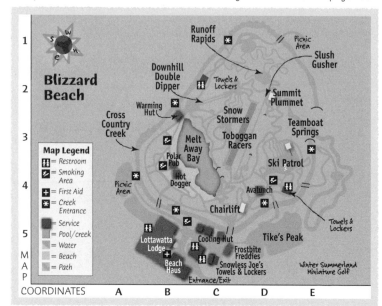

Charting the Attractions at Blizzard Beach

Deb Wills' Rating | Deb Koma's Rating | Readers' Rating

■ Summit Plummet [D-2]   🧍 | 1 | 5 | 9

The world's highest body slide, which drops 120 feet (36.5 meters) at 60 mph (96.5 kph)! Go feet first, cross your arms and ankles, and it's over in 8 seconds. Very steep drop! Must climb stairs to access entrance. **[A][U][C][♥][T][P][S][L]** Long wait times in peak seasons. **[A][U][C][F][♥][T][P][S]** May be too intense for some adults and children. **[C][♥][T][P][E][S]** Guests with these conditions should not ride. **[B]** Use Rider Switch. **[F]** Fast, straight, steep, long drop! **[M]** Not accessible by wheelchair/ECV. **[B][L]** 48 in./122 cm. height restriction.

Body Slide
E-Ticket
Ages 9 & up

■ Slush Gusher [D-2]   🧍 | 1 | 6 | 8

90-foot (27-meter) high double-humped slide. Wear one-piece suits! Go feet first, lay down, cross arms. **[A][U][C][♥][T][P][S][L]** Long wait times in peak seasons. **[A][U][C][F][♥][T][P][S]** May be too intense. **[C][♥][T][P][E][S]** Do not ride. **[B]** Use Rider Switch. **[F]** Fast, straight, steep, long drop! **[M]** No wheelchair/ECV access. **[B][L]** 48 in./122 cm. height restriction.

Body Slide
D-Ticket
Ages 8 & up

■ Downhill Double Dipper [C-2]   🧍 | 2 | 5 | 8

Side-by-side tube racing slides enclosed for part of the run. The slides are set up as a race and run straight down the hill. Travel up to 25 mph (40 kph). **[F]** Enclosed area midway. **[C][♥][T][P][E][S][M]** Must climb stairs to access slide. Guests with heart, back, or neck problems and pregnant women should not ride. **[B]** Use Rider Switch. **[M]** Not accessible by wheelchair/ECV. **[Q]** Dipper humps may bother those with motion sensitivity. **[B][L]** 48 in./122 cm. height restriction.

Tube Slide
D-Ticket
Ages 8 & up

■ Snow Stormers [C-2] | 7 | 6 | 8

Switchback slalom-style slides. Mat pickup at top of Mt. Gushmore. Family-friendly. **[C][♥][T][P][E][S]** Must climb stairs to access slide entrance. Guests with heart, back, or neck problems and pregnant women should not ride. **[M]** **[M]** Access via Mt. Gushmore Chairlift (see next page). Must transfer from wheelchair to foam mat for experience.

Mat Slide
C-Ticket
Ages 6 & up

■ Toboggan Racers [D-2] | 3 | 5 | 7

Eight-lane toboggan. Mat pickup at top of Mt. Gushmore. **[C][♥][T][P][E][S][M]** Must climb stairs to access slide; small step to get in and out. Guests with heart, back, or neck problems and pregnant women should not ride.

Mat Slide
D-Ticket
Ags 6 & up

■ Teamboat Springs [E-2] | 5 | 8 | 9

World's longest family raft ride for up to 6 people; 1,400 ft. (427 m.) along twisting ride. Family-friendly fun. **[A][U][C][♥][T][P][S][L]** Popular ride, long wait times during peak seasons. **[F]** May be combined with other groups to fill raft. **[M]** Access via Mt. Gushmore Chairlift. Water wheelchair can return in separate raft. **[Q]** May experience motion problems. **[L]** Only one plus-size person per raft.

Raft Slide
D-Ticket
Ages 4 & up

■ Runoff Rapids [D-2] | 5 | 6 | 7

Three different open and enclosed innertube runs. Two can share tube on open runs. Tube pickup at bottom of Mt. Gushmore. **[C][♥][T][P][E][S][M]** Guests with heart, back, or neck problems and pregnant women should not ride. **[M]** Access via Mt. Gushmore Chairlift (see next page).

Tube Slide
C-Ticket
Ages 6 & up

Planning | Special Challenges | Getting There | Staying in Style | Touring | Feasting | Resources | Index

Charting the Attractions at Blizzard Beach
(continued)

	Deb Wills' Rating	Deb Koma's Rating	Readers' Rating

☐ Cross Country Creek [Entry points: B-4, A-4, B-2, C-1, E-3, D-4] — **9 9 7**

Float around in tube along continuous flowing creek, encircling park. Tubes at each of the seven entrances. Waterfalls, snow-making machine, and shooting water along the way. Family-friendly fun. Children under 10 should be accompanied by adult. Weak swimmers should use personal floatation device or swimmer's aid. Current is strong at times. Water depth is 2 feet 6 inches (76 cm). There are a few tubes with bottoms for children who cannot hold themselves upright—request from a cast member. **[A][U]** Multiple entrances and exits, may be confusing to find way back. **[M]** Wheelchair/ECV accessible at the following landings: Manatee Landing next to the Warming Hut; Ice Gator Landing across from Avalunch; and Polar Bear Landing between the two main bridges. If you don't get out of the exit where your wheelchair/ECV is parked, you may have to go all the way around again, as water current pushes you in one direction. **[L]** People of larger size may be uncomfortable in tube. **[B]** Children in diapers must wear snug-fitting plastic pants of special swim diapers.	**Lazy River** D-Ticket Ages 2 & up 20 min.

☐ Melt Away Bay [D-4] — **7 7 7**

One-acre (4,046 sq. m.) wave pool at the base of Mt. Gushmore. Constant bobbing gentle waves. **[A][U]** Put your beach chair in the water and be up close to watch your child. **[M]** ECV users must transfer to a standard wheelchair to enter. Wheelchair users can enter from the pathway and zero-depth entry points across from the Warming Hut and from the ramp from the Boardwalk near the Iced Cappuccino wagon. Standard wheelchairs only permitted in the pool as far as the axle on the main wheels.	**Pool** C-Ticket All ages

☐ Ski Patrol Training Camp [D-3] — **7 6 7**

Preteen fun with floating icebergs, tube slalom, and slides. Ages 6–12.	**Playground**

☐ Tike's Peak [D-5] 🧍 — **6 6 7**

Miniature version of Blizzard Beach for those age 0–6 and their folks. **[A][F][I][U]** There are several spots where water is squirted on swimmers. **[B]** Children in diapers must wear snug-fitting plastic pants or special swim diapers. **[L]** Must be 48 in./122 cm. or shorter. **[M]** Wheelchairs can enter Tike's Peak wading pool via zero-depth entry points surrounding the area.	**Playground** C-Ticket

☐ Mt. Gushmore Chairlift [D-5] — **2 3 7**

Wooden bench-seat chairs take you up to Mt. Gushmore's family of rides. There is a special gondola to transport guests with a wheelchair and their companions. **[B]** Use Rider Switch—no infants or lap-seating allowed. **[F]** Heights, no lap bar, feet dangle, travel upward. **[♥][T][M][P][E][S]** Those with back or neck problems and expectant mothers should not ride. **[M]** Persons traveling in wheelchairs and one companion may access Mt. Gushmore via the lift. Enter to the right of the main queue, remainder of party proceed through standard queue. Transfer from ECV or electric wheelchair to water wheelchair (obtain it from cast member if available). Use chairlift to travel to observation deck or to access Runoff Rapids, Snow Stormers, and Teamboat Springs. This is a one-way trip—the only ways down are to slide or take the stairs. **[L]** Weight limit of vehicle is 375 lbs./170 kg.	**Lift to Rides** C-Ticket Ages 3 & up

Downtown Disney

Looking for a delightful break from the theme parks? **Downtown Disney** reigns as a shopping, dining, and entertainment mecca. With the world's largest Disney Store, a unique non-circus circus, and restaurants ranging, quite literally, from soup to nuts, you're sure to find something fun to do.

AMBIENCE

More than a pedestrian mall, Downtown Disney has **three unique districts**: The Marketplace, which is mostly shops and eateries; Pleasure Island, Disney's nightlife capital; and the West Side, with trendy shops and unique restaurants and entertainment venues. Downtown Disney offers the traveler with special challenges the chance to get away from the hectic pace of the parks. Here you can stop and grab a cappuccino, sit by the water, and people watch. Or, if you'd prefer, you can truly "shop 'til you drop."

GETTING THERE

By Car—From I-4, take exit 67, then take the first exit and turn right on Buena Vista Dr. Parking is free. The disabled parking spots are located right in front. Tip: The Downtown Disney Marketplace and Pleasure Island parking lots are often packed, especially on the weekends. Try the huge West Side parking lot and stroll/wheel over to the other end of Downtown Disney at your leisure.
By Bus—Buses are available from every Disney resort. From the Magic Kingdom, Epcot, Disney-MGM Studios, or Disney's Animal Kingdom, bus or monorail to a nearby resort and transfer.
By Boat—Resort guests at Port Orleans, Old Key West, and Saratoga Springs can take a boat to the Marketplace.
By Land—Guests at Saratoga Springs Resort, Old Key West, and Hotel Plaza Resorts may find it quicker to walk or wheel.

Admission to Downtown Disney is free, although there is admission charged to enter the clubs on Pleasure Island (see page 321-324).

Most areas in Downtown Disney are **wheelchair/ECV accessible**, and you can rent both wheelchairs and ECVs at Guest Relations at Downtown Disney Marketplace. Wheelchairs can be rented for $10/day with a credit card imprint for deposit; ECVs for $35/day with a $5 deposit and a credit card imprint. (When you return the ECV, the imprint is returned to you; otherwise, you will be charged $500!) You can also rent wheelchairs at the Guest Relations office on the West Side for the same charge. Wheelchairs cannot be rented on Pleasure Island.

Planning · Special Challenges · Getting There · Staying in Style · Touring · Feasting · Resources · Index

Making the Most of Downtown Disney

TIPS

Strollers cannot be rented on Pleasure Island, but can be rented from either Guest Relations location mentioned on the previous page (single strollers only, no doubles!). Cost is the same as for wheelchairs: $10/day with a credit card imprint.

To get from Pleasure Island to the West Side, avoid the steep stairs by using the **pathway** along the parking lot (near Planet Hollywood) or the elevator at the West End Stage (near the restrooms).

There's a **ramp** that leads along Rainforest Café in the Marketplace, down to Cap'n Jack's. There's another ramp leading up from the marina there that goes along the waterfront and leads up from the Dock Stage, making the area completely wheelchair/ECV accessible.

Companion-assisted restrooms are located behind Once Upon a Toy (Marketplace) and near the Pin Cart (West Side). There is also a companion restroom located in the Once Upon A Toy shop. Other restrooms scattered around Downtown Disney have at least one accessible stall. There are

Companion restrooms are roomy

© Debra Martin Koma

no large changing tables anywhere in Downtown Disney, however.

Text Typewriter TTY Phones are located on Pleasure Island near Motion, on the West Side near the AMC Movie Theatre, and near the restrooms outside Cirque du Soleil. And a multilingual information kiosk can be found at the West Side.

For **international visitors**, a prepaid international phone card vending machine is located near the Marketplace's Guest Relations office.

Kids love to frolic in the **water play fountain** (see page 268) near the Marketplace bus stop entrance and Once Upon a Toy.

Although most of the **restaurants** located at Downtown Disney are owned and operated by outside interests (Cap'n Jack's being the notable exception), most will still strive to accommodate special diets if they have adequate notice. Follow our procedures for making special dietary requests in chapter 2. We assess each of the eateries in Downtown Disney in chapter 6.

For **more information** and answers to questions, call Downtown Disney Guest Relations at 407-828-3150.

Making the Most of
Downtown Disney

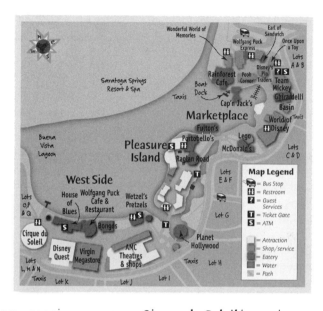

DOWNTOWN DISNEY MAP

ENTERTAINMENT

Planning Special Challenges Getting There Staying in Style Touring Feasting Resources Index

The new-age circus company **Cirque du Soleil** has a show on the West Side called La Nouba (from the French "to live it up"). It is a remarkable performance featuring acrobats, clowns, jugglers, dancers, aerialists, and original music (and not one animal!). While the bright lights and costumes and loud music may be overstimulating to some, it is still a fantastic 90 minutes worth experiencing if you can! Note that there are some strobe light effects at the beginning of the performance. The huge theater is accessible for wheelchairs and ECVs, as is the boutique located on the lower level. Remember to request wheelchair seating when purchasing your tickets. Note: There is only one set of elevators to the second level, so allow extra time for seating if you use a wheelchair/ECV. Shows are at 6:00 pm and 9:00 pm, Tues.-Sat. Tickets are $63–$112/adults and $50–$90/kids ages 3-9. Not recommended for very young children. Call 407-939-7600 or visit the box office on the West Side.

The **theaters** at the AMC 24 Theatres Complex sport stadium seating, most with retractable armrests. Theaters offer wheelchair seating. Some shows offer reflective or closed-captioning, assistive listening, or descriptive listening devices (which describe the action/scenes in a movie for people with vision impairment). Visit: http://moviewatcher.com/theatres/theatre_information.jsp?unit=572.

Shopping
at Downtown Disney

SHOPPING

Most **shops** in the Marketplace open at 9:30 am, while West Side shops open at 10:30 am. Closing is at 11:00 pm, with seasonal variations.

Just as at the theme parks, your Downtown Disney **purchases** (not including food and beverage) can be delivered to your Disney resort. In fact, at Once Upon a Toy, there are touch-screens near the cashier's desk that allow you to arrange for this service yourself.

While all of the shops in the Marketplace are accessible in theory, many are so **crammed with merchandise** that they are difficult to get around in. In addition, they all have heavy manual doors—no electric doors—making entry and exit awkward for someone in a wheelchair/ECV or struggling with a stroller. Some shops are also worth singling out for aspects that matter to special needs travelers:

Basin, which features bath and facial products, has many of its soaps and fragrances out in the open—if you are sensitive to strong scents, you may want to avoid this shop.

Once Upon a Toy is very accessible, as mentioned previously. Not only does this store have a companion restroom, all restrooms feature handrails, and there is Braille signage.

Lego Imagination Center has an extensive play area outside, perfect for letting off some steam. Small pieces scattered around the store make navigating in a wheelchair/ECV difficult.

Ronald's Fun House (a.k.a. McDonald's) also has a whimsical play area for kids.

World of Disney (the world's largest Disney Store), is huge—it's easy to get lost or disoriented when wandering around in here. This store houses the Bibbidi Bobbidi Boutique for little girls (and boys). There are multiple exits, and the store is very busy—agree on a meeting place in case members of your party get separated.

Goofy's Candy Company features some sugar-free choices.

West Side shopping is also mostly accessible. Some shops to note in this section for special needs considerations:

Disney's Candy Cauldron features some sugar-free items.

Hoypoloi is so crowded with merchandise that a wheelchair or ECV user would find it nearly impossible to maneuver. Also, merchandise is fragile and easily reached, so this is not recommended for those with impulse control issues. Some may enjoy it, though, as they often play calming new age music and feature activity items like Zen sand drawing.

Sosa Family Cigars often has the odor of cigar smoke emanating from its doors—those sensitive to smoke should avoid it.

Starabilias (collectibles) specifically requests that no strollers be brought into the store. Wheelchairs/ECVs are welcome, of course, but users might find it hard to navigate in narrow aisles.

DisneyQuest

DisneyQuest is an indoor "theme park" housed in a big, blue, five-story building at Downtown Disney West Side. It is very loud, with flashing lights and sounds coming from all directions. It can be extremely overstimulating. It features ride simulators, high-tech games, and hands-on activities for young and old alike. Attractions run the gamut from simple video arcade games to a build-your-own coaster simulator. Here's general information about DisneyQuest for the visitor with special challenges:

Hours vary by season. Peak season: 11:30 am–11:00 pm, Sundays–Thursdays, and 11:30 am–midnight on Fridays and Saturdays.

As with Disney's theme park admission, you pay a single all-day price and enjoy **unlimited use** of all rides, games, and activities (excluding games that award prizes—a 20-credit card costs $5). Adults pay $38.64 for a full day, and kids ages 3–9 pay $31.95 (includes tax). Children under 10 must be with an adult, but you can leave the older kids here while you shop elsewhere. Annual passes are available—see page 214. DisneyQuest admission is included in the Magic Your Way with Water Parks Fun and More option and Premium Annual Passes, but it is not an option on the old Park Hopper Plus passes. Discount admissions may be available after 10:00 pm. DisneyQuest will turn guests away when they reach maximum capacity.

Best times to visit are during the mornings and afternoons and on the weekends. It gets pretty busy in the evenings, after other parks are closed. Crowds are *huge* on foul-weather days. Least crowded days are great weather days, when most everyone else is outdoors. Waits can be very frustrating for children with special challenges—Guest Assistance Cards are not accepted here.

No strollers are allowed in the DisneyQuest building, unless it is a stroller being used as a wheelchair. Stroller parking is located right outside the main entrance, but most of the experiences here are for older children. This might be one time when it's better to leave Baby at home with a sitter.

Smoking is prohibited throughout the DisneyQuest building.

The main **Information Desk** is located on the first floor, to the left. This is also a Lost & Found. Coat check is on the opposite end of the first floor. There is a TTY phone located on the first floor along with the standard phone bank.

Restrooms are all wheelchair/ECV accessible, with at least one accessible stall, but there are no companion-assisted restrooms. Restrooms are located on the first, fourth, and fifth floors.

There is a **height measuring station** located on the first floor entrance—it's Genie from Aladdin. Measure before you start out, to avoid disappointment later.

Important Note: To purchase any of the Create Zone items (excluding Sticker Shot!), you must do so at the Guest Gallery within 10 minutes after making your creation.

Your adventure begins when you **board the "Cybrolator"** (elevator)—you're treated to a short film featuring the Genie, who briefs you on the experiences to come. These special effects could be frightening to some. When you reach the Ventureport on the third floor, you'll find you can enter four zones: Explore Zone, Score Zone, Create Zone, and Replay Zone. Each zone groups the attractions (described below) by theme.

Planning

Special Challenges

Getting There

Staying in Style

Touring

Feasting

Resources

Index

Making the Most of DisneyQuest

TIPS

Each zone spans at least two floors, with various stairs, elevators, and pathways linking them. This makes for a **bewildering maze**—study the map to orient yourself.

First-time visitors should **spend time exploring** the entire place before splitting up. While you're at it, choose a meeting place and time. The Wonderland Café is a good choice with places to sit, and the Ventureport on the third floor is highly visible.

Allow at least 4–5 hours to tour, more if you love arcades. Be sure to wear a wristwatch—it's easy to lose track of time! It's faster to use the stairs to go up or down one level, if you can. On the other hand, the elevators are less disorienting than the curving staircases.

Relatively quiet cool-down spots include VenturePort on level 3 and Wonderland Cafe and its Internet alcoves on level 4.

The Cheesecake Factory operates two accessible counter-service eateries in DisneyQuest. FoodQuest is located on the top floor (see page 364) with the Wonderland Café (see page 365) on the fourth floor.

Questions? Call 407-828-4600 or visit http://www.disneyquest.com. There's also a DisneyQuest kiosk in Downtown Disney Marketplace.

DisneyQuest Attractions With Restrictions/Warnings

RESTRICTIONS

Aladdin's Magic Carpet Ride	You should be free from a tendency toward motion sickness, dizziness, or sensitivity to flashing lights.
Buzz Lightyear's AstroBlasters	51 in. (130 cm.). You should be in good health and free from heart, back, or neck problems, motion sickness, or other conditions that could be aggravated by this adventure. Expectant mothers should not ride.
CyberSpace Mountain	51 in. (130 cm.). You should be in good health and free from heart, back, or neck problems, motion sickness, or other conditions that could be aggravated by this adventure. Expectant mothers should not ride.
Cybrolators	You should be free from claustrophobia and sensitivity to flashing lights.
Mighty Ducks Pinball Slam	48 in. (122 cm.). You should be in good health and free from heart, back, or neck problems, motion sickness, or other conditions that could be aggravated by this adventure. Expectant mothers should not ride.
Pirates of the Caribbean: Battle for Buccaneer Gold	35 in. (89 cm.). You should be in good health and free from heart, back, or neck problems, motion sickness, or other conditions that could be aggravated by this adventure. Expectant mothers should not ride.
Virtual Jungle Cruise	You should be in good health and free from heart, back, or neck problems, motion sickness, or other conditions that could be aggravated. Expectant mothers should not ride.
Ride the Comix	You should be free from a tendency toward motion sickness, dizziness, or sensitivity to flashing lights.

Charting the Attractions at DisneyQuest

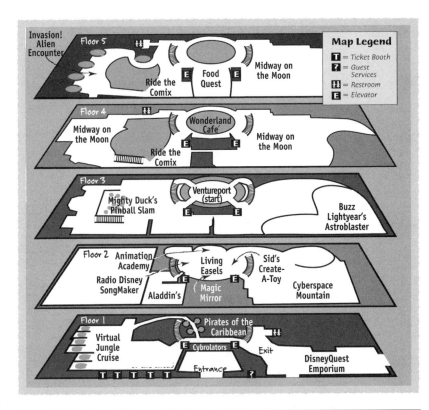

Map Legend
T = Ticket Booth
? = Guest Services
♯♯ = Restroom
E = Elevator

Floor 5 — Invasion! Alien Encounter, Ride the Comix, Food Quest, Midway on the Moon

Floor 4 — Midway on the Moon, Wonderland Café, Midway on the Moon, Ride the Comix

Floor 3 — Mighty Duck's Pinball Slam, Ventureport (start), Buzz Lightyear's Astroblaster

Floor 2 — Animation Academy, Living Easels, Sid's Create-A-Toy, Radio Disney SongMaker, Magic Mirror, Aladdin's, Cyberspace Mountain

Floor 1 — Virtual Jungle Cruise, Pirates of the Caribbean, Cybrolators, Exit, Entrance, DisneyQuest Emporium

---

■ Aladdin's Magic Carpet Ride [Floor 2, Explore Zone]   6 8 6

Don virtual reality goggles for a wild ride on Aladdin's magic carpet. Swoop through Agrabah and the Cave of Wonder to search for jewels and free the Genie. Seating is similar to sitting astride a motorcycle. **[Q]** *There's a real chance of motion sickness here, due to all the swooping and flying you do on your "carpet."* **[A][U][I]** *The noise level is high—could cause overstimulation. Also there are lots of bright, flashing lights.* **[A][U][C][♥][T][I][P][E][S][L]** *Often has long waits with few places to sit.* **[F][V]** *The area is very dark.* **[H]** *Closed-captioning available.* **[M]** *Wheelchair/ECV users may remain in chair, since the low seats can be adjusted.* **[V]** *You must wear special goggles to experience the effects of this ride.*

Virtual	
D-Ticket	
Ages 6 & up	
Dizziness	
4-min. ride	

■ Animation Academy [Floor 2, Create Zone]   6 6 6

Take your seat at a computer workstation as an instructor draws out your artistry. Hands-on lessons in drawing and/or animating characters. Several 20-minute lessons are offered. After the class, you can buy your creation. **[A][U][C][♥][T][I][P][E][S][L]** *Often has long waits with few places to sit and wait.* **[M]** *Wheelchair/ECV users may remain in chair.* **[V]** *May have difficulty viewing the computer screen images.*

Hands-On	
D-Ticket	
Ages 6 & up	
20 min.	

Charting the Attractions at DisneyQuest
(continued)

Deb Wills' Rating
Deb Koma's Rating
Readers' Rating

■ Buzz Lightyear's Astroblasters [Floor 3, Replay Zone] 🚶

5 9 7

Ride fully enclosed two-person bumper cars mounted with "cannons" that shoot large rubber balls. The driver pilots to scoop up ammo, and the gunner fires on other cars to make them spin out of control. You can ride solo, but it really is better with a companion. **[Q]** Motion sickness possible—bumper cars spin when hit by rubber balls. **[A][U][I]** The noise level is high—could cause overstimulation. Lots of flashing lights, too. **[♥][T][M][P][E][S]** Because the bumper cars collide frequently, you should be in good health and free from high blood pressure, heart, back, or neck problems. Expectant mothers should not ride. **[M]** Wheelchair/ECV users must transfer out to experience. **[F][S][V]** The area is very dark. **[F]** The cars have doors that close them in—can create a very claustrophobic feeling. **[S][L]** Enclosed cars may be difficult to get in and out of quickly. **[L]** 51 in./130 cm. height restriction.

Bumper Cars
D-Ticket
Ages 9 & up
Very bumpy

■ CyberSpace Mountain [Floor 2, Create Zone] 🚶

2 8 9

Design and ride your own coaster! Start by choosing a theme and designing the coaster tracks on a computer screen. Then get strapped into a two-person flight simulator (seats are very small!) to experience your coaster, or choose from a ready-made coaster program. Be prepared to be shaken, rattled, and rolled on a ride more dizzying than the real thing. Note: Anyone can create a coaster, but you must meet the height restriction to board the simulator. **[Q]** The simulator rotates a full 360 degrees, creating a sensation that you are inverting like a real coaster. Motion sickness potential is high. **[A][U][I]** The noise level is very high—could cause overstimulation. **[A][U][C][♥][T][I][P][E][S][L]** Often has long waits with few places to sit. **[♥][T][M][P][E][S]** You should be in good health and free from high blood pressure and heart, back, or neck problems. Expectant mothers should not ride. **[M]** You must be ambulatory to experience. There is a wheelchair lift to bring you to the ride simulators, but you must climb up and then down a couple of steps to get into the simulators themselves. **[F][V]** The area is very dark. In addition, the simulators are very closed in. If you have a fear of small spaces, you may not be comfortable, but there is a "panic button" that you can press at any time to stop the ride immediately. **[L]** 51 in./130 cm. height restriction. People of size may have trouble fitting comfortably in the simulator seats.

Simulator
E-Ticket
Ages 9 & up
Upside-down during inversions

■ Invasion! An ExtraTERRORestrial Alien Encounter [Floor 5, Score Zone]

2 5 5

Dash across the galaxy to rescue Earth colonists from an invading horde in this simulator ride that borrows characters and fun from the former Magic Kingdom attraction. One teammate pilots the rescue vehicle, while three other teammates keep the bad guys at bay. Great preshow film. **[Q]** Motion sickness warning. **[A][U][I]** The noise level is high—could cause overstimulation. **[A][U][C][♥][T][I][P][E][S][L]** Often has long waits with few places to sit. **[F][V]** The area is very dark. **[H]** Closed-captioning available. **[M]** Wheelchair/ECV users must transfer out to the "cockpit" to experience. **[S][L]** Enclosed cockpit may be difficult to get in and out of quickly.

Simulator
E-Ticket
Ages 7 & up
Violent theme

Planning
Special Challenges
Getting There
Staying in Style
Touring
Feasting
Resources
Index

Charting the Attractions
at DisneyQuest
(continued)

	Deb Wills' Rating	Deb Koma's Rating	Readers' Rating

☐ Living Easels [Floor 2, Create Zone] — 5 5 4

Use a touch-sensitive screen to draw animated landscapes. You can buy printouts of your finished product at the Guest Gallery. **[A][U][C][♥][T][I][P][E][S][L]** Often has long waits with few places to sit and wait. **[M]** Wheelchair/ECV users may remain in chairs. **[V]** May have difficulty viewing images on the screen.

Hands-On / **B-Ticket** / **Ages 3 & up**

☐ Magic Mirror [Floor 2, Create Zone] — 4 5 5

Turn a photo of yourself into a wacky portrait. You can buy your creation at the Guest Gallery. **[A][U][C][♥][T][I][P][E][S][L]** Often has long waits with few places to sit and wait. **[M]** Wheelchair/ECV users may remain in their chairs.

Hands-On / **B-Ticket** / **Ages 4 & up**

☐ Midway on the Moon [Floors 4 & 5, Replay Zone] — 7 8 5

Here you'll find Disney-themed versions of arcade games like Ursula's Whirlpool and traditional games like Skeeball. No additional charge. **[M]** Wheelchair/ECV users may remain in their chairs.

Arcade / **A-Ticket** / **Ages 5 & up**

☐ Classic Games [Floors 3 & 5, Replay Zone] — 7 8 5

Walk down Arcade Memory Lane, with games that were popular in years gone by, like Defender, Pac Man, and Donkey Kong. No additional charge. **[M]** Wheelchair/ECV users must be able to stand to access these older games.

Arcade / **A-Ticket** / **Ages 5 & up**

☐ Sports Arena Arcade [Floor 4, Replay Zone] — 6 6 5

Sports-themed arcade games. No additional charge. **[M]** Wheelchair/ECV users must be able to stand to access many of these games. Ages 5 & up.

Arcade / **A-Ticket**

☐ The Underground Arcade [Floor 3, Replay Zone] — 5 7 5

Popular video arcade games. No additional charge. **[M]** Wheelchair/ECV users must be able to stand to access many of these games. Ages 5 & up.

Arcade / **A-Ticket**

☐ Mighty Ducks Pinball Slam [Floor 3, Score Zone] 🕴 — 5 8 7

Imagine you're inside an old-style pinball machine and you have the idea behind this game. You stand on a platform with handles and use body motion/weight to move a "puck" around the huge screen. You must also "body check" opponents on this simulator. **[A][U][C][♥][T][I][P][E][S][L]** Very few places to sit and wait. **[A][U][I][S][♥][T][M][P][E][S]** Strenuous! You need to be able to rock your body back and forth and around to maneuver your "puck" on the screen. You may experience some sudden, sharp movements. You should be in good health, free from high blood pressure and, heart, back, or neck problems. Pregnant women should not ride. There is one stationary platform if you don't want to rock—if there are no kids waiting, you may be able to use it (ask a cast member). **[M]** Wheelchair/ECV users may remain in their chair. There is a wheelchair lift to get to the game floor, but it is enclosed and may cause claustrophic feelings, especially for those under 48 in. tall. **[Q]** Moving platform and wide-screen video may be disorienting. **[B][L][M]** 48 in./122 cm. height restriction. Those under 48" should talk to a cast member—there is one stationary platform with a joystick for guests who don't weigh enough to move the puck, yet still want to pretend they are playing.

Simulator / **D-Ticket** / **Ages 9 & up**

Planning • Special Challenges • Getting There • Staying in Style • Touring • Feasting • Resources • Index

Charting the Attractions at DisneyQuest
(continued)

Deb Wills' Rating
Deb Koma's Rating
Readers' Rating

Pirates of the Caribbean: Battle for Buccaneer Gold [Floor 1] 🧍

5 | **10** | **9**

You and up to four shipmates enter this 3-D simulated sea battle in quest of pirate gold. Fire virtual cannonballs against your foes and feel the deck shudder when hit. **[A][U][C][♥][T][I][P][E][S][L]** Lines can be very long, and there are very few places to sit. **[A][U][I][S][V]** You must wear special goggles to experience the 3-D effects. **[♥][T][M][P][E][C][S]** You need to move from cannon to cannon, pulling a cord to fire on the enemy ships. As your "ship" is hit, you feel the impact. The deck rocks like a real ship. Thus, you should be in good health and free from high blood pressure and, heart, back, or neck problems. Expectant mothers should not ride. **[F]** The attraction takes place in a darkened, enclosed booth. During the experience, buccaneer skeletons fly out at you. There are also many perilous situations—being shot at, boat sinking, etc. **[M]** ECV users must transfer into a standard wheelchair. The movement effects will be turned off for those in a wheelchair. **[Q]** Realistic film and moving deck create sensation of being on the water—motion sickness potential is high. **[B][L]** 35 in./89 cm. height restriction. **[S][V]** The booth is very dark, and as the motion simulator rocks back and forth, footing becomes unsteady.

Simulator
E-Ticket
Ages 7 & up
Violent theme

Radio Disney SongMaker [Floor 2, Create Zone]

5 | **5** | **4**

Create your own hit song in a soundbooth. Combine styles and lyrics for laughs. You can buy a CD of it. **[A][U][C][♥][T][I][P][E][S][L]** Often has long waits with few places to sit. **[M]** Wheelchair/ECV users may remain in their chairs.

Hands-On
D-Ticket
Ages 4 & up

Ride the Comix [Floors 4 and 5, Score Zone]

2 | **7** | **5**

Swing your laser sword to battle comic strip villains in this 3-D virtual reality game. **[A][U][I]** The noise level is high—could overstimulate. Lots of flashing lights/lasers, too. Violent theme. **[A][U][C][♥][T][I][P][E][S][L]** Long waits with few places to sit and wait. **[♥][T][M][P][E][C][S]** Strenuous! You battle with a heavy "sword." **[F]** Lots of scary monsters "attack" you. **[M]** Wheelchair/ECV users must be able to sit on a stool. **[Q]** High potential for motion sickness. **[S][V][C][T][P]** You must wear heavy virtual reality headgear to see the 3-D effect.

Virtual
D-Ticket
Ages 8 & up
May feel dizzy
4 min.

Sid's Create-A-Toy [Floor 2, Create Zone]

3 | **4** | **5**

Create a demented toy from spare toy parts—on a computer screen. You can buy a real version of your creation. **[M]** Wheelchair/ECV users may remain in chairs.

Hands-On
B-Ticket

Virtual Jungle Cruise [Floor 1]

5 | **9** | **6**

Board a raft, grab a paddle, and take a white-water river cruise back in time on this motion simulator ride. Dr. Wayne Szalinski guides you and your teammates on this riotous journey over waterfalls and into the age of the dinosaurs. **[A][U][I]** You occasionally get spritzed with water. **[♥][C][P][T][M][P][E][S]** You need to paddle as if on a raft—can be quite difficult. For this reason, you should be in good health and free from high blood pressure and, heart, back, or neck problems. Expectant mothers should not ride. **[F]** Lots of dinosaurs spring out at you. There are also many perilous situations—going over waterfalls, into fire, etc. **[M]** Wheelchair/ECV users must transfer out and board the raft to experience this. The raft on the far left is accessible. **[Q]** Realistic film of white-water rafting creates sensation of being on the water—motion sickness potential is high.

Simulator
E-Ticket
Ages 6 & up
Paddling

Pleasure Island

If you're looking for nightlife, **Pleasure Island** is the place. You can dance until 2:00 am or go for the gags at a comedy club. Located smack-dab in the middle of Downtown Disney, Pleasure Island is an entertainment extravaganza.

As of this writing, Pleasure Island is undergoing an extensive **renovation**. It is expected to be completed by the end of 2007.

A **Harley Davidson** shop is located near Mannequins Dance Club, but other stores at Pleasure Island have closed during its renovation.

By Bus—Frequent buses are available from Disney resorts. From a park, bus or monorail to a nearby resort and transfer to a Downtown Disney bus. Get off at the second Downtown Disney stop.
By Car—Follow signs to Downtown Disney. Parking is free. If you intend to drink, please designate a driver.
By Boat—From Port Orleans, Old Key West, and Saratoga Springs, take a boat to the Marketplace and walk or wheel.

Most Pleasure Island **clubs are open** from about 7:00 pm to 2:00 am most nights to guests 21 years and older (younger kids can come with a parent or legal guardian). You'll need a valid driver's license or state ID (with photo). They really do "proof" you at the door, and if you're over 21, you'll get a special wristband that allows you to imbibe. If you bring kids (they can only enter the Adventurers Club and Comedy Warehouse), be prepared for some good-natured ribbing from performers.

Time flies here, so **arrive early** in the evening to make the most of your visit. The clubs start hopping as soon as they open at 7:00-9:00 pm.

To escape the crowds and noise, consider the **Comedy Warehouse** during the busiest times of the evening—usually between 10:00 pm and midnight.

There is a **Braille map** of Downtown Disney located across from the entrance to Raglan Road.

© Debra Martin Koma

Babylonia at the Adventurers Club

Making the Most of
at Pleasure Island

TIPS

All Pleasure Island Clubs are now **nonsmoking**, though those sensitive to smoke may still detect it in some clubs.

Some dance clubs here use **flashing lights and/or strobe lights** on the dance floor.

Pleasure Island's streets are now **admission-free** at all times. Stroll through—some clubs may be open for a free "sample" and the live stage is rocking for all. Admission is checked at club entrances, and tickets can be bought at some shops as well as the ticket booths.

Pleasure Island **Multi-Club ticket** good for all clubs on the island for one evening: $22.32/person (adult or child). Pleasure Island Single-Club Ticket, good for only one club/evening (not including Comedy Warehouse or Adventurers Club): $10.60. Ask about discounts. Note: You must buy the Multi-Club ticket to enter the Comedy Warehouse or the Adventurers Club.

Alcoholic beverages are even served on the streets of Pleasure Island. Adults 21 and older get wristbands to show they can drink.

If you find the excitement too much or just want to go somewhere romantic with that special someone, head for the "**hidden patio**." Go down the stairs beside the Adventurers Club, or go down the stairs beside the West End Stage (or take the elevator) and turn right before the bridge for ramp access.

A **TTY phone** is located with standard phones near the Motion club.

All areas are **wheelchair accessible**. All clubs have elevators. There's a long, steep incline rising from the Hub Stage to the West End Stage.

Wheelchairs cannot be rented on Pleasure Island. You can rent both wheelchairs and ECVs elsewhere in Downtown Disney, however. Guest Relations at Marketplace rents both ECVs and wheelchairs; West Side rents only wheelchairs (see page 213 for details). Strollers cannot be rented on Pleasure Island, either, but can be rented from either Guest Relations location mentioned above (single strollers only, no doubles!).

Charting the Attractions at Pleasure Island

8Trax

9 8 6

Disco in all its Saturday Night Fever glory! The sound is classic '70s. (Thursday is '80s night; the floor is packed and illuminated, and dancers are enthusiastic!) **[A][U][C][♥][T][I][P][E][S][L]** *Lines for this popular nightspot can be VERY long, and there are very few places to sit and wait.* **[M]** *Wheelchair/ECV accessible.* **[S][V]** *The club is very dark, and the floor is uneven.*

Dance

C-Ticket

Adventurers Club

10 10 8

In all ways, this is the most "Disney" of the clubs on Pleasure Island (and our absolute favorite). Come with a sense of adventure and be ready to join in. You can be inducted into the fictitious club, learn the secret greeting, and sing the club song! Be prepared for the unexpected, the quirky, and the hilarious. In true Disney fashion, the décor matches the theme here perfectly. The walls are covered with trophies, mementos (some even talk!), and photos amassed by the club members! You may be greeted by the club's stoic butler, the matronly Club President, or even a French maid. Different shows are held throughout the night in the Mask Room, Treasure Room, and Library. Though the Adventurers Club can seem a little confusing at first, just wait a while—something's sure to happen wherever you are, when you least expect it. **[F]** *If you're shy, be aware that cast members do involve the audience in the improvisation here.* **[H]** *You can request sign language interpreting in advance. Call 407-939-4763 before your trip.* **[M]** *Wheelchair/ECV users may remain in their chair. Elevator is located immediately to the left after entering club. When club is crowded, it is difficult to maneuver from room to room.*

Comedy

E-Ticket

Shows run continuously from 8:00 pm to 1:00 am

Audience participation

Charting the Attractions
at Pleasure Island
(continued)

	Deb Wills' Rating	Deb Koma's Rating	Readers' Rating
BET SoundStage Club	5	5	4

Contemporary music and dancing for guests 21 and over. The club is one of the smaller ones, but the intimate atmosphere can be enjoyable. *[M]* Wheelchair/ECV accessible. *[S][V]* The club is very dark, and the floor is uneven.

Dance
C-Ticket

Comedy Warehouse	9	9	9

Houses the Who, What, and Wherehouse Players, a comedy improvisation troupe that delivers hilarious skits, standup acts, sketches, and adult humor "Disney-style." *[A][U][C][♥][T][I][P][E][S][L]* Lines for this popular nightspot can be VERY long if you've just missed a show, and there are very few places to sit and wait. *[F]* If you're shy, be aware that cast members do involve the audience in the improvisation here. To avoid being selected, stay away from the telephones on the wall. *[H]* You can request sign language interpreting in advance. Call 407-828-3150 before your trip. *[M]* Wheelchair/ECV users may remain in their chair. Accessible entrance is located on the left side as you're facing the Warehouse, down a long ramp. Ask a cast member for directions.

Comedy
D-Ticket
Rib-tickling

Mannequins Dance Palace	3	7	6

Voted the #1 dance club in the Southeast, this is the place for the hottest dance mix and the biggest sound and lighting system. Bouncers in tuxes proof you and let in a few people at a time. Very, very loud. *[A][U][C][♥][T][I][P][E][S][L]* Lines for this popular nightspot can be VERY long, and there are very few places to sit and wait. *[M]* Wheelchair/ECV accessible. *[S][V]* The club is very dark, and the floor is uneven.

Dance
E-Ticket
Must be 21+

Motion	4	6	7

A big dance floor and clean, open layout are all that distinguish this large club. Top 40 and alternative dance. *[M]* Wheelchair/ECV users may remain in their chair.

Dance
C-Ticket

Rock 'n' Roll Beach Club	7	7	6

Offers fans of classic and modern rock a crowded dance floor, live "cover" bands, and a DJ. You can also play pinball and munch out on nachos. *[M]* Wheelchair/ECV users may remain in their chair.

Dance
D-Ticket

Looking for Raglan Road? See our dining descripion on page 363.

Other Things to Do

Behind the Scenes Tours—Curious about how the magic is made at Walt Disney World? Want to learn more about your favorite park? Then perhaps you want to take one of the special tours offered at Walt Disney World. For a price, you can spend hours learning about the ins and outs of Future World, snorkel in the aquarium in The Seas with Nemo and Friends, take a full-day tour of the theme parks and backstage areas, or learn about the Magic Kingdom. Most tours have age requirements (usually 16 and up)—be sure to inquire before booking at 407-WDW-TOUR. **[G][D]** Some tours include a meal (such as the Keys to the Kingdom and Backstage Magic). If you have special dietary needs, make sure you mention this when booking the tour, or at least several days before you arrive. **[B]** Strollers provided for small children on the Behind the Seeds Tour. **[M]** Most tours are accessible by wheelchair/ECV. ECV users must transfer to standard wheelchair for Behind the Seeds Tour. Be sure to mention that you will have a wheelchair when booking. **[C][♥][T][M][P][E] [S][L][V]** Most tours require a great amount of walking outdoors. Tour participants should be in good health and free from heart, head, neck, and back ailments, or consider using an ECV. **[H]** The Wild by Design Tour in Disney's Animal Kingdom is presented with special amplifying headsets. **[X]** When making tour reservation, be sure to notify cast member if you will have a service animal so that they can make proper arrangements. **[E]** Pregnant women may not participate in the Segway Around the World tour or the Dolphins in Depth experience. **[L]** Most tours have no size requirements, but the Segway Around the World tour does have a 250 lb./113 kg. limit. **[V]** Special one-on-one guided tours for those with vision impairments can be arranged through Disney's VIP Tours at 407-560-4033. Other tours can accommodate those with vision impairments—just be sure to mention your requirements when booking. **[Ö]** Some foreign language tours may be arranged. Inquire at Guest Relations in the parks.

Peer Reviewer Masayo Kano points to greenhouse bananas during the Behind the Seeds Tour at Epcot

© Masayo Kano

BoardWalk—Pleasure Island doesn't have a monopoly on nightclubs in Walt Disney World—the BoardWalk resort has its own entertainment complex with clubs, restaurants, and entertainment. Jellyrolls is a dueling piano bar that serves drinks and free popcorn ($7 cover, 21 and up, smoking allowed). Atlantic Dance Hall serves specialty drinks while open-request DJ music lures you onto the floor (no cover, 21 and up, open Tuesday-Saturday). ESPN Club (see page 368) is a popular sports bar. Midway games and street performers add to the fun. For details and directions to the BoardWalk resort, see pages 131-134. **[R]** Several nightclubs here encourage the sale of alcoholic beverages. **[U]** Arcade and carnival-type games here are fun and good for blowing off steam. **[M]** Wheelchair/ECV users may remain in their chair, but some shops and restaurants have narrow entrances and are difficult to navigate. **[M][S][V]** The BoardWalk boards may be uneven in spots. **[G]** Smoking is permitted at Jellyrolls and ESPN Club's bar area. **[S]** Jellyrolls can get very loud. **[C][B][♥][T][M][P][E][S]** Jellyrolls is often standing-room only.

Planning | Special Challenges | Getting There | Staying in Style | Touring | Feasting | Resources | Index

Other Things to Do
(continued)

Golf—The Walt Disney World Resort boasts 99 holes of golf on five championship courses and one nine-hole course, and it consistently lands on a variety of prestigious "top golf resort" lists. All courses are open to the public and feature full-service facilities, including driving ranges, pro shops, cafes, and lessons. If you're staying at a Disney resort hotel, you'll get free transportation to the links for your scheduled tee times. For more details and to reserve tee times, call 407-WDW-GOLF. We also recommend Marc Schwartz's Unofficial WDW Golf Site at http://www.wdwgolf.com. Note: Eagle Pines and Osprey Ridge will be closing for good to make way for the new Four Seasons Resort opening in 2010. **[C][♥][T][I][M][P][S][L]** Courses are accessible for wheelchair/ECV users. If you can use a regular golf cart, Disney will give you a "limited mobility" flag that can be put on the cart to identify to other players that you may require more time than usual. If you cannot use a regular cart, there is <u>one</u> special golf cart available that enables you to rotate the seat to hit the ball without having to leave the cart. The golf bag is specially positioned for access to the clubs as well. The cart also has hand controls and a limited mobility flag. It is kept at the Lake Buena Vista golf course, but with at least a half-day notice, it can be moved to the other courses as required. Request this cart when you're arranging your tee time, then reconfirm a few days ahead of time by calling the golf event manager at the Lake Buena Vista course. For more information on rules for golfers with disabilities, visit http://www.usga.org/playing/rules/golfers_with_disabilities.html. **[S]** Seniors may enjoy a round of golf instead of another day at the parks!

Fort Wilderness—The campgrounds here offer a respite from the hubbub of the theme parks and get you back to nature with canoeing, boating, fishing excursions, biking, tennis, horseback trail rides, horse-drawn carriage rides, and hayride. The petting farm is free (pony rides cost $4), and so is a visit to the blacksmith shop. There's a nightly campfire program (with character visits and free movies). Trail ride at the resort's Tri-Circle D Livery is a good entry-level horseback riding experience for riders age 9 and up and costs $32. Phone 407-824-2832 for reservations. For more information on Fort Wilderness, see pages 147–150. **[A][U]** Lots of open spaces for running around and blowing off steam. **[G]** Animals, tree pollens abound. Allergy sufferers beware. **[C][B][♥][T][M][P][E][S][L]** Distances between points of interest can be great. **[F]** Lots of animals on the grounds—roaming lizards, raccoons, armadillos. **[M]** Wheelchair/ECV users may remain in their chair around the campgrounds. **[L]** Children (ages 2–8) must weigh no more than 80 lbs. (36 kg.) for pony rides. Riders on the horses must weigh no more than 250 lbs. (113 kg.).

Health Clubs & Spas—Many of the deluxe resorts have health clubs with exercise equipment—some even offer massage treatments, steam rooms, and saunas. If you're looking to relax, we recommend the Saratoga Springs Spa or the Grand Floridian Spa and Health Club. These world-class, full-service centers offer many beauty and wellness treatments, nutrition and fitness counseling, and lots of pampering. If you're hoping to keep up an exercise regimen, visit one of the health clubs located at the deluxe resorts. If you're a guest of that resort, your membership at the club is free. If you're staying elsewhere, you can still work out—you'll just be charged a fee. See our descriptions of the individual resorts starting on page 123 for more details on the health clubs and spas. **[M]** Wheelchair/ECV accessible. **[X]** Service animals may be permitted in some locations—ask in advance. **[♥][P]** Health clubs are great for keeping up exercise routines.

Other Things to Do
(continued)

Tennis—There are a number of courts are available around Walt Disney World. Call 407-939-7529. *[M]* Most tennis courts are wheelchair/ECV accessible. Ask for details about the individual resort's tennis court when making reservations.

Waterways, Boating, Fishing—If you love the water, you'll surely find something to do on it here. You can rent boats at nearly every deluxe and moderate resort and Downtown Disney. Probably the most popular rental craft are little, two-person speed boats called Sea Raycers. They're available at most marinas around Disney for about $23 per half-hour. Fishing excursions and cane pole rentals are also available in most of those same locations. You can also reserve two-

A Sea Raycer personal watercraft

hour, guided, catch-and-release bass fishing expeditions at many Disney marinas. All equipment is provided (even a digital camera to document your catch). Fishing licenses are not needed thanks to the state-licensed guide on board, and participants get a free subscription to Bassmaster Magazine. Excursions accommodate up to five guests and cost $200–$405. Kids 6–12 can go on special one-hour excursions for $30. Phone 407-WDW-BASS for reservations. *[L]* Sea Raycers have a weight limit of 320 lbs./145 kg. *[M][L]* At most rental locations, there's a docked Sea Raycer that you can practice getting into/out of. *[M][S][L]* You must step down into the watercraft. Likewise, getting out may be difficult. *[M]* The pontoon boats can accommodate some wheelchairs. If the chair fits through the gate of the boat railing, you can wheel a manual wheelchair for boarding, then leave it on the boat. The wheelchair user must sit in a boat seat for the ride. *[S]* Cruising on the waterways can be very relaxing.

Walt Disney World Speedway—Disney has its own speedway—a one-mile, tri-oval track for auto racing. The race track is home to the Richard Petty Driving Experience, in which participants get to drive or ride at speeds up to 145 mph (233 kph)! You don't really have to be a fan to get a thrill out of this experience. You must be at least 16 for the ride-along program—otherwise there are no health restrictions, but check first with your doctor if you have any concerns. You need to be at least 18 and have a valid driver's license to participate in the driving programs. Riders are subject to strong g-forces. Required to wear special coveralls and helmet in a high-temperature environment. Five-point lap and shoulder harness in vehicle. For Richard Petty Experience details, call 407-939-0130. *[L][M][S]* You need to be able to enter the race car through a window 15" (38 cm.) high by 30" (76 cm.) wide, which is 36" (91 cm.) from the ground. The car doors do not open. *[L]* Usually people who are less than 6' 8" (203 cm.) and 280 lbs. (127 kg.) can participate. However, these numbers can vary up or down according to an individual's flexibility and weight distribution.

Other Things to Do
(continued)

Disney's Wide World of Sports Complex—Disney's state-of-the-art athletic center features a 9,500-seat baseball stadium, a 30,000-square-foot fieldhouse, a track and field complex, volleyball, tennis, baseball, softball, football, and more. This complex is completely accessible, with Braille signage marking restrooms and floor numbers. Admission is $8.25/adults or $8.00/kids 3–9, tax included. The 200-acre center is also home to amateur and professional sports, including Atlanta Braves Spring Training and the Tampa Bay Buccaneers training camp. Call 407-828-FANS (407-828-3267), or visit http://www.disneyworldsports.com for more information. **[M]** Wheelchairs are available at the complex's turnstiles (no ECVs). There is no charge, but you must leave some valid form of ID as a "deposit." There is a companion restroom located near the First Aid Center in the baseball stadium, just under the archway for Sections 113–114. Also, there are special wheelchair/ECV seating areas located in the following sections of the stadium: 109 and 111-114 on the lower level; 208, 210, 212, 214, 216, 218, 220 on the upper level. Note that it's a long way up a steep ramp from the parking area to the turnstile and wheelchair rental location. During popular activities like Braves Spring Training games, most parking is in unpaved grassy fields. Guest drop-off area is near the entrance. **[H]** Assistive listening devices can be rented from D-Sport, just past the ticket booths, and may be used at several locations in Disney's Wide World of Sports, including the Baseball Stadium and the Field House. **[V]** Braille signage throughout stadium.

Miniature Golf—Yes, you can even play miniature golf at two themed locations at Disney. Tee times are available for play on the day of; however, you must make these in person. Cost is about $10.75 for adults and $8.50 for children, with discounts for Annual Passholders. Hours: 10:00 am to 11:00 pm. Disney's miniature golf courses are as follows:

Fantasia Gardens is located near the Walt Disney World Swan and offers two 18-hole courses. One course is whimsically based on the scenes, characters, and music of Disney's classic animated film, "Fantasia." The other is a "grass" course for the "pro" mini-golfer with wildly undulating par-three and par-four holes from 40 feet to 75 feet (12–23 meters) long. There's a companion restroom here, as well as a video game arcade. **[M]** The courses are very accessible by wheelchair; no steps involved. A sidewalk follows the perimeter of the course for those wanting surer footing or wheeling, and there are plenty of benches for sitting and resting. The more challenging course, Fantasia Fairways, may also be more difficult for those with mobility concerns due to its steeper slopes. **[V]** We asked about special "beeping balls" for those with vision impairments, but they are not available.

Winter Summerland is adjacent to Blizzard Beach water park and also offers two courses—one celebrates holidays in the tropics, the other snow! There's medium shade throughout the courses from very tall pine trees. There is no companion restroom here. The background music here gets you in the holiday spirit. **[M]** The courses are very accessible by wheelchair; no steps involved. A sidewalk follows the perimeter of the course for those wanting surer footing or wheeling. **[V]** No special "beeping balls" for those with vision impairments are available here either.

Your Touring Tips and Stories

When I was seven months pregnant, it was difficult for me to sit without back support. I did my research ahead of time and knew which attractions had backless seating. I brought my own stadium seat (with a back) and was able to enjoy the shows!

—contributed by Jill Blejwas

I highly recommend obtaining a Guest Assistance Card, which is available for people touring with someone with an [invisible] disability, such as autism. My son, Nick, is 4 years old, and that card was a godsend on more than one occasion. It is extremely difficult for Nick to wait for much of anything, let alone something that he values very highly. Being able to access the rides through the FASTPASS lanes or have an alternative waiting area that is not so insulting to one's senses was a complete necessity to avoid the meltdowns and tantrums. It was hard enough to have him wait the 5 to 10 minutes in the FASTPASS lanes, constantly talking him through the waiting. I know many people feel guilty about obtaining these cards, but every day, we devote our lives to children or adults who have disabilities, and I think that Disney is one of those places that recognizes those efforts. Disney goes out of its way to give guests with special needs a great vacation, as well as the families that are usually so in need of one. It is great that Disney offers a way for every one of us to experience the Magic. —Contributed by Tamara Osborne

My daughter is developmentally delayed (age 24) and is really challenged when it comes to walking far. She is also obese, which makes it too hard for me to push her in a wheelchair. What I've done the last four or five times we've visited Walt Disney World was to rent an ECV. I walk alongside her and control the throttle and steering for her. When we board the bus, I help her on, then I drive the ECV onto the bus and off again. —contributed by Maggie Ercoli

I am a rather large fellow at 6'8" and 275 lbs. Needless to say, every day at the parks, I get lots of looks and stares from guests and cast members alike. (This has never bothered me, and it is kind of fun when strangers ask me if I am or was an NBA player.) This last year, we decided to get a few photos with characters. We stopped at Disney-MGM Studios to get a picture with Sorcerer Mickey. He looked up at me and put both of his hands on his mouth with a look of puzzlement. It was a classic picture. We decided after that to have fun with the characters and my height. When we ran into Goofy at Epcot, he was really impressed that someone was taller than him. I placed both my arms on top of Chip and Dale, and they both laughed (so to speak, since they don't speak!). Minnie made my girlfriend "jealous", because she was "flirting" with me as I towered over her. We went out of our way to find character photo shoots and had a blast with it. It really made the parks much more fun. —contributed by Anonymous

My daughter has moderate autism, so when we are touring the parks, we always carry her sunglasses. This allows her to block out a lot of the colors and makes her feel safe in her own world. She may look silly to some, but it allows her participate in a world she is sometimes overwhelmed with. —contributed by Anonymous

Your Touring Tips and Stories
(continued)

Don't take anyone else's word that an attraction is fine for an individual with special needs. Try it yourself first if there is any question if the ride is too harsh/bumpy. You know your needs better than anyone else. One ride that is "too much" can ruin your trip for a day or longer. Cast members at the attractions will accommodate requests such as these without much delay, if any, in overall wait times.
—contributed by Anonymous

The accessible seats are not always the best view for little ones. We ask if we can park my 8-year-old daughter's pushchair (stroller) off to the side and claim it at the end. For example, in Turtle Talk with Crush, Emma will sit in her pushchair in line, and when we go in I'll park it out of the way; then Emma can sit on the floor with the other kids. Also, some of the handicapped entrances to the rides are not clearly defined, especially if the parks are crowded. We generally assume that we should wait in the same line as everyone else with Emma in her pushchair, but this can lead to difficulty. Even if you don't see a handicapped sign, confirm with a cast member before you get in line.
—contributed by Anonymous

I am large and I also have high blood pressure. I don't have any problems with most rides as long as I follow my doctor's orders—to make sure I take deep breaths during the ride (between screams, at least!). When I do this, I'm fine. When I don't, I end up with a headache. For example, I had minor problems on Rock 'n' Roller Coaster and Test Track because I kept forgetting to breathe and just screamed when necessary. But both were great rides, and the second time through them was much better than the first because I got some oxygen in my system.
—contributed by Ellen

Setting alone time boundaries before leaving is key. Some people don't ask for alone time until they REALLY need it and, by then, it is obvious that they are angry or frustrated. By making it just another part of the day, no one needs to feel rejected.
—contributed by peer reviewer Sandy Bostwick

We bring along Steve Barrett's "Hidden Mickeys" book on our visits. We have so much fun trying to find all of the Mickeys through all the parks and resorts. We even try to find Hidden Mickeys not in the book and take pictures of them and send to Mr. Barrett. Hunting for Hidden Mickeys has become such an obsession for us that when we travel with family and friends, they get caught up in the thrill of seeing or finding them. This is a great way to keep children going as they too love to find the Hidden Mickeys.
—contributed by peer reviewer Carol Scopa

People of size should always bring their sense of humor with them at the water parks. Attractions like Gangplank Falls, for example, are potentially embarrassing. Since the loading area is in a shallow pool of water and the 'family-sized' rafts have to be pushed up onto the slide surface, a large person will probably cause a portion of the raft to sink below the slide surface level. This makes it very difficult for the raft to be pushed up onto the slide surface. You may have to put your feet down and lift your derriere up off the floor of the raft for the cast members to be able to push your raft up onto the slide. Just be prepared for the possibility!
—contributed by peer reviewer Josh Olive

Dining
Your
Way

Can you believe that the Walt Disney World Resort has more than 300 places to eat? With that many choices, you're sure to find an eatery that meets your requirements, whatever they may be. If anything, there are *too* many choices! So how do you go about deciding which eateries are best for you? That's where we come in. We've been to nearly every restaurant on property at least once and probably several times. We've poured our experience into these pages to help you make the best dining decisions.

This chapter gives you an overview of all your dining options with a variety of special situations in mind so that you can make well-informed decisions. You'll find descriptions of nearly all table-service and counter-service restaurants at both the theme parks and resort hotels, as well as some of the snack shops and carts at the theme parks. Descriptions are organized alphabetically within each park and resort, so you are able to choose the eateries that best meet your needs.

As you make decisions about your meals, be sure to make note of those table-service restaurants for which advance reservations may be made. These restaurants are the ones that are best able to address your concerns, especially if your special needs are dietary.

Peer reviewer Elizabeth Shorten gets a special treat

Deciding on Dining

The first thing to do is **decide how often you want to eat out**. Depending on your situation, you may find it advantageous to bring or buy some food for snacks or meals in your room. Most Disney resorts supply a complimentary refrigerator (it's $10/day for value resorts), many include a coffeemaker, and Disney Vacation Club resorts have kitchen facilities.

Bright Idea: If you only have a few items to chill overnight (and no refrigerator), fill your room's ice bucket and place your items in plastic bags inside the ice.

You could, of course, eat out for every meal, but if you're traveling with children with ADHD or autism spectrum disorders, for whom long waits are difficult, or with a person who has diabetes or other special dietary needs, it might make sense to have some meals, particularly breakfast, in your room. Light breakfasts are the most practical and the easiest to prepare. It's easy enough to run to the resort's sundries shop and purchase bagels and cream cheese or some cold cereal and milk.

Bright Idea: Bring some favorite snacks/treats from home! Especially remember harder-to-find items like sugar-free candy, low-sodium pretzels or crackers, or dairy-free/gluten-free products. You can also ship snacks from home to arrive at your Disney resort when you do.

What Disney Does for Special Dietary Challenges

Disney revamped its menus to include healthier options for children. Disney also announced its commitment to eliminating all transfats and improving the nutritional value of all foods by the end of 2007. Also, a special line is included on all table-service menus: "We are happy to discuss with you and attempt to accommodate any special dietary requests." According to the official statement, all Walt Disney World Resort table-service restaurants that accept advance reservations offer "balanced menu choices, and will accommodate lifestyle dining options (such as no-sugar-added, low-fat, low-sodium, low-carb, vegetarian, or vegan)." Counter-service locations also offer balanced menu choices and can accommodate most lifestyle dining options. If a special menu request is needed, you should speak with a cast member. Note that dinner shows require 24-hour notice for any special menu request. Examples of Disney's enhanced options include: more vegetarian dishes; reduced-fat and reduced-calorie meals and snacks, and no-sugar-added items. Disney has also added low-fat milk, juice, and no-sugar beverages (Minute Maid Light Lemonade) as alternatives to soft drinks. Other special dietary needs: All Walt Disney World Resort table-service restaurants that accept advance reservations can accommodate special dietary needs (such as allergies to gluten or wheat, shellfish, soy, lactose or milk, peanuts, tree nuts, fish, or eggs). Special dietary needs can be accommodated if requested at least 72 hours in advance at 407-WDW-DINE (407-939-3463). Also see Kosher Meals on pages 338–339.

Advance Reservations

Nearly every table-service restaurant within Walt Disney World allows you to make advance reservations. Unlike traditional reservations, in which a table would be held for your party at a designated time, Disney's advance reservation system gives you the **first available table for your party size**. The only Disney table-service restaurants that don't accept advance arrangements are some Downtown Disney restaurants, Big River Grille and Brewing Works, and ESPN Club (see detailed listings in this chapter). Additionally, some restaurants DO take traditional reservations, such as Victoria & Albert's, the Swan & Dolphin restaurants (see pages 376–377), and the character meals at Cinderella's Royal Table and Akershus Royal Banquet Hall (see pages 381–382 for reservation details/policies).

Advance reservations can be **made before your trip** by calling 407-WDW-DINE (407-939-3463). Call up to 180 days in advance for reservations at most restaurants. (We note any different policies.) We suggest you visit Scott Thomas's handy Planning Strategy Calculator at http://pscalculator.net for more advance reservation details. Arrangements can also be made the same day in person at Guest Relations, a resort's Lobby Concierge, at any Disney table-service restaurant, or by touching *88 on any Disney pay phone or 55 on your Disney resort in-room phone. Be sure to mention if someone in your party uses a wheelchair/ECV or has special dietary concerns.

When you call, you will be asked to **supply the name of the Disney resort** at which you are staying and your date of arrival. If you aren't staying at a Disney resort, no problem—you'll simply need to provide a daytime phone number. Also note that some character meals and other special dining events require a credit card guarantee—in some cases (Cinderella's Royal Table, Hoop Dee Doo Musical Revue), your credit card will actually be charged when you make the reservation. You will receive a confirmation number for each successfully arranged reservation; be sure to bring it with you to the restaurant. If you are unable to get a reservation, call back about one week before the desired date.

Check in at the restaurant's podium **15 minutes before your seating time**. You may also need to wait (occasionally for quite a while) for a table to become available, depending upon how busy it is. Some restaurants issue a pager, and some have a comfortable waiting area or bar.

If you later decide not to eat at a particular restaurant, just call Disney again and **cancel your advance reservation**. In the case of the special dinner shows and those meals that require a credit card guarantee, however, be aware that there is a 48-hour cancellation policy.

Making Special Dietary Requests

As we mentioned in chapter 2, all Walt Disney World table-service restaurants that accept advance reservations (see page 333) try to meet your special needs if you give them adequate notice—at least 72 hours is required. In fact, even the counter-service eateries and resort food courts are happy to "take requests" with enough fair warning. And, as we found through talking with Disney chefs at various locations, the more warning they have, the better they are able to serve you. The key is to **plan ahead** when you're dealing with a special diet. Here's our step-by-step approach to making special dietary requests:

1. **Choose your restaurants**. A good way to determine your dining spots is to preview the menus. Most of the Disney eatery menus are available online at AllEars.net (http://allears.net/menu/menus.htm). Menus give you an idea of the prices and types of foods available, including many of the ingredients used.

2. Once you've decided on your meals, **make advance reservations** for as many eateries as possible. It's best to call (407-939-3463) before you leave for your trip. Tell the cast member you speak to about your specific dietary concerns and to make a notation on your record.

3. For information about special dining in the theme park restaurants, you can **call the park restaurant management** directly at the telephone numbers listed below. (If no one is available when you call, leave your name and telephone number so they can get back to you!)

   ✔ Magic Kingdom: 407-824-5967
   ✔ Epcot: 407-560-6395
   ✔ Disney-MGM Studios: 407-560-3551
   ✔ Disney's Animal Kingdom: 407-938-3288

   For more information on dining at a resort hotel, ask for the restaurant telephone number so you can speak to a chef or manager in advance.

4. If you are staying at a Disney resort hotel, **speak to a cast member** at the resort's Lobby Concierge desk upon your arrival to confirm that your specific dining needs have been noted on your dining arrangements. Ask that they call the restaurant for you, so you can speak to a chef. The more specific and individual your needs are, the more lead time the restaurant will require. If you are staying off Disney property, call the main switchboard (407-824-2222) and ask to be connected to the specific restaurant to confirm they are aware of your special needs.

Important Note: Don't forget to confirm your special dietary requests for any dinner shows you may plan to attend. Events like the Spirit of Aloha dinner require at least 24 hours' notice.

Planning

Special Challenges

Getting There

Staying in Style

Touring

Dining

Resources

Index

5. If you'll be dining at a resort's food court, visit it or phone during an off-peak time (after the lunch rush, for example) and ask to **talk to a chef**. We've found that most chefs are happy to answer all of your questions about how foods are prepared and which foods are available. Many, if not all, will even ask you specifics so that they can order any special items ahead of time. For example, many places keep a certain number of kosher meals on hand. If you have a large group, though, letting them know in advance allows them to order additional quantities and serve you exactly the foods you want.

6. **Visit theme park counter-service eateries** you want to dine at in the morning to make special requests, like kosher food or sugar-free desserts. Note that counter-service eateries have a book of ingredients used in their offerings—just ask a cast member. Ask to speak to the manager on duty if you have any additional concerns or questions.

7. Even with all these advance plans, however, the message sometimes fails to reach the restaurant or the chef. Be sure to **alert your server at the restaurant** to your special requirements. Most often, the chef will come to your table to discuss what your needs are and then prepare a dish or dishes to your specifications. Also, not all restaurants on Disney property are operated by Disney, so their guidelines on accommodating special dietary needs may be different.

Bright Idea: Disney sometimes changes vendors and recipes, so remember to get updated dietary information before every trip and even while at the restaurant during the visit.

⚠ Vegan Snacks

"Being a vegan doesn't mean missing all the fun at Walt Disney World. There are tasty snacks for us, too! Salty snacks like popcorn and soft pretzels are available in all four parks. Min and Bill's at Disney-MGM Studios even has an Apple Cinnamon Stuffed Dessert Pretzel. Roasted cashews and cinnamon-glazed almonds and pecans are also readily available. For something more substantial, the new Samosas at the Egg Roll Wagon in the Magic Kingdom are completely vegan. Kaki Goris from the Japan pavilion are a perfect treat on a hot day, as are juice bars and Itzakadoozies. While caramel apples do have dairy, the candy apples are safe. The Main Street Confectionery has a sticky treat called "Coconut Cashew Crisp," very similar in consistency to peanut brittle, but minus the peanuts and butter. There are also a number of prepackaged candies and cookies available in different shops throughout the resort. Some of my favorite finds include cookies in the Norway and Canada pavilions, and dark chocolate in the Germany pavilion, as well as some prepackaged taffy found in several locations. Just be sure to read the ingredients, as not everything is vegan, and products change from time to time. There are plenty of healthy snacks, too, but if you're looking to satisfy a vegan sweet tooth, you can certainly do that, too!"—contributed by peer reviewer Kitty Smith

Gluten-Free Dining

What does "gluten-free" mean? Gluten is a set of proteins found in wheat flour. (Only wheat is considered to have true gluten, but rye and barley have similar proteins. Oats are also often avoided due to potential cross-contamination during harvesting.) Some folks can't process these proteins properly and need to eliminate them from their diet. If you're one of those individuals, here are the counter-service eateries and snack places, and their foods, we've found around the theme parks that are **safe bets** (and some definite no-no's):

General Food Carts: The turkey legs, strawberry and orange juice bars, frozen lemonade, and Itzakadoozie bars are all gluten-free.

Disney's Animal Kingdom: On Discovery Island, Flame Tree Barbecue's ribs, chicken, and salad are all gluten-free. In Africa, there's fresh fruit at Harambe Market. Other gluten-free foods can be found in DinoLand at Restaurantosaurus (salad, french fries, hamburgers) and Petri-Fries (french fries).

In Epcot: The Liberty Inn sometimes has gluten-free pizza available; it contains milk, sunflower seeds, and soy. The meat in the beef burgers, chicken sandwich, and all-beef hot dogs are gluten-free, but the rolls are not. Sometimes gluten-free rolls/bread are available—ask to speak with a manager.

In Magic Kingdom: Cosmic Ray's has rotisserie chicken; El Pirata y el Perico has gluten-free nachos, taco shells, and salsa. Also gluten-free: Scuttle's Landing frozen beverages; ToonTown Farmer's Market and Liberty Square Market for fresh fruit; and Aloha Isle's Dole Whips (vanilla, chocolate, and pineapple). Main Street Ice Cream Parlor has gluten-free ice cream—ask for the manager, as it's kept in the back.

Disney-MGM Studios: Disney chefs do not recommend you order fries from the ABC Commissary—they are in very close proximity to the batter-dipped fish area. The counter-service areas can provide gluten-free pizza or pasta with advance notice.

You can also obtain current info on gluten-free dining by e-mailing Walt Disney World **Guest Communications** through the form on their web site at http://www.disneyworld.com.

Weight Loss Surgery

You should be so proud of yourself! With the help of a surgical procedure—either gastric bypass, lapband surgery, or some other surgical method—you've been able to lose a significant amount of weight. But now you're vacationing at Walt Disney World, and guess what? You can't eat as much as you used to—in fact, the surgery you've had physically restricts your stomach capacity, and you can only eat very small portions. Will you still be charged full price at the buffets or all-you-can-eat meals? Are there any alternatives to ordering full dinners? Will you be frowned upon for ordering light meals or special items?

While there is as yet **no official Disney policy** on dining for those who have had such weight loss surgery, most travelers we spoke to report having positive experiences at Disney restaurants.

Ask to **speak to a manager** when you arrive at the restaurant, particularly if it's an "all-you-can-eat" meal, and explain your situation—that your surgery physically limits the amount of food you can eat. Bring with you a personalized card or physician's note that states you've had the surgery.

Almost all restaurants at Disney will allow you to **share dishes** (although there may be a minimal plate charge). When eating at a counter-service restaurant, ask the cast member to provide you with a second plate and cut your sandwich or entrée in half so you can easily share it.

At the manager's discretion, many Disney buffets will only charge you the **kid's meal price**. Inquire into the restaurant's policy before you dine.

Some buffet restaurants, like Fresh at the Walt Disney World Dolphin, offer a continental breakfast (i.e., just fruit and baked goods) and/or a soup and salad bar buffet (again, no hot entrées) at a **reduced price**. This is generally not well-advertised, so ask the host/hostess, your server, or the manager.

If you cannot drink carbonated beverages, **bottled water** is widely available in the parks. Most Disney eateries also offer at least one sugar-free, non-carbonated soft drink, such as light lemonade. In addition, the sports drink PowerAde is available at many locations; other sugared drinks, such as lemonade, fruit punch, and iced tea, can also be found.

Other tips:
- ✔ When you make your advance reservations, be sure to have your surgery noted as a special dietary request on the reservation.
- ✔ Each park has at least one fresh fruit stand (see page 339).
- ✔ Ask your server if a grilled chicken breast is available, even if it's not on the menu.
- ✔ Consider ordering an appetizer in lieu of an entrée. Combine that with a beverage and a small dessert for a small meal instead of a full-course one.
- ✔ Remember to bring some good snacks with you in the parks!

Kosher Meals

Almost all Disney Resort table-service restaurants that accept advance reservations can accommodate kosher needs if requested at least 72 hours in advance at 407-WDW-DINE (407-939-3463). A credit card is required to guarantee the order, but will not be charged the full price of the meal(s) unless the reservation is canceled within 24 hours or the party is a no-show.

Important Note: Kosher meals are not offered at certain restaurants—we note them in the individual restaurant descriptions later in this chapter.

Kosher products offered at Walt Disney World are **Glatt Kosher** and are certified by the OK Kosher Certification Organization (http://www.okkosher.com). Entrées are plated on a three-compartment plastic dish, wrapped in a kosher labeled bag. Entrées include a vegetable and starch accompaniment, dinner rolls, and stainless utensils.

Pricing for kosher meals is as follows as of July 2007, but like everything at Walt Disney World, it is subject to change without notice:

Table-Service Restaurants	Dinner Shows	Buffets and All-You-Care-to-Eat Locations
Breakfast = $9.99 Entrée = $17.99 Kid's Meals = $5.99 Soup = $4.99 Dessert = $5.99	Regular current dinner show prices. You will only receive one meal, not all-you-can-eat, however.	Regular current buffet/all-you-care-to-eat price. You will only receive one meal, not all-you-care-to-eat, however. This includes character and fixed-menu meals.

Vacationers using a **Disney package** (Magic Your Way Plus Dining or Premium and Platinum packages) get the following as part of their kosher meal: one soup, one entrée, and one dessert per guest.

Kosher Meals Available Without Advance Notice

Theme Parks:
Disney's Animal Kingdom: Pizzafari
Disney-MGM Studios: ABC Commissary
Epcot: Liberty Inn at American Adventure
Magic Kingdom: Cosmic Ray's Starlight Café in Tomorrowland

Resort Hotels:
All-Star Food Courts: World Premiere (Movies), Intermission (Music), and End Zone (Sports)
Pop Century: Everything Pop
Port Orleans Riverside: Riverside Mill Food Court

As of February 2007, these are the **types of kosher meals available**. All come with kosher flatware pack, and items are subject to change at any time.

Breakfast:
- ✔ Cheese blintzes with hash browns, large twist rolls
- ✔ Cheese omelet with home fries, large twist rolls

Entrée:
- ✔ Beef brisket with brown gravy, oven-browned potatoes, mixed vegetables, and large twist rolls
- ✔ Honey glazed breast of chicken, toasted almond couscous, ratatouille, and large twist rolls
- ✔ Cheese lasagna, asparagus, and large twist rolls
- ✔ Baked fillet of salmon, baby carrots and rice medley, and large twist rolls

Kid's Meal:
- ✔ Kid's hot dog on bun with potato croquettes
- ✔ Kid's macaroni and cheese
- ✔ Chicken strips with potato croquettes

Soup:
- ✔ Matzo ball soup
- ✔ Garden vegetable soup

Dessert:
- ✔ Chocolate cake
- ✔ Apple strudel
- ✔ Non-dairy cheesecake

Special **Passover** meals, including a Seder plate, can also be prepared and are available for about a week around Passover.

Fresh Fruit Finds

Many counter-service restaurants offer fresh fruit cups, baby carrots, or whole fresh fruit. When buying a "combo meal," **ask if fruit or carrots can be substituted for fries**. The following spots have whole fruit or fruit cups on their regular menus.

Disney's Animal Kingdom: Harambe Fruit Market

Disney-MGM Studios: Anaheim Produce on Hollywood Blvd.

Epcot: Refreshment Outpost in World Showcase; Sunshine Seasons in The Land

Magic Kingdom: Toontown Farmer's Market; Liberty Square Market

All resort food courts/fast food areas

Fresh fruit at Refreshment Outpost in Epcot

© Debra Martin Koma

Dining Basics

Alcoholic Beverages—Most eateries serve alcoholic drinks, with the notable exception of those in the Magic Kingdom. Bars and lounges are located around the "World." Some areas sell alcohol in the walkways, such as Pleasure Island and Epcot. Legal drinking age is 21 and they do check your identification.

Character Dining—Dine with Disney characters! See pages 381–382.

Children's Meals—Nearly every eatery has a children's menu for ages 3-9 at parent-friendly prices. Perennial kid faves macaroni and cheese and chicken tenders can be found even at the most exotic of restaurants—ask your server. In addition, Disney recently revamped its children's menus to include "balanced meal" options with items from the five food groups. Although fries and soft drinks are not offered on some children's menus, they are available upon request. Note that counter-service eatery kids' meals are 10 percent to 28 percent smaller than adult portions.

Bright Idea: Remember if you need a high chair, just ask! They are available at all full-service restaurants and most counter-service spots, too.

Counter Service—This is essentially fast food. The quality varies, and so do the offerings. Most counter-service spots in the Magic Kingdom serve up the traditional burgers, dogs, and fries, while at Disney's Animal Kingdom, you'll find more unusual selections, such as barbecue.

© Debra Martin Koma

Dietary Requirements—Low-cholesterol, low-salt, low-fat, and/or vegetarian meals are a regular part of the menu in most restaurants. Look for special Mickey Apple icons on Disney menus for healthy or vegetarian options. With 72-hour advance notice, restaurants can meet kosher and other special dietary needs—see pages 334–335. At least one eatery in each theme park now has kosher items available without advance notice (see page 338)—ask if you don't see the menu posted.

Some counter-service registers are lower for easy accessibility

Dinner Shows—Disney offers several dinner shows, combining all-you-care-to-eat meals with live entertainment. Special dietary requests for these shows must be made at least 24 hours in advance. See pages 383–386 for Special Meals.

Disney Dining Plan—Available as an add-on to your Magic Your Way package, the 2007 plan costs $38.99/adult ($10.99/child) plus tax per person per night of stay and gives each person one table-service credit, one quick-service credit, and one snack credit per night of stay, including appetizer and gratuities. The plan changes in 2008 and costs $37.99/$9.99 plus tax per person per night of stay and gives the same credits, but without gratuities or appetizers. A Deluxe Dining Plan debuts in 2008 for $69.99/adult ($19.99/child) plus tax per person per night of stay and gives each person three meals (your choice of table service or counter service) and two snacks, plus a refillable mug for each person—table-service meals include appetizer but not gratuities. The Disney Dining Plan isn't as a great a moneysaver as in years past, but it may still be worth it for the convenience factor. For more details, visit http://www.allears.net/din/ddp.htm.

Dress—Casual clothing is appropriate for most restaurants except Victoria & Albert's in the Grand Floridian (see page 373) and Wolfgang Puck's upstairs dining room (see page 365). Several spots have a "business casual" dress code, which means no tank tops, cut-offs, or swimwear; collared shirts and nicer pants or shorts are preferred. We note these rules, when present, in an eatery's description later in this chapter.

Entertainment—Some restaurants supply entertainment (Restaurant Marrakesh, Biergarten, and Rose and Crown bar area) while others like the Whispering Canyon Cafe and 'Ohana provide activities for kids or server/guest interactions.

Menus—Most menus at counter-service locations are pictorial, so that foreign-speaking guests should have no trouble interpreting them. We have found no Braille menus at any Disney restaurant, presumably because they change so frequently. Many menus can be previewed, though, at Guest Services. Co-author Deb Wills' AllEars.net web site (http://www.allears.net) also has a nearly complete and very current collection of menus brought back by fellow vacationers.

Money—Cash, Disney Dollars, traveler's checks, the Disney Credit Card, Disney Visa Reward Cards, MasterCard, Visa, American Express, JCB, Discover, Diner's Club, and Disney Resort room charge cards are welcomed. Disney Gift Cards are also accepted; personal checks are not. Gratuities may be applied automatically to large parties.

Smoking—Florida law prohibits smoking in all enclosed restaurants and other indoor public spaces. Only outdoor establishments and freestanding bars (no restaurants or hotel lobbies allowed) can allow smoking, but Disney has chosen to ban smoking at most of these, too. Smoking is permitted inside Jellyrolls and at the bar in the ESPN Club (both on the BoardWalk).

For Particular Palates

Some children—and some adults as well—aren't the most adventurous eaters. In fact, they'll often only eat certain foods. We've found that many of these finicky eaters want one of several very simple dishes: peanut butter and jelly sandwich, macaroni and cheese, chicken nuggets, or a grilled cheese sandwich. Here's a sampling of what we found around the theme park counter-service spots—read the individual restaurant descriptions for more details:

Magic Kingdom:
Pinocchio Village Haus: mac and cheese, peanut butter and jelly
Columbia Harbour House: mac and cheese; chicken strips
Cosmic Ray's Starlight Cafe: chicken nuggets

Epcot:
Electric Umbrella: mac and cheese; chicken nuggets
Liberty Inn: chicken nuggets; peanut butter and jelly
Refreshment Port: McDonald's chicken nuggets
Sunshine Seasons: mac and cheese
Tangierine Cafe: pizza; chicken tenders

Disney's Animal Kingdom:
Pizzafari: peanut butter and jelly sandwich
Restaurantosaurus: McDonald's chicken nuggets (Happy Meal)

Disney-MGM Studios:
ABC Commissary: chicken nuggets
Backlot Express: chicken nuggets; chicken strips

Planning

Special Challenges

Getting There

Staying in Style

Touring

Dining

Resources

Index

Tips for Diners With Special Challenges

✔ Some counter-service eateries have **wheelchair-/ECV-accessible** cash registers, usually located on the far ends of the counter.

✔ Consider eating **earlier or later than traditional mealtime hours**. You'll be more likely to get a seat and be served quicker (if you haven't made advance reservations), or simply find the restaurant less crowded and noisy.

✔ Most items at counter-service eateries can be ordered **a la carte**. If you don't want fries with that burger "meal," just ask, and you'll usually pay a reduced price.

✔ Resort eateries are frequently **less crowded** than those in the parks, especially during lunch. Consider a visit to a nearby resort restaurant before, during, or after a park visit. The Contemporary, Polynesian, and Grand Floridian resorts are a short monorail ride from the Magic Kingdom, while the Yacht & Beach Club, BoardWalk, and Swan & Dolphin restaurants are near Epcot.

Bright Idea: Travelers with vision impairments may want to consider dining in a quieter eatery, as too much noise can be distracting.

✔ Some table-service eateries have a **separate vegetarian menu**—if you don't see it, ask!

✔ Most table-service restaurants have at least **one sugar-free or no-sugar-added dessert** on request.

✔ Most counter-service restaurants have an **ingredients list** behind the counter. If the cast member serving you doesn't know about it, ask to speak to a manager.

✔ Be sure to inquire about the **oil type** used and what items have been fried in that oil. Fryer oil for french fries, etc., is 100% soybean oil, but be sure to consider the potential for cross-contamination with other nearby food items, such as batter-dipped or seafood items. McDonald's fries may contain wheat, dairy, and beef flavoring.

✔ If you're traveling alone, cast members will **assist you with your tray** or with reading the menu—just ask!

✔ Special meals sometimes **take longer to prepare**, so allow extra time when dining.

✔ When dealing with buffets and family-style servings, **cross-contamination** is always a possibility. Talk with a chef—they may need to prepare a separate plate for you.

✔ Many **familiar chain restaurants** are located nearby, off Disney property. Consult the local telephone book for locations.

✔ If you require your foods to be **mixed in a blender**, just ask your server. Table-service restaurants can very easily handle this request. It may even be possible at counter-service eateries if you give them enough advance notice—stop by and speak to the manager several hours before you plan to dine.

✔ If for some reason your **intake of food is limited** in some way (e.g., you are fed through a gastric tube, or you've had gastric bypass surgery), be sure to speak to the manager, especially at an "all-you-can-eat" meal. Disney does not seem to have a set policy on charging in such cases—it's at the discretion of the individual restaurant manager. Be sure to ask before dining.

Bright Idea: Be sure to ask what "extras" may be placed next to or on top of the foods that you want to order. At the Garden Grill, for example, the turkey comes into contact with cranberry sauce piled on top. Request all extras on the side. When in doubt, ask about ingredients. Menu items change.

Understanding and Using the Eatery Descriptions and Ratings

Our capsule reviews of Disney eateries cover all table-service restaurants, as well as counter-service eateries at the parks, and most food outlets at the resorts. We even include most snack carts. We offer the information you need to know for your specific situation, plus our ratings.

Description Key

Ratings[6]

[1] **Eatery Name** [D-2[2]]	B/L/D/S[3]	$[4]	🕭[5]	#	#
Description offering an overview of the eatery, including comments on the theming, quality, and menu range. We try to give you an idea of what sort of foods you'll find at a particular eatery, along with our recommendations. We also include information on the availability of lighter fare, children's meals, and alcoholic beverages. Whenever possible, we describe the type of seating (tables, booths, etc.) and whether it is indoor or outdoor.				Type[7]
				Cuisine[7]
				Noise factor[7]
				Seating[7]
				Avg. wait[7]
				Hours[7]

[1] Each chart has an empty **checkbox** in the upper left corner—use it to check off the eateries that interest you (before you go) or those at which you ate (after your return).

[2] **Map coordinates**—match them up to park maps in chapter 5 for locations.

[3] Meals are indicated by letters: **B (breakfast), L (lunch), D (dinner), and S (snack)**.

[4] **Dollar figures** represent the average cost of a full adult dinner. Table-service meal costs include appetizer, entrée, dessert, soft drink, tax, and tip. Whenever possible, we also provide in parentheses the average cost of a lighter dinner, such as a sandwich, pizza, or entrée salad plus dessert, soft drink, tax, and tip. Average counter-service meal costs include entrée (with fries when appropriate), dessert, soft drink, and tax. Average counter-service snack prices include a snack, soft drink, and tax. Use these only as a guide.

[5] Eateries with a reasonable selection of healthy items (low-fat/low-sodium/low-calorie) are indicated with a **tape measure symbol**. These are also friendly to weight watchers!

[6] The two white boxes on the right show **ratings** on a scale of 1 (poor) to 10 (loved it!). The first rating is **Deb Wills'** and the second is Deb Koma's. We offer our personal ratings to show how opinions vary, even between two like-minded people. You can also use our ratings as a point of reference—Deb Wills likes eateries with extensive theming and foods that aren't too exotic or spicy. She also enjoys eating vegetarian meals, but avoids seafood—she has a severe shellfish allergy. Deb Koma's tastes run the gamut, from basic meat and potatoes to seafood to unusual, spicy dishes, but she tries to eat healthily, avoiding heavy sauces and overly rich desserts. Both authors consider it a real treat to relax with a glass of wine and a fine meal at the end of a tough day touring the theme parks.

© Deb Wills

[7] The boxes on the right beneath the numeric ratings give **basic information**: eatery type, cuisine, noise factor, seating, average wait time, and the eatery's hours.

No-sugar-added dessert at Citricos

Magic Kingdom Eateries

The Magic Kingdom may be magical in many ways, but dining with special needs is not one of them. There are several table-service restaurants in this theme park—all of them catering to a distinctly younger crowd—but most food served here comes from counter-service spots or even less sophisticated "quick-service" snack carts. On the plus side, though, for recovering alcoholics, this park serves no alcohol in any of its establishments.

Aunt Polly's Dockside Inn [B-3] S $5   6 6

Isolated over on Tom Sawyer Island, this little seasonal spot is great for getting away from the mania. Main items: snacks, cold drinks, and ice cream treats. **[A]** **[U]** Open-air environment is good spot for letting off steam. Can also be good quiet spot since eatery is often closed, but watch out for birds and the loud passing riverboat. **[M][Q][S][T][U][X]** Seating areas can be difficult to navigate. **[M]** The rafts to Tom Sawyer Island are not ECV accessible.	**Counter**
	American
	Quiet
	Outdoor seating

Casey's Corner [D-4]   L $10, D $10, S   4 6

Need a quick hot dog and fries? Casey's is the spot for a fast All-American lunch. Most seating is outdoors; indoor seating is at just a few small tables or on wooden bleachers. **[M][E][S][L][V][X]** Tables are very close together; seating areas can be difficult to navigate. **[F]** Birds of all types (sparrows, even ibises!) love to come and scrounge a fry or crumbs—if you have a fear of them, avoid the outdoor seating area. **[A][U]** Indoors features black-and-white Disney cartoons with a sports theme; outside often features an old-time piano player. **[M]** The first register on the left is wheelchair/ECV accessible. **[B]** Just around the corner from this eatery is the Magic Kingdom Baby Care Center.	**Counter**
	American
	Noisy
	Mostly outdoor seating
	Short waits
	11:00 am- park closing

Cinderella's Royal Table [D-3]   B $40, L $42, D $50   🍷   4 6

Everyone's a princess or prince inside Cinderella Castle! The character breakfast (adults $31.99/children 3-9 $21.99) here is ultra-popular, which means ultra-noisy. Lunch is also a character meal (adults $33.99/children 3-9 $22.99). Dinner's a fixed-price meal ($39.99/$24.99) with an appetizer, entree, dessert, and beverage. A premium of $2-$4 per person is charged during the holiday season. Also note that prices are scheduled to increase by $1-$2 per person on November 11, 2007. All meals include a photo package (your photo is taken before you're seated) and a gift for any prince or princess (child) in attendance. **[A][U]** Very noisy at breakfast, but character meals are better meet-and-greet opportunities than in the parks. **[R]** All-you-care-to-eat preplated breakfast and lunch. **[D]** A number of chicken and seafood entrées for health-conscious diets. Always offers at least one vegetarian selection, like cheese tortellini with vegetables. Important Note: We have found this restaurant to be inflexible at breakfast when it comes to accommodating special requests without advance notice. **[F]** Narrow winding stairs to get to restaurant, or take small elevator. Breakfast and lunch feature costumed characters who frequently make the rounds—if anyone has a fear of costumed characters, you may want to avoid. **[M]** Restaurant is on second floor; use elevator or walk up steep stairway. **[S]** Can be quite noisy with lots of children.	**Table Service**
	American
	Medium noise
	Reservations and payment in full at time of booking required for breakfast
	~8:00 am- 10:20 am, noon- 3:00 pm, 4:00 pm- park closing

Eatery descriptions and ratings are explained on page 343.

Magic Kingdom Eateries
(continued)

	Deb Wills' Rating	Deb Koma's Rating

Columbia Harbour House [C-2] L $12, D $12, S

	7	**8**

A seafarer's waystation, this is a cozy, nautically themed spot that has some unusual lunch offerings. Main items: Soups, sandwiches, fried chicken strips, and fish. **[M]** The first register on left is wheelchair/ECV accessible. Additional seating upstairs is via an elevator. **[M] [E] [S] [L] [V] [X]** The seating area can be difficult to negotiate. **[D]** Some vegetarian options are available, like vegetarian chili ($4.49). We recommend the Lighthouse Sandwich—hummus with tomato & broccoli slaw ($6.49). **[Ö]** Pictorial menu available for foreign-language speakers. **[A] [U] [B] [S]** Upstairs seating area is usually much quieter than downstairs. **[A] [U] [D]** Macaroni and cheese is available.

Counter
American
Med. noise
More seating upstairs
Short waits
11:00 am–1 hr. before closing

A Columbia Harbour House meal

© MediaMarx, Inc.

Cosmic Ray's Starlight Café [E-3] L $13, D $13, S

	5	**7**

Several different counters serve up a variety of meals in this space-age setting—burgers on one side, soup/salads on another, and chicken on the third. **[D]** Kosher menu items available without advance notice. Chicken and salad items for the health-conscious diner. No-sugar-added brownies are available ($2.49). Rotisserie chicken is gluten-free. Veggie burger ($6.19) may not be vegan—ask to see ingredient list. **[D] [G]** Gluten-free rotisserie chicken, fries, hot dogs, and hamburgers available. **[F]** Audio-Animatronics Sonny Eclipse performs in one corner—may be frightening to some. **[Ö]** Pictorial menu for foreign-language speakers. **[H]** Assistive listening offered for Sonny Eclipse's performance. **[M]** First register on left of Blast-Off Burgers and Starlight Soup-Salad-Sandwich and first register on right of Cosmic Chicken are wheelchair/ECV accessible.

Counter
American
Very noisy
Indoor seating
Avg. waits
10:00 am– closing

Crystal Palace [C-4] B $24, L $26, D $35

	8	**8**

All-day character buffet in a Victorian-era conservatory with hanging plants and stained glass windows. Breakfast is fairly typical bacon/eggs/waffles fare ($18.99 adults/$10.99 children 3-9). Main lunch/dinner items: carved meats, chicken, some fish and pasta items. (Adult lunch $20.99/dinner $27.99; children 3-9 $12.99.) Special kid's buffet with mac and cheese, chicken nuggets. **[A] [U]** Very noisy, but character meals are better meet-and-greet opportunities than in the parks. **[R]** All-you-can-eat buffet. **[D]** Some chicken and fish entrées on the buffet for health-conscious diets. Vegetarian offerings include cheeses, salads, grilled vegetables. **[M]** Entrance ramp located to the left of the main entrance. **[B]** Just around the corner from the Baby Care Center and First Aid. **[F]** All meals here feature Winnie the Pooh and friends, who frequently make the rounds—if little ones have fear of costumed characters, you may want to avoid. **[S]** Can be quite noisy.

Buffet
American
Very noisy
Reservations strongly suggested
Long waits
8-10:30 am, 11:30 am– 3:00 pm, 4:00 pm– park closing

El Pirata Y El Perico [A-4] L $10, D $10, S

	5	**6**

This seasonal spot, just a stone's throw from Pirates of the Caribbean, serves up out-of-the-ordinary fast food in a South of the Border atmosphere. Limited menu features tacos, taco salad, and beef empanada. Seating area shared with Pecos Bill's. **[D]** Nachos, taco shells, and salsa are gluten-free. **[Ö]** Pictorial menu for foreign-language speakers. **[V]** Dimly lit.

Counter
Mexican
Med. noise
In/Outdoor

At press time, Diamond Horseshoe was serving light fare like ham sandwiches and chips daily from 11:00 am to 4:00 pm. This may just be temporary to accommodate the busy summer season—we have no word on if the spot will revert to its meet and greet duties in the fall.

Planning · Special Challenges · Getting There · Staying in Style · Touring · Dining · Resources · Index

Magic Kingdom Eateries
(continued)

			Deb Wills' Rating	Deb Koma's Rating

■ Liberty Tree Tavern [C-3]   L/D $33 | 6 | 6 |

Colonial America is the theme at this warm and cozy tavern. All-you-can-eat character meal at dinnertime (adults $27.99/children 3-9 $12.99); no characters at lunch. Lunch menu features wider selection, including vegetarian and low-fat options. Main dinner items: turkey, flank steak, ham. Only restrooms here are very small and up a narrow staircase—must go outside and around corner to reach accessible restrooms. **[A] [U]** Very noisy, but character meals are better meet-and-greet opportunities than the parks. **[D]** Vegetarian selections include salads and "Amber Waves of Grain," a veggie/grain combo. Readers report that chefs here are particularly sensitive to guests with special diets. Mac and cheese available. **[M]** Ramp is located to the left of the lobby. Once inside, speak to a cast member for seating directions. **[F]** Dinner has costumed characters who make the rounds—avoid if you have a fear of costumed characters. **[R]** Dinner is an all-you-can-eat meal. **[S]** Can be quite noisy at dinner with lots of small children. **[S][V]** Low lighting and uneven flooring.	**Table**
	American
	Medium noise
	Advance reservations suggested
	Average waits
	11:30 am–3:00 pm 4:00 pm-park closing

■ Main Street Bakery [D-5]   B $11, L $11, S | 8 | 8 |

Just follow your nose to this mecca of all manner of fresh baked goodies—but be aware it's very crowded at park opening as everyone else is doing the same. Also serves up specialty sandwiches and coffees. **[D]** Specialty sandwiches include vegetarian selections such as tomato-mozzarella with basil. No-sugar-added selections available, as well as fresh fruit. **[M]** Queue is difficult to navigate in wheelchair/ECV.	**Counter**
	American
	Med. noise
	Outdoor
	Med. waits
	Open all day

■ Pecos Bill Café [A-4]   L $12, D $12, S   🍴 | 7 | 6 |

Rustic cowboy hangout with standard fast food—it even has an expanded fresh fixings bar, which sets it apart from its counterparts. Lots of seating—try the area in back for fewer crowds/less noise. Some seats are backless but padded. Main items: burgers, hot dogs, fresh chicken salad. **[D]** A few low-fat options, such as chicken salad and chicken wrap. Salad available without chicken or cheese, making it a good vegan choice. **[F]** Beware of the low-flying birds outdoors, which may swoop down and take food off trays! **[Ö]** Pictorial menu for foreign-language speakers. **[M]** Two registers in middle are wheelchair/ECV accessible.	**Counter**
	American
	Noisy
	In/Outdoor
	Med. waits
	10:00 am–1 hour before closing

Eatery descriptions and ratings are explained on page 343.

⚓ Best Bets in Magic Kingdom for Special Dietary Needs

✔ The table-service restaurants (Liberty Tree Tavern, Crystal Palace, Tony's Town Square, and Cinderella's Royal Table), for their ability to take advance reservations and advance special requests.

✔ Cosmic Ray's Starlight Café, for its no-advance-notice kosher menu.

✔ Toontown Market, for its variety of fresh fruit.

✔ Pecos Bill Café, for its health-conscious salad and wrap offerings.

✔ Columbia Harbour House, for its vegetarian options, including its vegetarian chili.

Magic Kingdom Eateries
(continued)

	Deb Wills' Rating	Deb Koma's Rating

☐ Pinocchio Village Haus [D-1]   L $13, D $13, S | 6 | 7 |

The Swiss chalet setting of this counter-service eatery is charming although the menu is all Italian, featuring pizza and panini sandwiches. One unique thing—you have a view down into "it's a small world" from here! Seating is on wooden chairs indoors and metal chairs outdoors. **[M]** Third register from left is wheelchair/ECV accessible. **[A][U]** Mac and cheese and peanut butter and jelly sandwich available for kids.	**Counter** Italian Noisy 11 am–1 hour before closing

☐ Plaza Restaurant [E-4]   L $21, D $21, S | 6 | 7 |

The old-fashioned ice cream parlor feel is captured in this eatery's cozy decor. Main items: Reuben sandwiches ($10.79), club sandwiches ($10.89), burgers. No restrooms here; you need to exit to go to the restrooms next door. Some seating is on padded benches. **[D]** A chicken and strawberry salad ($10.29) and a vegetarian sandwich ($9.39) are nods to health-conscious diets. Some no-sugar-added ice cream available. **[M] [E] [S] [L] [V] [X]** Very crowded conditions in this small space make it difficult to navigate. **[F]** Can feel very closed in.	**Table** American Reservations suggested 11 am–1 hour before closing

☐ Tomorrowland Terrace Noodle Station [E-4]   L $12, D $12, S | 6 | 6 |

This seasonal terrace eatery is also a shortcut between Main Street and Tomorrowland. Seating is covered, but not enclosed—and not exactly air-conditioned. Menu includes Asian-inspired dishes like a chicken or vegetarian noodle bowl or teriyaki chicken. **[G]** Request "no MSG" if sensitive. Note that peanut oil may be used in some cooking here. **[Ö]** Pictorial menu for foreign-language speakers. **[M]** First register on the left is wheelchair/ECV accessible.	**Counter** Asian Outdoor, covered 11 am–1 hour before closing

☐ Tony's Town Square Restaurant [E-6]   L $31, D $47, S | 5 | 4 |

Italian cuisine in a setting straight out of Disney's animated classic "Lady and the Tramp." Limited outdoor seating. Main items: Pasta, veal dishes, strip steak ($25.49). **[D]** A few chicken and seafood entrées for health-conscious diets. At least one vegetarian selection, like Eggplant Rotini ($19.49), is also available. **[D] [G]** Some gluten-free pasta available—ask to speak to the chef. **[M]** Ramp located to far right, near Main Street Station tunnel.	**Table** Italian Reservations suggested 12–3 pm 5 pm-closing

Selected Magic Kingdom Snack Shops and Carts

Name	Specialties
Main Street Ice Cream Parlor	Ice cream treats; sugar-free/fat-free/dairy-free
Aloha Isle	Dole Whips (gluten-free)
Sunshine Tree Terrace	Citrus Swirl (orange juice/soft-serve)
Frontierland Fries	McDonald's fries
Liberty Square Market	Fresh fruit
Enchanted Grove	Strawberry Swirl
Sleepy Hollow	Ice cream; funnel cake
Mrs. Potts' Cupboard	Ice cream treats
Scuttle's Landing	Frozen drinks (gluten-free); chips; cookies
Auntie Gravity's	Ice cream treats; smoothies; reduced-fat ice cream
The Lunching Pad	Turkey legs; frozen drinks
Toontown Market	Fresh fruit
Village Fry Shoppe	McDonald's fries

Planning · Special Challenges · Getting There · Staying in Style · Touring · Dining · Resources · Index

Planning
Special Challenges
Getting There
Staying in Style
Touring
Dining
Resources
Index

Epcot Eateries

Epcot offers a **smorgasbord of tastes and cuisines**. We know of few places where you can dine in Mexico, Norway, the United Kingdom, China, and Morocco all on the same day (if you so desire). And when it comes to special dietary needs, you'll find some places incredibly accommodating.

Many Disney guests find Epcot *the* **place to dine in the evening** with the variety of choices available. The restaurants are extremely popular, especially during the holiday Candlelight Processional season, and long waits are the norm—advance reservations are highly recommended.

Alcohol is served in all table-service and most counter-service restaurants in Epcot, as well as from kiosks located along the walkways and shops in World Showcase. During Epcot's Food & Wine Festival (see 355), alcohol is at just about every outside booth throughout World Showcase.

Gluten-free breads, as well as special desserts, are available at most full-service restaurants, but be sure to give the chefs 72 hours' notice.

Soft pretzels and chocolate chip cookies at Epcot counter-service eateries are processed in a plant that contains **peanuts and tree nuts**, so be careful!

Fresh fruit cups are sold at all counter-service venues. Some counter-service eateries will substitute fruit or carrots for fries.

⬜ **Akershus Royal Banquet Hall** [B-3] B $29, L $31, D $36	6	7

	Preplated
*Home of the Princess Storybook Dining Experience, this replica Norwegian palace hosts royalty all day long. Characters visit your table. The preplated breakfast is basic American fare with scrambled eggs, bacon, sausage, pastries, and hash browns ($22.99/$12.99). Lunch ($24.99/$13.99) and dinner ($28.99/$13.99) have family-style appetizers and individual entrée selections. Ask for ingredients of desserts! Unless you have to see the Princesses, we don't recommend dining here at breakfast. Be sure to bring your reservation number with you, especially for early breakfast. **[A] [U]** Very noisy, but character meals are better meet-and-greet*	Norwegian
	Noisy
	Reservations recommended
	Med. waits
	Call 180 days

opportunities than in the parks.
***[G] [D]** Preplated food means little accommodation possible at the last minute. Be sure to request special meals 72 hours in advance!*
***[F]** Costumed characters make rounds—if anyone has fear of characters, consider avoiding this.*
***[C][T][M][P][S][L][V]** There are several rooms of tables and some can be very close together, making maneuvering difficult.*

8:30 am–
10:10 am,
11:40 am–
2:50 pm,
4:20 pm–
8:20 pm

© MediaMarx, Inc.

Chef Wade at Akershus Royal Banquet Hall

Epcot Eateries
(continued)

Deb Wills' Rating · Deb Koma's Rating

■ Alfredo's / Tutto Italia [C-1]	L $47, D $51	?	?

Alfredo's closed at the end of August and reopened September 1 under the management of the Patina Restaurant Group as a temporary Italian eatery, Tutto Italia. A new restaurant will debut in the fall of 2008.

Table
Italian
Call 180 days

■ Biergarten [B-1]	L $25, D $35	6	8

Oktoberfest is the setting for this buffet restaurant, complete with large wooden tables and live entertainment, including an oompah band and Alpenhorns! Buffet includes sausages, pork schnitzel, kraut, pasta salads, vegetable salads, and seafood salads. A fish entrée is added at dinner ($23.99 adults/$11.99 children 3-9). Lunch is $19.99/$11.99. **[A][U][F]** May be seated with other parties; request separate table if desired. **[A][U][T][I][S]** Can be very noisy—could cause overstimulation. However, those who respond to music and rhythmic movement might find the entertainment a treat. **[L][M][E][V][X]** Tables are very close together and seating is on several different levels, making maneuvering difficult. **[R]** All-you-care-to-eat buffet. **[C][L]** Wooden chairs, no arms. **[V]** Low lighting with entertainment. **[Ö]** Most servers here are from Germany and/or speak German. **[H]** Assistive listening devices work for the live performances held here. **[D]** Peer reviewer Amy Stoll notes, "We found the chefs here very accommodating to dietary needs—one chef cooked an entirely separate lunch for a person in our party."

Buffet
German
Very noisy
Reservations recommended
Call 180 days
Short waits
Noon–3:45 pm,
4:00–8:30 pm

© Debra Martin Koma

Co-author Deb Koma with peer reviewer Lydia Economou and their families

■ Bistro de Paris [F-2]	D $64	8	8

On the second floor above Chefs de France is the quieter, more elegant, and pricier Bistro de Paris. The restaurant is accessible via a winding staircase or elevator. Offerings include delicacies such as pan-seared foie gras, truffles, grilled lobster, and roasted quail. The Dover sole ($24) is first rate. Desserts are outstanding ($6.50-$8.00). Ask for a window seat and linger until IllumiNations. No tank tops are allowed. **[A][U][B][S]** Quiet, elegant atmosphere. **[D]** No vegetarian items on regular menu, but ask! No sugar-free dessert, but artisan cheese plate is good alternative. **[D][♥]** Many rich, high-fat foods. **[C][F][♥][T][M][P][S][L][V]** Elevator available; ask cast member. **[L]** Some tables have padded bench seating. **[Ö]** Many servers here speak French.

Table
French
Very quiet
Reservations strongly recommended
Call 30 days
6:00 pm–8:45 pm

■ Boulangerie Patisserie [F-2]	L $12, S	9	9

Great French pastries and sandwiches; always crowded. Very limited indoor/outdoor seating, some covered. Indoor seating across the way at Galerie les Halles. **[D]** Nothing low-fat or low-cal here! Cheese plate for low-carb diets. **[A][F][U][M][L][V][X]** Very small inside area, usually very crowded.

Counter
French
Long waits
~11 am-closing

Epcot Eateries
(continued)

Deb Wills' Rating | Deb Koma's Rating

☐ Cantina de San Angel [B-4]   L $13, D $13, S   ♀ | 5 | 6

	Counter

Open-air dining with tacos and burritos. Tables have umbrellas and offer some shade and a great view of World Showcase Lagoon. Recent reports indicate there are no accommodations for special dietary requests. We hear that the cantina will soon be expanded to offer more World Showcase Lagoon viewing and will have a new menu by summer 2008. **[R]** Outdoor margarita and beer bar. **[D]** Burritos ($7.75), nachos ($7.25), and taco salad ($8.50) can be made vegetarian upon request. **[U][B][F][I][S]** Beware of seagulls and other low-flying birds in this immediate area. They have been known to swoop down and take food off trays! **[C][L]** Outdoor seating, wood chairs (no arms) and benches (no backs), neither moves.

Counter · Mexican · Med. noise · Med. waits · Outdoor seating · ~11 am–closing

☐ Les Chefs de France [F-2]   L $32, D $52 | 4 | 6

A little taste of France in America. Typical items: escargot ($9), French onion soup ($5.25), beef au poivre ($28) sautéed sole ($25), and duck with cherries ($25). Seating is on chairs and in half-booths. **[A][U][T][I][S]** Very noisy—could cause overstimulation. **[D]** At least one vegetarian option (like lasagna, $16). Lunch offers lighter fare including salads. No special requests, even with advance notice—not accommodating at all. **[Ö]** Many servers here speak French.

Table · French · Reservations recommended · Noon–3 pm · 5 pm–closing

☐ Coral Reef [D-7]   L $45, D $54   ♀ | 7 | 8

Incredible tile work and a wonderful view of the Living Seas Aquarium make this a most unique dining experience. Primarily seafood entrées; chicken and beef are also offered. Inquire about fixed-price lunch. Spotty service. **[A][U]** The aquarium keeps kids and adults entertained for much of your meal. Ask to be seated on the lower level if you want a close-up look at the fish. If seated further away, kids may be tempted to go up to the glass for a close look, which could disturb other diners. **[G]** Allergy alert: edible playdough for kids is made with peanut butter. This is primarily a seafood restaurant, so those with fish/shellfish allergies may want to avoid. **[D]** A number of fish entrées for health-conscious diets. At least one vegetarian entrée, such as Vegetable Strudel ($16) and other veggies, on menu. **[F]** An occasional shark and rays swim by in the aquarium. **[L]** Wooden chairs no arms. **[V]** Low lighting, seating on several levels.

Table · Seafood · Noisy · Reservations recommended for dinner · Call 180 days · Med. waits · 11:30–3 pm, 4:40–8:00 pm

☐ Electric Umbrella [C-6]   L $10, D $10, S   ♀ | 6 | 7

This bustling counter-service spot serves up good food fast. Basic burgers and deli sandwiches, plus a fixin's bar. Quieter seating available upstairs. Indoor/outdoor seating. Good fixings bar. **[D][♥]** Healthier fare includes chicken salad. **[D]** For vegetarians: vegetarian chili ($4.29). Turkey pinwheels and macaroni and cheese available. **[F]** Beware of birds and squirrels if eating outside. **[M]** Ask cast member to operate elevator for upstairs seating. You will also have to find a cast member to return to the main floor.

Counter · American · Med. noise · Short waits · 11:30 am–7:00 pm

☐ Fountainview Bakery [D-6]   B $6, S | 8 | 7

Baked goods, pastries, sweet treats, as well as specialty coffees. Limited indoor/outdoor (covered) seating. On breezy days, the spray from the Fountain of Nations may get you wet. **[D]** Sugar-free cheesecake offered. **[M][V]** Stairs in front, ramp access from inside on left. Queue area is small, difficult to maneuver.

Counter · American · Limited hours; seasonal

Eatery descriptions and ratings are explained on page 343.

Epcot Eateries
(continued)

Deb Wills' Rating
Deb Koma's Rating

Planning

Special Challenges

Getting There

Staying in Style

Touring

Dining

Resources

Index

☐ **The Garden Grill Restaurant** [F-6] **L $26, D $38**   🍴 | 5 | 6 |

This Land pavilion restaurant serves lunch (adults $20.99/children 3–9 $11.99) and dinner (adults $27.99/children 3–9 $11.99). Meals served "family style" with rolls, mashed potatoes, cornbread stuffing, flank steak with mushrooms, fried catfish, and roast turkey with cranberry sauce. Dessert is bread pudding; no-sugar-added ice cream is available. Character dining with semicircular booth seating—each booth looks out. First tier has better ambiance. Second tier seating is table and chairs—wheelchair/ECV seating is on this level. Restrooms located outside restaurant and down the hall. **[A][U]** We recommend this character meal—much better than meet-and-greet opportunities in the parks; much less confusion and noise. **[D]** Chefs here are very accommodating if you have special dietary requests. "We've had amazingly healthy platters that were made for our family, plus almost all the vegetables used are organic!"—peer reviewer Betsy Hicks **[Q][U]** Restaurant rotates slowly and overlooks part of the Living With the Land boat ride. **[L][M][S][V]** Seating areas close together. **[M][V]** Restaurant has two tiers of seating (a couple steps up or ask for ramp). **[U]** Sound effects from boat ride below may be bothersome.

Table
American
Med. noise
Reservations not always needed
Call 180 days
Short waits
11:00 am–3:00 pm, 4:30–closing

☐ **Kringla Bakeri og Kafé** [B-3] **L $12, D $12, S $6** | 8 | 8 |

Pastries and Norwegian sandwiches; limited outdoor seating is covered. Long waits. **[D]** Fruit cup, sugar-free Jello-O available. **[M][L][V][X]** Very small space inside, usually very crowded.

Counter
Norwegian
~11 am–9 pm

☐ **Le Cellier Steakhouse** [E-4] **L $50, D $53** | 8 | 9 |

This is a very popular steakhouse located in a "stone cellar," featuring red meat and seafood paired with the wines and beers of Canada. The restaurant does not sell mixed drinks—only beer and wine. **[D]** Lots of rich sauces on the dishes—tell server if you don't want them. Good menu for low-carb diners. At least one vegetarian entrée (like Grilled Portobello and Sweet Potato Stack, $16) is offered. **[F]** This is a dark restaurant with no windows—possible claustrophobia alert. **[L]** Chairs with no arms. **[S][V]** Low lighting with no natural sunlight. **[Ö]** Some servers here speak French. **[L][M][S][V][X]** Tables close together. Also difficult to maneuver wheelchair/ECV in these restrooms.

Table
Canadian
Med. noise
Reservations a must
Long waits
Noon–3 pm 4:00–closing

☐ **Liberty Inn** [C-1] **L $12, D $12, S** | 5 | 4 |

Bright and busy fast food, with lots of seating indoors and out. Main items: hamburgers, hot dogs, and chicken strips. Good fixin's bar. **[D][W]** Kosher meal available without advance notice. **[D]** French fries and hot dogs are gluten-free. Gluten-free bread also available. Grilled chicken sandwich is marinated in canola oil and Italian spices, garlic, salt, and pepper. Gluten-free pizza may be on hand in the freezer. No-sugar-added ice cream and dairy-free ice cream also available. **[Ö]** Pictured menu items. **[L]** Outdoor seating has padded seats without arms.

Counter
American
Med. noise
Short waits
Indoor/outdoor seating
~11 am–closing

☐ **Lotus Blossom Café** [B-3] **L $12, D $12, S** | 4 | 7 |

Renovated in 2007, this is a Chinese counter-service eatery with offerings that include stir fry, egg rolls, and a daily special. Limited covered seating. Ask to see the ingredients list. **[D]** Chicken stock and fish paste used in many dishes. Vegetable lo mein made with chicken stock. **[D][G]** Avoid this eatery if you have nut allergies, as peanut oil is used in cooking. **[G]** Request "no MSG" if sensitive.

Counter
Chinese
Med. noise
Med. waits
~11 am–closing

Epcot Eateries
(continued)

	Deb Wills' Rating	Deb Koma's Rating

■ Restaurant Marrakesh [F-1]　　L $43, D $48　　💀　| 5 | 8 |

Traditional Moroccan cuisine and live entertainment, including a belly dancer, in a beautiful Middle Eastern setting. Main items: lamb ($25), chicken ($23), couscous. Great desserts. We have found this restaurant to be inflexible in accommodating special requests, even for a simple grilled chicken meal. **[D]** Vegetable couscous (not vegan). **[F]** Diners can be invited up to dance with belly dancer. **[L]** Wooden chairs without arms. **[W]** There is a designated meditation/prayer room open daily from 11:00 am to 9:00 pm located nearby (inside the museum); small rugs are available for use. **[Ö]** Many servers here speak Arabic.

Table
Middle Eastern
Noisy
Reservations not usually req.
11:30 am–3:45 pm, 4 pm–closing

■ Nine Dragons [B-3]　　L $37, D $40　| 6 | 5 |

This elegant dining room serves standard Chinese fare. Various regions of China are represented in the food offerings. The food is of average quality. At press time, Nine Dragons was scheduled to close in early 2008 for renovations, which will include an exhibition kitchen. Reopening date is not known. **[D]** Chicken stock and fish paste are used in many dishes. Gluten-free soy sauce available for food preparation and table use upon request. **[D][G]** Avoid this eatery if you have nut allergies, as peanut oil is used in cooking. **[G]** Request "no MSG" if sensitive. **[Ö]** Many servers here speak Chinese. **[L]** Wooden chairs without arms.

Table
Chinese
Reservations suggested
12 pm–4:30 pm, 4:45 pm–9 pm

■ Rose & Crown Pub and Dining Room [E-3]　　L $37, D $40, S　| 6 | 6 |

A bit of Merry Olde England in our midst! Convivial atmosphere with Harry Ramsden's famous fish and chips ($16), bangers and mash ($16), grilled steak ($24), and ale! Live entertainment includes pub pianist or magician (pub hours: 11:30 am–park closing). Some outdoor seating, perfect for viewing IllumiNations, as long as the wind is blowing in the other direction! Outdoor seating on a cool night can be damp and windy. **[A][U][T][I][S]** Indoors can be very noisy—could cause overstimulation. **[D]** At least one vegetarian offering (such as curried vegetables and tofu for $13). Ask about soup bases. **[M][L][V][X]** Indoor seating is close together; difficult to maneuver.

Table
English
Very noisy
Reservations strongly recommended
Noon–4:00 pm, 4:30 pm–close

■ San Angel Inn [B-4]　　L $35, D $42　　💀　| 6 | 6 |

Your table sits in a dimly lit romantic setting of Mexican twilight, while a volcano steams in the distance. Sit by the railing and watch the boats go by. Typical menu items: beef tenderloin with black beans ($27) and mole poblano ($20). **[A][U][T][V]** Cool, nighttime atmosphere can provide relief to those sensitive to light and heat. **[D]** Ask for vegetarian menu. **[C][L]** Wooden chairs without arms. **[M]** Tight space; hard to maneuver a wheelchair here. Ramp is left of check-in near Gran Fiesta Tour. Ask cast member for assistance. **[M][V][X]** Very low lighting. Tables are _very_ close together—hard to manuever around. **[Ö]** Many servers here speak Spanish. **[U][F]** May be troubled by close seating or sound effects from volcano.

Table
Mexican
Noisy
Reservations strongly recommended
11:30 am–4:00 pm

Epcot Eateries
(continued)

	Deb Wills' Rating	Deb Koma's Rating

Sommerfest [B-1] **L $13, D $13, S**	4	5
Very limited quick food menu of bratwurst ($6.39) and frankfurters ($6) with sauerkraut. Limited covered seating can be crowded. Noisy eatery. **[R]** Emphasis on German beer and schnapps. **[M]** Very tight area for maneuvering wheelchair/ECV.	**Counter** German 11 am–closing	

Sunshine Seasons [F-6] **B $14, L $14, D $14, S** 🎗	6	7
Sunshine Seasons is a "fast-casual" dining area, combining the convenience of a counter-service spot with unusual menus more typically found at table-service restaurants. Limited breakfast; typical lunch/dinner menu items include roasted beet and goat cheese salad ($7), grilled salmon ($9), and smoked turkey sandwich ($7). Also a bakery station with pastries, special coffees, and ice cream. Each station also offers vegetarian and children's options, as well as prepackaged "grab 'n' go" items. **[D]** Vegetarian-friendly, with items like vegetarian noodle bowl with tofu and grilled Cuban veggie sandwich. Sugar-free Jello available. **[G]** Avoid Asian station if you have nut allergies, as peanut oil may be used in cooking. Request "no MSG" at Asian station if sensitive. **[Ö]** Video menu screens used to identify items. Sushi rolls available. **[U]** Very noisy, lots of people crowding around.	**Counter** Various cuisines Noisy Med.–long waits 9:00am–park closing	

Tangierine Café [E-1] **L $17, D $17, S**	7	7
Chicken, lamb, hummus, and couscous in an open-air café serving traditional Middle Eastern cuisine. Great place for a healthy lunch without feeling stuffed! Desserts are yummy, but not lo-cal at all! Indoor/outdoor seating. **[D]** Vegetarian-friendly. Vegetarian platter ($8) is vegan. **[C][T][M][P][S][L][X]** Tables and chairs are close together and difficult to maneuver with wheelchair/ECV. **[Ö]** Many servers speak Arabic.	**Counter** Middle Eastern Med. noise Noon–closing	

Eatery descriptions and ratings are explained on page 343.

⚠ Best Bets in Epcot for Special Dietary Needs

✔ Sunshine Seasons—The Land
✔ Liberty Inn—American Adventure, for all the special products kept on hand, including kosher meals available with no advance notice and many gluten-free items.
✔ Tangierine Café—Morocco

Important Note: San Angel Inn (Mexico), Chefs de France (France), Restaurant Marrakesh (Morrocco), and the new restaurant in Italy are operated by third parties (not Disney) and are not always the most flexible and accommodating when it comes to special orders.

Epcot Eateries
(continued)

Deb Wills' Rating
Deb Koma's Rating

☐ Teppan Edo [E-1]   L, D   ? | ?

Teppan Edo will replace the very popular Teppanyaki Dining Room in fall 2007. The basic concept of the restaurant, with seats surrounding teppan grills, will remain the same. Seafood, beef, chicken, veggies, and rice are prepared with panache in front of you on a hot Teppan grill. Seated around the grill at tables that fit up to eight—your table may include other parties. See AllEars.net for details after opening. [G] Avoid if you have nut allergies, as peanut oil may be used in cooking. Request "no MSG" if sensitive. [D] Great for low-carb diets. Beware of sugar content in some sauces. If you have seafood or other allergies, notify your server so your food can be cooked first or separately. [M] Located on second floor above Mitsukoshi Department Store—the elevator is to the left of store entrance. [Ö] Many servers here speak Japanese.

| Table |
| Japanese |
| Noisy |
| Advance reservations a must |
| Call 180 days |
| Long waits |
| 12-3:45 pm, 4:30 pm-park closing |

☐ Tokyo Dining [E-1]   L, D, S   ? | ?

Tokyo Dining will open fall 2007 in the Japan pavilion, replacing Tempura Kiku and Matsunoma Lounge. This eatery will showcase the traditional cuisine of Japan with an emphasis on sushi [G] Avoid if you have nut allergies, since peanut oil may be used in cooking. Request "no MSG" if sensitive. Also avoid if you have shellfish allergies. [M] Located on second floor above Mitsukoshi—the elevator is to the left of store entrance. [Ö] Many servers here speak Japanese.

| Table |
| Japanese |
| Advance reservations recommended |

☐ Yakitori House [D-1]   L $14, D $14, S   6 | 7

Quick-service eatery offering items like teriyaki chicken (all dark meat on the entire menu), sukiyaki beef, shrimp tempura, udon noodles, and miso soup. Indoor/outdoor tables. [G] Avoid if you have nut allergies, as peanut oil is used in cooking. Request "no MSG" if sensitive. [D] Udon noodles usually made with wheat flour, salt, and water—ask about ingredients. [M] Located across the courtyard, with steps in front. Use the ramp through the garden instead. [V] Nearby restroom is very dark.

| Counter |
| Japanese |
| Med. noise |
| Long waits |
| ~11 am-closing |

☐ Yorkshire County Fish Shop [E-3]   L $11, D $11, S   6 | 8

Harry Ramsden's fish and chips ($8) are the only order of the day, every day! Outdoor patio seating is available to the right rear, overlooking the World Showcase Lagoon. Some tables are shaded with umbrellas. [D] Very limited menu of fried fish. [U][B][F][I][S] Beware of seagulls and other low-flying birds in this immediate area—they have been known to swoop down and take food off trays!

| Counter |
| English |
| Outdoor seating |
| ~11 am-closing |

Eatery descriptions and ratings are explained on page 343.

Selected Epcot Snack Shops and Carts

Treat	Found at
Fresh fruit	Outpost (between Germany and China)
Rice cream with strawberry topping	Norway (Kringla Bakeri og Kafé)
Kaki Gori (fruit-flavored shaved ice, vegan)	Japan (along promenade)
McDonald's fries	Refreshment Port (near Canada)

Planning
Special Challenges
Getting There
Staying in Style
Touring
Dining
Resources
Index

Epcot Food & Wine Festival

Each fall, Epcot is host to the **International Food & Wine Festival**. Small food and beverage booths are set up all along the World Showcase Promenade offering appetizer portions ($2–$6) of a wide variety of cuisines from around the world, including Peru, Greece, South Africa, and Poland, to name but a few. Small glasses of wines, beers, champagne, ports, and cognac are also available for purchase. Most special dieters will find something of interest here, but be sure to inquire about an ingredients list at the booths! Other than leaving off a sauce/topping or side, no special orders here!

Special food and wine **"hard-ticket" events** (that means you have to buy a separate entry ticket) are plentiful during the Festival, some costing as much as $195 a person. As a rule, no special dietary requests are available—in fact, they don't even make a special menu (or offer a reduced price) at these events for children. We have found an alternative entrée offered at some events, but don't count on it. Check in early and let the host/hostess know of your dietary needs. It is possible that your special requests may be honored (although there's no guarantee). The bottom line is, due to the expense of these events, be wary of going with restricted dietary concerns or picky palates, as you may leave disappointed—not to mention hungry.

The one exception to the above is the very popular **Party for the Senses**, with numerous areas set up with appetizer portions of gourmet foods, wines, and even a beer and scotch table! Low-carb diners should have no problem with the expansive cheese table, fish, poultry, and meat offerings. Food is prepared right in front of you, so you can ask the chef for a sauce or side to be left off, but basically, what is offered is what's available. The chefs who prepare the food are right at the table, so you can easily find out the ingredients of any dish you are curious about. These events are not very vegan friendly, but we did find a good number of vegetarian options at the 2006 parties. The menus are set, and no special requests are available.

© Deb Wills

Co-author Deb Koma talks to Mark Newman at Party for the Senses

Disney-MGM Studios Eateries

Where the Magic Kingdom and Disney's Animal Kingdom may be lacking in dining options for the traveler with special needs, Disney-MGM Studios makes up for their shortages. Several table-service restaurants **accommodate special diners with sufficient notice**, and even the counter-service spots offer many good alternatives. A few of the restaurants have very special themes—be sure to check them out before you go to be sure that they're up your alley.

ABC Commissary [C-3] B $13, L $13, D $13, S `4` `7`

Nicer than any true movie set commissary, this art deco spot features television monitors plugging the latest ABC-TV shows. Plentiful indoor seating on padded chairs and in banquettes (long padded benches); some outdoor seating, too. **[D]** International cuisine features vegetarian as well as low-fat selections. Fries here may be gluten-free—chance for cross-contamination with deep fryers. **[D] [W]** Kosher meals on regular menu without advance notice. **[Ö]** Pictorial menu for foreign-language speakers. **[L]** Chairs have arms and are not made for large bottoms. **[M]** First register on left is wheelchair/ECV accessible. **[H]** Television monitors are captioned.

Counter · Multi-ethnic · Indoor seating · Med. noise · Med. waits · Open all day

Backlot Express [C-5] L $13, D $13, S `7` `7`

A great place for standard fast food fare, this place gives you a behind-the-scenes look at a movie set, complete with props. Main items: burgers, hot dogs, sandwiches, chicken strips. Indoor/outdoor seating, with some high stools in upper seating area. **[D]** Vegetarian sandwich offered ($7). Also grilled turkey sandwich ($6.59) for lighter fare. **[Ö]** Pictorial menu for foreign-language speakers. **[M]** Use ramp on far right.

Counter · American · In/Outdoor · Noisy · 11 am-closing

Catalina Eddie's [G-3] L $13, D $13, S `5` `5`

Part of the outdoor food court known as the Sunset Ranch Market, Eddie's specializes in pizzas with side salads. Gets very crowded and noisy at peak mealtimes. Short waits. Outdoor seating at picnic tables with backless benches. **[D]** Garden salad is the only vegetarian selection available. **[M][V][X]** Hard to maneuver around picnic tables. **[B][C][E][S][♥]** No indoor seating—can be quite uncomfortable on hot, humid days.

Counter · American · Med. noise · 11 am-closing

'50s Prime Time Cafe [E-5] L $35, D $36 `8` `8`

A '50s-style diner with an interactive twist: the servers are all one big, happy family and often chide patrons to eat all their veggies or keep the elbows off the table. Main entrées: meat loaf, fried chicken, pot roast (each $13). Our readers report the chefs here are very accommodating! **[A][U][I][S]** Can be very noisy—could cause overstimulation. Televisions scattered throughout restaurant play old TV clips on a continuous loop. **[D]** A number of low-fat entrées (grilled chicken, tuna, salmon) for health-conscious diets. At least one vegetarian selection available, such as stuffed pepper ($12.49). **[F]** Cast members frequently put diners "on the spot" as part of the role-playing here. Be sure to tell them if you want to be left alone.

Table · American · Noisy · Reservations a must · Call 180 days · Long waits · 11 am-4 pm, 4:00 pm-park closing

Eatery descriptions and ratings are explained on page 343.

Disney-MGM Studios Eateries
(continued)

	Deb Wills' Rating	Deb Koma's Rating

☐ Hollywood & Vine [E-5]   B $29, L $31, D $30 | 7 | 7 |

This '40s-style cafeteria with art deco decor and stainless steel touches is home to a buffet character breakfast and lunch. "Play 'n' Dine at Hollywood & Vine" features Disney Channel stars JoJo and Goliath and the Little Einsteins. Breakfast is $22.99/adults ($12.99/kids 3-9) and lunch is $24.99/$13.99. There is also a non-character buffet at dinner ($23.99/$11.99). Ask about the Fantasmic! Dinner Package, which offers special seating at Fantasmic! (see below). **[A][U][I][S]** Can be very noisy—could cause overstimulation. **[R]** All-you-can-eat buffet. **[D]** A number of turkey, chicken, and fish entrées are on the buffet. Vegetarian selections, like vegetable lo mein and pasta salads, also available.	**Buffet** American Noisy Reservations recommended Call 180 days 4 pm-closing

☐ The Hollywood Brown Derby [E-3]   L $41, D $50   🍸 | 9 | 9 |

A chic spot of brass and mahogany, the Brown Derby recalls the bygone era of the silver screen. Caricatures of old-time celebrities adorn the walls, while white-coated servers take your order. Main entrées: pork tenderloin ($22), seafood, famous Cobb Salad ($13, enough for two!). Ask about the Fantasmic! Dinner Package available here, which offers special seating at Fantasmic! without the long waits (see below). **[D]** A number of chicken and seafood entrées for health-conscious diets. At least one vegetarian selection, like Thai noodle bowl with tofu ($17), is also available.	**Table** American Med. noise Reservations recommended Call 180 days 11:30 am-3 pm 3:30 pm-close

⚠ What is the Fantasmic! Dinner Package?

The Fantasmic! Dinner Package includes dinner at one of the participating Disney-MGM Studios restaurants and reserved seating for Fantasmic! (see page 280). This means that instead of waiting in line for 60-90 minutes outside the theater, you can walk into the theater 30-45 minutes before show time (no waiting in line!) and still have a seat.

There is no additional charge for the package itself. Just call 180 days in advance and book your reservation at one of the participating restaurants. Your credit card will be charged at the time of booking—there is a 48-hour cancellation policy (with a $10/person fee). As of this writing, only Brown Derby, Mama Melrose's, and Hollywood & Vine participate. Prices (not including admission, tax, gratuity, or alcoholic beverages) for the fixed-price dinners are as follows:

Hollywood Brown Derby—$43.99 adult/$11.99 child (3-9). Your choice of appetizer, soup, or salad; entrée; and dessert from menu. Adult price increases to $46.99 on November 5, 2007.

Mama Melrose's—$32.99 adult/$11.99 child (3-9). Your choice of appetizer, entree, dessert, and non-specialty, nonalcoholic beverage from the regular menu.

Hollywood & Vine—$24.99 adult/$11.99 child (3-9). All-you-care-to-eat buffet.

Report to your restaurant 10 minutes before your Fantasmic! Dinner Package reservation, and you'll receive your special Fantasmic! seating pass at that time. You'll also receive instructions on where and when to enter the amphitheater. Although you do not have a reserved seat with this package, you have access to the reserved section, which is on the far right (the Witch section) of the amphitheater. Seating is on a first-come, first-served basis. The amphitheater is set up so that there really are no "bad" seats, except you will get wet if you sit in the first few rows. Note that this package must be guaranteed with a credit card.

Disney-MGM Studios Eateries
(continued)

Deb Wills' Rating | Deb Koma's Rating

☐ Mama Melrose's Ristorante Italiano [A-4]   L $33, D $40   ♥ | 8 | 8 |

Hollywood Italian—need we say more? Main entrées: wood-fired flatbreads ($12), pasta, chicken parmesan ($16). Ask about the Fantasmic! Dinner Package available here, which offers special seating at Fantasmic! without the long waits (see page 357). **[D]** A number of chicken and seafood entrées for health-conscious diets. At least one vegetarian selection (like Eggplant Napoleon, $15) is also available. **[D] [G]** Gluten-free pasta available; speak to the chef.

Table
Italian
Reservations suggested
Noon–3 pm 3:30 pm–close

☐ Rosie's All-American Cafe [G-3]   L $12, D $12, S | 5 | 5 |

Part of the outdoor food court called Sunset Market Ranch, Rosie's is your basic burger stand. Area gets very crowded and noisy at peak mealtimes. Main items: hamburgers, cheeseburgers, chicken strips, fries. Outdoor seating at picnic tables with backless benches. **[D]** Vegetarian burger on menu ($5.69). **[M]** First register on right is wheelchair/ECV accessible. **[B][C][E][S][♥]** No indoor seating—can be quite uncomfortable on hot, humid days.

Counter
American
Med. noise
Med. waits
11 am–closing

☐ Sci-Fi Dine-In Theater Restaurant [C-4] L/D   L $34, D $35 | 5 | 7 |

Designed to resemble a drive-in theater, diners sit in reproductions of vintage cars while watching clips from black and white sci-fi films. A sample car sits outside the restaurant so you can see if you'd prefer table seating. Main items: Pasta, fish, ribs ($16). **[D]** A number of seafood entrées for health-conscious diets. At least one vegetarian selection, like Vegetable Potato Bake ($14), is also available. **[M] [L] [S]** "Car" tables may be awkward; request standard table seating. (Regular table seating is limited; may increase your wait time.) Picnic table in rear should accommodate all. **[A] [U] [I] [F]** Very dark setting, with potentially scary movie scenes on the screen. **[V]** Very dimly lit—may be difficult for those with vision impairments. **[H]** Assistive listening devices can be used here. **[X]** Close tables leave limited room for service animals.

Table
American
Noisy
Reservations strongly recommended
Call 180 days
Med. waits
11 am–4 pm 4 pm–closing

☐ Starring Rolls Cafe [E-3]   L $10, D $10   ♥ | 8 | 8 |

This former bakery features specialty sandwiches and salads, mini-desserts, gourmet chocolates, and a fresh-roasted house-blend coffee. Outdoor seating. **[D]** Turkey on focaccia, vegetarian pita (both $7), and smoked salmon on a bagel ($5.79) are among the items for health-conscious diets. **[M]** First register on left is wheelchair/ECV accessible.

Counter
American
Noisy
Med. waits
10 am–closing

Eatery descriptions and ratings are explained on page 343.

🔔 Best Bets in Disney-MGM Studios for Special Diets

✔ The table-service restaurants (Hollywood Brown Derby, Mama Melrose's Ristorante Italiano, 50s Prime Time Café, Sci-Fine Dine-In Theater, and Hollywood & Vine), for their ability to take advance reservations and advance special requests.

✔ ABC Commissary, for its no-advance-notice kosher menu.

✔ Anaheim Produce, for its variety of fresh fruit.

✔ Starring Rolls, for its health-conscious salad and sandwich offerings.

Disney-MGM Studios Eateries
(continued)

	Deb Wills' Rating	Deb Koma's Rating

◼ Studio Catering Flatbread Grill [C-4]   L $13, D $13, S   6 | 6

The menu at this open-air, counter-service spot includes BBQ pulled pork subs ($6.49), grilled chicken ($6.49), and Greek salad ($5.99). The kids' menu includes grilled chicken wrap and peanut butter & jelly sandwich. Seating is under shade but not air-conditioned, on padded chairs without arms. **[D] [G]** Gluten-free items available on request. **[M]** Register on far right is accessible.

Seating at Studio Catering
© Debra Martin Koma

Counter
Mixed
Outdoor seating
Med. noise
Average waits
11:00 am– park closing

◼ Toluca Legs Turkey Co. [G-3]   L $9, D $9, S   4 | 3

Part of the outdoor Sunset Ranch Market mini food court on Sunset Blvd. As you may have guessed, you can get a turkey leg ($4.69) to munch on. You can also get foot-long hot dogs with chili and/or cheese ($3.69–$4.89). Seating is outdoors at covered, backless picnic benches. Other stands nearby offer burgers, chicken strips, soup, ice cream, McDonald's fries, and fresh fruit. **[B][C][E][S][♥]** No indoor seating–can be quite uncomfortable on hot, humid days.

Counter
American
Noisy
Med. waits
11:00 am– closing

◼ Toy Story Pizza Planet [B-5]   L $12, D $12, S   5 | 6

Pizza and salads in a spot patterned after the kids' eatery in the original Toy Story movie. Seating is available both indoors (wide open upstairs area) and outside. Game arcade adjacent to first-floor seating area. **[A][U][I][S]** Can get very noisy due to arcade. **[D]** Veggie pizza ($5.99) available. **[D][G]** Also has gluten-free pizza available (not on the menu, just ask!). **[Ö]** Pictorial menu for foreign-language speakers. **[M]** First register on right is wheelchair/ECV accessible. Reach second-floor seating via elevator located in arcade area.

Counter
American
Very noisy
Long waits
11:00 am– 1 hour before park closing

◼ Writer's Stop [A-4]   B $8, L $8, S   7 | 6

Book shop and coffee bar, featuring fresh-brewed java and iced concoctions, plus baked goodies. **[M]** Wheelchair/ECV accessible, but difficult to negotiate around displays and seating. **[B]** Usually quiet, with comfy sofas, for discreet nursing.

Counter
American
Avg. noise

Selected Disney-MGM Studios Snack Shops and Carts

Treat	Found at
Ice cream treats	Dinosaur Gertie's
Stuffed pretzels, drinks	Min & Bill's Dockside Diner
Nonalcoholic beverages	Peevy's Polar Pipeline
Lounge with specialty drinks	Tune-In Lounge
Fresh fruit	Anaheim Produce
Ice cream treats; sugar-free/fat-free/dairy-free	Hollywood Scoops
McDonald's fries	Fairfax Fries
Smoothies, coffees	KRNR The Rock Station

Planning Special Challenges Getting There Staying in Style Touring Dining Resources Index

Disney's Animal Kingdom Eateries

Disney's Animal Kingdom has a **limited number of places to eat** compared to the other theme parks. Luckily "Yak and Yeti," a brand new full-service restaurant, is scheduled to open in fall 2007 in Asia to join the Rainforest Café, located at the park entrance.

For the safety of the animals here, **no straws or lids are available** with your beverages, although you can purchase an Animal Topper Sports Bottle for $6.79 (comes with beverage).

Beer is sold at some counter- and quick-service spots, and the Dawa Bar and Rainforest Café offer **full bar service**.

Bright Idea: Strawberry juice bars and "Itzakadoozie" ice pops found at many snack carts are all gluten-free.

Flame Tree Barbecue [E-4]	**L $13, D $13, S**	7	7
The place for BBQ ribs ($8.49) or smoked beef ($7.29), chicken ($7.99), and pork ($7.29). Also serves up sandwiches, salads and fries. Shaded outdoor seating, some areas even semi-secluded and quiet. [A][U][T][S] There are some very nice quieter areas with shade—you'll just need to walk a little to find them. Follow the signs for additional seating. [D] Ribs, chicken, and salad are gluten-free and dairy-free. Tortilla shells on the salad contain gluten; request without the tortilla shells. Fruit plate with honey ($7). [F] Birds and small animals may be found in seating areas. [G][D][♥] BBQ chicken salad ($7) and fruit plate ($7) offered for lighter/veggie fare. [M] Signs point to wheelchair accessible seating.		**Counter** American/ Barbecue Quiet Med. waits 10:00 am-5:00 pm	

Pizzafari [B-4]	**L $12, D $12, S**	7	7
Beautifully painted eatery with themed rooms serving pizza, deli sandwiches, and salads. Frozen lemonade available for hot days, but beware of sugar content. [A][U][T][I][S] Very noisy—could cause overstimulation. Look for less crowded room near back. [D][W] Kosher items without advance notice. [D] Grilled chicken Caesar salad for lighter fare ($6.39). Plain pizza ($5.59) is the only vegetarian option. Sugar-free Jell-O available. [Ö] Cashier has menu in Japanese.		**Counter** Italian Very noisy Seating in/outdoors 10 am-5pm	

Selected Disney's Animal Kindom Snack Shops and Carts

Treat	Found at
Full bar	Dawa Bar
Fresh fruit; juices	Harambe Fruit Market
Baked goods; special coffees	Kusafiri Coffee Shop and Bakery
Ice cream; smoothies	Tamu Tamu Refreshments
Popcorn	Harambe kiosk
Gluten-free/dairy-free ice cream	Dino Bite Snacks
Ice cream, drinks	Dino Diner
McDonald's fries	Petrifries

Tip: All Animal Kingdom ice cream carts sell a fat-free, no sugar added ice cream cup ($2.50).

Disney's Animal Kingdom Eateries
(continued)

	Deb Wills' Rating	Deb Koma's Rating

▪ Rainforest Cafe [B-7]   B $15, L $52, D $51, S   🎗   6   5

Similar to Downtown Disney Rainforest Cafe, this one serves breakfast as well as lunch and dinner. Access this restaurant from inside or outside of theme park. Very themed dining areas with lots of sounds, lights, and movement, including a thunderstorm and gorilla beating his chest. Huge menu that should satisfy most needs. Food portions large. **[A][U][T][I][S]** Can be very noisy. **[F]** Some effects might be scary—lightning, loud thunder, animatronic animals. **[D]** Portobello and veggie sandwich ($11.99) for vegetarian diets; other items (such as Hong Kong Stir-fry) may be available sans meat. **[M][V][X]** Tables are very close together, maneuvering can be tricky. **[V]** Dimly lit.

Table
American
Noisy
Reservations recommended
8:30–10 am, 10:30 am–1.5 hours after park closing

▪ Restaurantosaurus [E-6]   B $24, L $11, D $11, S   5   6

Up until November 5, 2007, this eatery will continue to hold Donald's Breakfastosaurus in the mornings—a character buffet with the Duck, Mickey, Goofy, and Pluto ($18.99/adults, $10.99/kids 3–9). After November 2007, a new character breakfast will be featured in the Tusker House restaurant (see below). Lunch/dinner menu includes McDonald's burgers, fries, salads, and Happy Meals. There is indoor and outdoor seating. **[A][U][T][I]** Can be very noisy—could cause overstimulation. Small, quieter rooms are farther away from main serving area. **[R]** Breakfast (until Nov. 2007) is all-you-can-eat buffet. **[D]** Veggie burger on menu ($6.29). **[D][G]** Gluten-free burgers (not buns) available. Salad can be made gluten-free on request. Dairy-free ice cream on request.

Counter
American
Very noisy
Reservations at breakfast
8:00–10:30 am
11:30–3:30 pm
(opens at 10:30 am after Nov. 2007)

▪ Tusker House Restaurant [B-2]   🎗   ?   ?

Our favorite counter-service spot in Disney's Animal Kingdom closed in August 2007 to be converted into a buffet. When it reopens in mid-November 2007, Tusker House will offer a character breakfast buffet called Donald's Breakfast Safari, featuring Donald, Mickey, Daisy, and Goofy (subject to change). The restaurant will also have a non-character buffet at lunch and dinner. Lots of indoor seating; some outside available, too. At press time, we had no information on menu or prices, but we expect that many of the same circumstances found at other character buffets will apply. **[A][U][T][I]** Can be very noisy—could cause overstimulation. **[R]** All-you-can-eat buffet. **[F]** Breakfast features costumed characters—if you are afraid of characters, you may want to avoid. **[S]** Can be quite noisy at breakfast with lots of small children.

Buffet
American
9:30 am–10:30am,
11:00 am–varies

🛈 Best Bets in Animal Kingdom for Special Dietary Needs
- ✔ Dino Bites, for its gluten-free/dairy-free ice cream.
- ✔ Harambe Fruit Market, for its fresh fruit items.
- ✔ Pizzafari, which has kosher items without advance notice.

🛈 Yak & Yeti Restaurant
Coming in 2007! Yak & Yeti is a new restaurant scheduled to open in Asia in fall 2007. The Asian-themed eatery will offer both table service and counter service, as well as a shop selling items that fit with the Asian theme.

Downtown Disney Marketplace Eateries

Cap'n Jack's Restaurant   L $38, D $49   🎗   3   3

A casual nautical restaurant overlooking Lake Buena Vista. Menu includes crab cakes, shrimp, salmon, chicken and ribs. Advance reservations are not accepted. Limited flexibility in accommodating special dietary requests. **[G]** Primarily a seafood restaurant—those with seafood/shellfish allergy may want to avoid. **[D]** Grilled portobello mushroom sandwich ($9) at lunch; no vegetarian entrées on regular dinner menu.

Table
Seafood
Short waits
11:30 am–10:30 pm

Earl of Sandwich   B/L/D/S $10   8   7

Hot sandwiches, salads, wraps and "grab and go" food. Limited breakfast items, kids' selections. Open 8:00 am–11:00 pm. Limited indoor/outdoor seating—can get very crowded. No restroom—must go out to Marketplace area. **[D]** Tuna, fruit, and chicken salad. Hot Caprese sandwich ($5) for vegetarians. Vegan salad made upon request. **[M]** Ordering and pickup queues may be hard for wheelchair/ECV users.

Counter
American
Noisy
8:00 am–11:00 pm

Ghirardelli Soda Fountain & Chocolate Shop   S $8   9   10

Straight from San Francisco comes this famous chocolate maker! Best hot fudge sundaes at Disney. Sundaes, shakes, and malts. On cold nights, stop in for a hot chocolate. Noisy. Limited tables and counter/stools. Indoor/outdoor seating. Fri./Sat. hours: 9:30 am–midnight. **[D]** Sugar and fat-free ice cream available. **[M]** Wheelchair/ECV accessible, but difficult to negotiate displays and seating.

Counter
American
Long waits
10:30 am–11:00 pm

Rainforest Cafe   L $52, D $52, S   6   5

Similar to Disney's Animal Kingdom's Rainforest Cafe, with very themed dining areas that have lots of sounds, lights, and movement, including a thunderstorm and gorilla beating his chest. There's even a volcano that periodically "erupts!" Huge menu should satisfy most needs—food portions here are large. Open until midnight on Fridays and Saturdays. Visit Animal Kingdom location for lighter crowds at lunch. **[A][U][F][T][I][S]** Very noisy—could cause overstimulation. Some effects might be scary—dark, flashes of lightning, loud thunder, animatronic animals. **[D]** Hong Kong stir fry and Plant Sandwich ($11.99) for vegetarian diets; other items may be available sans meat. **[D][W]** Kosher items not available here. **[V]** Dimly lit. **[M][X]** Dark and crowded seating areas may be difficult to negotiate.

Table
American
Noisy
Call for reservations: 407-827-8500
Very long waits
11:30–4 pm, 5–11 pm

Ronald's Fun House (McDonald's)   B $6, L $6, D $6, S   2   4

This is your basic McDonald's burger joint, just like at home. **[A][U][T][I][S]** Can be very noisy—could cause overstimulation. **[A][U]** Outdoor play area. **[D]** High-calorie, high-fat foods. Go with salads and use lemon for dressing if you're looking for light eating. **[D][G]** McDonald's web site at http://www.mcdonalds.com/usa/eat/nutrition_info.html has information on gluten-free items, ingredient lists, and allergens . Gluten-free items include burger patty (no bun), fries, apple dippers with caramel, and side salads.

Counter
American
Very noisy
Med. waits
8:00 am–1:00am

Wolfgang Puck Express   B $11, L $11, D $11, S   6   6

Fast food for the upscale set. Inside and outside dining. Features pizzas, pastas, soups, and salads. Some sushi and sandwiches prepackaged. Drink homemade lemonade, frozen cafe mocha, wines by the bottle and glass, and beer on tap. Dine outside or take out. Limited indoor seating—very crowded. **[M][X]** Queues and indoor/outdoor seating areas are tight for guests using wheelchairs/ECVs.

Counter
American
Noisy
8:30 am–10:00 pm

Downtown Disney Pleasure Island Eateries

Planning

Special Challenges

Getting There

Staying in Style

Touring

Dining

Resources

Index

Cookes of Dublin	**L $13, D $13, S**	7	7

Small fast food shop next to Raglan Road specializing in fish and chips. Limited outdoor seating. **[G]** Ask about cross-contamination with fryers. Noisy.

Counter
3 pm–11 pm

Fulton's Crab House	**L $42, D $59**	🎗	7	8

Owned and operated by the Levy Corporation, Fulton's is housed in a beautiful, old-style steamboat and serves up a variety of seafood specialties, like Cioppino ($19), fresh fish, crab legs, and lobster dishes. Advance reservations are accepted and suggested. **[D]** Non-seafood entrées include filet mignon ($36) and free-range chicken breast ($18). **[D][W]** Kosher items are not available here. **[G]** Primarily a seafood restaurant—those with seafood/shellfish allergy may want to avoid this restaurant. **[F][M][V]** Must cross gangplank to enter boat. Uneven flooring. Request seating on main floor if stairs are a concern, although there is an elevator.

Table
Seafood
Med. noise
Avg. waits
11:30 am–4:00 pm, 5:00 pm–11:00 pm

© Deb Wills

New Zealand Orange Roughy with Shrimp ($30)

Portobello Yacht Club	**L $41, D $53**	🎗	7	7

Upscale Italian in a club atmosphere. Owned and operated by the Levy Corporation, which also runs the neighboring Fulton's Crab House and Wolfgang Puck's. Main menu items: pasta, veal, seafood. Reservations accepted. **[D]** A number of chicken and fish entrées for health-conscious diets. **[D][W]** Kosher items not available here. **[M]** Wheelchair/ECV accessible, but difficult to negotiate around seating.

Table
Italian
Med. noise
Avg. waits
11:30 am–11 pm

Raglan Road	**D $48**	7	7

This authentic Irish pub and restaurant offers traditional and contemporary Irish fare, as well as music, storytelling, and dance. Typical menu items include salmon, lamb shank, and beef stew. Pleasure Island club admission not required for entry into the pub. **[D]** At least one vegetarian dish is offered, like Raglan Risotto ($14.95). **[R]** Pub atmosphere encourages alcohol consumption. **[D][W]** Kosher items not available.

Table
Irish
Noisy
Med. waits
3:00 pm–11:00 pm

Eatery descriptions and ratings are explained on page 343.

T-Rex: A Prehistoric Family Adventure, A Place to Eat, Shop, Explore and Discover is set to open in Downtown Disney in early 2008. It will be home to life-sized Audio-Animatronic dinosaurs, a dig site, and much more, including shopping and hands-on activities. Guests will be able to pan for precious stones and use interactive "Paleo" screens. The table-service restaurant will feature waterfalls and geysers and the Kitchen of Fire, which will have a wood-burning pizza oven and rotisseries surrounded by live flames. Food will feature themed items like Triassic Tortellini and Bronto Burgers. **[A][U][F][T][I][S]** Very noisy—could cause overstimulation. **[F]** Live fire in the kitchen cooking area, Audio-Animatronic dinosaurs.

Downtown Disney West Side Eateries

▪ Bongos Cuban Cafe — L $35, D $42 — 🏆 7 | 7

Table
Cuban
Very noisy
No advance reservations
Long waits

Latin flavor in the kitchen and in the theming of Gloria Estefan's beautifully decorated restaurant. Salads, sandwiches for lunch; salads, seafood, chicken, and beef for dinner. Additional seating upstairs is open mainly during dinner. Hours: 11:00 am–10:30 pm at restaurant, 10:30 am–11:00 pm at express window. **[A][U][F][L][M][X]** Tables and chairs very close together. **[D]** Salads for lighter fare. Special vegetarian plate ($14) available. **[H]** Tile floors and walls create lots of echoes; very noisy environment. **[L]** Padded metal chairs with no arms.

▪ FoodQuest — L $12, D $12, S — 🏆 10 | 6

Counter
American
Noisy
Med. waits
11:30 am–10:30 pm

When hunger pangs hit you at DisneyQuest, run up to this fast food place. Co-author Deb Wills thinks it's the best counter-service spot at Walt Disney World! (Must have DisneyQuest admission to enter.) Several counters serve up different items—pizza, pasta, sandwiches, salads, hot and cold wraps. Limited flexibility, but very willing to accommodate however possible. **[D]** Several vegetarian options available, including spinach/artichoke dip with chips ($6.50), pasta with marinara (meatless) sauce ($6.50), pizza. Herbal teas available. **[M]** Lines to get food can wind around and be difficult to negotiate. Located on upper level of DisneyQuest—take the elevator.

▪ House of Blues — L $46, D $46 — 5 | 5

Table
American
Very noisy
Reservations for dinner
Long waits
11 am–11 pm (open later on Tue.-Sat.)

American food with a Cajun flair offering traditional foods plus gumbo, jambalaya, and etouffée. Food quality and service low. Located near Cirque du Soleil and DisneyQuest, "HOB" looks like a weatherbeaten wharfside dive. Inside is an equally aged interior with comfy booths. Live blues bands keep the joint cookin' (and make conversation difficult). Headliners play at the concert hall next door. A Gospel Brunch (disappointing) is held every Sunday. Open to midnight Tue.-Wed., and until 2:00 am Thu.-Sat. **[A][U][T][I][S]** Can be very noisy—could cause overstimulation. **[D]** Few items on the light side. **[D][W]** Kosher items are not available here.

▪ Planet Hollywood — L $47, D $47 — 🏆 4 | 5

Table
American
Very noisy
Long waits
11:00 am–1:00 am

The big blue world planted outside of Downtown Disney's West Side is the Orlando outlet of this global chain that features movie and TV memorabilia as it serves up sandwiches and burgers, entrée salads, pasta, and more. Portions are generous, but quality is just so-so. **[D][W]** Kosher items are not available here. **[A][U][H][T][I][S]** Can be very loud. **[M][S][V]** Steep, spiral staircase can be difficult to climb. Elevator is available. **[F]** Request to be seated on ground level if you have fear of heights. **[V]** Dimly lit.

▪ Wetzel's Pretzels — S $4 — 5 | 5

Counter
American
Med. noise

Gourmet pretzels with dips, hot dogs, and Haagen Dazs Ice Cream. A second kiosk in the Marketplace. Indoor seating. Open 10:30 am–11:00 pm Sun-Thu, 10:30–midnight Fri-Sat (West Side), and 10:30 am–11:30 pm (Marketplace). **[D]** Sorbet, frozen lemonade, and granitas available.

Eatery descriptions and ratings are explained on page 343.

Downtown Disney West Side Eateries
(continued)

Deb Wills' Rating
Deb Koma's Rating

Planning

Special Challenges

Getting There

Staying in Style

Touring

Dining

Resources

Index

☐ **Wolfgang Puck Grand Cafe**　L $52, D $52	7	7

Hearty soups, wood-fired pizzas, salads, pasta, rotisserie, grill, sushi, and sashimi (that's raw fish to you and me!). Seating is available inside, at the bar, and outside. Seating is crowded. Try for a late lunch instead of dinner. **[A][U][T][I][S]** This restaurant can be very noisy—could cause overstimulation. **[D]** Turkey burger ($11) as well as other lighter options are on menu. Some vegetarian choices, like pumpkin ravioli ($14) and penne with spinach and goat cheese ($14). **[L]** Tables for two are very small.	**Table** American Very noisy Reservations for dinner Very long waits 11:30 am–11 pm

☐ **Wolfgang Puck Dining Room**　D $66	8	8

Puck's Dining Room is upstairs, upscale, and pricey. Noise carries up from the café downstairs. Seafood, duck, lamb, beef, and risotto. Reservations recommended. Open 6:00 pm–10:30 pm. Dress code is "business casual" (no swimwear/tank tops/flip-flops) and is strictly enforced. **[G][D]** Be sure to call in advance for special dietary concerns. **[V]** Dimly lit.	**Table** American Long waits

☐ **Wolfgang Puck Express**　L $12, D $12, S	6	6

Fast food for the upscale set. Inside and outside dining. Features pizzas, pastas, soups, and salads. Some sushi and sandwiches prepackaged. See page 362 for the Marketplace location. Open 11:00 am–11:00 pm. **[M]** Shop and the outdoor seating are tight for wheelchair/ECV users.	**Counter** American Med. noise

☐ **Wonderland Cafe**　S $8	9	6

Located inside DisneyQuest (admission required), this is the spot for a quick pick-me-up or a sweet treat. Lots of gorgeous desserts (the place is run by the Cheesecake Factory, after all) and specialty coffees. Comfy seating in tables and booths. Several booths have Internet access. **[D]** Herbal teas available. **[M]** Located on upper floor of DisneyQuest—just take the elevator!	**Counter** American Noisy 11:00 am–11:45 pm

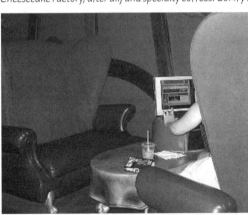

© Debra Martin Koma

An Internet station at the Wonderland Cafe

Resort Dining

There's a number of really good restaurants at the resorts—in fact, resort restaurants are **generally much better** than those found in the theme parks. That said, there are a few things to keep in mind when dining at your Walt Disney World resort:

Some **kosher items** (usually chicken and hot dogs) are available in the food courts of some of Disney's value and moderate resort hotels. But be sure to give 24 hours' notice if you'll have a group dining or if you're at a deluxe resort.

Most resorts have at least one **microwave** available for warming foods, located in their food court or counter-service area.

In addition to the prepackaged "grab and go" items found in most of the food courts, the resort general stores **sell some food items**. You'll find the most variety at the Disney Vacation Club resorts, since their units have kitchen facilities. Staples such as bread, milk, donuts, and cereal are generally available—remember, though, that you'll pay a premium. We have found the Hess Express gas stations on Disney property to be less expensive than the resort general store on many items. See page 128 in chapter 4 for a table listing food items generally available at the resort shops.

Bring any **specialty items** you don't want to do without, like sugar-free syrup, specific sugar substitutes, and low-sodium salt. These types of items are sometimes provided, but may not always be available. We have seen Lactaid or soy milk in most food courts, but not all, for example. Each venue decides what to offer (such as Splenda), so just because you find an item one place doesn't mean you'll find it everywhere.

© MediaMarx, Inc.

Everything Pop is the food court and general shopping area at Pop Century Resort

Planning

Special Challenges

Getting There

Staying in Style

Touring

Dining

Resources

Index

Resort Eateries
(All-Star Resorts and Disney's Animal Kingdom Lodge)

Deb Wills' Rating

Deb Koma's Rating

All-Star Resorts Eateries

End Zone, Intermission, World Premiere B $13, L $13, D $13, S		5	5
Food courts offering typical fast food fare. Breakfast items include eggs and bacon, waffle platter ($5.69). Lunch/dinner serve up burgers, hot dogs, sandwiches, pizza. Grab'n'go items, salads, pastas, and hand-dipped ice cream. Indoor seating with limited outdoor seating. **[D][W]** Kosher meals available without advance notice. Inquire about gluten- and dairy-free items. **[Ö]** Video screen menu aids foreign-language speakers. **[M]** Special seating areas designated.	**Counter** American Very noisy 6 am-12 am		

Disney's Animal Kingdom Lodge Resort Eateries

Boma–Flavors of Africa B $21, D $32, S		8	7
A unique dining experience in one of Disney's most unusual resorts. Boma features a wide variety of foods for every taste and a kitchen staff that goes out of its way to be accommodating. Breakfast ($16.99 adults/$9.99 children 3-9) items include standard fare, roasted meats and a few South African favorites. At dinner ($25.99/$11.99), don't miss the hearty soups, smoked meats, grilled fish, and desserts. **[A][U][T][I][S]** Can be very noisy—could cause overstimulation. **[R]** All-you-care-to-eat buffet. **[D]** Open kitchen right behind food stations make chefs very accessible for questions and requests. Huge selection of vegetarian and vegan items included in buffet. **[L]** Heavy wooden chairs, most with no arms. **[Ö]** Traditional Japanese breakfast available upon request. Peer reviewer Masayo Kano says, "Boma's Japanese breakfast is great—not perfect, but still good to have."	**Buffet** African Very noisy Reservations a must Call 180 days Long waits 7:30 am-11:00 am, 5:00 pm-10:00 pm		

© Deb Wills

Boma

Jiko–The Cooking Place D $55		10	10
Africa meets Asia meets California—fusion cooking reigns supreme in this stylish restaurant! Flatbreads, dips, soups, salads, and creative entrées. Relaxed atmosphere, knowledgeable servers. No tank tops/swimwear—dress is "business casual." On crowded nights you may be seated in the Cape Town Lounge and Wine Bar located at the entrance to the restaurant. Wine list boasts incredible South African wines. **[D]** Fish and vegetarian selections standard. Don't miss the spicy tandoori tofu with grains and veggies ($19). Many menu items are gluten-free. We've found this restaurant to be very accommodating to special diet requests with several special diet menus available. Artisan cheese plate available in lieu of sugar-free dessert. **[V]** Dimly lit.	**Table** African Med. noise Reservations a must Call 180 days Med. waits 5:30 pm-10:00 pm		

The Mara B $10, L $13, D $13, S		8	8
The only option open for lunch at Animal Kingdom Lodge offers grilled items, salads, soups, baked goods, and some "grab 'n' go" items. TV plays in the corner. During busy times, you may have to wait for food to be prepared. **[A][U][I][S]** Can be quite noisy. **[L]** Chairs are armless, but very uncomfortable. There is banquette seating on two walls—tables move, so a larger person can sit more comfortably there. **[Ö]** Video screen menus aid foreign-language speakers.	**Counter** African Very noisy 6:00 am-11:30 pm		

Resort Eateries
(BoardWalk Inn & Villas Resort)

Deb Wills' Rating / Deb Koma's Rating

BoardWalk Inn & Villas Resort Eateries

■ Big River Grille & Brewing Works   L $35, D $40   5 | 5

Brewpub with ordinary sandwich/salad fare. Typical items: burgers, steaks, ribs ($19.99), chicken Caesar salad ($10.99). Brewery stays open later than restaurant; last call 1:00 am. Indoor/outdoor seating. **[R]** Recovering alcoholics should be aware that this is a brewpub, with beer made on the premises. **[D]** Some chicken and fish entrées (grilled salmon $18.99) geared to health-conscious diets. No specific vegetarian entrée offered. **[M][V][X]** Crowded tables make navigating indoors difficult. Consider sitting outside, weather permitting.

Table
American
Noisy
Reservations
407-560-0253
11:30 am–
11:00 pm

■ BoardWalk Bakery   B $10, L $10, S   7 | 7

Those yummy aromas emanating from the BoardWalk area in the morning are probably coming from the ovens here! Fresh baked goods, specialty coffees, breakfast burritos, and light lunches. Limited outdoor seating. **[D]** Whole fresh fruit is available, as is a mixed fruit bowl ($3.59). Peanut butter and jelly. Fat-free muffins ($2.29). **[L]** Armless chairs available. **[M][L]** Space inside shop is small, hard to navigate. **[A][U][F]** Birds love to hang out here and try to grab a crumb or two from you. **[S]** Peaceful here in the mornings overlooking Crescent Lake.

Counter
Bakery
Long waits in
the morning
6:30 am–
11:00 pm

■ ESPN Club   L $42, D $42   4 | 4

The ultimate sports bar, with television screens everywhere—even in the restrooms—all showing some type of athletic endeavors. Seating is cramped—there are booths, tables, and high bar stools. Usual bar fare. Typical items: burgers, grilled meat, sandwiches, and salads. **[A][U][T][I][S]** Can be very noisy—could cause overstimulation. **[R]** Recovering alcoholics should be aware that this is largely a sports bar environment. In addition, those recovering from or with a gambling addiction should be aware that more than 100 televisions fill this restaurant, all televising sporting events. **[D]** A few chicken and fish options are concessions to health-conscious diets. A few vegetarian selections (veggie burger $7.99, portobello sandwich $8.99) are also available. **[G]** Smoking is allowed in the bar area.

Table
American
Very noisy
No
reservations
Med. waits
Indoor seating
11:30 am–1 am
(Open until
2:00 am on
weekends)

■ Flying Fish Cafe   D $70   9 | 9

This beautifully appointed restaurant on the BoardWalk serves up some of the freshest, most inventively prepared seafood we've ever had. Menu changes seasonally, but typically includes several non-seafood choices (veal chop $39, steak $38) in addition to its wide variety of fish and shellfish. No tank tops/swimwear—dress is "smart casual." **[G]** Primarily a seafood restaurant—those with seafood/shellfish allergy may want to avoid. **[D]** Fish entrées for health-conscious diets. At least one vegetarian selection, like Fondutta Ravioli ($21), is also available. **[A][U][I][S]** Crowds can be noisy—for a quieter experience, ask to be seated in the back under the "canopy."

Table
Seafood
Very noisy
Reservations
strongly
recommended
Med. waits
5:30–10 pm

Resort Eateries
(BoardWalk Resort and Caribbean Beach Resort)

BoardWalk Inn & Villas Resort Eateries *(continued)*

Seashore Sweets	S $6		7	7

*Just the place for your candy or ice cream fix, this old-style shop also has a display of memorabilia from the Miss America beauty pageant, traditionally held in Atlantic City (hence the BoardWalk connection). Hard and soft-serve ice cream in cones, waffle cones, or bowls, shakes and floats, as well as coffee, soft drinks, bulk and packaged candy, including mix-your-own-colors M&Ms. **[D]** Sugar-free candy available. **[L]** Armless chairs available outside on the BoardWalk. **[M][L][V][X]** Space inside shop is small, hard to navigate. **[A][U][F]** Birds love to hang outside here and try to grab a crumb or two from you.*

Deb Wills' Rating / Deb Koma's Rating

Counter
Ice cream
Limited
Outdoor
Seating
Med. waits
1:00–
11:00 pm

Spoodles	B $15, D $48	🎗	7	7

*This popular eatery features fresh seafood, grilled meats, flatbreads, and pastas with Italian, Greek, and Spanish flavors. Breakfast features American food as well as frittatas (open-faced omelets). Indoor seating. Outside pizza window open noon–midnight. **[G]** Current breakfast flatbread made with wheat flour. **[D]** A number of low-fat entrées, including fresh fruit plate ($8.99) at breakfast, for health-conscious diets. Vegetarian selections include gnocchi with mushrooms ($18) and four-cheese flatbread ($7).*

Table
Mediterranean
Reservations
suggested
Med. waits
7:30–11 am
5–10 pm

Caribbean Beach Resort

Old Port Royale	B $14, L $14, D $14, S		6	6

*A collection of fast food stations with standard pizza, pasta, burgers, rotisserie items, and a grab'n'go area. Extensive indoor seating. Some outdoor seating, but beward of birds! **[D]** Vegetable platter ($6.99) available at Bridgetown Broiler. Mac and cheese for kids. **[D][W]** Kosher selections available without advance notice. **[L]** Chairs without arms available.*

Counter
American
6:30 am–
11:00 pm

Shutters	D $45	🎗	6	6

*Caribbean Beach Resort's only table-service restaurant offers American cuisine with Caribbean flavors. This eatery is open only for dinner. Entrees include pan-seared salmon ($17), roasted chicken ($16), penne pasta with shrimp ($17, also available as a vegetarian option for $13.50). Average fare. Spotty service. **[D]** No vegetarian items on menu; be sure to ask server. **[C][L]** Heavy wooden armless chairs with backs.*

Table
American
Reservations
suggested
5:30 pm–
10:00 pm

© Debra Martin Koma

Shutters

Eatery descriptions and ratings are explained on page 343.

Planning / Special Challenges / Getting There / Staying in Style / Touring / Dining / Resources / Index

Resort Eateries
(Contemporary Resort)

Deb Wills' Rating
Deb Koma's Rating

Contemporary Resort Eateries

California Grill	D $64		10	10

The magnificent view alone would draw you to this top-notch restaurant at Disney. Open kitchen keeps restaurant noise level constantly high. Main items: Sushi, flatbreads, seafood, and meats—well-known for its pork tenderloin ($22.75) and beef filet ($34.50). Menu changes weekly. No tank tops/swimwear—dress is "smart casual." Check-in at this restaurant is on the second floor—you're escorted upstairs via private elevator. Wait for your table in the lounge area at the restaurant's entrance in overstuffed chairs looking out at the Magic Kingdom below. On crowded nights, you may be seated in the lounge area. **[D]** Veggie appetizers, pumpkin lasagna ($20) entrée—vegetarian options specifically indicated on the menu. We've found this restaurant to be particularly accommodating to special needs diners, but forget their sugar-free desserts—order the cheese platter instead! **[L]** Chairs with no arms in dining room. Cocktail chairs with arms in lounge. **[F]** Request seat away from window if you have a fear of heights.

- Table
- American
- Noisy
- Reservations recommended
- Call 180 days
- Med. to long waits
- 5:30 pm-10:00 pm (Lounge is 5:30 pm-midnight)

Chef Mickey's	B $23, D $35		7	7

Located on the fourth-floor concourse, with the monorail occasionally gliding by overhead, this is a character dining experience with lots of energy, good food, and fun. Standard breakfast ($17.99 adults/$9.99 children 3-9) fare. Dinner ($26.99/$11.99) is also standard American fare: beef, chicken, pasta, seafood. Kids have their own buffet. Make your own sundae bar a splurge! Restaurant is open—ceiling is ten stories overhead. **[A][U][T][I][S]** Can be very noisy—often there's loud music and napkin twirling as the characters make the rounds. Could cause overstimulation. **[F]** Meals feature costumed character—avoid if afraid. **[R]** All-you-can-eat buffet. Waiting area is part of Outer Rim cocktail lounge. **[D]** Call in advance for special needs. Ask available chefs for ingredients' details.

- Buffet
- American
- Very noisy
- Reservations suggested
- Med.-long waits
- 7-11:30 am, 5:00-9:30 pm

Concourse Steakhouse	B $18, L $41, D $43		5	6

This is an open restaurant adjacent to Chef Mickey's—sometimes it's hard to tell where one restaurant ends and the other begins. Not only does the noise filter in, but overflow guests do, too. Breakfast has omelets, pancakes, waffles, and a fruit plate. Lunch features pizza, salads, soups, and sandwiches. Dinner offers ribs, steak, shrimp, and salmon. Solid quality at breakfast and lunch, but spotty for dinner. There are much better steaks at Disney than at this eatery! At press time, this restaurant is scheduled to close in spring 2008, to be converted into a quick-service spot, set to open mid-August 2008. **[A][U][T][I][S]** Can be very noisy—could cause overstimulation. **[D]** Be sure to call well in advance with any special dietary needs. **[L]** Chairs without arms are available.

- Table
- Steakhouse
- Noisy
- Reservations suggested
- 7:30-11 am, noon-2:00 pm, 5:30-10 pm

Food & Fun Center			?	?

The Food and Fun Center closed in July 2007 to be converted to a new table-service restaurant called The Wave (tentatively set to open in spring 2008). A temporary quick-service restaurant called Tempo Grab and Go is operating near the Outer Rim lounge on the fourth floor.

- Counter
- American

Eatery descriptions and ratings are explained on page 343.

Resort Eateries
(Coronado Springs and Fort Wilderness Resorts)

Deb Wills' Rating
Deb Koma's Rating

Coronado Springs Resort Eateries

Maya Grill — B $17, D $49 — 7 | 6

Maya Grill

As the name implies, Mayan architecture inspired the décor and design of this restaurant that holds a daily breakfast buffet ($16.95 adults/$9.95 children 3-9). In the evenings, it becomes a fairly typical steakhouse that caters to the large amount of convention trade that Coronado Springs hosts. Usual dinner items include steaks, ribs ($19), and salmon. *[R]* Breakfast is an all-you-care-to-eat buffet. *[D]* Some lighter fare is available, such as seafood and grilled chicken breast entrées. Vegetarian selections are available upon request, but are not on regular menu. *[V]* Low lighting.

Buffet/Table
American
Med. noise
Reservations suggested
Short waits
7:00 am-11:00 am, 5:00 pm-10:00 pm

Pepper Market — B $8, L $8, D $8 — 8 | 7

This is a unique food court with freshly made items. Go from station to station to choose which foods you want—hot entrées are made to order. Stations include: Mexican, stir fry, American, pasta, pizza, bakery, and a kid's station. Note there is a 10 percent gratuity automatically applied to your bill. *[D]* Chicken and fish entrées available for health-conscious diets. Vegetarian selections also available—ask the chef at the particular station. *[G]* Avoid the wok station if you have nut allergies—peanut oil used in cooking.

Counter
Multi-ethnic
Noisy
Indoor seats
Med. waits
7 am-11 pm

La Tienda — B $8, L $8, D $8 — 6 | 6

This little convenience store is located next to Pepper Market—a great place to grab a light snack or sandwich on the run. Take your food back to your room or outside, where you can sit at umbrella tables overlooking Lago Dorado. *[D]* Whole fresh fruit and juices are available. Also offered are prepackaged sandwiches, including turkey and chicken wraps.

Counter
American
Med. noise
Short waits
6 am-12 am

Fort Wilderness Resort & Campground Eatery

Trail's End Restaurant — B $17, L $19, D $25 — 7 | 7

One of the best values on Disney property, this homey restaurant offers standard buffet fare prepared in a no-nonsense manner. Breakfast ($11.99/$7.99), lunch ($12.99/$8.99), and dinner ($17.99/$9.99) are all served from a buffet. Typical lunch/dinner items include: carved meats, fish, ribs, and chicken. Pizza is available for take-out next door. You must exit this restaurant to use the restrooms. *[R]* All-you-care-to-eat buffet. *[D]* A number of chicken and fish entrées are on the buffet for health-conscious diets. Soup and salad bar special ($11.50) for lighter eaters. *[D][W]* Kosher meals and other special requests are available with advance notice. *[L]* Chairs without arms are available.

Buffet
American
Noisy
Indoor seating
Med. waits
7:30-11 am, noon-2:30 pm, 4:30-9:30 pm

See also Hoop Dee Doo Revue (page 383) and Mickey's Backyard BBQ (page 382).

Planning | Special Challenges | Getting There | Staying in Style | Touring | Dining | Resources | Index

Resort Eateries
(Grand Floridian Resort)

Grand Floridian Resort Eateries

Deb Wills' Rating   Deb Koma's Rating

☐ Cítricos   D $61   9 | 9

This elegant restaurant combines the simple and fresh cooking flavors from the south of France with some unusual dishes. Tables are well-spaced. Typical entrées: grilled fish, lamb chops ($29), filet ($33). Closed Mondays and Tuesdays. No tank tops/swimwear—dress is "smart casual." Indoor seating. **[D]** A number of fish entrées for health-conscious diets. At least one vegetarian selection, such as Braised Autumn Vegetables ($21), is also available on the menu. We found the chefs and servers very accommodating to special requests!	**Table**
	Mediterranean
	Med. noise
	Reservations suggested
	5:30–10 pm

☐ Garden View Lounge   S $25   8 | 9

Elegant lounge with starched linens and fine china, offers daily English tea for a quiet mid-afternoon break. Special tea (chocolate milk!) for children also available. Also hosts "My Disney Girl's Perfectly Princess Tea Party" (see character dining on page 382). **[D][G]** Gluten-free sandwiches may be available with sufficient advance notice. **[D][W]** Kosher items are not available here. **[S]** Seniors looking for a quiet break will enjoy a relaxing, refined afternoon tea.	**Table/Bar**
	English tea
	Quiet
	Reservations
	Med. waits
	2–6 pm

☐ Gasparilla's Grill   B $14, L $14, D $14, S   5 | 7

This counter-service spot offers all-day dining, adjacent to a game arcade. Typical offerings include breakfast croissants and french toast sticks for breakfast; pizza, sandwiches, burgers, and hot dogs for lunch and dinner. Indoor/outdoor seating available. (Note that outdoor seating overlooking marina is an even quieter option.) **[D]** Vegetarian entrée ($6.99), tabbouleh wrap ($6.59), and fattoush green salad ($7.49) available. Ingredients for many items prominently posted. **[D][W]** Kosher foods are available with advance notice. **[A][U][T][I][S]** Can be very noisy due to the arcade nearby—could cause overstimulation. **[C][L]** Wooden chairs with backs are bolted in place.	**Counter**
	American
	Med. noise
	Med. waits
	Open 24 hours

☐ Grand Floridian Cafe   B $30, L $37, D $39   5 | 5

An upscale café, this spot has a surprisingly extensive menu. Breakfast features the usual suspects (pancakes, eggs, sausage), but also corned beef hash and eggs ($10.99) and eggs benedict ($10.99). Typical lunch/dinner items: sandwiches, fish, steak, and prime rib. **[D]** Chicken and fish entrées for health-conscious diets. At least one vegetarian selection (e.g., Asian Noodle Bowl for $12.99) also available. This eatery also offers a special Berry Pyramid for fat-free/no-sugar-added diets. The chef here is very accommodating to special diets. **[L]** Armless chairs available. **[Ö]** Traditional Japanese breakfast ($19.99) available.	**Table**
	American
	Very noisy
	Reservations suggested
	Med. waits
	7–11 am, 11:45 am–2 pm, 5–9 pm

Eatery descriptions and ratings are explained on page 343.

Resort Eateries
(Grand Floridian Resort)

Grand Floridian Resort Eateries (continued)

Narcoossee's   D $69   7 | 9

Located on the Seven Seas Lagoon, this casual restaurant reflects the relaxed atmosphere of Florida living, featuring seafood and its famous Key Lime crème brulee. Wait for your table in the lounge—you can also order appetizers and/or desserts here. If you time it right, you can see the Magic Kingdom fireworks and the Electrical Water Pageant from window seats or the verandah overlooking the water. **[C][♥][M][E][S][L]** This restaurant is located a few minutes' walk away from the main building. **[G]** Primarily a seafood restaurant—those with seafood/shellfish allergy may want to avoid.

Table
Seafood
Noisy
Reservations recommended
Indoor seats
Short waits
6–10 pm

1900 Park Fare   B $24, D $36   8 | 7

This gorgeous Victorian restaurant features lively character meals, enhanced by the piping of Big Bertha—the gigantic player organ that goes off periodically. Breakfast ($18.99/$10.99) with Mary Poppins, Alice in Wonderland, and the Mad Hatter is fairly typical fare: bacon and eggs, waffles, cereals, and danish. Dinner ($28.99/$13.99) with Cinderella and friends has items that vary widely from the norm: carved meats, paella, mussels, and chicken piccata. This spot also is home to the Wonderland Tea Party for kids—see page 382. **[A][U][T][I]** Can be very noisy—could cause overstimulation. **[R]** All-you-care-to-eat buffet. **[D]** A number of chicken and fish entrées are on the buffet for health-conscious diets. Several vegetarian selections, like vegetable lo mein and roasted vegetables, also available. Kosher meals and other special requests with advance notice. **[F]** Breakfast and dinner feature costumed characters who frequently make the rounds—if anyone has fear of costumed characters, you may want to avoid. **[S]** Can be quite noisy and overrun with small children.

Buffet
American
Very noisy
Advance reservations strongly recommended
Indoor seating
Short waits
8:00–11:10 am 4:30–8:20 pm

Victoria & Albert's   D $150   10 | 10

Disney's five-star dining experience. Five-course prix fixe menu ($125) changes daily. This is the place for extra-special occasions. Very quiet and romantic, with a harp to serenade you. All your servers are either "Victoria" or "Albert." Dress code requires eveningwear for women, jacket for men. Reservations are required—call 407-824-1089 up to 180 days in advance. **[G][D]** Special dietary requests must be made in advance. Call 24 hours in advance to confirm.

Table
French
Quiet
Short waits
5:45 pm & 9:00 pm

⊕ Eating 24/7!

Most quick-service areas at the resorts close somewhere between 10:00 pm and midnight, but there are a few places that are open 24 hours. All grills close by midnight, though, so only grab 'n' go, prepackaged foods are available throughout the night.

- ✔ Picabu—Walt Disney World Dolphin
- ✔ Captain Cook's—Polynesian
- ✔ Gasparilla's Grill—Grand Floridian Resort & Spa
- ✔ Hess Station near Magic Kingdom

Planning · Special Challenges · Getting There · Staying in Style · Touring · Dining · Resources · Index

Resort Eateries
(Old Key West and Polynesian Resorts)

Deb Wills' Rating   Deb Koma's Rating

Old Key West Resort Eateries

Olivia's Cafe	B $18, L $35, D $43	🏅	8	7

A diamond in the rough where you'll find locals enjoying a good meal at reasonable prices. Kitchen does best with simpler entrées. Lunch menu offers half salad/sandwich with soup. Indoor seating; outdoor covered seating sometimes available—check with a cast member. Many menu items are available for takeout—order here, pick up at Goods to Go. **[D]** Salads, chicken, and fish offer lighter fare. **[L]** Chairs with arms.

- Table
- Floridian
- 7:30-10:30 am, 11:30 am-5 pm, 5-10 pm

Goods to Go	B $10, L $10, D $10, S	5	5

This counter-service spot offers fast food from ordinary (burgers and sandwiches) to the unusual (conch fritters!). Continental breakfast foods are available in the morning. **[D]** A fruit plate ($5.89) is available.

- Counter
- American
- 7:30 am-10 pm

Polynesian Resort Eateries

See pages 385-386 for the Spirit of Aloha dinner

Kona Cafe	B $17, L $32, D $42	🏅	9	8

This popular, innovative eatery offers American cuisine with Asian influences. Breakfast includes the famous "Tonga Toast," a banana-stuffed version of French toast ($8.99). Typical lunch and dinner items: Mahi Mahi, filet, pasta, and teriyaki. Indoor seating. **[D]** Many fish and lighter dishes for health-conscious diets. Vegetarian selections, such as vegetable rice bowl ($14.49), are also available. Chefs here are particularly agreeable to accommodating special requests, especially for vegetarian/vegan diners. **[G]** Peanut oil may be used in some cooking, stir fry here—be sure to ask! Request "no MSG" if sensitive. **[L]** Armless chairs available.

- Table
- Asian-inspiried
- Med. noise
- Reservations suggested
- Short waits
- 7:30-11:30 am, noon-3:00 pm, 5-10 pm

'Ohana	B $22, D $31	6	7

This popular restaurant features an all-you-care-to-eat meal brought to your table. Breakfast features standard bacon and eggs, Mickey waffle fare ($18.99 adult/$10.99 child). Dinner features: skewered grilled meats and fish. Kids parade around the dining area periodically with servers or characters ($25.99 adult/$11.99 child). **[R]** All-you-care-to-eat buffet. **[G]** Beware of cross-contamination! Talk to your server/manager in advance—meats and fish are taken off the skewer with the same implements and are brought to the table touching each other. Open fire pit can be smoky at times. **[D]** Vegetarian selections are not on the regular menu but are available if you ask. **[F]** Breakfast features costumed characters who frequently make the rounds—if anyone has a fear of costumed characters, you may want to avoid. **[L]** Chairs have low arms, which can be uncomfortable. **[M]** Companion restroom located just outside restaurant entrance. **[S]** Can be quite noisy at breakfast. Dinner, too, can be noisy with the interactive activities featured.

- Table
- Polynesian
- Noisy
- Reservations strongly recommended
- Indoor seating
- Med. waits
- 7:30 am-11:00 am, 5:00 am-10:00 pm

Captain Cook's Snack Co.	B $10, L $10, D $10, S	5	5

Open all day, this recently renovated spot is the place to get a bite to eat on the run. Grill closes around 11:00 pm, but a good selection of prepackaged foods (salads, wraps, sandwiches) is always available. Indoor/outdoor seating. **[D][W]** Kosher meals only available with advance notice. Grilled cheese for kids.

- Counter
- American
- Noisy
- 24 hours

Resort Eateries
(Pop Century, Port Orleans, and Saratoga Springs Resorts)

Deb Wills' Rating / Deb Koma's Rating

Pop Century Resort Eatery

Everything Pop	B $10, L $12, D $12, S	6	5

A food court offering typical fast-food fare. Breakfast platter is eggs, biscuit, potatoes, and bacon ($5.59/$3.59). Burgers, dogs, sandwiches, and pizza at lunch and dinner. Also has wide selection of prepackaged foods, such as salads, bagels, and desserts. **[D]** Vegetable frittata at breakfast ($4.99). **[D][W]** Kosher meals available without advance notice. **[G]** Asian foods may have peanut oil and MSG—be sure to ask. **[Ö]** Video screen menu. **[♥]** Pan-seared fish ($8.99).

Counter / American / Noisy / 6:00 am–midnight

Port Orleans Resort Eateries

Boatwright's Dining Hall	B/D	$38	5	7

A southern flavor pervades the atmosphere here—there are hearty breakfasts of sweet potato cakes ($7.29) and banana-stuffed french toast ($7.99), plus Cajun cooking featured at dinner. Typical dinner items: blackened fish, bourbon-glazed chicken ($14.59), ribs ($18.59), and jambalaya ($16.99). **[D]** A number of chicken and fish entrées for health-conscious diets. Some vegetarian selections, such as four cheese ravioli ($14.29) or summer vegetable medley ($13.99). **[D][W]** Kosher meals available without advance notice. Other special requests with advance notice.

Table / American / Med. noise / Indoor seats / Short waits / 7:30–11:30 am, 5–10 pm

Riverside Mill	B $13, L $13, D $13, S	7	7

Recently renovated food court with Riverside Market and Deli, Bleu Bayou Burgers and Chicken, Southern Bakery, and pizza. Broiler closes at 10:00 pm. **[D]** Lighter entrées for health-conscious diets. Vegetarian sandwich ($5.59). Special requests with advance notice. Chefs seem very willing to accommodate special diets. Grilled cheese and mac and cheese available for kids. **[D][W]** Kosher meals available without advance notice. **[Ö]** Pictorial menu for foreign-language speakers.

Counter / American / Noisy / Indoor seats / Short waits / 6 am–midnight

Sassagoula Floatworks and Food Factory	B $13, L $13, D $13, S	7	7

Typical Disney food court. Dinner served until 10:00 pm (pizza and bakery open to midnight). **[D]** A number of lighter entrées for health-conscious diets. Vegetarian chili $4.99. Chefs seem very willing to accommodate special diets. **[D][W]** Special requests with advance notice. **[Ö]** Pictorial menu for foreign-language speakers.

Counter / American / Noisy / Med. waits / 6 am–midnight

Saratoga Springs Resort Eatery

Artist's Palette	B $14, L $14, D $14	5	6

Prepackaged items along with a limited selection of made-to-order menu items, in an airy setting resembling an artist's workspace. Main items: flatbreads (pizzas), wraps, and salads. **[D]** A number of turkey, chicken, and fish entrées for health-conscious diets. Fruit and cheese plate ($6.29) is available. Macaroni and cheese is available for kids.

Counter / American / Med. noise / Short waits / 7:30 am–11 pm

Turf Club Bar and Grill	L $37, D $41	7	7

A converted lounge, this eatery offers American fare with a flair. Entrees include Angus chuck cheeseburger ($11.49), BBQ spareribs ($17.99), and penne pasta with shrimp ($16.49). Indoor/outdoor seating. Short waits.

Table / American / Noon–9 pm

Planning / Special Challenges / Getting There / Staying in Style / Touring / Dining / Resources / Index

Resort Eateries
(Swan and Dolphin Resorts)

Swan and Dolphin Resort Eateries

	Deb Wills' Rating	Deb Koma's Rating

☐ Cabana Bar and Grill (Dolphin)   L $13, D $13, S   🎗

	6	8

Pool bar for refreshments alfresco. Mostly lighter fare and finger foods. Grill closes at 5:00 pm. **[D]** A number of tuna, chicken, and fish items for health-conscious diets. Fresh fruit plate is also available. Vegetarian wrap ($8.50) and veggie burger ($8.95) on menu, as well as low-carb chicken wrap ($9.75).

Counter
Snacks
Noisy
11 am-7 pm

☐ The Fountain (Dolphin)   L $18, D $18, S   🎗

	7	7

Burgers and homemade ice cream in a spot recently renovated with chic decor! **[D][W]** Kosher items available with at least 24-hour notice. **[D]** Veggie burger ($7) on the menu. Special treat: Billy D. Lite ($4.25), a fat-free vanilla yogurt blended with skim milk, strawberry sauce, and a fresh banana. Medium noise.

Table
American
Indoor seats
11 am-11 pm

☐ Fresh (Dolphin)   B $22, L $34   🎗

	9	8

A Mediterranean-style market that features American foods with flavor. Food prepared as you order, in many cases. In addition to regular buffet, you can order a "continental breakfast" buffet for a lower price. It includes the baked goods, but not the hot foods. "The Market Room" across the hall is often used for business breakfasts, but you can sometimes be seated here with a regular a la carte breakfast menu. **[D]** A number of chicken and fish entrées are on the buffet for health-conscious diets. Vegetarian selections, like lentil and tomato soup or roasted red peppers stuffed with goat cheese, are also

Buffet/Table
Mediterranean
Medium noise
Indoor seats
Med. waits
6:30-11 am, 11:30 am-2 pm

available. Many items made to order, so ask the chefs if you have questions about the ingredients. Don't miss the fresh-squeezed juices. **[R]** All-you-can-eat buffet, although there is an a la carte menu to order from for lunch. **[D][W]** Request kosher items or other special dietary requirements 48 hours in advance.

© MediaMarx, Inc.

The chefs at Fresh are always on hand to answer questions

☐ Garden Grove Cafe/Gulliver's Grill (Swan)   B $17, L $33, D $49 🎗

	7	6

Monday through Friday (8:30 am-11:00 am), this spacious restaurant offers a breakfast buffet (adults $13.95; children 3-9 $8.50) and even a Japanese breakfast ($17.95). On weekends, though, it hosts a character breakfast with Pluto and Goofy ($16.95/$8.50). And characters attend nightly at dinner, which features family-style themed buffets ($26.95/$10.95) as well as an a la carte menu. Weekend breakfast is 8:00 am-11:00 am. **[R]** Breakfast and dinner are all-you-can-eat buffets. **[S]** Can be quite noisy during the character meals and overrun with small children. **[D][W]** Kosher items available with at least 24-hour notice. **[D]** No vegetarian selections on regular menu—ask! **[Ö]** Traditional Japanese breakfast available. **[F]** Some meals feature costumed characters—if you are afraid of characters, you may want to avoid this restaurant.

Buffet/Table
American
Indoor seats
Med. waits
Noisy
6:30 am-11:30 am, 11:30-2 pm, 5:30-10 pm

Eatery descriptions and ratings are explained on page 343.

Resort Eateries
(Swan and Dolphin Resorts)

Swan and Dolphin Resort Eateries *(continued)*

☐ Il Mulino New York (Swan) D $50

	Deb Wills' Rating: 5	Deb Koma's Rating: 8

Open in February 2007, this trattoria replaced former Swan restaurant, Palio, with fresh, chic decor and a new menu that features a wide range of Italian favorites. **[D][W]** Kosher items available with at least 24-hour notice. **[D][G]** No cheese platter available. No pastry chef on premises. No sugar-free or no-sugar-added desserts. Heavy on sauce.

Table / Italian / Quiet / Med. waits / 6–11 pm

☐ Kimonos (Swan) D $46, S ♻ 7 5

Sushi, Asian appetizers, and cocktails served with a healthy dose of karaoke singalong. **[D]** A number of fish items for health-conscious diets. Some sushi items (like asparagus roll, $4, and ichiban roll, $5) are vegetarian; there are also items like edamame ($5). **[S]** Can be quite noisy with karaoke. **[G]** Those with seafood/shellfish allergies might want to avoid. Request "no MSG" if sensitive. **[M]** Difficult to navigate with ECV/wheelchair.

Table / Japanese / Noisy / Med. waits / 5:30 pm–1 am

☐ Shula's Steakhouse (Dolphin) D $79 7 8

Masculine décor in dark woods reveals this expensive restaurant for what it is—a throwback to the old-fashioned, expense-account-type steakhouse. Direct reservations line is 407-934-1609. **[D]** Few concessions to lighter fare—a few chicken and fish entrées. No vegetarian items on the regular menu—ask if they'll accommodate you! **[D][W]** Kosher items with at least 24-hour notice.

Table / Steakhouse / Quiet / Short waits / 5–11 pm

☐ Splash Grill & Deli (Swan) L $13, D $13, S ♻ 6 7

Poolside treats at the main pool area connecting the Swan and Dolphin resorts. Mostly lighter fare and finger foods. Grill closes at 5:00 pm. **[D]** A number of tuna, chicken, and fish items for health-conscious diets. Fresh fruit plate is also available. Vegetarian wrap ($8.50) and veggie burger ($8.95) on menu, as well as low-carb chicken wrap ($9.75). **[A][U][H][T][I][S]** Can be very noisy, as it is located near the main pool.

Counter / Snacks / Very noisy / Outdoor seats / Short waits / 11 am–7 pm

☐ Todd English's bluezoo (Dolphin) D $67 ♻ 6 9

One of the newest additions to Walt Disney World, this celebrity chef brings his unique take on fresh seafood dishes. Very trendy décor. No tank tops—dress is "smart casual." You may also dine at the raw bar or in the cafe—order items by the piece. **[G]** Primarily a seafood restaurant—those with fish/shellfish allergies may want to avoid. **[D]** Plain grilled fish entrées for health-conscious diets. Vegetarian selections are also available on request, but not particularly accommodating to other special requests. **[D][W]** Kosher items with at least 24-hour notice. **[S][V]** Very dimly lit—may be difficult for those with vision impairments.

Table / Seafood / Quiet / Reservations in main room; none in cafe / 5–11 pm

☐ Picabu (Dolphin) L $10, D $10, S ♻ 8 9

A combination cafeteria/convenience store, this 24-hour stop in the lower level of the Dolphin has it all—from healthy fruit and juice to sandwiches and pizza to Krispy Kreme donuts. **[D][W]** Kosher items with at least 24-hour notice. **[D]** Whole fruit available. Fruit plate ($4.95) and veggie burger ($7) are good vegetarian options. Grilled cheese and peanut butter and jelly sandwiches for kids.

Counter / American / Med. noise / Short waits / Open 24 hours

Side tabs: Planning · Special Challenges · Getting There · Staying in Style · Touring · Dining · Resources · Index

Resort Eateries
(Wilderness Lodge and Yacht and Beach Club Resorts)

Wilderness Lodge Resort Eateries

Artist Point — D $59 — 🎗 — 7 | 9

Beautifully appointed restaurant with Mission-style seating and flavorful contemporary fare from the Pacific Northwest—it's not uncommon to find game and other uncommon entrées (buffalo, venison, duck) on the menu. Menu changes seasonally. Signature dish is cedar-planked roasted salmon ($32). Don't miss the berry cobbler ($8)! No tank tops/swimwear—dress is "smart casual." Wait for your table in the adjacent Territory Lounge, where appetizers are available. **[D]** Be sure to call in advance for special dietary requests. At least one vegetarian option on the menu (e.g., Potato Chive Pot Stickers, $21). **[M]** Ramp to restaurant located to the left of check-in desk.

Table
Pacific Northwest
Med. noise
Reservations suggested
Med. waits
5:30–10 pm

Roaring Fork — B $10, L $10, D $10, S — 6 | 6

This quick-service dining spot is open all day—it's a great place to get a bite to eat on the run. Small area—gets crowded. **[D] [W]** Kosher meals available with 24-hour notice; ask for manager. **[D]** Veggie pizza ($6.59) at lunch. Peanut butter and jelly sandwiches are available.

Counter
Snacks
Noisy
6 am–midnight

Whispering Canyon Café — B $22, L $31, D $41 — 7 | 8

A hearty BBQ restaurant that bellows occasionally into the cavernous lobby of the Wilderness Lodge. Servers all take on personas from the Wild West, and engage diners in good ol' fun. It's not uncommon for servers to yell across the restaurant. Periodic kid races with stick ponies. All-you-care-to-eat skillets or a la carte. Breakfast skillet $9.69; lunch $13.99; dinner $21.99. **[A][U]** Lincoln Logs available while waiting. **[A][U][T][I][S]** Can be very noisy—could cause overstimulation. **[D]** Call in advance for special dietary requests. Fruit plate ($6.29) available for breakfast. **[F]** Servers will interact with you, so if you don't wish to partake, be sure to let your greeter and server know right from the start.

Table
Barbecue
Very noisy
Reservations suggested
Long waits
7:30–11 am, noon–3 pm, 5–10 pm

Yacht and Beach Club Resort Eateries

Beaches and Cream — L $28, D $28, S — 🎗 — 8 | 8

Patterned after an old-time soda shop, complete with jukebox, this spot features some of the best burgers on Disney property. It also has some of the greatest ice cream treats to be found anywhere! Seating available via booth, high stools, or tables. Very small indoor area and small outdoor seating that is covered.

Connected to arcade. **[A][U][H][T][I][S]** Very noisy—located near pool, plus there is a jukebox in the restaurant. **[D]** Several light entrées for health-conscious diets. Veggie burger is $7.49. Kosher meals and other special requests may be available with advance notice. **[D][G]** Dairy-free ice cream available on request. **[F]** Ordering the Kitchen Sink will draw lots of attention—if this bothers you, avoid. **[C][T][M][P][S][L][X]** Small space with tables close together—maneuvering is difficult.

Table
American
Very noisy
Indoor/ outdoor seats
No advance reservations
Long waits
11 am–11 pm

Stool seating at Beaches and Cream

© MediaMarx, Inc.

Deb Wills' Rating
Deb Koma's Rating

Resort Eateries
(Yacht and Beach Club Resorts)

Deb Wills' Rating
Deb Koma's Rating

Yacht and Beach Club Resort Eateries *(continued)*

▢ Beach Club Marketplace   B $12, L $12, S

	7	7

Located just off the lobby of the Beach Club, this shop offers prepackaged and made-to-order items, great for a bite on the go. Breakfast croissant, sandwiches, wraps, salads; fresh-made gelato. Limited seating in marketplace—try the nearby Breezeway. [D][G] Grilled veggie wrap ($4.99) at lunch. Peanut butter & jelly sandwiches are available. Homemade gelato also available.

Counter
American
Med/noise
8 am-11 pm

▢ Cape May Cafe   B $24, D $35

	6	8

Character breakfast buffet $18.99/$10.99; clambake buffet dinner $25.99/$11.99. [A][U][T][I][S] Can be very noisy—could cause overstimulation, especially during character breakfast. [R] All-you-can-eat buffet. [G] Dinner buffet features lots of seafood—those with shellfish/fish allergies may want to avoid. [D] Some vegetarian choices on buffet. Kids' buffet has mac and cheese. [F] Breakfast features costumed characters who frequently make the rounds—if anyone has fear of costumed characters, you may want to avoid. [S] Can be quite noisy at breakfast.

Buffet
American
Noisy
Reservations
strongly
suggested
7:30-11 am,
5:30-9:30 pm

▢ Hurricane Hanna's Grill   L $10, S

	6	8

This counter-service spot is operated seasonally and offers fairly typical pool bar food, such as burgers, hot dogs, salads, and sandwiches. It's located next to Stormalong Bay. [D] Vegetable wrap is $6.59; fruit boat is $3.99. [R] This grill offers a good selection of nonalcoholic drinks.

Counter
American
Noisy
Outdoor seats

▢ Crew's Cup   L $15, S

	8	7

This is a cozy bar that shares the kitchen with the next-door Yacht Club Galley, featuring a light lunchtime menu. Beer and ale are available from around the world, and you can order light appetizers until 10:00 pm. [D] Some salads are available. [L] Seating is in booths or lounge-type chairs.

Table
American
Med. noise
Noon-mid.

▢ Yacht Club Galley   B $22, L $32, D $39

	7	7

This casual eatery with a nautical theme serves up great grub for a reasonable price. Breakfast buffet ($15.99/adults and $8.99/kids) or a la carte, sandwiches, and entrées. This eatery is quieter and less hectic than other restaurants. [D] A number of lighter entrées for health-conscious diets are available. Tomato and mozzarella ciabatta ($9.19) at lunch; Roasted Portobello Mushroom Salad as entrée ($13.99) at dinner.

Buffet/Table
American
Short waits
7:30 am-11 am,
11:30 am-2 pm,
5:30-9:30 pm

▢ Yachtsman Steakhouse   D $72   🍬

	6	7

One of the better steakhouses on Disney property, this light, airy restaurant has a varied menu that also includes seafood and vegetarian options. [D] A few lighter entrées for health-conscious diets. At least one vegetarian selection, e.g., Winter Squash Ravioli ($21), is available. Be aware that the chefs here seem to go heavy on the seasonings! [F] To the left of the podium is a meat case with the beef that is to be cooked—If you're squeamish about seeing raw meat, avoid that area.

Table
Steakhouse
Noisy
Reservations
suggested
Med. waits
5:30-9:45 pm

Sidebar tabs: Planning, Special Challenges, Getting There, Staying in Style, Touring, Dining, Resources, Index

Room Service

Most Disney resorts have their **own version of "room service,"** from simple pizza delivery at the value resorts to full dinner entrées at the deluxe resorts. Room service menus are placed in each room (look by the TV, on the table, or in the nightstand), and most phones have a Room Service button on them. Although we have found the room service at the Walt Disney World Swan and Dolphin to be far superior in food quality than at the other Disney resorts, the food at the other resorts is perfectly adequate for those times when you don't want to or can't leave your room. It's not for the budget-conscious, though—room service meals are not only taxed with an automatic 18%–20% gratuity, but there is also a delivery charge, which may be a set fee or a percentage.

Important Note: Special requests may or may not be honored at the time of ordering. The best thing is to ask!

Available Room Service

Disney's Animal Kingdom Lodge (kosher meals available with 24 hours' notice)	6:00 am—midnight
All-Star Resorts—limited pizza, subs, beer, salads	4:00 pm—midnight
Boardwalk Inn/Villas	6:00 am—midnight
Caribbean Beach—pizza	4:00 pm—11:30 pm
Contemporary Resort	24 hours a day
Coronado Springs—limited full-day service	7:00 am—11:00 pm
Grand Floridian Resort & Spa	24 hours a day
Pop Century—limited pizza, subs, beer, salads	4:00 pm—midnight
Port Orleans—pizza, beer, wine, sodas	4:00 pm—midnight
Old Key West—pizza, beer, wine, sodas	4:00 pm—midnight
Polynesian Resort	6:30 am—midnight
Shades of Green	7:00 am—11:00 am and 4:00 pm—11:00 pm
Walt Disney World Swan and Dolphin	24 hours a day
Wilderness Lodge	7:00 am—11:00 am and 4:00 pm—midnight
Yacht and Beach Club	24 hours a day

Note that the following resorts offer room service **24 hours/day**: Contemporary, Grand Floridian, Walt Disney World Swan and Dolphin, and Yacht and Beach Club.

No room service/delivery is available at Fort Wilderness Resort & Campground or at Saratoga Springs Spa & Resort.

Character Meals

Disney offers many opportunities to dine with characters, both those in full guise (like Mickey Mouse) and "face characters" in costume (like Cinderella). While they don't actually sit with you throughout your meal, they roam around the restaurant and visit your table for autograph signing and picture-taking. Character meals are generally higher priced than regular meals (usually $17–$35 for adults and $9–$18 for kids ages 3–9), but the chance to meet the characters in an unhurried atmosphere makes it worthwhile, especially for those who can't tolerate waiting in the typically long "meet and greet" lines you find in the theme parks.

Even if meeting the characters isn't on your agenda, character dinners are a **good value** when you consider all the other factors—the cost of these buffets and family-style meals is usually less than comparable full-service meals when you factor all costs. Character meals are extremely popular—make arrangements as far in advance as possible (up to 180 days) at 407-939-3463. Remember to bring your camera and an autograph book!

Be aware that there's a **mad rush** for advance reservations at Cinderella's Royal Table in the Magic Kingdom. Folks start phoning at 7:00 am Eastern time, exactly 180 days prior to their desired date, and tables are often gone in a matter of minutes. This may be alleviated a bit with the recent addition of a character lunch at the restaurant, but we expect that will be popular as well. Payment in full at the time of booking is required for all meals at Cinderella's Royal Table. If you miss out, don't despair. Try again once you get to Walt Disney World. Cancellations are common, so it never hurts to ask for a table, even as you're walking through Cinderella Castle. If you are set on dining with a princess, try the Princess Storybook Dining at Akershus Royal Banquet Hall—now three meals with the princesses a day—or the character dinner at 1900 Park Fare. Chef Mickey's character meals also tend to sell out quickly.

✔ Some character breakfasts start prior to park opening. All Disney resorts offer special Disney bus transportation to the early character breakfasts. Be sure to allow plenty of travel time. Look for a special entrance designated for breakfast reservations. A cast member with clipboard will check off your name, allowing you to enter the turnstiles.

✔ Character meals at the resorts are typically less crowded than those at the theme parks. Consider the Cape May Cafe at breakfast or 1900 Park Fare for dinner.

✔ For the best experience, dine off-hours. While Mickey may only do a quick hello during busy mealtimes, you might end up with a close relationship when tables are empty.

✔ Don't forget to make any special dietary requests in advance! These character meals are preplated or buffets and so are not as flexible when it comes to special requests, unless the kitchen has had adequate advance notice.

✔ Don't be shy, grown-ups! Even if you aren't dining with kids, the characters visit your table. If you'd rather sit things out, though, simply indicate this, and they will simply give you a nod or handshake as they pass by.

✔ The "head" characters don't speak, but that doesn't mean you have to keep quiet. Talk to them and they'll pantomime and play along. They are especially good with special guests—we've seen them treat foreign-language speaking visitors like visiting royalty!

✔ Theme park admission is required for character meals in the parks.

Available Character Meals

(alphabetical by park, then by resort)

First price is for an adult, followed by a child ages 3–9.

"Chip and Dale's Harvest Feast" Garden Grill   Epcot (The Land)
Lunch ($19.99/$10.99) and dinner from 4:30 pm to 8:00 pm ($24.99/$10.99).

"Princess Storybook Dining"   Epcot (Norway's Akershus)
Breakfast ($21.99/$11.99) are 8:30 am–10:10 am; lunch ($23.99/$12.99) and dinner($27.99/$12.99).

"Donald's Breakfastosaurus"   Disney's Animal Kingdom
Daily at Restaurantosaurus in DinoLand U.S.A. $17.99/$9.99. Ends in Nov. 2007.

"A Buffet With Character"   Magic Kingdom (Crystal Palace)
Breakfast is from 8:00 am to 10:30 am ($17.99/$9.99), lunch is from 11:30 am to 3:00 pm ($19.99/$10.99), and dinner is from 4:00 pm and varies with park closing ($24.99/$10.99).

"A Fairytale Lunch at Cinderella's Royal Table" Magic Kingdom
Noon to 3:00 pm daily at Cinderella's Royal Table. $23.99/$12.99. Reservations required.

"Goofy's Liberate Your Appetite Dinner"   Magic Kingdom
At the Liberty Tree Tavern, featuring Minnie Mouse, Goofy, Pluto. $24.99/$10.99.

"Once Upon a Time Breakfast"   Magic Kingdom
At Cinderella's Royal Table, featuring Cinderella. $23.99/ $12.99. Reservations required.

"Beach Club Buffet"   Beach Club Resort
Breakfast ($17.99/$9.99) with Goofy and friends, daily at the Cape May Cafe.

"Chef Mickey's Fun Time Buffet"   Contemporary Resort
Daily from 7:00 am to 11:30 am ($17.99/$9.99) and from 5:00 to 9:30 pm ($26.99/ $11.99).

"Mickey's Backyard BBQ"   Fort Wilderness Resort
Offered from March to December only, held Tuesday and Thursday nights only from 6:30 pm to 9:30 pm. Cost is $44.99/$26.99 (tax and gratuity included).

"Supercalifragilistic Breakfast"   Grand Floridian Resort & Spa
At 1900 Park Fare with Mary Poppins and friends. $17.99/$10.99.

"Cinderella's Gala Feast"   Grand Floridian Resort & Spa
At 1900 Park Fare with Cinderella and her Storybook Friends. $27.99/$12.99.

"My Disney Girl's Perfectly Princess Tea Party" Grand Floridian Resort & Spa
At the Garden View Lounge on Sunday, Monday, Wednesday, Thursday, and Friday from 10:30 am to noon. One adult and one child (ages 3–9) is $200, including gratuity. Extra adult $65; extra child $135. 72-hour cancellation policy.

"Wonderland Tea Party"   Grand Floridian Resort & Spa
Hosted by Alice in Wonderland and friends, held at 1900 Park Fare. For children ages 4–10 only. Price $28.17 per child; available Monday through Friday at 1:30 pm.

'Ohana Best Friends Breakfast   Polynesian Resort
Served family style at 'Ohana from 7:30 am to 11:00 am daily. $17.99/$9.99.

"Good Morning Character Breakfast"   Walt Disney World Swan
At Garden Grove on Saturday and Sunday from 8:00 am to 11:00 am. $16.95/$8.50

Gulliver's Grill Character Dinner   Walt Disney World Swan
Disney characters nightly from 5:30 pm to 10:00 pm. $24.99/$10.95. A la carte service. Reservations accepted. Call 407-934-3000, ext. 1618.

Special Meals

Hoop Dee Doo Musical Revue

The Hoop Dee Doo Musical Revue, Walt Disney World's longest-running dinner show, will have you **doubled over with laughter and groans** and enjoying plain old country-style fare in spite of yourself.

Performed three times nightly in Pioneer Hall, the Hoop Dee Doo is well-known and beloved by many for its **vaudeville-style shtick**—no joke too slapstick, no pun too lame, for the cast of six players. But even if this singing and dancing, hootin' and hollerin' is not usually your cup of tea, we think you'll find yourself enjoying the show, along with an abundance of salad, fried chicken, barbecued ribs, corn, baked beans, and strawberry shortcake.

There's no plot to the show, and it's not sophisticated humor by any stretch—this is just an **old-fashioned, G-rated, good ol' time**. Before you're shown into the hall, you'll have your photo snapped (servers will come around during your meal to give you the chance to purchase). Once the doors open and everyone's seated, you have a chance to start on the salad and rolls with honey-sweetened butter. The performers introduce themselves with a rousing opening number and mingle a bit with the audience. After another number, they leave the stage and dinner is served.

The **all-you-care-to-eat dinner** is slammed on your table in old-fashioned pails—the fried chicken is moist, the ribs a bit smoky. Side dishes are served in the same way—slow-cooked baked beans and corn seasoned with onion and green pepper bits. For choosier children, the servers are more than happy to bring a variety of kid-tested fare—macaroni and cheese, hot dogs, and even peanut butter and jelly sandwiches are available upon request.

If the tall Mason jars filled to the brim with icy water aren't enough to slake your thirst, your server brings you the **beverage of your choice**: lemonade, milk (white and chocolate), soft drinks, iced tea, coffee, beer, or wine (cabernet, white zinfandel, chardonnay, or sangria) are all included.

As the main course draws to a conclusion, the **entertainment swings into high gear**. The performers return to engage the audience in celebrating birthdays and anniversaries and mingle once again with the crowd, not forgetting those seated at the upstairs tables. Finally, a rousing rendition of Woody Guthrie's "This Land Is Your Land" gets the audience really cheering, twirling their red gingham napkins wildly overhead.

Reader Tip: "The only time I really had to make a special request regarding a menu was when I took my son to the Hoop Dee Doo show, because he would never touch fried chicken or ribs. I gave them about 48 hours' notice, and they gladly provided him with exactly what he wanted: grilled cheese, apple sauce, broccoli, and apple juice, certainly not their regular fare. They were very accommodating and helpful; just give them enough notice."—contributed by Peter Johnson

Planning

Special Challenges

Getting There

Staying in Style

Touring

Dining

Resources

Index

Special Meals (continued)

After one more song, dessert is brought out amongst much fanfare and chorus-line-style high leg kicks—even the servers get into the act! Dishes of delectable **strawberry shortcake** smothered with whipped cream are plonked on the table, and as you gobble up this grand finale (with coffee if you want it), the players enact theirs—a tribute to Davy Crockett that includes the participation of several audience members. As the show draws to its end, servers run through and distribute washboards for the final number so that everyone can join in and make as much ruckus as possible.

Maybe this show is **not for everyone**, but for those who don't mind their ribs barbecued, their chicken southern-fried, and their humor corned, the Hoop Dee Doo is a must-do.

Special Diets: The Hoop Dee Doo Revue will accommodate your special dietary requests (vegetarian, diabetic, etc.) if you call at least 48 hours in advance. Make your requests at 407-824-2803. When you call, be prepared to answer questions about accommodations you need for your meal. Unlike other special requests (which will just alert the restaurant to be prepared for you to show up), when you call regarding this show they generally want to offer you suggestions and have you pick your substitutions on the spot. If you are calling for someone else, be sure you know exactly what they would prefer.

Pricing/Seating: The Hoop Dee Doo Musical Revue dinner show began new tiered pricing on January 1, 2007. Category 1 seats (first floor level with your table near the stage and in the middle of the action) are $58.99/adult and $29.99/kid age 3–9; category 2 seats (either first floor or in the center of the balcony) are $54.99/$26.99; category 3 seats (right or left side of the balcony) are $50.99/$25.99 (all prices include tax and gratuity; kids under 3 are no charge). Guests in need of wheelchair accessibility may only be seated in category 1; guests in category 2 or 3 may be required to ascend one flight of stairs. Discounts are sometimes available for annual passholders, Disney Vacation Club members, and Disney Visa card holders. Disney Dining Plan may be used for the Hoop Dee Doo for categories 2 and 3 only—two table-service credits will be deducted for this show. Shows are held at 5:00 pm, 7:15 pm, and 9:30 pm. Call 407-939-3463 for reservations. Reservations may be made 180 days in advance. Your credit card will be charged at the time the reservation is made. There is a 48-hour cancellation policy.

Bright Idea: Shows can sell out during busy times of the year. Be sure to request any special requirements at time of booking, but you'll need to reconfirm a day or two before your show.

How to Get There: Fort Wilderness guests board the internal bus to the Settlement Depot. You can also drive (and then transfer to an internal bus), take the boat from Contemporary, Wilderness Lodge, or the Magic Kingdom, or take a bus from the Transportation & Ticket Center or any park.

Looking for information on dining on the Disney Cruise Line? See pages 191.

Spirit of Aloha (Polynesian Luau)

Aloha! Presented nightly in Luau Cove, an open theater on the Seven Seas Lagoon, the Spirit of Aloha dinner show is everything that you'd expect from a **traditional luau**—women in "grass" skirts, men in face paint, fire dancers, traditional music, and a little bit of Elvis, as they all relate the modern Hawaii seen in Lilo and Stitch. Your hostess for the evening, Auntie Wini, invites you for a celebration of the cultures of Tahiti, Samoa, Tonga, New Zealand, and Hawaii, while you dine on a feast inspired by the flavors of Polynesia. Before the night is over, you'll learn all about their traditional values, including 'ohana (family).

Upon arrival, guests are presented with a complimentary lei and entertained in the garden before dinner. While you wait for the show, you can buy drinks and souvenirs and have a family photo taken. Guests are seated at long, wooden tables that fan out from the stage, all under shelter in the event of rain. The tables are long, so you may be seated with diners from another party. The **all-you-care-to-eat meal**, served family-style for your party, includes salad, fresh pineapple, roasted chicken, bbq ribs, rice, and sautéed vegetables, with a special "volcano dessert" (the name is the most exciting part). Included with your meal is your choice of unlimited soda, coffee, iced tea, milk, beer, and wine. Specialty drinks are extra. The show begins after dinner with Hawaiian music and South Seas dancing by both men and women. Children are quite welcome at the Luau. Although it's not as kid-friendly as the long-departed Mickey's Tropical Luau, the Lilo and Stitch tie-in helps, and the young ones will be invited on stage for a special dance. Photos can be picked up after the show. Shows are held at 5:15 pm and 8:00 pm, Tuesdays through Saturdays. We prefer the later seating as the darkness adds to the mystique and romance of the show. Annual passholders may get a discount on the late show (ask when you call). In the cooler months, the late show may be canceled. We highly recommend you make your reservations 180 days in advance or as early as possible. Travel directions are detailed on the next page.

Special Diets: The Spirit of Aloha show will accommodate your special dietary requests (vegetarian, diabetic, etc.) if you call at least 48 hours in advance. Make your requests at 407-824-2803. When you call, be prepared to answer questions about what you want as your meal. Unlike other special requests (which will just alert the restaurant to be prepared for you to show up), the chefs for this show generally want to offer you suggestions and have you pick your substitutions on the spot. If you are calling for someone else, be sure you know exactly what they would prefer.

Reader Tip: "Be sure to make your reservations for the Hoop Dee Doo Revue and the Spirit of Aloha shows as far in advance as possible, and have any accessibility needs noted on your reservation. There are no elevators at the Hoop Dee Doo for upstairs seating, but there is a special entrance for wheelchairs/ECVs at both shows."—contributed by peer reviewer Chet McDoniel

Planning

Special Challenges

Getting There

Staying in Style

Touring

Dining

Resources

Index

Special Meals (continued)

Pricing/Seating: The Spirit of Aloha dinner show began new tiered pricing on January 1, 2007. Category 1 seats (lower level, front and center) are $58.99/adult and $29.99/kid age 3–9; category 2 seats (lower level, either left or right side) are $54.99/$26.99; category 3 seats (lower level on extreme far right, or upper level) are $50.99/$25.99 (all prices include tax and gratuity; kids under 3 are no charge). Discounts are sometimes available for annual passholders, Disney Vacation Club members, and Disney Visa card holders. Disney Dining Plan may be used for the Spirit of Aloha—two table-service credits will be deducted for this show. Shows are held at 5:15 pm and 8:00 pm, Tuesday–Saturday. Call 407-939-3463 for reservations. Reservations may be made 180 days in advance. Your credit card will be charged at the time the reservation is made. There is a 48-hour cancellation policy.

How to get there: To get to the Polynesian Luau, you can drive directly to the Polynesian Resort. From the Magic Kingdom, take the resort monorail. From other parks, bus to the Polynesian. From other resorts, bus to the Magic Kingdom and take the monorail (daytime) or bus (evening) to Downtown Disney and transfer to a Polynesian bus. Once inside the resort, follow signs to Luau Cove. Allow plenty of time for travel, especially from a resort.

House of Blues Gospel Brunch

If you're looking for something other than the run-of-the-mill Sunday brunch, head on over to the House of Blues at Downtown Disney's West Side. Twice each Sunday (at 10:30 am and 1:00 pm), this casual eatery, famous for its live entertainment, serves up 90 minutes of **grub and gospel revue**. You get about 45 minutes to sample the buffet, which consists of many of the usual brunch suspects mixed with some more Southern-inspired fare: pastries, breads, sausage, bacon, grits, prawns with cocktail sauce, smoked catfish, assorted salads, barbecued chicken, and chicken jambalaya, as well as roasted meats, made-to-order omelets, and desserts. After brunch, you're treated to 45 minutes of uplifting music and entertainment from a rotating cadre of gospel performers.

Special Needs Considerations: Seating in the front section nearest the stage is at long communal tables, on hard, narrow, wooden folding chairs. There is not much room to move, and once the show begins, with folks getting up and sitting down, it is fairly awkward. Seating around the back and sides of the restaurant and up in the balcony is at tables or booths, with some cocktail tables and stools. Lighting in the restaurant is very dim. Special diets can be accommodated with at least 72 hours' notice.

Ticket prices, as of February 2007: $32.50/adults; $16.25 children 3–9; under 3 free. Inquire about discounts for Annual Passholders or Disney Vacation Club members. For reservations, call 407-934-BLUE (2583).

How to get there: Follow the directions for getting to Downtown Disney in chapter 5 on page 311.

IN FOCUS: Traveling With Special Dietary Concerns

When Lydia Economou was planning her family's first trip to Walt Disney World, her biggest concern was for her son Andrew, who is lactose intolerant.

"I was afraid he would get sick from the milk products and then not be able to enjoy the park, making it a wasted trip," she recalls. "I was also concerned that the parks might have snacks that were lactose-free, but still not be snacks that I approve of—like ones that are mostly sugar."

What Lydia found, though, was that if they went to the table-service restaurants and let the servers know about her son's issues, they almost always had a chef come out to speak to them. "That was always a great comfort," Lydia notes. "They told us specifically what he should or should not eat. Also, main dishes are usually less of an issue since the milk is usually added to sauces or vegetables. So the restaurants can and did prepare the meat or vegetable free of milk products."

Still, she found that lactose-free desserts were limited, no matter where they went. On top of that, she was dealing with a picky child, so that sometimes he did without, and very unhappily. That is when they would try to track down the shaved ice (Kaki Gori) in Japan in World Showcase, one of his favorite desserts.

What helped, Lydia says, was carrying some of her own snacks that she knew Andrew could eat so they didn't need to wait until they could find an acceptable place.

They've returned to Walt Disney World several times since that first trip, and now that Andrew is older and able to take a lactase pill that allows lactose-intolerant people to ingest dairy products more easily, things are a lot better. Lydia's also found that even though more places carry lactose-free milk now, it is mostly fat-free, which is not so desirable, as they would like Andrew to gain weight.

© Lydia Economou

"Our solution," she says, "is to make sure we rent a car, so we can pick up some special milk ourselves and keep it in the room fridge."

Andrew Economou

·········>

Planning

Special Challenges

Getting There

Staying in Style

Touring

Dining

Resources

Index

Quick Bites: Special Tips From Our Peer Reviewers

Peer reviewer Susie Koppel advises, "**Certain dietary items can be delivered** with enough advance notice, even to counter-service spots. For instance, I called and requested dairy-free margarine at Flame Tree Barbecue for a particular date and approximate time. It was there waiting for my son to enjoy his corn on the cob. They have a list available for items they can deliver to counter-service places with advance notice."

Peer reviewer Michelle Hohmann says, "**Coral Reef at Epcot is the favorite restaurant** of my daughter, who has ADHD/Asperger's Syndrome. I can't tell you how many times we've enjoyed a great lunch because she could finally sit still and be mesmerized by the fish and by trying to match the fish on the card they gave us to what was in the aquarium. A tip: Arrive at least 10 minutes early for the first lunch seating of the day so you can ask for the coveted aquarium-side seats."

Peer reviewer Kitty Smith comments, "**Kona Café is a favorite restaurant for this vegan.** The Stir-Fried Asian Noodles dish is available as a vegan entrée without prior notice, and it's very tasty! Also, I was able to get soy milk instead of creamer, for a wonderful cup of their special coffee!"

Peer reviewer Kathy Sauviac notes, "**People with noise sensitivities** should be aware that the Hoop Dee Doo Revue may be a lot to deal with, especially the loud banging of buckets on the table and the 'washboard' activity. Consider bringing earplugs for children or avoid the show altogether for cases that are severe."

Peer reviewer Blossom Zell says, "**Dine at the buffet meals!** After a long day of touring, the kids get very, very hungry, tired, and irritable. With any kind of behavioral issue, being hungry and tired equals a lack of tolerance. With a buffet, you can be seated and they can start their meal almost immediately. The addition of some characters keeps everyone busy and happy. Many times we've started out with grumpy people, but after Chip and Dale came by, everyone was smiling! It's the definition of magic!"

Peer reviewer Carol Scopa advises, "**Have a fruit or food gift basket sent to your room.** This way you have fresh fruit and snacks for breakfast, snack, or a light lunch. Call the Disney Florist at 407-827-3505 or ask the front desk for a local florist that may deliver."

© Debra Martin Koma

Expert peer reviewer Masayo Kano (right) and friends at 'Ohana character breakfast

Dining Tips and Stories

Whenever I travel, I carry a few "Special Dietary Needs" cards with me. They are business card size. I can make them at home or order them. I include my food allergies (onions, aspartame, nuts, dairy, etc.) as well as a "special salad" recipe that is my favorite: plain, not marinated, chicken, iceberg and romaine lettuce, black olives, and red roasted peppers. I give the card to the server who in turn gives it to the chef. The staff always appreciates that it is spelled out exactly for them. I have never been disappointed. This one simple idea has saved me time and time again. It is so easy and efficient."   —contributed by Anonymous

Our two oldest sons are lactose intolerant, so we and the boys are used to making dietary adjustments to accommodate them. Last weekend we had lunch at The Liberty Tree Tavern in the Magic Kingdom, one of our favorite stops. When the waiter raised an eyebrow at our orders of cheeseless pizzas for the kids, I mentioned the lactose intolerance. Minutes later, the chef himself came to our table with a notepad and said the chef will always come out to the table whenever there is any dietary concern or allergy, to ensure safety and guest satisfaction! The chef suggested alternative sides to replace the salad with ranch dressing, and mentioned that if we ordered dessert, they had a lactose-free ice cream!   —contributed by Mary Mahaney

When I travel with a group of special needs adults, it's difficult for them to stand in line and wait to see characters in the parks. You never know when the characters will be whisked off without notice, and the guys wouldn't understand that Mickey had to go to the washroom and might not be back for some time, so we're basically out of luck! So I make character breakfast reservations for the latest possible time (usually 9:45 a.m.) and we do it as a brunch. The guys I support are guaranteed to see the characters, get a photo taken, and an autograph. Since it's so late, the characters are just hanging around and they aren't rushed to move on to the next table, so I've found that they have lots of patience.   —contributed by Anonymous

We did a three-day Disney Cruise with my three children, one of whom has severe food allergies. Do not be afraid to let your child go into any of the kids' clubs—mine did, had a ball, and had NO problems. All it took was a little planning on my part. He did fine, and then the staff at the kids' club got him his own special dinner so that he could eat with the other kids ... very accommodating and never a worry. Also, at Walt Disney World, don't hesitate to quiz the servers about what is in the foods. If they don't know, they will ask the chef. Frequently, the chef has come out to talk to us about the menu, either what my son can have or what is in the buffet that he can have. I have also found that if I ask the chef for something he can have and likes they will make it for him! At Tony's Town Square this trip, the chef made meatballs without egg or milk products in them—just meat and seasonings, because that was the way my son could eat it and that was the way he liked it! Disney is by far the easiest place to go with my son who has multiple severe food allergies.   —contributed by Renee Kilgarriff

I put all the phone numbers of the eateries we eat at in my cell phone. I use these numbers to call the eateries about one hour prior to our dining reservation so preparations could begin for our special dietary meals. I also entered the four theme park phone numbers for special diets in case I needed to check a food or have a question. And don't forget Disney's main number (407-824-2222) to contact whatever you may have forgotten.   —contributed by peer reviewer Susie Koppel

Dining Tips and Stories
(continued)

My son, Nick, is 4 years old and has autism. Prior to going to Walt Disney World, I checked all of the menus on AllEars.net to determine which restaurants my picky family would like. I called Disney Dining (407-939-3463) and obtained reservations for all of our sit-down plans to reduce any wait time for Nick, as he has trouble waiting for anything. For my trip coming up this year, I have called to make my reservations and asked if I could request seating in a booth if available. They told me that I could request that when I arrive. Nick is easier to handle sitting in a booth as he is contained to some degree, as opposed to a chair which he can escape from on either side.   —contributed by Tamara Osborne

Send an adult to a counter-service eatery ahead of the group to order a special food item. We ordered a low-allergen meal ahead of time so that our special needs child does not have to wait and everyone can eat together. Our system worked great. It was such a breeze! The chefs were all very well educated in our dietary needs, and they were incredibly friendly. This ease of feeding my daughter on our trip is what truly made our vacation a magical experience. I loved the simplicity and availability, but most importantly, I loved that she was never left out anywhere we went. She was always included, never left to stare longingly at everyone else's plates. She loved every eatery we visited on our Disney vacation, and we can't wait to go back!—contributed by Laura Schmitt

I keep Glatt kosher and my family and I have traveled numerous times to Walt Disney World. With enough planning, you can have a completely Glatt kosher vacation, even enjoying many of the restaurants and shows that everyone else enjoys. The first thing to decide is how many meals you want to eat out. Then you can decide what food you need to either bring, ship, or shop for. We usually do a combination of all three. We ship nonperishables, we bring some perishables, and shop for the rest. The Publix on Orange Lake Boulevard has the most expansive kosher groceries available in the immediate area. You can make advance dining reservations for most Disney restaurants, but you'll be getting prepackaged food that is double wrapped. I have found that the servers' knowledge and sometimes even the chef's knowledge varies tremendously and you might need to tell them what you want, e.g., not to open up the double sealed meals or bread, to give you "to go" cups instead of the regular cups, etc. The food is not fine dining quality but you are at Disney and want to soak up the Disney atmosphere, so fine dining is not the top priority. For breakfast, there are only two choices: cheese blintzes and cheese omelets. Both are acceptable but are problematic for those with dairy allergies. I have contacted Weberman Foods (the provider of the kosher meals) and they informed me that they will be coming out with meals that are allergen-free. At all of our breakfast buffets, we found that the staff was very helpful and allowed us to take fresh fruit from the buffet without any problem. Lunch and dinner are the same at all table-service restaurants: brisket, glazed chicken breast, salmon, or cheese lasagna for adults; breaded chicken strips, hot dog, or macaroni and cheese for kids. Meals are accompanied by desserts if you are doing a buffet or the Disney Dining Plan. We enjoy being able to dine with characters or being able to see the Hoop Dee Doo Revue. If anyone in your family does not eat sugar, there are no sugar-free desserts available. Weberman's told me that they will consider the idea of adding a sugar-free alternative to the kosher menu, but until then, you will have to satisfy your sweet tooth with fresh fruit, which luckily is quite abundant. The bottom line is that you can really enjoy Disney while maintaining your kosher standards.   —contributed by Joy Jacobs

Finding Pixie Dust and Resources

We've told you the whos, whats, whens, wheres, hows, and even the whys of staying at Walt Disney World and cruising aboard the Disney Cruise Line, but would you believe there's still more we could tell? We've been on countless Disney vacations, and there's still more to do each time we go. In this chapter, we've added a few things that are sort of the "icing on the cake"—a little pixie dust that adds to the magic of a Disney vacation.

Is a member of your group celebrating a birthday or anniversary? We tell you what you can do to ring in your special day in grand style! Are you hoping to tie the knot? We'll point you in the right direction for planning a wedding or even a vow renewal. Looking for a night out without the kids? We explain various childcare options, including alternatives for families traveling with special needs children. Planning to attend (or maybe avoid) a special Disney event? We provide you with a calendar of Disney's upcoming festivals, holiday celebrations, and other special activities.

Even if you don't have a special event to celebrate, you can enhance your trip by trying some of the other ideas you'll find in this chapter. If you're with someone who gets bored easily or doesn't tolerate standing in lines well, searching for the Hidden Mickeys or coin press machines we discuss here will keep their active minds (and bodies) busy. Hunting for and finding the Disney characters can be another adventure, while collecting autographs and/or photographs is a special activity in and of itself. Use or adapt the suggestions we've made in this chapter to your benefit ... and let us know what others you come up with!

Finally, even a book of this size may leave you with some unanswered questions. We've compiled a list of resources that we think will be helpful to travelers with special challenges—they certainly came in handy for us as we developed this book! In addition, we've added numerous other resources—web sites, magazines, and other programs—contributed by our expert peer reviewers. These are tried-and-true resources that have proven valuable to travelers with a variety of special challenges. We hope you'll find them useful as well.

Planning

Your Special Need

Getting There

Staying in Style

Touring

Dining

Resources

Index

Making Pixie Dust

Time to Celebrate

There are plenty of ways to make a birthday special at Walt Disney World. Stop at Guest Relations in any of the theme parks and ask for a **"Today's My Birthday" button** for the birthday boy or girl to wear. You'll be surprised at the special treatment you get! (On a recent trip, Deb Wills encouraged a group of her friends to sing Happy Birthday to a girl she spotted wearing the button in Epcot!) Even if you're too shy to wear the button, dial "0" from a Disney resort phone and ask to hear the special birthday message. Oh, and be sure to mention the birthday to restaurant servers, too!

Authors Deb and Deb show off their special birthday dessert at Narcoossee's

Bright Idea: Disney recently changed the special event buttons they hand out, and there are now buttons for other special occasions, too! Ask for a "1ˢᵗ Visit," "Congratulations," or "Happy Anniversary" button, if the occasion fits. Several of the new buttons have a space in which you can write your name for an even more personalized experience.

If you want a **birthday party** for your child, there are a number of alternatives. For kids 4–12, contact one of the childcare clubs (see next page). For other parties or birthday cruises on Walt Disney World's waterways, contact Disney directly at 407-WDW-PLAY (407-939-7529).

Another idea is to have an outside outfit, such as Gifts of a Lifetime, **decorate your hotel room** while you're at a park or create a special birthday treasure hunt or anniversary vow renewal event. For details, visit http://www.giftsofalifetime.com.

Celebrating a birthday onboard

On the **Disney Cruise Line**, mention your birthday or anniversary at the time you reserve your cruise, and remind your servers again when you board. Cruisers celebrating birthdays and anniversaries get a special cake at dinner and a serenade from their dining room servers. You can also bring or purchase decorations for your stateroom! Consider decorating your stateroom while the birthday boy or girl is eating lunch on embarkation day; then when the room is seen for the first time, it'll be all decked out for the special event!

Grown-Ups Need a Night Out … Alone!
Taking a night out on the town without the kids may be a bit difficult for families with a special needs child. Several Disney resorts offer childcare clubs, but they will only accept children 4–12 who are potty-trained. In addition, these childcare clubs won't accept children who require specialized one-on-one attention. If, however, your child will be fine on his/her own, you can make arrangements at 407-WDW-DINE (407-939-3463) in advance.

Important Note: There have been reports that occasionally, Disney's childcare club will take a special needs child, providing parents with a beeper so they can be called on to change diapers or assist the child with toileting. Be honest when you make your childcare club reservation regarding the child's needs. The cast members at the childcare club will make the final determination.

Here's a list of **Disney's child care clubs**:
- ✔ Camp Dolphin (Dolphin hotel)
- ✔ Simba's Cubhouse (Animal Kingdom Lodge)
- ✔ Mouseketeer Club (Grand Floridian)
- ✔ Cub's Den (Wilderness Lodge)
- ✔ Never Land Club (Polynesian)
- ✔ Sandcastle Club (Yacht & Beach Club)

Rates are about $11/hour per child, and some clubs have a minimum stay. Parents are given pagers so they can be reached if there's a problem.

If your child has special needs, **in-room babysitting** is another option. Kid's Nite Out (407-828-0920) offers Disney-sanctioned, private babysitting 24 hours a day. Two other independent childcare agencies, Fairy Godmothers (407-275-7326) and All About Kids (407-812-9300), offer similar services. With advance notice, the professional sitters will watch infants and children with some special needs. The sitters are bonded, insured, and well-trained and come equipped with games and activities. Rates vary, depending on the age and number of the children.

If your child requires **other medical care** that the babysitters are unable to provide, such as help with gastric feeding tubes (g-tubes), you may want to contact the Visiting Nurse Association at Orlando Regional Health Care Systems at 407-854-3100 for additional options.

Will You Marry Me?
Some people come to Walt Disney World to get engaged; others come for their anniversaries or honeymoons, still others come for the Big Event—the wedding itself! In fact, Disney's Fairy Tale Weddings department will plan your special occasion, whether it's a wedding or a vow renewal, from intimate to blow-out celebration. For details, call 321-939-4610 or visit http://www.disneyweddings.com.

A Disney wedding

Making Pixie Dust (continued)

What's a Hidden Mickey?

They can take many forms, but the traditional two circles (ears) on top of a larger circle (Mickey's head), make a Hidden Mickey. Sometimes you'll even find Mickey's profile or his whole body! Once an inside joke for Imagineers and cast members, Hidden Mickeys are now popular with guests. There are hundreds scattered throughout Walt Disney World and the Disney Cruise Line, and trying to spot them can be a great diversion for an antsy child (or adult). You can find them everywhere: your resort bedspread, designed into furniture, on the wall of an attraction—you never know where they will turn up. To help get you started, check out the "Hidden Mickeys" guide by Steven M. Barrett (Intrepid Traveler), available in bookstores, many stores around Disney, and on the PassPorter web site. He also has a web site at http://www.hiddenmickeysguide.com.

© Debra Martin Koma

A Hidden Mickey at Maharajah Jungle Trek

Press a Penny

Looking for an inexpensive souvenir? Make a pressed coin. The machines can be found all over the parks and resorts. For 51 cents (pressed penny) or $1.25 (pressed quarter), you get a flattened coin that sports designs of Disney characters, the attractions, and a variety of Disney logos. Peer reviewer Josh Olive advises, "Keep your pressed pennies in a sealed bag on water rides—a bit of moisture will turn your newly pressed coins green!"

Bright Idea: Use shiny pennies from 1985 or earlier, as they have less zinc in them. When they are pressed, they make a more uniform copper-colored penny.

Take a Tour

Disney offers guided tours and behind-the-scenes peeks—see page 325.

Meet a Character

For kids young and old, being at Disney is all about seeing the characters. And we've heard from many relatives of Disney-goers with special challenges that spending time with the characters has done them a world of good, from simply boosting their spirits to even encouraging them to try new words. So how do you find the characters? They're all around the Disney theme parks and on the cruise ships. The best way to find them is to check with Guest Relations when you first get to the park. If you have a specific character that you simply *must* see, ask a cast member—they have a special phone number they can call to find out such information. You can also consult the theme park's times guide (or cruise's Navigator) to find out the times and locations of meet and greet spots. Be sure to arrive early—lines form fast. If you're after an autograph, have a thicker pen and your autograph book at the ready. If you're hoping for a photograph, too, keep your camera handy.

Special Events

Every month of the year, there is **something special happening** at Walt Disney World. Just about every holiday has a special event, and Christmas and Halloween even have their own special "parties" at the Magic Kingdom. Here's just a sampling of what you can expect. For more information on these events, visit http://www.allears.net or check our *PassPorter's Walt Disney World* guidebook.

From now through December 31, 2007, Walt Disney World and Disneyland are celebrating **The Year of a Million Dreams** with the Disney Dreams Giveaway promotion, during which more than a million extra-special dreams are being randomly awarded. A Dream Squad cast member might tap you on the shoulder and announce that you've been invited as a special guest of the princess herself to enjoy a stay that night in the all-new Cinderella Castle Suite in the heart of the Magic Kingdom. You may receive a DREAM FASTPASS badge to enjoy some of the most popular Disney attractions with little or no wait. Or a cast member might even let you know you've been selected to win a Grand Marshal World Tour trip to Disney Parks around the globe.

January–March: Run, walk fast, or wheel fast in the **Walt Disney World Marathon** and Half Marathon in January (http://www.disneysports.com). Celebrate Mardi Gras, Valentine's Day, and St. Patrick's Day with special activities at Pleasure Island, and in March, watch the Atlanta Braves work out the kinks in spring training at Disney's Wide World of Sports. The **Pirate and Princess Party** in the Magic Kingdom (extra charge) may also take place during this time frame.

April–June: Epcot leads the way with the six-week **International Flower & Garden Festival** and Flower Power Concert series. The Disney-MGM Studios hosts Star Wars Weekends, Grad Nights take over the Magic Kingdom for several evenings, and then there's Mother's Day!

July–August: The summer heats up with amazing fireworks displays celebrating **Independence Day**. Professional football's Tampa Bay Buccaneers hold training camp at Disney's Wide World of Sports. The **Pirate and Princess Party** in the Magic Kingdom (extra charge) may also take place during this time frame.

September–December: **Nights of Joy** in September bring some of the biggest talents in Christian rock. **Epcot's International Food & Wine Festival** offers free and ticketed seminars and dining events, as well as a smorgasbord of ethnic cuisines in food booths located around the World Showcase Lagoon. **Mickey's Not-So-Scary Halloween Party** brings happy haunts to the Magic Kingdom on selected nights. Sports fans will enjoy the **Funai Classic** golf tournament. **ABC Super Soap Weekend** features your favorite daytime TV stars for a few days of autographs and fun. And the December holidays are observed in style with a variety of annual events: The Candlelight Processional is a moving show filled with music and the narration of the Christmas story. The Osborne Family Spectacle of Lights dominates the Studios. **Mickey's Very Merry Christmas Party** is held on certain nights in the Magic Kingdom, complete with hot cocoa and "snow" on Main Street, U.S.A. And what better place to celebrate New Year's Eve than Walt Disney World?

Resources

Our research journey for this guidebook introduced us to many informative resources. And our expert peer reviewers submitted their favorite sites to help special travelers, too. These resources range from those specifically about an individual special need to those that arrange for rental equipment or actual vacations for special travelers. We hope that you will find some of these sites useful, too.

General Information

Deb's Unofficial Walt Disney World Information Guide:
http://www.allears.net

Walt Disney World Disabilities Guide:
http://disneyworld.disney.go.com/wdw/common/Plain?id=PlainHomePage

National Institutes of Health:
http://health.nih.gov

Council for Exceptional Children:
http://www.cec.sped.org

Centers for Disease Control:
http://www.cdc.gov/travel

TSA (Transportation Security Administration):
http://www.tsa.gov/travelers/index.shtm

Federal Aviation Administration:
http://www.faa.gov/passengers/

Canadian Transportation Agency Air Travel Accessibility Regulations:
http://www.cta-otc.gc.ca/access/regs/air_e.html

Information for Guests with Disabilities:
http://www.disneyworld.com *(click on Disabilities link at bottom of page)*

Society for Accessible Travel and Hospitality:
http://www.sath.org

ABLEDATA (information on assistive technology):
http://www.abledata.com
8630 Fenton Street, Suite 930, Silver Spring, MD 20910
800-227-0216 or 301-608-8998; TTY: 301-608-8912

Special Message Boards or Areas

Our own PassPorter Forum for Vacationing With Special Needs:
http://www.passporterboards.com/forums/vacationing-your-way-your-special-needs

DIS Boards disABILITIES forum:
http://www.disboards.com/forumdisplay.php?f=20

MousePlanet.com Theme Park Access Guide:
http://mousepad.mouseplanet.com/forumdisplay.php?f=16

Special Needs Sites

ADHD [A]
ADHD/ADD and related disorders (they also have a magazine):
http://www.additudemag.com

CHADD—Children and Adults With Attention-Deficit/Hyperactivity Disorder:
http://www.chadd.org/

Answers to your questions about ADD:
http://addvance.com

National Institutes of Mental Health:
http://www.nimh.nih.gov/publicat/adhd.cfm

Attention Deficit Disorder Association:
http://www.add.org

Addiction Recovery [R]
Addiction Recovery Guide:
http://www.addictionrecoveryguide.org

Alcoholics Anonymous:
http://www.alcoholics-anonymous.org

Alcoholics Anonymous Orange County, FL meetings:
http://aaorlandointergroup.org

Alcoholics Anonymous Osceola County, FL meetings:
http://osceolaintergroup.org

Gamblers Anonymous:
http://www.gamblersanonymous.org

Planning
Your Special Need
Getting There
Staying in Style
Touring
Dining
Resources
Index

Resources (continued)

Narcotics Anonymous:
http://www.na.org

Overeaters Anonymous:
http://www.oa.org

Allergies/Asthma [G]
Local pollen reports and forecasts (Walt Disney World's ZIP code is 32830):
http://www.pollen.com

Asthma and vacations
http://www.asthma-education.com/info16.html

Allergy and Asthma Network Mothers of Asthmatics:
http://www.breatherville.org

Asthma resources for parents:
http://www.keepkidshealthy.com/asthma

Corn Allergens:
http://www.cornallergens.com

Latex Allergy Resources:
http://www.latexallergyresources.com

Autism Spectrum Disorders [U]
Autism Society of America:
http://www.autism-society.org

Autism One Radio, a web-based broadcast:
http://www.autismone.org

Autism Research Institute:
http://www.autismwebsite.com/ari/index.htm

Asperger Syndrome:
http://www.udel.edu/bkirby/asperger

Autism Speaks:
http://www.autismspeaks.org

Chronic Fatigue Syndrome and Fibromyalgia [C]
Chronic Fatigue Syndrome:
http://www.niaid.nih.gov/factsheets/cfs.htm

Chronic Fatigue and Immune Dysfunction Syndrome (CFIDS) Association:
http://www.cfids.org

National Fibromyalgia Association:
http://fmaware.org

National Fibromyalgia Research Association:
http://www.nfra.net

Diet [D]
The Food Allergy and Anaphylaxis Network:
http://www.foodallergy.org (English and Spanish)

Celiac Disease and Eating Gluten-Free:
http://www.celiac.com

Gluten Intolerance Group of North America:
http://www.gluten.net

Vegetarian/vegan message board:
http://www.veggieboards.com/boards/index.php

Vegetarian- and vegan-friendly restaurants, resorts, and shops:
http://vegetarianusa.com

National Institutes of Health—Food Allergies:
http://www.niaid.nih.gov/factsheets/food.htm

Food and Drug Administration: Information about food allergens:
http://www.cfsan.fda.gov/~dms/wh-alrgy.html

Peanut Allergy—information and discussion boards:
http://www.peanutallergy.com

Vegan and vegetarian articles, recipes, message boards:
http://www.vegsource.com

Gluten-Free Casein Free Diet for Autistic Spectrum Disorders
http://www.gfcdiet.com

Vegetarian Resource Group:
http://www.vrg.org

Planning

Your Special Need

Getting There

Staying in Style

Touring

Dining

Resources

Index

Resources (continued)

Down Syndrome, Fragile X, and Other Cognitive Disabilities [I]
National Fragile X Foundation:
http://www.nfxf.org

The Fragile X Research Foundation:
http://www.fraxa.org

National Down Syndrome Society:
http://www.ndss.org (English and Spanish)

Fears [F]
National Library of Medicine Phobias/Anxiety:
http://www.nlm.nih.gov/medlineplus/phobias.html

Teen Health—Fears and Phobias:
http://kidshealth.org/teen/your_mind/mental_health/phobias.html

Foreign Language [Ö]
USA Tourist: French, Spanish, German, Japanese:
http://www.usatourist.com

Currency Exchange:
http://www.oanda.com/convert/classic

Universal Currency Converters:
http://www.xe.net/ucc
http://content.virgin.net/uk.vnetuk/travel/travelcurrency.htm

Hearing [H]
National Association of the Deaf Air Travel:
http://www.nad.org/airtravel

Able Access Travel—TTY numbers:
http://www.access-able.com/relay.html

Heart Health [♥]
National Heart and Lung Blood Institute:
http://www.nhlbi.nih.gov

American Heart Association:
http://www.americanheart.org

Women's Heart Foundation:
http://womensheartfoundation.org

Healthy Heart Guide:
http://www.healthy-heart-guide.com

Infants *[B]*
Centers for Disease Control: Traveling with infants and children:
http://www.cdc.gov/travel/child_travel.htm

Abilitations (products for children with special needs):
http://abilitations.com

Gabby's Swim Diapers:
http://www.gabbys.net

Medical Treatment *[T]*
Epilepsy and seizure information for patients and health professionals:
http://www.epilepsy.com

Epilepsy Foundation:
http://www.epilepsyfoundation.org

American Diabetes Association:
http://www.diabetes.org

Diabetes and More (information, supplies and accessories):
http://www.diabetesandmore.com

American Sleep Apnea Association (has a Spanish message board):
http://www.sleepapnea.org

Spina Bifida Association (has latex info; in English and Spanish):
http://www.sbaa.org

Juvenile Diabetes Research Foundation International (traveling):
http://www.jdrf.org/index.cfm?page_id=103441

Companies that rent medical equipment (in addition to renting wheelchairs/ECVs as mentioned in chapter 5, Wheels section):

Apria Healthcare (407-291-2229):
http://www.apria.com

CARE Medical (800-741-2282):
http://www.caremedicalequipment.com

The Neuropathy Association:
http://www.neuropathy.org

Reflex Sympathetic Dystrophy Syndrome:
http://www.rsds.org

Sensory Processing Disorder Community Network:
http://www.sinetwork.org

Planning

Your Special Need

Getting There

Staying in Style

Touring

Dining

Resources

Index

Resources (continued)

Dialysisfinder (dialysis center locator service)—Walt Disney World's ZIP code is 32830:
http://www.dialysisfinder.com

Medical Travel, Inc.:
http://www.medicaltravel.org

Medical Travel, Inc. caters to patients with special medical needs and can arrange vacations for dialysis patients, wheelchair users, those requiring oxygen, and others. They also can arrange wheelchair-accessible villa rentals just four miles from Walt Disney World. 5184 Majorca Club Drive, Boca Raton, FL 33486. 800-778-7953

Mental Health *[T]*
Child & Adolescent Bipolar Foundation—For families of children and adolescents with bipolar disorder and professionals who serve them:
http://www.bpkids.org

National Mental Health Association (English and Spanish):
http://www.nmha.org

NAMI (formerly National Alliance for the Mentally Ill):
http://www.nami.org

Healthyplace.com:
http://www.healthyplace.com

A parent's guide to helping kids with learning difficulties:
http://www.schwablearning.org

Tourette Syndrome Online:
http://www.tourette-syndrome.com

Tourette Syndrome Association, Inc.:
http://www.tsa-usa.org

Mobility *[M]*
Cerebral Palsy:
http://www.ucp.org

Motion Sensitivity [Q]
American Academy of Otolaryngology (Head and Neck Surgery) Dizziness and Motion Sickness:
http://www.entnet.org/healthinfo/balance/dizziness.cfm

Motion Sickness:
http://www.nlm.nih.gov/medlineplus/motionsickness.html

Seasickness:
http://www.seasickness.co.uk

Sean's Seasickness:
http://www.seasickness.org

Physical Therapy [P]
American Physical Therapy Association:
http://www.apta.org/Consumer

Pregnancy/Fertility [E]
Pregnancy Travel
http://www.babycenter.com/pregnancy/pregnancytravel/index

American Pregnancy Association
http://www.americanpregnancy.org

Religion [W]
Kosher travel:
http://www.kashrut.com

Kosher restaurant database:
http://www.shamash.org

First Baptist Church of Kissimmee:
http://www.fbckissimmee.com

Mary, Queen of the Universe Roman Catholic Shrine:
http://www.maryqueenoftheuniverse.org

Celebration Presbyterian Church:
http://www.commpres.org

Islamic Society of Central Florida:
http://www.iscf.org

Celebration Jewish Congregation:
http://www.jrf.org/cjc/index.htm

Planning

Your Special Need

Getting There

Staying in Style

Touring

Dining

Resources

Index

Planning

Your Special Need

Getting There

Staying in Style

Touring

Dining

Resources

Index

Resources (continued)

Seniors *[S]*
Association for Advancement of Retired Persons (AARP):
http://www.aarp.com

Sensory Sensitivities, Behavior, and Attention Challenges *[A][U][T]*
Henry Occupational Therapy Services, Inc. (articles, stories, workshops, and sensory products):
http://www.ateachabout.com

Service Animals *[X]*
Commonly asked questions about service animals:
http://www.usdoj.gov/crt/ada/svcanimb.htm

International Association of Assistance Dog Partners:
http://www.iaadp.org

Human-Animal Health Connection:
http://www.deltasociety.org

Paws With a Cause:
http://www.pawswithacause.org

Size *[L]*
Size Wise—Your World Your Size:
http://www.sizewise.com

AmpleStuff (travel products for people of size):
http://amplestuff.safeshopper.com/21/cat21.htm?691

National Association to Advance Fat Acceptance:
http://www.naafa.org/

Vision *[V]*
Blind Children's Resource Center:
http://www.blindchildren.org

Travel tips for people who are blind or visually impaired:
http://www.access-able.com/tips/braille.htm

Center for the Partially Sighted:
http://www.low-vision.org

Magazines

ABILITY Magazine (949-854-8700):
http://www.abilitymagazine.com

Emerging Horizons: Accessible Travel Information (209-599-9409):
http://www.emerginghorizons.com

Exceptional Parent Magazine (800-EPARENT or 800-372-7368):
http://www.eparent.com

Living Without Magazine (food allergies/preferences, 847-480-8810):
http://www.livingwithout.com

Spectrum Magazine for Autism Spectrum Disorders:
http://www.spectrumpublications.com

ADDitude (888-762-8475):
http://www.additudemag.com

Travel Sites

Centers for Disease Control's Traveler's Health:
http://www.cdc.gov/travel

FAA information for passengers with disabilities:
http://www.faa.gov/passengers

Guide to airline seating (covers most airlines)
http://www.seatguru.com

Canadian Transportation Agency (English and French):
http://www.cta-otc.gc.ca

MossRehab Resources Net:
http://www.mossresourcenet.org

Society for Accessible Travel and Hospitality:
http://www.sath.org

Gimp on the Go—Wide range of special needs covered:
http://www.gimponthego.com

Planning

Your Special Need

Getting There

Staying in Style

Touring

Dining

Resources

Index

Resources (continued)

Special Programs

If your special traveler is severely or terminally ill, you may also want to contact the following:

Make a Wish Foundation (800-722-WISH or 800-722-9474):
http://www.wish.org

Dream Factory (800-456-7556):
http://www.dreamfactoryinc.org

Give Kids the World (800-998-KIDS):
http://www.gktw.org

Starlight Starbright Children's Foundation:
http://www.starlight.org

Children's Wish Foundation of Canada:
http://www.childrenswish.ca

Dream Foundation for Terminally Ill Adults:
http://www.dreamfoundation.com

Fairy Godmother Foundation (for adults):
http://www.fairygodmother.org

Make a Wish Japan:
http://www.mawj.org

A Special Wish:
http://www.spwish.org/

Orlando Area Facilities

If your special need requires a hospital facility—say you need periodic dialysis—you'll need to make arrangements in advance. Your best bet is to contact a local hospital. Here is a list of several local medical facilities that should be able to arrange a variety of services and therapies for you (contact numbers current as of July 2007). For additional details on medical emergencies, see the sidebar on page 64.

Celebration Hospital is the closest hospital to the Walt Disney World Resort. It accepts all medical plans for emergency care.
Phone: 407-303-4000

Florida Hospital Medical Center
601 E. Rollins Street, Orlando, FL 32803
Phone: 407-897-1985 or 407-303-6611

Florida Kidney Center
4301 Vineland Road South, Suite E-17, Orlando, FL 32811
Phone: 407-425-4415

Orlando Regional Medical Center
1414 Kuhl Ave., Orlando, FL; Phone: 407-896-6611 or 407 841-5111

Florida Children's Hospital:
Phone: 407-553-KIDS (407-553-5437) or toll-free 800-553-KIDS

Arnold Palmer Hospital for Children
92 West Miller Street, Orlando, FL 32806; Phone: 407-841-5111

Ask-a-Nurse for doctor referrals or general information:
Phone: 407-303-1700

Centra Care In-Room Services:
Phone: 407-238-2000

Doctors on Call Service (DOCS):
Phone: 407-399-3627

EastCoast Medical—Call Center staffed by Registered Nurses and medical ancillary staff 24 hours a day:
Phone: 407-648-5252

Celebration Dental Group—For dental emergencies:
Phone: 407-566-2222

If you need to get a prescription refilled, Turner Pharmacy (407-828-8125) on S.R. 535, in the Centra Care Building, is open 8:00 am to midnight Monday–Friday and 8:00 am to 8:00 pm weekends. Delivery is available to resort guests for $5. Orders are left with the Lobby Concierge and are charged to your account. Turner Pharmacy will not bill your insurance—you must pay full price. The price can be charged to your resort account or you can provide your credit card number and have it charged directly to your credit card. If you have a vehicle, you can get prescriptions refilled at Orlando-area discount stores, such as Walgreens, Wal-Mart, Target, or Costco. Consult the phone book or web site (see below) for locations.

Area grocers and/or pharmacies (visit the web sites for store locations):
Albertson's: http://www.albertsons.com
Costco: http://www.costco.com
CVS: http://www.cvs.com
Goodings: http://www.goodings.com
K-Mart: http://www.kmart.com
Kash n' Karry: http://www.kashnkarry.com
Publix: http://www.publix.com
Sam's Club: http://www.samsclub.com
Target: http://www.target.com
Walgreens: http://www.walgreens.com
Wal-Mart: http://www.wal-mart.com
Winn Dixie: http://www.winndixie.com

Planning

Your Special Need

Getting There

Staying in Style

Touring

Dining

Resources

Index

IN FOCUS: Traveling With Epilepsy

Peer Reviewer Amy Warren Stoll has been a frequent guest at Walt Disney World since 1996. She's made more than 20 visits and taken several Disney cruises, many of them on her own, participated in the last two Disney Half Marathons, and has wowed friends and strangers alike with her fantastic voice when she's taken center stage for Karaoke Night at Kimonos in the Swan Resort. You'd probably never guess that she has epilepsy.

Amy has never let this "invisible challenge" keep her from enjoying her favorite vacation destination or from riding her favorite thrill rides.

"Having a seizure during a trip can certainly put a damper on things," Amy admits. "But I've learned through experience how to minimize the risks. I've also learned what to do if I should find myself waking up to discover the Reedy Creek emergency medical team hovering over me."

Amy offers this advice for travelers who have a seizure while on a Disney vacation:

1. My first piece of advice: Don't worry! Even if you do everything you can, sometimes, because of the unpredictability of epilepsy, you'll still have a seizure. It's not an uncommon occurrence at Walt Disney World. If you're traveling with friends or family, they can assist you and let cast members know whether a call to Emergency Medical Services (EMS) is necessary. If you're traveling alone, then a cast member will most likely call EMS as soon as they become aware that a guest is having a seizure. Again ... don't worry. As long as you begin to wake and reorient, Reedy Creek Fire Department (Walt Disney World's EMS) will not haul you off to a hospital emergency room without your consent. From personal experience, I have found them to be very sensitive to the desire of most seizure patients to not go to the emergency room for every seizure. They'll determine whether you're able to make an informed decision, then after discussing the risks with you, you will be allowed to leave on your own if you wish. If you are staying on Disney property, they may even be able to arrange for alternate transportation back to your resort, rather than using Disney transportation, getting you back to your room for a good rest as quickly as possible.

2. If a trip to the hospital is necessary—then what? Florida Hospital at Celebration is the closest hospital to Walt Disney World, and Reedy Creek can transport you there. You'll then need to take a taxi back to your resort after you've been treated. The cost is reasonable, less than $20 to most resorts. Note: Disney doesn't charge for its emergency medical services. That's quite a perk when you realize that an ambulance trip to the hospital at home could easily cost you more than $350!

© Amy Stoll

3. Don't think the fun and magic have to end just because you've had a seizure. After a good rest, don't be afraid to get back out to the theme parks. If you've had seizures for most of your life, then you know what you're capable of. Take stock of what happened. Think about what the possible triggers could have been: dehydration, lack of food or sleep, illness? Then try to take steps to prevent another seizure.

Amy notes that while traveling away from your "comfort zone" can be daunting for a person with epilepsy, with planning, Walt Disney World and the Disney Cruise Line can be ideal vacations. They are especially places where she feels she can celebrate her "me, me, all for me" solo trips, assured that she's going to be safe.

Your Resources

Note here the helpful resources and phone numbers you discover to keep your information in the same place.

Resource	Site Address/Phone Number

Planning

Your Special Need

Getting There

Staying in Style

Touring

Dining

Resources

Index

Planning

Your Special Need

Getting There

Staying in Style

Touring

Dining

Resources

Index

Readers' Tips and Stories

Don't let any handicap hold you back! Do and see whatever you can. You might surprise yourself and encourage someone else at the same time. I always wanted to swim with the dolphins, but being in a wheelchair, it was always harder for me to be in the water. But this year, I called Disney's Dolphins in Depth Tour, and they said it would be no problem for me to do this. They had me transfer into one of their wheelchairs, which is easier to move around in the water, and since the water is very salty, they put a weight across my lap to keep me from floating and help keep my legs down. The water is only waist deep for a standing person, so it came up to my mid-chest. One of the trainers stayed with me the whole time, and I was able to pet the dolphins and have my picture taken. I really enjoyed this. They took good care of me, and I felt really safe. It was one of the best experiences that I have had so far at Disney. If you haven't tried this tour because you were worried or afraid because of a handicap, don't be! I look forward to doing this again.   —contributed by Cheryl Giffear-Sywkiw

We chose not to do any character greets at the Magic Kingdom to avoid long lines. We went first thing to the Character Connection (in Innoventions) at Epcot. We told the first handler about our son's autism and she (very discreetly) made sure that all the photographers, handlers, and characters knew without our having to repeat the information. The handler went a step ahead of us to Mickey and adjusted his tie as she told him about our son. No one else would have known what she was telling him. The handlers and characters are wonderful—they were very tolerant of my son playing with the faces of their costumes.   —contributed by Sam and Spring Slagle

We will be traveling in a group of nine this year. Two people in our party are elderly and three are in their 20s. I know this group won't be together all the time, but we do have meals planned together. I made up itineraries for each member of the group with all our meal times, places, and reservation numbers, along with places to meet up during the day. This way no one will be lost or confused. I have also included our resort info and highlights of events for each day on the itineraries. All the planning should make our family gathering a Magical event.   —contributed by peer reviewer Deb Kendall

It is fun to celebrate special occasions at Walt Disney World. My husband and I have done birthdays there as seniors and had a great time. Our birthdays are only a day apart, so we both get special attention from one trip! Also, it has become a tradition for us to celebrate our wedding anniversary at the Brown Derby. The server recognizes the event with champagne, special dessert, and/or a phone call from Goofy with the phone brought right to the table.   —contributed by peer reviewer Jean Miller

Another great way to add a little bit of pixie dust to a vacation and get a little more individualized attention might be to go on one of the many guided tours they offer at the parks. For an animal lover who needs a little slower pace, the Backstage Safari at Disney's Animal Kingdom or the Dolphins in Depth program at Epcot is a really good way to view the parks. Kids with autism spectrum disorders, particularly Asperger's, who are fascinated with animals, would be thrilled to see animals up close, get in-depth information on how Disney takes care of them, etc. Also, I know a child with Asperger's who has memorized just about everything there is to know about boats; a child with a similar love of trains would probably be happy to go on the train tour in the Magic Kingdom. It costs a little extra to do these things, but depending on the person, they could turn out to be priceless experiences and memories.   —contributed by peer reviewer Joshua Olive

Index

Planning

Your Special Need

Getting There

Staying in Style

Touring

Dining

Resources

Index

Planning

Your Special Need

Getting There

Staying in Style

Touring

Dining

Resources

Index

Planning

Your Special Need

Getting There

Staying in Style

Touring

Dining

Resources

Index

Planning · Your Special Need · Getting There · Staying in Style · Touring · Dining · Resources · Index

Planning

Your Special Need

Getting There

Staying in Style

Touring

Dining

Resources

Index

Planning · Your Special Need · Getting There · Staying in Style · Touring · Dining · Resources · Index

Notes

....

....

....

....

....

....

....

....

....

....

....

....

....

....

....

....

....

....

....

....

....

....

Notes

....

....

....

....

....

....

....

....

....

....

....

....

....

....

....

....

....

....

....

....

....

....

....

Planning

Your Special Need

Getting There

Staying in Style

Touring

Dining

Resources

Index

Register Your PassPorter

We are <u>very</u> interested to learn how your vacation went and what you think of this guidebook, how it worked (or didn't work) for you, and your opinion on how we could improve it! We encourage you to register your copy of PassPorter with us—in return for your feedback, we'll send you **two valuable coupons** good for discounts on PassPorters and PassHolder pouches when purchased directly from us. You can register your copy of PassPorter at http://www.passporter.com/register.asp, or you can send us a postcard or letter to P.O. Box 3880, Ann Arbor, Michigan 48106.

Report a Correction or Change

Keeping up with the changes at Walt Disney World is virtually impossible without your help. When you notice something is different from what is printed in PassPorter or you just come across something you'd like to see us cover, please let us know! You can report your news, updates, changes, and corrections at http://www.passporter.com/wdw/report.htm.

Contribute to the Next Edition of PassPorter

You can become an important part of our next edition of *PassPorter's Open Mouse for Walt Disney World and the Disney Cruise Line!* The easiest way is to rate the resorts, rides, and/or restaurants at Walt Disney World at http://www.passporter.com/wdw/rate.htm. Your ratings and comments become part of our reader ratings throughout the book. Want to get more involved? Send us a vacation tip or story—if we use it in a future edition of PassPorter, we'll credit you by name in the guidebook and send you a free copy! Visit http://www.passporter.com/customs/tipsandstories.asp.

Get Your Questions Answered

We love to hear from you! Alas, due to the thousands of e-mails and hundreds of phone calls we receive each week, we cannot offer personalized advice to all our readers. But there's a great way to get your questions answered: Ask your fellow readers! Visit our message boards at http://www.passporterboards.com, join for free, and post your question. In most cases, fellow readers and Disney fans will offer their ideas and experiences! Our message boards also function as an ultimate list of frequently asked questions. Just browsing through to see the answers to other readers' questions will reap untold benefit! This is also a great way to make friends and have fun while planning your vacation. But be careful—our message boards can be addictive!

PassPorter® Online

A wonderful way to get the most from your PassPorter is to visit our active web site at http://www.passporter.com. We serve up valuable PassPorter updates, plus useful Disney and general information and advice we couldn't jam into our book. You can swap tales (that's t-a-l-e-s, Mickey!) with fellow Disney fans, play contests and games, find links to other sites, get plenty of details, and ask us questions. You can also order PassPorters and shop for PassPorter accessories and travel gear! The latest information on new PassPorters to other destinations is available on our web site as well. To go directly to our latest list of page-by-page PassPorter updates, visit http://www.passporter.com/customs/bookupdates.htm.

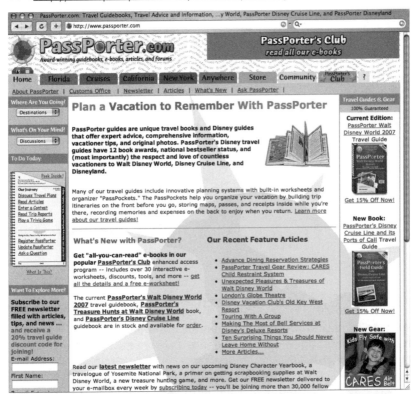

PassPorter Web Sites	Address (URL)
Main Page: PassPorter Online	http://www.passporter.com
Open Mouse Section	http://www.passporter.com/wdw/openmouse/guidebook.asp
PassPorter Message Boards	http://www.passporterboards.com
Book Updates	http://www.passporter.com/customs/bookupdates.htm
Rate the Rides, Resorts, Restaurants	http://www.passporter.com/wdw/rate.htm
Register Your PassPorter	http://www.passporter.com/register.asp

Planning · Your Special Need · Getting There · Staying in Style · Touring · Dining · Resources · Index

AllEars.net®

AllEars.net® is one of the web's most popular Disney-related sites, consistently drawing hundreds of thousands of visitors each month to its unique blend of up-to-the-minute news and detailed information about Walt Disney World in Orlando, Florida. The Wall Street Journal, The Unofficial Guide to Walt Disney World, and even Disney's own Disney Magazine have all singled out AllEars.net® as a top resource for vacation planners, and countless individuals on Internet discussion forums recommend the site for all kinds of Disney vacation information.

AllEars.net® is as comprehensive as possible, with information that is relevant to not only the traditional family, but to singles, couples, travel professionals, first-timers, seasoned Walt Disney World veterans, those with special touring or dietary needs, and international travelers.

AllEars.net® also encompasses the free electronic newsletter ALL EARS®, which is sent via e-mail to more than 90,000 subscribers weekly. The newsletter, which is entering its ninth year of publication, provides entertaining features, current news, reader-submitted tips, and commentary, all about Walt Disney World, with a dose of information on Disneyland and the Disney Cruise Line thrown for good measure.

Visit AllEars.net® at http://www.allears.net.

AllEars.net® and ALL EARS® are owned and operated by RYI Enterprises, LLC (Deb Wills, president).

PassPorter Goodies

PassPorter was born out of the necessity for more planning, organization, and a way to preserve the memories of a great vacation! Along the way we've found other things that either help us use the PassPorter better, appreciate our vacation more, or just make our journey a little more comfortable. Others have asked us about them, so we thought we'd share them with you. Order online at http://www.passporterstore.com, call us toll-free 877-929-3273, or use a photocopy of the order form below.

PassPorter® PassHolder is a small, lightweight nylon pouch that holds passes, ID cards, passports, money, and pens. Wear it around your neck for hands-free touring and for easy access at the airport. The front features a clear compartment, a zippered pocket, and a velcro pocket; the back has a small pocket (perfect size for FASTPASS) and two pen slots. Adjustable cord. Royal blue. 4 $^7/_8$" x 6 $^1/_2$"

Quantity:
____ x $7.95

PassPorter® Badge personalized with your name! Go around the "World" in style with our lemon yellow oval pin. Price includes personalization with your name, shipping, and handling. Please indicate pin name(s) with your order.

Quantity:
___ x $4.00

Name(s): _____

PassPorter® Pin is our collectible, cloissone pin. Our pin (shown at left) depicts the colorful PassPorter logo. Watch for new pins to be introduced each year!

Quantity:
___ x $6.00

Please ship my PassPorter Goodies to:

Name ....

Address ....

City, State, Zip ....

Daytime Phone..

Payment: ❏ check (to "MediaMarx") ❏ charge card

❏ MasterCard ❏ Visa ❏ American Express ❏ Discover

Card number ....Exp. Date. ....

Signature ....

Subtotal:

Tax*:

Shipping**:

Total:

* Please include sales tax if you live in Michigan.
**Shipping costs are:
$5 for totals up to $9
$6 for totals up to $19
$7 for totals up to $29
$8 for totals up to $39
Delivery takes 1-2 weeks.

Send your order form to P.O. Box 3880, Ann Arbor, MI 48106, call us toll-free at 877-WAYFARER (877-929-3273), or order online http://www.passporterstore.com.

Planning

Your Special Need

Getting There

Staying in Style

Touring

Dining

Resources

Index

More PassPorters

You've asked for more PassPorters—we've listened! We've added several new PassPorters since the first release of this book, all designed to make your Disney vacation the best it can be. And we also have our best-selling, award-winning general purpose guidebooks to both the Walt Disney World Resort (see below) and the Disney Cruise Line (see right). To learn about these and other PassPorters, visit http://www.passporter.com.

PassPorter's Walt Disney World Spiral Edition

It all started with Walt Disney World (and a mouse)! Our general Walt Disney World guidebook covers everything you need to plan a practically perfect vacation, including fold-

out park maps; resort room layout diagrams; KidTips; descriptions, reviews, and ratings for the resorts, parks, attractions, and restaurants; and much more! This edition also includes 14 organizer pockets you can use to plan your trip before you go, hold papers while you're there, and record your memories for when you return. Learn more and order at http://www.passporter.com/wdw, or get a copy at your favorite bookstore. Our Walt Disney World guide is available in a spiral-bound edition (2008 edition ISBN-13: 978-1-58771-049-0 or 2009 edition ISBN-13: 978-1-58771-060-5) and a Deluxe Edition (see below)—both have 14 PassPockets.

PassPorter's Walt Disney World Deluxe Edition

Design first-class vacations with this loose-leaf ring binder edition. The Deluxe Edition features the same great content as the general PassPorter Walt Disney World spiral guide. Special features of the Deluxe Edition include ten interior storage slots in the binder to hold guidemaps, ID cards, and a pen (we even include a pen). The Deluxe binder makes it really easy to add, remove, and rearrange pages ... you can even download, print, and add updates and supplemental pages from our web site, and refills are available for purchase. Learn more at http://www.passporter.com/wdw/deluxe.htm. The Deluxe Edition is available through bookstores by special order—just give your bookstore the ISBN for the 2008 Deluxe Edition (978-1-58771-050-6) or our 2009 Deluxe Edition (978-1-58771-061-2).

Wondering why PassPorter's Open Mouse isn't available in a deluxe edition? The answer is simple—it's just too big to fit in the deluxe binder! If you must have a binder, consider getting a binder with just PassPockets (available on our web site) and use both the binder and this book to plan your vacation!

Even More PassPorters

PassPorter's Disney Cruise Line and Its Ports of Call

Completely updated annually! Includes complete itinerary and port-of-call descriptions for all upcoming itineraries.

Get your cruise plans in shipshape with our updated field guide! Authors Jennifer and Dave Marx cover the Disney Cruise Line in incredible detail, including deck plans,

stateroom floor plans, original photos, menus, entertainment guides, port/shore excursion details, and plenty of worksheets to help you budget, plan, and record your cruise information. Currently in its fifth edition, this is the original and most comprehensive guidebook devoted to the Disney Cruise Line! Learn more and order your copy at http://www.passporter.com/dcl or get a copy at your favorite bookstore. The paperback version without PassPockets is ISBN-13: 978-1-58771-037-7 (5th Ed.) or ISBN-13: 978-1-58771-055-1 (6th Ed.). Also available in a Deluxe Edition with organizer PassPockets with ISBN-13: 978-1-58771-038-4 (5th Ed.) or ISBN-13: 978-1-58771-056-8 (6th Ed.).

PassPorter's Disneyland Resort and Southern California Attractions

PassPorter tours the park that started it all! California's Disneyland Park, Disney's California Adventure, and Downtown Disney get PassPorter's expert treatment, and we throw in Universal Studios Hollywood, Knott's Berry Farm, Hollywood and Downtown Los Angeles, San Diego, SeaWorld, the San Diego Zoo and Wild Animal Park, LEGOLAND, and Six Flags Magic Mountain. All this, and PassPorter's famous PassPockets and planning features. Whether you're making the pilgrimage to Disneyland Resort or planning a classic Southern California family vacation, you can't miss. Learn more at http://www.passporter.com/dl, or pick it up at your favorite bookstore (ISBN-13: 978-1-58771-042-1). Also available as a Deluxe Edition in a padded, six-ring binder (ISBN-13: 978-1-58771-043-8).

PassPorter's Treasure Hunts at Walt Disney World

Have even more fun at Walt Disney World! Jennifer and Dave's treasure hunts have long been a favorite part of PassPorter reader gatherings at Walt Disney World, and now you can join in the fun. Gain a whole new appreciation of Disney's fabulous attention to detail as you search through the parks and resorts for the little (and big) things that you may never have noticed before. Great for individuals, families, and groups, with hunts for people of all ages and levels of Disney knowledge. Special, "secure" answer pages make sure nobody can cheat. Prepared with plenty of help from Jeff and Jen Carter, famous for their all-day, all-parks scavenger hunts. Learn more about this fun book and order at http://www.passporter.com/hunts or get a copy at your favorite bookstore (ISBN-13: 978-1-58771-026-1).

To order our guidebooks, visit http://www.passporterstore.com/store or call toll-free 877-929-3273. PassPorter guidebooks are also available in your local bookstore. If you don't see them on the shelf, just ask!

Note: The ISBN codes listed here apply to our 2007–2009 editions. For the latest edition, ask your bookstore to search their database for "PassPorter."

PassPorter E-Books

Looking for more in-depth coverage on specific topics? Look no further than PassPorter E-Books! Our e-books are inexpensive (most just $4.95) and available immediately as a download on your computer (Adobe PDF format). If you prefer your books printed, we have options for that, too! And unlike most e-books, ours are fully formatted just like a regular PassPorter print book. A PassPorter e-book will even fit into a Deluxe PassPorter Binder, if you have one. We offer seven e-books at press time, and have plans for many, many more!

PassPorter's Cruise Clues: *First-Class Tips for Disney Cruise Trips*
Get the best tips for the Disney Cruise Line—all categorized and coded—as well as cruise line comparisons, a teen perspective, and ultimate packing lists! This e-book is packed with 250 cruiser-tested tips—all edited by award-winning author Jennifer Marx.

PassPorter's Disney 500: *Fast Tips for Walt Disney World Trips*
Our most popular e-book has more than 500 time-tested Walt Disney World tips—all categorized and coded! We chose the best of our reader-submitted tips over a six-year period for this e-book and each has been edited by author Jennifer Marx.

PassPorter's Disney Character Yearbook
Who, What, and Where at Walt Disney World, Disneyland, and the Disney Cruise Line
A compendium of all the live Disney characters you can find at Walt Disney World, Disneyland, and on the Disney Cruise Line. Also includes tips on finding, meeting, photographing, and getting autographs, plus a customizable autograph book to print!

PassPorter's Disney Speed Planner: *The Easy Ten-Step Program*
A fast, easy method for planning practically perfect vacations—great for busy people or those who don't have lots of time to plan. Follow this simple, ten-step plan to help you get your vacation planned in short order so you can get on with your life. It's like a having an experienced friend show you the ropes step by step—and have fun doing it!

PassPorter's Free-Book
A Guide to Free and Low-Cost Activities at Walt Disney World
It's hard to believe anything is free at Walt Disney World, but there are actually a number of things you can get or do for little to no cost. This e-book documents more than 150 free or cheap things to do before you go and after you arrive. It's the most comprehensive collection!

PassPorter's Sidekick for the Walt Disney World Guidebook
An interactive collection of worksheets, journal pages, and charts
This is a customizable companion to our general Walt Disney World guidebook—you can personalize worksheets, journals, luggage tags, and charts, plus click links to all the URLs in the guidebook and get transportation pages for all points within Walt Disney World!

PassPorter's Walt Disney World for Brit Holidaymakers:
Brits, you can get super in-depth information for your Walt Disney World vacation from fellow Brit and PassPorter feature columnist Cheryl Pendry. More than 300 pages long!

Learn more about these and other titles and order e-books at:
http://www.passporterstore.com/store/ebooks.aspx

PassPorter's Club

Do you want more help planning your Walt Disney World vacation? Join the PassPorter's Club and get all these benefits:

✔ "All-you-can-read" access to EVERY e-book we publish (see current list on the previous page). PassPorter's Club passholders also get early access to these e-books before the general public. New e-books are added on a regular basis, too.

✔ Interactive, customizable "e-worksheets" to help make your trip planning easier, faster, and smoother. The worksheets are electronic and can be printed for a truly personalized approach! We have more than 35 worksheets, with more on the way. You can see a sample e-worksheet to the right.

✔ Access to super-sized "e-photos" in the PassPorter Photo Archives—photos can be zoomed in up to 25 times larger than standard web photos. You can use these e-photos to see detail as if you're actually standing there—or use them for desktop wallpaper, scrapbooking, whatever!

✔ Our best discount on print guidebooks ... 35% off!

There's more features, too! For a full list of features and current e-books, e-worksheets, and e-photos, visit http://www.passporter.com/club. You can also take a peek inside the Club's Gallery at: http://www.passporterboards.com/forums/passporters-club-gallery. The Gallery is open to everyone—it contains a FREE interactive e-worksheet to try out!

Price: A PassPorter's Club pass is only $4.95/month, or the cost of just one e-book!

How to Get Your Pass to the PassPorter's Club

Step 1. Get a free community account. Register simply and quickly at http://www.passporterboards.com/forums/register.php.

Step 2. Log in at http://www.passporterboards.com/forums/login.php using the Member Name and password you created in step 1.

Step 3. Get your pass. Select the type of pass you'd like and follow the directions to activate it immediately. We currently offer monthly and annual passes. (Annual passes save 25% and get extra perks!)

Questions? Assistance? We're here to help! Please send e-mail to club@passporter.com.

You may also find many of your questions answered in our FAQ (Frequently Asked Questions) in the Gallery forum (see link above).

Planning

Your Special Need

Getting There

Staying in Style

Touring

Dining

Resources

Index

Vacation at a Glance

You have our permission to make a copy of the worksheet below and create an itinerary overview. You can then make copies of it and give one to everyone in your traveling party, as well as to those who stay behind.

Name(s):	
Departing on: Time: #:	
Arriving at:	
Staying at: Phone:	

Date:	Date:
Park/Activity:	Park/Activity:
Breakfast:	Breakfast:
Lunch:	Lunch:
Dinner:	Dinner:
Other:	Other:

Date:	Date:
Park/Activity:	Park/Activity:
Breakfast:	Breakfast:
Lunch:	Lunch:
Dinner:	Dinner:
Other:	Other:

Date:	Date:
Park/Activity:	Park/Activity:
Breakfast:	Breakfast:
Lunch:	Lunch:
Dinner:	Dinner:
Other:	Other:

Date:	Date:
Park/Activity:	Park/Activity:
Breakfast:	Breakfast:
Lunch:	Lunch:
Dinner:	Dinner:
Other:	Other:

Date:	Date:
Park/Activity:	Park/Activity:
Breakfast:	Breakfast:
Lunch:	Lunch:
Dinner:	Dinner:
Other:	Other:

Departing on: Time: #:	
Returning at:	